# THE PAPERS OF ALEXANDER HAMILTON

Alexander Hamilton, 1792. Painting by John Trumbull
New York State Chamber of Commerce

# THE PAPERS OF

## *Alexander Hamilton*

VOLUME X

DECEMBER 1791–JANUARY 1792

HAROLD C. SYRETT, EDITOR

JACOB E. COOKE, ASSOCIATE EDITOR

*Assistant Editors*

JEAN G. COOKE      CARA-LOUISE MILLER

DOROTHY TWOHIG      PATRICIA SYRETT

 COLUMBIA UNIVERSITY PRESS

NEW YORK AND LONDON, 1966

FROM THE PUBLISHER

The preparation of this edition of the papers of Alexander Hamilton has been made possible by the support
received for the work of the editorial and research staff
from the generous grants of the Rockefeller Foundation, Time Inc., and the Ford Foundation, and by the
far-sighted cooperation of the National Historical Publications Commission. To these organizations, the publisher expresses gratitude on behalf of all who are
concerned about making available the record of the
founding of the United States.

The Alfred P. Sloan Foundation, through a special
grant, has enabled the Press to publish this volume.

# ACKNOWLEDGMENTS

SINCE the publication in 1965 of Volumes VIII and IX of *The Papers of Alexander Hamilton*, the editors have incurred new obligations which they wish to take this opportunity to acknowledge. Miss Priscilla Ohler, who joined the staff in 1965, has performed a variety of tasks with unfailing good humor and grace. Of the many individuals who generously shared their specialized information or provided assistance in locating elusive documents, the editors are especially indebted to

Professor Bernard Bailyn, Harvard University

Mr. Edmund Berkeley, Jr., Senior Assistant in Manuscripts, University of Virginia Library

Mr. George R. Beyer, Assistant Archivist, Division of Public Records, Pennsylvania Historical and Museum Commission, Harrisburg

Mrs. Mary Givens Bryan, Director, Department of Archives and History, Atlanta, Georgia

Mr. Geoffrey Clifford, Curator, Oneida Historical Society, Utica, New York

Miss Doris E. Cook, Manuscripts Cataloger, Connecticut Historical Society, Hartford

Mrs. George Cunningham, Librarian, Pennsylvania Division, Carnegie Library of Pittsburgh

Mr. John Daly, Archival Examiner, Department of Records, City of Philadelphia

Mr. S. L. deVausney, Vice President and Secretary, Bank of New York

Mr. Frank B. Evans, Archivist and Chief, Division of Public Records, Pennsylvania Historical and Museum Commission, Harrisburg

Mr. Edward M. Graf, Curator, The Passaic County Historical Society, Lambert Castle, Paterson, New Jersey

Mr. Harold Hazleton, Librarian, New York Genealogical and Biographical Society, New York City

Miss Sandra M. Kamtman, Manuscripts Assistant, Maryland Historical Society, Baltimore

Mr. John D. Kilbourne, Librarian, Maryland Historical Society, Baltimore

Miss Mary Jo Kline, Assistant Editor, John Jay Papers, Columbia University

Mr. John Lindenbusch, Manuscripts Librarian, New Hampshire Historical Society, Concord

Professor Abraham P. Nasatir, San Diego State College, California

Mr. James W. Patton, Director, Southern Historical Collection, University of North Carolina Library, Chapel Hill

Mrs. Thomas D. Phillips, Marietta, Ohio

Mr. Morris L. Radoff, Archivist, Hall of Records, Annapolis, Maryland

Mr. Gust Skordas, Assistant Archivist, Hall of Records, Annapolis, Maryland

Mr. B. A. Sorby, Librarian, Hunterdon County Historical Society, Flemington, New Jersey

Mr. David Syrett, London

Miss Prudence B. Trimble, Librarian-Editor, The Historical Society of Western Pennsylvania, Pittsburgh

Mr. William J. Van Schreeven, State Archivist, Virginia State Library, Richmond.

# PREFACE

THIS EDITION of Alexander Hamilton's papers contains letters and other documents written by Hamilton, letters to Hamilton, and some documents (commissions, certificates, etc.) that directly concern Hamilton but were written neither by him nor to him. All letters and other documents have been printed in chronological order. Hamilton's legal papers are being published under the editorial direction of Julius Goebel, Jr., George Welwood Murray Professor Emeritus of Legal History of the School of Law, Columbia University. The first volume of this distinguished work, which is entitled *The Law Practice of Alexander Hamilton,* was published by the Columbia University Press in 1964.

Many letters and documents have been calendared. Such calendared items include routine letters and documents by Hamilton, routine letters to Hamilton, some of the letters or documents written by Hamilton for someone else, letters or documents which have not been found but which are known to have existed, letters or documents which have been erroneously attributed to Hamilton, and letters to or by Hamilton that deal exclusively with his legal practice.

Certain routine documents which Hamilton wrote and received as Secretary of the Treasury have not been printed. The documents that fall within this category are warrants or interest certificates; letters written by Hamilton acknowledging receipts from banks, endorsing margins of certificate of registry, and enclosing sea letters; letters to Hamilton transmitting weekly, monthly, and quarterly accounts, or enclosing certificates of registry and other routine Treasury forms; and drafts by Hamilton on the treasurer. Statements of facts from the judges of the District Courts on cases concerning violations of the customs laws and warrants of remission of forfeiture issued by Hamilton have generally been omitted unless they pertain to cases discussed in Hamilton's correspondence.

The notes in these volumes are designed to provide information concerning the nature and location of each document, to identify Hamilton's correspondents and the individuals mentioned in the text, to explain events or ideas referred to in the text, and to point out textual variations or mistakes. Occasional departures from these standards can be attributed to a variety of reasons. In many cases the desired information has been supplied in an earlier note and can be found through the use of the index. Notes have not been added when in the opinion of the editors the material in the text was either self-explanatory or common knowledge. The editors, moreover, have not thought it desirable or necessary to provide full annotation for Hamilton's legal correspondence. Perhaps at this point it should also be stated that arithmetical errors in Hamilton's reports to Congress have not been corrected or noted. Finally, the editors on some occasions have been unable to find the desired information, and on other occasions the editors have been remiss.

# GUIDE TO EDITORIAL APPARATUS

## I. SYMBOLS USED TO DESCRIBE MANUSCRIPTS

| | |
|---|---|
| AD | Autograph Document |
| ADS | Autograph Document Signed |
| ADf | Autograph Draft |
| ADfS | Autograph Draft Signed |
| AL | Autograph Letter |
| ALS | Autograph Letter Signed |
| D | Document |
| DS | Document Signed |
| Df | Draft |
| DfS | Draft Signed |
| LS | Letter Signed |
| LC | Letter Book Copy |
| [S] | [S] is used with other symbols (AD[S], ADf[S], AL[S], D[S], Df[S], L[S]) to indicate that the signature on the document has been cropped or clipped. |

## II. MONETARY SYMBOLS AND ABBREVIATIONS

| | |
|---|---|
| bf | Banco florin |
| V | Ecu |
| f | Florin |
| ₶ | Livre Tournois |
| medes | Maravedis (also md and mde) |
| d. | Penny or denier |
| ps | Piece of eight |

| £ | Pound sterling or livre |
| Ry | Real |
| rs vn | Reals de vellon |
| rdr | Rix daller |
| s | Shilling, sou or sol (also expressed as /) |
| sti | Stiver |

### III. SHORT TITLES AND ABBREVIATIONS

*Annals of Congress*, I, II, III — *The Debates and Proceedings in the Congress of the United States; with an Appendix, Containing Important State Papers and Public Documents, and All the Laws of a Public Nature* (Washington, 1834–1849).

*Arch. des Aff. Etr., Corr. Pol., Etats-Unis* — Transcripts or photostats from the French Foreign Office deposited in the Library of Congress.

*Archives Parlementaires* — *Archives Parlementaires de 1787 à 1860* (Paris, 1868–        ).

*ASP* — *American State Papers, Documents, Legislative and Executive, of the Congress of the United States* (Washington, 1832–1861).

Barton, *The True Interest* — [William Barton], *The True Interest of the United States, and particularly of Pennsylvania, considered; with respect to the advantages resulting from a State Paper-Money: with Some Observations on the subject of a Bank and on Agriculture, Manufactures and Commerce. By an American* (Philadelphia: Printed by Charles Cist, at the Corner of Fourth and Arch-streets, 1786).

Boyd, *Papers of Thomas Jefferson* — Julian P. Boyd, ed., *The Papers of Thomas Jefferson* (Princeton, 1950–        ).

Brymner, *Canadian Archives*, 1890

Douglas Brymner, ed., *Report on Canadian Archives*, 1890 (Ottawa, 1891).

Clark, *State Records of North Carolina*

Walter Clark, ed., *The State Records of North Carolina* (Goldsboro, North Carolina, 1886–1907).

Clavière, *Considerations on America*

Etienne Clavière, *Considerations on the Relative Situation of France, and the United States of America: Shewing the Importance of the American Revolution to the Welfare of France: Giving also An Account of their Productions, and the reciprocal Advantages which may be drawn from their Commercial Connexions: And Finally, Pointing Out the Actual Situation of the United States. Translated from the French of Etienne Clavière, and J. P. Brissot De Warville* (London: Printed at the Logographic Press, and Sold by Robson and Clarke, New Bond Street; T. Longman, Pater-Noster-Row; and W. Richardson, Royal-Exchange, 1788).

Coxe, *Address*

Tench Coxe, *An Address to an Assembly of the Friends of American Manufactures, Convened for the Purpose of establishing a Society for the Encouragement of Manufactures and the useful Arts, read in the University of Pennsylvania, on Thursday the 9th of August 1787, by Tench Coxe, Esq. and Published at their Request* (Philadelphia: Printed by R. Aitken & Son, at Pope's Head in Market Street, 1787).

Coxe, *Brief Examination*

Tench Coxe, *A Brief Examina-*

Ford, *Writings of Jefferson*

Freeman, *Washington*

*GW*

Hamilton, *History*

Hamilton, *Intimate Life*

Hamilton, *Life*

*HCLW*

Hogan, *Pennsylvania State Trials*

Hume, *Political Discourses*

Hutcheson, *Coxe*

Isambert, *Recueil Général des Anciennes Lois Françaises*

de *L'Imprimierie Nationale, Par Baudouin, et Du Bulletin des Lois* (Paris, 1824).

Paul Leicester Ford, ed., *The Writings of Thomas Jefferson* (New York, 1892–1899).

Douglas Southall Freeman, *George Washington* (New York, 1948–1957). Volume VII of this series was written by John Alexander Carroll and Mary Wells Ashworth.

John C. Fitzpatrick, ed., *The Writings of George Washington* (Washington, 1931–1944).

John C. Hamilton, *Life of Alexander Hamilton, a History of the Republic of the United States of America* (Boston, 1879).

Allan McLane Hamilton, *The Intimate Life of Alexander Hamilton* (New York, 1910).

John C. Hamilton, *The Life of Alexander Hamilton* (New York, 1840).

Henry Cabot Lodge, ed., *The Works of Alexander Hamilton* (New York, 1904).

[Edmund Hogan], *The Pennsylvania State Trials: Containing the Impeachment, Trial, and Acquittal of Francis Hopkinson, and John Nicholson, Esquires . . .* (Philadelphia, 1794).

David Hume, *Political Discourses* (Edinburgh: Printed by R. Fleming, for A. Kincaid and A. Donaldson, 1752).

Harold Hutcheson, *Tench Coxe, a Study in American Economic Development* (Baltimore, 1938).

*Recueil Général des Anciennes Lois Françaises, Depuis L'An*

420 Jusqu'à La Révolution de 1789, par MM. Jourdan, Docteur en droit, Avocat à la Cour royale de Paris; Isambert, Avocat aux Conseil du Roi et à la Cour de Cassation; Decrusy, ancien Avocat à la Cour royale de Paris (Paris, 1827).

JCC — Journals of the Continental Congress, 1774–1789 (Washington, 1904–1937).

JCH Transcripts — John C. Hamilton Transcripts. These transcripts are owned by Mr. William H. Swan, Hampton Bays, New York, and have been placed on loan in the Columbia University Libraries.

JCHW — John C. Hamilton, ed., The Works of Alexander Hamilton (New York, 1851–1856).

Johnson, Greene — William Johnson, Sketches of the Life and Correspondence of Nathanael Greene, Major General of the Armies of the United States, in the War of the Revolution (Charleston, 1822).

Journal of the House, I — Journal of the House of Representatives of the United States (Washington, 1826), I.

Mayo, Instructions to British Ministers — Bernard Mayo, ed., "Instructions to the British Ministers to the United States, 1791-1812," Annual Report of the American Historical Association for the Year 1936 (Washington, 1941), III.

"Minutes of the S.U.M." — MS Minutes of the Society for Establishing Useful Manufactures, City of Paterson, New Jersey, Plant Management Commission, Successors to the Society for Establishing Useful Manufactures.

Mitchell, Hamilton — Broadus Mitchell, Alexander

Montesquieu, *The Spirit of Laws*

Moreau de St. Méry, *Loix et Constitutions des Colonies Françoises de l'Amérique sous le Vent*

Necker, *Finances of France*

Necker, *Œuvres*

New York Assembly *Journal,* 1792

Postlethwayt, *Universal Dictionary*

*Hamilton* (New York, 1957–1962).

Charles Louis de Secondat, Baron de la Brede et de Montesquieu, *The Spirit of Laws,* trans. Mr. Nugent (3d ed.; 2 Vols.; London: Printed for J. Nourse and P. Vaillant in the Strand, 1758).

Mederic Louis Elie Moreau de St. Méry, *Loix et Constitutions des Colonies Françoises de l'Amérique sous le Vent* (Paris, 1784–1790).

Jacques Necker, *A Treatise on the Administration of the Finances of France. In Three Volumes. By Mr. Necker. Translated from the genuine French Edition, 1784, by Thomas Mortimer, Esq.* (London: Printed at the Logographic Press, 1785).

Jacques Necker, *Œuvres de M. Necker* (A Lausanne: Chez J. P. Heubach et Compagnie, 1786).

*Journal of the Assembly of the State of New York. Fifteenth Session* (New York, 1792).

Malachy Postlethwayt, *The Universal Dictionary of Trade and Commerce, Translated from the French of the Celebrated Monsieur Savary, Inspector-General of the Manufactures for the King, at the Custom-house of Paris; With Large Additions and Improvements, Incorporated throughout the Whole Work; Which more particularly accommodate the same to the Trade and Navigation Of these Kingdoms, And the Laws, Customs, and Usages, To which all Traders are subject. Second*

PRO: F.O., or PRO: C.O.

*edition* (London: Printed for John Knapton, in Ludgate-Street, 2 vols., 1757).

Transcripts or photostats from the Public Record Office of Great Britain desposited in the Library of Congress.

PRO: F.O., or PRO: C.O. (Great Britain)

Public Record Office of Great Britain.

"Reynolds Pamphlet"

Alexander Hamilton, *Observations on Certain Documents Contained in No. V and VI of "The History of the United States for the Year 1796," in which the Charge of Speculation against Alexander Hamilton, Late Secretary of the Treasury, is Fully Refuted. Written by Himself* (Philadelphia: Printed for John Fenno, by John Bioren, 1797).

Saintoyant, *La Colonisation Française pendant la Révolution*

J. Saintoyant, *La Colonisation Française pendant la Révolution, 1789–1799* (Paris, 1930).

Smith, *Wealth of Nations*

Adam Smith, *An Inquiry into the Nature and Causes of the Wealth of Nations. By Adam Smith, LL.D. and F.R.S. of London and Edinburgh: One of the Commissioners of His Majesty's Customs in Scotland; and Formerly Professor of Moral Philosophy in the University of Glasgow. The Fourth Edition, With Additions. In Two Volumes* (Dublin: Printed for W. Colles, R. Moncrieffe, G. Burnet, W. Wilson, C. Jenkin, L. White, H. Whitestone, P. Byrne, J. Cash, W. M'Kenzie, 1785).

1 Stat.

*The Public Statutes at Large of the United States of America* (Boston, 1845).

6 *Stat.*      *The Public Statutes at Large of the United States of America [Private Statutes] (Boston, 1856).*

Steuart, *Political Economy*      Sir James Steuart, *An Inquiry into the Principles of Political Œconomy: Being an Essay on the Science of Domestic Policy in Free Nations. In Which Are Particularly Considered Population, Agriculture, Trade, Industry, Money, Coin, Interest, Circulation, Banks, Exchange, Public Credit, and Taxes. By Sir James Steuart, Bart. . . . In Two Volumes* (London: Printed for A. Millar, and T. Candell, in the Strand, 1767).

Vattel, *Law of Nations*      Emeric de Vattel, *Law of Nations; or Principles of the Law of Nature Applied to the Conduct and Affairs of Nations and Sovereigns* (London, 1759–1760).

## IV. INDECIPHERABLE WORDS

Words or parts of words which could not be deciphered because of the illegibility of the writing or the mutilation of the manuscript have been indicated as follows:

1. ⟨-----⟩ indicates illegible words with the number of dashes indicating the estimated number of illegible words.
2. Words or letters in broken brackets indicate a guess as to what the words or letters in question may be. If the source of the words or letters within the broken brackets is known, it has been given a note.

## V. CROSSED-OUT MATERIAL IN MANUSCRIPTS

Words or sentences crossed out by a writer in a manuscript have been handled in one of the three following ways:

1. They have been ignored, and the document or letter has been printed in its final version.
2. Crossed-out words and insertions for the crossed-out words have been described in the notes.
3. When the significance of a manuscript seems to warrant it, the crossed-out words have been retained, and the document has been printed as it was written.

## VI. TEXTUAL CHANGES AND INSERTIONS

The following changes or insertions have been made in the letters and documents printed in these volumes:

1. Words or letters written above the line of print (for example, 9<sup>th</sup>) have been made even with the line of print (9th).
2. Punctuation and capitalization have been changed in those instances where it seemed necessary to make clear the sense of the writer. A special effort has been made to eliminate the dash, which was such a popular eighteenth-century device.
3. When the place or date, or both, of a letter or document does not appear at the head of that letter or document, it has been inserted in the text in brackets. If either the place or date at the head of a letter or document is incomplete, the necessary additional material has been added in the text in brackets. For all but the best known localities or places, the name of the colony, state, or territory has been added in brackets at the head of a document or letter.
4. In calendared documents, place and date have been uniformly written out in full without the use of brackets. Thus "N. York, Octr. 8, '99" becomes "New York, October 8, 1799." If, however, substantive material is added to the place or date in a calendared document, such material is placed in brackets. Thus "Oxford, Jan. 6" becomes "Oxford [Massachusetts] January 6 [1788]."
5. When a writer made an unintentional slip comparable to a typographical error, one of the four following devices has been used:
   a. It has been allowed to stand as written.

   b. It has been corrected by inserting either one or more letters in brackets.
   c. It has been corrected without indicating the change.
   d. It has been explained in a note.
6. Because the symbol for the thorn was archaic even in Hamilton's day, the editors have used the letter "y" to represent it. In doing this they are conforming to eighteenth-century manuscript usage.

# THE PAPERS OF ALEXANDER HAMILTON

# 1791

## Report on the Subject of Manufactures

[Philadelphia, December 5, 1791]

*Introductory Note*

Like Hamilton's other major state papers, the "Report on Manufactures" is distinguished not so much by originality of thought as by the cogency and persuasiveness of its arguments, its far-reaching implications, and its ennobling vision of the destiny of the United States. Indeed, it contains few, if any, specific proposals that even the most enthusiastic supporters of Hamilton could maintain were original. In this sense, the Report is as much a product of its times as the creation of its author, for many of the ideas which it contains had been debated for decades on both sides of the Atlantic. During the second half of the eighteenth century western Europe and America provided in varying degrees an economic climate which was conducive to discussions of questions concerning national economic growth and the role of manufacturing in the economy.

For many years preceding the preparation of Hamilton's Report, leading French and English politicians and students of national economic policy had devoted considerable attention to such matters as the relative economic advantages of agriculture and manufacturing, machinery and manual industry, bounties and restrictions on imports, and colonial and domestic trade. In England before the outbreak of the American Revolution statesmen and writers who were concerned with imperial problems had considered the American potential for economic growth and the possibility of America's achieving self-sufficiency in manufacturing. There is ample evidence, moreover, that for several years before he joined the new government Hamilton had studied the writings of such leading political and economic theorists as Jacques Necker, David Hume, Malachy Postlethwayt, Adam Smith, and Sir James Steuart.[1] Despite the fact that these men ranged

1. See the introductory notes to "Report Relative to a Provision for the Support of Public Credit," January 9, 1790; "Second Report on the Further Pro-

over a number of diverse topics, each was concerned in different ways
with some of the subjects contained in the "Report on Manufactures."

Hamilton could draw on American as well as European experiences
and ideas in the preparation of his Report. Although he refers only
incidentally in the Report to attempts to promote industry during
the American Revolution, some of the arguments for domestic manufacturing advanced during the war are similar to those later used by
Hamilton. After the Revolution, Americans of necessity increasingly
turned their attention to questions concerning the need for manufacturing, economic independence, tariff policy, and the role of invention and technology in the economy. The interest in these and related
matters during the seventeen-eighties is indicated in part by the
increasing number of pamphlets and articles in periodicals that discussed such subjects, by the founding of associations and societies for
the encouragement of American manufactures, and by petitions to
Congress and debates in that body on the desirability of Federal
support of manufacturing. Hamilton, however, was not satisfied with
the existing body of available material on manufacturing, for while
preparing this Report he solicited information from various Americans on both manufacturing and agriculture.[2] In addition, through
his connection with the Society for Establishing Useful Manufactures
he had acquired firsthand knowledge of the problems involved in the
formation of a large-scale manufacturing company. Finally, and
perhaps most important, the subject of this Report was not new to
Hamilton in 1791, for his earlier writings reveal a continuing interest
in the part that manufacturing should play in the nation's economy.

The encouragement of manufactures, as the "next great work to be
accomplished," was an integral part of Hamiltonian finance. In the
Report Hamilton defends the financial policies already in effect that
had been subjected to strong criticism. The Bank of the United States
and the funding system had been the targets of mounting opposition

vision Necessary for Establishing Public Credit (Report on a National Bank),"
December 13, 1790; and "Report on the Establishment of a Mint," January 28,
1791.
    2. See H to Benjamin Lincoln, January 25, 1790; circular letter of May 11,
1790, signed by Tench Coxe, quoted in H to Lincoln, January 25, 1790, note 4;
"Treasury Department Circular to the Supervisors of the Revenue," June 22,
1791; and "Treasury Department Circular," August 13, 1791.

in the wake of increased speculation in public funds and bank scrip, and the market break of August, 1791, had given additional support to those who contended that all "paper" produced "bubbles." In the "Report on Manufactures" Hamilton reiterates his view of the public debt as an acquisition of artificial capital available for the promotion of manufactures, and, as in his "Report on Public Credit," he attempts to dissociate his views from the opinions of those who regarded every increase in the public debt as an unmitigated public blessing.

The "Report on Manufactures" cannot be divorced from Hamilton's view of public credit and banking, but an equally close relation exists between this Report and his attitude toward foreign policy. It is possible that Hamilton's views might have aroused less opposition in Congress if he had suggested that the encouragement of American manufactures could be used as a lever to bring a change in European trade policy—especially that of Great Britain. In a conversation with George Beckwith, unofficial British representative in the United States, he had said that American manufacturing efforts would be proportioned to British conduct.[3] But although there is evidence that Hamilton attempted to gain support both from free traders and from those who desired greater accommodation for France, he did not attempt to appeal to anti-British groups in the United States by emphasizing that the growth of manufactures might serve as a device for twisting the lion's tail.

In an evident attempt to avoid unnecessary opposition from those more favorably disposed to the French Revolution and free trade, he deleted outspoken criticism of the French assignat policy and equally outspoken praise for mercantilism. In a marginal query in his fourth draft he asked whether even the support for self-sufficiency in necessaries might not contradict what had previously been stated in favor of free trade. Necker's "either-or" contrast between agrarian law and commercial restrictions was omitted, as was the view of Hume and Steuart that subsistence farmers were of no use to a state either for revenue or for defense.[4]

On points of policy, however, Hamilton gave no ground. For example, the Report does not share the ambiguity of many con-

3. "Conversation with George Beckwith," October, 1789.
4. Necker, Œuvres, IV, 34-35; Hume, Political Discourses, 13-14; Steuart, Political Economy, I, 88, 136

temporary American essays concerning the improvement of either agriculture or manufactures. Hamilton left no doubt of his support for commercial farming and factory production. He gave little space to household industry or manufactures associated with agriculture, and in the discussion of bounties he distinguished clearly between factory production and handicrafts related to self-sufficiency. He emphasized the increased profits to the landholder from intensive farming, but omitted the corollary which Steuart drew that, while manufactures aid commercial agriculture, they hurt subsistence farming.[5]

By 1791 European trade policies had helped to create an attitude among Americans which Hamilton had every reason to believe would prove favorable to the encouragement of manufactures in the United States. A commercial treaty with Britain after the Revolution had failed to materialize, and Orders in Council closing the West Indies trade had been a source of irritation for the better part of a decade.[6] A greater cause for surprise and irritation came from French commercial policies, some of which Hamilton noted in his second and third drafts of this Report.[7] Some Frenchmen in the period between 1783 and 1791 had emphasized the possibilities of Franco-American trade, but the policies of the French government caused almost as much ill feeling in 1791 as the highhanded attitudes of the British government and press. Even Jefferson, inveterate foe of American manufactures and stanch friend of France, commented in June, 1791:

"Very considerable discouragements are recently established by France Spain & England with respect to our commerce: the first as to whale oil, tobacco, & ships, the second as to corn, & the third as to corn & ships. Should these regulations not be permanent, still they

5. Steuart, *Political Economy*, I, 103–05.
6. The irritation caused by French and British restrictions was increased by uncertainty. For example, although on February 14, 1791, Washington had reported to Congress that there was little hope for a British commercial treaty (*Journal of the House*, I, 377–78), a report in the *National Gazette* stated that Britain had opened the West Indian ports to American vessels on the same basis as that enjoyed by British ships ([Philadelphia] *National Gazette*, November 14, 1791).
7. William Short repeatedly gave H information on the changes in French policies and politics. See Short to H, February 7, March 4, March 11, and June 3, 1791.

add to the proofs that too little reliance is to be had on a steady & certain course of commerce with the countries of Europe to permit us to depend more on that than we cannot avoid. Out best interest would be to employ our principal labour in agriculture, because to the profits of labour, which is dear this adds the profits of our lands which are cheap. But the risk of hanging our prosperity on the fluctuating counsels & caprices of others renders it wise in us to turn seriously to manufactures; and if Europe will not let us carry our provisions to their manufactures we must endeavor to bring their manufacturers to our provisions." [8]

In his final version of the "Report on Manufactures" Hamilton deleted specific references to the regulations of England and France respecting American commerce, but the risk of foreign commercial restrictions was a stronger argument for the encouragement of manufactures in the minds of many Americans than Hamilton's critique of laissez-faire theory.

Pamphlets as well as government regulations reflected British and French concern over the effect of political independence on the course of American trade with Europe. At the close of the American Revolution Lord Sheffield wrote a pamphlet [9] which contained the economic policies he thought Great Britain should pursue toward the United States and which clearly indicated his contempt for the economic power of the new nation. Lord Sheffield's pamphlet elicited extensive criticism in American periodicals; especially exasperating to his American contemporaries were his views that a commercial treaty was not necessary, since American products could be obtained from other countries, and that the superiority of British manufactures would ensure their predominance in the American market. Although official British policy coincided with the views of Lord Sheffield, his ideas were criticized in England as well as in the United States. The final volume of the three-volume book of travels of Jean Pierre Brissot de Warville, written in collaboration with Etienne Clavière,

8. See Jefferson to David Humphreys, June 23, 1791 (ALS, letterpress copy, Thomas Jefferson Papers, Library of Congress).
9. Lord Sheffield, *Observations on the Commerce of the American States with Europe and the West Indies; including the several articles of import and export; and on the tendency of a bill now depending in Parliament* (London: J. Debrett, 1783).

made clear to Americans the possibilities of French trade and cautioned them against the waste and social evils which would surely attend the development of manufacturing. Clavière wrote:

"Europe has the spirit of manufactures; independent America ought to have that of cultivating lands. . . . I do, and ought to insist upon these observations, because the reading of American papers proves to me, that notwithstanding general insights, enough is not yet known in the United States, neither of the principles which must form connexions with Europe, nor of the terrible inconveniencies attached to manufactures. . . . The same arguments which prove the necessity of making stockings, family linen, &c. at home, are applied without distinction to cloths, silks, and the most complicated and pernicious manufactures." [10]

Other views from Europe were more favorable to American economic prospects. Théophile Cazenove, who was serving as an agent in America for a group of Dutch bankers, wrote to Hamilton that in his opinion manufactures would have a favorable effect on the American balance of trade, the value of the debt, and the ease with which loans could be obtained abroad.[11] Necker discussed American economic prospects and predicted the downfall of the French monopoly of her own colonial trade as well as the probable elimination of the favorable balance of trade enjoyed by France:

"The commerce carried on with its manufactures, and with its American commodities, make three-fourths of the exports of the kingdom [of France]. The knowledge of this fact cannot but occasion some uneasiness, for both these branches of commerce are liable to revolutions. . . . works of industry and ingenuity are not like the

10. Clavière, *Considerations on America*, 157–58. First published in France in March, 1787, this work was translated and published in London the following year. Clavière, a Genevan banker, had moved to Paris during the seventeen-eighties. His assistance to Brissot, his acquaintance with Crèvecœur, his later position in the French government, and his partnership with various individuals ranging from William Duer and Daniel Parker to Théophile Cazenove, the Willinks, and others who were interested in the American public debt ensured American interest in his work. For example, Jefferson's familiarity with Clavière's work, which "reveals many traces of TJ's influence," is discussed in Boyd, *Papers of Thomas Jefferson*, X, 263–64.

Although parallels might be drawn between H's Report and the writings of the Physiocrats, which *Considerations on America* reflects in some respects, there is no reason to believe that H had read the works of Quesnay, Turgot, or others of the "économistes."

11. Cazenove to H, April 1, 1790.

privileged gifts of soil and climate, men in every part of the globe are capable of ingenious labour; . . . in a word, that species of industry which springs up and strengthens itself in the bosom of civil liberty, and of a fruitful territory, will in time make a considerable progress in the extensive republic just formed upon the continent of America; and this new power will one day, participate in some measure, in supplying the West India islands, and the Spanish West India settlements. Let it not be objected, that they will find it more to their advantage to till their lands; the more they are cultivated the greater will be the quantity of subsistence, and this abundance will, sooner or later, invite arts and industry, whenever the government takes care to second the efforts of private interest." [12]

The "Report on Manufactures" contains considerable evidence of Hamilton's reliance on those European writers from whom he had drawn material in some of his earlier papers and reports. Several scholars have noted the close similarity between sections of the Report and parts of Adam Smith's *The Wealth of Nations*,[13] and the footnotes to the Report in this edition of Hamilton's papers make it clear that there can be little doubt concerning the source to which the Secretary of the Treasury turned for the free-trade views which he refuted in the Report. More in sympathy with the general tenor of the Report were the conclusions of Necker and Steuart, for both shared Hamilton's views concerning the relation between manufactures and the power and prestige of a state. Although Malachy Postlethwayt's *Universal Dictionary*, which Hamilton had repeatedly used in his earlier writing, was perhaps of less assistance in this Report, Postlethwayt's views on manufactures and modern society nevertheless correspond in many respects to those of Hamilton. Among other European writers who may have influenced Hamilton's thinking some mention should be made of Vattel, who conceded that moderate commercial restrictions did not constitute violations of natural law; [14] Montesquieu, who maintained that freedom of commerce did not

12. Necker, *Finances of France*, II, 148–49.

13. Mitchell, *Hamilton*, II, 144, 146, 149; Louis M. Hacker, *Alexander Hamilton in the American Tradition* (New York, 1957), 11–12, 150, 168–70, 182–83; Edward G. Bourne, "Alexander Hamilton and Adam Smith," *The Quarterly Journal of Economics*, VIII (April, 1894), 328–44; Ugo Rabbeno, *The American Commercial Policy* (London, 1895), 313–18.

14. Vattel, *Law of Nations*, I, 40.

preclude commercial restrictions;[15] and Hume, who along with several other eighteenth-century writers argued that the growth of manufacturing was desirable in that it would increase the market for agricultural products.[16]

Of the many sources used by Hamilton, *The Wealth of Nations* in many respects provides the most interesting case study. According to one biographer, Hamilton had prepared a critique of *The Wealth of Nations* during his service in the Continental Congress.[17] No trace of this document, however, has been found, and the student must turn to the "Report on Manufactures" to discover those points on which Hamilton and Smith either agreed or disagreed. Hamilton's respect for some of Smith's views is revealed by his reliance on *The Wealth of Nations* for his discussion of the division of labor and for the direct quotation taken from the same book to describe the advantages of transportation facilities. He also paraphrased Smith's statement and criticism of the Physiocratic classification of manufactures as unproductive labor. On the other hand, he could not accept Smith's notion of the superior productivity of agriculture, and he criticized Smith's view that private interest was led by an invisible hand to support the type of activity most beneficial to society. Hamilton may also have entertained much the same doubts concerning the labor theory of value as those expressed by Thomas Pownall.[18] In his third draft of this Report Hamilton speaks of the "practical estimate of value" in determining the relative productivity of agriculture and manufactures.

A study of the "Report on Manufactures" clearly reveals the influence of Jacques Necker on Hamilton's thinking. A statement which Hamilton inserted (and then deleted) in his third draft of this Report indicates that he, like Necker, was opposed to the assignat policy.[19] There is also a similarity between some of the arguments used in the Report and those in Necker's discussion of the grain trade and in his eulogy of Colbert.[20] Hamilton's views correspond

15. Montesquieu, *The Spirit of Laws*, II, 11.
16. Hume, *Political Discourses*, 11-12.
17. Hamilton, *History*, II, 514.
18. Thomas Pownall, *A Letter from Governor Pownall to Adam Smith, L.L.D. F.R.S. Being an Examination of Several Points of Doctrine, Laid Down in His "Inquiry into the Nature and Causes of the Wealth of Nations"* (London: Printed for J. Almon, opposite Burlington-house, in Piccadilly, 1776).
19. When the National Assembly in 1790 voted to issue additional assignats, Necker resigned as Director-General of Finances.
20. Necker, *Œuvres*, III, 179-314; IV, 1-292.

to those of the French Minister in his discussion of the penalties which would be incurred by one nation attempting to institute free trade in a world of mercantilist economic policies.[21] Finally, both men agreed that a diversified, self-sufficient economy would gain a more favorable balance of trade than one which depended upon agricultural exports alone.[22] Although scholars have emphasized the similarity of expression between statements in the Report and *The Wealth of Nations*, it is difficult to overlook the fact that the general conclusions of the Report are closer to those of Necker than to those of Smith.

But if Hamilton shared Necker's opposition to unqualified statements of free-trade views, his respect for the "liberal doctrine" was similar to that of William Pitt and his associates. One commentator has suggested:

"Pitt was not merely being polite when he acknowledged Adam Smith as his master. . . . Perhaps owing partly to his example, the influence [of *The Wealth of Nations*] had its fashion in Government circles. . . . There is no need to underestimate the general stimulus thus provided. It could also be usefully invoked when required for persuasion or support. . . . The word 'liberal' was liberally used, when it was convenient. . . . There was nothing insincere in the use of the word to denote an acknowledgment of industrial facts by men who rightly regarded themselves as being abreast of the times. To Governments as to men of business, freedom of trade meant freedom to trade. But perhaps it did not mean much more than that." [23]

In America as well as in Europe manufacturing and its relation to the government were subjects that were frequently discussed from a variety of viewpoints in official and unofficial circles for several years before Hamilton's Report was presented to Congress in 1791. During the Revolution difficulties encountered in obtaining supplies had called the attention of the Continental Congress to the desirability of domestic manufactures, and as early as 1775 Benjamin Rush gave a speech on the possibilities open to American manufactures.[24] Members of the First Congress of the new government considered the advisability of protecting domestic manufactures in the course of

21. Necker, *Œuvres*, III, 260–61.  22. Necker, *Œuvres*, IV, 32, 34, 89.
23. John Ehrman, *The British Government and Commercial Negotiations with Europe, 1783–1793* (Cambridge, 1962), 178–80.
24. JCC, III, 268–69; VI, 1072–73. Rush's speech was reprinted in *The American Museum*, V (June, 1789), 581–84.

their debates over the revenue and tonnage acts, and the question of extensive government intervention in the economy was raised in debates over the act establishing the Bank of the United States.[25]

One of the most frequently cited sources for the "Report on Manufactures" consists of the information that Hamilton received from various individuals in reply to his requests for facts concerning the current state of American agriculture and manufacturing. Although Hamilton made use of some of the material which was sent to him from various correspondents,[26] the information which he appeared most anxious to obtain was not readily available. The reports of his correspondents on prices and profits of farms, wages and profits in Britain, European regulations, and even the costs and profits of American factories fell far short of his requests. Manufacturers were either unable or reluctant to disclose their full financial operations, and the records kept by farmers were so inadequate that it was impossible to make a valid comparison between the profits of agriculture and those of manufacturing. But the information that Hamilton did receive at least gave an indication of the extent of manufactures, the problems in establishing them, and the attitude toward government encouragement of manufacturing.

Tench Coxe was perhaps the best-known American advocate of manufactures in the years immediately preceding 1791, a fact that may in part account for his appointment by Hamilton as Assistant Secretary of the Treasury.[27] Coxe's influence on the "Report on

25. See *Annals of Congress*, I, 106–26, 129–48, 150–77, 180–240, 243–56, 261–76, 282–301, 303–30, 337–80; II, 1941–2012.

26. See note 2. For examples of replies to H's requests for information from manufacturers, see Samuel Paterson to H, February 10, 1791; Nathaniel Hazard to H, March 9, 1791; Samuel Breck to H, September 3, 1791; Daniel Stevens to H, September 3, 1791; George Cabot to H, September 6, 1791; Aaron Dunham to H, September 9, 1791; Edward Carrington to H, October 4, 1791; John Chester to H, October 11, 1791; Nathaniel Gorham to H, October 13, 1791; and John Dexter to H, October, 1791.

For examples of replies concerning agriculture, see Richard Peters to H, August 27, 1791; Henry Wynkoop to H, August 29, 1791; Timothy Pickering to H, October 13, 1791; John Neville to H, October 27, 1791; and John Beale Bordley to H, November 11, 1791.

27. In May, 1790, H described Coxe as a man "who to great industry and very good talents adds an extensive theoretical and practical knowlege of Trade" (H to Timothy Pickering, May 13, 1790). See also H to Coxe, May 1, 1790.

Manufactures" has been suggested by both contemporary observers and recent scholars,[28] and there is little question that he was of great assistance to Hamilton in obtaining and compiling information concerning manufactures received from various individuals. Although Hamilton devoted little space in the Report to household manufactures or to "manufactures associated with agricultural pursuits," Coxe placed greater emphasis on both types of manufacturing. In an enlarged version of his *A Brief Examination of Lord Sheffield's Observations on the Commerce of the United States*, Coxe appended a "Supplementary Note" concerning household manufactures compiled from the results of inquiries made in preparation for the "Report on Manufactures." [29]

In recent years scholars have speculated on the importance of Coxe's part in the preparation of this Report, but the fact that Coxe's papers were not available to them precluded any definitive statement concerning his role.[30] Through the courtesy of Mr. Daniel M. Coxe a draft of the Report in Coxe's handwriting has been made available to the editors of *The Papers of Alexander Hamilton* and is printed in this volume as "Tench Coxe's Draft of the Report on the Subject of Manufactures." [31] That Coxe's contribution was not limited to his own draft is suggested by a note which Coxe wrote to the clerk who copied part of Hamilton's first draft, for the material to which the note refers does not appear in the Coxe draft.[32] In addition, there is

28. James Kent noted in his copy of the "Report on Manufactures": "Mr. *Coxe* seems to have led the way in vindicating the Utility of American Manufactures, & many of his Ideas have been used in the following Report. See various Parts of his View of the U States, & particularly pa. 55" (*Report of the Secretary of the Treasury of the United States, on the Subject of Manufactures. Presented to the House of Representatives. December 5, 1791* [n.p.: Printed by Childs and Swaine, n.d.]; Kent's copy is now in the possession of the Columbia University Libraries). In 1794 Coxe collected and published several of his papers in the *View*. Although some of these papers had been written before the "Report on Manufactures" was submitted to Congress, the material cited by Kent, which appears on page 55 of the *View*, did not appear before 1794.

See Hutcheson, *Coxe*, vii–viii. See also Dorfman, *The Economic Mind*, I, 290.

29. Coxe, *Brief Examination*, 113–20.

30. Hutcheson, *Coxe*, vii–viii.

31. The editors also wish to express their indebtedness to Mr. Nicholas Wainwright, Director of the Historical Society of Pennsylvania, for making it possible for them to examine Coxe's draft of the Report.

32. See note 62.

always the possibility that further material relevant to the "Report on Manufactures" may come to light when scholars have unlimited access to the Coxe Papers.[33]

Hamilton's first draft of this Report is considerably longer than Coxe's, but it is equally significant that Hamilton incorporated a major part of Coxe's draft in his own first draft. A study of Coxe's draft helps not only to clarify Coxe's contribution to this Report but also to illustrate some of the differences between Hamilton's views on manufacturing and those of Coxe. In his first draft Hamilton deleted Coxe's proposals for a land premium, for the introduction of new and useful machinery, and for the abolition of tonnage duty on coasting vessels.[34] Hamilton's additions indicate a greater interest in questions of economic theory, a lively awareness of the position of the United States among the competing trading nations of Europe, and a more outspoken advocacy of late eighteenth-century European mercantilist views. Coxe's contribution to the "Report on Manufactures" should not, however, be underestimated. In addition, any student seeking to compare the views of Coxe and Hamilton should keep in mind that Coxe's draft was prepared over a short period of time, while Hamilton's final version was the product of almost a year's intermittent work. At the same time Hamilton's final version of this Report differs markedly in both emphasis and substance from Coxe's draft and from Coxe's other writings on manufactures.

William Barton and Mathew Carey, like Coxe, were known to favor the encouragement of manufactures. Barton's "Remarks on the state of American manufactures and commerce" was printed in *The American Museum*,[35] and a copy is in the Hamilton Papers at the

33. In this connection it should be noted that the Tench Coxe Papers, on deposit at the Historical Society of Pennsylvania, are not open to the public. The MS of Coxe's draft of the Report was discovered by the staff of the Historical Society of Pennsylvania and was made available through the generosity of Mr. Daniel M. Coxe for publication in this edition of Hamilton's papers.

34. The importance which Coxe attached to the first two of these proposals is indicated in his letters to James Madison and Thomas Jefferson (Coxe to Madison, March 21, 1790 [ALS, James Madison Papers, Library of Congress] and Coxe to Jefferson, March 5, 1791, with enclosure in Coxe's handwriting [AL, Thomas Jefferson Papers, Library of Congress]).

35. *The American Museum*, VII (June, 1790), 285–92.

Library of Congress. Carey had expressed his opinions through the selection and publication of material in *The American Museum* and by occasional annotation of material in that magazine.

Although George Washington's influence on this Report cannot be precisely ascertained, there can be no doubt concerning his interest in manufacturing. In 1789 he indicated his willingness to support the establishment of a woolen factory in Virginia, and in the same year in a letter to Jefferson he mentioned the "Measures taken by the different States for carrying the new government into execution" and continued: "Exclusive of these things, the greatest and most important objects of internal concern, which at present occupy the attention of the public mind, are manufactures and inland navigation. Many successful efforts in fabrics of different kinds are every day made. . . . A desire of encouraging whatever is useful and œconomical seems now generally to prevail. Several capitol artists, in different branches, have lately arrived in this Country." [36] What may have been a draft of Washington's first inaugural address provides evidence of the first President's belief that manufacturing was essential to the nation's well-being.[37] It may also be significant that in October, 1791, he wrote to Hamilton suggesting bounties on hemp and cotton.[38] Finally, it should be remembered that the occasion for the House order requesting this Report was an address from the President opening the second session of the First Congress. In a section devoted to provision for the common defense, Washington said: "A free people ought not only to be armed but disciplined; to which end a uniform and well digested plan is requisite: And their safety and interest require, that they should promote such manufactories, as tend to render them independent on others for essential, particularly for military supplies." [39]

Parallels between Hamilton's statements in the Report and those made by other Americans and Europeans should not obscure the fact that Hamilton himself had displayed a sustained interest in manufacturing for several years. To a certain degree he was one of his own best sources. In *A Full Vindication* he had emphasized the high prices

36. Boyd, *Papers of Thomas Jefferson*, XIV, 546–47.
37. *GW*, XXX, 305–06.  38. Washington to H, October 14, 1791.
39. *GW*, XXX, 491–92.

which would be paid to farmers who supplied the raw materials used in the manufacture of clothing.[40] This argument was repeated in his pamphlet *The Farmer Refuted*,[41] where he maintained that an agricultural country was of necessity politically dependent on manufacturing nations, that a variety of products would stimulate a mutually beneficial commerce, and that internal commerce promoted national stability. In a letter to Robert Morris in 1781 he had emphasized the importance of a habit of industry, and four months later he had stated that the first essential power which should be given to Congress should be "THE POWER OF REGULATING TRADE, comprehending a right of granting bounties and premiums by way of encouragement, of imposing duties of every kind, as well for revenue as regulation, of appointing all officers of the customs, and of laying embargoes, in extraordinary emergencies." [42]

The intellectual origins of the "Report on Manufactures" have attracted the attention of countless scholars. Ugo Rabbeno, Edward G. Bourne, and Louis M. Hacker have written on the relation between ideas in *The Wealth of Nations* and those in the Report.[43] Arthur H. Cole has indicated specific instances in which points made in the Report are similar to those raised by Hamilton's correspondents.[44] Joseph Dorfman and Joseph Stancliffe Davis, among others, have discussed some of the ideas in the Report which were shared by Hamilton's contemporaries and which had their origins in European experience and theory.[45] These examples by no means exhaust the list of those who have studied the genesis of the "Report on Manufactures," and it seems likely that the subject will continue to fascinate historians and economists.

In annotating the "Report on Manufactures," the editors of *The Papers of Alexander Hamilton* can make no claim to being either

40. *A Full Vindication of the Measures of the Congress, &c.*, December 15, 1774.
41. *The Farmer Refuted, &c.*, February 23, 1775.
42. H to Morris, April 30, 1781; "The Continentalist No. IV," August 30, 1781.
43. See note 13.
44. Arthur Harrison Cole, *Industrial and Commercial Correspondence of Alexander Hamilton Anticipating His Report on Manufactures* (Chicago, 1928), 5, 14, 46, 64, 65, 72, 95, 112, 193–94.
45. Dorfman, *The Economic Mind*, I, especially Chapters XII and XIII; Davis, *Essays*, I, 349–89, II, 255–90.

exhaustive or definitive. On the other hand, some precedents for material in the Report from sources with which Hamilton is known to have been familiar are indicated in the footnotes to his final version, and wherever possible other substantive footnotes have been provided for this version. In addition, in Coxe's draft and Hamilton's four drafts there are some substantive footnotes for material which Hamilton did not include in his final version. Statute references are given in all drafts and in Hamilton's final version of the Report. Notes 46, 59, 107, and 123 explain the editorial devices used to indicate the different handwritings that appear in Coxe's draft and in Hamilton's first and fourth draft and in his final version. No attempt has been made, however, to identify the individuals who made marginal comments or interlineations in Hamilton's drafts of the Report, for the number of people Hamilton may have consulted and the brevity of the material that was added in any one instance have convinced the editors that they lacked both the temerity and the ability to identify the handwriting of each of these anonymous contributors.

## TENCH COXE'S DRAFT OF THE REPORT ON THE SUBJECT OF MANUFACTURES [46]

Treasury Department
the        [47] 1790

The Secretary of the Treasury, in obedience to the order of the house of Representatives of the fifteenth day of January last, has applied his attention, at as early a period as his other duties would permit, to the subject of manufactures, and particularly to the means of promoting such as will tend to render the United States independent on foreign Nations for military and other essential supplies.

The expediency of encouraging manufactures in the United States, tho recently deemed very questionable, appears at this time to be generally admitted. The advantages of the Landholder in furnishing

46. ADf, deposited in the Historical Society of Pennsylvania, Philadelphia, and printed by permission of Mr. Daniel M. Coxe, Philadelphia.

There are two small portions of this draft which are in a clerk's handwriting and which are printed in italics.

47. Space left blank in MS. Internal evidence indicates that this draft was written during the fall of 1790.

raw materials, subsistence, fuel and other supplies to the workmen—
the support which the fisheries derive from them by their consumption of articles drawn from the ocean—the assistance given to external
commerce by promoting the importation [48] of raw articles and furnishing manufactured commodities for exportation—their favorable
effects on population by inducing the emigration of foreign artists
and laborers—the introduction of money by offering a new & promising field to capitalists of other nations—the promotion of individual
industry & œconomy which naturally result from manufactures and
particularly when engrafted upon an extensive agriculture—their encreasing and rendering more certain the means of defence and other
articles of prime necessity and lastly the Reduction of the prices of
convenient & essential supplies for public & private use, which has
already taken place on the appearance of competition from the American manufacturer are among the considerations, which have produced more favorable opinions concerning this object.

Among the means devised by the European nations to encourage
manufactures protecting duties have been very generally adopted. It
cannot be unobserved by those, who are engaged in these pursuits nor
will it escape the notice of those capitalists, and workmen who may
intend to transfer their property and business to the United States,
that the duties already imposed by the legislature,[49] tho principally for

48. The remainder of this paragraph does not appear in H's first draft of the
Report.
49. This is a reference to Section 1 of "An Act making further provision for
the payment of the debts of the United States," which reads in part as follows:
"Section 1. *Be it enacted by the Senate and House of Representatives of the
United States of America in Congress assembled,* That from and after the last
day of December next, the duties specified and laid in and by the act aforesaid,
shall cease and determine; and that upon all goods, wares and merchandise (not
herein particularly excepted) which after the said day shall be brought into the
United States, from any foreign port or place, there shall be levied, collected
and paid the several and respective duties following, that is to say: . . . molasses,
per gallon, three cents; beer, ale and porter in casks, per gallon, five cents; beer,
ale and porter in bottles, per dozen, twenty cents; . . . cocoa, per pound, one
cent; loaf sugar, per pound, five cents; brown sugar, per pound, one and a half
cent; other sugar, per pound, two and a half cents; candles of tallow, per pound,
two cents; candles of wax or spermaceti, per pound, six cents; . . . cotton, per
pound, three cents; nails and spikes, per pound, one cent; bar and other lead, per
pound, one cent; steel unwrought, per one hundred and twelve pounds, seventy-
five cents; hemp, per one hundred and twelve pounds, fifty-four cents; . . . malt,
per bushel, ten cents; coal, per bushel, three cents; boots, per pair, fifty cents;
shoes, slippers and goloshoes, made of leather, per pair, seven cents; shoes and
slippers, made of silk or stuff, per pair, ten cents; wool and cotton cards, per

the purposes of Revenue, afford very considerable and certain advantages to the American manufacturer. Tho it may be very doubtful whether general addition to these duties be necessary further to encourage the Manufactures of the United States, yet it is humbly conceived a few articles may be very properly aided by a moderate encrease. Among those in View is Sail Cloth which is important to defence, to domestic & foreign commerce, the fisheries &, as it relates to the raw materials, to agriculture likewise.

Prohibitions of rival articles, or duties equivalent, frequently present themselves in the laws of foreign nations. Tho this measure, in most instances, may be of doubtful propriety in the United States, it appears to merit consideration in regard to particular Articles. From the present flourishing condition of some manufactories of military supplies, such as Gunpowder, leaden & iron ball, iron cannon & cartridge paper it may not be deemed hazardous, in a season of profound peace, to encrease the duty so as to prevent the Importation of them. Besides warlike stores there are certain Articles manufactured from materials with which the United States abound, that do not appear unfit Subjects of excluding duties. Among the objects here contemplated are Malt liquors, spirits made from grain of every sort & from fruit, (exepting that made of the grape) the oils of sea and land animals & of flaxseed, the spirits of turpentine, snuff, chewing & smoking tobacco, starch and other things manufactured from

---

dozen, fifty cents; . . . all China ware, looking glasses, window and other glass, and all manufactures of glass, (black quart bottles excepted) twelve and an half per centum ad valorem; . . . blank books, writing paper, and wrapping paper, paper hangings, pasteboards, parchment and vellum . . . oil, gun-powder . . . ten per centum ad valorem; cabinet wares . . . saddles, gloves of leather, hats of beaver, felt, wool, or a mixture of any of them, millinery ready made, castings of iron, and slit and rolled iron, leather tanned or tawed, and all manufactures of which leather is the article of chief value, except such as are herein otherwise rated, canes, walking sticks, and whips, clothing ready made, brushes, anchors, all wares of tin, pewter, or copper, all or any of them . . . carpets and carpeting, all velvets, velverets, satins and other wrought silks, cambrics, muslins, muslinets, lawns, laces, gauzes, chintzes, and colored calicoes, and nankeens, seven and an half per centum ad valorem. . . . and five per centum ad valorem upon all other goods, wares and merchandise, except . . . tin in pigs, tin plates, old pewter, brass teutenague, iron and brass wire, copper in plates, saltpetre . . . wool, dyeing woods, and dyeing drugs, raw hides and skins, undressed furs of every kind, the sea stores of ships or vessels, the clothes, books, household furniture, and the tools or implements of the trade or profession of persons who come to reside in the United States, philosophical apparatus, specially imported for any seminary of learning . . ." (1 Stat. 180–81 [August 10, 1790]).

such productions of the Earth & of the fisheries as are constantly exported in large quantities which are encreasing on our hands, and for which a sufficient vent is consequently difficult to procure. The wisdom of the house however will render them duly aware of the injuries, that may be occasioned by an indiscriminate & too extended an application of duties equivalent to prohibitions should they be induced to impose them in favor of certain manufactures necessary for defence, or highly and universally beneficial to the landed interest.

*Pecuniary bounties upon home made articles have been tried in several European countries with great success. The linen branch in Ireland is a well known instance. [But under the present]* [50] *circumstances of this country the Secretary cannot discover sufficient inducements to these expensive encouragements to justify a [strenuous] recommendation of them to the consideration of the legislature. This aid to manufactures however is less necessary at [the present moment] in the United States than in any European country, because their fabrics, being generally wanted for hom⟨e consumption, are free from the heavy expences of importation, which rival foreign⟩* [51] *goods sustain to the amount of [fifteen, ⟨twenty⟩ and twenty five]* ₱ Cent *on their Value according to their* bulk. But if it should on consideration be deemed inexpedient to grant bounties in money to encourage manufactures it may nevertheless appear adviseable to reward certain great and useful promoters of them by other means. The United States having a very large quantity of unappropriated lands the Secretary humbly submits to the house the propriety of setting apart the quantity of five hundred thousand acres, of good quality and advantageously situated, for the purpose of rewarding the first introducers or establishers of new and useful manufactories, arts, machines, & secrets not before possessed, known or carried on in the United States. The objects here contemplated, and the mode of applying this landed fund will be more clearly explained by the plan contained in the paper (A) [52] which accompanies this report. A measure of this nature would

50. The material within brackets in this paragraph is in Coxe's handwriting.
51. Material within broken brackets in this draft has been taken from H's first draft of the Report.
52. Coxe is referring to the following document, which may be found in the Hamilton Papers, Library of Congress:
"A.
"A Plan for creating a landed fund to be granted in premiums to the Intro-

evince to the manufacturers of Europe the disposition of the legislature to encourage and reward them, and would afford to persons, who
may transfer their capitals and establishments ⟨to the United States, a
certain⟩ tho ⟨not⟩ an immediate compensation ⟨even in unsuccessful⟩
instances.

In addition to these rewards for the Importation of manufacturing
Machinery, and secrets of great value, acts may be passed, if sufficiently warranted by the extraordinary utility of the object and the
difficulty of attaining it, granting to the introducers such exclusive
privileges for a term of years as would have been secured by patent,
had they been the inventors. Public Advantage, if derived from each
in an equal degree, will justify this favor to the one as well as to the
other, and the successful practice of the principal manufacturing nations of Europe establishes the prudence of the measure.

As a substitute for pecuniary bounties on particular articles, sufficiently beneficial to the landed interest to merit that expensive and
inconvenient encouragement, the revenue may be calculated to assist
them by diminishing the use of rival, tho in some instances different,
commodities. Thus the Duties on ardent spirits may be rendered a
virtual bounty on beer, ale & porter & the impost on foreign spirituous

---

ducers, Inventors and Establishers of manufactories, machinery and secrets in
the useful Arts.

"There being six great staple raw materials, silk, cotton, wool, hemp, flax and
iron, that are deemed capable of being maunfactured by water they may be
considered as forming

| | |
|---|---:|
| the 1st. Class, which may be encouraged by a grant of 30,000 Acres of Land to the persons who shall introduce the Model and the com-pletest foreign mill for each. This will require | Acres 180,000 |
| The 2d. Class will be more numerous. Let it be supposed that it may contain ten objects, but being individually less important 15,000 Acres are proposed. This will require | 150,000 |
| The 3d. Class will be still more numerous, but of less individual im-portance. Let it be supposed that it may contain 17 objects each to be rewarded by 10,000 Acres. This will require | 170,000 |
| | 500,000 |

"The above premiums may be applied indiscriminately to reward Introduc-
tions, or native Inventions, which will not yield an immediate or adequate
benefit to the Inventor.

"The management and distribution of this fund it is conceived would be most
beneficially conducted under the direction of the President of the United States.
The principles of the distribution being fixed by the Law, the application of

the fund to the several cases ~~would~~ might be most conveniently left in the judgment
and discretion of the President."

liquors and encouragement to those made at home. By careful attention to regulations of this nature, it is believed very effectual aid may be given to our manufactures without any hazard of public inconvenience or injurious frauds. An examination of the Articles imported for consumption in the United States, and of the capacity of our manufacturers to make succedance for them out of our own produce, and imported raw Materials will suggest many objects, to which, it is supposed, this Idea may be advantageously applied.

*A drawback of the amount of the duty on the raw Material on the ex⟨portation of manufactured Articles⟩ is a measure recommended by ⟨policy,⟩ and ⟨rendered in some degree necessary⟩ by the practice of nations, who will hold a competition with us in foreign Markets. The duty on Molasses, if the idea here suggested should meet the approbation of the legislature, might be allowed on the exportation of American rum—that on Muscovado sugars on the exportation of refined—that on Cocoa on the exportation of Chocolate and in such other instances as shall admit of due security against deception &*
*fraud* the danger of which is the only objection that occurs to this mode of encouragement.

⟨The promotion of friendly intercourse and fair trade with the indian Tribes will have a favorable effect upon some valuable branches of Manufacture, the raw materials for which are derived from the western Country. Towards these ends the wisdom⟩ of the Legislature and of ⟨the Chief Magistrate⟩ have been already successfully directed; but some objects of great consequence to the Indian trade & consequently to the Manufactures dependent on it remain to be obtained. The pursuit of them however rests upon considerations of so much more Importance than any which arise on the present topic, that it is sufficient merely to present them to the attention of the house, as connected with the subject of this report.

Facility of communication, and cheapness of transportation are matters of primary importance in the business of every country; but under the existing circumstances of the United States they call for the earliest & most efficient exertions of government. The good condition of the post roads, especially where they happen to connect places of landing on the rivers & bays, and those which run into the western country, will conduce exceedingly to the cheapness of transporting and the facility of obtaining raw materials, fuel & provisions.

But the most useful assistance perhaps, which it is in the power of the legislature to give to manufactures and which at the same time will equally benefit the landed & commercial interests, is the improvement of inland navigation.

Three of the easiest and most important operations of this kind are the improvement of the communication between New York, Connecticut, Rhode Island & Boston by cutting a passage thro the penninsula of cape Cod, the Union of Delaware and Chesapeak bays by a canal from the waters of the former to those of the latter, and the junction the Chessapeak bay & Albermarle sound by uniting the Elizabeth and the          .[53] The accomplishment of these and other objects of the same nature seem likely to afford greater & more various aids to our growing manufactures than any other measure, that has occured to the Secretary in the investigation, which he has been directed to make.

A further ⟨measure⟩ to promote the cheap transportation of raw materials & provisions presents itself in the abolition of the duty of Tonnage imposed on coasting vessels.[54] This appears to be a burden on the produce of lands, as substantial as if it were imposed on working waggons, and seems hardly consistent with sound policy.

The principal productions of the fisheries may not improperly be considered as articles of the nature of manufactures, & the remainder are of great Utility as raw materials or cheap & wholesome food but as the means of encouraging that important branch of trade have been refered by the house to the Secretary of State,[55] it is unnecessary and improper to enlarge upon it here.

The regulation of inland bills of exchange, so as to ensure due caution in drawing them and strict punctuality in paying them, must have a favorable effect on the purchases of raw materials &

53. Space left blank in MS.
54. The current tonnage was imposed under "An Act imposing duties on the tonnage of ships or vessels" (1 *Stat.* 135–36 [July 20, 1790]).
55. On August 9, 1790, the House had "*Ordered*, That the representation from the General Court of the Commonwealth of Massachusetts, on the subject of the Whale and Cod Fisheries, together with the several papers accompanying the same, which lay on the table, be referred to the Secretary of State, with instruction to examine the matter thereof, and report his opinion thereupon to the next session of Congress" (*Journal of the House*, I, 296).

Jefferson's report on the fisheries was not submitted until February 4, 1791 (*Journal of the House*, I, 370).

sales of manufactured Articles in a country so extensive as the United States.

The ability to place funds with celerity and ease in every part of the Country for the purchase of raw materials and provisions is a matter of great importance to the manufacturer. To afford the accommodation of a general paper circulation of the nature of Bank Notes, payable with absolute certainty in specie on demand, is therefore very desirable. This benefit will immediately result from a national bank, & from ⟨such arrangements⟩ of Government with that ⟨Institution as soon⟩ as it shall be erected, as may give an universal circulation to their cash notes.[56]

The want of sufficient capital being deemed one of the principal difficulties, in a national view, with which the manufactures of the United States have at this time to contend a steady pursuit of such measures as will give full and unfluctuating value to the public funds appears of the utmost importance to the increase and prosperity of American Manufactures. Having enlarged upon the beneficial circulation that ever grows out of a well founded national debt in the report upon public credit, which he had the honor to make in January last, the Secretary conceives it sufficient at this time to repeat his thorough convictions of what is therein stated on that point.

The ⟨Importation of⟩ raw materials and ingredients, and of colors, drugs & other articles necessary to complete manufactures, free of duty, is an encouragement of obvious propriety, generally considered; but when it is remembered, that the principal nations of Europe afford this aid to their manufactories, and that we are to meet them, as competitors, in our own and in foreign markets, it appears to be almost indispensible. Proceeding, it is presumed, on these principles the legislature have been pleased to exempt from impost a number of articles of the nature above described,[57] thereby giving their sanction to the principle here contemplated. An extension of this exemption further than has yet taken place particularly to include, cotton &

56. At this point Coxe wrote several additional sentences which because of the disintegration of the MS cannot be read.

See "Second Report on the Further Provision Necessary for Establishing Public Credit (Report on a National Bank)," December 13, 1790. "An Act to incorporate the subscribers to the Bank of the United States" was not approved by the President until February 25, 1791 (1 *Stat.* 191–96).

57. See note 49.

hemp, the Secretary humbly conceives to be necessary to success in the business of manufactures.

The particular value to the U.S. of improved implements and machinery for manufacturing, and the inducements to export those we have already obtained or may hereafter procure, which the interest of our competitors obviously creates, ⟨seem to⟩ render a penalty for such exportations an eligible m⟨easure.⟩ It is manifestly proper to guard carefully against extending this ⟨fur⟩ther than is absolutely necessary to prevent a deprivation of any particular implement or machine, lest in the formation of the law, the export trade of well known articles, applicable in manufactures, may be unfavorably affected.

Besides the measures for the encouragement of manufactures, which it appears eligible that the legislature should pursue there are some of considerable importance which fall more immediately within the sphere of the other branches of government and on which for obvious reasons arising out of the nature of those measures, the Secretary refrains from enlarging.[58]


## ALEXANDER HAMILTON'S FIRST DRAFT OF THE REPORT ON THE SUBJECT OF MANUFACTURES [59]

Treasury Department ⎱ [60]
the          1790.  ⎰

The Secretary of the Treasury, in obedience to the order of the house of Representatives of the fifteenth day of January last, has

[to be left out—or pro last read 1790]

58. This paragraph does not appear in H's first draft of the Report.
59. Df, Hamilton Papers, Library of Congress.
Approximately one third of this draft is a clerk's copy of Tench Coxe's draft of this Report. Several additional pages are also in the clerk's handwriting. There are queries and comments in the margin and additions and interlineations to the text in H's handwriting and in an unidentified handwriting, possibly that of Tench Coxe. All material in H's handwriting is printed in italics; that in an unidentified handwriting is bracketed.
Words which were underlined for emphasis in the MS are printed with underlines in this draft of the Report.
60. Internal evidence indicates that H's additions and corrections for this draft were prepared between January 27, 1791, and February 4, 1791.

applied his attention, at as early a period as his other duties would permit, to the subject of Manufactures, and particularly to the means of promoting such as will tend to render the United States independent on foreign Nations for military and other essential supplies.

*Stands*

The expediency of encouraging manufactures in the United States,

*Stands*

                                                  *pretty*

'tho recently deemed very questionable, appears at this time to be ^generally admitted.[61] *There are nevertheless still persons, who* ~~entertain a less favourable opinion of them than~~ *are less inclined to affording them patronage than may perhaps consist with real good policy.* ~~It is~~ *Their*

                       [most proper ~~fittest~~]

*argument against it is—that Agriculture is* ~~the true~~ *object of pursuit in the United States; that labour laid out in the improvement of our waste lands will be more productive than in any other way—that it is always best to leave human industry to its natural course; that* ~~to attempt to~~

                                            *an*

~~divert it from the channel in which would flow of itself into any~~ ^*other*

                       ~~naturally~~ ^*of itself*

~~is to turn it more~~ *it will* ~~always~~ *flow* ^*into that channel where it finds*

             *employment    consequently*

*the most profitable* ^~~objects~~*; that* ^*all attempts to divert it from this to another tend to divert it from* ^*more to less beneficial objects; that manufactures can only grow out of a full population and that the high price of labour in this Country, from an opposite situation, forbids an advantageous competition with foreigners in the article of manufactures; which therefore can only succeed if at all by such restrains & burthens on foreign importation as will give them a virtual monopoly;*

              *the*

          *is* ^*for* ~~the~~ *community*

*that it* ^*better* ^*to procure* ~~from foreigners~~ *manufactured articles from*

*other countries*                     *its*

~~foreigners~~ *with the* ~~prof~~ *surplus products of* ~~our~~ *soil at the cheapest*

                                            *its*

*rate than to give a higher price for them to workmen of* ~~our~~ *own, who would be more* ~~usef~~ *usefully employed in producing the materials of exchange from the* ~~land~~ *cultivation of the earth.*

                                         *attentive*

*There is so much of* ~~trut~~ *truth in these positions that an* ~~careful~~ *eye*

---

61. At this point a page has been inserted, at the top of which H wrote and crossed out: "The objections usually opposed to the encouragement of manufactures."

*ought to be had to them in every step of our progress towards*
[the Attainment of manufactures.]
~~becoming a manufacturing people~~. *But though they are very proper*
*considerations to moderate; they are not such as ought to extinguish*
        *political*     *in the main,*
*a zeal for manufactures. All* ‸*theories, however true* ‸*become perni-*
                 *numerous*
*cious when pushed to an* ~~certain~~ *extreme. They all admit of* ~~certain~~ *ex-*
*ceptions and qualifications; in discerning which the wisdom of a*
    [manifested.]
*government* ~~it~~ *is* ~~shown~~

 *It is true for instance that agriculture, the best object of the atten-*
*tion of almost every country is peculiarly so of ours; but it does not*
[it should be our sole pursuit, nor that]
*follow that* ‸*it will be* ~~will~~ *injured or impeded nor that it may not*
       ~~prudent~~
*even be promoted by a reasonable attention to manufactures.*

 *A principal mean of promoting agriculture is to extend and as far*
      *extensive*
*as possible to render steady and certain the demand for that* ~~sup~~ *sur-*
*plus which the labour of the farmer is capable of producing. This*
*demand must depend on two circumstances; the wants of those classes*
*of our own*
*of* ‸*citizens who are not engaged in the culture of the soil; and the*
*wants of foreigners. The first, as far as it goes, is a certain dependence;*
    *a*     *one*
*the last is* ‸*more precarious* ‸. *To increase that* ~~source of~~ *demand, which* [dele:
*is the most certain is evidently desireable; and the most direct mean* source of]
*to this end is to multiply the number of manufacturers. These must*
*of course derive their subsistence fuel, and the raw materials for*
*their various fabrics from the cultivators of land. Provisions, Flax,*
*hemp, wool, cotton, iron and a variety of other articles will find* *particularly*
*their*     *uniform*    *in*    ~~wool and~~
~~then~~ *most constant and most* ~~certain~~ *vent* ~~in in~~ ‸*an extensive scene of* *cotton*
*domestic manufactures. Perhaps indeed it may be affirmed that the*
*abundant*
~~extensive~~ ‸*production of some of these articles must grow out of*
*such a sience.*

 *It has been observed, that the foreign demand for the surplus pro-*
     [in some degree]
*ductions of our soils is to be regarded as* ‸*a precarious one. This arises*

*from an ~~very~~ obvious cause. It is a ~~prima~~ primary object of the policy*

themselves
*of ~~every~~ most nations to be able to supply ~~itself~~ with subsistence for*

their own          for
*~~its~~ inhabitants and raw materials ~~in~~ their own workmen. And it is presumeable from the ~~app~~ manifest propriety of this policy, that it will obtain more and more. Already the demand for foreign supply of such articles in several countries is rather casual and occasional than usual or constant. How far ~~it~~ or how soon it may become ~~in~~ the case*

It is not ~~dissented~~     however
*in others is not ~~easily~~ to be foreseen. ~~nor will it be~~ affirmed ˄ that we have at any time heretofore experienced ~~a stagnation~~ from the opera-*

an injurious
*tion of that principle ˄ ~~an~~ stagnation in the demand for ~~some of~~ the*

particular inconvenience
*staple commodities of our country ~~and~~ nor that any ~~thing~~ of the kind*

in future.
*is seriously ~~to be~~ apprehended ˄ ~~hereafter~~. Nevertheless, the fact which has been remarked is of a nature to beget reflections ~~calculated to~~*

leading to a
*~~inspire~~ ˄ ~~a desire~~ desire of diversifying the objects of our labour and industry; and, as it applies to ~~of~~ our agricultural interest, of increasing*

internal       of
*the sources of ~~domestic~~ consumption ~~for~~ the products of our ~~soil~~ lands.*

the of our present citizens
*It is likewise perhaps true in a general sense that ˄ labour ˄ employed in converting waste lands into cultivated farms is more profitably employed than in other ways. Yet this is hardly to be admitted as universally true. There are certain fabrics in which a given capital*

bestowed on
*and a given quantity of labour will produce more than if ~~employed in~~ Agriculture. And when the variety of human talent is ~~considered~~*

strongest and
*adverted to—when it is considered that minds of the ˄ most active powers for their proper objects fall below mediocrity and labour*

if              results
*without effect ~~when~~ confined to incongenial pursuits; that the ˄ ~~effects~~ of human enterprise and exertion are immensely augmented by the*

their objects;
*diversification of ~~its objects pursuits~~; that there is a reciprocal reaction*

*upon each other*
of the various species of industry ˄ mutually ~~beu~~ benefical ~~to each other~~
and conducive to general prosperity ~~it is natural to conclude~~ it must
appear probable that the interest of a community will ~~mo~~ be most
effectually promoted by diversifying the industrious pursuits of its
*members*
~~citizens~~; and by so regulating the political œconomy as that those who
have been peculiarly qualified by nature for arts and manufactures
may find the encouragement necessary to call forth and reward their
peculiar talents. It is a position which seems to carry its own evidence,
*along*
with it, that the Nation whose citizens have attained to eminence and
perfection in the greatest number of useful employments will be
found at once the most independent and the most respectable.

~~The positions positions which suppos~~
The considerations which recommend the leaving the industry of
a people to its natural course are so far just that they ought to serve
as cautions to every government to refrain from endeavouring by
violent efforts or expedient, to produce an artificial change. ~~But they~~
~~are so far it would be to allow them an undue weight~~ But they ought
not to deter from pratronising ~~the~~ and ~~encourageme~~ encouraging by
moderate methods the introduction of any branch of industry for
              *an*        ~~a natural tendency~~
which there is discovered to be ~~a particular~~ aptitude ˄ in the situation
of a country. Men are so much governed by habit and a spirit of imi-
   *is*              *induce*
tation that it ˄ not always easy to ~~make~~ them to adopt the simplest and
most obvious improvements in the ~~m instruments and~~ means which
*are accustomed to*
they ˄ employ in their ordinary occupations. And how much less is
    *counted upon*
it to be ~~expected that they will of themselves without invitation and~~
                            *spring up*
~~encouragement turn to new and untr~~ that new arts will ~~be introduced~~
                          *from*
~~into~~ a community as early as may be its interest, ~~by~~ the voluntary
movements of individuals, without invitation or encouragement from
the government. Distress from want of employment in other ways
may after ~~a~~ length of time beget them; but the progress towards the
desireable changes would probably be slower than they ought to be.

                               *make*

*This may not only be inferred from the natural* ^*byass* *of the human mind but it would be to be looked for from the actual state of things*

                              *certain        in*

*in other respects. The progress made by* ~~particular~~ ^*nations* ~~by~~ *arts and manufacturing and the free intercourse established by commerce*

                *them & those*

*between* ~~different~~ *countries in which the like arts & manufactures do*

     *prevail*

*not* ~~obtain~~ *would preclude their introduction into the latter without the aid of their governments. Every attempt towards it would be defeated by the impracticability of maintaining a competition with*

              *had        acquired*

*those who* ^*already* ~~possessed~~ *so great a superiority in the business. Hence the expediency and necessity of the interposition of Government in certain cases to give a new and more beneficial direction to the* ~~de~~ *industry of its citizens.*

    *The objection deductd from the high price of labour in this*

                                 *one,    especially*

*Country against our success in manufactures is a weighty,* ~~perhaps~~

                               *costly*

~~decisive~~ *when applied to the finer and most* ^~~precious~~ *kinds. But there are circumstances which diminish its weight and seem to afford an assurance that many very* ~~extensive~~ *useful and extensive ones may be prosecuted with advantage.*

     *growing      raw materials*

    *The* ^*cheapness of* ~~provisions which is likely to increase the growing cheapness also of raw materials~~ *the trivial taxes* ~~and duties~~ *(compared*

     *those of*

*with* ^*other countries)* ~~which an American workman pays, the exemption from tythes and from corporation restraints~~ *which are paid by the Citizens of the United States; the exemption from tythes and corporation restraints* ~~and the heavy charges of importing rival the~~

                  *great    labour-saving*

~~extensive ac~~ *the* ^*agency of* ^~~labour saving~~ *machines, which has been so much extended by late inventions and improvements and which by diminishing the necessity of manual labour materially lessens the effect of disproportion in the prices of it—& the heavy charges of importing rival articles from abroad, even independent of the duties* ~~are~~ *laid on their importation—are circumstances which go far towards counterballancing the advantage of the superior cheapness of labour*

*in*
~~in the e~~ other countries.

There are other considerations which may serve to shew that the
rate of labour is less likely to be an obstable to the success of manu-
                         supposed          Some
factures than may have been ~~apprehended~~. ~~Many~~ branches of them
are conducted wholly or in a great degree in the U States and in other
countries in private families and at hours that would otherwise be
unemployed. And in this respect there is an advantage in favour of
                                  [of the]                [the body of]
                            [of a part, less luxurious habits]    ~~remainder of~~
this country arising from the more easy situation of its yeomanry   [less
                           [stronger dispositions]                  luxurious
~~which~~ affording greater leisure for collateral pursuits: ~~And~~, in other   habits]
branches, in certain parts of the Union, wages very little, if at all
exceed the rates, which successful manufacturers in Europe pay in   Qr
                              And it
the same business. ~~Women also are known to It~~ may ~~also~~ be added
that women in ~~the~~ some kinds of fabrics perform at a cheap rate the
work which in other parts of the world is executed by men. Nor has
it been found impracticable in some cases to substitute ~~with adv~~
*with*
~~to~~ ~~good~~ effect the services of Children. It is one and no inconsiderable
                                                                  the
recommendation of manufactures that they give occasion to exertion
of a greater quantity of industry, even by the same number of persons, inhabitating a place, in which they prevail, than if they did not
                       [peculiarly]
exist; and from that cause alone promote the wealth of a community.
                                  produce
They in many instances ~~rate~~ rather ~~promote~~ additional effort than
change the course of labour.

                                     addition
There are two ~~general~~ reflections which occur, in ~~relation~~ to what
has been said, on the point in question. One is that there are certain
                                       [populated]
parts of the United States which are becoming thickly inhabited and
the inhabitants of which increase notwithstanding emigrations to
other parts. It may be expected that the increasing populousness of
        ~~regions~~
those districts cooperating with the cheapness of subsistence will
every day lessen the force of the objection drawn from the price of

*labour as it applies to them. The other reflection is, ~~that a strong~~*
*~~expectation may reasonably be entained~~ that if this country should*
prosecution of
*exhibit the countenance of a serious ~~encouragement to~~ manufactures*
*there is room for a strong expectation that considerable numbers of*
*European workmen will be induced to transplant themselves to the*
*United States. The higher price of labour, where it exists, ~~would be~~*
*~~a material inducement~~; the superior cheapness of provisions, the com-*
*paritive lightness of taxes would tend to render their condition here*
it
*so much preferable to what is, that it can only be required to make*
*the advantages of it known and to afford a certain prospect of em-*
foreign
*ployment, to secure a numerous accession of valuable artists. ~~from~~*
*~~abroad~~.*

*~~If experience be consulted~~*

*In this circumstance also may be perceived a considerable resource*
*for obtaining the hands necessary for manufactures without diminish-*
naturally
*ing the number of those which would ~~otherwise~~ be employed in*
~~which they are calculated to afford to~~ by the demand they create for
*Agriculture. The advantages of the Landholder ~~in furnishing~~ raw*
manufacturer—
materials, subsistence, fuel and other supplies to the ~~workmen~~ the
are in habit of giving
they ~~tend to give~~ to                          by promoting the
support which the fisheries ~~derive from them by their~~ consumption
which is to be derived from them
of articles drawn from the ocean—the assistance given to external
their inducing
commerce by ~~promotoing~~ the importation

Should the United States decline or omit to encourage manufactures their local situation will subject them to some peculiar disad-
[productions of their soil,]
vantages. Their ~~commodities~~ which are generally very bulky, will
sustain, in the freight and other charges of exportation to their distant
foreign Consumers, a proportionate deduction; and, as the equality
[settlements of ~~the~~]
and moderation of individual property and the ~~great of certain of~~ unimproved lands occasion an unusual demand for coarse manufactures,
a corresponding weight of expence will be imposed on all their sup-

plies. In seasons of profound peace these circumstances occasion an immense annual deduction from the gross value of their productions; but in the time of a war, that shall involve their principal carriers, the charges of exportation on some of the most bulky raw materials, perhaps the most profitable, must become a grievous burden to the farmer, if the introduction of factories should not be previously effected.

~~It is unnecessary to suggest to the~~ [~~wisdom of the~~] ~~house~~ The
                                              [in employment]
~~sound~~ policy of pursuing such measures as will retain‸at home the active capital, which will certainly flow, with due œconomy, out of
                        [intelligent]   *cannot admit of question.*
the affairs of an industrious, and‸~~sensible~~ people,‸That Manufacturing, in a considerable degree, is necessary to this purpose appears, highly probable, since we know not of any great maunfacturing nation, however inconsiderable its agriculture may be, that does not abound with money; nor is there any instance of a country which does not manufacture, that can retain its specie, however blest its
                                        *The importations*
soil or abundant its sources of the precious metals. ~~The reason is~~
                                        *invariably*
~~obvious. The importations~~ of manufactured supplies‸~~incessantly~~ drain the merely agricultural people of their wealth. Hence it is that the West India islands, the soils of which are the most fertile; and the
*which* [in the greatest degree]      [and Bullion;]            [almost]
Nation ~~that~~‸supplies Europe with Coin‸enchange to a loss with‸every country in the world. In further illustration of this point it may be observed, that undisputed Statements [62] in a principal manufacturing Country of Europe render it more than probable that their exports
                      [have not for many years]
including their various fabrics‸~~never~~ exceeded one third of the gross

62. On a separate sheet of paper in the MS of this draft there is a note in Coxe's handwriting which reads:

"* this note is not to be copied.

"Mr. Pitts Statement to the house of commons in May 1790 placed the exports of G. B. at £ 18,513,000 of wch. British Mans., he said, were £ 13,494.000. The imports he said were £ 17,828,000. The Duke of Portlands Statement in 1783 was £ 54,000,000 as the Value of all the Manufs. made, i.e consumed & exported. There is no doubt of their increase since 1783."

The material to which this note refers is not found in Coxe's draft of the Report. Under the circumstances it seems logical to assume that Coxe's draft does not constitute his only substantive contribution to this Report.

value of their Manufactures. Had they entirely neglected this domestic branch of trade, and had they as freely consumed foreign articles
*presumeable that their*
similar to those they make for themselves, it is ~~evident that national~~ *situation would exhibit a very different aspect from that which it now wears.* ~~and individual poverty~~ must ~~have been the consequences~~. That the
[have]                                    *such a*
United States ʌheretofore felt the inconvenience of ~~that~~ situation in a very great degree is a matter of notoriety. To prevent the increase,
[among]
and gradually to diminish the evil was ʌthe objects of the house, it is humbly presumed, in the resolution, which calls for this report.

[See after] Altho agricultural employments are, generally speaking, the most proper for the great body of the inhabitants of these states, yet when the variety of human talent is duly remembred, and it is considered, that minds, of the strongest and most active powers for their proper objects, may fall below mediocrity, or labour without effect, if confined to incongenial pursuits, it will appear unwise so to arrange our political œconomy, as to impel to agriculture the whole body of the people. It is interesting to the prosperity and advancement of the United States that those, who have been peculiarly qualified by
[and manufactures,]
nature for ~~the useful~~ arts ʌshould find the encouragement necessary
[and reward]
to call forth ʌtheir various talents. All employments, that are compre-
[organized]
hended in the general plan of a well-~~formed~~ community, were doubtless intended to be pursued, and that nation, whose citizens have attained to facility and eminence in the greatest variety, will be found at once the most independent and the most respectable.

If ~~a~~ doubts should remain of the expediency of encouraging manufactures in the United States an appeal to the ~~substantial~~ Evidence of facts may be safely made. The house may be respectfully reminded, that those parts of the Union, in which Manufactures have most strikingly encreased, have recovered in the greatest degree from the injuries of the late war, and that those states, which have given the most liberal encouragement to this branch of trade, are now among
[which]
the most flourishing. Nor is this less manifest in the states, ~~that~~ ʌpossess extensive bodies of vacant Land, than in those that are most numerously populated.

*It And with regard to*

~~It may be usful in a survey of this subject to advert~~ to the capacity
of the United States in the business of Manufactures, ~~especially as it
was the opinion of a former period, not very remote, that they were
incapable of any thing considerable in this branch of trade. To a body~~

*a strong argument may be drawn from the*

~~as accurately informed as the honorable house it is unnecessary to
adduce proofs, that a very~~ considerable number of Manufacturers,

*who*

in a great variety of branches have already established themselves
in the United States, not a small part of whom carry on branches
depending entirely on manual labor. It may be reasonably argued that
what has succeeded in so many instances, notwithstanding the disadvantages supposed to exist, may succeed in many more. ~~The cheapness
of provisions, which is likely to encrease, the trivial taxes and internal~~   [introduced before]

[an American]

~~duties (compared with those of other countries) which a workman
pays, the exemption from tythes and from corporation restraints, the
growing cheapness of raw materials, together with the heavy charges
of importing rival Articles, have produced this success, and promise
the same advantage to all prudent and oeconomical attempts to~~

[factories]

~~establish even handicraft manufactures of articles in general Use. But
when it is remembred, that the great objection to American manufac-~~

[of the]

~~tures (the price of labor) is in the most valuable branches obviated
by the agency of fire or by that of water, or by that of labor saving~~

[except in fabrics of the finest kinds,]

~~machines moved by fire, water, or hand a doubt of success cannot
be entertained~~.

But the rate of labor, it is believed, will not be found on considera-   [before]
tion so weighty an objection, as it is by some supposed to be. Many
branches are conducted wholly or in a great degree in the United
States and all other countries by the thrifty industry of private
families, in hours that would otherwise be unemployed. The wages

[branches]

in others, do not exceed, in some parts of the Union, the rates which

[business.]

successful manufacturers in Europe pay in the same branches. Women

the

are known to perform the work, in making of some kinds of fabrics, which in other parts of the world, is executed by men. This useful

*may be added.*

habit may be extended, and the labor of Children It is moreover a reasonable expectation, that European workmen will be induced; by the supposed high rates of labor, wherever they really exist, to transplant themselves from that consideration to the United States.

[transpose]
[error—introduced afterwards in its proper place]

After these preliminary observations, which have been rendered as brief as the nature of the subject would admit, the immediate object of the Resolution of the honorable house remains to be considered.

Capitals it is urged are wanting in this young country for manufacturing establishments. This seems to be no more, than an unduly confined assertion of an obvious and comfortable truth—that the opening affairs of this rising country afford profitable objects for more capital than it has yet acquired. It is true as well with regard to

do

foreign Commerce as Manufactures else why the American Merchants import so largely upon credit. That it is also true with regard

[actual]

to agriculture, our millions of uncultivated acres fully prove. The past

nevertheless

success of many branches of manufacture shew that our own industry and funds, if wisely directed, may be advantageously applied to them. But when the European Manufacturer and Capitalist shall be ac-

[present & encreasing]

curately informed of the situation of this country, of the cheapness of provisions and raw materials, of the duties on the importation of his European fabrics and the exemption of our own, of the cheapness of mill-seats and building—when he shall advert to the expences of freight and insurance with which his commodities are loaded and the facility of establishing the great labor-saving-works by water and fire, he must be convinced that no profit can accrue in Europe adequate to what must follow a well conducted establishment with a suitable capital in many parts of the United States. [After these preliminary observations, which have been rendered as concise as the nature of the Subject would admit, the immediate Object of the resolution of the house remains to be considered.] *Hence an accession of foreign Capital may be expected in aid of our own. But it ought*

the account

*also to be taken into acco that a new and very considerable Capital has been brought into activity by the* ~~means which have been adopted for~~ *provision which has been made for the public Debt.*

*It remains at present to take into view the particular means by which the* ~~reference~~ *intention of the House in their reference on the subject of this report may be fulfilled.*

Among the means devised by the European nations to encourage manufactures <u>protecting duties</u> have been very generally adopted. It cannot be unobserved by those, who are engaged in these pursuits, nor will it escape the notice of those capitalists, and workmen who may intend to transfer their property and business to the United States, that the duties already imposed by the legislature 'tho principally for the purposes of revenue, afford very considerable and certain advantages to the American Manufacturer. Tho it may be ~~very~~ doubtful whether general additions to these duties be necessary further to encourage the manufactures of the United States, yet, it is humbly conceived, a few articles may be very properly aided by a moderate encrease. Among those in View is Sail Cloth which is important to defence, to domestic and foreign commerce, the fisheries
[the source of]
and, as ~~it relates to~~ ∧the raw materials, to agriculture likewise.

<u>Prohibitions of rival articles,</u> or duties equivalent, frequently present themselves in the laws of foreign nations. Tho this measure, in most instances, may be of doubtful propriety in the United States, it appears to merit consideration in regard to particular Articles. From the present flourishing condition of some manufactories of military supplies, such as Gunpowder, leaden and iron ball, iron cannon and cartridge paper it may not be deemed hazardous, in a season of profound peace, to encrease the duty so as to prevent the Importation of them. Besides warlike stores there are certain Articles manufactured from materials with which the United States abound, that do not appear unfit subjects of excluding duties. Among the objects here contemplated are <u>Malt liquors,</u> spirits made from grain of every sort *Qr.* and from fruit, (excepting that made of the grape,) the oils of sea (1) and land animals and of flaxseed, the spirits of turpentine, snuff, chewing and smoking tobacco, starch and other things manufactured
                                    the
from such productions of ∧Earth and of the fisheries as are constantly exported in large quantities, which are encreasing on our hands, and for which a sufficient vent is consequently difficult to procure. The

wisdom of the house however will render them duly aware of the injuries, that may be occasioned by an indiscriminate and too extended ~~an~~ application of duties equivalent to prohibitions, should they be induced to impose them in favor of certain maunfactures necessary for defence, or highly and universally beneficial to the landed interest.

<u>Pecuniary</u> <u>bounties</u> upon home made articles have been tried in several European countries with great success. The linen branch in Ireland is a well known instance. But under the present circumstances of this country the Secretary cannot discover sufficient inducements to these expensive encouragements to justify a strenuous recommendation of them to the consideration of the legislature. This aid to manufactures however is less necessary at the present moment in the United States than in any European country, because their fabrics, being generally wanted for home consumption, are free from the heavy expences of importation, which rival foreign goods sustain to the amount of fifteen, twenty and twenty five per Cent on their value according to their bulk. But if it should on consideration be deemed inexpedient to grant bounties in money to encourage manufactures it may nevertheless appear adviseable to *devise some other method of aiding pecuniarily new undertakings, and to institute rewards and other* encouragements for the introducers ~~introduction~~ of new and useful ~~inventions~~ A ~~m~~ manufactories arts machines and secrets, not before carried on or known ~~known or~~ possessed in the United States. ~~reward certain great and useful promoters of them by other means. The United States having a very large quantity of unappropriated lands the Secretary humbly submits to the house the propriety of setting apart the quantity of five hundred thousand acres of good quality and advantageously situated for the purpose of rewarding the first introducers or establishers of new and useful manufactories, arts, machines, and secrets not before possessed, known or carried on in the United States. The objects here contemplated and the mode of applying this landed fund will be more clearly explained by the plan contained in the paper [A]~~ [63] ~~which accompanies this report. A measure of this~~ Something of this kind besides its more direct effects nature would evince to the manufacturers of Europe the disposition

63. See note 52.

of the legislature to encourage and reward them, and would afford
to persons, who may transfer their capitals and establishments to the
United States, a certain tho not an immediate compensation even in
unsuccessful instances. *The manner in which this may be done will
be submitted ~~in the~~ hereafter.*

In addition to ~~these~~ rewards for the Importation of manufacturing
Machinery, and secrets of great value, acts may be passed, if suf-    (3)
ficiently warranted by the extraordinary utility of the object and the
difficulty of attaining it, *and* ^*if*^ *within the compass of the powers of
the government* granting to the introducers such exclusive privileges
for a term of years as would have been secured by patent, had they
been the inventors. Public advantage, if derived from each in an equal
degree, will justify this favor to the one as well as to the other, and
the successful practice of the principal manufacturing nations of
Europe establishes the prudence of the measure.

As a substitute for pecuniary bounties on particular articles, sufficiently beneficial to the landed interest to merit that expensive and
inconvenient encouragement, the revenue may be calculated to assist
them by diminishing the use of rival, tho in some instances different,
commodities. Thus the duties on ardent spirits may ~~be rendered~~ ^serve as^ a
virtual bounty on beer, ale and porter and the impost on foreign
spirituous liquors ^as^ an encouragement to those made at home. By careful attention to regulations of this nature, it is believed, very effectual
aid may be given to our manufactures without any hazard of public
inconvenience or injurious frauds. An examination of the Articles imported for ~~circumspection~~ ^[consumption]^ in the United States, and of the capacity of our manufacturers to make succedance for them out of
our own produce, and imported raw Materials will suggest many
objects, to which, it is supposed, this idea may be advantageously
applied.

A drawback of the amount of the duty on the raw Material on the
exportation of manufactured Articles is a measure recommended by
policy, and rendered in some degree necessary by the practice of ^those^
nations, who will hold a competition with us in foreign Markets.

*This idea has been pursued in the bill*[64] *which lately passed the H of R in re-*
ᴧThe duty on Molasses, ~~if the idea here suggested should meet the~~
*spect to*
~~approbation of the legislature, might be allowed on the exportation~~
*It may perhaps be extended to*
~~of American rum~~, that on Muscovado Sugars on the exportation of
    to                                          to
refined;ᴧthat on Cocoa on the exportation of Chocolate and ~~in~~ such
other instances as shall admit due security against deception and
fraud, the danger of which is the only objection that occurs to this
mode of encouragement.

The admission of the tools and implements of their trade and the
household furniture of manufacturers, free from import duty, is a
regulation, which the legislature have already been pleased to make
in their favor,[65] in common with other emigrants. The continuance
                             [highly]
of this exemption appears to be perfectly safe andᴧpolitic.

The promotion of friendly intercourse and fair trade with the
indian Tribes will have a favorable effect upon some valuable
branches of Manufacture, the raw materials for which are derived
                                     *as well*
from the western Country. Towards these ends the wisdom ~~of the~~
                   *as of the Legislature*
~~legislature and~~ of the Chief Magistrateᴧhave been already ~~successfully~~
*and will doubtless continue to be so till they are completely attained.*

[ (the<br>western<br>posts) ]

directed; ~~but some objects of great consequence to the indian trade~~
~~and consequently to the manufactures dependent on it remain to be~~
~~obtained. The pursuit of them however rests upon considerations of~~
~~so much more Importance than any which arise on the present topic,~~
          *intimate the relation between those objects &*
~~that~~ It is sufficient merely to ~~present~~ them ~~to the attention of the~~
~~house, as connected with~~ the subject of this report.

Facility of communication, and cheapness of transportation *are ob-*
*jects which concern all the domestic interests of a community; but*
*they may perhaps be mentioned without impropriety as* ~~immediately~~
*connected with the prosperity of manufactures.* ~~are matters of pri-~~

---

64. On January 27, 1791, a bill, entitled "An act repealing, after the last day
of June next, the duties heretofore laid upon distilled spirits, imported from
abroad, and laying others in their stead; and also upon spirits distilled within the
United States, and for appropriating the same," passed the House of Representatives (*Journal of the House*, I, 365). During the following spring it became
law (1 *Stat.* 199–214 [March 3, 1791]).
65. See note 49.

~~mary importance in the business of every country: but under the~~
~~existing circumstances of the United States they call for the earliest~~
~~and most efficient exertions of government.~~ The good condition of
the post roads, especially ~~places of landing~~ where they happen to
[places of landing]
connect ͟on the rivers and bays, and those which run into the western
country, will conduce exceedingly to the cheapness of transporting
and the facility of obtaining raw materials, fuel and provisions. But the
most useful assistance perhaps, which it is in the power of the legislature to give to manufactures and which at the same time will equally
benefit the landed and commercial interests, is the improvement of  (4)
inland navigation. Three of the easiest and most important operations
    *which occur at this time*
of this kind ͟are the improvement of the communication between
New York, Connecticut, Rhode Island and Boston by cutting a
passage thro the peninsula of cape Cod, the Union of Delaware and
Chessapeak bays by a canal from the waters of the former to those of
                                    *of*
the latter, and the junction ͟the Chessapeak bay and Albermarle sound
by uniting the Elizabeth and [Pasquotank rivers.] The accomplishment of these and other objects of the same nature seem likely to afford greater and more various aids to our growing manufactures than
                *than can perhaps be devised.*
any other measure, ~~that has occured to the Secretary in the investiga-~~
~~tion, which he has been directed to make~~.

    A further measure to promote the cheap transportation of raw
materials and provisions presents itself in the abolition of the duty of
Tonnage imposed on coasting vessels.[66] This appears to be a burden
on the produce of lands, as substantial as if it were imposed on working waggons, and seems hardly consistent with sound policy.
        ~~Other~~
    *And however*
    ~~However~~ ͟true it may be that other ~~most~~ *more urgent provisions*
*ought to postpone awhile enterprises of this nature; it seems not un-*
*useful to contemplate them in advance as means to be resorted to as*
*early as circumstances shall permit.*

    Several ~~The~~ productions of the fisheries ͟may not improperly be
considered as articles of the nature of manufactures, and the remainder are of great utility as raw materials or cheap and wholesome

66. See note 54.

food. [Whalebone cutters, the makers of whips, umbrellas, stays, millenary, fishing tackle and philosophical apparatus consume whalebone, Ivory turners use the seahorses teeth, druggists, chemists, instrument makers, hatters, tanners, watchmakers, sadlers and shoemakers work up the skins and furs of various sea animals, shipbuilders, riggers, soap & candle makers, and leather dressers consume the oils or spermaceti, and the workmen and manufacturers are enabled to observe a more beneficial œconomy by the use of the oils in lighting their shops and houses and of the fish in their sustenance. Aiding the
[among the]
fisheries therefore appears to be a very safe and efficient methods of promoting manufactures.] but as the means of encouraging that im-
[specially]
portant branch of trade have been refered by the house to the Secre-
[would be]
tary of State,[67] it is unnecessary and improper to enlarge upon it here.

The establishment of impartial and judicious inspections, by which frauds upon consumers at home and exporters to foreign countries might be prevented and proper standards might be ascertained, would have a favorable effect upon the quality and character of our manu-
*The reputation of*                               *the*
factures. Flour in some ports and reputation of Pot-ash in others
*has*
have been established by that method. The same good name may be derived to those articles by similar means in all the ports of the
*are*          *the*      *laws*
United States from whence they usually shipt; and inspection may be advantageously extended to other commodities. The manufactory of Gun Powder, it is conceived, is now in a train to be perfected by placing it under this wholesome regulation and it is not to be doubted
*probably*
that reflection and time will suggest other objects.

The regulation of inland bills of exchange, so as to ensure due caution in drawing them and strict punctuality in paying them, must have a favorable effect on the purchases of raw materials and sales of manufactured Articles in a country so extensive as the United States.

The ability to place funds with celerity and ease in every part of the Country for the purchase of raw materials and provisions is a matter of great importance to the manufacturer. To afford the accom-

67. See note 55.

modation of a general paper circulation of the nature of Bank Notes, payable with absolute certainty in specie on demand, is therefore very desirable. This benefit will ~~immediately~~ result from a National Bank,
[that]
and from such arrangements of Government with ∧Institution, as soon as it shall be erected, as may give an universal circulation to their cash notes.[68]

The want of sufficient capital being deemed one of the principal difficulties, in a national view, with which the manufactures of the United States have at this time to contend a steady pursuit of such measures as will give full and unfluctuating value to the public funds
ut
appears of the ∧most importance to the increase and prosperity of American manufactures. Having enlarged upon the beneficial circulation that ~~ever~~ grows out of a well founded national debt in the report upon public credit, which he had the honor to make in Janu-
reiterate his
ary last, the Secretary conceives it sufficient at this time to ~~repeat his~~
the truth
~~thorough~~ convictions of ∧what is therein stated on that point.

The Importation of raw materials and ingredients, and of colors, drugs and other articles necessary to complete manufactures, free of duty, is an encouragement of obvious propriety, generally considered; but when it is remembered, that the principal nations of Europe afford this aid to their manufactories, and that we are to meet
[not only]        [but]
them, as competitors, ∧in our own ∧~~and~~ in foreign markets, it appears to be almost indispensible. Proceeding, it is presumed, on these principles the legislature have been pleased to exempt from impost a number of articles of the nature above described,[69] thereby giving their sanction to the principle here contemplated.

*It is worthy of consideration whether this exemption ought ~~to~~ not*
*Hemp*
*to extended to other articles and among the rest to Iron ∧Cotton ~~Hemp~~*
*bar*
*and raw silk. Our manufactories of ∧Iron seem to have attained a*
*degree of Maturity which leave them ~~nothing~~ in no danger of being*
*and may derive more*
*subverted by foreign Competition. They also derive aid ∧from the*

68. See note 56.        69. See note 49.

*extension of demand which is created by the effect of the encourage-
ments already given and those which may still be given to various
manufactures of iron and by the outlet for that article which is afforded by the East India trade. Accordingly the price of Iron has*
[in our lowest markets]
*risen of late years ,from sixty five to Eighty Dollars per Ton. It is
therefore presumeable that sufficient profi̶t̶s̶ will remain, if foreign
Iron is admitted into our market free of duty. While great additional*
by it
*encouragement will be given ,to the manufactures of that article.*

*The h̶e̶a̶v̶y̶ motive to the heavy duty which has been laid upon
Cotton professedly is to encourage the growth of it. But this pre-*
in
*supposes an internal demand for what is raised. While t̶h̶e̶ ,fact i̶s̶ t̶h̶a̶t̶*
very inconsiderable
*little if any such internal demand exists; s̶c̶a̶r̶c̶e̶l̶y̶ a̶n̶y̶ progress having*
yet
*been ,made in manufactures of Cotton except in private families in
the parts of the Country where it is raised for their own use. That*
[may retard & may even]
*duty consequently o̶n̶l̶y̶ t̶e̶n̶d̶s̶ t̶o̶ prevent the introduction of Cotton
manufactories without answering the purpose for which it is laid. It
even operates against that purpose; since it prevents the creation of*
such
*that internal demand m̶u̶ which must be an effect of p̶r̶e̶e̶x̶i̶s̶t̶i̶n̶g̶ manu-
factories. The way to the encouragement of the growth of the commodity seems to be first to encourage the establishment̶s̶ of m̶a̶n̶u̶-
f̶a̶c̶t̶o̶r̶i̶e̶s̶ o̶f̶ i̶t̶ those manufactories and to this a cheap & plentiful
supply of the raw material in the first instance is indispensable.*

*The same observations apply to Hemp, in a degree, & to raw silk
intirely. To Hemp, they apply with less force because there already
exist respectable manufactories of that material and because it is now
extensively cultivated so as to afford a more immediate prospect of
adequate and cheap supply. It is however probable that eventually the
growth of it will be most effectually encouraged by promoting a rapid
and vigorous extension of the manufacture of it. A̶n̶ e̶x̶t̶e̶n̶s̶i̶o̶n̶ o̶f̶ t̶h̶i̶s̶
e̶x̶e̶m̶p̶t̶i̶o̶n̶ f̶u̶r̶t̶h̶e̶r̶ t̶h̶a̶n̶ h̶a̶s̶ y̶e̶t̶ t̶a̶k̶e̶n̶ p̶l̶a̶c̶e̶, p̶a̶r̶t̶i̶c̶u̶l̶a̶r̶l̶y̶ t̶o̶ i̶n̶c̶l̶u̶d̶e̶,*
raw-silk,
*i̶r̶o̶n̶ ,c̶o̶t̶t̶o̶n̶ a̶n̶d̶ h̶e̶m̶p̶, t̶h̶e̶ S̶e̶c̶r̶e̶t̶a̶r̶y̶ h̶u̶m̶b̶l̶y̶ c̶o̶n̶c̶e̶i̶v̶e̶s̶ t̶o̶ b̶e̶ n̶e̶c̶e̶s̶-
s̶a̶r̶y̶ t̶o̶ s̶u̶c̶c̶e̶s̶s̶ i̶n̶ t̶h̶e̶ b̶u̶s̶i̶n̶e̶s̶s̶ o̶f̶ m̶a̶n̶u̶f̶a̶c̶t̶u̶r̶e̶s̶.*

(5)

The particular value to the United States of improved implements and machinery for manufacturing, and the inducements to export those we have already obtained or may hereafter procure, which the interest of our competitiors obviously creates, seem to render a pen-   ~~Quare?~~

[In doing this it]
alty for such exportations an eligible measure. ~~It~~ is manifestly proper
[regulation]
to guard carefully against extending the ‸ further than is absolutely necessary to prevent a deprivation of any particular implement or machine, lest in the formation of the law, the export trade of well
[un]
known articles, applicable in manufactures, may be ‸ favorably affected.

~~Under the existing circumstances of this Country~~ The foregoing
[are ~~suggested~~ detailed] *as introductory to more specific suggestions relatively to* ideas ~~are respectfully submitted as the constituent parts of a general~~
*in such particulars as appear*
[the]       [~~that shall be~~ adapted to the circumstances of the Country.]
~~plan for the~~ encouragement of ~~national~~ manufactures ‸ . The requisite aid to those ~~particular~~ branches, which are necessary for defence, or which may be deemed most essential to the Government and citizens
[may, after the preceding survey, be more accurately]
of the United States ~~are yet to be considered~~. [digested.]

The manufactory of Gunpowder has been rapidly advanced, and principally by individual exertions, within the few last years. Tho
[high]
it may be considered as established, yet its ‸ importance renders its extension through the Union very desireable. Sulphur, which is a ~~very~~ considerable ingredient in its composition, has been made liable to the non enumerated duty of five ℔ Cent.[70] No quantity of that article has yet been produced from internal sources. The addition of sulphur to the class of free goods appears therefore to merit consideration. It may be further observed, that another principal use of this commodity is in finishing the bottoms of Ships, a manufactory that cannot be deemed secondary to that of gunpowder, they being at once powerful instruments of defence, and the necessary vehicles of all the productions and all the supplies of the United States.

The annual importation of a certain quantity of Salt petre rough   *Qu:* (6)

70. See note 49.

[it is said,]
or refined, has been made,‸an indispensible obligation on one of the most successful East India companies of Europe.[71] This, it is understood, has been required with a view to assisting the manufacturers of gun Powder. The trade to China being now well established, a moderate regulation of this nature, duly proportioned to the Tonnage of each vessel, might perhaps be conveniently enacted. The United
ies
States not having factors established in other parts of the East Indies the requisition could not be reasonably extended to Vessels from any other than the port of Canton.

Leaden Ball and Shot employ but few hands and require little skill
[reasonably]
to make them, and therefore may be‸expected to succeed. To aid the exertions of the owners of lead mines the foreign commodity has been charged with a duty of one cent per pound, which may be safely extended, it is believed, to shot, ball and all the manufactures of this article. These are liable at present to the lowest rate of duty,[72] tho the foreign raw material is subjected to one of the highest, which
[directly]                                    the
operates‸to encourage the importation of‸foreign manufactures.

The brass founderies, that are already introduced into the United States, tho at present confined to common wares, may be considered as furnishing the future means of manufacturing ordinance of that
'tho
metal. In the new impost law,[73] iron Castings, and copper wares are rated at seven and one half per cent, those of brass are included in the non enumerated class, which pay the lowest duty. If this raw material
ingredient
be continued among the free articles, and copper (the principal‸in
[& lapis calaminaris (the component ingredients of brass) should]
brass) in pigs and bars‸should‸be added to that class, there appears to be perfect safety in placing manufactured brass in the list of wares subject to the duty of seven and one half per Cent. This metal being

71. The requirement covering the importation of saltpeter dates back to the founding in 1702 of the United Company of Merchants Trading to the East Indies (1 Ann., Stat. I, C. 12 [1702]). In subsequent years laws to extend and amend this requirement were enacted.
72. Before the "Report on Manufactures" was submitted to Congress, this recommendation was carried into effect by "An Act to explain and amend an act intituled 'An act making further provision for the payment of the debts of the United States'" (1 Stat. 198 [March 2, 1791]).
73. See note 49.

also used in the manufactory of some kinds of small arms, of instruments in the Arts and Sciences, and other useful articles the influence of the duty, which cannot be deemed high, will be extensive.

Musquets and all the class of small fire arms, swords and other military weapons of that nature, and the connected articles of surgical instruments and cutlery<sub>∧</sub>[in general] might be rated, it is conceived, without injury at seven and one half per C̶e̶n̶t̶<sub>∧</sub>[centum], Iron and Steel of which they are made, being among the most abundant p̶r̶o̶d̶u̶c̶t̶i̶o̶n̶s̶ o̶f̶<sub>∧</sub>[commodities in] the United States.

The several species of wood and timber, ordinarily used in cabinet work and ship building, are free of duty in foreign Countries, when imported in their national Vessels. Cabinet wares being in general use, and frequently exported; and the manufactory of ships being the most perfect in the United States, it appears both safe and politic to give the workers in wood that support, which other nations have universally extended to them. A further inducement to this regulation arises from its favorable tendency in regard to our Magazines of Ship timber. The encreasing scarcity and the growing importance of that article in the European countries admonish the United States to commence and systematically to pursue measures for the preservation of their stock.

In the enumeration of<sub>∧</sub>the several kinds of paper which are subjected to a duty of seven and one half ⅌ Cent, sheathing and cartridge paper are omitted. Being the most simple manufactures of that nature, and necessary to military supply, as well as the national shipping the addition of these to the specification appears to be<sub>∧</sub>re-commended by all the considerations that apply to the other articles.

The duty on nails, and spikes, however various in size and value is laid upon their weight. The effect of this is to reduce the impost on the smallest kind<sub>∧</sub>[nearly] [to the rate of non enumerated<sub>∧</sub>,] [goods] while the larger pay a considerable advalorem duty. Of the persons employed in this branch a great proportion are boys, whose early habits of industry are of importance to the community, to the present r̶e̶l̶i̶e̶f̶<sub>∧</sub>[support] of their families, and to their own future comfort. The raw material is a native

production of almost every state—the necessary fuel is abundant in
all. The addition [of a duty] ^Therefore of ~~74~~ ₱ ~~Cent~~ upon the value of
nails only, does not appear unworthy of consideration. *Upwards of a million & a half pounds of this article were imported in a year ending the 30th of Sepr last.*

Glue, Starch, hair powder, and wafers are left in the mass of non enumerated articles at five ₱ Cent. No manufactures are more simple. The first, like paper, is an entire œconomy of materials, which if not manufactured, must be left to perish. The three last are made, with the utmost ease, from the most abundant productions of the Earth. They all appear suitable additions to the class of Articles rated at 12½ ₱ Cent. In Europe they are generally objects of excluding duties, or expressly prohibited.

[qu:]

(7)

The progress, which has been made within a few years in the manufactory of Sail Cloth and other coarse linen articles, their importance in the equipment of fleets and in the appointment of armies, the universal capacity of the states to produce the raw materials, both flax and hemp, and the precious effects of the linen branch upon individual industry and domestic œconomy recommend all the fabrics of that kind, in a peculiar degree, to the protection of the legislature. To these considerations may be added the example of a more encouraging duty upon the principal maunfactures of cotton, which are rated, and with sound policy, it is conceived, at seven and a half ₱ Cent. There appears to be no hazard of injury from placing a little above non enumerated goods, two descriptions of merchandize, ~~the~~ cotton and ~~the~~ linens *of the coarser kinds*^ capable of being manufactured by the great labor-saving machines. *The sail cloth manufactured at Boston is said to be of a quality superior ~~quality~~ to any imported: And there is a respectable maunfactory of the same article at New London. Tow linnens and other household linnens are ~~pro~~ made in such abundance in different parts of the U States as already to maintain a successful competition with the rival foreign articles & to ~~to~~ occasion a diminution of their prices.*

It is not possible to do ~~complete~~ justice to the subject of this report without bringing into the view of the house those great instruments

74. Space left blank in MS.

of manufacture in the European Nations, labor-saving Machines. The United States, by the bountiful distribution of mill seats over the face

*the uncommon turn for mechanic arts observable in their citizens*

of their Territories and by~~their skill in mechanism~~, are peculiarly qualified for these profitable modes of manufacture. A fitness, no less peculiar, arises from the State and nature of their population. By the

[& climate] [by]

qualities of their soil~and~the activity of their Merchants they can

[~~obtain~~ procure]

~~command~~~the raw materials to which these machines best apply, on the most advantageous Terms. The requisite machinery is already

b

obtained: ~~But~~ the enterprise has hitherto appeared ~~appeared~~ too novel for individuals. The capital required is not inconsiderable and the risque of injury in the attempt consequently greater than a private person has yet ventured to encounter. Tis seldom adviseable for a government to interest itself in these undertakings, however promis-

[may be]

ing the calculations~, because they too often suffer in the execution of projects that would have been profitable to individuals. It is also true that a loan of capital to individuals, even upon indubitable

[which] [and cautiously]

security, is a measure, ~~that~~ should be very rarely~adopted, and that such aid should never be extended to objects of confined Utility. Yet there may be cases of such obvious safety & from which such extensive national benefits will certainly result, as to justify a deviation from those rules, by which a wise government will circumscribe itself in all ordinary instances.

*ation*

*It is submitted to the Consider~~able~~ of the House, whether it may not be expedient to institute some proper Board (which if judged*

*pre-*

*adviseable may consist of~existing officers of the Government) and*

*place in their disposal* ~~may~~

*to ~~vest in them all~~ the product of all such duties ~~as shall be laid either pursuant to the suggestions of this report or otherwise with a view to the~~ as it may be thought proper to lay with a view ~~not to revenue but~~ to the encouragement of manufactures only, to be applied by*

*such shall be generally*

*them to that purpose, in ~~such modes as in certain~~ ways ~~to~~ as be~desig-*

*to that*

*nated~~~to them~~ by ~~the~~ law.*

The species of encouragements, which are contemplated, are, to procure at the public expence for a limited time skilful manufacturers from ~~in~~ Europe ~~to be Europe~~ to be employed^ in aid of ^~~the~~ manufactories
                                                      the first or early attempts of the

                              r                in the U States. ~~first~~
which have been of^ shall be established ~~in their commencements~~.

~~There is g or first at in their first or early attempts~~ to ~~rew~~ induce the
                                                                proper
introduction of new inventions and improvements by ^~~rewards prop seasonably affording in~~ holding out competent rewards well timed and in the ways best calculated to give then effect— ~~&~~ to encourage
                                                                  endeavours
by premiums both honorary and lucrative, ~~to excel exertions~~^ to excel
                                              fabrication
in the production of raw materials and in the ^~~workmanship~~ of manu-
                                to undertakers^
factures: & perhaps to afford loans ^at a moderate rate of interest upon good security.

There is ~~good~~ reason to believe that the failure or slow progress of particular manufactures has been owing to the want of skill in the workmen employed; and it is not common for the capitals engaged
                    purpose of
to be equal to the ^procuring from abroad workmen of a superior kind. Here the auxiliary agency of Government seems to be wanting and in all probability would be very useful.

The idea of rewarding the introduction of useful inventions will probably be embraced without difficulty. But the success of attemps ~~int~~ in this way will evidently depend in a great degree upon the manner of conductin them. It is ~~conceiving~~ conceived that the placing them under some discretionary direction where they may be accompanied by collateral expedients will serve to give them the surest efficacy. It seems ~~scarcely~~ impracticable to apportion by general rules specific rewards for discoveries & improvements of unknown and disproportionate utility.

                                                          may be
The usefulness of premiums would probably be greater than can
readily
well be imagined. Their effect under the direction of private societies,
              confined
upon a very ~~narrow~~ scale, is known to have been considerable in a
                              then  ~~then~~
variety of instances. How much more ^may ^reasonably be hoped

*from them, proceeding upon public and more ample ~~extensive~~ funds,
under a judicious and liberal management. Premiums are of a nature
essentially different from bounties. The latter are applicable to the*
a correspondent degree of
*whole quantity of an article produced and involve ^proportionable
expence. The latter are confined to some particular excellence or
superiority either in relation to quantity or quality and ~~operable~~
operate only in a few cases; while at the same time they have the effect
of producing a general effort. They are therefore a cheap mean of*
whole
*stimulating the enterprise and emulation of a ^community.*

*With regard to loans they will serve to aid a defect of Capital, till
a manufacture shall have acquired maturity enough to ~~aid it~~ support
itself. While the public money so employed will neither be given*
rendered
*away nor ^unproductive to the govert.*

*All which is hum sum*

~~Whether that now contemplated may be deemed of a nature, that
will warrant the advancement of an adequate capital, is humbly submitted with the other suggestions in this report by~~

Alexander Hamilton
Secy. of the Treasury.

## ALEXANDER HAMILTON'S SECOND DRAFT OF THE REPORT ON THE SUBJECT OF MANUFACTURES [75]

The Secretary of the Treasury in obedience to the order of the
House of Representatives of the fifteenth day of January 1790 has
applied his attention, at as early a period as his other duties would
permit to the subject of Manufactures and particularly to the means
tend to
of promoting such as will ^render the United States, independent on
foreign nations, for military and other essential supplies.

The expediency of encouraging manufactures in the United States,
~~though~~ not long since deemed very questionable, appears at this time

75. ADf, Hamilton Papers, Library of Congress.
Words which were underlined for emphasis in the MS are printed with underlines in this draft of the Report.

to be pretty generally admitted. The embarrassments, which have obstructed the progress of our foreign Trade, have led to serious reflections on the necessity of enlarging the sphere of our domestic commerce, and the success which has attended, ~~in certain valu~~ manufacturing enterprise, in ~~certain~~ some valuable branches, has evinced that ~~greater and more various success ought not to be despaired of~~ the obstacles to the extension of this species of industry are not so formidable as they have been apprehended to be.

There are nevertheless still patrons of opinions unfavourable to the encouragement of manufactures. The arguments which support these opinions are of the following nature.

In every country, Agriculture is the most beneficial and productive object of human Industry. In the United States this position derives ~~great~~ additional force from the immense tracts of waste lands still uninhabited and unimproved. Nothing can afford so advantageous an employment for capital and labour as the conversion of this wilderness into cultivated farms. Nothing can contribute so much as this, to the rapid increase of the population and real riches of the Country.

To ^endeavour to^ promote ~~and foster~~ the growth of manufactures by the ^extraordinary^ ~~particular particular~~ patronage and favour of the government is to endeavour by a misjudged and artificial ^misapplied^ ~~policy to turn aside the course~~ ^impulse to^ ~~of in~~ change the natural current of Industry from a more to a less ~~not~~ beneficial channel. It can scarcely ever be wise in ^a^ government to attempt to give a direction to the industry of its citizens. This, if left to itself, will under the guidance of individual ^private^ interest, naturally make its way wherever it can find ~~out its way to~~ the most profitable employment; and by such employment alone will ~~be~~ the public prosperity be most effectually advanced. The safest and soundest policy therefore is to leave it to itself.

This policy is not only recommended to the United States by considerations applicable to all ~~countries~~ ^nations^, but in a manner dictated to it by ~~an~~ the invincible force of ^a very^ peculiar situation. The smallness

of their population compared with their territory; the continual
allurements to emigration from the settled to the unsettled parts of
the country, the facility with which the less independent situation of   artificer
an artisan can be exchanged for the more independent situation of a
                            and other similar
farmer—these ~~circumspence~~ circumstances conspire to produce and
                                                            occasion
for a great length of time must necessarily continue to ~~produce~~ a
scarcity of hands for manufacturing occupations; and a correspondent
dearness of labour. These impediments, combined with a deficiency
of capital, forbid a successful competition with the manufacturers of
Europe. Extensive manufactures can only be the offspring of a re-
                                      the latter
dundant, at least of a full population. 'Till ~~that~~ shall characterise the
situation of this country, tis vain to hope for the former.

   If contrary to the natural and salutary course of things, a premature
                                                      fabrics
and artificial spring should be given to certain ~~manufactures~~, by ~~force~~
heavy duties, prohibitions, bounties or by any other forced and
violent expedients, this will only be to sacrifice the interests of the
community to those of particular classes. Besides the misdirection of
                                      the persons
labour, a virtual monopoly will be given to ~~those~~ employed on such
fabrics; and an enhancement of price, the inevitable consequence of
every monopoly, must be defrayed at the expence of all others. It
is far better that those persons should be employed in the cultivation
of the Earth, and that we should procure with the surplus products
of our soil ~~at the cheapest~~ the commodities with which foreigners are
                   on better terms
able to supply us ~~at a cheaper rate~~ and of superior quality.

   This theory has so much of truth in it, that its principles ought
                out
never to be ~~ought~~ of the view of the Legislators of this Country. And
while its extremes ought to be qualified in practice by the exceptions
to which every general ~~theory~~ theory is subject, its maxims ought to
                                        any other
serve as cautions against all ~~its~~ extremes of ~~a different~~ kind. If they
                                  countenance
do not persuade, ~~us~~ that all legislative ~~aid~~ ought to be witheld from
particular branches of industry which appear to stand in need of it

pursuits

—they ought at least to inculcate, that it should be afforded with moderation and measures—that the real aptitudes in the state of things

and ameliorations
for particular improvements ʌ should be carefully consulted—and that

ʌ nurtured
these should be ʌ developped by gradual systematic and progressive

gigantic
sanguine
excessive

vehement
efforts rather than forced into maturity by violent and disproportioned exertions.

In order to a right judgment of the policy, which ought to

govern
be pursued in relation to the encouragement of manufactures in the

take a concise view of

take as con-
cise a view
as may con-
sist with
perspiccuity

United States, it will be useful to pass in review the considerations
which serve to limit the generality of the maxims that stand opposed
to it.

must without hesitation            readily to be
In the first ʌ place, though it is will readily ʌ be ʌ admitted that if a

supply
Nation Agriculture, as the great and primary basis of national ʌ prosperity, as the immediate source of subsistence and nourishment to

fountain
man, as the origin of those materials, which principally give employment and support to other kinds of labour, as involving, perhaps,
a state most favourable to the freedom and independence of the

science
human mind is intitled to the first a preeminence in the system of
political œconomy; yet it is not equally evident that this species of

is, as alleged,
industry ʌ as alleged, is more productive in any substantial meaning of

The reality of this
the term, more productive than every other. It is not verified by

ʌ accurate                        An a general argument
any ʌ detail of facts and calculations; & The argument, commonly
made use of to prove it, is rather quaint than satisfactory. It is said
that in the productions of the soil nature cooperates with man and

the labour of
that the effect of their joint labour must be greater than that of ʌ man
alone. But this appears by no means a necessary inferen inference. It

a work
is very conceivable that the labour of man alone bestowed upon ʌ an
object requiring great skill and art to bring it to perfection, may in

the estimate of value, be more productive, than the labour of nature and man combined, when directed towards more simple operations and objects. And ~~accordingly~~ when it is considered to what an extent the ~~mechanical~~ <sup>mechanical</sup> powers ~~of mechanism~~ are rendered ~~auxiliary~~ <sup>subservient</sup> to the prosecution of manufactures, little more than the quaintness of the hypothesis remains. ~~Accordingly it~~ It is certain, that higher wages are given to workmen in most manufactures, than to labourers employed in Tillage, and that in a ~~greater~~ number of cases the undertaker enjoys <sub>a larger</sub> ~~greater~~ profit upon his Capital than the ~~landho~~ proprietor of land upon his; both which are indications of superior productiveness. And it is not less certain that nations which have <sub>arrived to eminence</sub> ~~made a considerable progress~~ in manufactures abound more in wealth and resources than those which have made little progress in them.

In the second place it may be observed that nothing can be a greater error than to consider ~~manu~~ Agriculture and manufactures as standing in opposition to each other ~~or~~ <sub>inferring</sub> ~~and to suppose~~ <sub>and to suppose</sub> that the growth of the one will impede the progress of the other.

If a country were to be ~~supposed~~ <sup>imagined</sup>, having a <u>given</u> extent of territory, requiring a given number of persons to cultivate it, <sub>possessing exactly that number of inhabitants,</sub> and intirely shut out from foreign Trade there could be little room for question that it would be more its interest <sub>and more for the advantage of agriculture</sub> to have <sub>the necessary</sub> ~~the requisite such a~~ proportion of its inhabitants employed <sub>exclusively</sub> in furnishing manufactures for the whole society ~~as were requisite for that purpose~~, than to have them all employed as cultivators. ~~and there would be as little room~~ <sub>for doubt</sub> ~~that its agriculture that the mass~~

This would not arise, either, from ~~the~~ <sup>an</sup> absolute impracticability ~~of~~ <sup>to</sup> the cultivators of land to procur~~ing~~<sup>e</sup> ~~those manufactures for themselves; for it is very conceivable~~ by their own labour, the manufactures of which they might stand in need: For it is <sub>supposeable</sub> ~~conceivable~~ that the same persons in each family might till the ground and make the

fabrics ~~which were~~ requisite to the supply of indispensable wants:
Or if there are exceptions to the possibility of doing this, they are not
numerous.

But ~~it w~~ <sup>in any country, it is evident that its</sup> if such a state of things existed ~~any where, it would
quickly be discovered that it was the interest~~ expedient ~~to change it
—The~~ lands ~~in a country so situated~~ would be wretchedly cultivated
and the whole community <sub>miserably</sub> ~~badly~~ supplied. The want of a <sup>proper division</sup> ~~subdivision~~
of labour would prevent improvement and skill in every thing—
Husbandry would be in a rude state and the arts in a still ruder. The
inducements to make the land productive would be circumscribed to
the necessary subsistence of each family. ~~in the simplest The~~ Neither
the gratification of those appetites & inclinations which are incident
to a state of greater improvement nor the desire of accumulating
wealth, by the exchange of ~~thos~~ a surplus <sup>won by hard labour</sup> produced from the soil,
would prompt exertions to obtain such a surplus. ~~While~~ The inter-
ruptions and delays arising from the necessity of passing <sub>frequently</sub> <sup>~~continually~~</sup> from one
kind of labour to another and the want of <sub>that</sub> skill in execution which
can only be acquired by a continual application to the same ~~object~~
business ~~renders~~ <sub>would</sub> diminishes the effect of it in every operation to
which it <sub>was</sub> ~~is~~ applied: ~~All~~ <sub>And</sub> the important inventions, by which machinery is made to abridge and perfect labour, would be excluded;
~~from~~ <sup>through</sup> the want of adequate motives to excite ~~the~~ a spirit of discovery
and contrivance.

It is readily perceived, that in ~~a country so situated~~ <sup>such a state of things</sup> not only the
total mass of labour would be much less than if its inhabitants were
subdivided in due proportions into cultivators <sup>and Artizans</sup> mechanics and manufacturers—but the mass of agricultural industry would also be incomparably less—The superior cultivation of so much of the soil
as was ~~cultivated~~ <sup>occupied</sup> in one case would greatly overballance in produc-

ness
tivel the intire quantity occupied in the other, ~~ease~~ under circumstances of very inferior cultivation.

Whence are to
~~And from hence~~ the following inferences ~~may~~ be drawn—that it
be and consequently having waste and occupied lands
may the interest even of a state not fully peopled, to have a part of
withhold withdrawn the soil
its inhabitants ~~abstracted~~ from the cultivation of ~~land~~ to be employed
in mechanic and manufacturing ~~occupu~~ occupations and that the
withdrawing of such a state
~~abstraction of the~~ a part of the inhabitants ~~of a state, not fully~~ peopled
and consequently having waste and unoccupied lands, from agricul-
to those occupations only not
tural ~~pursuits~~ is not, necessarily injurious to agriculture but may be
also be affirmed
essential to its prosperity. And it may be ~~safely presumed~~ that in a
country situated as has been supposed the natural interests of the
community would of themselves subdivide it into the different classes
of cultivators mechanics and manufactures.

Accordingly ~~shewn~~ history and experience shew that in very early
stages of national progress ~~long before the land~~ mechanic and manufacturing arts grow up. Villages are formed from distance to distance
by the collection of in which collect
~~in which~~ those who devote themselves to such arts, ~~collect~~, for the
supply of the neighbouring country, which repays their industry with
produce
the ~~progress~~ of the soil. ~~And it is~~ This takes place from two causes
the palpable advantages of a ~~subdivision~~ separation and distribution of
in the faculties
industrious pursuits and the diversity of dispositions and ~~talents of
mankind~~ of the human mind. The importance of giving scope to this
diversity, ~~by varying the objects~~ by diversifying the objects of national industry will deserve particular notice in another place.

long standing parts of a country
It is a remark of ~~all time~~ that the ~~country~~ in the vicinity of ~~a~~ manufac-
manufacturing towns are much better cultivated and more thriving tures occa-
for ~~great~~ sion calls fo.
than those remote from them; which is to be accounted by the facil- new objects
on better terms of Agricul-
ity of obtaining those supplies for which the husbandman has occasion ture

Elsewhere

and
ˌby the advantage of a near market for the sale of whatever surplus he may have to dispose of. This fact no affords no inconsiderable illustration of the beneficial influence which the industry of the towns has upon that of the country or in other words which the ~~progress~~ establishment of manufactures has upon the progress of agriculture.

It ~~were a~~ is manifestly an error to consider the prosperity of Agriculture as in proportion to the quantity of land occupied or even to the number of persons who occupy it or to both. It is rather to be considered as in a compound ratio to the quantity of lands occupied and to the degree of improvement.

But a reflection naturally arises here, that ~~although~~ however true
                                vacant & fertile            is
ˌwhich possessing large tracts of ~~uncultivated~~ territory ~~was~~ at the same time
it may be that a state ˌsecluded from foreign Commerce would find
                                                    diverting
its interest and the interest of Agriculture in ~~devoting~~ a part of its
                                        from
population, ~~which might be find employment in~~ tillage, to manufac-
es
tur~~ing pursuits~~ —yet ~~wil~~ it will not follow that the same thing can be advantageous to a community ~~in~~ which having such tracts of
                at the same            ˌat the same
vacant territory, ~~can also have the benefit of~~ ˌtime by means of
external
~~foreign~~ commerce procure ~~from~~ foreign nations on good terms all
                        of        ˌhas
the fabrics ~~necessary for~~ which it ~~may have~~ ˌoccasion.

This point requires therefore a further and more particular examination.

If the free system were the prevailing system of nations, if industry and commerce were generally left to their natural course, the arguments which dissuade a Country situated like the United States
        eager
from the ˌpursuit of manufactures would be more difficult to combat than they now are. It is not certain that they might not safely be permitted to serve as a rule of conduct. Each Country would then have the full benefit of its peculiar advantages to compensate for its disadvantages. That which was invited by its particular situation to direct its attention exclusively to agriculture would be able to furnish the products of the earth on so much better terms than the coun-

try which was engaged in an extensive scene of manufactures as to
be able to maintain a beneficial exchange of subsistence and raw
materials for manufactured articles.

But this natural ballance is disturbed and in great measure destroyed by the general policy of nations. The spirit of monopoly
which ~~governs most countries~~ is the governing one interrupts that
free exchange which would distribute to each party its proportion
of benefits; and seconded in some instances by a great superiority
                            ^pecuniary
~~bet~~ both of industrious skill and of ^capital would subject any nation
which should implicity follow the dictates of the opposite system
to disadvantageous very incompatible with its property. It has, with
regard to a Country situated like the United States, in a great degree,
the same effect, as an exclusion from foreign commerce.

England, for instance, from which we derive our principal supplies
of manufactured articles forbids the importation of our grain into
her home market except when its price there is beyond ~~what is con-
sidered~~ what is considered as its average or ordinary rate; [76] and thus
                     constantly
while we ~~continually~~ take from her her manufactures, she only occasionally takes from us our grain.

Again she excludes us either from bringing from her West Inia
possessions those products which we stand in need of from thence or
from carrying thither those of our products of which they stand in
                                                            her
need. ~~thus not only ex~~ It is true that she brings to us in ~~our~~ own ships
all the different articles produced in her Islands and takes from us
              likewise
in her own ships ^all ~~the articles of the~~ our productions requisite to
their supply; but by preventing us from being our own carriers,[77]
she reduces us in this branch of trade to a commerce merely passive,
deprives us of all ~~her~~ share in the profits of the carrying trade whatever they may be and substantially of a participation in the profits
of the advanced price both of the commodities of her Islands in our
markets and of our commodities in the markets of her Islands. While

76. The most recent British regulation regarding the importation of grain
was contained in 31 Geo. III, C. 30 (1791).

77. 28 Geo. III, C. 6 (1788) confirmed earlier Orders in Council regarding
trade with the West Indies.

in the trade between her European dominions and the United States she shares fully with us in every species of advantage.

With regard to the fisheries which from situation may be considered as the staple of a part of the United States, ~~such~~ the British regulations amount to a prohibition of all but the finer oils ~~of w~~

notwithstanding the heavy

which find admission into Great Britain ~~in spite of the enormous~~ duty of        78

If from England our eyes are turned towards France we shall not see a more favourable Picture. It ~~is the standing~~ has been long the

wheat &

standing policy of France to exclude the introduction of ^ flour into every part of her dominions. Relaxations in this policy from particular exigencies occasionally take place but it is the prevailing

e

one.[79] And th~~is~~ exportation of this great staple of our country meets with with a still more formidable bar from the regulations of France than of Britain.

France permits us to bring from her Islands in our own ships Rum melasses          and to carry thither in our own ships          but

78. This and subsequent spaces left blank in MS by H.

Jefferson had described these regulations in the report on the fisheries which he had communicated to Congress on February 4, 1791 (*ASP, Commerce and Navigation*, I, 8–22). According to the 1787 consolidated table of rates (27 Geo. III, C. 13 [1787]), foreign train oil, blubber, or fish oil paid £18 3s. per tun of 252 gallons, whereas the same quantity from the British fisheries paid £1 15s. 3d. British spermaceti was entered duty free, while that of foreign fisheries paid 17s. 8d. per hundredweight if "coarse and oily," and 8d. per pound if fine.

79. The policy of temporary suspension of impost restrictions in favor of necessary provisions was stated in Article 17 of the decree concerning the French colonies that was passed by the National Assembly on March 28, 1790, and published by royal proclamation on April 9, 1790. Article 17 states: "Examinant les formes suivant lesquelles le pouvoir législatif doit être exercé relativement aux colonies, elles reconnoîtront que les lois destinées à les régir, méditées & préparées dans leur sein, ne sauraient avoir une existence entière & définitive, avant d'avoir été décrétées par l'Assemblée nationale & sanctionnées par le Roi; que si les lois purement intérieures peuvent être provisoirement exécutées avec la sanction d'un gouverneur, & en réservant l'approbation définitive du Roi & de la Législature française, les lois proposées qui toucheraient aux rapports extérieurs, & qui pourraient en aucune manière changer ou modifier les relations entre les colonies ou la métropole, ne sauraient recevoir aucune exécution, même provisoire, avant d'avoir été consacrées par la volonté nationale; n'entendant point comprendre sous la dénomination des lois les exceptions momentanées relatives à l'introduction des substances qui peuvent avoir lieu à raison d'un besoin pressant, et avec sanction du gouverneur" (Duvergier, *Lois*, I, 164–65).

our
~~flour or~~ wheat & flour cannot be admitted there either in ~~our~~ our own or in French bottoms—~~nor~~ more than Sugar Coffee or Cocoa can be brought to us in the one or in the other.[80]

Our ~~The~~ fisheries by a late edict of the National Assembly are placed on a footing still more disadvantageous than that upon which it stands in respect to Great Britain.[81]

And though
yet being charged with a duty of          per quintal, which amounts to ₱ a prohibition ~~since~~ this apparent distinction in our favour is merely nominal. The state of things in France is not likely to afford us the same advantage with regard to our fine oils as results from the state of things in Great Britain.

Another Regulation of the National Assembly of France has placed our Tobacco Trade upon a very disadvantageous footing.[82]

80. After the American Revolution, regulations concerning the commerce of the United States with the French West Indies were established by the "Arrêt du conseil concernant le commerce étranger dans les îles françaises de l'Amérique" of August 30, 1784. Section 1 of the *arrêt* opened new entrepôts to foreign ships. Sections 2 and 3 stipulated the products which might be imported into these entrepôts. These sections read in part as follows:
"2. Permet S. M. . . . aux navires étrangers, du port de soixante tonneaux au moins, uniquement chargés de bois de toute espèce, même de bois de teinture, de charbon de terre, d'animaux et bestiaux vivants de toute nature, de salaisons de bœufs et non de porcs, de morue et poisson salés, de riz, maïs, légumes, de cuirs verts en poil ou tannés, de pelleteries, de résines et goudron, d'aller dans les seuls ports d'entrepôt désignés par l'article précédent, et d'y décharger et commercer lesdites marchandises.
"3. Il sera permis aux navires étrangers qui iront dans les ports d'entrepôt, soit pour y porter les marchandises permises par l'art. 2, soit à vide, d'y charger pour l'etranger, uniquement des sirops et taffias, et des marchandises venues de France." (Isambert, *Recueil Général des Anciennes Lois Françaises*, XXVII, 460.)
81. On January 24, 1791, during discussion of the general tariff act, the National Assembly adopted the rate of five livres per quintal for fish oils from America whether in French or American ships. Later the same day this was amended and a rate of twelve livres per quintal was substituted. On March 2, 1791, the question was raised again, and a tariff of six livres per quintal assessed (*Archives Parlementaires*, XXII, 470–71, 475; XXIII, 602, 611).
82. Discussions concerning a new decree adjusting the duties on tobacco began in the National Assembly in February, 1791. The decree, passed March 1, 1791, is printed in *Archives Parlementaires*, XXIII, 595. According to this decree the duty on tobacco imported into France in foreign ships was twenty-five livres per quintal, while the duty on tobacco imported in French ships was eighteen livres, fifteen sous. This duty was incorporated into the "Tarif des Droits d'Entrée" passed by the National Assembly on March 2, 1791 (*Archives Parlementaires*, XXIII, 618–19).

The Tobacco of the United States may be carried to France in French or American bottoms but if carried in the former, it is liable to a duty of only          if carried in the latter it is liable to a duty of          a difference which prohibits its exportation in vessels of the United States; and by narrowing the field of commercial enterprise and substituting a less eligible mode of transportation is calculated to incumber and injure the trade in that article.

Upon the whole it may be affirmed that ineligible as is the footing upon which our Trade with Britain is carried on it stands‸ at this time upon a still less eligible footing in regard to France.

Spain too and Portugal have regulations injurious to our Trade in Grain. Flour

With regard to the Northern Powers of Europe they are in general our competitors in furnishing the articles which constitute our Agricultural staples.

And as to the most Southern ~~Powers~~ parts of Europe, the avenues to them have been almost intirely closed by the hostile dispositions of the Barbary Powers.

This view of our external situation is not designed by way of complaint of the policy by which our trade ~~it~~ is embarrassed. It is the right of every independent nation, where not restrained by Treaty, to pursue its own interest, in its own way; so that it does not violate any positive right of another. Tis for itself to judge how far its ~~meer~~ practice may counteract its own object, and, by aiming at too much, may occasion the loss of advantages actually possessed‸ or easily attainable and which by a more natural policy might have been long preserved ~~as~~ in the one case, and with certainty acquired ~~for~~ in the other.

Its sole intention is to shew that the policy of other countries interferes ~~withou~~ our deriving the full benefit of our Agricultural Industry, ~~placing~~ places us under serious disadvantages in exchanging the surplus of our soil for those foreign productions and manufactures of which we‸ now stand in need, and renders more precarious than might be wished the obtaining‸ ~~of a regular~~ in foreign markets a ready and regular vent for that immense increasing surplus which ~~the inevitable progress~~ must result from the inevitable progress of population and settlement in the United States.

 though                                        ought to be
And ~~while~~ no overweening anxiety for the future ~~is~~ indulged—
though                          even
~~while~~ the experience we have had of an‸increasing demand ~~even for~~ ~~those very staples with w~~ for some of our principal productions ought to guard us against a degree of solicitude, which might mislead
                                  powerful causes
—though we ought fully to appreciate those‸which counteract, in our favour, ~~those~~ the regulations tending to abrige the advantages of
                                          the U States
our situation and which are likely to continue to render ~~us~~ the granary of Europe in those emergencies which ~~its~~ the interests and passions of its various subdivisions will not fail to reiterate—Yet it
          us
~~ere~~ becomes‸to consider seriously of the means of rendering our prosperity less dependent on the projects and vicissitudes of foroegn Politics.

It is a consolation that, already the measures which have borne hard upon our Trade have accelerated internal improvements which
                              condition
upon the whole have bettered our situation. To diversify, develope and extend those improvements is the surest and safest method of indemnifying ourselves for any inconveniences which those or similar measures have a tendency to occasion, and will be found the most effectual retaliation for any unkindness of disposition (if any there
                        dictated
has been) which may have produced them. If Europe will not take the products of our soil, upon such terms as we ought to expect, let us endeavour as fast as possible to cease to have occasion for her manufactures. These considerations shew that in pursuing the free system we should not have the full benefit of its principles from the want of reciprocity—and the policy of foreign countries has in a great measure the effect of an exclusion from foreign Trade.

The best of all expedients for the encouragement of Agriculture
                  a certain & sufficient
is to secure ~~an extensive home~~ market for that surplus ~~which~~ produced by the labour of the farmer which remains after supplying the wants of himself and family.

The foreign market is necessarily a precarious dependence for the
vent of this
∧surplus. It is the effort of every nation to be able to supply itself
                                                    relate to
with articles of prime necessity, particularly those which∧ ~~constitute~~
its subsistence. Hence most nations ~~supply~~ ~~themselves~~ in ordinary
          furnish
times ~~supply~~ themselves with ~~aut~~ the principal products of the earth.
            extraordinary
Seasons of ~~particular~~ scarcity and times of war only oblige them to
resort to foreign ~~supply~~ assistance. And hence also the demand for
the surplus of a country merely Agriculture must be liable to injurious stagnations. Plentiful harvests and a state of pretty general peace
in the countries with which its Trade is carried on
∧are always likely to interrupt it. And while the wants of such a
country for manufactured supplies are pretty constant and uniform,
the demand for the commodities which it has to give in exchange is
liable to frequent fluctuations. And this will account for the fact
which has been already remarked namely that countries merely
Agricultural have seldom much active wealth being continually
of what they acquire
drained∧by those manufacturing countries with which they trade.

This being the case it is consequently of the highest importance to
secure an extensive domestic market for that surplus. The superior
steadiness and certainty of such a market by rendering the reward
of the farmer more certain is the strongest incement to his industry.

Towards the creation of this domestic market the establishment
and extension of manufactures ~~is~~ are indispensable. The manufacturer is a certain customer to the farmer for what he can spare and
in return furnishes him with what he wants. This is not the least of
the circumstances by which manufactures promote the interest of
Agriculture.

Another respect in which they do it is this—They not ~~not~~ only
render the demand for the surplus productions of the soil in general
                          or extend
more certain but they create∧a demand in cases in which [83]

83. No further material for this draft has been found. There are, however,
four pages of an outline in H's handwriting in the Hamilton Papers, Library of
Congress, which H apparently intended as a recapitulation of his second draft
and as an outline for his third draft of this Report. This outline reads as follows:

"Points

1 Agriculture most productive kind of Industry} Answered fully
  Not unproductive
  Society more revenue with manufactures than without it

2 Wrong for government to give a direction to interest *Private* interest will do all that is necessary } To be answered
  *This is to be deferred*

3 Obstacles to manufacturing in this country—
  1 Scarcity of hands (full population)    To be answered
  2 dearness of labour

4 Attempt would give an injurious *monopoly* causing enhancement of price. better to purchase *with surplus*    To be answered

Objections

Not true with regard to a County which has external Commerce } Answered (Monopolising system of Europe)

Conversion of wastes into cultivated felds must eventually be most advantageous Though revenue in the interval less capital in the end greater } To be answered

United States cannot succeed
  scarcity of hands
  dearness of labour
  want of Capital } To be answered
  Scarcity of Hands—
  Some districts populous
  women and children
  Machines
  occasional employment to classes otherwise occupied
  foreign emigrants

Create injurious monopoly better to purchase
  Cheaper augment value of surplus of land } To be answered

General position that (priv)ate Interest will do all. wrong to attempt to give a direction to Industry } To be answered

General Considerations

Advantange to Trade from more various market
Independence from possessing all necessary means internally

Particular consideration

Distance from Europe
Bulk of Commodities &c.

Kinds of manufactures which
U States ought to *aim at*

Usual means employed for encouragt
of manufactures

Specific means proper
*to be taken*

Manufactures tend to increase the mass of productive labour
  1 by promoting the division of it
  2 by giving an occasion to the extension of the artificial powers of machinery
  3 by enlarging the sphere of income out of which savings can be made to increase the national capital and the number of persons by whom they are to be made."

## ALEXANDER HAMILTON'S THIRD DRAFT OF THE REPORT ON THE SUBJECT OF MANUFACTURES [84]

The Secretary of the Treasury in obedience to the order of the House of Representatives of the fifteenth day of January 1790 has applied his attention, at as early a period as his other duties would permit, to the subject of manufactures; and particularly to the means of promoting such as will tend to render the United States, independent on foreign nations for military and other essential supplies.

The expediency of encouraging manufactures in the United States, which was, not long since, deemed very questionable, appears, at this time, to be pretty generally admitted. The embarrassments, which have obstructed the progress of our foreign trade, have led to serious reflections on the necessity of enlarging the sphere of our domestic commerce; and the success which has attended manufac-
                                                                            evinced,
turing enterprise in some valuable branches th has ~~evinced~~ that the obstacles to the growth of this species of Industry are, ~~at least~~, not insurmountable.

There are neverthess, still, respectable patrons of opinions, unfriendly to the encouragement of manufactures. The arguments, with which they support these opinions, are substantially of the following nature—

I       In every Country, say they, Agriculture is the most beneficial and productive object of human ~~labour~~ Industry. This general position, in its application to the United States, derives peculiar emphasis from their immense trats of land, still uninhabited and unimproved. Nothing can afford so advantageous an employment for capital and labour, as the conversion of this wilderness into ~~fruitful and~~ cultivated farms. Nothing, so much as this, can contribute to the population and real riches of the Country.

To endeavour therefore to accelerate the growth of manufactures,
                                                the
~~force and~~   by ~~an~~ extraordinary patronage of government is, in fact, to en-
~~art~~

84. ADf, Hamilton Papers, Library of Congress.
Words which were underlined for emphasis in the MS are printed with underlines in this draft of the Report.

deavour, by ^an ~~artificial~~ ~~power,~~ ~~or~~ ~~impulse,~~ ~~to~~ ~~change~~ ^force and art, to transfer the natural current of Industry from a more to a less beneficial channel. ^Whatever has such ~~This~~ a tendency must necessarily be unwise. ~~certainly~~ ~~certainly~~ ~~cannot~~ ~~be~~ ~~wise.~~ Indeed, it can scarcely ever be wise in government to attempt to give a <u>direction</u> to the Industry of its citizens. This, if left to itself, will under the ~~sharp~~ ^quick -sighted guidance of private interest naturally find its way^to wherever there is the most profitable employment; and by such employment ~~only~~ ^alone will the public prosperity be most effectually promoted. To leave it to itself ~~is~~ ^is, consequently,^ in almost every ~~situation~~ ^case the safest and ^the soundest policy.

This policy is not only recommended to the United States, by considerations, which^apply to ~~affect~~ all nations, but is, in a manner, dictated ^to them ^to ~~it~~, by the^ ~~invincible~~ ^irresistible force of a very peculiar situation. The smallness of their population compared with their territory—the continual allurements to emigration from the settled to the unsettled parts of the country—the facility with which the less independent situation of an Artizan can be exchanged for the more independent situation of a Farmer—these and similar causes conspire to produce, and, for a great length of time, must continue to occasion a scarcity of hands for manufacturing occupations, and ~~a~~ dearness of labour generally. ^A deficiency of Capital combining itself, ^With these impediments ~~a~~ ~~deficiency~~ ~~of~~ ~~Capital~~ ~~combines~~ ~~to~~ forbids a successful competition with the manufacturers of Europe. Extensive manufactures can only be the offspring of a redundant, at least of a full population. 'Till the latter shall characterize the situation of this country, 'tis vain to hope for the former.

^unseasonable and
If contrary to the natural course of things, an^ premature spring can be given to certain fabrics, by heavy duties, prohibitions, bounties, or other forced expedients, this will only be to sacrifice the interests of the community to those of particular classes. Besides the misdirection of labour, a virtual monopoly will be given to the persons employed on such fabrics; and an enhancement of price, the in-

evitable consequence of every monopoly, must be defrayed at the expence of all others. It is far preferrable, that those persons should be employed in the cultivation of the earth, and that we should procure with the surplus of our soil, the commodities, with which foreigners are able to supply us, in greater perfection, and upon better terms.

This mode of reasoning is founded upon principles just in the main; but frequently carried by those who ~~adopt~~ espouse them to an erroneous extreme. Carefully ~~guarding~~ attending to the exceptions by which they are qualified and limited, they ought to serve as cautions against extremes of an opposite kind. If they do not tend to convince, that all legislative aid should be withheld from particular branches of industry, which appear to require it, they at least inculcate, forcibly, that it ought to be afforded with moderation and measure—that the real aptitudes in the state of things for particular improvements and undertakings should be consulted with circumspection and care, and that even these should be unfolded, by gradual, systematic and progressive efforts rather than impelled into maturity by ~~violent~~ precipitate and ~~disproportioned~~ violent exertions.

But in order to an accurate judgment of the true weight of the objections which ~~oppose~~ are urged against ~~restrict~~ the encouragement of manufactures in the United States, it is necessary to take a concise view of the circumstances and considerations ~~which seem capable~~ which are to be found in the contrary scale.

Though it is readily to be admitted that Agriculture, as the primary and most certain source of national supply—as the immediate source of subsistence and nourishment to man—as the principal source of those materials, which give employment and support to other kinds of labour, as involving a state most favourable to the freedom and independence of the human mind, perhaps most conducive to one the multiplication of the human species, has intrinsically a strong claim to preeminence over ~~every~~ other kinds of industry; yet it is not equally evident that it is (as

in any substantial meaning of the term
~~has is~~ alleged) more <u>productive</u> than every other kind. The reality
of this suggestion has not been verified by any accurate detail of facts

the                                                are
and calculations; and ~~a~~ the general arguments which ~~is~~ are made use of to

are      subtil and paradoxical than solid or
prove it ~~is~~ rather ~~quaint than~~ satisfactory. ~~It is to this effect—that in~~
~~the productions of the earth nature cooperates with man, and that the~~
~~joint result of their united labour must be greater than the result of~~
~~the labour of man alone.~~

~~But this does, by no means, appear to be a necessary inference. It is~~
~~very conceivable that the labour of man alone bestowed upon a~~
requiring
~~work, of great skill and art to bring it to perfection may, in the~~
~~practical estimate of value, be more productive than the labour of~~
~~nature and man combined; when directed towards more simple opera-~~
~~tions and objects. And when it is considered to what an extent the~~
~~mechanical powers are rendered subservient to the prosecution of~~
~~manufactures, little more than the quaintness of the argument remains.~~
These may be divided into such as are made use of to ~~produce~~ prove
that the labour of ~~of~~ artificrs & manufactures is wholly unproductive
and                                   only
~~and that the labour~~ such as are designed to ~~the~~ shew that it is less
productive than that of Farmers or Cultivators. Of the first kind the
The principal of these
principal ~~They~~ are in substance to this effect—"Labour, which is
bestowed upon the cultivation of land, produces enough not only to
replace all the necessary expences incurred towards carrying it on and
to maintain those employed in the work—but to afford together with
the <u>ordinary</u> <u>profit</u> on the stock employed by the ~~favour~~ farmer, ~~to-~~
~~gether with the~~ a clear <u>nett</u> <u>surplus</u> or <u>rent</u> for the landlord or proprietor of the soil. But the labour of Artificers and manufactures does
nothing more than <u>replace</u> the stock which employs them, or in other
words, which furnishes materials tools and wages, and yield the
<u>ordinary</u> profit upon that stock. It ~~procures~~ produces nothing equiva-
lent to the rent of the landlord. Neither does it add any thing to the
value of the <u>whole</u> <u>annual</u> <u>produce</u> of the <u>land</u> or to the <u>annual</u> <u>value</u>
land and
of the <u>whole</u> <u>produce</u> of the labour of the country. Whatever additional value is given ~~into~~ to those parts of the produce of land which are

wrought into manufactures is counterballanced by the value of those other parts of that ~~produced~~ which are consumed by the manufacturers. It can only therefore be by <u>parsimony</u> not ~~but~~ <sup>by</sup> the positive
<u>productiveness</u> of their labour that the classes ~~and~~ of Artificers and
manufactures can in any degree add to the Revenue of the ~~country~~ <sup>community</sup>.

~~It cannot appear extraordinary~~ <sub>either,</sub> ~~that agriculture should be more productive than any other species of Industry, when it is considered that
in <u>that</u>, nature cooperates with man. The result of their joint labour~~ <sup>efforts</sup>
~~must be greater than that of the efforts of man alone"~~
which affirms the total unproductiveness of m ∽ labour

To this system <sub>it</sub> it has been ~~very properly~~ answered—that inasmuch
as manufacturing labour reproduces an equal value with that which
is consumed in carrying it on, and continues in existence the stock
or capital employed <sub>for that purpose</sub> ~~in it~~, it ~~cannot~~ <sup>ought not to</sup>, on that account alone, be considered as <sub>wholly</sub> unproductives:—That though it were admitted to be true,
as the system, <sub>in question</sub> supposes, that the ~~annual~~ consumption of the products
of the soil ~~was exactly~~ by the classes of <sub>artificers and</sub> manufacturers was exactly
equal to the additional value given by their labour to the materials
upon which it was bestowed; yet it would not thence follow that it
added nothing to the revenue of the Society or to the total value of
the annual produce of its land or labour. If the consumption ~~during~~ <sup>for</sup>
any given period ~~be stated at~~ <sub>amounted to</sub> a given sum and the additional ~~value~~
value of produce manufactured <sub>in the same ~~period~~</sub> ~~during that~~ period ~~at an equal sum~~ <sup>to a like sum,</sup>
the total amount in value of what was ~~produc~~ consumed and pro-
duced during that period, would be equal to the two sums, and consequently double the value of the ~~produce~~ agricultural produce
consumed. And though the value of what the Artificer or Manufacturer produces should at no time exceed that of his consumption,
yet there would be at every moment, in consequence of his labour, a
greater value of goods in the market, than would exist independent

of it. That ~~it ough~~ instead of saying that the consumption of Artificers
and manufacturers is equal to what they produce, it would be more
accurate to say that their revenue, or the fund acquired by the ~~value
of the~~ product of their labour and destined for their consumption was,
in an ordinary way, not more than equal to it. And, thence, it would
follow that all the savings of the more thrifty and parsimonious, and <sub>from</sub>
~~all~~ the surplus acquisitions of superior skill would be positive augmentations of the real ~~ven~~ wealth or capital of the community—ready to
give employment to a greater quantity of useful labour. That it is
only by similar savings that the cultivators of land can augment the
real revenue of a country: For the annual produce of the land and
labour of a society can be increased only in two ways—either by
some improvement in the productive powers of useful labour actually
existing <sub>within it</sub> or by some ~~augment~~ increase of its quantity. And since the
labour of artificers and manufactures, from being capable of greater
subdivision and ~~greater~~ simplicity of operation is ~~on those accounts~~
more susceptible of improvement in its productive powers, than that
of the cultivators of land, whether it be considered with regard to
~~either as it respects increase of skill in the results from an augemt~~ augmentation of skill or the facility of applying Machinery, ~~than that of
the cultivators of land~~ it will follow that the labour employed in Agriculture can in this respect have no advantage over that employed in
manufactures. And as far as concerns an ~~enlargement~~ <sub>increase</sub> of the quantity
of useful labour, this must depend essentially upon an increase of
Capital—which again must depend upon the savings <sub>that are made</sub> ~~of those of a~~ out
of the revenue of those who ~~manage or~~ furnish <sub>or manage</sub> that which is at any
time employed; whether in Agriculture or in manufacturing or in
any other way.

But while it has been thus contended that the labour of Artificers
and manufactures ought not to be considered as wholly barren and
unproductive it has been, at the same time conceded that it is not
equally productive with that of husbandmen ~~and~~ <sub>or</sub> cultivators; a position which has ~~had~~ <sub>obtained</sub> no inconsiderable currency in this country and

of
which being ~~in great~~ importance ~~as it~~ in its relation ~~of~~ to maxims of
                                                        distinct
public administration ~~effec~~ is not unworthy of ~~an~~ ᴧexamination of the
grounds on which it rests. One of the arguments made use of in
support of it is of so sufercial a nature that it shall be little more than
mentioned. It is to this effect. ~~That in nature~~ In the productions of the
soil nature (~~it is said~~) cooperates with man; and that the effect of their
joint labour must be greater than that of the labour of man alone. ~~But~~
It is sufficient to say that this
~~this~~ appears by no means to be a necessary inference. It is very conceivable that the labour of man alone bestowed upon a work requiring
great skill and art to bring it to perfection may in the practical
estimate of value be more productive than the labour of nature and
man combined when directed towards more ⟨si⟩mple operations and
objects. And when it is considered to what extent the mechanical
powers are made subservient to the prosecution of manufactures little
more remains than the quaintness of the hypothesis remains.

Another and the principal argument for the superior productiveness of Agricultural labour turns upon a concession of the fact that
manufacturing industry yields nothing equivalent to the Nett surplus
or rent of land.

In investigating this point
                  that which        in this inquiry is that it
~~The first thing which strikes the attention~~ᴧis the circumstance
at once strikes the attention that
which is supposed to constitute the superior productiveness of Agricultural labour seems to turn upon a distinction purely verbal. This
species of labour, it is said, besides replacing the expences of carrying
on the business, yields the ordinary profit of stock to the farmer (by
whom is ʈo be understood the actual tenant of the land) and a nett
surplus or rent to the landlord (who is the ultimate proprietor)—
                                of the business carried on together
While manufacturing labour only replaces the necessary expencesᴧ
                                      the
with the ordinary profits ofᴧstock employed, but without any such
nett surplus as is produced from land.
                                                          ᴧunder
But in fact, what is separated into two parts in the first case ~~and~~ᴧ
the heads of the ordinary profit of stock to the farmer and rent to
                                            second case
the landlord are nothing more than what in the ~~first place~~ is called

simply and singly "the ordinary profits of stock." To illustrate this idea, let it be supposed that there are two persons—one having, in money, Eight hundred Dollars the other two hundred dollars—Let it
further be supposed that the first with his eight hundred dollars purchases
a ~~farm~~ piece of land and lets it to the second, for a certain annual rent, who with his two hundred dollars ~~purchases~~ procures the requisite stock and utensils and hires the necessary labours for tilling and planting the ground ~~the land~~. Here it is evident that the whole Capital employed in order to the cultivation of this farm though belonging to two different persons is 1000 Dollars
—the surplus which remains to the tenant after defraying all ex- or ~~replacing~~ reimbursing pences, is the ordinary profit of ~~Stock or Capit~~ his stock or Capital of two hundred dollars and the rent which is paid to the landlord is the ordinary profit of his stock or Capital of 800 dollars: both to- gether are the ordinary profit of a capital of 1000 Dollars employed towards the cultivation of ~~the~~ a farm. ~~All fallacy or confusion~~ This conclusion becomes palpable if instead of considering that sum as an aggregate Capital ~~as divided into~~ consisting of two parts and belonging to two persons, it is considered ~~as one intire~~ under the aspect of one intire capital belong- ing to one person, who ~~himself cultivates the f~~ is at once the Owner, and cultivator of the farm; an ~~union~~ association of character common in the United States.

Let it on the other hand be supposed that one person having in money a thousand dollars employs it in a particular manufacture. If the manufacture succeed it will defray or reimburse the expences of carrying it on and will yield the ordinary profit of a stock or capital of one thousand dollars employed in that way. If this capital had been owned by two persons who had united it in the prosecution of the same object, the profit ~~as in the case of landlord and tenant~~ would ~~have been~~ divided ~~been~~ between the two and would resemble what takes place in the other case, in relation to the landlord and tenant. Perhaps however a more exact similitude may be found in the case of two persons—one ~~who who is~~ being the lender of money to another who is the undertaker of a manufacture. What ever profit is made by the undertaker over and above the interest paid by him on the sum

borrowed and upon ~~whatever~~ <sup>any</sup> addition of capital which he may have
been able from his own resources to apply to the undertaking would
be the ordinary profit of his own labour skill and capital and the
interest paid to the lender would be equivalent to the rent paid to the
landlord. ~~In~~ The interest in one case and the rent in the other are the
ordinary profits of different stocks or capitals furnished <sub>one in land the other in money</sub> for carrying
on different businesses— ~~one in land the other in money~~ <sub>In one case,</sub> Land is the
Organ; ~~in one case~~ <sub>in the other</sub> gold and silver. ~~in the other.~~

The rent therefore of the Landlord so far from being a test of
~~superior~~ <sup>exclusive</sup> productiveness is not even a test of superior productiveness.
This <sup>last</sup> is a question of fact. To decide it <sup>it</sup> ~~it see~~ is necessary to examine
whether a given capital emplowed towards the <u>purchase</u> and <u>culture</u>
of a piece of land yields a greater surplus, ~~after defraying all expences~~,
than a like capital employed towards carrying on a particular manufacture, defraying in each case all necessary expences. This examination indeed is not a very simple or easy one. It involves details
numerous and complicated. But there is reason to believe that it
would not issue in a demonstration of the superior productiveness of
Agricultural industry.

In England the rent of the landlord is computed at about 3 ₱ Cent
on the value of his landed capital, which is itself computed at about
one third the gross product of the land. In the same country ~~it is~~
~~affirmed that~~ the average <sup>nett</sup> profit of manufacturing Capital is <sup>usually estimated at</sup> <sub>^</sub>ten per
Cent; which if true would be a <sup>strong symptom</sup> ~~proof~~ that manufacturing industry is <sup>there</sup>
more productive than Agricultural. This qualified mode of expression
is used because


~~A partial investigation~~
~~A slight investi~~
The <sup>result</sup> ~~relation~~ of a slight investigation of this point in relation to

in reference
particular parts of the United States and ^to land owned and culti-
^on the one hand
vated by the same person ^and ~~the brew~~ brueries of Malt liquors
^on the other,
prosecuted upon a large scale ^, is that the gross annual produce of the
Capital employed in the first case is at the rate of [85] and the
of the Capital
gross annual produce ^employed in the second case at the rate of
the nett produce in the first case at the rate of ~~and~~ and
the nett produce in the second case at the rate of This comparison as far as it can be relied upon is strongly in favour of the
superior productiveness of manufacturing industry; but it is acknowleged that it has not been extended far enough nor made with
sufficient precision to justify a positive inference of that kind. ~~An-
other argument which has been made use of to prove the superior
productiveness of agricultural labour is of the following~~. But there
are a variety of other lights in which the subject presents itself tending to shew that manufacturing labour is not only not unproductive;
render
but that the establishment of manufactures tends to ~~increase~~ the total
mass of the useful & productive labour of a community greater even
than it could be without them and even to augment the productiveness of Agriculture.

In tracing the topics which warrant such a conclusion it will be
and review
necesary to resume ^some of the points that have been already
touched.

^maintained by
As incident to the general doctrine one of the positions ^~~which~~
denies the productiveness of M Indy
^which ~~that which that~~ is
~~belongs to~~ the system ^~~which~~ has been stated ~~maintains also~~ That the
^total value of the
labour of Artificers and Manufactures adds nothing ^to the ^whole
or revenue of the society
annual produce ^~~of the land and labour of a country, asserting that~~
(it is alleged) ~~in value~~
~~they~~ ^consume ^as much ^~~of the produce of the land as they furnish in~~
as they produce

Connec-
tions obser-
vation more
particularly
examined

85. This and subsequent spaces left blank in MS.

The answer which has been noted as one that has been given to this position is ~~certainly~~ conclusive and satisfactory. The revenue of the society is ^evidently^ increased by the whole additional value given to the ^raw^ materials which are ~~manufactur~~ manufactured.

To render this idea more obvious and ~~favour~~ familiar it may be ^somewhat to dilate it &^ perhaps ^even^ to ~~place~~ put it ^even^ of use ^to place it^ into another ~~light.~~ form ~~The consumption of a cou~~ ~~country together with the~~ ^yearly current^ ~~savings or accumlations of the industrious~~ ~~and industrious or thrifty may be stated as corresponding with its~~ ~~revenue or income. That consumption~~ ^The Consumption of a Country has~~ ~~principally~~ relation does not ~~consist merely of the~~ ~~immediate productions of the earth in a compound of articles of~~ sub- ^to^ ^principally to^ sistence ~~all articles of~~ cloathing ~~articles of~~ furniture ~~and equita~~ equipage, ~~houses for~~ habitation. ~~Though~~ Some of these objects, particularly ~~to~~ the last, have a degree of permanency, which seem to render it scarcely proper to class them among those of a consumeable nature; yet the gradual wear to which they are subject ~~will justify~~ and which ~~requires~~ occasions a continual expence in reparations appears to justify their being included—at least for the purpose for which it is done. It is however not material to the argument, whether they are included or not. The value of all these articles in the state in which they are consumed, not in the ^primitive^ condition of raw materials determines ^consequently,^ the total amount in value of the consumption of the society. ~~And for~~ ~~the same~~ The value which each raw material acquires from its conversion ~~it~~ into a fabric enters into the estimate. And by the same rule it constitutes an increase of the Revenue of the Society. The consumption of a community ^together with^ ~~and~~ the savings of the ~~industry~~ industrious and thrifty (which go towards increasing the mass of the national capital) may be said in a general sense to correspond with its revenue or income.

Admitting it to be true that the manufacturer consumes exactly as much ^in value^ of the produce of land as he adds to the value of the raw material which he manufactures, ~~it this~~ would be no more ~~a~~ reason <sub>there</sub> <sub>on this account,</sub>

for considering his labour as unproductive ~~it~~ would be to consider <sub>than there</sub>

that of the cultivator ~~to be unproduct~~ which ~~produces~~ the surplus <sub>provides</sub>
he exchanges with the manufacturer, as unproductive, because he
consumes the fabric, which he receives in exchange for his provisions
and raw materials.

The allegation that the Manufacturer consumes as much of the
produce of land as he adds to the value of the raw materials is of no <sub>which he manufactures</sub>
more force to prove that his labour is unproductive than would

To say that the labour of the Artificer or Manufacturer is unproductive, because he consumes as much of the produce of the land, as
he adds in value to the raw materials, which he manufactures, is as
inconclusive, as it would be to say that the labour of the farmer which
~~produces~~ the materials exchanged with the manufacturer is unpro- <sub>furnishes</sub>
ductive; because he consumes an equal amount in value of manufac-
tured articles. Each furnishes a certain ~~proportion~~ of the product of <sub>quantum</sub>
his labour to the other ~~of a given value~~ and each destroys ~~an equal~~ <sub>or consumes</sub>
~~proportion or~~ correspondent quantum of the labour of the other. <sub>a</sub>
~~The~~ maintenance of two citizens in the mean time, instead of one, <sub>But the</sub>
is going on; and they together consume at least double the value of
what is produced from the land.

If instead of a farmer the artificer, there was a farmer only he
would be obliged to devote a part of his labour to producing cloathing and other articles which in the other case he ~~would~~ procure of <sub>would</sub>
the artificer. He would of course produce proportionably less from
his land. And the whole quantity of his production, in this case, in
provisions raw materials and manufactures, would not exceed in value
~~would be would~~ produced in the other case in provisions and raw <sub>what would be</sub>
materials only.

If there was an artificer as well as a farmer, the latter would be left at liberty to apply his whole labour to the cultivation of his farm. A greater quantity of provisions and raw materials would consequently be produced; equal as has been observed to the whole amount ~~of provisions raw~~ in value of ^the^ provisions raw materials, and manufactures which would be produced on the other supposition. The artificer, or manufacturer, at the same time, would produce ~~in manufactured articles~~ ^a^ like amount in value in manufactured articles (deducting the first cost of the materials) a part of which he would give in exchange for the ~~surplus~~ provisions and materials of the farmer, and the remainder he would apply to his own consumption and use. Here then would be two quantities, or values, instead of one, and the revenue and consumption would be double in one case what it would be in the other.

If in place of both these suppositions, there were two farmers, and no artificer, ^each of^ whom applied a part of ~~their~~ ^his^ labour to the culture of ~~the~~ land and another part to the fabrication of ~~the~~ manufactures ~~of which they might stand in need~~ ^he^, the portion of the labour of each bestowed ~~on~~ ^upon^ land would produce the same quantity of provisions and materials ~~would~~ as would be produced in the last case by the intire sum of the labour of one applied in the same manner and the portion of the labour of each bestowed upon manufactures would produce the same quantity of manufactures as would be produced in the ~~same~~ ^like^ case by the intire sum of the labour of one applied in the same manner. Hence the value of the labour of the two farmers would not be more than equal to that of the labour of the farmer and artificer and hence it is perceived that the labour of the artificer as well as that of the ~~favour~~ ^farmer^ is positively productive occasionning ~~a a~~ ^a^ real ^an^ augmentation of the revenue of the community.

The labour of the Artificer replaces to the farmer ~~the~~ that portion of his labour with which he produces the materials ~~which he~~ ^of^ exchange with the Artificer and which he would otherwise have been obliged

to bestow upon manufactures; and while the Artificer thus ~~purch~~
                                                    industry
enables the farmer to enlarge his stock of agricultural ~~labour~~ of which
he purchases a portion for his own use, he also <u>furnishes</u> <u>himself</u> with
                                                        for
the manufactured articles, ~~of~~ which he has ~~himself~~ occasion. Thus he
                        ₍and gives₎
not only produces ₍ₐ₎an equivalent for the labour of the farmer which
he consumes but he produces an <u>additional</u> <u>supply</u> of manufactured
articles for his own own consumption & use.

In the course of these illustrations the labour of the Artificer and
farmer are considered as equal to each other. But while this method
of speaking was necessary to ~~the~~ simplicity and perspicuity it will
not be understood that it is intended to state equal quantities of the
two kinds of labour as precisely equal in value. That of the Artificer
may be somewhat less or more valuable without affecting the ~~maid~~
main scope of the argument which only aims at shewing that it occasions a positive augmentation of the produce or revenue of the
Society.

From what has been already ~~it~~ said it appears clearly that the labour
of the Artificer more than replaces that portion of the labour of the
farmer which he consumes; namely by producing an additional supply
of manufactured articles for his own use. But it does still more than
this. It furnishes a surplus which compensates for the advance of
capital either by himself or some other person towards his own maintenance and the providing of materials for his work. This is the
                                    ₍carrying on₎
ordinary profit on the stock employed in ₍ₐ₎the business and is as effective an addition to the income or revenue of the society as the rent
of land. Hence the labour of the Artifcer may be regarded as consist-
                    value of the provisions purchased of the farmer & of the
ing of three parts that which ~~pl~~ replaces the ~~so be labour of the farmer~~
materials of agricultural labour employed in the fabric that which
furnishes the Artificer with cloathing and other necessaries of which
~~in~~ he stands in need and that which constitutes the nett profit on the
                                                intirely
Stock employed. The two last portions seem to have ₍ₐ₎lost sight of in
the ~~assertion~~ ~~that~~ ~~ma~~ doctrine ~~do~~ which maintains that the produce of
the labour of the Artificer does no more than replace the produce of
the land which he <u>consumes</u>.

☞
               a variety of
~~But there are~~ ^other~~ considerations from, which it may be inferred~~
                     in a country
the establishment of ~~manufactures~~ ^not only        ~~not only~~
~~that manufacturing artificers and manufacturers The following~~ But
there remain to be enumerated a variety of important circumstances
by which extensive manufacturing establishments contribute to the
positive              a           rendering it in fact
^augmentation of the Revenue of ~~the~~ Society; ~~but in fact rinders it it~~
              ^can
greater than it ^~~could~~ possibly be without them.

     These ~~considerations~~ relate to

1   The Division of Labour
2   The extension of the powers of machinery
                               to
3   The furnishing to ~~classes not principally~~ ^other classes of the
     community additional employment.
4   The promoting of emigration from foreign countries
5   The giving ~~a~~ greater scope to the difference of talents and
                   among
     dispositions ~~of~~ mankind

~~cheapness of~~
~~articles raises~~
~~the~~ ~~value~~ ~~of~~
~~land~~

6   The furnishing a more ample and various field ~~for~~ enterprise
     creating in some instances a new &
                   in all
7   The ^securing ^a more certain and steady demand for the
     surplus
     ^produce of the soil

☞

8   The furnishing a more various and abundant market to
     foreigners.

These arti-
cles to be
taken up
elsewhere
Quare?

{ 9   The enlargement of the ~~spere~~ sphere ~~in ought~~ out of which
     parsimonious savings may be made to increase the permanent
     capital of the Nation.

     There is scarcely any thing of greater importance in the œconomy
of a nation than the proper division of labour. The separation of
different occupations causes each to be carried to a much greater
perfection than it could possibly acquire if they ~~b~~ were blended. This
arises ~~prin~~ principally from three causes—1   the greater skill and
               naturally
dexterity which ^result from an undivided and constant application to
the same, ~~object~~ and a single object. It is evident, that these qualities
must increase in proportion to the separation and simplification of

objects and the steadiness of the attention which is bestowed upon
or be less
~~them~~ each—and must ~~be~~ decrease ˄in proportion to the complication
of objects and the ~~division of the attention~~ number among which the
by
attention is divided.  2   The saving of time, ~~which arises from~~ ˄avoid-
the
ing ~~a~~ loss of it incident to a frequent transition from one operation
to another of a different nature. This depends on various circumstances—the transition itself—~~the putt~~ the arrangements requisite to
implements
order, in regard to the ˄~~tools~~ machines or other means employed on
the operation which is to be ~~req~~ relinquished—the preparations which
must precede the commencement of a new one—the interruption of
the impulse ~~or momentum~~ which the mind of the workman derives
from ~~having~~ being actually engaged in ~~it~~ a particular operation—the
mind,
dissipation of the ˄—the hesitations reluctances and saunterings which
commonly
~~often~~ attend the passage from one kind of business to another.  3   An
increase of the use of Machinery. A man engaged in a single operation
will naturally be more led and will have it more in his power to
exercise his imagination ~~and~~ in inventing methods to facilitate and
independent distinct and dissimilar
abrige labour than if he is distracted and harrassed by a variety of ˄
operations. The invention and application of machines will of course
be necessarily more multiplied and extended in the former than in the
latter case. This will happen too from another cause. The fabrication
trade,
of machines, in various instances, becoming itself a distinct ~~trait~~ the
has
Artist employed in it ~~act under under~~ all the advantages ~~which have~~
~~been noticed noted att~~ which have been enumerated to lead him to
improvements in his particular Art.
    Thus it is evident, that the mere division of labour; or the siparation
of the calling of the farmer from that of the Artificer or manufacturer has the effect of ~~rendering increases~~ augmenting the productive
powers of labour and consequently ~~its~~ the total mass of the produce or
˄of the subject
revenue of ~~a~~ a ~~Country~~ community. And in this ~~sim~~ single view ˄the

as contradistinguished from cultivators
utility of artificers or manufacturers to that end ₍is₎ obvious.

could

If the Cultivators of land ~~were~~ themselves ~~to~~ be the fabricators of those manufactured articles, of which they stand in need, the state

husbandry     of the arts

both of ~~agriculture~~ and ~~manufactures~~ would be incomparably worse than ~~under a different the opposite~~ ~~arrangement~~. in the opposite

**Elsewhere**

system. ~~The inducements to make the soil productive~~ The quantity of every species of industry would be less and the quality much inferior —the manufactures produced would be ~~coas cour~~ less abundant coarse and bad—the lands ~~would be~~ ill cultivated and the whole community ill supplied. In regard to Agriculture in particular, not only the advantages resulting from the division of labour would be lost, but the inducements to render the land productive would be ~~sup~~ circumscribed ~~to~~ within the narrowest limits. They would be limited to the maintenance of each family in the simplest manner. Neither the ~~gratification of the manu inclinations which are incident to a state of greater improvement, nor the desire of~~ desire of multiplying enjoyments nor of accumulating wealth, by ~~the~~ an exchange of surplus productions of the soil would prompt to exertions for obtaining such a surplus.

~~Their utility to the same end is not less obvious as it relates to an extension of the powers of machinery in the industry.~~

The second circumstance which has been mentioned, namely the extension of the Powers of Machinery by manufacturing establish-

in part        be ~~viewed~~

ments has been ₍anticipated₎. But it deserves to ₍viewed₎ in one or two additional lights.

A substitute for domestic manufactures is the existence of foreign ones the products of which can be ~~exten~~ obtained in exchange for

by this substitute

~~those~~ the domestic products of the soil. But ~~Since~~ ₍a₎ very great advantage for the increase of the industry of a country is transferred. It ~~is certain that~~ appears not to admit of dispute that manufacturing

are susceptible of the application

~~and~~ pursuits ₍admit of the use₎ of machinery in much greater extent and variety than Agricultural ones. The reality of this fact must be

this

referred to observation—nor can ₍it can₎ appear extraordinary, when it is considered how few and simple are the operations of agriculture and

how numerous and complicated are those of ~~Agriculture~~ manufactures. If true, all

the difference ~~in the degree~~ is lost to the ~~country~~ community, which instead of

manufacturing for itself procures the ~~manufactured produce for~~ fabrics necessary to the supply of its

~~which it has occasion~~ wants from other countries. The circumstance of the

employment of ~~Mech~~ Machinery ~~froms forms a weight~~ from an item

of prodigious importance in the general mass of national industry. Tis an

artificial force brought in aid of the ~~for~~ natural force of man and is

to all the purposes of labour an increase of hands an accession of strength. ~~Hence~~ Those occu-

pations therefore ~~in which in can be exerted to most advantage other~~

~~things being equal must be most~~ conducive ~~conduce to the augmentation~~ which

give the greatest scope to it add proportionably to the aggregate

momentum of industrious effort and consequently to the aggregate

product of industry.

The furnishing to other classes of the community additional em-

ployment is another ~~and a very valuable effect of the~~ mean and a very valuable mean by which the establishment

of manufactures tends to increase the mass of Industry and the Reve-

nue of the Society. In towns and neighbourhoods ~~were~~ where manu-

factures are established besides those who are regularly ~~and constantly~~

~~engaged in them~~ bred to them they adopt ~~occasional~~ & give employment to many

persons who would otherwise be idle, either from the ~~bent~~ byass of their

dispositions, the habits they may have acquired infirmity of body or

some other cause indisposing or disqualifying them for the toils of

the country; and they give occasional employments also to ~~families~~ industrious

families who ~~devote the leisure~~ are willing to ~~emplo~~ devote the leisure,

which the intermission of their ordinary occupations allows them, to

collateral pursuits by which they can increase their acquisitions or

their enjoyments. ~~The two classes of~~ Women and Children particularly are ren-

dered more useful and more early useful by means of manufactures than they could otherwise be. Of the number of persons employed in the Cotton manufactories of Great Britain it is computed that nearly ⁴/₇ are women and children—of whom the greatest proportion are children. Thus it is one of the recommendations of manufactories that that they give ~~M~~ occasion to the exertion of a greater quantity of industry even by the same number of persons inhabiting a place in which they prevail than if they did not exist—another circumstance by which they serve to increase the sum of the produce & revenue of the society.

Of a similar nature is their tendency to draw emigrants from foreign ~~country~~ commonly countries. Men are ~~generally~~ reluctant to quit ~~the one~~ ~~to whie~~ course of occupation and livelihood for another unless invited to it by very apparent and proximate advantages. Many who would resolve to go from one country to another, if they had a prospect of pursuing with more benefit the callings to which they have been educated will often not be tempted to change their situation by the prospect of doing better in some other way. ~~This consideration is of great importance~~ Manufacturers, who listening to the invitations of a better price for their fabrics or their labour, of ~~greater~~ greater ~~abundance and~~ cheapness ~~of subsistence~~, both of provisions and raw materials of an exemption from the greater part of the ~~burthens~~ taxes and burthens which they endure throughout ~~Europe~~ the old world of greater personal independence under the operation of a more equal government would flock from Europe to the United States to pursue their own trades and professions, if they were once made to understand the advantages with an assurance of ~~countenance and encoura~~ countenance and employment will not readily be persuaded to ~~transa~~ transplant themselves for the ~~pup~~ purpose of becoming cultivators and husbandmen. If it be true (as it is presumed to be) that it is the interest of the United States to open all the sluices of European emigration ~~and~~ a powerful argument may be derived from this source in favour of the encouragement of manufactures. It will probably be found a fruitful mean of augmenting the population, and with it the useful and productive labour of the country. Here we perceive a resource for the prosecution of manufactures without deducting materially from the hands which would ~~naturally~~ otherwise be drawn to tillage

Quare

48.

the society.

Of a similar nature is their tendency to draw emigrants from foreign ~~country~~ countries. Men are ~~generally~~ commonly reluctant to quit ~~one~~ the one course of occupation and ~~livelihood~~ for another unless invited to it by very apparent and proximate advantages. Many who would resolve to go from one country to another, if they had a prospect of pursuing with more benefit the callings to which they have been educated will often not be tempted to change their situation by the prospect of doing better in some other way. ~~This consideration is of great importance.~~ Manufacturers, who ~~listening~~ to the invitations of a ~~little~~ ~~greater price for their fabric~~ and cheapness ~~&~~ ~~of~~ labour, of greater abundance and ~~cheapness~~ ~~of an exemption from the greater part of the hardships and burthens which they endure throughout~~ ~~the old world~~ ~~Europe~~ of greater personal independence under the operation of a more equal government — would flock from Europe to the United States to pursue their own trades and professions, if they were once made to understand the advantages with an assurance of ~~countenance and encoura~~ countenance and employment will not readily be persuaded to ~~transpose~~ transplant themselves for the ~~pur~~ purpose of becoming cultivators and husbandmen. If it be true (as it is presumed to be) that it is the interest of the United States to open all the sluices of European emigration — a powerful argument may be derived from this source in favour )

A Page from Hamilton's Third Draft of the "Report on the Subject of Manufactures"

the
~~and we perceive~~ and even for indemnification of agriculture for those
                withdrawn or
who might be ^witheld from it. Many whom manufacturing views
                                    afterwards
would in the first instance bring over would ^~~after their arrival~~ yield
to the ~~temptations~~ temptations ~~wh~~ which the particular situation of
this country holds out to Agricultural pursuits. And while Agriculture would derive many positive and ~~unqualif~~ unmingled advantages
from the growth and progress of manufactures in the United States,
        even
it is ^a problem whether it would gain or lose ~~even~~ in the ~~particular~~
article of the number of persons who would be employed in carrying
it on.

                    diversity
    The giving scope to the ~~variety~~ of talents and dispositions which
~~distinguinsh mankind~~ discriminate men from each other is a much
more powerful mean of augmenting the fund of National Industry
                            an        ^not less just than common
than may at first sight appear. It is ~~a common~~ observation ^that minds
of the strongest and most active powers for their proper objects fall
below mediocrity and labour without effect, if confined to uncongenial pursuits. Whence it will follow that the results of human ~~enter-
prise and~~ exertion must be immensely augmented by the diversifica-
        its            all the                    prevail
tion of ~~their~~ objects when ~~every~~ different species of industry ~~exists~~
in a community each ~~citizen is~~ individual ~~each citizen~~ is then able to
                                            into activity
find his ~~proper~~ natural element and can ~~there~~ call ^~~forth~~ the whole
            nature.
vigour of his ~~genius~~. And the community is benefitted by the services
of each of ~~the~~ its members in the way in which he can serve it with
most effect.

    If there be any thing in a remark which is every where ~~m~~ to be met
                                of the people of
with, namely that there is a peculiar aptitude in the genius of ^this
country for mechanic inventions and improvements it ~~will add great
weight to the general reasoning~~ —would afford a strong argument for
                        to the operation of that
giving opportunities ~~for that~~ propensity by the encouragement of
manufactures.
        effects
    The ~~benefits~~ of enlarging the field of enterprise, by varying the

industrious pursuits of a community, are of a nature ~~allied~~ closely allied to those which have been just ~~attributed~~ ascribed to ~~ex~~ an extension of the opportunities for exercising the different talents and dispositions of men. That a ~~general~~ spirit of enterprise is a fruitful source of national wealth is readily admitted as a general proposition; but the vast differences which are made in the aggregate of public prosperity by situations more or less favourable to it are not easy even to be conceived. Every new sience which is opened to the busy nature of man to rouse and exert itself is the addition of a new energy to the general stock of effort. It might be compared with the discovery of some new power in mechanics. This most useful and prolific spirit must necessarily be contracted or extended in proportion to the simplicity or variety of the occupations which obtain in a society. A nation of mere cultivators will ~~experiene~~ possess less of it ~~an~~ than a nation of cultivators and Merchants—and a nation of culti-
                                                                artificers
vators and merchants than one of cultivators ˄ ~~manufacturers~~ and merchants.

One of the great arts of enriching a nation is to ~~stipul~~ cherish and stimulate the activity of the human mind by multiplying its objects. Things even in themselves not positively advantageous ~~be~~ often be-
                    increase                    within due limits,
come so by their tendency to ˄ ~~promote greater~~ exertion. This idea ˄ is well worthy of the attention of ~~the~~ Legislators. ~~of a Country~~.

To create in some instances a new and to secure in all a more steady demand for the surplus produce of the soil—This is another and a very principal mean by which the establishment of domestic manufactures tends to augment the produce or revenue of a Country. It is evident that the exertions of the husbandman will be steady or fluctuating feeble or vigorous in proportion to the steadiness or fluctuation adequateness or inadequateness of the market to which he can send the surplus produce of his lands; and consequently their produce will be greater or less in the same proportion. A domestic market is for this purpose infinitely more desireable than a foreign one because in the nature of things it is infinitely more to be relied upon. It is a primary object of the policy of most nations to be able to supply themselves with subsistence; and manufacturing nations endeavour as far as circumstances permit to procure from their own soil the raw materials which are necessary for their own workmen. This disposition is not only carried to what may be deemed a reasonable ~~extent~~ and salutary

extent; but the spirit of ~~money~~ <sup>monopoly</sup> in many cases<sub>∧</sub> ~~carries it to~~ <sup>begets</sup> an extreme,

which defeats the end aimed<sub>∧</sub><sup>at.</sup>. It seems not to be recollected that na-

tions which have<sub>∧</sub><sup>no</sup> ~~not mi mines can only procure the precious metals in~~

~~exchange for the products of their industry — that those which have~~

~~not manufactures can only~~ <sup>mor no</sup> neither mines nor manufactures can only

procure the manufactured articles of which they stand in need by an
exchange of the products of the soil; and that if those nations who
can best furnish them with manufactures are not willing, to give a
free course to the exchange of those products, they must of necessity
endeavour to manufacture for themselves. The consequence of which

must be that<sub>∧</sub><sup>the</sup> manufacturing nations ~~will~~ abrige the advantages of
their situation because they are unwilling to permit the Agricultural
ones to reap the benefits of theirs. They lose the substance in the vain
project of selling every thing and buying nothing.

But the effect of the policy which has been stated is, that the<sub>∧</sub><sup>foreign</sup>
demands for the products of the soil of Agricultural ~~country~~ coun-

tries<sub>∧</sub><sup>(provisions especially)</sup> is rather casual and occasional than usual or constant. To what
degree ~~any~~ injurious interruptions of the demand for the staple com-

modities of the United States may have been experienced<sub>∧</sub><sup>on this account</sup> must be
referred to the judgment of those who are engaged in carrying on the

commerce of the country. But<sub>∧</sub><sup>it is presumed</sup> it may be taken for granted that such
interruptions have been severely felt; ~~either in a want~~ and that markets

have either been wanting or<sub>∧</sub><sup>in</sup> so low<sub>∧</sub><sup>a state</sup> as to oblige to rumours sacrifices

in<sub>∧</sub> ~~the~~ <sup>respect to</sup> price.

When it is considered how ~~much~~ <sup>fast</sup> the increasing settlements of the

United States must augment the surplus product of ~~the~~ <sup>their</sup> soil and when

the<sub>∧</sub><sup>inauspicious</sup> symptoms which have appeared in some late regulations of

Europe are duly attended to (however the necessary force of circumstances may be counted upon for counteracting an artificial
policy and for ~~repelling~~ silencing an overweening anxiety for the issue) ~~prudence~~ we shall be naturally led to regard the foreign demand for

error to contrast manufactures & Agriculture as rivals

that, surplus as too precarious a dependence and to a serious consideration of the means of finding a substitute in an extensive domestic market.

To have such a market, it is evident, there is no other ~~other~~ way than to promote extensive manufacturing establishments. Artificers and manufactures are the principal consumers of the surplus produce of the soil.

This idea of ~~a se~~ an extensive domestic market for the ~~sup~~ surplus produced by the labour of the country is of the greatest importance. It is of all things, that which will conduce most to a flourishing and vigorous state of Agriculture. As far as the number of hands who would be employed in tillage may be diminished by being drawn to manufactures it might possibly occasion a less quantity of lands to be under culture but those which were so would be much better improved and far more productive. And while the condition of each individual farmer would be meliorated ~~the~~ the total mass of Agricultural production would probably be increased. This evidently depends, as much perhaps more ~~as well~~ upon the degree of improvement as upon the quantity of land improved.

The ~~establishment~~ existence, establishment of domestic manufactures ~~depends~~ not only
~~occasions~~ furnishes a market ~~wh~~ for those articles which have been accustommed to be produced in abundance in a particular, country but it creates a demand for ~~the~~ others which either have not been accustomed to be produced before or in much smaller quantity. Thus the ~~production~~ culture of silk & the ~~cult~~ production of wool now circumscribed within very ~~nam~~ norrow limits in the UStates would not fail to grow with the growth of manufactures of those articles. ~~A Animals Plants minerals and other fossils are produced and brought into use which were before neglected and~~ Supplies are called for both from the surface and from the bowels of the earth which were before neglected. Animals plants

& minerals ~~each earths stones are produced~~ acquire an utility and value
which were before unknown. ~~to them~~.

The result of the whole ^is^ not only an increase of the total mass of
productive labour, but an improvement in the state of Agriculture,
certainly an amelioration of the condition of those who are employed
in it.

The furnishing a more various and abundant market to foreigners
—in consequence of the establishment of manufactures ~~is of a nature~~
~~simil~~ is attended with effects similar to those which have been ascribed  Stet
to the securing an extensive domestic market for the surplus of the
soil. But as there are many additional considerations involved in this
circumstance which would be improperly ~~anticapt~~ anticipated ^here^ it will
be more properly enlarged upon in another place.

The foregoing considerations seem sufficient to satisfy the mind
that, in the abstract, it is the interest of ~~every~~ communities to diversify the industrious pursuits of the citizens—and that the establishment of manufactures has a tendency not only to increase the ~~total~~
general stock of useful and productive labour; but even ~~the~~ to improve the state of Agriculture, certainly to ameliorate the condition
of those who are employed in it. There are other ~~as~~ views of the
subject which it is presumed will confirm this inference; previous
to which it will be useful to see what can be said against the ~~general~~
^arguments which have been used particularly in^
~~doctrine~~ in relation to a Country circumstanced like the United
States.

It ~~may~~ ^might^ be observed with considerable force that however true it
may be that a state which possessing large tracts of vacant and fertile
territory is at the same time secluded from foreign commerce would
find its interest and the interest of Agriculture in diverting a part of
its population from tillage to manufactures; yet it will not follow
that the same thing can be advantageous to a country which having
^at the same time^
such vacant territory is ^in^ a situation by means of external commerce
to procure on good terms from foreign nations all the fabrics which
^at least secures all the advantages^
it may want. This ~~all the effects~~ of a division of labour leaving the
farmer at liberty to pursue exclusively the culture of his land and
~~to procure the~~ enabling him to procure the manufactured articles

requisite
~~required~~ for his use ~~with the surplus of its produce~~ in exchange for its produce. And however true it may be that in settled countries the ~~existin~~ diversification of industry increases the total mass and augments the Revenue of the Society, it can hardly be conceivable that any thing can be of such permanent advantage to an unpeopled country as to turn its wastes into fertile fields. Though the revenue in the mean time may be less the capital must ultimately be greater. ~~And it may be added that as far as foreigners can supply those articles cheaper than citizens, the difference is an enhancement of the value of Agricultural labour; a smaller portion of which will then command a greater quantity of manufactured produce~~.

This objection is worthy of a particular examination.

If the free system were the prevailing system of Nations—if industry and commerce were every where left to their natural course, the considerations which dissuade a Country in the predicament of the United States from the zealous pursuit of manufactures would doubtless have very considerable weight. It will not be affirmed that they
be ^with few exceptions,
might not ~~be trusted~~ with a great degree of safety ^permitted ^to serve as a rule of national conduct; ~~and that the ultimate~~ though some very important advantages might in consequence of it be relinquished or postponed to a distant day. In such a state of things each country would have the full benefit of its peculiar advantages to compensate
disadvantages or
for its ^deficiences. ~~or d~~ If one was in condition to produce and supply manufactured articles on better terms than the other the latter might be able to supply the produce of the soil on better terms than the former. And a free exchange mutually beneficial would be carried on between them supporting in full vigour the industry of each. And though the circumstances which have been mentioned and others which will be added render it ~~prop~~ probable that ~~the~~ Nations merely Agricultural would not enjoy the same degree of opulence in proportion to their numbers as those which were both Agricultural and manufactural; yet the progressive improvement of the lands of the former might in the end ~~in~~ compensate for an inferior degree of opulence in the mean time; and in a case where considerations are pretty equally ballanced the option ought perhaps always to be ~~in favour~~ in favour of leaving industry to its own direction.

But such a ~~perform~~ <sup>perfect</sup> freedom of intercourse ~~is~~ very far from <sub>^</sub>~~being the being~~ <sup>has been</sup> the <sup>characterising</sup> policy of Nations. And to judge from recent events the contrary spirit would seem rather to gain than to lose ground.

The consequence of it is that the United States are in a great measure in the situation of a Country secluded from foreign commerce. They ~~may~~ <sup>can</sup> indeed obtain ~~with ease~~ from abroad without difficulty the manufactured articles which they require; but they experience numerous and very injurious impediments to the <sup>emission</sup>^ outlet and vent of their own commodities. Nor is this the case in reference to one foreign Nation only—The regulations of different countries with whom we have the most extensive intercourse, ~~Great Britain France~~ ~~Portugal and Spain~~^ <sup>& Portugal</sup> <sup>several of the</sup> throw serious obstructions in the way of the^ principal staples of the United States.

The Corn laws of Great Britain [86] shut the European market against^ <sup>our grain</sup> except in rare and extraordinary cases; and ~~by a late ex ex~~ intirely against the products of our fisheries.[87] The markets of her Islands are indeed open to all our commodities (except        ) but it is under the disadvantage of an exportation in her own ships.[88]

France also excludes from her European market our        and from her West India markets all ~~her grain~~ our grain except rice and Indian corn and our Pork.[89] In particular emergencies the exclusion is suspended or relaxed but it is the general policy. ~~Our Tobacco~~ A serious obstacle has also been thrown in the way of the importation of our Tobacco into France by a difference of duties on the article imported in French or American bottoms, which can only not amount to a prohibition of the importation in our own vessels by ~~an absolute~~ a deficiency of French Vessels.[90]

In such a ~~posture~~ <sup>position</sup> of things the United States cannot exchange ~~commodities~~ with Europe

~~In such a state of things the want of reciprocity would render the principles~~

86. See note 76.    87. See note 78.    88. See note 77.
89. See notes 79 and 80.    90. See note 82.

upon equal terms and the want of reciprocity would render them in a
great measure the victim of a system which ~~is calculated~~ persuades them to confine
their views to ~~Agri~~ Agricultural Industry and to refrain from
attempting a progress in ~~any other species.~~ and increasing manufactures. A constant
necessity on their part for the ~~the~~ commodities of Europe and only
on occasional ~~and~~ or partial demand for their own could not but
check the progress of their Industry and leave them in a state of impoverishment compared with the degree of ~~opulance~~ opulence to
which ~~their faculties and resources ought to lead them~~ and the natural ~~give them a~~
~~right~~ their political and natural advantages give them a right to aspire ~~pre-~~
~~tend.~~

~~It is not meant by what has been said to~~ complain heap censure on the ~~stigmatise the policy~~ of
~~conduct of any other nations towards the United States~~ regulations
~~other nations.~~ What has been remarked with regard to the ~~conduct~~ of
certain foreign nations is ~~not~~ designed neither for complaint nor censure. 'Tis for them to judge whether by grasping at too much they do
not lose ~~the advantages~~ more than they gain; defeating ~~the~~ advantages
which relative situations and a more natural policy would secure
and long preserve ~~to them~~. 'Tis for the United States to consider by
what means they can ~~best indemnify themselves for the impediments~~
~~to their external course b commerce by giving a new direction to~~
~~their pursuits and by opening new domestic resources.~~ render their
prosperity least dependent on the projects and vicissitudes of foreign
policy.

It is no small consolation that already the measures which have embarrassed our Trade have accelerated internal improvements which
upon the whole have bettered our condition. To diversify develope
and extend these improvements is the surest and safest method of
indemnifying ourselves for any inconviences which those or ~~in~~ similar
measures have a tendency to occasion & will be found the most effectual retaliation, for any unkindness of disposition (if any there has
been) which may have dictated them. If Europe will not consent to
take from us the products of our soil upon terms consistent with our
interest let us contract as fast as possible our wants of her.

The transformation of their waste into cultivated lands is certainly
an idea of great weight and importance in the œconomical calculations of the United States. But the ~~more~~ degree in which this may
possibly be retarded‸does not appear to counterballance the powerful considerations ~~in favour of the encouragement of manufactures~~
which operate in favour of their encouragement.

It is ~~pretty evd~~ evident that ~~the~~‸interest of a community ~~even con-
fining the question~~ viewing the question only in relation to ~~the state
of~~ its Agriculture to have such of its lands as are under cultivation
well cultivated than to have a greater quantity under inferior cultivation. The ~~product of~~ total amount of the product of its soil may even
be greater in the first case than in the last. And if manufacturers for
the reasons which have been assigned should promote a more steady
and vigorous cultivation of the lands occupied than might otherwise
be the case, they might abundantly indemnify for any ~~progress~~
diminution of the progress of new settlements. Not only the income
but the ~~Capi~~ real capital of the nation ~~may~~ might be ~~greater~~ increased
by them. The smaller quantity of lands under good cultivation might
be truly worth more than the greater‸under bad or indifferent culture; independent of the increase of active capital which naturally
results from manufacturing industry.

But it does by no means follow that even the progress of new
settlements would be retarded by the extension of manufactures. The
desire of being a ~~propriet~~ ~~propriety~~ depends upon such strong principles in the human breast, that where the opportunity of acquiring
is so easy as it is in the United States the proportion must be small
of those, whose circumstances would otherwise lead to it, that would
be diverted from the pursuit toward manufactures. And it is very
probable‸that the accessions from Europe of persons who originally
drawn over by manufacturing views would abandon them for Acri-
cultural ones would more than compensate for those of our own
citizens who might happen to be detained from them.

It is ~~any~~ idea of great consequence to the affairs of this Country
to open as many avenues as possible to European emigration; which

said before will best be affected by multiplying the objects upon which the industrious of all descriptions can be employed. The overflowing of these
streams can ͜hardly fail in the result to benefit Agriculture, ~~which is very~~
the common center of attraction ~~and~~ as well as
~~justly~~ ~~considered~~ ~~as~~ the predominant interest of the United States.

The objections which ~~consider~~ represent an impracticability on
the part of the United States to make any considerable progress in
manufactures require next to be examined. These relate to three points
—the scarcity of hands—the consequent dearness of labour—the want
of Capital.

The ~~circum~~ two first circumstances are in a considerable degree
real and ought to be admitted within due limits as obstables to our
success in manufactures; especially those of the finer and most costly
kinds. But there are various considerations, which diminish their
weight, and ~~seem~~ seem to afford an assurance that many very useful and
extensive manufactories may be prosecuted with advantage.

First with regard to the scarcity of hands—The fact itself must
be applied with material qualifications to certain parts of the United
States. There are large districts of country which may be considered
as pretty fully peopled; and ͜in which numerous flourishing and increasing towns have grown up; and this notwithstanding a continual
drain for distant settlement. If these districts have not already arrived
at the point at which the complaint of a scarcity of hands ceases, they
appear, at least, to be not very remote from it, and to be ~~still~~ approaching ~~to~~ towards it. ͜And ͜Not being equally happy in agricultural advantages
with some other parts of the United States they exhibit a proportionably stronger tendency towards other kinds of industry. In these
districts ~~there~~ may be discerned no inconsiderable maturity for manufacturing establishments.

But there are circumstances which have been already noticed with
another view that lessen the effect of this scarcity every where.
These circumstances are—the extensive use which can be made of
women and children, on which point, a very ͜pregnant & instructive fact has been
stated: the vast ͜extension ~~employment~~ which late improvements have given to

the employment of machines which substituting the agency of firer ~~to that of manual labour~~ and water‸has prodigiously lessened the necessity for manual labour. Of this, the mill for spinning Cotton invented in Great Britain within the last seventeen years is a signal example. In consequence of it, the preparation of ~~the~~ Cotton for spinning and the spinning of it into yarns are performed by the mere force of machinery‸with‸a to a very great extent ~~only~~ very ~~very~~ small number of persons to attend the process. ~~and collect the results~~ Whence it has happened that Great Britain is ~~not~~ able not only to supply herself with the cotton manufactures which she formerly procured from India, but ~~probably the rest~~ to export any quantity for which a demand can be found.

Fustians
Jeans
Bed ticking
Muslins
Coarse
Striped Cottons
Jerseys

Handkerchief B
Ribbands
Buttons imp  } Silk

The ~~employmen occasional~~ employment of persons engaged in other occupations during the hours or seasons of leisure. This ~~is not only a resource for procuring an additional supply of labour, but as has been remarked in another give place gives~~ besides giving occasion to the exertion of a greater quantity of labour by the same number of persons and increasing the general stock of labour (as has been remarked in another place) ~~is a material~~ may also be mentioned as a resource for ~~carrying on manufactures and~~ obviating the inconveniences of a scarcity of hands for the prosecution of manufactures; though it is of less importance than any other.

The attraction of foreign emigrants—This is a very important and efficacious resource for remedying the defect ~~whi~~ of hands. Whoever examines with a careful eye the composition of the population of our towns will be convinced how much this resource may be relied upon. This presents a large number of ingenious and valuable artists and mechanics, who, by expatriating from the old world, have essentially materially bettered their own condition and‸added to the industry and wealth of the new. It is demonstrated by the ~~fact~~ experience already had, that if the United States should exhibit the countenance of a serious prosecution ~~encouragement~~ of manufactures, considerable numbers of European workmen will be induced to transplant themselves to the United

91. See Constant Southworth to William Williams, September 1, 1791, printed as an enclosure to John Chester to H, October 11, 1791.

States. How indeed should it be otherwise, considering the numerous and powerful attractions which the situation of this country presents and which address themselves to so many strong passions & interests?

The ~~personal~~ equality and independence of ₍the condition₎ ~~its citizens~~ ₍the superior price of labour₎—the actual abundance and cheapness of provisions—the growing abundance and cheapness of raw materials—the lightness of taxes—the exemptions

Qr

from <u>tythes</u> & corporation restraints, ~~would~~ ~~furnish~~ <u>differ</u> ~~allurements to different descriptions of person~~ these and other circumstances, operating differently indeed upon different descriptions of personals but powerfully upon each, would present to foreign Artists & manufacturatures prospects too alluring to be resisted when it was once clearly understood ~~when~~ that the state of things here afforded a certainty of employment in their respective branches.

It may be said therefore, in respect to hands for carrying on manufactures, that we should in a great measure trade upon a foreign stock, reserving our own for the cultivation of our lands; as far ~~as~~ as character and circumstances might dictate.

Secondly. ₍With regard to₎ The dearness of Labour—This depends essentially on two circumstances, ~~that which which has been just discussed namely the scarcity of hands~~ one that which has been just discussed, or the ~~dearness of labour~~, scarcity of hands—the other the greatness of profits.

As far as it ~~depends on the~~ is a consequence of the scarcity of hands, all the circumstances which lessen ~~that~~ ₍this₎ inconvenience have a similar effect upon the other.

The ~~disparity~~ ₍indeed, real disparity indeed₎ which exists in this respect between certain parts of Europe and certain parts of the United States is not so considerable as may have been imagined. And the effect of this disparity in the final result is ~~evidently~~ diminished in proportion to the use which can be made of machines. To illustrate this idea let it be supposed that the difference of price in two countries of a given quantity of ~~labour~~ manual labour requisite to the fabrication of a particular commodity is as 10—and that some <u>mechanic power</u> is substituted in both, which performing half the requisite labour leaves only half to be done by hand, it is evident that the difference ~~of~~ in the ~~price~~ [cost of the fabrication] of that commodity ~~produced~~ in each country, as far as it is connected with the price of labour, will be reduced to five instead of 10 as [it] would ~~if~~ have been ~~the case~~, independently of the employment of that <u>Power</u>. To procure all such [Machines as are known] ~~as are made use of~~ in any part of Europe can only require the necessary pains. ~~And some of them~~ To prepare them here is in most cases practicable on nearly equal terms. As far as they depend on water some peculiar advantages may be claimed from the [uncommon] variety of situations adapted to mill seats with which ~~this~~ many parts of the U States abound.

As far as the dearness of labour is a consequence of the greatness of Profits, in any ~~undertaking~~ branch of business, it is no obstacle to its ~~see~~ success, ~~but~~ because the Undertakers can ~~well~~ afford to pay the Price.

There appears to be no doubt that undertakers of manufactures in this Country [at this time] can afford to pay higher wages to the workmen they may employ than are paid to similar workmen in Europe. ~~Generally~~ ~~speaking~~ [The component parts of] The prices of manufactured articles ~~in this country~~ [foreign] in the market of the United States [which will for a long time regulate those of domestic manufacture,] may be considered as compounded of these ingredients—the first cost of the materials, ~~wa the wages of the workmen~~ including the taxes ~~w~~ if any, which are ~~laid~~ [paid] upon them, the expence of ~~tools and~~ machinery & tools the wages of the workmen by whom they are fabricated, the profits of the ~~stock of the Undertak~~ capital or stock employed in the business, the commissions of an Agent to purchase them where they are made, the expence of transportation from thence to the United States including the taxes if any which are paid upon exportation, ~~the the~~ the taxes or duties on importation—the profits of the [importing] Merchants ~~who import the articles~~.

As to the first ~~article~~ item, the ~~cost first~~ cost of ~~the~~ raw materials, the advantage upon the whole is on the side of the United States and in a little time might be rendered much more so. Qr

As to the second, the wages of ~~the~~ ~~m~~ workmen, the comparison is to the disadvantage of the United States; though as already remarked, not in so great a degree as has been commonly supposed.

the

As to the profits of ᴧstock employd in the manufacture these are alike applicable to the domestic as to the foreign manufacture and must be excluded from the calculation.

But as to all the succeeding items they are alone applicable to the foreign ~~nat~~ manufacture and constitute a mass of extra charge upon

it which cannot be ~~les~~ computed at less than 40 or 50 per Cent on the Cost at the foreign factory and which ~~must~~ ~~much~~ ~~more~~ ~~than~~ ~~counterb~~ in the competition between domestic and foreign manufactures must be much more than a counterpoise for the difference in

the price of labour. The statement of the amount of these charges

the

will not appear high when it is considered that Commissions of Agents & expence of transportation alone amount on different articles from 15 to    per Cent.

Domestic manufactures therefore can well sustain the extra price

as far as it is real,

of labour ᴧand prosper in defiance of it.

Thirdly. With regard to a want of capital—This objection is of a nature rather indefinite, one which it is ~~not~~ easy neither to maintain

to

nor ᴧrefute. It is not ~~easy~~ possible to pronounce any thing ~~cert~~ precise

or moneyd

concerning the extent of the active ᴧcapital of the United States, still

that

less concerning the proportion which it bears to the objects ~~which~~ require ~~Capital~~ and invite the employment of Capital. Why might ~~it~~ not ~~as~~ ~~well~~ ~~be~~ ~~objected~~ the same objection be made to foreign Commerce: since it is ~~event~~ evident that our immense tracts of uncultivated land ~~would~~ ~~give~~ ~~employment~~ ~~to~~ ~~more~~ are capable of giving

is

employment to a larger capital than ᴧare actually bestowed upon them? It is certain that the United States offer a boundless field to the advantageous employment of Capital. But it does not follow that

successful

there will not be found a sufficiency for the ᴧprosecution of any species of Industry, which is likely to prove really beneficial.

The Effect of money as Capital, or in other words as a medium for putting in motion and circulating the industry of a country may be compared with the momentum of heavy bodies and may be said to be in a compound ratio ration to the quantity and velocity. Every new impulse therefore

~~In every such Question~~

It is not easy to pronounce how far the effect of any given quantity of money as capital or in other words as a medium for circulating the industry of a country may be multiplied or extended by the very ~~si~~ circumstance of giving to it ~~new~~ additional motion by new objects of employment. It is very certain that that effect may in many   Qr. respects be compared with the momentum of descending bodies, and

                              mass

may be regarded as in a compound ratio to quantity and velocity. A given sum of money in a situation unaided by the quick impulses of commercial activity would be found inadequate to the circulation of as great a quantity of industry and property as in one in which it felt the full influence of that activity.

The establishment and increase of Banks in the United States will tend powerfully to obviate the objection under consideration.

The aid of foreign Capital also, in every question of this nature may
  and with considerable latitude
be safely ⌄admitted into the calculation. It has been long experienced
                        a
in our external commerce in the shape of ~~the~~ credit ~~given~~ to our merchants. And it begins to be perceived in various other modes. ~~Not~~   Persons who
                            think it an
                      of late     evil—~~Nat~~
~~only our funds, but our Agriculture~~ Its operation has ⌄reached not   Approbation
only our funds; but our Agriculture and other internel improvements   of our Government
                       our
—in a few instances it has even extended to ~~particular~~ manufactures.

It is a well known fact, that there are parts of Europe which have
      ·                  domestic
much more Capital than profitable ⌄objects of employment. Hence
  public
the ⌄loans continually made to foreign States. And it is equally certain that the capital of other parts may find more profitable employment

                              are
in the United States than at home. And ~~that~~ though there ⌄many   defect
weighty considerations which induce men to prefer the employment   material difference

Whatever attracts money once introduced may be turned elsewhere good way to detain it is to multiply objects.

~~advantage of encouraging manufactures to the fisheries~~

of their capital in their own country ~~even~~ at less profit to ~~a distant~~ employment of it in foreign countries at greater profit; yet those considered give way, either where there is ~~and~~ an absolute deficiency of employment or where the difference in ~~employment~~ profit is material. As well the former cause as the latter have operated in relation to us. Tis certain that various objects in this Country invite foreign Capital by much greater profits than can be made at home; and under the increasingly favourable impressions which are entertained of our Government the attraction will be [92]

One or two points of view only remain, in which to consider the expediency of the encouragement of manufactures in the U States, previous to a discussion of the means, by which it is to be effected.

It is not uncommon to meet with an opinion that though the promoting of manufactures may be the interest of a part of the United States, it is contrary to that of another part. The Northern and Southern regions are sometimes represented as having a ^an opposite^ ~~distinct~~ interest in ^this^ ~~that~~ respect. Those are called manufacturing states, these Agricultural—and a species of opposition and contradiction is imagined to subsist between the manufacturing and Agricultural interest.

It is not to be denied that particular encouragements of particular manufactures may be of a nature to sacrifice ^certain interests^ ~~the interest~~ of the Landholder to those of the Manufacturer—~~And hence it can~~ of which ~~examples~~ there are not wanting examples in manufacturing countries. And hence it cannot be admitted as ~~us~~ universally true ⟨that⟩ the interests of Agriculture and manufactures ⟨are⟩ the same, a position which has been in many ⟨in⟩stances abused. But there is no maxim ~~bet~~ ⟨bet⟩ter established by experience or more generally ⟨ac⟩knowleged where there has been sufficient experience, than that the <u>aggregate</u> prosperity of manufactures and the <u>aggregate</u> prosperity of Agriculture are intimately connected. And it is relied upon that the truth of this maxim has been demonstrated by a variety of ^important^ considerations in the course of the preceding discussion,—of which the ^superior steadiness of the^ ~~steady~~

92. At this point in the MS three or more pages are missing.

demand of a domestic market for the surplus products of the soil is alone a convincing argument.

The idea of a contrariety of interests between the Northern & Southern regions of the United States ought to be ~~treated without mercy~~ exploded as often as it appears. It is as unfounded as it is mischievous. The diversity of circumstances on which it is ~~founded~~ predicated authorises a directly contrary conclusion. Mutual wants constitute one of the strongest links of political connection and ~~these are the reas~~ the extent of these ~~is in~~ bears a proportion to the diversity in the objects of supply.

If there ~~are~~ have been appearances of a struggle between contending interests in any cases ~~they~~ it may be confidently affirmed that they have proceeded from erroneous opinions on one part or on the other. It ought to be the effort of patriot⟨ism⟩ to suppress the suggestions, proceeding from the suppos⟨ition of a different⟩ interest. It will be the effort of ⟨enlightened⟩ patriotism to extinguish a spirit ⟨as unfriendly to⟩ ~~a concentration of efforts~~ a steady ⟨pursuit of one⟩ great common cause and to the ⟨perfect harmony of⟩ [93] all the parts.

In proportion as the mind is accustomed to ~~contemplate~~ trace the intimate ~~u union and~~ connection of interest; between all the parts of a Society, united ~~one~~ under one and the same government—the infinite variety of channels, through which the prosperity of each circulates to and through the rest, will it be little disposed to respect ~~little~~ the ideas of a jealous discrimination. It is a truth as important as it is ~~solid, that~~ consoling as profound as it is simple that every ~~every~~ thing which tends to establish substantial & permanent order in the affairs of a country, to increase the ~~great~~ total mass of industry and opulence is ultimately beneficial to every part of it. ~~On the credit of this consol-~~ truth as profound as it is simple & On the credit of this great Truth ~~ing and invaluable precept may be~~ an acquiescence be safely given from every quarter to every institution and arrangement which promises a confirmation of public order and an augmentation of national resource.

93. Words within broken brackets in this paragraph have been taken from H's fourth draft of this Report.

~~Encouragement to Fisheries arising from manufactures~~

~~This great truth, as profound as it is simple & consoling cannot be too deeply impressed on the minds of all those who are entrusted with the care of the public welfare. It teaches that~~

But there are more particular considerations which serve to ~~shew~~
idea
confirm the ~~belief~~ that the encouragement of manufactures is the
interest of all parts of the Union. If the Northern and middle states
should be the principal scenes of such establishments, they would
immediately benefit the more Southern by creating a demand for productions; some of which they have in common with the other states
and others of which are either peculiar to them or ~~of better quality~~
more abundant or of better quality than elsewhere. These productions principally are, Timber, flax, hemp, cotton, wool, raw silk,
indigo, iron, lead, furs, hides, skins and coal. Of these articles, cotton
altogether                                              hitherto
and Indigo are peculiar to the Southern states, ~~and~~ as are in a great
measure lead and coal. Flax and Hemp are or may be raised in greater
abundance there than in the more Northern States. And the wool
produced in certain parts of Virginia is said to be of better quality
than that which is raised in other parts of the United States; a circumstance which is rendered the more probable by the reflection that
Ex        the finest wool country of Europe is in the same latitude with that
cultivation
state. The extensive propagation of Cotton in particular can perhaps
hardly be expected, but from the previous establishment of domestic
manufactories of that article, and the surest encouragement and vent
~~fro~~ for the others would result from similar establishments in relation to them.

The last remark which remains previous to a specification of the
objects to be encouraged & the means of encouragement is this—That
the present is the critical moment for entering with zeal upon the
important business. Two circumstances conspire to make it so—A
and increasing
considerable influx of ~~Capital~~ money from foreign speculations in the
public Debt, the disorders in Europe.
not only
~~When~~ The first circumstance facilitates the execution of manufacturing projects but it indicates them as a necessary mean to render it
an advantage and prevent its being ultimately an evil. It is of great
moment to find useful employt. for the increase of ~~num~~ money resulting from foreign purchases of our debt else it will be reexported in
consequence of an increased consumption of foreign luxuries and we

must suffer hereafter distressing drains of our specie to pay the interest and finally the principal of the purchased debt.

This useful employment too must be of a nature to produce solid
~~dome~~ and permanent domestic improvements. If it merely gives an
            additional spring
~~increased activity~~ ᵥto foreign commerce, as it ~~is not~~ cannot procure
            outlets
new and lasting <u>sources of demand</u> for the products of our country,
            durable
it will be of no real or ~~lasting~~ advantage. In Agricultural ameliorations
as far as it may find its way, it will ~~be~~ prove of solid utility—but it is
to be doubted whether in this channel it would find sufficient employment & still more whether many of those who possess it would be
            to
as readily attached ᵥobjects of this nature as to those of a manufacturing kind which bear greater analogy to their accustomned pursuits.

To open the one field as well as the other will at least ~~afford~~ secure
a better prospect of useful employment for whatever accession of
money their either has been or may be.
                    a certain fermentation of mind
                    a certain
This is at the present juncture ~~an~~ activity of speculation and enter-
                                                    very
prise, which if properly directed may be turned to ~~the~~ beneficial
purposes but if left wholly to itself may be attended with many
pernicious effects.

The present disturbed state of Europe inclining its citizens to emigration, the requisite manufacturers will be the more easily acquired
at this juncture and the opening new means of employment to them
by giving a new impulse to the current may increase the extent of
valuable acquisitions to our population & to our industry in every
branch.

In entering upon a designation of the species of manufactures,
which may appear to claim, in a peculiar manner, the encouraging
hand of government, it occurs both as an indication of aptitudes in
the state of things, and as an assurance of the probability of success,
in manufacturing attempts, that already a considerable progress has
been made in manufactures of the following kinds—~~Distill Distilleries
of~~ ardent spirits, ~~breweries of~~ malt liquors, ~~various art~~ various articles

of iron ~~particularly~~ (including the ~~preparation~~ extraction & preparation of the metal itself) particuly steel, muskets nails      various

Lead
Cotton
Wool
Stocking,
Glass
Books
Oils & paints

~~kinds of le~~ articles of ~~which~~ leather ~~is the basis~~, particularly, ~~sala~~
sadlery, shoes
Paper and paper hangings—Sail Duck and some other linnens of the
coarser kind—Hats—Gunpowder, Carriages, Cordage, Books
                  beginnings have also been made
Some promising ~~attempts are also going on~~ in other branches, ~~in Cott~~
                                                              acquired
in fabrics of cotton wool lead glass but as yet these have ~~attained to~~
little maturity or extent. An association however has lately been set
on foot to carry on the cotton branch with a force of capital and
means which with the due countenance of government can hardly
fail of success and which promises an acquisition of incalculable value
to the United States.
            selection
    In the ~~section~~ of ~~the~~ proper objects of encouragement the follow-
ing circumstances deserve peculiar attention—the aptitudes of the
country for furnishing the raw material—the degree to which a sub-
stitude for manual labour may be found in machinery, the facility of
executing the manufacture—the extent of the usues to which it is
~~applied~~ applicable.

Where these circumstances unite in favour of a particular object they
plead for its encouragement with irresistible force.
    ~~Son~~
    The following manufactures are particularly recommended by
some or all of the considerations which have been noticed. ~~Of Iron~~
~~particularly of~~ Of ~~spirits~~ ardent spirits and malt liquors—~~Of iron~~
~~particularly~~
These relate immediately to the principal and most valuable staples
                        Fruits also are to be comprehended.
of the country, grain of different kinds ^—It is peculiarly worthy of
the cares of the legislature to ~~promote and~~ multiply the means of a

See what has
been said on
other occa-
sions as to
ardent spirits

profitable disposition of that increasing surplus which is resulting
from the improvements in agriculture and the continual progress of
new settlements in the immense territory of the U States. Of the two
objects which have been mentioned malt-liquors are in various lights
intitled to a preference; but ~~ardent spirits~~ the domestic manufacture

of ardent spirits will deserve encouragement in competition with those of foreign countries. As far as the habits of the country lead to the use of them, it is desirable that they should be of our own making & from our own materials.

    Of Iron particularly

Here the raw material is an abundant production of our country.<sub>∧</sub> Numerous &
flourishing foundries are established
The process in many particulars is not difficult and it gives occasion
to ~~an exten~~ a considerable employ~~ed~~<sub>∧</sub>ment of machinery & in some cases
may be performed by Children.

    Of lead particularly

It is known to the Legislature that Mines of lead have begun to be worked, and it is ascertained, that ~~copiedus~~ copious supplies are to be had in various parts of the United States.

    Of Leather particularly

~~It is needless to observe that we produce a~~
The plentiful production of ~~the~~ the raw material ~~of the manufactures~~
among ourselves, the simplicity of the process, ~~the~~ e in many cases—
the extensive uses of ~~ar~~ the article and the maturity which the manu-
facture<sub>∧</sub>of it in certain branches ~~of it~~ has acquired indicate it as one of the
best objects of industrious pursuit & public patronage.

    Of paper, paper hangings,

~~The manufacture of pape~~ Manufactories of paper are numerous extensive and have nearly attained to perfection. An encouraging prog-
ress<sub>∧</sub>has been made in paper hangings, and nothing but adequate skill in the conductors of it is requisite to complete success. In viewing the growth of this manufacture it is a pleasing reflection that the materials of it are
an absolute saving of what would otherwise be lost<sub>∧</sub>while the demand for them ~~and~~ contributes to the support of the indigent. It is also presumeable that it will be found practicable with advantage to employ in this way the raw

materials of linnens in their primitive shape; thus giving a new aid to agriculture.

       & coarse linnens

Sail ~~Duck~~ Cloth<sub>^</sub>. The progress which has been made within a few years in the manufacture of sail Cloth and in other coarse linnen

to navigation,

articles, their importance<sub>^</sub>in the equipments of fleets and in the appointment of ~~arti~~ armies, their general use ~~as materia~~ for the purposes of apparel, the universal capacity of the States to produce the raw materials, the precious effects of the linnen branch upon individual industry & domestic œconomy recommend all the fabrics of that kind in a peculiar manner to the protection of the Legislature. ~~These~~

Hemp & flax

~~fabries are intitled to peculiar attention. The raw~~ materials<sub>^</sub>~~are our~~

be

~~own and may increased ↑ø with vast advantage to our agriculture~~

  requisite        in each kind       Some

~~to~~ any<sub>^</sub>~~necessary extent~~. The process<sub>^</sub>is simple and easy. ~~Several~~ of

~~them are now carried on with great advantage and success in private~~

already                 considerable

~~families. Sail Duck~~ is<sub>^</sub>made ~~in sev~~ different ~~places in a~~<sub>^</sub>~~great degree~~

~~of perfection. The interests of our nav navigation are materially concerned in the extension~~ growth ~~of this manufacture~~. Manufactories of Sail are prosecuted with spirit & success at Boston New London & other places: That which is made at Boston is asserted to be of a quality superior to any imported. New York and Baltimore have each an association occupied principally in linnen fabrics. And tow and other household linnens are ~~already~~ made in such abundance in different parts of the U States as alredy to maintain a successful competition with ~~rep~~ rival foreign articles & to occasion a diminution of their prices.

~~The like~~

Similar considerations apply to Cordage. But it is the less necessary to dwell upon this article as it is one which has for some time been in a very prosperous train.

Hats:   the manufacture of this article as well of wool as of beaver ~~exists in an extent~~ has succeeded in an extent which leaves no doubt of the possibility of carrying it on to a degree completely adequate to the wants of the country. The materials of both kinds are our own and the utility is general.

Carpets and blankets particularly the latter.   Manufactories of the

first exist but not under the most ~~fav~~ <sup>presages</sup> favourable circumstances. It is

not known that any of the latter are made in the United States. ~~the~~

But the essential ~~nature, the extensive~~ <sup>& general</sup> utility<sub>∧</sub> <sup>of the article</sup>—the facility of its fabri-

cation, the certainty of being able<sub>∧</sub> <sup>with due exertion</sup> to supply ourselves with the raw

material—are circumstances which strongly recommend an encour-

agement of the manufacture of it.

Carriages   The manufacture of these is in a train that leaves little

more to be desired.

Glass:   The chief ingredients<sub>∧</sub> <sup>the kinds of Earth & Stone called Tarson & the sea Weed called Kali or Kelp</sup> and it is believed, of a proper kind,

for the manufacture of this article are to be found in the ~~us~~ United

States, and the abundance of fuel is particularly favourable to its

success. But the result of the ~~experiments~~ <sup>essays</sup> hitherto made is not flatter-

ing—and it is a question whether future attempts are likely to be more

so. The process is difficult and<sub>∧</sub> <sup>arduous</sup> ~~labourious   depending altogether to~~

~~a very mu requisi~~ requiring too an unusual portion of ~~manuf~~ manual

labour; which is in this country the principal obstacle to success in

manufactures. Without despairing wholly of ~~the success of~~ manufac-

tories of this article there is no room in indulge such expectations as to

authorise anticipations by the ~~Govurme~~ Goverment. It will be time

enough to aid when future experiments shall afford better hopes; in

which event the vast importance & general usefulness of the manu-

facture will plead powerfully for all reasonable cooperation.

Gunpowder.   ~~The progress which has already been made in this~~

~~article is an earnest of its complete sulphur I success. It is not to be~~

~~doubted that surpl sulphure a principal ind ingredient in its composi-~~

~~tion is to be found in sufficient quantity in the United States~~ The

manufactory of this article has been rapidly advanced, and principally

by individual exertions within the few last years. Though it may be

considered as established yet its importance renders its extention very

desirable. Sulphur a considerable ingredient in its composition, it is

~~presumeable~~ <sup>probable</sup> will hereafter be found in sufficient quantity in the

United States; but hitherto ~~no material~~ internal resources have afforded but an insignificant supply. The deficiency may easily be supplied from other quarters. And means may be taken to facilitate the introduction of the other ingredients.

Muskets<sub>∧</sub> ~~Respee~~ and other fire arms This article might have been properly referred to under the head of manufactories of iron; but its importance intitles it to a distinct ~~view~~ place. Manufactories of it exist & the ~~specifi~~ specimens of work which ~~n~~ have been furnished assure success to ~~an~~ attempts to extend them.

Books    The two last mentioned articles concern so immediately the defence of the country, that they claim the serious attention of the Governments upon considerations not merely relative to the national advantage but to ~~the~~ national safety.

next paper    Books.   The printing and binding of books has of late considerably increased. It is evident however that much more might be done in this business than is at present done. The manufactories of paper furnish the principal material to ourselves and the vast number of printing presses disseminated throughout the Union leave no doubt of ~~the~~ adequate means of execution.

Cotton Goods.   The manufacture of these generally will deserve the particular patronage of the government. The Southern States supply the raw material; and though it is questionable whether that which they produce will answer for the coarser kind of goods, those in most general use, the staple being short and fine, yet there is reason to believe that it will be very serviceable and even preferable to the West India Cotton, in fabrics of the finer kind. And the French Spanish Dutch & Danish West Indies as well as the East Indies will abundantly supply any deficiency in the Material. The reasons which particularly recommend fabrics of this article, are the very great use which can be made of machinery, women and Children in carrying them on. This circumstance has been remarked and dwelt upon in another place. ~~The peculiar texture of~~ It depends on the peculiar texture of the material. An association has lately been formed for carrying on the manufacture of this article with a force of Capital that with the due countenance of government, seems to ensure success, promising an acquisition of incalculable value to the Union.

In addition to the foregoing objects, there are others which will be mentioned in the subsequent part of this report as requiring some favouring regulations, which it is unnecessary to present here in a ∧distinct perspective.
~~distant view~~

                                                        resorted
In order to a judgment of the means proper to be ~~employed~~ by the United States for the encouragement of manufactures, it will be useful to advert to those which have been employed with success in other countries. The principal of these are

1  Protecting duties—or duties upon those foreign articles which ⟩ Beging
t are the rivals of the domestic ones intended to be encouraged.
                                amount to
Duties of this nature ~~are~~ evidently ∧a virtual bounty on the domes-
                                           ∧since
tic fabrics; ~~enab giving these as~~ ∧by enhancing the charges on foreign │ A
articles, they enable the national manufacturers to undersell their
foreign competitors. The propriety of this species of encouragement │ No. II
need not be dwelt upon; as it is not only a clear result from the numer-
            ∧suggested        ~~entered upon~~
ous topics which have been ∧~~discussed~~ but is sanctionned by the laws
of the United States in a variety of instances. ~~Indeed~~ It has the addi-
                                        re
tional recommendation of being a source of revenue. Indeed all the
            on imported articles,                    of revenue,
duties imposed ∧though with an exclusive view to the object ∧have the
effect in contemplation, and ~~wear~~ except where they fall on raw
            wear  ∧beneficial
materials ~~have~~ ∧a ∧~~benignant~~ aspect towards the manufactures of the
country.                                                            │ End

2  Prohibitions of rival articles, or duties equivalent to prohibitions. ⟩ Beginning
                              ∧giving a monopoly of the │ No. III
This is another and an efficacious mean of encouraging national
home market to those who are engaged in them.      ∧fit    em-
manufactures; ∧~~it is one however~~ But in general it is only ∧to be ∧~~re~~-
ployed
~~sorted to~~ when a manufacture has made such a progress and is in so
            ∧a due competition and an adequate        ~~for~~
many hands, ~~as~~ as to insure ∧a ~~competent~~ supply, ~~in the home market,~~
on reasonable terms. Of duties equivalent to prohibitions, there are
examples in the laws of the United States—such are those on      94

94. At this point in the MS H wrote "blank of two lines."

—and there are other cases to which the principle may be advantageously extended, but they are not numerous.

Considering a monopoly of the domestic market to its own manufacturers as the ~~rei~~ reigning policy of ~~corre~~ manufacturing nations, a similar policy on the part of the United States, in every proper instance is dictated ~~by considerations~~ it might almost be said by the principles of distributive justice ~~by the desire or self preservation and the principles of Justice to its own Citizens.~~ ~~of securing to their own citizens retaining~~ certainly by the duty of endeavouring to ~~It is dictated by the necessity of aiming at a reciprocity of advantages.~~ secure to their own citizens a reciprocity of advantages.

**End**

IV ~~3~~ Pecuniary bounties on home made articles—

This has been found one of the most efficacious means of encouraging manufactures; and it is in ~~many~~ some respects the very ~~views the~~ best; though it has not ~~yet been practiced upon~~ ~~been resorted to~~ by the government of the U States (unless the allowance on the exportation of dried & pickled fish & salted ~~pro~~ meat [95] could be considered in that light) and though it is less favoured by public opinion, than some other modes ~~kinds~~.

Its advantages are these.

It is a species of encouragement more positive and direct, than any other, and for that very reason, it has a more immediate tendency to promote and support new enterprizes; increasing the chances of profit, and diminishing the risks of loss, in first attempts. ~~indemnifying~~ ~~wholly or in part~~ them ~~for the first losses which are~~ commonly ~~usually attend them.~~

It ~~steers clear of~~ either avoids steers clear of the inconvenience of a temporary increase of price, which is incident to ~~the~~ other modes, ~~that have been mentioned~~ ~~because~~ or it produces it in a less degree; ~~by~~ either by not increasing the charges on the foreign rival article ~~similar to that to be manufactured~~ or by increasing them in a ~~less~~ smaller proportion. ~~degree~~. The first happens when the fund for the

95. H is referring to the drawback given under Section 4 of "An Act making further provision for the payment of the debts of the United States" (1 *Stat.* 181–82 [August 10, 1790]).

derived
bounty is ~~drawn~~ from ~~another~~ a different object in which case, however, it may or may not increase the price of some other article ac-
the fund
cording to the nature of the object; the second when ~~it~~ is derived
or a similar object ˰manufacture. per
from the same ˰of foreign ˰~~production~~. One ~~per Cent du shilling~~ ˰cent
article
duty on the foreign ˰converted into a bounty on the domestic will
have ~~t~~ an equal effect with two per Cent duty on the foreign articlle
exclusive of commodity
~~without~~ ˰such bounty; and the ~~charge first~~ price of the foreign ~~article~~ ˰
is ~~on~~ raised in the one case, in the proportion of one per cent, in the
other, of two per Cent. Indeed the bounty when derived from another
˰a diminution of price
source promotes ˰~~cheapness~~ because without laying any new charges
on the foreign article, it increases the ~~quan~~ total quantity of the article
A
in the market. ~~and even where the duty is~~ The bounty has also less
tendency to occasion scarcity, ~~of which there is greater danger from~~ ˰
than protecting duties; ˰if high
~~high protecting duties. An increase of price~~ which ˰may for a time
˰of the articles upon which they are laid:
interfere too much with the profits to be gained on the importation ˰~~of~~
~~an~~ immediate
~~the article.~~ For an increase of price is not always the ˰~~effect of a new~~
commonly
though it is ~~generally~~ the ultimate effect of ~~a new~~ an additional duty,
manufacture
where the progress of a domestic ~~article~~ ˰does not counteract the rise.
    Bounties are sometimes not only the best but the only proper mean
˰that of
of uniting the encouragement of a new object of manufacture with ˰a
new object of agriculture. It is the interest of the farmer to have the
production of a raw material encouraged—of the manufacturer, to
domestic
have the raw material cheap. If prior to a ~~sufficient~~ production of ~~the~~
the ·
~~domestic~~ ˰raw material in sufficient quantity to supply the manufacturer on cheap ~~tern~~ terms, a duty is laid on the foreign raw material
with a view to the encouragement of its cultivation at home, it equally
counteracts the purpose of the ~~farmer and of~~ the manufacturer and of
the farmer. By raising the price of the raw material to the former it

to            ^incapacitates    e
^~~disables~~ him ~~from~~ prosecut~~ing~~ with success the manufacture—and
                                    latter; because
thus defeats the object of the ~~farmer, for~~ there being no domestic
manufacture to create a demand for his commodity, it is in vain that
the competition of the foreign article may have been destroyed. The
true way to conciliate both interests is to lay a duty on foreign <u>manu-</u>
<u>factures</u> of the raw material in question and to apply the product of
that duty, in a bounty either immediately upon the production of the
                    the exportation or
article or upon ^the manufacture of that which is produced at home.
In this case the manufacturer undertakes his enterprise under every
                                        ^quantity & the
advantage he can desire as far as respects the ^price of the raw material
                                                                to
—and where the bounty is directly to the farmer, he can afford ^~~the b~~
undersell the foreign material, or where it is to the manufacturer, on
                            (prices being equal)
the domestic material he has ^a motive of interest to prefer the use of
it. ~~prices being equal~~.

{ Qr }    The linnen branch in Ireland is a well known instance of the effect
of this species of encouragement. And the Cotton branch in England
is a no less signal example. At this moment there is a bounty on
certain kinds of cotton goods of ~~not~~ about 12½ per Cent.[96]
                            in respect for which there are transcendent local advantages
Except in the simplest and most ordinary kinds of manufactures ^—
pecuniary bounties are ~~a~~ in most cases indispensable to the introduction of a new branch. A stimulous and a support not less powerful and
direct is essential to the overcoming of the obstacles arising from the
competitions of ~~the~~ superior skill and maturity in foreigners. It is
especially essential in those cases where they are themselves in the
practice of granting bounties.
                            ~~a~~ pecuniary ies
The continuance of ^~~a~~ bount~~y~~ on ~~a~~ manufactures long established
                                    utility
would be in most cases of questionable ^policy; because a presumption
                                    inherent            their
would arise that there were natural and intrinsic impediments to ~~its~~
                                            ^often
success—but in new undertakings they are ^not only justifiable but

96. See 29 Geo. II, C. 15 (1756), continued by 28 Geo. III, C. 23 (1788).

necessary. And it would be a highly misplaced parsimony to withold them.

There is nevertheless a prejudice with <sub>some</sub> against bounties which may be traced to a misconstrued appearance of giving away the public money to individuals without an immediate consideration—and to a supposition that it is rewarding a particular class at the expence of the community.

But neither of these objections on cool examination ~~can be deemed~~ will appear to have much weight. There can be no purpose to which public money can be more beneficially applied that to the acquisition of a new and beneficial branch of Industry. And as to the last objection, as far as it is founded it equally lies against all the other modes of encouragement. A duty on the foreign article, by raising the price on the community creates to it an extra expence for the benefit of the manufacturer. A bounty does no more—But it is the interest of the community to submit to this expence which is in its nature temporary, because it is more than indemnified in the variety of ways which have been delineated ~~and among the rest in the even~~ in a general increase of industry and of wealth, in an agmentation of its resources and independence—and in what is a more direct compensation, though perhaps an inferior consideration, in the circumstance of eventual cheapness. The Govert. too will find ample retribution for its disbursements in a multiplication of the means from which future supplies are to arise.

This mode of encouragement, nevertheless, may perhaps be moderated, in its ~~qua~~ degree, by the consideration of the heavy expences, which the distance of the U States from the manufacturing countries of Europe imposes on the introduction of foreign supplies—amounting to 15, 20 & 25 ℔ Cent on their value according to their bulk. ~~Questions have been made concerning the right of the U States to adopt this mode of encouraging the industry of the Society. But.~~

No. IV

~~The~~

4 V Premiums.

These are of a nature allied to bounties, though materially ~~in some respects~~

*[margin notes:]* Qr. if nothing elsewhere contradictory

Qr. how far elsewhere

distinguishable from them ^in some important features. Bounties are applicable to the whole quantity of an article produced, or manufactured, or exported, and involve a correspondent expence. Premiums serve to reward some particular excellence or superiority, some extraordinary exertion or ~~extraordinary~~ skill; and are dispensed only in a small number of cases. But their effect is to ~~ex~~ ^stimulate ~~stimulate~~ general effort. ~~Being so contin~~ Contrived so as to be ~~both~~ honorary ^both ~~as well as~~ ^and lucrative they ^address themselves to ~~touch different chords and excite different put in motion~~ different passions, touching the chords as well of emulation as of avarice. They are accordingly a very œconomical mean of exciting the enterprise of a whole community.

There are various societies in different countries, ~~the U States included~~, whose object is the dispensation of premiums for the encouragement of agricuture arts ~~and~~ manufactures ^and Commerce;; and though they are for the most part, voluntary associations, with comparatively slender funds, their utility has been immense. Much has been done ^by this mean ~~in this way~~ in Great Britain: Scotland ^in particular owes materially to ~~this cause~~ ^it a prodigious ~~mal~~ amelioration of ~~its~~ ^her condition. From A similar establishment ^in the U States ~~in the United States~~ supplied and supported by the Government of the Union vast benefits might reasonably be expected. Some ^further ideas on

End of IV
this head ^shall accordingly be submitted in the ~~will~~ conclusion of this report.

5 Drawbacks of the duties ^which are imposed on f ~~the raw~~ ^the materials of Manufactures—

~~These~~ ^This constitutes another and an obviously proper method of encouraging ^them ~~manufactures~~. It is in general good policy to forbear ~~the~~ lay taxing ~~of~~ ^the materials of manufactures ~~raw materials~~; but there are ~~expect~~ exceptions to the rule. Of these the following are ^examples ~~instances~~. Where the ~~raw~~ material is itself an ~~immediate~~ object of general ^or extensive consumption, and a fit and

productive source of revenue. ⟨Such is the article of molasses: As a
        too
sweet ^ it is just that the consumers of it ~~as~~ should pay a duty as well
                                    ^the article is in fact
as the consumers of Sugar.⟩ Where ^ ~~the material it has assumed the~~
                    ^though of a simpler kind
~~shape of~~ a munufacture ^, (of which it is proper to prevent a competition with some similar ~~national~~ domestic manufacture) and is yet
capable of a further process, by which it may be converted into a
manufacture of a different kind which it is ~~desired~~ desireable to encourage. Such may be deemed cottons and linnens in their white
states, ~~proper for the purpose of being converted into Callicoes~~. A
                                          ^is
duty upon them as an article of consumption ^ ~~would be~~ proper to
favour the manufacture of the article in the same ~~state~~—A drawback
                is                    to            e
of that duty ^ ~~would be~~ proper ~~for~~ ^ encouragi~~ng~~ the printing and
staining of them at home.
        expediency of such
The ^ ~~propriety of~~ drawbacks is enforced in ~~similar cases~~ by the
consideration, that it is the practice of nations who may be our competitors either in the domestic or in foreign markets. The ideas has
        by the U States,                      it will probably be found that
been pursued ^ in respect to the article of molasses [97] & ^ it may be
advantageously extended to other articles.
        6
VI   6   The exemption of the materials of manufactures from duty.
The expediency of this policy has been already noticed with the
exceptions of which it admits. ~~No species of en~~ Nothing certainly can
be more obviously proper in itself—and the necessity of it is enforced
by the same consideration which has been remarked in relation to
Drawbacks namely that it is the practice of the principal manufacturing nations: those whom we are to meet as ~~our~~ competitors both in

97. The drawback on molasses was allowed under Section 51 of "An Act repealing, after the last day of June next, the duties heretofore laid upon Distilled
Spirits imported from abroad, and laying others in their stead; and also upon
Spirits distilled within the United States, and for appropriating the same," which
reads in part as follows: "*Be it further enacted*, That if any of the said spirits . . .
shall, after the last day of June next, be exported . . . there shall be an allowance
to the exporter . . . by way of drawback . . . upon spirits distilled within the
United States, from molasses . . . three cents per gallon . . ." (1 *Stat*. 210–11
[March 3, 1791]).

our own and in foreign markets. This policy has been pursued by the
U States in relation to a number of articles but it will <sub>probably</sub> be found
adviseable to extend it to others. Of a nature somewhat allied to this
is the exempting from duty the tools and implements ~~of foreign artists~~ <sup>of their trade</sup>
& the household furniture of foreign artists who come to <sup>settle in</sup> the United
States; an advantage which has been already secured to them in com-
mon with other emigrants—and which it will be in every view proper
to continue.[98]

    VIII ¶ <sup>8</sup> The encouragement of new inventions ~~of machine~~ and
improvements at home ~~and~~ (particularly in the article of machinery)
and <sup>of</sup> the introduction of such as have been made abroad.
    This is among the most important <sub>and unexceptionable</sub> of the aids ~~that~~ <sup>which</sup> can be given

**Inspections**    to manufactures. The <sup>most usual</sup> means of encouragement are pecuniary rewards and, for a time, exclusive privileges. For the last as far as regards
**Patent Act** [99]  "Authors and Inventors" provision has been made. ~~in the existing laws~~.
But in respect to ~~some~~ improvements and secrets of extraordinary
utility and value it might be found advantageous to extend them to
introducers, though not authors nor inventors, that is, when brought
from abroad. But in this as in some other cases there is cause to regret
that there is room for ~~qu~~ a question whether the constitutional authority of the United States is competent to the good which might be
done by aiding ~~the~~ industry ~~of the Country~~ and promoting a variety
of ~~domestic~~ <sup>internal</sup> improvements of primary magnitude.
    It ought not to pass unnoticed here that it is a ~~customary~~ policy
customary with manufacturing nations to prohibit, under severe
penalties, the exportation ~~of those implemen~~ implements and machines
which they have either invented or improved. ~~Similar regulations in
the U States~~ There are already proper objects of a similar regulation
in the U States & ~~they will be multiplied~~ others will doubtless occur
from time to time. The adoption of it is dictated by the principle of

---

98. For these exemptions, see note 49.
99. H is referring to "An Act to promote the progress of useful Arts" (1 *Stat.*
109-12 [April 10, 1790]).

reciprocity. Greater liberality in such respects would be more con-
genial with the general spirit ~~which prevails~~ <sup>prevailing</sup> in this Country; but a
jealous policy every where ᵥ<sup>else</sup> will often forbid the indulgence of that
spirit.

X ~~8~~ The ~~facility~~ <sup>facilitating</sup> of pecuniary remittances from place to place. | No. V

~~This~~ <sup>I</sup> is a point of considerable ~~consequence~~ <sup>moment</sup> to trade in general, and
to manufactures in particular; by facilitating the purchase of raw
materials and provisions and the payment for manufactured supplies.
As general circulation of Bank paper which is to be expected from
the institution lately established will be a most valuable mean to this
end. ~~proposed~~. But much good ᵥ<sup>would</sup> also ~~would~~ accrue from some addi-
tional ~~sanctions to the circulation of~~ <sup>provisions</sup> ~~concerning~~ <sup>respecting</sup> ᵥinland bills of exchange. If those
drawn in one state payable in another were made negotiable, every
where, and interest and damages allowed in case of protest, it would
greatly promote the reciprocal negoti ᵥ<sup>ati</sup> ons between the citizens of different states, by rendering them more secure; and, with it, the convenience and advantage of the merchants ~~of all~~ & manufacturers of
each. ~~A law of the These will~~ <sup>which</sup> ᵥ<sup>accordingly</sup> ~~be submitted in their proper place~~

| ~~to make bills drawn in one state payable in another negotiable & to allow interest & damages~~

XI ~~9~~ The ~~facility of communication and the ease and cheapness of~~ <sup>facilitating of the</sup> transportation of commodities. | No. VI

Improvements favouring ᵥ<sup>this</sup> ~~these~~ objects intimately concern all the
domestic interests of a community; but they may without impro-
priety be mentioned as having an important ᵥ~~reference~~ <sup>relation</sup> to manufactures. There is perhaps scarcely any thing which has ᵥ~~had a more~~ <sup>been better</sup>
~~beneficial influence upon~~ <sup>calculated to ~~fr~~ assist</sup> manufactures of Great Britain than the
ameliorations of the public road of that Kingdom, and the ~~vast~~ <sup>great</sup>
progress which has been ~~latel recently~~ <sup>of late</sup> ᵥmade in opening canals. Of
the former the United States stand ~~greatly~~ <sup>much</sup> in need & for the latter

they present uncommon facilities. The symptoms of attention to ^the improvement of inland Navigation ^this great object which have appea lately appeared in some quarters and ^especially particularly in the state of Pensylvania, must fill with pleasure every breast warmed with a true zeal for the prosperity of the Country. The example it is to be hoped will be extended ^so as to and will stimule the exertions of the government and the citizens of every state. There can certainly be no object more worthy of the cares of the local administrations; and it were to be wished that there was no doubt of the power of the national Government to lend its aid direct aid ^on a comprehensive plan. This is one of those. There are improvements of this nature which could certainly be prosecuted with more efficacy by the whole than by any part or parts of the Union. Indeed There are cases in which the general interest will be ^in danger too likely to be sacrificed to the collision of some supposed adverse local interests. Jealousies in matters of this kind are as apt to exist as they are apt to be erroneous.

The following remarks are sufficiently judicious and applicable ^pertinent to deserve a literal quotation "Good roads canals and navigable rivers (says a judicious writer) [100] by diminishing the expence of carriage, put the remote parts of a country more nearly upon a level with those in the neighbourhood of the town. They are upon that account the greatest of all improvements. They encourage the cultivation of the remote which must always be the most extensive circle of the country. They are advantageous to the Town by breaking down the monopoly of the country in its neighbourhood. They are advantageous even to that part of the country. Though they introduce some rival com-

100. At the bottom of this MS page H wrote and crossed out "(Smith W of Nations 1 Vol P 219)." The edition from which H is quoting is *An Inquiry into the Nature and Causes of the Wealth of Nations. By Adam Smith, LL.D. and F.R.S. Formerly Professor of Moral Philosophy in the University of Glasgow. In Three Volumes. Vol. I* (Dublin: Printed for Messrs. Whitestone, Chamberlaine, W. Watson, Potts, S. Watson, Hoey, Williams, W. Colles, Wilson, Armitage, Walker, Moncrieffe, Jenkin, Gilbert, Cross, Mills, Hallhead, Faulkner, Hillary, and J. Colles. 1776).

References which H made to Smith, however, in other documents in the Hamilton Papers, Library of Congress, do not coincide with the pagination of this edition of *The Wealth of Nations*.

modities into the old market, they open many new markets to its produce. Monopoly besides is a great enemy to good management, which can never be universally established but in consequence of that free and universal competition which forces every body to have recourse to it for the sake of self defence. It is not more than fifty years ago that some of the Counties in the neighbourhood of London petitioned the Parliament against the extension of the turnpike roads into the remoter counties. Those remoter counties, they pretended, from the cheapness of labor would be able to sell their grass and corn cheaper in the London Market than themselves, and would thereby reduce their rents and ruin their cultivation. Their rents however have s risen and their cultivation has been improved, since that time."

Specimens of a ~~similar~~ spirit similar to that which governed the counties here spoken of present themselves too frequently to the eye of an impartial observer, and ~~m~~ render it a wish of patriotism that the body in this country ‸ whose councils ‸ so partial a spirit is least likely to predominate were at liberty to ‸ ~~pursue the public good~~ interest in those ~~instaces~~ instances in which there might be danger of the inter-ference ‸ ~~from that~~ spirit.

*(interlineations: "in" / "a local or" above "whose councils so"; "pursue & promote the general" above "pursue the public good"; "of such a" above "from that")*

But if there should be a doubt of the power of the ~~National~~ Government to embrace the whole subject, there is none of its ~~right~~ to a provision for the improvement of the Post roads; an object which merits and will doubtless occupy an early attention of the ~~national Government~~ Legislature of the United States.

*(interlineation: "competency" above "right")*

It remains to s designate some specific means for the encouragement of specific objects of manufacture in the U States.

1   of Ardent Spirits

The differences in the rates of duties heretofore laid on imported and home made spirits [101] afford considerable advantage and encouragement to the latter; yet there appears to be a strong impression on the minds of those who are concerned in distilleries, ~~that~~ even the

*(marginal notes:* No. VI *;* No. VI *;* ~~Intercourse with Indians Inspections~~ *)*

101. The differences are given in Sections 1, 14, and 15 of "An Act repealing, after the last day of June next, the duties heretofore laid upon Distilled Spirits imported from abroad, and laying others in their stead; and also upon Spirits distilled within the United States, and for appropriating the same" (1 *Stat.* 199–214 [March 3, 1791]).

most candid, that still greater differences are requisite completely to secure the success of the business; and there are reasons which recommend an attention to this impression. ~~are reasons~~ which plead for ~~which to render still greater differences.~~ ~~expedient~~ It ~~has~~ is agreed that the price of molasses for some years past has been ~~gra~~ successively rising in the West India ~~(to~~ Market putting out of the question the temporary dearness and scarcity ~~arising from~~ occasioned by the existing disturbances in the French ~~colonies~~ Islands) which together with the duty of 3 Cents on Molasses, renders it difficult for the makers of spirits from that article to maintain with adequate profit a competition with the rum brought from the West Indies, the quality of which is ~~naturally~~ considerably superior.

Experiment only could perhaps decide, with certainty, the point—but ~~it~~ it in so important a branch of manufactures, it would be inexpedient to hazard an unfavourable issue, and better to err on the side of too great than too small a difference in the particular in question.

~~The differ~~

The object to be ~~obtained~~ accomplished may be obtained either by raising the duties on foreign spirits or diminishing ~~that on those made at home~~ those on spirits made at home. The experience of other countries demonstrates that duties on distilled liquors may be advantageously carried much further than they at present are in the United States; yet it may be a question whether it can be done; with perfect safety, under a system of collection ~~not more coerciv offe~~ secured by no greater precautions, than that which has been devised—a doubt which ~~recommends~~ conspiring with other inducements recommends ~~a diminution~~ the alternative of a diminution of the ~~spe~~ duties on home made spirits.

It is therefore proposed that there be an abatement ~~of~~ in the duties on spirits distilled within the U States; whether from foreign or domestic materials ~~of~~ at the rate of one cent ℔ Gallon of the lowest class of proof and in proportion upon the higher classes of proof.

It is probable too that some modification in the form of the duties on spirits made of domestic materials may be found expedient and convenient—but the nature of such modification is not yet sufficiently indicated by experience to be here submitted.

2   of Malt Liquors.

It has been truly observed that Malt liquors have a title to encour-
<sub>beverage</sub>
agement superior to ardent spirits—They constitute a national drink
<sub>it is</sub>
as wholesome and invigorating as ̭ palatable—leadly rarely to intoxi-
cation; while they ~~also give vent to the products of the soil~~ also
promote a demand for the surplus productions of ~~the ear~~ Agriculture.

There are materials for a tolerable conjecture ~~that~~ (though not an exact computation) that about two thirds of the malt liquors consumed in the United States are the product of domestic breweries—   Qr
the remaining third being imported. This conjecture has reference to the importation of a year ending ~~in~~ the ~~30th~~ 30th of September 1790.[102]
It is desireable and attainable that the whole consumption should be supplied by ourselves.

A considerable part of the Malt liquors imported is not superior in
<sub>those        are</sub>
quality ~~th~~ to ~~thats~~ which ~~is~~ made at home; and ~~if the same can~~ though the same cannot with truth be said of the whole, yet there is no natural impediment to the attainment of equal perfection throughout. The progress already made is an earnest of what may be accomplished. The growing competition is an assurance of improvement. This will be accelerated by measures tending to invite ~~Capital~~ a
<sub>channel</sub>
greater capital into this mode of employment.

An ~~increase of the duty~~ addition to the duty heretofore laid will conduce to this end. Instead of the existing rates it is presumed that it will be found safe and expedient to lay 8 Cents per Gallon generally.   Qr
<sub>It is to be hoped that this will</sub>
~~This will probably~~ banish from the market foreign malt liquors of
<sub>and that the best</sub>
inferior quality; ~~The better~~ kind only will continue to be imported, till it shall be supplanted by the efforts of equal skill or care at home.

102. See "Report on Imports for the Year Ending September 30, 1790," Novem-
ber 18, 1791. The enclosures to this report may be found in *ASP, Commerce and Navigation*, I, 35–43.
    The tariff rates in effect, to which H is referring here and in the remainder of this section, are cited in note 49.

~~And~~ Till then it will ~~tend to excite exertion to improve~~ be an useful stimulus to improvement. And in the mean time the payment of the increased price, for the enjoyment of a luxury, in order to the encouragement of an useful branch of domestic industry cannot reasonably be deemed a hardship.

bounty of 2 Cent ⅌ Gall on such as being made in one state shall be exported to another

## Iron

The importance of encouraging manufactures of this article and the probability of success have been strongly insisted upon.

The first of these manufactures which presents itself is steel. A considerable progress has already been made ^in^ ~~of~~ it and new undertakings are on foot. There is ^at present^ a duty ~~of~~ upon its importation of 75 ~~⅌ Ct~~. ^Cents ⅌ Cwt^ which is about 7½ ⅌ Cent on the value. It is conceived that this duty may be ^safely &^ advantageously increased to 100 Cents—And it is desireable to ensure by decisive arrangements the success of the efforts which are making ^or may be made^ to extend so useful a branch. As an auxiliary to this ^manufacture^ it is not perceived that there is any good objection to classing surgical instruments and cutlery ^generally^ among the articles which are rated at 7½ ⅌ Cent.

Qr. as to bounty on steel exportation

~~The~~ Nails ^& spikes^ next present themselves to consideration. This manufacture has already attained very considerable maturity. Several of the states almost wholly supply themselves and furnish a surplus to the others. There is no doubt that the U States are completely adequate to their own supply in this article. And it is one for which they ought to depend on no other nation.

Qr.

It appears that the importation of this article for a year ending the last of September 1790 was 1579947 lb a quantity which though far f short of the total consumption of the country is too great to be permitted to continue.

The present duty is of 1 Cent ⅌ lb generally on Nails and spikes which appears not to be sufficient and is perhaps not in the best ^form^ there the                    of the article.

being a very great inequality in the value of ˄different kinds Twenty

℔ Cent ad valorem while it obviated this objection would probably

be found adequate to the end proposed.

Various other manufactures of iron and to a considerable extent
are carried on in the U States. The addition of iron wares generally
to the class of articles rated at 7½ ℔ Cent would have a very beneficial effect for the manufacture and is in other respects liable to no
material objection.

It may also be expedient to grant a bounty on the implements of
husbandry made in the United States, namely Scythes

Pickaxes

spades

shovels

hoes

which may be regulated suficicially according to a ratio of 2 ℔ Cent
of their value. This would have the double effect of promoting their

of

manufacture and ˄~~favouring husbandry~~ indemnifying agriculture for
the increase of duty on the imported article. A bounty likewise on

home made

the exportation of ˄Nails ~~m~~ might be found to have a beneficial tendency. ~~The~~ The rate may be ~~5 ℔ Cent~~ 50 cents ℔ hundred weight.

It will moreover deserve the serious consideration of the Legislature
whether the importation of Iron in ~~gu~~ pigs and bars ought not to be
permitted free of duty. It now pays 5 ℔ Cent. This would certainly
tend to encourage manufactures of the article. The doubt only is
whether it may not interfere with the production of it, which is
certainly of far greater importance. The following circumstances
abate if they do not remove apprehension on this score. The price of
iron has ~~risen~~ of late years risen in the lowest markets of the United
States from 65 to 80 Dollars ℔ Ton. It is therefore presumeable that
sufficient profit will remain if foreign Iron is admitted free of duty.

also

The increase of demand ˄will ~~also~~ serve to counteract the ~~effect of a~~

iron,

reduction of price from the competition of foreign below the desireable level. ~~This~~ An augmentation of demand has already ~~taken place~~
proceeded from the Trade to the East Indies and progress of domestic

---

Qr

quare if not
2 Cents ℔
lb or 25 ℔ Ct
at valorem

~~Note boun-
ties given by
Eng & Ire-
land on Iron
Wares~~

note all
bounties to
be on public
factories—

manufactures. The regulations here proposed for their further encouragement will necessarily promote a greater augmentation.

Muskets and small fire arms of every kind.
It would appear adviseable to impose on these a specific duty according to the following rates
    For every musket
        Fusee
        Fowling piece
        Blunderbuss
        Carbine
        p pistols
And it would assist the manufacture to allow a bounty on the exportation of such as are made in the U States which may be regulated according to
~~upon~~ the ratio of     ℔ Centum of the value.

If in addition to this it were ~~establ~~ provided by law that a certain number annually of muskets manufactured in the U States should be purchased on the account of the government at a liberal determinate price, towards the formation of magazines it would have a considerable effect as a mode of encouragement, by producing a certainty of demand to a given extent. ~~The price~~    ℔ Musket would be not an extravagant price and it would ~~answer~~ be an adequate one for the manufacturer.

### Gun Powder

This article is already rated at 10 ℔ Ct. on its importation from abroad. There is no need of any further duty. There seem but ~~three~~
success
things requisite to complete its ~~progress~~ which is already consider-
~~which is~~ (a principal ingredient in its composition)
able. One is to rank surphur ∧ among ~~the free articles~~ free goods. Of this article no great quantity has yet been produced in the United States—Another is to establish proper regulations for its inspection; and a third which will deserve to be considered is a bounty on its exportation. For this purpose a dollar ~~for~~ ℔ hundred weight ~~will~~ may be the proper standard. Great Britain allows in the like case 4/6 Stg.[103]

103. This bounty, given in 4 Geo. II, C. 29 (1731), had been extended by various acts and was repealed by 31 Geo. III, C. 42 (1791).

The bounty by promoting a foreign demand for the article will tend to ensure the demand necessary to its support.

~~The It is said~~

     an
It is said to be ∧injunction on the British East India Company to import annually a certain quantity of salt Petre rough or refined in order to assist the manufacture of Gunpowder.[104] A similar regulation with regard to Ships trading to China from the U States proportioned to the Tonnage of each may ~~be~~ perhaps be enacted without inconvenience. No American factories being established in other ~~pla~~ parts

             ∧if made
of the East Indies ~~the reason requisition~~ a requisition of this nature∧

     vessels from
ought to be confined to∧the Port of Canton.


    Sail Cloath and other coarse Linnens
  Considering that Great Britain grants a bounty of 2d. Sterling pr.

            about
ell on the exportation of British Made sail Cloth and of ∧12½ pr Cent ad valorem upon an average on all British made linnens of ~~the~~ value ~~of~~

not exceeding
~~not less than~~ ⅙ Stg. ℗ yard, and that Ireland grants a still greater bounty on the exportation of her sail Cloth & similar bounties on that of other coarse linnens,[105] it ~~is ess~~ appears necessary to the complete success of similar manufactures in the United States that further encouragements should be given.

  First by an increase of duty. It is consequently submitted that the present duty of 5 ℗ Cent be raised to ten on the following articles

      Sail Cloth
      Oznaburghs
      Ticklenburghs
and upon all other linnens which cost at the place of exportation a rate
~~and under~~ pr. yard not exceeding 35 Cents.       18d. Stg

---

104. See note 71.
105. The sailcloth bounty, instituted in Great Britain under 12 Ann., Stat. I, C. 16 (1714), had been extended by several acts, the most recent of which was 29 Geo. III, C. 54 (1789). The linen bounty of 1 1/2d. per yard on all British and Irish linens twenty-five inches in width and between the value of 6d. and 1s. 6d. per yard had been given under 29 Geo. III, C. 15 (1756); its most recent extension was made under 28 Geo. III, C. 23 (1788). The Irish bounties were granted under 19 and 20 Geo. III, C. 33 (1779–80) and were subsequently reenacted at each session of the Irish Parliament.

home made                    Factory        2̶
Secondly   By a bounty on˄sail Cloth at the m̶a̶n̶u̶f̶a̶c̶t̶u̶r̶e̶, of 5̶1
of 5 ₩ Cent ad valorem
Cents per yard, and a s̶i̶m̶i̶l̶a̶r̶ bounty˄on all linnens of the above
descriptions made in the U States, upon their exportation to foreign
Countries.

The bounty on sail Cloth will not only promote the fabric but will
be favourable to navigation by counteracting the influence of the
upon
increased duty t̶o̶ ̶r̶a̶i̶s̶e̶ the price of the article.

## Cotton Goods

A Bounty similar to that on linnens and within the same limits as to
value                                    the exportation of
P̶r̶i̶c̶e̶ is allowed in Great Britain upon˄Cotton goods, or goods of
cotton & linnen mixed and which are either printed painted stained
or dyed; [106]

The same reason therefore which applies to linnens calls for a like
arrangement in respect to such goods.

## ALEXANDER HAMILTON'S FOURTH DRAFT
## OF THE REPORT ON THE SUBJECT
## OF MANUFACTURES[107]

Treasury
The Secretary of the˄in obedience to the order of the House of
Representatives, of the 15. day of January 1790, has applied his attention, at as early a period as his other duties would permit, to the
subject of manufactures and particularly to the means of promoting
˄tend to
such, as will˄render the United States independent on foreign nations,
for military and other essential supplies: And he thereupon respectfully submits the following report.

The expediency of encouraging manufactures in the United States,

106. See 23 Geo. III, C. 21 (1783).
107. ADf, Hamilton Papers, Library of Congress.
Small sections of this draft of the Report are in a clerk's handwriting and
are printed in italics. Interlineations and marginal comments or queries in an
unidentified handwriting have been bracketed.
Words which were underlined for emphasis in the MS are printed with underlines in this draft of the Report.

which was not long since deemed very questionable, appears at this
time to be pretty generally admitted. The embarrassments, which

been imposed upon _____ external
have ^obstructed the progress of our ^~~foreign~~ trade, have led to serious
reflections on the necessity of enlarging the sphere of our domestic

in foreign markets
commerce: the restrictive regulations, which ^abrige the vent of the

increasing
^surplus of our Agricultural produce, ~~in foreign markets, naturally~~

an earnest
serve to beget ~~a~~ ^desire, that a more extensive demand for that surplus
may be created at home: And the complete success, which has rewarded manufacturing enterprise, in some valuable branches, ~~con-~~

conspiring
~~curring~~ with the promising symptoms which attend some less mature

justify
essays, in others, ~~authorise~~ a hope, that the obstacles to the growth

~~encourage~~
~~prompt~~
~~embolden~~
~~justify~~

less than
of this species of industry are ~~not so~~ ^formidable, ~~as~~ ^they were appre-

it is not difficult to find in its further extension a full
hended to be; and that ^~~in its extension, may be found, an~~ ^indemnifica-

for any external disadvantages
tion ^~~for the effects of those external impediments which resist the~~

~~obstruct~~ which are or may be experienced; as well as an
~~tide of our prosperity, and~~ ^an accession of resources, favourable to
national independence and safety.

There still are nevertheless, respectable patrons of opinions, unfriendly to the encouragement of manufactures. The following are,
substantially, the arguments by which ~~support~~ these opinions are ~~sup-~~

defended
~~ported.~~

(say those who entertain them)
"In very country ~~('tis alleged)~~ ^Agriculture is the most beneficial

generally if not
and productive object of human industry. This position ^universally
true, applies with peculiar emphasis to the United States, on account

fertile territory
of their immense tracts of ^uninhabited and unimproved. Nothing
can afford so advantageous an employment for capital and labour,

[extensive] rude
as the conversion of ~~so~~ this ^~~vast~~ wilderness into cultivated farms. Qr 4
Nothing, equally with this, can contribute to the population strength
and real riches of the country."

"To endeavour, by the extraordinary patronage of Government, to
accelerate the growth of manufactures, is <sub>in fact,</sub> to endeavour, by force
and art, to transfer the natural current of industry, from a more to
a less beneficial channel. Whatever has such a tendency must necessarily be unwise. Indeed, it can hardly ever [be proper] wise in a government to
attempt to give a direction to the industry of its citizens: This, under
the quick-sighted guidance of private interest, will, if left to itself,
infallibly find its own way to wherever it can meet with [into channels where] the most
profitable employment: and 'tis by such employment, that the public
prosperity will be most effectually promoted. To leave industry to
itself, therefore, is in almost every case the soundest as well as the
safest of the simplest policy."

"This policy is not only recommended to the United States, by
considerations which affect all nations—it is, in a manner, dictated
to them by the imperious force of a very peculiar situation. The
smallness of their population compared with their territory—the
constant allurements to emigration from the settled to the unsettled
parts of the country—the facility, with which the less independent
situation condition of an artisan can be exchanged for the more independent condition of a farmer—these and similar causes conspire to
produce, and for a length of time, must continue to occasion, a
scarcity of hands for manufacturing occupations, and dearness of
labour generally. To these disadvantages for manufactures, a deficiency of capital being added, the prospect of a successful competition with the manufacturers of Europe must be regarded as desperate.
Extensive manufactures can only be the offspring of a redundant, at
least of a full population. Till the latter shall characterise the situation
of this country, 'tis vain to hope for the former."

"If contrary to the natural course of things, an unseasonable and
premature spring can be given to certain fabrics, by heavy duties,
prohibitions, bounties, or by other forced expedients; this will only
be to sacif sacrifice the interests of the community to those of particular classes. Besides the misdirection of labour, a virtual monopoly

will be given to the persons employed on such fabrics; and an enhancement of price, the inevitable consequence of every monopoly,
must be defrayed at the expence of the other parts of the society. It
is far preferable, that those persons should be engaged in the cultivation of the earth, and that we should ~~produe~~ procure, ^in exchange for ~~with~~ its
productions, the commodities, with which foreigners are able to
supply ^us in greater perfection, and upon better terms."

This mode of reasoning is founded upon facts and principles, ~~and
is espoused~~ which have certainly ~~very~~ respectable pretensions. If it
had governed the conduct of nations, more generally than it has done,
there is room to suppose, that it ^might ~~would~~ have carried them faster to
prosperity and greatness, than they have attained, by the pursuit of
maxims too ^widely ~~far~~ opposite. Most general theories, however, admit of
numerous exceptions; and there are few ^if any of the political kind, which
do not blend a considerable portion of error, with the truths they
~~contain~~ inculcate. ~~That, which has been stated, does not, it is presumed, steer clear of this imputation. In order to an accurate judgment how far this may be the case, it is necessary to advert to the
considerations which are to be found in a contrary scale, and which
appear to recommend the positive and special encouragement of
manufactures in countries where they do not happen to prevail and
particularly in the United States.~~

In order to an accurate judgment how far that which has been
just stated ought to be deemed liable to a similar imputation, it is
necessary to advert ^carefully to the considerations which plead in favour of
manufactures, and which, appear to recommend the special and positive encouragement of them; in certain cases, and under certain reasonable limitations.

It ought readily to be conceded that the cultivation of the earth—
as the primary and most certain source of national supply—as the
immediate and chief source of subsistence to man—as the principal
source of those materials which ^constitute ~~are~~ the nutriment of other kinds of
labour—as including a state most favourable to the freedom and inde-

pendence of the human mind—one, perhaps, most conducive to the multiplication of the human species, has <u>intrinsically</u> <u>a</u> <u>strong</u> <u>claim</u> <u>to</u> <u>pre-eminence</u> <u>over</u> <u>every</u> <u>other</u> <u>kind</u> <u>of</u> <u>industry</u>.

But that it has a title to any thing like an exclusive predilection in any country, ought to be admitted with great caution—That it is even more productive than every other branch of Industry requires more evidence than has yet been given, in support of the position—

That its ^real interests, ^precious and important as, without the help of ^they truly are, ~~may be~~ will be advanced rather than injured by the due en-couragement of manufactures, may, it is ^believed ~~presumed~~, be ~~fairly~~ ^[~~clearly~~] satisfactorily demon-strated—And ^it is also ~~it is~~ believed that the expediency of such encouragement, ^in a general view may be shewn to be ~~resulting~~ recommended ~~in other respects by~~ ^and persuasive ~~from the~~ by the most cogent ^motives of national policy, ~~may be placed in a light, which it is believed, can leave little room for question or doubt.~~

It has been maintained, ~~not only~~ that Agriculture is, not only, the most productive, but the only productive species of industry. The reality of this suggestion ^in either aspect has, however, not been verified by any accurate detail of facts and calculations; and the general arguments, which are adduced to prove it, are rather subtil and paradoxical than solid or convincing.

Those which maintain its exclusive productiveness are to this effect—

Labour, bestowed upon the cultivation of land, produces enough, not only to replace all the necessary expences incurred in the business, and to maintain the persons ^who are employed in it, but to afford, together with the <u>ordinary</u> <u>profit</u> on the stock or capital ^of ~~employed by~~ the Farmer, a nett surplus, or <u>rent</u> for the landlord or proprietor of the soil. But the labour of Artificers does nothing more, than replace the stock which employs them (or which furnishes materials tools and wages) and yield the <u>ordinary</u> <u>profit</u> upon that stock. It ^yields ~~yields~~ nothing equivalent to the <u>rent</u> of land. Neither does it <u>add</u> any thing to the ^total value of the <u>whole</u> <u>annual</u> <u>produce</u> of the land and labour of the country. The additional value given to those parts of the produce of

land, which are wrought into manufactures, is counterballanced by
the value of those other parts of that produce, which are consumed
by the manufacturers. It can therefore only be by saving, or parsimony, not by the positive productiveness of their labour, that the
Qr.

                                                                   nett
classes of Artificers can in any degree augment the revenue or income
of the Society.

    To this system, it has been answered—

I. That inasmuch as it is acknowleged, that manufacturing labour
reproduces a value equal to that, which is expended or consumed in
                                        original
carrying it on, and continues in existence the stock or capital em-
      ought,
ployed—it on that account alone, ought to escape being considered
as wholly unproductive: That though it should be admitted, as
alleged, that the consumption of the produce of the soil, by the classes
                                        ex
of Artificers or manufacturers, is exquactly equal to the value added
                                            exerted
by their labour to the materials upon which it is bestowed; yet it
would not thence follow, that it added nothing to the Revenue of
the Society, or to the aggregate value of the annual produce of its
land and labour. If the consumption for any given period amounted
                                            the
to a given sum and the increased value of produce manufactured, in
the same period, to a like sum, the total amount of the consumption
and production, during that period, would be equal to the two sums,
and consequently double the value of the agricultural produce con-
                      increment of
sumed. And though the value of produced by the classes of Artificers
should at no time exceed the value of the produce of the land consumed by them, yet there would be at every moment, in the market
consequence of their labour, a greater value of goods in the market,
than would exist independent of it.

       as far as
    That it is true that the labour of of Artificers can

                                    m
II. That the position, that Artificers can augment the nett revenue of
a Society, only by parsimony, is true in no other sense than in one
                             Husbandmen or
which is equally applicable to the Cultivators. It may be alike affirmed
    all
of these different classes, that the fund acquired by their labour and

destined for their support is not, in an ordinary way, more than equal

to it. And hence it will follow, that augmentations of the ₍wealth or₎ capital ~~or~~
~~wealth~~ of the community ₍(except in the instances of some extraordinary dexterity or skill)₎ can only proceed, with respect to any of
them, from the savings of the more thrifty and parsimonious. ~~ext~~
~~except in the instances of some extraordinary dexterity or skill.~~

[~~profits may~~
~~arise from~~
~~Sales to for-~~
~~eign Na-~~
~~tions~~]

III. That the annual produce of the land and labour of a country
can only be increased in two ways—by some improvement in the
<u>productive powers</u> of the useful labour, which actually exists within
it, or by some increase in the <u>quantity</u> of ~~that~~ ₍such₎ labour: That with regard to the first, the labour of artificers being capable of greater
subdivision and simplicity of operation than that of cultivators, ₍it₎ is
susceptible, in a proportionably greater degree, of improvement in
its <u>productive powers</u>, whether to be derived from an ₍accession₎ ~~increase~~ of
skill or ₍from₎ the ~~applicable~~ application of ingenious machinery; in which
particular, therefore, the labour employed in the culture of land can
pretend to no advantage over that engaged in manufactures: That
with regard to an augmentation of the quantity of useful labour, this,
excluding adventitious circumstances, must depen~~ding~~ essentially
upon an increase of <u>capital,</u> which again must depend upon the savings
made out of the revenues of those, who furnish or manage <u>that,</u> which
is at any time employed, whether in Agriculture, or in Manufactures,
or in ~~some~~ ₍any₎ other way.

But while the <u>exclusive</u> productiveness of Agricultural labour has
been thus denied₍and refuted,₎ the superiority of its productiveness has been conceded without hesitation. As ~~the prevalent opinion in this country~~
~~corresponds with~~ this concession, ~~and as it~~ involves a point of considerable magnitude, in relation to maxims of public administration, ~~it~~
~~seems nece~~ the grounds on which it rests ₍are worthy of₎ ~~seem to require~~ a distinct
and particular examination.

One of the arguments made use of, in support of the idea ₍may be₎ ~~is not~~
~~less~~ ₍pronounced both₎ quaint ~~than~~ ₍and₎ superficial. It amounts to this—That in the produc-

tions of the soil, nature cooperates with man; and ~~it is inferred~~, that the effect of their joint labour must be greater than that of the labour of man alone.

This however is far from being a necessary inference. It is very conceivable, that the labour of man alone ~~bestowed~~ <sup>laid out</sup> upon ~~an~~ a work, ~~art and ingenuity~~ requiring great skill and art to bring it to perfection, may be more productive <sup>in</sup> value, than the labour of nature and man combined, when directed towards more simple operations and objects: And when it is recollected, to what an extent the agency of nature, in the application of the mechanical powers, is made auxiliary to the prosecution of manufactures, ~~little more than the quaintness of the suggestion remains~~ the suggestion, which has been noticed, loses even the appearance of plausibility.

It might <sup>also</sup> ~~even~~ be observed, with a contrary view, that ~~in Agriculture~~ the labour ~~of man~~ employed in ~~Agree~~ Agriculture is in a great measure periodical and occasional, depending on seasons, ~~and~~ liable to various and long intermissions; while that occupied ~~in~~ <sup>many</sup> manufac <sup>tures</sup> is constant, ~~incessant~~ <sup>and regular,</sup> extending through the years, embracing in some instances night as well as day. It is also probable that there are among the cultivators of land more examples of remissness than among artificers. The farmer, ~~may~~ from the peculiar fertility of his land or some other <sup>favourable</sup> circumstance may frequently obtain a livelihood, even with a considerable degree of carelessness in the mode of cultivation; but the Artisan ~~Greater ingenuity as well as steadiness~~ can with difficulty effect the same objects ~~unless~~ <sup>without</sup> exerting himself pretty equally with all those who are engaged in the same pursuit. And if it may likewise be assumed as a fact, that manufactures open a wider field to exertions of ingenuity than agriculture, it would not be a strained conjecture, that the labour employed in the former, being at once more constant <sup>more uniform</sup> and more ingenious, than that which is employed in the latter, will be found at the same time ~~most pro~~ <sup>more</sup> productive.

But it is not meant to lay ~~great~~ stress on observations of this nature

—they ought only to serve ~~to~~ as ^a counter ballance to^ ~~a counter~~ those of a similar complexion. Circumstances so vague, and general, as well as so abstract, can afford little instruction, in a matter of this kind. ~~light~~

Another, and ^that^ which seems to be the principal argument, ~~that has been~~ offered for the superior productiveness of Agricultural Labour, turns upon the allegation, that labour employed in manufactures yields nothing equivalent to the rent of land; or to that nett surplus, as it is called, which accrues to the proprietor of the soil.

But this distinction, important as it has been deemed, appears rather verbal than substantial. To bring it under a more precise ^view^ ~~inspection~~, it may be of use ~~of~~ in this place to restate the proposition, which is to be examined. It is this—"Labour employed in Agriculture, besides replacing the expences of the business, and yielding the ordinary profit on the stock or capital of the ~~farmer or~~ tenant, yields also a nett surplus or rent to the ~~landlord or~~ owner of the land. But the labour employed in manufactures only replaces the expences of the business, and yields the ordinary profit on the stock or Capital of the Undertaker." [108]

It is easily discernible, that what in the first ^instance^ ~~case~~ is divided into two parts under the denominations of the ordinary profit of the stock of the farmer and rent to the landlord is, in the second ^instance^ ~~case~~ united under the ~~simple~~ ^general^ appellation of the ordinary profit ^on^ ~~of~~ the stock of the Undertaker; and that this ^formal or^ verbal distribution constitutes the whole difference in the two cases. It seems to have been overlooked, that the land is itself a stock or capital, advanced or lent by its owner to the occupier or tenant, and that the rent he receives is only the ordinary profit of a certain stock in land, not managed by the proprietor himself, but by another to whom he lends or lets it, and who ^on his part^ advances a second capital to stock and ^improve^ ~~cultivate~~ the land, upon which he also receives the usual profit. The rent of the landlord, and the profit of

108. This quotation is a paraphrase from Smith, *Wealth of Nations*, II, 179–80.

the farmer are therefore nothing more than the <u>ordinary</u> <u>profits</u> of <u>two</u> capitals, belonging to <u>two</u> different persons, and united in the cultivation of a farm: As in the other case, the surplus which arises upon any manufactory, after replacing the expences of carrying it on, ~~corresponds with~~ answers to the ordinary profits of <u>one</u> or <u>more</u>
<sub>such</sub>
capitals engaged in the prosecution of ~~a~~ manufactory. It is said, one or more capitals; because in fact, the same thing which is contem-
<sub>that of</sub>
plated in the case of the farm, sometimes happens in ~~respect to~~ ₍a₎
<sub>a part of</sub>
manufactory. There is one who ~~lends~~ furnishes ₍the₎ capital, or lends a part of the money, by which it is carried on, and another, who carries it on, with the addition of his own capital. Out of the surplus,
<sub>remains</sub>                                                    money–
which ₍~~arises~~₎, after defraying expences, an interest is paid to the₍₎ lender for the portion of the capital ~~adv~~ furnished by him which
<sub>exactly agrees with</sub>
~~corresponds with~~ ₍the₎ rent paid to the landlord; and the residue of that surplus constitutes the profit of the ~~undertaking undertaken ee~~
<sub>and</sub>
undertaker or manufacturer, ~~which~~ ₍agrees₎ with what is denominated
<sub>make</sub>
the ordinary profits on the stock of the farmer. Both together ₍~~amount~~₎ ~~to~~ the <u>ordinary</u> <u>profits</u> of <u>two</u> <u>capitals</u> employed in a manufactory; as in the other case the rent of the landlord and the revenue of the
<sub>compose</sub>
farmer ₍~~constitute~~₎ the ordinary profits of two capitals employed in the cultivation of a farm.

The rent therefore accruing to the proprietor of the land, far from being a criterion of <u>exclusive</u> productiveness as has been argued, is no criterion even of superior productiveness. The question must still be, whether the surplus, after defraying expences, of a <u>given</u> <u>capital</u> em-
<sub>and</sub>
ployed in the <u>purchase</u> ~~or~~ <u>improvement</u> of a piece of land is greater or less than that of a like capital employed in the prosecution of a
<sub>whole</sub>
manufactory: or whether the <u>value</u> <u>produced</u> from a <u>given</u> <u>capital</u> and a <u>given</u> <u>quantity</u> <u>of</u> <u>labour</u>, employed in one way, be greater or less, than the ~~value~~ whole ~~net~~ value <u>produced</u> from an <u>equal</u> <u>capital</u> and an <u>equal</u> <u>quantity</u> <u>of</u> <u>labour</u> employed in the other way: or rather,

                                               that of
perhaps, whether the business of Agriculture or͜Manufactures will
yield the greatest product, according to a compound ratio of the
quantity of Capital & the quantity of labour, ~~employed~~ which are
                                        in
employed in the one or͜ the other.

   The solution of either of these questions is not easy; it involves
numerous and ~~capit~~ complicated details, depending on an accurate
knowlege of the objects to be compared. It is not known that the
comparison has ever yet been made upon sufficient data properly
                 on the present occasion with satisfactory precision, ~~and certainty~~,
ascertained and analized. To ~~do~~ be able to make it͜ would ~~req~~ demand
       ͜previous
more͜ inquiry and investigation than there has been hitherto either
leisure or opportunity to accomplish. ~~Some essays however have been
made towards acquiring the requisite information; the result of which
does b by no means confirm the hypothesis of the superior productiveness which is under examination.~~

   Some essays however have been made towards acquiring the
requisite information; which have rather served to throw doubt
upon, than to confirm the hypothesis, under examination. But it ought
[~~remissness~~
Skill
~~cases~~
~~mode~~] ☞
to be acknowleged, that they have been too little diversified, and are
too imperfect, to authorise a definitive conclusion either way; leading
rather to probable conjecture, than to certain deduction. They render
                              various
it probable, that there are͜ ~~some~~ branches of manufactures, in which
a given Capital will yield a greater total product, and a considerably
greater nett product, than an equal capital invested in the purchase
and improvement of lands; ~~in an already establ~~ which are ~~under
previous cultivation~~, and that there are also some branches, in which
both the gross and the nett produce will exceed that of Agricultural
industry, according to a compound ratio of capital and labour. But
it is on this last point, that there appears to be the greatest room for
                          infer
doubt. It is far less difficult to ~~decide~~ generally, that the nett produce
           engaged
of Capital ~~invested~~͜ in manufacturing enterprises is greater than that
of Capital engaged in Agriculture.

   ~~But~~ In stating these results, the purchase and improvement of lands, under previous cultivation ~~is~~ ^are^ alone contemplated. The comparison is more in favour of Agriculture, when it is made with reference to the settlement of new and waste ~~of~~ lands; but an argument drawn ^from so^ ~~for~~ temporary a circumstance could have no weight in determining the ~~course~~ general ~~merits of the~~ question concerning the ^permanent relative^ ~~comparative~~ ^the two species^ productiveness of ^of^ ~~Agricultural and manufacturing~~ industry. How far it ought to influence the policy of the United States, on the score of particular situation, will be adverted to in another place.

vide

The foregoing ^suggestions^ ~~conjectures~~ are not designed to inculcate ^an opinion^ ~~a supposition~~ that manufacturing industry is <u>more</u> productive than that of Agriculture. They are intended rather to shew that the ^re^ ~~converse~~ of this proposition is not ascertained; ~~and~~ that the general arguments which are ^brought^ ~~used~~ to establish it are not satisfactory; and ^consequently^ that a supposition of the superior productiveness of Tillage ought to be no obstacle to listening to any substantial inducements to the encouragement of manufactures, ~~m~~ which may be otherwise perceived to exist; ~~on the~~ ~~as having a~~ ^through an apprehension that they may have a^ ~~ground~~ ~~if~~ ^its^ tendency to divert labour from a more to a less profitable employment.

It is extremely probable, that on a full and accurate developpement of the ~~manner~~ matter, on the ^ground^ ~~basis~~ of fact and calculation, it would be discovered, that there is no material difference between the aggregate productiveness of the one and of the other kind of industry ~~in question~~; and that the propriety of the encouragements, which may in any case be proposed to be given to either ought to be determined upon considerations ^irrelative to any^ ~~exclusive of all~~ comparison of that nature.

But without contending for the superior productiveness of Manufacturing Industry, ^it may conduce to a better judgment of the policy which ought to be pursued,^ ~~it would be to omit doing justice to the subject not to place it in some farther light under~~ respecting its encouragement, to ^to contemplate^ ~~view~~ the subject under some additional aspects, tending ~~not~~

[~~The two employments will regulate themselves~~ ~~If manufactures will consume produce, Agriculture must produce for Manufactures.~~]

~~in respect to~~ respecting its encouragement to view the subject

ₐnot only to confirm the idea
ₐ~~still further~~ that this kind of Industry
~~only to evince still further not only that it~~ has been improperly repre-
ₐto evince in addition ~~to fur shew~~
sented as unproductive in itself; but ₐ~~that the establishment~~ of manu-
~~likewise~~ that the establishment and diffusion
factures have the effect of rendering the total mass of ~~the~~ useful and
productive labour, in a community, <u>greater</u> than <u>it</u> <u>would</u> <u>otherwise</u>
<u>be.</u> In prosecuting this discussion, it may be necessary briefly to
resume and review some of the topics which have been already
touched.

To affirm that the labour of the Manufacturer is unproductive,
because he consumes as much of the produce of land, as he adds value
to the raw materials, which he manufactures, is not better founded,
that it would be to affirm, that the labour of the farmer, which furnishes materials to the manufacturer, is unproductive <u>because</u> he <u>con-</u>
<u>sumes</u> <u>an</u> <u>equal</u> <u>value</u> <u>of</u> <u>manufactured</u> articles. Each furnishes a
ₐportion
certainₐ~~quantum~~ of the produce of his labour to the other and each
ₐportion          ₐproduce of the
destroys a correspondentₐ~~quantum~~ of theₐlabour of the other. In the
mean time, the maintenance of two citizens instead of one is going on,
the state has two members instead of one; and they together consume
twice the value of what is produced from the land.

If instead of a farmer and artificer, there were a farmer only, he
would be under a necessity of devoting a part of his labour to the
fabrication of cloathing and other articles, which he would procure
ₐin the case of there being
of the artificer ~~if there were~~ₐsuch a person; and of course he would
be able to devote less labour to the cultivation of his farm, and would
ₐproduct.
draw from it a proportionably lessₐ~~quantity of produce~~. The whole
quantity of production, in this state of things, in provisions raw
materials and manufactures, would certainly not exceed in value the
amount of what would be produced in provisions and raw materials
only, if there were an artificer as well as a farmer.

Again—if there were both an artificer and a farmer, the latter
would be left at liberty to pursue exclusively the cultivation of his
farm. A greater quantity of provisions and raw materials would of
course be produced—equal at least, as has been already observed, to

the whole amount of the provisions raw materials and manufactures which would exist on a contrary supposition. The artificer, at the same time, would be going on in the production of manufactured
<sub>commodities,</sub>
~~articles~~ to an amount sufficient not only to repay the farmer, in those commodities, for the provisions and materials which were procured from him, but to furnish the Artificer himself with a supply of similar commodities for his own use. Thus then, there would be two
<sub>in existence</sub>
quantities or values<sub>^</sub>instead of one; and the ~~income~~ revenue and consumption would be double in one case, what it would be in the other.

If in place of both these suppositions, there were supposed to be two farmers, and no artificer, each of whom applied a part of his labour to the culture of ~~his~~ land and another part to the fabrication of
<sub>both ~~which was~~</sub>
manufactures—in this case, the portion of the labour of<sub>^</sub>~~each~~ bestowed upon land would produce the same quantity of provisions and raw materials only as would be produced by the intire sum of the labour of one applied in the same manner, and the portion of the labour of both ~~which was~~ bestowed upon manufactures, would pro-
<sub>only</sub>
duce the same quantity of manufactures<sub>^</sub>, as would be produced by the intire sum of the labour of one applied in the same manner. Hence the ~~value of the~~ produce of the labour of the two farmers would not be greater than ~~that of~~ the produce of the labour of the farmer and
<sub>results</sub>
artificer; and hence, it<sub>^</sub>~~is manifest~~, that the labour of the artificer is as positively productive as that of the farmer, and, as positively, augments the revenue of the Society.

The labour of the Artificer replaces to the farmer that portion of his labour, with which he provides the materials of exchange with the Artificer, and which he would otherwise have been compelled to apply to manufactures: and while the Artificer thus enables the farmer to enlarge his stock of agricultural industry, a portion of which he purchases for his own use, <u>he also supplies himself with the manufactured articles of which he stands in need</u>. ~~thus producing over and above the equivalent which he gives to the farmer~~.

He does still more. Besides this equivalent which he gives for the portion of agricultural labour consumed by him and this supply of manufactured commodities for his own <sub>^</sub>use—he furnishes <sub>^</sub>a surplus, which compensates for the use of the Capital advanced either by himself or some other person, for carrying on the business. This is the ordinary profit of the stock employed in the manufactory, and is in every <sub>^</sub>respect as effective an addition to the income of the Society as the rent of land.

The produce of the labour of the Artificer, consequently, may ~~justly~~ be regarded as composed of three parts; one by which the provisions for his subsistence and the materials for his work are purchased of the farmer, one by which he supplies himself with manufactured necessaries, and a third which constitutes the profit on the Stock employed. The two last portions seem to have been overlooked in the system, which represents manufacturing industry as ~~an~~ barren and unproductive.

In the course of the preceding illustrations <sub>^</sub>equal quantities of the labour of the farmer and artificer have been treated as <sub>^</sub>equal to each other. ~~Simplicity and perspicuity required this mode of expression, but it will not be understood as being indicating an intention to assert an exact equality in the value of the produce of~~ But this is not to be understood as intending to assert any such precise equality. It is merely a manner of expression adopted for the sake of simplicity and perspicuity. Whether the <sub>^</sub>produce of the labour of the Farmer be some what more or less than that of the Artificer is not material to the main scope of the argument which <sub>^</sub>only aimed at shewing, that the one, as well as the other, occasions a positive augmentation of the total produce and revenue of the Society.

It is now ~~the~~ proper to proceed a step ~~a~~ further, and to enumerate the principal circumstances, ~~whence~~ it may be inferred—That manufacturing establishments not only occasion a positive augmentation of the ~~Rev~~ Produce and Revenue of the Society, but <sub>^</sub>contribute essentially to rendering them greater than they could possibly be, without such establishments. These circumstances are—

1  The ~~effects of~~ a division of Labour
2  An extension of the use of Machinery
3  ~~The~~ Additional employment to classes of the community not ~~regularly~~ ordinarily engaged in the business
4  The promoting of emigration from foreign countries
5  The furnishing greater scope for the diversity of talents and

   which are to be found

   dispositions ~~among the citizens of a Country~~ which discriminate men from each other.
6  The affording a more ample and various field for enterprize.
7  The creating in some instances a new, and securing in all, a
   more certain and steady demand for the surplus produce of the
   soil.

[~~and the ac-
quisition of
foreign Capi-
tal~~]

Each of these circumstances has a considerable influence upon the
total mass of industrious effort in a community: Together, they ~~in-~~

energy

~~crease it and enhance~~ add to it a degree of ~~force~~ and effect, which are

comments

not easily conceived. Some ~~remarks~~ upon each of them in the order
in which they have been stated may serve to explain their importance.

   I   As to the Division of Labour.

   It has justly been observed, that there is ~~sae~~ scarcely any thing of

moment,                    a

greater ~~importance~~ in the œconomy of nations, than the proper division of labour. The separation of occupations causes each to be carried ~~on~~ to much greater perfection, than it could possibly acquire, if
they were blended. This arises principally from three circumstances—

   1 ~~One~~ The greater skill and dexterity naturally resulting from a

application

constant and undivided ~~attention~~ to a single object. It is evident that
these properties must increase, in proportion to the separation and
simplification of objects and the steadiness of the attention devoted to
each; and must be less, in proportion to the complication of objects,
and the number among which the attention is destracted.

the

   2 ~~Another is~~ The œconomy of time—by avoiding ~~that~~ loss of it,
~~which is naturally~~ incident to a frequent transition from one operation to another, of a different nature. This depends on various circumstances—the transition itself—the ~~ordinary~~ orderly disposition of the
implements, machines and materials employed in the operation to be

relinquished—the preparatory steps to the commencement of a new one—the interruption of the impulse which the mind of the workman acquires from being engaged in a particular operation—the distractions hesitations and reluctances, which ~~are apt to~~ attend the passage from one kind of business to another.

3 ~~The third is~~ An extension of the use of machinery. A man occupied on a single object will have it more in his power, and will be more naturally led to exert his ^imagination, ~~invention~~ in devising methods to facilitate and abrige labour, than if he were perplexed by a variety of independent and dissimilar operations. Besides this, the fabrication of machines, in numerous instances, becoming itself a distinct trade, the Artist who follows it, has all the advantages which have been enumerated, for improvement in his particular art; and, in both ways the invention and application of machinery are extended.

And from these causes united, the ~~mere~~ [mere] separation of the occupation of the Cultivator, from that of the Artificer, has the effect of augmenting the <u>productive</u> <u>powers</u> of labour, and with them, the total mass of the produce or revenue of a Country. In this single view of the subject, therefore, the utility of Artificers or Manufacturers, towards promoting an increase of productive industry, is apparent.

II   As to an extension of the use of Machinery: a point which has ^been already, ~~in part~~ ^though partly anticipated, ~~but which~~ requires to be placed in ~~some~~ ^one or two additional lights.

The employment of Machinery ~~seems to~~ forms an item of great importance in the general mass of national industry. 'Tis an artificial

force brought in aid of the natural force of man; and, to all the proposes of labour, is an increase of hands; an accession of strength^. <u>unincumbered</u> <u>too</u> <u>by</u> <u>the</u> <u>expence</u> <u>of</u> <u>maintaining</u> <u>the</u> <u>labourer.</u>
May it not therefore be fairly inferred, that those occupations, which give greatest scope to the use of this auxiliary, contribute most to the general stock of industrious effort, and, in consequence, to the general product of Industry?

It shall be taken for granted, and the truth of the position referred to observation, that manufacturing pursuits are ~~more~~ susceptible ^in a greater degree ^of the application of Machinery, ~~for~~ than those of Agriculture. If so, all

the difference is lost to a ^community, ~~country~~ which, instead of manufacturing
for itself, procures the fabrics requisite to ~~the~~ supply ^its ~~of its wants~~, from other countries. The substitution of foreign for domestic manufactures is a transfer to foreign nations of the advantages accruing from the employment of Machinery in the modes, in which it is capable of being employed, with most utility and to the greatest extent.

The Cotton Mill invented in England, within the last twenty years,  is a signal illustration of the general proposition, which has been just advanced. In consequence of it, all the different processes for spining cotton are performed by means of machines, which are put in motion by water and attended chiefly by women and children; ~~the~~ ^a very small number of whom compared with the number requisite in ^the ordinary mode of spining, suffices. And it ^n ^is an advantage of great moment that the operations of this mill continue ^with convenience during the night, as well as through the day. The prodigious effect of such a machine is easily conceived. To this invention is to be attributed ^essentially the ~~vast~~ ^immense progress, which has been so suddenly made in great Britain, in the ~~rela~~ various fabrics of cotton.

III   As to the additional employment of classes of the community, not ordinarily engaged in the particular business—

This is not among the least valuable of the means, by which manufacturing institutions contribute to augment the general stock of industry and production. In ^places ~~two towns and neighbourhoods~~, where those institutions prevail, ~~they give employment~~ besides the persons regularly engaged in them, they afford occasional and extra employment to industrious individuals and families, who are willing to devote the leisure resulting from the intermissions of their ordinary ~~occupa-tions~~ pursuits to collateral labours, as ^a resource for ~~the mean of~~ multiplying their acquisitions or their enjoyments. The Husbandman himself experiences a new source of profit and support ~~to himself and family~~ from the increased industry of his wife and daughters invited and stimulated by the demands of the ^neighbouring manufactories. ~~in his vicinity~~.

a Cotton mill

Besides this advantage of ~~additional~~ occasional employment to classes ~~other-~~
~~wise occupied~~ having different ~~other~~ occupations, there ~~are others~~ is another of a nature
allied to it, and ~~which have~~ of a similar tendency. This is the employ-
ment of persons, who would otherwise be idle (and in many cases
a burthen on the community); ~~who~~ either from the byass of temper,
habit, infirmity of body, or some other cause, indisposing, or disqualifying them for the toils of the Country. ~~and of Children at an~~
~~earlier period~~ It is worthy of particular remark that in general Women and
Children are rendered more useful and the latter more early useful
by manufacturing establishments than they would otherwise be. Of
the number of persons employed in the cotton manufactories of Great
Britain it is computed that 4/7 nearly are women and children, of
whom the greatest proportion are children and many of them of a very
tender age.

And thus it appears to be one of the attributes of manufactures, and
one of no small consequence, ~~importance~~ to give occasion to the exertion of a
greater quantity of Industry, even by the <u>same</u> <u>number</u> of persons,
~~wherever~~ they happen to prevail, than would exist, if there were no
such establishments.

IV   As to the promoting of emigration from foreign Countries.
Men reluctantly quit one course of occupation and livelihood for
another, unless invited to it by very apparent and proximate advantages. Many,
who would go from one country to another, if they had a prospect of
continuing with more benefit the callings, to which they ~~are~~ have
been educated, will often not be tempted to change their situation by
the ~~possibility~~ hope of doing better, in some other way. Manufacturers,
who listening to the powerful invitations of a better price for their
fabrics or their labour, of greater cheapness of provisions and raw
materials, of an exemption from the chief part of the taxes burthens
~~with which they are vexed~~
and restraints, which they endure in the old world, of greater personal
independence and consequence, under the operation of a more equal

what is far more precious than mere
and of ~the more than~ religious toleration—a perfect equality of religious
government ^—would probably flock from Europe to the United
privileges;
States to pursue their own trades or professions, if they were once
made sensible of the advantages they would enjoy, and were inspired
with an assurance of encouragement and employment, will, with
difficulty, be induced to transplant themselves, with a view to becoming Cultivators of land.

then,
If it be true ^that it is the interest of the United States to open every
it ~well~ affords a
possible avenue to emigration from abroad ^~a procee~ weighty argument for the encouragement of manufactures; which for the reasons
just assigned will have the strongest tendency to multiply the inducements to it.

is
Here ~are~ perceived ~not only~ an important resource, not only for
extending the population, and with it the useful and productive labour
of the country, but likewise for the prosecution of manufactures,
without deducting from the number of hands, which might otherwise
be drawn to Tillage; and even for the indemnification of agriculture
for such as might happen to be diverted from it. Many, whom manufacturing views would ~originally~ induce to emigrate, would afterwards yield to the temptation which the particular situation of this
Country holds out to Agricultural pursuits. And while Agriculture
would in other respects derive many signal and unmingled advantages
from the growth of manufactures, it is a problem whether it would
persons
gain or lose, as to the article of the ~nu~ numbers of ^~hands~ employed in
carrying it on.

V   As to the furnishing greater scope for the diversity of talents
and dispositions, which discriminate men from each other.

~It is a s~
This is a much more powerful mean of augmenting the fund of
national Industry than may at first sight appear. It is a ~true~ just observation, that minds of the strongest and most active powers for their
proper objects fall below mediocrity and labour without effect if
confined to uncongenial pursuits. And it is thence to be inferred, that

the results of human exertion may be immensely increased by diversifying its objects. When all the different kinds of industry obtain in a community, each individual can find his proper element, and can call into activity the whole vigour of his nature. And the community is benefitted by the services of its respective members, in the manner, in which each can serve it with most effect.

If there be any thing in a remark often to be met with—namely that there is, in the genius of the people of this country, a peculiar aptitude for mechanic improvements, it would operate as a forcible reason for giving opportunities to the exercise of that species of talent, by the propagation of manufactures.

VI   As to the affording a more ample and various field for enterprise.

This also is of greater consequence in the general scale of national ~~use~~ exertion, than might perhaps on a superficial view be supposed, and has effects not altogether dissimilar from those of the circumstance last noticed. To cherish and stimulate the activity of the human mind, by multiplying the objects of enterprise, is not among the least considerable of the expedients, by which the wealth of a nation may be promoted. ~~Things~~ Even things, in themselves not positively advantageous, sometimes become so, by their tendency to ~~excite~~ provoke exertion. Every new scene which is opened to the busy nature of man to rouse and exert itself is the addition of a new energy to the general stock of efforts.

The spirit of enterprise, useful and prolific as it is, must necessarily be contracted or expanded in proportion to the simplicity or variety of the occupations and productions, which are to be found in a Society. It must be less in a nation of mere cultivators, than in a nation of cultivators and merchants; less in a nation of cultivators and merchants than in a nation of cultivators, artificers, and merchants.

VII   As to the creating, in some instances, a new, and securing in all a more certain and steady demand for the surplus produce of the soil—

This, is among the most important of the ~~of all the~~ circumstances, which have been indicated, ~~stated is the~~ ~~is perhaps~~ ~~most important~~. It is a principal mean, by which the establishment of manufactures contributes to an augmentation of the produce or revenue of a country; It ^and has in particular an immediate and direct influence upon relation to the prosperity of Agriculture.

It is evident that the exertions of the husbandman will be steady or fluctuating, vigorous or feeble, in proportion to the steadiness, or fluctuation, adequateness, or inadequateness of the markets on which he must depend, for the vent of the surplus, which may be produced by his labour; and that ^[such] that surplus in the ordinary course of things, will be greater or less in the same proportion.

For the purpose of this vent, a domestic market is greatly to be preferred to a foreign one; because it is in the nature of things, far more to be relied upon.

It is a primary object of the policy of nations, to be able to supply themselves with subsistence from their own soils; and manufacturing nations, as far as circumstances will permit, endeavour to procure, from the same source the raw materials necessary for their own fabrics. This disposition, urged by the spirit of monopoly, is some-times even carried to an ^injudicious injurious extreme. It seems not always to be recollected, that nations, who have neither mines nor manufactures, can only obtain the manufactured articles, of which they stand in need, by ^means of an exchange of the products of their soils; and that, if those who can best furnish them with such articles are unwilling to give a due course to this exchange, they must of necessity ^make every possible effort to manufacture for themselves; the effect of which is that the manufacturing nations abrige the natural advantages of their situation, through an unwilling-ness to permit the Agricultural ^[countries] ones to enjoy the ^advantages benefits of theirs, and sacrifice the interests of a mutually ^beneficial beneficial intercourse to the vain project of <u>selling</u> <u>every</u> thing and <u>buying</u> <u>nothing</u>.

But it is also a consequence of the policy, which has been noted, that the foreign demand for the products of agricultural and countries, is, in a great degree, rather casual and occasional, than certain or constant. To what degree extent injurious interruptions of the demand for some of the staple commodities of the United States, may have been experienced, from that cause, must be referred to the judgment of those who are engaged in carrying on the commerce of the country; but it may be safely affirmed, that such interruptions are at

~~cases occur in which~~

times very inconveniently felt, and that ~markets are frequently either wanting, or so narrowed restricted narrowed, as to be very unequal to the supply are much too few and too circumscribed for the supply, which is to be disposed of~~ cases not unfrequently occur, in which

*abundant seasons! Independly likewise*

markets are so confined and restricted, as to render the demand very unequal to the supply.

impediments, which are created by

Independently likewise of the artificial ~diminution of demand, which result from~~ the policy ~~that has been mentioned~~ in question,

tending

there are natural causes ~~which serve~~ to render the external demand

nations a

for the surplus of Agricultural ~~countries~~ ~precarious ~~and flu~~ reliance.

*the changes on this account very disadvantageous to Agriculture* ☞

are the consumers,

The differences of seasons, in the countries, which ~~usually buy~~, make imense differences in the produce of their own soils, ~~and the degree~~ in

degrees of their necessity for

different years; and consequently in the ~~ir wants of~~ foreign supply.

similar ones occur at the same time

Plentiful harvests with them, ~~and~~ especially if ~~they happen~~ in the countries which are the furnishers, ~~neces~~ occasion of course a ~~distressing~~ glut of produce in the markets of the latter.

Considering how fast and how much the ~~rapid~~ progress of new

~~Considering how fast the increasing~~ ~settlements ~~of the United

must ~~fast~~ increase

States must increase~~, in the United States ~the surplus produce of the

weighing

soil, and ~~adverting to the inauspicious symptoms which characterise some late~~ commercial ~~regulations~~ in various attending seriously

tendency

to the ~~spirit of the system which ~~has hitherto governed the~~ prevails among most of the commercial nations of Europe; whatever dependence may be placed on the force of natural circumstances to

fi

counteract the effects of an arti~cial policy; there appear strong rea-

the

sons to regard ~~a foreign demand for that surplus as too uncertain a reliance, and to desire a substitute for it in an extensive domestic market.

To secure such a market there is no other expedient, than to promote manufacturing establishments. Manufacturers, who ~~very~~ constitute the most numerous class, after the cultivators of land, ^are^ ~~must~~ for that reason, ~~be~~ the principal consumers of the surplus of their labour.

This idea of an extensive domestic market for the surplus produce of the soil is of the first consequence. It is of all things, that which ~~best~~ most effectually conduces to a flourishing state of Agriculture. If the effect of manufactories should be to detach a portion of the hands ~~of~~ which would otherwise be engaged in ~~Agriculture~~ Tillage, it might possibly cause a smaller quantity of lands to be under ^cultivation;^ ~~cul~~ ~~ture,~~ ^but by^ ~~but it would also a by~~ their tendency ^to~~ ~~secure a steady~~ ^procure a more certain^ demand for the surplus produce of the soil, they would, at the same time, cause the lands which were in cultivation to be better ~~cultivated~~ ^improved^ & more productive. And ~~in~~ while ^by their influence,^ the condition of each individual farmer would be meliorated ~~by this circumstance~~, the total mass of agricultural production, would ~~be~~ probably be increased: For this must ^evidently^ ~~doubtless~~ depend as much, ~~if not more~~ ^if not more^, upon the degree of improvement, ~~as~~ ^than^ upon the ~~quantity~~ ^number^ of acres under culture.

It merits particu⁓ observation, that The multiplication of manufactories not only furnishes a market for those articles which have been accustomed to be produced, in abundance, in a country; but it likewise creates a demand for such as were either unknown ^before,^ or produced in ^inconsiderable^ ~~inferior~~ quantities. The bowels as well as the surface of the earth are ransacked for articles which were ~~before~~ ^formerly before^ neglected. Animals plants and minerals acquire ^a^ utility and value ^which were unexplored.^ before ~~unknown.~~     ~~earth   fossils~~

The foregoing considerations seem ~~alone~~ sufficient to establish, as ~~a~~ general propositions, That it is the interest of nations to diversify the industrious pursuits of ^the^ individuals ^who compose them—^ That the establishment of manufactures is calculated not only to increase the general stock of

useful and productive labour; but even to improve the state of Agriculture in particular; certainly to advance the interests of those who
are engaged in it. There are other views ₍that will be hereafter taken₎ of the subject, which, it is conceived, will serve to confirm these inferences. Previously to a ₍a further₎ ~~prosecution of~~ discussion of the ~~remaining~~ objections to the encouragement of manufactures, which have been stated, ~~previously to entering upon them~~, it will be of use to see what can be said, in reference to the particular situations of the United States, against the conclusions ₍appearing₎ ~~which appear~~ to result from ~~the considerations that have been stated; and in the next place~~ ~~which~~ what has been already offered.

It may be observed ₍and the Idea is of₎ ~~with~~ no inconsiderable weight, that however ~~tur~~ true it ₍might₎ ~~may~~ be, that a state, which possessing large tracts of vacant and fertile territory, was at the same time secluded from foreign commerce, would find its interest and the interest of Agriculture, in diverting a part of its population from Tillage to Manufactures; yet it will not follow, that the same is true of a state, which having such vacant and fertile territory, has at the same ~~abundant~~ time ample opportunity of procuring from ₍abroad₎ ~~foreigners~~, on good terms, all the fabrics of which it ~~may~~ stands in need, for the supply of its inhabitants. The power of doing this at least secures the ~~principal~~ ₍great₎ advantage of a division of labour; leaving the farmer free to pursue exclusively the culture of his land, and enabling him to procure with its ₍products₎ ~~fruits~~ the manufactured supplies requisite either to his wants or to his enjoyments. And though it should be true, that in settled countries, the diversification of Industry is conducive to an increase in the productive power of labour and to an augmentation of revenue and capital, yet it is scarcely conceiveable that there can be any thing of ₍so₎ ~~such~~ solid and permanent advantage to an uncultivated and unpeopled country, as to convert its wastes into ~~fertile fields and its deserts into~~ ₍fruitful₎ ₍cultivated and₎ ~~inhabited~~ inhabited districts. If the Revenue, in the mean time, should be less, the Capital, in the event, must be greater.

To these observations, the following appears to be a satisfactory answer—

1  If the ~~fu~~ system of perfect liberty to industry and commerce were the prevailing system of nations—~~if they were every where left to their natural course~~, the arguments which dissuade a country, in the predicament of the U States, from the zealous pursuit of manufactures would doubtless have great force. It will not be affirmed, that they might not be permitted, with few exceptions, to serve as a rule of national conduct. In such a state of things, each country would have the full benefit of its peculiar advantages to compensate for its
deficiencies or disadvantages. If one nation ~~was~~ were in condition to supply manufactured articles on better terms than another, that other might find an abundant indemnification in a superior capacity to furnish the produce of the soil. And a free exchange, mutually beneficial, of the commodities which each was able to supply, on the best terms, might be carried on between them; supporting in full vigour the industry of each. And though the circumstances which have been mentioned and others which will be unfolded hereafter render it probable, that nations merely Agricultural would not enjoy the same degree of opulence, in proportion to their numbers, as those which united manufactures with agriculture; yet the progressive improvement of the lands of the former might, in the end, atone for an inferior degree of opulence in the mean time: and in a case, in which opposite considerations are pretty equally balanced, the option ought perhaps always to be, in favour of leaving Industry to its own Direction.

But the system, which has been mentioned, is far from characterising the general policy of Nations. ~~and to judge from some recent symptoms, the contrary spirit would seem rather to gain than to lose ground~~.

The consequence of it is, that the U States are to a certain extent in the situation of a country precluded from foreign commerce. They can indeed, without difficulty, obtain from abroad the manufactured
supplies, ~~for~~ of which they are in want; but they experience numerous and very injurious impediments to the emission and vent of their own
commodities. Nor is this the case in reference to ~~one~~ [any a single] foreign nation only ~~only~~. The regulations of several countries, with which we have the

most extensive intercourse, throw serious obstructions in the way of the principal staples of the United States.

In such a position of things, the United States cannot exchange with Europe on equal terms ~~on equal terms~~; and the want of reciprocity would render them the victim of a system, which should induce them to confine their views to Agriculture and refrain from manufactures. A constant and increasing necessity on their part, for the commodities of Europe, and only a partial and occasional demand for their own, in return, could not but expose them to a state of impoverishment, compared with the opulence to which their political and natural advantages authorise them to aspire.

Remarks of this kind are not made in the spirit of complaint. 'Tis for the nations, whose regulations are alluded to to judge for themselves, whether by aiming at too much, they do not lose more than they gain. 'Tis for the United States to consider by what means they can render themselves least dependent on the <sub>combinations,</sub> ~~calculations~~, right or wrong, of foreign policy.

It is no small consolation, that already the measures which have embarrassed our trade have accelerated internal improvements, which upon the whole have bettered our affairs. To diversify and extend these improvements is the <sub>surest and safest</sub> ~~best~~ method of indemnifying ourselves for any inconveniences which those or similar measures have a tendency to beget, and will at ~~the same time be found the most efficacious retaliation for any unkindness of disposition (if any there has been) which may have dictated them~~. If Europe will not take from us the products of our soil, upon terms consistent with our interest, ~~tis our our remedy is~~ the natural remedy is ~~duty to ourselves~~ to contract as fast as possible our wants of her.

2   The conversion of their waste into cultivated lands is certainly a point of great moment in the political calculations of the United States. But the degree in which this may be possibly be retarded by the ~~establishment~~ encouragement of manufactories does not appear to counteract the powerful inducements to affording that encouragement.

An observation made in another place is of a nature to have great influence upon this question. If it cannot be denied, that the interests even of Agriculture may be advanced more by having such of

[Quere]

the lands of a state as are occupied, under good cultivation, than by
having a greater quantity occupied, under ~~very defective~~ ₐa much inferior cultivation;
and if manufactories, for the ₐreasons assigned, must be admitted to have a
tendency to promote a more steady and vigorous cultivation of the
lands occupied, than would happen without them, it will follow, that
they are capable of indemnifying a country for a diminution of the
progress of new settlements; and may serve to ₐincrease ~~render~~ both the capital
value and the income of ₐits ~~the~~ lands, ~~of a nation, greater~~ ₐeven though they
should ~~even~~ abrige the number of acres under Tillage.

But it does, by no means, follow, that the progress of new settlements would be retarded by the extension of manufactures. The desire of being an independent proprietor of land is founded on such
strong principles in the human breast, that where the opportunity of
becoming so is as great as it is in the United States, the proportion
will be small of those, whose situations would otherwise lead to it,
~~wou~~ who would be diverted from it towards manufactures. And it
is highly probable, as already intimated, that the accessions of foreigners, who originally drawn over by manufacturing views, would
afterwards abandon them for Agricultural, would ₐbe more than ₐan equivalent ~~com-
pensate~~ for those of our own citizens, who might happen to be detached from them.

The remaining objections to a particular encouragement of manufactures in the United States now require to be examined.

One of these turns on the proposition, that Industry, if left to itself, will naturally find its way to the most useful and profitable
employment: hence it ~~may be~~ is inferred that manufactures, without
the aid of government, will grow up as soon and as fast as the ₐnatural ~~actual~~
state of things and the increase of the community may require.

Against the solidity of this hypothesis, ~~man~~ in the full latitude of
the terms, very cogent reasons may be offered. These have relation to
—the strong influence of habit and the spirit of imitation—the fear
of want of success in untried enterprises—The ₐintrinsic difficulties ~~necessarily~~
incident to ~~the~~ first essays towards a competition with those who

have previously attained to perfection in the business to be attempted —the bounties premiums and other artificial encouragements with which foreign nations second the exertions of their own citizens in the ~~very~~ branches, in which they are to be rivalled.

Experience teaches, that men are often so much governed by what they are accustomned to see and practice, that the simplest and most obvious improvements, in the most ordinary occupations, are adopted with hesitation reluctance and by slow gradations. ~~The adopting of~~ ~~To substitute~~ ~~adopt new pursuits~~ _by a considerable_ ~~in a community~~ The spontaneous _transition to_ ~~introduction of~~ new pursuits ~~into~~ a community long habituated to different ones _may be expected to_ ~~must~~ be attended with proportionably greater difficulty. When former occupations ceased to yield a profit adequate to the ~~bare~~ subsistence of their followers, ~~and~~ or when there was an absolute deficiency of employment in them, owing to the superabundance of hands, changes would ensue; but these changes would be likely to be more tardy than might consist with the interest either of individuals or of the society. In many cases they would not happen, while a bare ~~livlihoo~~ support could be _ensured_ ~~secured~~ by an adherence to ancient courses; though a resort to more profitable employment might be practicable. ~~It may~~ To produce the desireable changes, as early as may be expedient, may therefore require the ~~invitation and~~ incitement and patronage of government.

The ~~dread~~ apprehension of failing in new attempts is perhaps a more serious impediment. There are dispositions apt to be attracted by the mere novelty of an undertaking—but these are not always those best calculated to give it success. To this, it is of importance, that the confidence of _cautious_ sagacious capitalists _both citizens and foreigners_ should be excited. And to inspire [~~both citizens & foreigners~~] this description of persons with confidence, it is essential that they should be made to see in any project, which is new, and for that reason alone, if, for no other, precarious, the prospect of such a degree of countenance and support from government as may be capable of overcoming _the_ obstacles, inseparable from first experiments.

The superiority antecedently enjoyed by nations, who have preoccupied and perfected a branch of Industry, constitutes a more formidable obstacle, than either of those, which have been mentioned, to the introduction of the same branch into a country in which it did not before exist. To maintain, between the recent establishments of one country and the long matured establishments of another country, a competition upon equal terms, both as to quality ˄and ~~of~~ price, is in most cases impracticable. The disparity in the one or in the other or in both must necessarily be so considerable as to forbid a successful rivalship, without the extraordinary aid and protection of government.

But the greatest obstacle of all to the successful prosecution of a new branch of industry in a country, in which it was before unknown, ~~on~~ consists as far as the instances apply, in ~~those~~ the bounties premiums and others aids which are granted, in a variety of ~~instances~~, cases by the nations, in which ~~it is previously established~~ the establishments to be imitated are previously introduced. It is well known (and particular examples in the course of this report will be cited) that certain nations grant bounties on the exportation of particular commodities to enable their own workmen to undersell and supplant ˄all competitors in ˄those commodities ˄~~those of~~ the countries to which ~~they~~ ˄are sent. Hence the undertakers of a new manufacture have to contend not only with the natural disadvantages of a new undertaking, but with the gratuities and remunerations ~~wit~~ which other governments bestow. To be enabled to contend with success, it is evident, that ~~the~~ ~~positive~~ ˄the ~~some~~ interference and aid of their own government are indispensable.

Combinations by those engaged ~~in gen or parti~~ in a particular branch of business in one country to frustrate the first efforts to introduce it into another, by temporary sacrifices, recompensed perhaps by extraordinary indemnifications of the government of such country, are believed to have existed, and are not to be regarded as destitute of probability. The existence or assurance of aid from the government of the country, in which the ~~new~~ business is to be introduced, may be essential to fortify adventurers against the dread of such combinations—to defeat their effects, if formed, and to prevent their being formed by demonstrating that they must in the end prove fruitless.

Whatever ˄room ~~ground ground~~ there ˄may ~~might~~ be for an expectation that ˄the

upon equal terms
Industry of a people, under the direction of private interest, will ^find

the
out ~~its~~ ^most beneficial ~~course upon equal terms~~ employment for it-

none                    will            the force of
self, there is ~~no room~~ for a reliance, that it ^struggle against ^unequal
terms, or will of itself surmount all the adventitious ~~and artificial~~

^barriers
~~impediments~~ ^to a successful competition, which may have been

from
erected ~~by an artifice~~ either by the advantages naturally acquired ^~~by~~
practice and previous possession of the ground, or by ~~by~~ those which
may have sprung from positive regulations and an artificial policy.

^general            ^alone
This ^reflection ~~alone~~ might ^suffice as an answer to the objection,

^examination;
~~exclus~~ under ^~~consideration~~; exclusively of the weighty considerations
which have been particularly urged.

The ~~remaining~~ objections to the pursuit of manufactures in the
^which next present themselves to discussion, ~~than and peculiar~~
United States ^~~are of a nature more local~~ ^those ~~which have been
hitherto discussed. They~~ represent an impracticability of success,
arising from ~~these~~ three causes—scarcity of hands—dearness of labour
—want of capital.

The two first circumstances are to a certain extent real, and, within
due limits, ought to be admitted, as obstacles to the success of manu-
[~~factories actually manual~~]
facturing enterprise in the United States. But there are various con-

tend
siderations, which ~~greatly~~ lessen their force, and ^~~seem~~ to afford an
assurance, that ~~many~~ they are not sufficient to prevent the advantageous prosecution of many very useful and extensive manufactories.

With regard to scarcity of hands, the fact itself must be applied
with no small qualification to certain parts of the United States. There
are large districts, which may be considered, as pretty fully peopled;
and ~~in~~ which, notwithstanding a continual drain for distant settle-

^are thickly interspersed with
ment, ~~numerous~~ ^flourishing and increasing towns. ~~are to be~~ If these
districts have not already reached the point, at which the complaint
of scarcity of hands ceases, they are not remote from it, and ~~they~~ are
approaching fast towards it: And ~~being being~~ having perhaps fewer

<sub>attractions to</sub>
~~advantages~~ agriculture, than some other parts of the Union, they
exhibit a proportionably stronger tendency towards other kinds of
industry. In these districts, may be discerned, no inconsiderable
maturity for manufacturing establishments.

But there are circumstances, which have been already noticed with
another view, that materially diminish every where the effect of a
scarcity of hands. These circumstances are—the great use which can
be made of women and children; on which point, a very pregnant
and instructive fact has been mentioned—the vast extension ~~which~~
given by late improvements to the employment of machines, which
substituting the agency of fire and water, has prodigiously lessened
the necessity for manual labour—the employment of persons ordinarily engaged in other occupations, during the seasons, or hours of
leisure; which, besides giving occasion to the exertion of a greater
quantity of labour by the same number of persons, and thereby increasing the general stock of labour, as has been elsewhere remarked,
may also be taken into the calculation, as a resource for obviating the
<sub>lastly</sub>
~~inconvenience~~ ~~deficienc~~ scarcity of hands— the attraction of foreign emigrants. Whoever inspects with a careful eye the composition
of our towns will be made sensible to what an extent this resource
may be relied upon. This exhibits a large proportion of ingenious
~~mechanics~~ and valuable workmen, in different arts and trades, ~~by~~
who, by expatriating from Europe, have improved their own condition and added to the industry and wealth of the United States. It is
<sub>already</sub> <sub>as soon as</sub>
a natural inference from the experience we have had that ~~if~~ the
United States shall present the countenance of a serious prosecution
of manufactures—as soon as foreign artists shall be made sensible that
the state of things here affords a moral certainty of employment and
encouragement—competent numbers of European workmen will
<sub>ensure</sub>
transplant themselves, effectually to ~~second~~ ~~and~~ ~~execute~~ ~~secure~~ the
success of the design. How indeed can it otherwise happen considering the various and powerful inducements, which the situation of this
country ~~pres~~ offers; addressing themselves to so many strong passions
<sub>and feelings,</sub>
to so many general and particular interests?

It may be ^affirmed ~~inferred~~ therefore, in respect to hands for carrying on manufactures, that we shall in a great measure trade upon a foreign stock; reserving our own, for the cultivation of our lands and the manning of our ships; as far as character and circumstances ^shall ~~may~~ incline. It is not unworthy of remark that the objection to the success of manufactures deduced from the scarcity of hands ~~seems~~ ^is alike applicable to Trade and navigation; and yet these are perceived to flourish without any sensible impediment from that cause.

As to the dearness of labour (another of the obstacles alleged) this has relation principally to two circumstances, one that which has been just discussed, or the scarity of hands, the other, the greatness of profits.

As far as it is a consequence of the scarcity of hands, it is mitigated by all the considerations, which have been adduced as lessening that deficiency.

It is certain too that the disparity in this respect between ^some of the most manufacturing ~~certain~~ parts of Europe and ~~certain parts~~ a large proportion of the U States is not nearly so great as is commonly imagined. It is also much less in regard to Artificers and manufacturers, than in regard to country labourers. And while a careful comparison shews that there is in this particular much exaggeration; ^it is also evident that ~~and~~ the effect of the ^degree of disparity which does truly exist is diminished in proportion to the use which can be made of machinery.

To illustrate this last idea, ~~which is one worthy of particular attention~~ Let it be supposed, that the difference of price, in two countries, of a given quantity of ^manual labour requisite to the fabrication of a ~~certain~~ ~~manufacture~~ ^given article is as 10; and that some <u>mechanic power</u> is introduced into both countries, which performing half the necessary labour, leaves only half to be done by hand; it is evident, that the difference in the cost of the fabrication of the article in question, in ^the two ~~each~~ countries, as far as it ~~w~~ is connected with the price of labour, will be reduced from 10 to 5, in consequence of the introduction of that <u>power.</u>

This circumstance is worthy of the most particular attention. It diminishes ~~in~~ immensely one of the objections most strenuously urged,

against ^the success of^ manufactures in the United States.

To procure all such machines, as are known in any part of Europe, can only require ~~due pains~~ a proper provision and due pains. The knowlege of several of the most important of them is already possessed. The preparation of them here, is in most cases, practicable on nearly equal terms. As far as they depend on Water, some superiority of advantages may be claimed, from the uncommon variety ^and greater cheapness^ of situations adapted to Mill seats, with which different parts of the U S abound. [& ~~cheapness~~]

So far as the dearness of labour may be a consequence of the greatness of profits in any branch of business, it is no obstacle to its success. The Undertaker can afford to pay the price.

There are grounds to conclude that undertakers of manufactures in this country can at this time afford to pay higher wages to the workmen they may employ than are paid to similar workmen in Europe. The prices of foreign fabrics, in the markets of the United States, which will for a ^long^ time regulate the prices of the domestic ones, may be considered as compounded of the following ingredients—The first cost of materials, including the taxes, if any, which are paid upon them, ^where they are made ~~in Europe~~^ —the expence of ^grounds buildings^ machinery and tools—the wages of ~~workmen~~ the persons employed in the manufactory—the profits ^on^ ~~of~~ the capital or stock employed—the commissions of Agents to purchase them where they are made—the expence of transportation to the U States —the taxes or duties, if any, which are paid on their exportation—the taxes or duties, which are paid on their importation—the profits of the importing Merchants.

As ^to^ the first of these items, the cost of materials, the advantage upon the whole, is at present on the side of the United States, and the difference in their favour must increase in proportion as a certain and extensive ^domestic^ demand shall induce the proprietors of land to devote more of their attention to the production of those materials. It ought

                         ^in a comparison on this point,
not to escape observation^that that some of the principal manufacturing
                        ^much more dependent
countries of Europe are^obliged on foreign supply for ~~a great part of~~
                          ~~than would be~~          than would be
the materials of ~~most of~~ their ~~principal~~ manufactures;^ while the U
                 are capable of supplying
States, who ~~can easily supply~~ themselves, with ~~the greatest part if~~
a ~~fra~~ greater abundance as well as a greater variety of the requisite materials.
~~not the whole of those which they may require.~~

As to the second item, the expence of grounds buildings machinery
and tools, an equality at least may be assumed; since advantages on
                                            ^temporary
[~~temporary~~]  some particulars will counterballance^disadvantages in others.

As to the third item, ~~the wages of the pers~~ or the article of wages,
the comparison certainly turns against the U States; though as before
observed, not in so great a degree as is commonly supposed.

~~It is not un-~~     The fourth item is alike applicable to the foreign and to the
~~worthy of~~     domestic manufacture. It is indeed more properly a result, than a
~~remarked~~     particular, to be compared.
~~that the ob-~~
~~jection to~~         ^respect
~~the suce~~     But with ~~regard~~^ to all the remaining items, they are alone applicable
to the foreign manufacture, and in the strictest sense extraordinaries;
                 ^sum
constituting a^ ~~mass~~ of extra charge on the foreign fabric, which
cannot be estimated, at ~~leas~~ less, than        [109] per Cent on the cost
                 ^manu
of it at the^factory. ~~This estimate will not appear high when it~~
~~is considered that~~

~~amount of to not less than from          to       per Cent.~~

                 sum
This ~~amount~~ of extra charge may confidently be regarded as more
                            the real
than a counterpoise for ~~any real~~ difference ~~which exists~~ in the price of
labour; and is a satisfactory proof that ~~domestic~~ manufactures may
                       [in the United States.]      allegation,
prosper in defiance of it^. To the general ~~observation~~ connected with
the circumstances of scarcity of hands and dearness of labour, ~~namely~~
that extensive manufactures can only grow out of a redundant or
full population, it will be sufficient to answer generally, that the fact

109. This and subsequent spaces left blank in MS.

has been otherwise. That the situation, alleged to be an essential

condition of success, ~~was not~~ has not been that of several nations, at ~~a~~ periods,
when they had already ~~made a very considerable progress in~~ attained to maturity in a variety of manufactures.

The supposed want of Capital for the prosecution of manufactures
in the U States is the most indefinite of the objections which are
usually opposed to it.

It is very difficult to pronounce any thing precise concerning the
real extent of the monied capital of ~~the~~ a Country, and still more concerning ~~the~~ the proportion, which it bears to the objects, that invite
the employment of Capital. It is not less difficult to pronounce how
far the <u>effect</u> of any given quantity of money, as capital, or in other
words, as a medium for circulating the industry and property of a nation ~~country~~, may
be increased by the very circumstance of the additional motion,
which is given to it, by new objects of employment. That effect, like
the momentum of descending bodies, may not improperly be represented, as in a compound ratio to <u>mass</u> and <u>velocity.</u> It seems pretty
certain that a given sum of money, in a ~~situated~~ situation, in which
the quick impulses of commercial activity were little felt, would
appear inadequate to the circulation of as great a quantity of industry and property, as in one, in which their full influence was
experienced.

It is not obvious, why the same objection might not as well be made
to ~~foreign~~ external commerce, as to manufactures; since it is manifest that our
immense tracts of land ~~cultivated~~ occupied and ~~uncultivated~~ unoccupied are capable of
giving employment to more capital than is actually bestowed upon them. It
is certain, that the U States offer a vast field for the advantageous
employment of Capital; but it does not follow, that there will not be
found, in one way or another, a sufficient fund for the successful
prosecution of any species of industry, which is likely to prove
truly beneficial.

The following considerations are of a nature to remove all inquietude on the score of want of Capital.

[~~The same
remark ap-
plies ⟨to⟩ the
hands em-
ployed in
trade ⟨or⟩
navigation~~]

The introduction of Banks as has been shewn on another occasion has a powerful tendency to extend the active capital of ~~the~~ a Country. ~~Institutions of this kind is are becoming~~ Experience of the utility of these institutions is multiplying them in the U States. It is probable that they will be established wherever they can exist with advantage; and wherever they can be supported, if administered with prudence, they will add new energies to all pecuniary operations.

The aid of foreign Capital may safely, and, with considerable latitude, be taken into the calculation. Its instrumentality has been long experienced in our external commerce; and it has begun to be felt in various other modes. Not only our funds, but our agriculture and other internal improvements have been animated by it. It has in a few instances ~~even~~ extended even to our manufactures. ~~and may be expected to do it hereaf~~

It is a well known fact, that there are parts of Europe, which have more capital, than profitable domestic objects of employment. Hence, among other proofs, the large loans continually furnished to foreign states. And it is equally certain that the capital of other parts may find more profitable employment in in the United States than at home. And ~~though~~ notwithstanding there are weighty inducements to prefer the employment of capital at home, even at less ~~less~~ profit, to an investment of it abroad ~~in foreign countries~~, though with ~~somewhat~~ greater gain; yet these inducements are overruled either by a deficiency of employment or by a very material difference in profit. Both these causes operate ~~to~~ to produce a transfer of foreign capital to the U States. 'Tis certain that various objects, in this country, hold out advantages which are ~~the temptations of greater~~ with difficulty to be equalled elsewhere; and under the increasingly favourable impressions, which are entertained of our government, the attractions will become more and more strong. These impressions will prove a rich mine of prosperity to the country, if they are confirmed and strengthened by the progress of our affairs. And to secure this advantage, little more is now necessary than to foster industry and

[and ~~peace at home & abroad~~] ~~peace~~ at home and abroad.

^cultivate                              ^tranquillity
^~~cultivate internal~~ order and ^~~tranquillity~~.

that
It is not impossible ^there may be ~~Whatever may be the objects which~~
~~It is possible~~ [~~may be~~] [disposed to]

~~There are~~ ^persons, ^~~who~~ look with a jealous eye on the introduction of foreign capital, as if it were an instrument to deprive our own
citizens of the profits of our own industry. But perhaps there never
[could be]
~~was~~ ^a more unreasonable jealousy. Instead of being viewed as a rival,
it ought to be considered as a most valuable auxiliary; conducing to
put in motion a greater quantity of productive labour and a greater
portion of useful enterprise than could exist without it. It is at least
evident, that in a country situated like the U States, with an infinite

[~~dormant~~]    [yet to be unfolded,]
fund of ~~undisplayed~~ resources ^every farthing of foreign capital,
which is laid out in internal amelioration and in industrious establishments of a permanent nature is a precious acquisition.

unexplained
undevel-
loped

And whatever be the objects which originally attract foreign Capital, when once introduced, it may be directed towards any purpose
of beneficial exertion, which is desired. And to detain it among us,
effectual
there can be no expedient so ~~beneficial~~ ^as to enlarge the sphere,
may                                      ^merely
within which it ^~~can~~ be usefully employed. Though introduced ^with
views to speculations in the ~~publie~~ funds, it may afterwards be
rendered subservient to the interests of Agriculture commerce and
Manufactures.

[~~If and~~]
But the attraction of foreign Capital, ~~wer~~ for the direct purpose of
manufactures, ought not to be deemed a chimerical expectation. There
are already examples of it, as remarked in another place; and the
can hardly fail to
examples, if the desposition, be cultivated, ~~will~~ ^multiply. ~~This expectation will appear the more likely to be fuffilled.~~

|Facts
in\ relation
~~which~~ to in-
land naviga-
tion &
Bridges /&
~~manufac-
tures~~ which
have already
taken place
at once sug-
gest & con-
firm these
expecta-
tions]

of
instances ^another kind,
~~And~~ There are also ~~examples of a~~ different which serve to
strengthen the ~~same~~ expectation. Enterprises for improving the public communications, ~~by opening new channels of~~ by cutting canals,
opening the obstructions in rivers and erecting bridges over them

                    ^very material
have received^important aid from the same source.

When the Manufacturing Capitalists of Europe shall advert to the many important advantages, which have been intimated, in the course of this report, he cannot but perceive very powerful inducements to a transfer of himself and his Capital to the United States. Among the reflections, which a most interesting peculiarity of situation ~~suggests~~ is calculated to suggest, it cannot escape his observation,
                                        ^in the calculation,
as a circumstance of ~~very great~~ moment^that the progressive population and improvement of the United States ensure a continually increasing domestic demand for the fabrics, which he shall produce—
       to
not^be affected by any external casualties or vicissitudes.

~~There is~~

But while there are circumstances sufficiently strong to authorise a considerable degree of reliance on the aid of foreign Capital, towards the attainment of the object in view, it is satisfactory to have
  ^good                              ^there are
^grounds of assurance that^domestic resources, of themselves, adequate to it. It happens that there is a species of capital actually existing within the United States, which relieves from all inquietude on the score of wan~~ted~~ of Capital. This is the funded debt.

*Quare*

The effect of a funded debt, as a species of Capital, has been noticed upon a former occasion; but a more particular elucidation of the point seems ~~here~~ to be required by the stress, which is here laid
                  accordingly
upon it: This shall^be attempted.

Public funds answer the purpose of Capital, from the estimation in which they are usually held by monied men; and consequently from the ease and dispatch with which they can be turned into money. This capacity of prompt convertibility into money causes a transfer of stock to be in a great number of cases equivalent to^a payment in coin. And where it does not happen to suit the party, who is to

[~~bank note or to~~]

[~~receiving~~]
receive, to accept a transfer of stock, the party who is to pay, is never at a loss to find elsewhere a purchaser of his stock, who will
                                        ^coin
furnish him in lieu of it, ~~of~~ with the^~~money~~, of which he stands in need.

Hence in a sound and settled state of the public funds, a man possessed of a sum in them, can embrace any scheme of business, which offers, with as much confidence, as if he were possessed of an equal sum in coin.

This operation of public funds, as capital, is too obvious to be denied; but it is objected to the idea of their operating as an augmentation of the Capital of the community, that they ₍serve to₎ occasion the destruction of some other capital to an equal amount.

The capital which alone they can be supposed to destroy must consist of—The annual revenue which is applied to the payment of t̶h̶e̶ d̶e̶b̶t̶ interest on the debt, and ₍to₎ the ₍gradual₎ redemption of the principal—And the amount of the coin which is employed in circulating the funds, or ₍i̶n̶₎ ₍in other words, in effecting₎ the different alienations which they undergo.

But the following appears to be the true and accurate view of this matter—

1  As to the Point of the Annual Revenue requisite for payment of interest and redemption of principal—

As a determinate proportion will tend to perspicuity in the reasoning, let it be supposed, that the annual revenue to be applied, corresponding with the modification of the 6 per Cent stock of the U States, is in the ratio of Eight ₍upon the₎ t̶o̶ ̶a̶ hundred, that is in the first instance, six ₍on account of₎ f̶o̶r̶ interest and two ₍on account₎ f̶o̶r̶ t̶h̶e̶ ̶r̶e̶d̶e̶m̶p̶t̶i̶o̶n̶ of principal.

Thus far it is evident, that the capital destroyed to t̶h̶a̶t̶ the capital created, would bear no greater proportion than 8 to 100. There would be withdrawn from the total mass of other capitals a sum of Eight dollars to be paid to the public Creditor; a̶n̶d̶ ₍while₎ he would be p̶u̶t̶ ̶i̶n̶ ̶p̶o̶s̶s̶e̶s̶s̶i̶o̶n̶ possessed of a sum of 100 dollars ₍ready₎ to be applied to any purpose, to be embarked in any enterprise, which might appear to him eligible. Here then the augmentation of Capital, or the excess of that which is produced ₍beyond₎ t̶o̶ that which is destroyed is a̶s̶ equal to 9̶6̶ ₍92₎ dollars. ₍not obvious₎

To this conclusion it may be objected that the sum of Eight dollars is to be withdrawn, annually, until the whole hundred is extinguished;

and it may be inferred ~~the from this~~, that in process of time ~~as great~~
a capital will be destroyed ~~as~~ equal to that which is at first created.

the answer to this objection is
But ~~however true this may be, in an absolute sense—in a relative~~

it is nevertheless true
~~one the it is equally true~~, that ~~to~~ during the whole of the interval,
between the ~~creation of the capital of 100~~ creation of the capital of

and its reduction                that of
100 Dollars ~~until it is reduced~~ to a sum not greater than the annual
revenue, appropriated to its redemption, ~~and its final extinguish-~~

in existence          been contracted.
~~ment~~, there will be a greater active capital than if no debt had ~~existed~~.
The sum drawn from other capitals on <u>any</u> <u>one</u> <u>year</u> will not exceed
eight dollars; but there will <u>be</u> <u>at</u> <u>every</u> <u>instant</u> <u>of</u> <u>time</u>, during the

                     ing
whole period, in question, a sum ~~which will~~ correspond<del>ings</del> with <u>so</u>
<u>much</u> <u>of</u> <u>the</u> <u>principal</u>, as <u>remains</u> <u>unredeemed</u>, in the hands of some
person, or other, employed, or ready to be employed in some prof-
itable undertaking. There will therefore constantly be more capital,
in capacity to be employed, than capital taken from employment.

                               92
The excess for the first year has been stated to be ~~96~~ Dollars; ~~in the~~

                             until
~~second~~ it will diminish yearly, but there always will be an excess ~~and~~

                        redeeming
the principal of the debt is brought to a level with the annuity, that
in the case which has been assumed by way of example
is to Eight dollars.

The reality of this excess
~~The idea intended to be established~~ becomes palpable, if it be sup-

            in reality
posed, as often happens, that the Citizen of a foreign Country, imports into the U States 100 Dollars for the purchase of an equal sum
of public debt. Here is an absolute augmentation of the mass of circulating coin to the extent of 100 Dollars. At the end of a year, the
foreigner is ~~to~~ presumed to draw back Eight dollars on account of
his principal and interest; but he still leaves 92 of his original deposit
in circulation; ~~At the end of another year he draws back another~~
~~Eight dollars, leaving still 84 dollars of the primitive contribution to~~

                      in like manner leaves
~~animate the industry of the Country~~ as he does 84 at the end of the

second year drawing back then also the annuity of 8 Dollars. And ˄the ˄thus
matter proceeds; the capital left in circulation ~~yearly~~ diminishing˄ ˄each year
and coming nearer to the level of the annuity drawn back. There
are ˄some differences in the ultimate operation of the part of the debt, ˄however
which is purchased by foreigners, and that which remains in the hands
of citizens. But the general effect in each case, though in different
~~in~~ degrees, is to add to the active capital of the Country.

Hitherto the reasoning has proceded on a concession of the ˄~~prin-~~ ˄position
~~ciple~~, that there is a destruction of some other capital, to the extent
of the annuity appropriated to the payment of the interest and the
~~gradual~~ redemption of the principal of the debt. But˄ too much has ˄in this
been conceded. There is at most a temporary transfer of some other
capital, to the ˄annuity, from those who pay to the Creditor who ˄amount of the
receives; which he again restores to the circulation to ~~invigorate for~~
resume the offices of a capital. This he does either immediately, by
employing the money in some branch of industry, or mediately by
lending it to some other person, who does so employ it, or by spending it on his own maintenance. In either supposition, there is no destruction of Capital; there is nothing more than a suspension of ˄~~it~~ for ˄its motion
a time that is, while it is passing from the hands of those who pay into
the public coffers, and thence, through the public Creditor into some
other channel of circulation. When the payments of interest are ~~quick~~
~~and~~ periodical and quick, and made by the instrumentality of banks,
the <u>division</u>˄ of Capital ~~is very temporary indeed~~. may almost be de- or suspension
nominated momentary. Hence the deduction on this account is far
less than ~~has~~ it at first sight appears to be.
There is evidently˄ no destruction nor ~~even~~ transfer of any other ˄as far as regards the annuity ~~rather~~
Capital, than that portion of the income of each individual, which
goes to make up the annuity. The land, which furnishes the farmer
~~contributory~~˄ the sum which he˄ contributes ˄the like may be observed is to
with ~~his contribution, share~~˄ remains the same; and s˄ of other capitals.

Indeed as far as the tax, which is the object of occasions the contribution (as dou<sub></sub>t-less frequently happens, when it does not oppress by its weight) may have been a motive to greater exertion in any occupation, it may even serve to increase the contributory Capital. This idea is not without importance in the general view of the subject.

It remains to see what further deduction is ought to be made from the increase of Capital which is created by the debt existence of the debt, on account of the coin, which is employed in the its circulation. of the debt. This is susceptible of much less precise calculation, than the article which has been just discussed. It is impossible to say what proportion of coin is carried or necessary to carry on the alienations, which any species of property usually undergoes. The quantity indeed varies, according to circumstances. But it may always still without hesitation be pronounced, from the quickness of the roat rotation, or rather of the transitions, that the medium of circulation always bears but a small proportion to the amount of the property circulated. And it is thence satisfactorily deducible, that the coin employed in the negotiations of the funds, and which serves to give them activity, as a capital, is incomparably less than the sum of the debt negotiated for the purposes of business.

It ought not however to be omitted, that the negotiation of the funds becomes itself a distinct business; which employs, and by employing diverts, a portion of the circulating coin from other pursuits. But making due allowance for this circumstance, there is no reason to conclude that the amount effect of the diversion of coin in w the whole operation, is an bears any considerable proportion to the amount of the capital in debt, to which it gives activity. The sum of the debt in circulation is continually at the command of any useful enterprise; the coin itself, which circulates it, is only from moment never more than momentarily to moment suspended from its ordinary functions. It ine experiences an incessant and rapid flux and reflux to and from the channels of industry to those of negotia speculations in the funds.

There are strong circumstances in confirmation of this theory. The
~~money~~ ~~moned~~ ₍monied₎
force of ₍₎Capital, which has been displayed in Great Britain, and the
height, ~~w~~ to which every species of industry has grown up under it,
defy a solution, from the quantity of coin, which that kingdom has
                                                              its
ever possessed. Accordingly it has been, coeval with ~~the~~ funding sys-
                                        ~~her~~ the
tem ~~of~~ ~~that~~ ~~Country~~, the prevailing opinion of ₍₎men of business and
                    the                          ₍of that Country₎
of the ~~the~~ generality of ~~her~~ most sagacious therorists ₍₎that the operation of the public funds as Capital has contributed to the effect, in
                                 ₍appearances₎
question. Among ourselves ₍₎~~experience~~ ~~has~~ thus far ~~favours~~ the same
conclusion. Industry in general seems to have been reanimated. There
are symptions indicating an extension of our commerce. Our ~~nag~~ navi-
                                             ₍And₎         appears
gation has certainly of late had a considerable spring. ₍₎There ~~seems~~
to be in many parts of the Union a command of Capital which till
                                 was
lately, since the revolution at least, ~~has~~ ~~been~~ ₍₎unknown. But it is at the
same time to be acknowleged, that other circumstances have ₍₎con-
[ (and in a ~~very~~ great degree) ]
curred ₍₎in producing the present state of things, and that the appearances are not yet sufficiently decisive to be intirely relied upon.

Quare this
last sen-
tence [110]

In the question under discussion, it is important to distinguish between an absolute increase of capital, or an accession of real wealth,
and an artifical increase of capital, as an Engine of business, or as an
instrument of industry and commerce. In the first sense a funded debt
has no pretensions to being deemed an increase of Capital; in the
last, it has pretensions which are not easy to be controverted. Of a
similar nature is bank credit, and in an inferior degree, every species
of private credit.

But though a funded debt is not, in the first instance, an absolute
increase of capital, or an augmentation of real wealth; yet by serving
as a new power in the operations of industry, it has, within certain
bounds, a tendency to increase the real wealth of a community; ~~as~~
~~more~~ in like manner, as money borrowed by a thrifty farmer, to be

110. In the margin below this query made by H, there is a crossed-out comment
written in an unknown handwriting which is illegible.

add to his stock
laid out in the improvement of his farm, may, in the end, ~~add furnish~~ ∧
~~an addition~~ of real riches.

respectable individuals
There are ∧ ~~persons~~ who from a just aversion to an accumulation of
public debt are unwilling to concede to it any kind of utility; who can
discern ~~in it~~ no good to alleviate the ill, with which they suppose it
pregnant; who cannot be persuaded, that it ought in any sense to be
more debt the
viewed as an increase of Capital, lest it should be inferred, that the ∧
more capital, the ~~mo~~ greater the burthens the greater the blessings
of the community.

But it interests the public councils to estimate every object as it
truly is; to appreciate how far the good in any measure is compensated by the ill or the ill by the good. Either of them is seldom unmixed.

Neither will it follow, that an accumulation of debt is desireable,
because a certain degree of it operates as capital. There may be a
plethora in the political as in the natural body. There may be a state
of things, in which any such artificial Capital is unnecessary. The debt
too may be swelled to such a size, as that the greatest part of it may
cease to be useful as a capital, serving only to pamper the dissipa-
and dissolute
tion of idle ∧ individuals; as that the sums required to pay the interest
upon it may become oppressive, and beyond the means, which a government can employ, consistently with its tranquillity to raise them;
that
as ∧ the resources of taxation, to face the debt, may have been strained
too far to admit of extensions adequate to exigencies, which regard
the public safety.

Where this critical point is cannot be pronounced; but it is impossible to believe that there is not such a point. ~~There exists a case, happily not in this Country, in which certain certain violent and almost
convulsive expedients, seem to indicate a near approach to it.~~

And as the vicissitudes of Nations beget a perpetual tendency to the
accumulation of debt, there ought to be, in ~~a~~ every government, a
perpetual anxious and unceasing effort to reduce that, which at any
time exists, as fast as shall be practicable consistently with integrity
and good faith.

Qu:
☞

Reasonings on a subject, comprehending ideas so abstract and com-
plex, so little reducible to precise ^calculation, as those which enter into the ~~subject~~ question
just discussed, are always attended with a danger of running into
fallacies. Due allowance ought therefore to be made for this possibility. But as far as the nature of the subject admits of it, there appears
to be satisfactory ground ~~to conclude~~ for a belief, that the public
funds operate as a resource of Capital to the citizens of the United
States; and, if they are a resource at all, it is an extensive one.

To all the arguments which are brought to evince the impracticability of success in manufacturing establishments in the U S it might
have been a sufficient answer to have referred to the experience of
what has been already done. It is certain that several important
branches have grown up and flourished with a rapidity which surprises; affording an encouraging assurance of success in future
attempts. Of these, it may not be improper to enumerate the most considerable.

II { Barr ~~iron~~ and sheet iron
Enumeration
of Iron
~~of Iron particularly~~ ^steel, Nails rods & nails,
implements of husbandry, stoves pots and
the steel and iron work of
other household utensils, ~~the materials for~~
for
carriages and ^shipbuilding, ~~and~~ anchors, ~~the~~
scale beams and weights & various
^tools of Artificers: ~~also~~ arms of different
kinds; though the manufacture of these has
of late diminished for want of demand.

I { 2 ~~Of leather particularly~~ Tanned and tawed
leather dressed Skins, shoes boots and slip-
~~Hides of~~
~~Leather &~~
harness & Sadlery of all kinds
pers ^~~harness of all kinds and other leathern~~
~~Skins~~
~~materials for carriages~~, Saddles ~~bridles and~~
of Skins
in general,
~~other sadlery articles of~~ sadlery, ^Portman-
leather
teaus and trunks, ^breeches, gloves, muffs
Parchment &
and tippets. ^Glue.

~~Ships~~
~~source of~~
~~Gold~~       IV A
~~Silver~~                    A  { 3

,flax &
Of ,hemp

3   ~~Ships~~ SailCloth ~~Sail and tow Cloth,~~ ,sewing thread
    ,Cables ,Cordage ,twine and packthread ,sail
                        ~~Sail Cloth~~ ,shirtings
    ~~cloth tow cloth, coarse~~ ,white and checked,
    ~~shirtings, coarse towelling, bedticks, hosiery.~~

Hats Higher
duty Choco-
late do—
Gold & sil-
ver & plated
ware

VII A

                                    stockings
4   ~~Woollen hats,~~ ,hosiery, ~~cloths, coatings,~~
                                    r
    ~~serges and flannels, chiefly coa,se, some~~
    ~~casimirs, linsey woolsey and negro cloth in~~
    ~~large quantities.~~ Hats of furr & Wool and
    of mixtures of both.

~~Cotton~~  VII B      5   Womens stuff & silk shoes.

~~Womens~~
~~stuff &~~
~~silk shoes~~
            VI         6   Writing & printing
                           ,Paper, ~~paper hangings~~, sheathing
                           and wrapping paper, paste-boards, fillers or
                           press papers, paper hangings.

            VIII       7   Refined Sugars

            III        8   ,Ships              ,Wool & Cotton Cards & other
            Of Wood ,V     ,Cabinet wares ,and Turnery. ,Machinery
                                                        ,Mathematical
                           for manufactures and husbandry ,and of ~~late~~
                           ~~musical~~ instruments. Coopers wares of every
                           kind.

            X          9   Copper and brass wares particularly utensils
                           for distillers, ~~brew~~ sugar refiners and brew-
                                   and for ~~household use~~ and of the articles for
                           ers, ~~Tea~~ kettles, and Irons ,shovels ~~and~~
                           Household use,
                           ~~tongs~~ ,pile philosophical apparatus.
                                   and
            XI         10  Tin ,wares for most purposes of ordinary
                           use.

            V ~~III~~      ~~11~~  Ardent spirits and malt liquors

| XIV | 12 | Starch & hair powder |
| IX | 13 | Oils of animals and seeds, Soap Spermaceti & Tallow Candles |
| XVI | 14 | Gunpowder. |
| B | | |
| IV | | ~~Pottery~~, bricks and coarse tiles & Potters Wares |
| XII | 16 | Carriages of all kinds |
| XV | 7 | Lampblack & other painters colours    Qr. |
| | 18 | ~~Pot ash & Pearl ash~~ |
| | 19 | ~~Tarr & Turpentine~~ |
| XIII | 20 | Snuff chewing & smoking Tobacco. |

Besides manufactories of these articles, which are carried on, as
regular ₍Trades and₎ ~~businesses and may~~ have attained to a considerable degree of
maturity, there is a vast scene of ~~hos~~ household manufacturing, which
contributes more largely to the supply of the community, than could
₍be₎ ~~have been~~ imagined ~~without making it an~~ [~~who have not made~~] ₍without having made it an₎ object of particular inquiry. ~~It is a~~ ₍This observation is the₎ pleasing result of the investigation ₍which~~ has been occa-~~₎
~~sioned by~~ ₍has led and is applicable as well to ~~some of~~₎ the subject of this report ₍~~that as~~ ~~well in~~ ₍to₎₎ the Southern as ~~in~~
₍the middle and Northern states. Great quantities of coarse ₍cloaths₎,
coatings serges and flannels, linsey woolseys, Hosiery of wool cotton
& thread ~~and even silk~~, coarse fustians ~~and~~ jeans and muslins, ~~cotton~~
checked and ~~stip~~ striped
cotton and linnen goods,
bed ticks coverlets and counterpanes
Tow linnens, ~~towelings~~, ₍coarse₎ shirtings, sheetings, toweling, ₍& table linnen₎ ~~bed ticks cov-~~
~~erlets counterpanes and some other articles~~ and various mixtures of
wool and cotton ₍and of₎ cotton and flax, are made in the household way and
in ~~some~~ ₍many₎ instances to an extent not only sufficient for the supply of the
families, in which they ₍are₎ made, but for sale, and even in some cases

from one State to another and

for exportation ~~to foreign countries~~. It is computed in a number of districts that ⅔ ¾ & even ⅘ of all the cloathing of the inhabitants are made by themselves. The importance of so great a progress as appears

family

to have been made in ~~household~~ manufactures within a few years, both in a moral and political view, renders the fact highly ~~satisfactory~~ interesting.

Neither does the above enumeration comprehend all the articles

that                     Trades

~~which~~ are manufactured as regular ~~businesses~~. Many others occur, which are equally well established but which not being of equal importance have been omitted. And there are many attempts still in their infancy, which though ~~they were~~ attended with very favourable appearances, could not have been properly comprised in an enumera-

already established. are to

tion of manufactories ~~which may~~ be ~~considered as having already succeeded~~.

~~Those manufactures also~~ There are other ~~manufactures also of the first importance which have been omitted as not being relative~~

of great importance

articles also which though strictly speaking manufactures, are omitted as being immediately connected with husbandry; such are flour Pot & Pearl Ash, Pitch Tar & Turpentine and the like.

to the encouragement of manufactures

There remains to be noticed an objection of a nature different *from those which question the probability of success. This is derived from its supposed tendency to give a monopoly of advantages to particular classes at the expence of the rest of the community, who, it is assumed, would be able to procure the requisite supplies of manufactured articles on better terms from foreigners than from our own Citizens, and who, it is alleged, are reduced to a necessity of paying an enhanced price for whatever they want by every measure which*

the            of

*obstructs free competition ~~and~~ foreign commodities.*

*It is not an unreasonable supposition that measures which serve to abrige the free competition of foreign articles have a tendency to occasion an enhancement of prices, and it is not to be denied that such is the effect in a number of cases; but the fact does not uniformly*

*correspond with the theory: A reduction of prices has in several in-*
*stances immediately succeeded the establishment of a domestic manu-*
*facture. Whether it be that foreign manufacturers endeavour to sup-*
*plant by underselling our own or whatever else be the cause, the*
*effect has been such as is stated, and the reverse of* what *might have been*
*expected.*

*But though it were true that the immediate and certain effect of*
[~~native or national~~]
*regulations controuling the competition of foreign with domestic* ∧
*fabrics was an increase of price, it is universally true that the contrary*
*is the ultimate effect with every successful manufacture. When a*
[~~native~~]
*domestic manufacture has attained to perfection ~~and has attained to~~*
*~~perfection~~ and has engaged in the prosecution of it a competent num-*
*ber of persons it invariably becomes cheaper. Being free from the*
*heavy charges which attend the importation of foreign commodities,*
*it can be afforded and accordingly seldom or never fails to be sold*
*cheaper in process of time than was the foreign article for which it is*
*a substitute. The internal competition which takes place soon does*
*away any thing like monopoly, and by degrees reduces the price of*
*the article to the minimum of a reasonable profit on the capital em-*
*ployed. This accords with the reason of the thing and with experience.*

*Whence it follows that it is the interest of a community with a*
*view to eventual and permanent œconomy to encourage the growth of*
*manufactures. In a national view a temporary enhancement of price*
*must always be well compensated by a permanent reduction of* ~~the posterior~~ *it.*

*It is a reflection which may with propriety be indulged here; that*
eventual
*this ~~material~~ diminution of the prices of manufactured Articles which*
internal
*is the result of ~~domestic~~* ∧*manufacturing establishments has a direct*
*and very important tendency to benefit agriculture. It enables the*
*farmer to procure with a smaller quantity of his labor the manufac-*
*tured produce of which he stands in need and consequently increases*
*the value of his income and property.*

The objections, which are commonly made to the expediency of
encouraging, and to the probability of succeeding in manufacturing

pursuits, in the United States, having now been discussed; the considerations, ~~recommending that species of industry to the patronage of the Government~~, which have appeared in the course of the discus-
recommending that species of industry to the patronage of the Government
                                                                    particular
sion ͺwill be materially strengthened by a few general and some ͺtopics
        have been naturally reserved ~~for~~ for subsequent Notices.
which ͺ~~not being connected with the answers that naturally suggested~~
                                        been
~~themselves to those objections, have reserved themselves for sub-~~
                Notice.
~~sequent Attention.~~

I    There seems to be a moral certainty, that the trade of a country, which is both manufacturing and Agricultural, will be more lucrative and prosperous, than that of a country, which is merely Agricultural. ~~This depends on several circumstances.~~
        One reason for this is found in
            ~~of these circumstances is,~~            which has been mentioned
~~One~~ ͺThat general effort of Nations ( ͺalready ~~taken notice of~~) to procure, from their own soils, the articles of prime necessity requisite
and which serves to ~~rendering~~ their demand for a foreign supply of such articles
to their own consumption and use, ~~whence it happens, that a foreign~~
                                        and precarious only. and contingent.
~~or external demand for articles in~~ in a great degree occasional ͺ~~and~~
~~fluctuating.~~ Hence while the necessities of ~~the mearly Agricultural~~
                                                Agriculture
~~State for the fabrics~~ a nations exclusively devoted to ͺ~~the cultivation~~
~~of the soil,~~ for the fabrics of ~~the~~ manufacturing states, ~~from which its~~
~~supplies~~ are constant and regular, the wants, ~~of the latter of which~~
                                for
of the latter ~~experienced of~~ ͺthe products of the former are liable to
    ͺconsiderable fluctuations              great
very ͺ~~great~~ ͺ~~inequalities~~ and interruptions. The ͺinequalities, resulting from difference of seasons, have been elsewhere remarked. This uniformity of demand, on one side, and unsteadiness of it, on the other, must necessarily have a tendency to cause the ~~course of~~ general course
                                                        turn to the
of the exchange of commodities between the parties to ͺ~~prove highly~~
            of
~~disadvantageous to~~ the merely Agricultural States. Peculiarity of situation, a ~~soil and~~ climate and soil adapted to the production of peculiar commodities may sometimes ~~produce a contrary effect~~ contradict the

rule; but there is every reason to ~~conclude~~ believe, that it will be found, in the main, a just one.

Another ~~of the~~ circumstances ~~alluded to as giving~~ which gives a superiority of commercial advantages to states ~~which~~ that manufacture, as well as cultivate, consists in the more numerous attractions, which a more diversified market offers to foreign customers, and in the greater scope, which it affords to mercantile enterprise. It is a position of indisputable truth in commerce, depending too on very obvious reasons, that the greatest resort will ever be to those marts, where commodities, while equally abundant, are most various. Each difference of kind holds out an additional inducement ~~while a general assortment of ⟨tra⟩de can be the more easily ⟨ex⟩cited~~: And it is a position not less clear, that the field of enterprise must be enlarged to the Merchants of a Country in proportion to the variety as well as the abundance of ~~domestic~~ commodities which they find at home for exportation to foreign markets.

A third ~~and perhaps~~ circumstance perhaps not inferior to either of the other two, ~~asserting conferring~~ conferring the superiority which has been stated ~~of either of the other two in question~~, has relation to the stagnations of ~~pr~~ demand for certain commodities which ~~are from time to time experienced~~ at some time or other interfere more or less with the sale of all. The Nation which can bring to market but few articles is likely to be more quickly and sensibly affected by such stagnations than one which is always possessed of a great variety of commodities. The former frequently finds too great a proportion of its stock of materials, for sale or exchange, lying on hand—or is obliged to make injurious sacrifices to supply its wants of foreign articles, which are <u>numerous</u> and <u>urgent,</u> in proportion to the smallness of the number of its own. The latter commonly finds itself indemnified, by the high prices of some articles, for the low prices of others; ~~while~~ and the prompt and advantageous sale of some articles enables its merchant the better to wait for a favourable change in respect to those which happen not to be in demand. There is ground to believe that a difference of situation in this particular has immensely different effects upon the wealth and prosperity of Nations.

From these circumstances collectively, two important inferences are to be drawn— ~~Th~~ one that there is always a higher probability of a favourable ballance of Trade, in regard to countries, in which manufactures, founded on the basis of a thriving Agriculture, flourish, than in regard to those, which are confined wholly or almost wholly to Agriculture; ~~and~~ the other, ~~the~~ (which is also a consequence of the former first) that countries of the ~~first~~ description are likely to possess more pecuniary wealth, or money, than those of the latter.

Facts appear to correspond with this conclusion. ~~Let the~~ The importations of manufactured supplies seem invariably to drain the merely Agricultural people of their wealth. Let the situation of the<sub>^</sub> manufacturing countries of Europe ~~which m~~ be compared in this particular, with ~~the~~ that of countries ~~situation of those~~, which only cultivate, and the disparity will be striking. Other causes, it is true, help to account for this disparity between some of them; and among these causes, the relative state of others Agriculture; but between ~~some~~<sub>^</sub>of them the most prominent circumstance of dissimilitude ~~were~~ arises from the comparative state of manufactures. In<sub>^</sub> ~~confirmation~~ corroboration of the same idea, it ought not to escape remark, that the West India Islands, the soils of which are the most fertile, and the Nation, ~~of Europe~~ which in the greatest degree supplies the rest of the world, with the precious metals, exchange to a loss with almost every other Country.

Stands
Qr.
~~Authentic statements in Great Britan render it more than probable~~ ~~that their exports including their various fabrics have not for many~~ ~~years exceeded a third of the total value of their manufactures. This~~ ~~illustrates the immense importance of the manufactures of that Coun-~~ ~~try as a cause of national wealth. Had they neglected this important~~ ~~branch of domestic industry and consumed foreign articles, in place~~ ~~of those they now make for themselves, it need not be said how differ-~~ ~~ent an aspect their case situation would exhibit from that which it at~~ ~~present wears.~~

As far as experience at home may guide, it will ~~furnish a confirma-~~ ~~tion~~ lead to the same conclusion. Previous to the revolution, the quantity of coin, possessed by the colonies, which now compose the

United States, appeared to be inadequate to their circulation: and their debt to Great Britain was progressive. Since the Revolution, the States, in which manufactures have most increased, have recovered fastest from the injuries of the late war; and abound most in pecuniary resources.

It ought to be admitted however, in this as in the preceding case, that causes ~irrelative to~ foreign from the state of manufactures account, in a degree, for the phenonema remarked. The continual progress of new settlements has a natural tendency to occasion s an unfavourable ballance of trade; though it indemnifies for the inconvenience, by that increase of the national capital, which flows from the conversion of waste into improved lands: And the different degrees of external commerce, which are carried on by the different states, may make material differences in the comparitive state of their wealth. The first circumstance has reference to the deficiency of Coin and the increase of debt, previous to the revolution; the last to the advantages which the most manufacturing states appears to have enjoyed, over the others, since the termination of the late war.

But the uniform appearance of an abundance of specie, as the con-c-omitant of a flourishing state of manufactures, and of the reverse, where they do not prevail, afford a strong presumption of their favourable operation upon the wealth of a Country.

Not only the wealth; but the independence and security of a country appear to be materially connected with the prosperity of manufactures. Every nation, with a view to those great objects, ought to endeavour to possess within itself all the essentials of national supply. These comprise the means of subsistence habitation cloathing and defence.

The possession of these is necessary to the perfection of the of the body politic; to the safety as well as to the welfare of the society. The want of either is the want of an important organ of political life and motion; and in the various crises which await a state, it must severely feel the effects of any such deficiency. The extreme embarrassments of the United States, during the late war, from an incapacity of supplying themselves ~common~ are still matter of keen recollection: A fu-

See if this is not contradicted where a free Trade is spoke of

                        ₐmight be expected
ture warₐ ~~could not fail~~ again to exemplify the mischiefs and dangers
               ₐthat incapacity is still in too gret a degree
of a situation, to whichₐ ~~it is~~ applicable; unless changed by timely and
vigourous exertion.

           effect
    To ~~work~~ₐ this change, as fast as shall be prudent, merits all the at-
                                    'Tis
tention and all the zeal of our public councils. ~~It is~~ the next great work
to be accomplished.

                                ₐas long as it shall continue must
~~Quaere?~~    The want of a Navy to protect our external commerceₐ ~~renders~~ it
a peculiarly precarious reliance, for the supply of essential articles,
    ₐmust serve
andₐ to ~~strengthens~~ prodigiously the arguments in favour of manufactures.

    To these ~~more~~ general considerations are added some of a more par-
ticular nature.

    Our distance from Europe, the great fountain of manufactured
supply, subjects us, in the existing state of things, to inconvenience
and loss, in two ways. The bulkiness of those commodities, which
are the chief productions of the soil, necessarily imposes very heavy
charges on their transportation to distant markets. These charges, in
the cases, in which the nations, to whom our products are sent, main-
                                     with us
tain, ~~with their own commodities~~, a competition, ~~with our~~ in the
supply of their own markets, principally fall upon us; ~~who furnish~~
                           form         deductions from
~~them to the extent of their deficiency~~, andₐ ~~materially diminish~~ the
primitive value of the articles furnished. The charges on manufactured supplies, brought from Europe, are ~~enhanced~~ greatly enhanced
by the same circumstance of distance. ~~particularly as to the coarser~~
               ₐagain,
~~and more bulky kinds~~. These chargesₐ in the cases, in which our own
                                 own
industry maintains no competition in our ~~own~~ₐ markets, also principally fall upon us, and are an additional cause of extraordinary deduction from the primitive value of our own products; these being the
materials of exchange for the foreign fabrics, which we consume.

    The equality and moderation of individual property, and the grow-
ing settlements of new ~~lands~~ districts, occasion in this country an

unusual demand for coarse manufactures; the charges of which being greater in proportion to their greater bulk augment the disadvantage, which has been just described.

As in most countries, domestic supplies ~~occasion~~ ^maintain^ a very consider-able competition with ^such^ foreign productions of the soil as are imported for sale; if the extensive establishment of manufactories in the United States does not create a similar competition in respect to manufactured articles, it appears to be clearly deducible from the considerations which have been mentioned, that they must sustain a double loss, in their exchanges with foreign nations; strongly conducive to an unfavourable ballance of Trade and very prejudicial to their Interests.

These disadvantages press with, no small weight, on the ^landed interest^ ~~proprietors~~ of the Country.

~~of land.~~ In seasons of peace, they cause a serious deduction from the intrinsic value of the products of the soil. In the time of a war, which should either involve ourselves, or another nation, possessing a considerable share of our carrying trade, the charges on the transportation of our commodities, bulky as most of them are, could hardly fail to prove a grievous burthen to the farmer; while obliged to depend in so great a degree as he ^now^ does, upon foreign markets, for the vent of the surplus of his labour.

As far as the prosperity of the Fisheries of the United States is impeded by the want of an adequate market, there arises another special reason for desiring the extension of manufactures. Besides the fish which in many places would be likely to make a part of the subsistence of the persons employed; it is known that the oils ^bones and skins^ of marine animals ~~is extensively~~ ^are^ of extensive use in various manufactures. Hence ^the prospect of^ ^an additional demand for the produce of the Fisheries.

[~~The fur~~
~~the bone~~
~~spermaceti~~
~~Skins~~]

One ~~or two~~ more points of view only remains, in which to consider the expediency of ~~the~~ encouragement ~~of~~ ^ing^ manufactures, in the United States; ~~previous to~~ ^a general^ ~~dis~~ discussion ~~of the means, by which it is to be~~

effected, and ~~a specification of the objects, to which it would seem~~ ^to ^most
proper to direct it, in the ^present ~~actual~~ state of the Country, and the particular measures which may be adviseable in respect to each.

It is not uncommon to meet with an opinion, that though the promoting of manufactures may be the interest of a part of the Union, it is contrary to that of another part. The Northern and Southern Regions are sometimes represented as having ^hostile ~~opposite~~ ^adverse interests in this respect. Those are called Manufacturing, these Agricultural states; and a species of opposition is imagined to subsist between the Manufacturing and Agricultural interests.

This idea of an opposition between those two interests is the common error of the early periods of every country; but experience gradually dissipates it. Indeed they are perceived so often to ^succour and befriend each other, that they come at length to be considered as one; a supposition which has been frequently abused, and is not universally true. Particular encouragements of particular manufactures may be of a nature to sacrifice the interests of landholders to those of Manufactures. But ^it is nevertheless a maxim, well established by experience and generally acknowleged, where there has been sufficient experience, that the <u>aggregate</u> prosperity of manufactures, and the <u>aggregate</u> prosperity of Agriculture are intimately connected. In the course of the discussion, which has had place, ~~a variey of~~ ^various weighty considerations have been adduced, ~~which~~ operating in support of that maxim. Perhaps the superior steadiness of the demand of a domestic market for the surplus produce of the soil is alone a convincing argument of its truth.

Ideas of a contrarity of interests between the ^Northern & ~~Northern and~~ Southern regions of the Union ~~ought always to~~ be ~~indulged with great~~ ~~caution. They~~ ^as often as they occur are in the main as unfounded as they are mischievous. The diversity of circumstances, on which such contrariety is usually predicated, authorises a directly contrary conclusion. Mutual wants constitute one of the strongest links of political connection; and the

Or what other

natural
extent of these bears a ˄proportion to the diversity in the ~~mutual~~ means
mutual
of ˄supply.

~~It ought~~

~~Ought it not to be the effort of enlightened patriotism to suppress~~
of an opposite ~~tendency~~ complexion
Suggestions ˄~~founded on the supposition of a different interest be-~~
[~~Interest~~ cause]
~~tween the states~~ are ever to be deplored; as unfriendly to the steady
pursuit of one great common ~~cause,~~ ˄and to the perfect harmony of
all the parts.

In proportion as the mind is accustommed to trace the intimate
a
connection of interest, which subsists between all the parts of ˄Society,
united under ~~one and~~ the same government—the infinite variety of
channels which serve to circulate the prosperity of each to and
through the rest in that proportion will it be little apt to be disturbed
by the solicitudes and apprehensions which originate in local discrimi-
apt              listen to
nations. ~~disposed to~~ ˄be ~~influenced by the surmises of a spirit of~~
                              pleasing encouraging
~~jealous locality~~. It is a truth as important, as it is agreeable, ~~as pro-~~
˄and
~~found as it is simple,~~ ˄one to which it is not easy to imagine ~~an~~ exceptions, that every thing tending to establish substantial and permanent
a
order, in the affairs of country, to increase the total mass of industry
and opulence, is ultimately beneficial to every part of it. On the credit
of this great ~~and precious~~ truth, an acquiescence may safely be accorded, from every quarter, to all institutions and arrangements,
which promise a confirmation of public order, and an augmentation
of National Resource.

by the solici-
tudes arising
from local
jealousies
spirit of
locality

But there are more particular considerations which serve to fortify
the idea that the encouragement of manufactures is the interest of all
parts of the Union. If the Northern & Middle states should be the
principal scenes of such establishments, they would immediately
benefit the more Southern by creating a demand for productions;
some of which they have in common with other states, and others of
which are either peculiar to them, or more abundant, or of better

quality than elsewhere. These productions principally are Timber, flax, hemp, cotton, wool, raw silk, indigo, iron, lead, furs, hides, skins, and coals. Of these articles, Cotton and Indigo are peculiar to the Southern States; as are hitherto <u>lead</u> and <u>coal</u>. Flax and Hemp are or may be raised in greater abundance there than in the more Northern states. And the wool ~~produced in certain parts~~ of Virginia is said to be of better quality, than that ~~which is raised in~~ of any other state; a circumstance rendered the more probable by the ~~accou~~ reflection that Virginia embraces the same latitudes with the finest wool country of Europe. The ~~extensive cultivation~~ climate of the South is also

better adapted to the <sub>^</sub>production ~~culture~~ of silk. ~~The extensive cultivation of cotton can perhaps~~

The extensive cultivation of cotton can perhaps hardly be expected, but from the previous establishment of [~~native~~] <sub>^</sub>domestic manufactories of the article; and the surest encouragement and vent, for the others would result from similar establishments in respect to them.

If, then, it satisfactorily appears, that it is the interest of the US, generally, to encourage manufactures; it merits particular attention, that there are circumstances which render the present a critical

moment for entering<sub>^</sub> with zeal upon the important business. The effort cannot fail to be materially seconded by a considerable and increasing influx of money in consequence of foreign speculations in the funds—and by the disorders, which exist in different parts of Europe.

The first circumstance ~~not~~ not only facilitates the execution of manufacturing enterprises; but it indicates them, ~~them~~ as a necessary mean, to turn the thing itself to advantage, and to prevent its being eventually an evil. If useful employment be not found for the money

of foreigners brought to the country to be invested in ~~the~~ pur~~poses~~ chases of

the<sub>^</sub> public debt, it will quickly be reexported to defray<sub>^</sub> the expence of an extraordinary consumption of foreign luxuries; and distressing drains of our specie may hereafter be experienced to pay the interest and redeem the principal of the purchased debt.

The useful employment too<sub>^</sub> ought to be ~~must~~ be of a nature to produce solid and permanent ~~domestic~~ improvements. If the money merely serves to give ~~and~~ a temporary spring to foreign commerce; as it cannot procure new and lasting outlets for the products of the country; there will be no real or durable advantage gained. ~~In Agricultural ameliorations~~ As far as it shall find its way, in Agricultural ameliorations, in opening ~~new or improving~~ old canals, and in similar improvements,

it will <sub>be</sub> productive <sub>of</sub> substantial utility. But there is reason to doubt whether in such channels it is likely to find sufficient employment and still more whether many of those who possess it would be as readily attracted to objects of this nature, as to manufacturing pursuits; which bear greater analogy to those to which they are accustomed, and to the spirit generated by them.

To open the one field, as well as the other, will at least secure a better prospect of useful employment, for whatever accession of money, there has been or may be.

There is at the present juncture a certain fermentation of mind, a certain activity of speculation and enterprise, which, if properly directed, may be made subservient to useful purposes; but which, if left intirely to itself, may be attended with pernicious effects.

The disturbed state of Europe inclining its citizens to emigration, the requisite workmen will be ~~the~~ more <sup>easily</sup> ~~easily~~ acquired than at another time; and ~~if~~ the ~~effecting~~ of multiplying the ~~objects~~ <sup>opportunities m</sup> of employment to those who emigrate, <sup>may be an</sup> ~~should be to~~ increase <sup>of</sup> the number of emigrants and extent of valuable acquisitions to the population arts and industry of the Country. To ~~take~~ <sup>find</sup> pleasure in the calamities of other nations would be criminal; but to benefit ourselves, by opening an asylum to those who suffer, in consequence of them, is as justifiable as it is politic.

A full view having now been taken of the inducements to the <sup>promotion and</sup> ~~encouragement~~ of manufactures, in the United States, accompanied with an examination of the principal objections, which are commonly urged <sup>[in opposition, there]</sup> ~~against it~~—it is proper, in the next place, to consider the means, by which it may be effected, as introductory to a specification of the objects which in the present state of things appear the most fit to be encouraged and of the particular measures which it may be adviseable to adopt in respect to each.

In order to a better judgment of the means proper to be resorted to by the United States, it will be of use to advert to those, which have been employed with success in other countries. The principal of these are—

No II

I  Protecting duties—or duties on those foreign articles, which are the rivals ~~ones~~ of the domestic ones, intended to be encouraged.

*Duties of this nature evidently amount to a virtual bounty on the domestic fabrics; since by enhancing the charges on foreign Articles they enable the National manufacturers to undersell their foreign competitors. The propriety of this species of encouragement need not be dwelt upon; as it is not only a clear result from the numerous topics which have been suggested but is sanctioned by the laws of the United States in a variety of instances. It has the additional recommendation of being a resource of Revenue. Indeed all the duties imposed on imported articles, though with an exclusive view to ~~the object of~~ Revenue, have the effect in contemplation, and except where they fall on raw materials wear a beneficent aspect towards the manufactures of the Country.*

No III

II  Prohibitions of ~~Rival~~ rival articles or duties equivalent to prohibitions.

*This is another and* ^an^ *efficacious mean of encouraging national manufactures. But in general it is only fit to be employed when a manufacture has made such* ^a^ *progress and is in so many hands as to insure a due competition and an adequate supply on reasonable terms. Of duties equivalent to prohibitions, there are examples in the Laws of the United States—such as those on*

malt liquors
loaf Sugar
Carriages
Candles

*and there are other cases to which the principle may be advantageously extended, but they are not numerous.*

*Considering a monopoly of the domestic market to its own manufacturers as the reigning policy of manufacturing nations, a similar policy on the part of the United States, in every proper instance, is dictated, it might almost be said, by the principles of distributive justice; certainly by the duty of endeavoring to secure to their own Citizens a reciprocity of advantages.*

III   Prohibitions of the exportation of ~~actual staples~~ the materials of ~~domestic~~ manufactures.

<sub>certain</sub> appears above "actual staples"

The desire of securing a cheap and plentiful supply for the national workmen, and, where the article is either peculiar to the country, or of peculiar quality ~~there~~, the jealousy of enabling foreign workmen to rival those of the nation, with its own materials, are the leading motives to this species of regulation. It ought to be affirmed that it is ~~nev~~ in no ~~case~~ proper; but it is certainly one which ought to be adopted with great circumspection and only in very plain cases. It is seen at once, that its operation, ~~is~~, ~~by exclusion at least~~, is to abrige the demand and keep down the price of the produce of some other branch of industry; generally speaking of Agriculture, to the prejudice of those, who carry it on; and though ~~it is certain that as far~~ ~~as it is~~ essential to the prosperity of any very important national manufacture, it may happen that those who are injured in the first instance may be eventually indemnified, by the superior steadiness of an extensive domestic market, depending on that prosperity; ~~if the manufacturing~~ yet in a matter, in which there is so much room for nice and difficult combinations, in which such opposite considerations combat each other, prudence seems to dictate, that the expedient in question ought to be ~~adopted~~ with a sparing hand.

Interlinear insertions: "there" above "there"; "not" above "ought"; "instance" above "case"; "immediate" above "its"; "if it be really" above "as it is"; "indulged" above "adopted"

IV   Pecuniary bounties

This has been found one of the most efficacious means of encouraging manufactures; and it is, in some views, the best—though it has not yet been practiced upon, by the Government of the United States, (unless the allowance on the exportortation of dried and pickled fish and salted meat could be considered as bounty) [111] and though it is less favoured by public opinion than some other modes. Its advantages are these—

Marginal note: [~~on the manufacture or on the raw material~~]

Interlinear insertion: "a" above "as"

111.  H is referring to the drawback given under Section 4 of "An Act making further provision for the payment of the debts of the United States" (1 *Stat.* 181–82 [August 10, 1790]).

1    It is a species of encouragement more positive and direct than any other, and, for that very reason, has a more immediate tendency to stimulate and uphold new enterprises; increasing the chances of profit, and diminishing the risks of loss, in the first attempts.

2    It avoids the inconvenience of a temporary augmentation of price, which is incident to some other modes, or it produces it ~~in~~ <sup>to</sup> a less ~~extent~~ <sub>degree</sub>; either by making no addition to the charges on the rival foreign article, as in the case of protecting duties, or by making a smaller addition. The first happens when the fund for the bounty is derived from a different object (which may or may not increase the price of some other article according to the nature of that object), the second when the fund is derived from the same or a similar object of foreign manufacture. One per cent duty on the foreign article, converted into a bounty on the domestic, will have an equal effect with a duty of two per Cent exclusive of such bounty: and the price of the foreign commodity is liable to be raised, in the one case, in the proportion of 1 ℔ Cent, in the other, in that of two per Cent. Indeed the bounty when drawn from another source is calculated to promote a reduction of price; because without laying any new charge on the foreign article, it serves to introduce a competition with it, and to increase the total quantity of the article in the market.

3.    Bounties have ~~less tenden~~ not like high protecting duties, ~~at~~ tendency to produce scarcity. An increase of price is not always [~~native~~] the immediate, though, where the progress of a domestic manufacture does not counteract a rise, it is commonly the ultimate effect of an additional duty. In ~~such an~~ <sup>the</sup> interval between the laying of the duty and a proportional increase of price, it may discourage importation, by interfering with the profits to be expected from the sale of the article.

4    Bounties are sometimes not only the best, but the only proper expedient, for uniting the encouragement of a new object of agriculture, with that of a new object of manufacture. It is the interest of the farmer to have the production of the raw material promoted, by <sup>counteracting</sup> ~~restraining~~ the interference of the foreign material of the same kind. It is the interest of the manufacturer to have the material abundant

and cheap. If prior to ~~a~~ the domestic production of the Material, in sufficient quantity, to supply the manufacturer on good terms—a duty be laid upon the importation of it from abroad, with a view to promote the raising of it at home, the interests both of the Farmer and Manufacturer will be disserved. By either destroying the requisite supply, or raising the price of the article beyond what can be afforded to be given for it by the ~~undertaker~~ Conductor of an infant manufacture, it is abandonned or fails; and there being no domestic manufactories to create a demand for the raw material, which is raised by the farmer, it is in vain, that the competition of the like foreign article may have been destroyed. It cannot escape notice, that a duty upon the importation of an article can no otherwise ~~promote~~ ^aid the domestic production of it, than by giving the latter greater advantages in the home market. It can ^have no influence, upon ~~foreign markets~~ the advantageous sale of the article produced, in foreign ~~mater~~ markets; no tendency, therefore, to promote its exportations.

The true way to conciliate these two interests is to lay a duty on foreign <u>manufactures</u> of the material, the growth of which is desired to be encouraged, and to apply the produce of that duty, by way of bounty, either upon the production of the material itself, ~~or upon its exportation to foreign countries~~, or upon its manufacture at home, or upon both. ^~~any or all of them~~. In this disposition of the thing, the Manufacturer commences his enterprise, under every advantage ^which is attainable, ~~he can desire~~, as to quantity, or price of the raw material: And the farmer, if the bounty be immediately to him, is enabled by it, ~~by~~ ^to enter into a successful competition with the foreign material; if ^the bounty ~~it~~ be to the manufacturer on ~~the~~ so much of the domestic ~~materials~~ as he consumes, the ^operation ^is nearly the same; he has a motive of interest to prefer the domestic commodity, if of equal quality, even at a higher price than the foreign, ~~if~~ ^so long as the difference of price ^is ~~be~~ any thing short of the bounty,   ☞ which is allowed ~~him~~ upon the article.

Except the ~~most~~ simple and ordinary kinds of ^household manufactures, or

those for which there are very commanding local advantages, pecuniary bounties are in most cases indispensable to the introduction of a
new branch. A stimulous and a support, not less powerful and direct,
is generally speaking essential to the overcoming of the obstacles, ~~in~~
which arise from the competitions of ~~the~~ superior skill and maturity

Bounties are                              in regard to articles      ~~those~~ upon

elsewhere. ~~It is~~ especially essential ~~in the cases, in which~~ foreigners,

which, those

who have been accustommed to supply a country, are in the practice

them

of ~~allowing~~ granting ~~the identical species of encouragement~~.

The continuance of bounties on manufactures long established must
almost always be of questionable policy; ~~but~~ because a presumption

every

would arise in such case, that there were natural and inherent impediments to success. But in new undertakings, they are as justifiable, as
they are oftentimes necessary. ~~And wherever they appear to be
really necessary~~

There is a degree of prejudice against bounties, from an appearance
of giving away the public money, without an immediate consideration, and from a supposition, that they serve to enrich particular
classes, at the expence of the community.

But neither of these sources of dislike will bear a serious examination. There is no purpose, to which public money can be more beneficially applied, than to the acquisition of a new and useful branch of
industry; no consideration more valuable, than a permanent addition

the

to general stock of productive labour.

As to the second source of objection, it equally lies against other
modes of encouragement, which are admitted to be eligible. As often
as a duty upon a foreign article makes an addition to its price, it
causes an extra expence to the community, for the benefit of the
domestic manufactures. A bounty does no more. But it is the interest
of the Society, in each case, to submit to a temporary expence; which

its

~~we~~ is more than compensated, by an increase of industry and wealth,

and      ~~very~~

by an augmentation of ~~its~~ resources and independence; by the cir-

ic

cumstance of eventual cheapness, which has been not ed in another
place.

~~The species of encouragement, however, may in the United States~~
It would deserve attention, however, in the ~~at the~~ employment of
this species of encouragement, in the U States, as a reason for moderating the degree of it, in the instances in which it might be deemed
<br>       of this country      ~~nations~~
eligible, that the~~se~~ great distance from ~~the manufacturing countries~~
<br>          charges
~~of~~ Europe imposes ~~a~~ very heavy ~~expence~~ on all the ~~foreign~~ fabrics
which are brought from thence, amounting from fifteen to 25 per
Cent on their value, according to their bulk.       Qr—

### V ~~Premiums~~

            constitutional
A Question has been made concerning the right of the ~~United
Sta~~ Government of the United States to apply this species of encouragement. But there is certainly no good foundation for such a
question. The National Legislature has ~~plenary~~ express authority ~~to~~
"To lay and collect taxes duties ~~and~~ imposts and excises, to pay the
debts and provide for the common defence and general welfare" with
no other qualifications than that "all duties imposts and excises shall
be uniform throughout the United States" that "no capitation or
other direct tax shall be laid, unless in proportion to numbers ascertained by a census or enumeration taken on the principles prescribed
in the Constitution" and that "no tax or duty shall be laid on articles
exported from any state." These three qualifications excepted, the
power to raise money is plenary and indefinite; and the objects to
which it may be appropriated are no less comprehensive than the
payment of the public debts and the providing for the common
defence and "general welfare." The terms "general welfare" were
doubtless intended to signify more than ~~were~~ was expressed or imported in those which preceded; otherwise numerous exigencies incident to the affairs of a nation would have been left without a provi-
<br>            any that
sion. The phrase is as ~~compreh~~ comprehensive ~~an one~~, as could have
been used; because it was not fit, that the constitutional authority of
the Union, to appropriate its revenues, should have been restricted
within narrower limits, than the "general welfare" and because this
necessarily embraces a vast variety of particulars, which are susceptible neither of specification nor of definition.

<u>wisely and</u>
It is therefore ᴧof necessity left to the discretion of the national Legislature, to pronounce upon the objects, which concern the general welfare, and for which, under that decription, an appropriation of money is requisite and proper. And there seems to be no room for a doubt, that whatever concerns the general interests of <u>learning,</u> of <u>agriculture,</u> of <u>manufactures</u> and of <u>commerce,</u> are within the
sphere                                                    ᴧregards
<u>purview</u> of the national councils, <u>as far</u> as ᴧ<s>concerns</s> an <u>application</u> of <u>money.</u>

The only qualification of the generality of the phrase, in question, which seems to be admissible, is this—That the object<s>ion</s> to which an appropriation of money is to be made be <u>general</u> and not <u>local;</u> its operation extending, in fact, or by possibility, throughout the Union, and not being confined to a particular spot.

No objection ought to arise to this construction from a supposition
               ᴧdo
that it would imply a power to ᴧwhatever ese should appear to
ᴧconducive
Congress ᴧto the general welfare. A power to appropriate money with this latitude (<s>and</s> which is granted too, in express terms) would not
                                          ᴧin the constitution
carry a power to do any other thing not <s>granted</s> authorised ᴧeither expressly or by fair implication.


## V  Premiums

*These are of a nature allied to bounties, though distinguishable from them, in some important features. Bounties are applicable to the whole quantity of an article produced, or manufactured, or exported, and involve a correspondent expence. Premiums serve to reward some particular excellence or superiority, some extraordinary exertion or skill; and are dispensed only in a small number of cases. But their effect is to stimulate general effort. Contrived so as to be both honorary and lucrative, they address themselves to different passions;*
                                          ᴧInterest. [<s>interest</s>]
*touching the chords as well of emulation as of ᴧ<s>avarice.</s> They are accordingly a very œconomical mean of exciting the enterprise of a whole community.*

*There are various societies in different countries, whose object is the dispensation of premiums for the encouragement of <u>agriculture</u>*

No. IV

*arts manufactures and commerce; and though they* <sup>are</sup> *for the most part,*
*voluntary associations, with comparatively slender funds; their utility*
*has been immense. Much has been done by this mean in great Britain:*
*Scotland in particular owes materially to it a prodigious amelioration*
*of condition. From a similar establishment, in the United states, sup-*
*plied and supported by the Government of the Union, vast benefits*
*might reasonably be expected. Some further ideas on this head shall*
*accordingly be submitted in the conclusion of this report.*

VI   The exemption of the Materials of manufactures from duty.   & implements

The policy of ~~such an~~ that exemption, as a general rule, ~~is obvious,~~
particularly in reference to new establishments is obvious. ~~Nothing~~
~~can be more unwise than to impede a~~ It can hardly ever be adviseable
to add the obstructions of fiscal burthens to the difficulties ~~to~~ which
naturally embarrass a new manufacture; and where is matured and
in condition to become an object of revenue, it is generally speaking
better that the fabric, than the material should be the subject of taxation. Ideas of proportion, between the quantum of the tax and the
value of the article can ~~better~~ be more easily adjusted in the former
than in the latter case. An argument for exemptions of this kind in the
United States, is to be derived from the practice (as far as their necessities have permitted) of those nations,
whom we are to meet as competitors in our own and in foreign
Markets ~~which~~ is ~~conformable to the principle of such ext exemptions,~~
~~as far as their necessities have admitted.~~

There are however exceptions to ~~the principle~~ of which some
examples will be given under the next head.

The laws of the Union afford instances of the observance of the
policy here recommended [112] but it will probably be found adviseable
to extend it to some other cases.

Of a nature, bearing some affinity ~~to~~ the ~~exemptions under considera-~~
~~tion is that regulation~~ to that policy, is the regulation ~~th~~ which
exempts from duty the tools and implements, as well as the books cloaths and
household furniture ~~furnis~~ of foreign artists, ~~to~~ who come to reside in the U States; an

112. For the free list and enumerated duties in effect, see note 49.

advantage already secured to them by the laws of the Union, and
~it is [is~ ~conceived~ ~to~ ~be,]~
which~ ~it~ ~is~ in every view, proper to continue.

[on~ ~raw]~
on
VII   Drawbacks of the duties, which are imposed ~by~ the Materi-
[on~ ~the~ ~exportation]~
als ~of manufactures.

It~ ~follows~
~that~ ~when,~   It has already been observed, as a general rule, that duties on those
~for~ ~special~   materials of manufacture, ought, with certain exceptions to be fore-
~reasons,~                                       three cases occur, which ~will~ may
~duties~ ~are~   borne. Of these ~exceptions~ exceptions ~the~ ~following~ ~examples~ ~kinds~
~laid~ ~on~ ~such~   ~deserve~ ~our~ serve as
~articles~   ~occur~ ~by~ ~way~ ~of~ ~examples—one where the material is itself ~and~
or
object of general, ~and~ ~extensive consumption, and a fit and productive source of revenue—[113]

VIII   The encouragement of new inventions and discoveries, at
home, and of the introduction into the United States, of such as may
have been made in other countries; ~Machinery~ particularly those,
which relate to machinery.

This is among the most useful and unexceptionable of the aids,
which can be given to manufactures. The usual means of that encouragement are pecuniary rewards, and, for a time, exclusive privileges.
The first must be employed, according to the occasion, and the utility

so
~or~ ~importance~ of the invention or discovery: For the last, ~as~ far as
respects "authors and inventors" provision has been made by law.[114]
~in regard to improvements & secrets of extraordinary value
But it is desireable ~to be able to extend the same benefit to ~the~ Intro-
also,            as well as Authors and Inventors; ~at~ ~least~
ducers, ~as~ ~well~ ~as~ ~the~ ~Authors~ ~or~ ~Inventors,~ ~in~ ~regard~ ~to improvements and ~secrets~ ~of~ ~extraordinary~ ~value~; a policy which has been
practiced with advantage in ~some~ other countries. Here, however,
as in some other cases,
~there is cause to regret, that the competency of the authority of the
National Government to the good, which might be done, ~it~ ~at~ ~least~
~questionable~ is not without a question. Many aids might be given to
industry; many internal improvements of primary magnitude might

113. At this point a page or pages are missing in MS.     114. See note 99.

be promoted, by an authority ^operating ~~extending~~ throughout the Union, which cannot be effected, as well, if at all, by an authority confined within the limits of a single state.

But if the legislature of the Union cannot do all the good, that might be wished, it is at least desireable, that all may be done, which is practicable. Means for promoting the introduction of foreign improvements though less efficaciously than might be ~~done~~ ^accomplished with more ^adequate ~~competant~~ authority, will form a part of the plan intended to be submitted in the close of this report.

It is customary with manufacturing nations to prohibit, under severe penalties, the exportation of implements and machines, which they have either invented or improved. There are already objects for a similar regulation in the United States; and others may be expected to occur from time to time. The adoption of it seems to be dictated by the principle of reciprocity. Greater liberalty, in such respects, might better comport with the general spirit of the Country; but a selfish and exclusive policy ^in other quarters ~~every where else~~ will not always permit the free indulgence of ~~that~~ ^a spirit, which would place us upon an unequal footing. As far as ~~such~~ prohibitions tend to prevent foreign competitors from deriving the benefit of ^the ~~such~~ improvements ^made at home, they tend to increase the advantages of those by whom they may have been introduced; and ~~so far~~ operate as an encouragement to exertion.

IX   Judicious regulations for the inspection of ^manufactured commodities.

This is not among the least important of the means, by which the prosperity of manufactures may be promoted. It is indeed in ~~some~~ ^many cases ^one of ~~among~~ the most essential. ~~To prevent frauds upon consumers~~ ~~Tending~~ ^Contributing to prevent frauds upon consumers at home and exporters to foreign countries—to improve the quality and preserve the character of the national manufactures, it cannot fail to aid the ~~rea~~ expeditious and advantageous sale of them, and to serve as a guard against successful competitions from ~~some~~ other quarters. The reputation of ^the flour  [& lumber]

の the          of
of some ~~ports~~ states and of ₍Potash ~~in~~ others has been established by
an attention to this point. And the like good name might be procured
                    ₍wheresoever produced,
for those articles₍ ~~in all parts of the Union~~ by a judicious and uniform
system of Inspection, throughout the ports of the United States. A
like system might also be extended with advantage to other commodities.

~~As the immediate obj~~
~~It is presumed that~~
X

No V

X    The facilitating of pecuniary remittances from place to place—
    is
*Is₍ a point of considerable moment to trade in general, and to manufac-*
                    [rendering more easy]
*tures in particular; by ~~facilitating~~₍ the purchase of raw materials and
provisions and the payment for manufactured supplies. A general cir-*

s

*culation of Bank paper, which is to be expected from the institution₍
lately established will be a most valuable mean to this end. But much
good would also accrue from some additional provisions respecting
inland bills of exchange. If those drawn in one state payable in another
were made negotiable, every where, and interest and damages allowed
in case of protest, it would greatly promote negociations between
the citizens of different States, by rendering them more secure; and,
with it the convenience and advantage of the merchants and manufacturers of each.*

No. VI

XI    The facilitating of the transportation of commodities—
*Improvements favoring this object intimately concern all the do-
mestic interests of a community; but they may without impropriety
be mentioned as having an important relation to manufactures. There
is perhaps scarcely any thing which has been better calculated to
                                            the
assist the manufactures of Great Britain than the ameliorations of₍
public roads of that Kingdom, and the great progress which has been
of late made in opening canals. Of the former, the United States stand
much in need, and for the latter they present uncommon facilities.
The symptoms of attention to the improvement of inland Navigation
which have lately appeared in some quarters ~~and especially in the
State of Pensylvania~~, must fill with pleasure every heart warmed with
a true Zeal for the prosperity of the country. These examples, it is to*

*be hoped, will stimulate the exertions of the Government and the citizens of every State. There can certainly be no object more worthy of the cares of the local administrations; and it were to be wished, that there was no doubt of the power of the national Government to lend its direct aid, on a comprehensive plan. This is one of those improvements which could be prosecuted with more efficacy by the whole than by any part or parts of the Union. There are cases in which the general interest will be in danger to be sacrificed to the collision of some supposed local interests. Jealousies, in matters of this kind, are as apt to exist, as they are apt to be erroneous.*

*The following remarks are sufficiently judicious and pertinent to deserve a literal quotation—"Good roads, canals and navigable rivers, by diminishing the expence of carriage, put the remote parts of a country more nearly upon a level with those in the neighborhood of the town. They are upon that account the greatest of all improvements. They encourage the cultivation of the remote, which must always be the most extensive circle of the country. They are advantageous to the Town by breaking down the monopoly of the country in its neighborhood. They are advantageous even to that part of the Country. Though they introduce some rival commodities into the old Market they open many new markets to its produce. Monopoly besides is a great enemy to good management, which can never be universally established, but in consequence of that free and universal competition, which forces every body to have recourse to it for the sake of self defence. It is not more than Fifty years ago that some of the Counties in the neighborhood of London petitioned the Parliament, against the extension of the turnpike roads, into the remoter*
Those remoter counties,
*counties. they pretended, from the cheapness of labor, would be able to sell their grass and corn cheaper in the London Market than themselves, and they would thereby reduce their rents and ruin their cultivation. Their rents however have risen and their cultivation has been improved, since that time."* [115]

*Specimens of a spirit, similar to that which governed the counties here spoken of, present themselves too frequently to the eye of an impartial observer, and render it a wish of patriotism, that the body in this Country, in whose councils a local or partial spirit is least likely*

115. See note 100.

*to predominate were at liberty to pursue & promote the general*
*interest, in those instances in which there might be danger of the*
*interference of such a spirit.*

*But if there should be a doubt of the power of the Government to*
*embrace the whole subject, there is none of its competency to a provi-*
*sion for the improvement of the Postroads, an object which merits*
*and will doubtless occupy an early attention of the Legislature of*
*the United States.*

The foregoing are the principal of the means, by which manufac-
                                          is ordinarily promoted.
turing countries promote the growth of manufactures. It is, how-
              merely                                              have
ever, not only necessary, that the d measures of government, which
a direct view to manufactures, should be calculated to assist and
                                    only
protect them, but that those which relate collaterally affect them, in
the general course of the administration, should be guarded from any
peculiar tendency to injure them.

There are certain species of taxes, which are apt to be oppressive to
different parts of the community and among other ill effects have a
very unfriendly aspect towards manufactures. All Poll or Capitation
taxes are of this nature. They either proceed, according to a fixed rate
                                                    [industrious]
which operates unequally, and injuriously to the labouring poor; or
they vest a discretion, in certain officers, to make estimates and assess-
        which are
ments necessarily vague conjectural and liable to abuse. They ought
therefore to be abstained from in all but cases of distressing emergency.
      such taxes (including all
All taxes on occupations) unless regulated in the degree by sal
                       to the amount of
which proceed according the capital supposed to be employed in a
business, or of profits supposed to be made in it, are unavoidably
oppressive and hurtful to industry. It is in vain, that the evil may be
endeavoured to be mitigated by leaving it, in the first instance, in the
option of the party to be taxed, to declare the amount of his Capital
or profits. Men engaged in any trade or business have commonly
                 avoid from
weighty reasons to forbear disclosures, which would expose, with
                                                    most frequently
any thing like accuracy, the real state of their affairs. They had rather

~~risk will oftenest~~ find it better to risk oppression, than to avail themselves of so inconvenient a ~~remedy~~ refuge. And the consequence is, [an alterna-
tive]
that they often suffer ^oppression ~~it. The public Those who~~

When the disclosure too, if made, is not definitive, but controulable
by the discretion, or in other words, by the passions and prejudices of
the ~~public~~ ^Revenue officers, it is not only an ineffectual protection, but the
possibility of its being so is an additional reason for not resorting to it.

Allowing to the public officers the most equitable dispositions;
yet ^wherever ~~where~~ they are to exercise a discretion, without certain data, they
cannot fail to be often misled by appearances. The quantity of business, which seems to be going on, ~~will be a usual criterion~~ is, in a vast
number of cases, a very deceitful criterion of the profits which are
made; yet it is perhaps the best they can have, and it is the one, on
which they will ^most naturally rely. A business therefore which ^may rather
requires aid, from the government, than be in a capacity to be contributory to it, may find itself crushed by the mistaken conjectures of
the Assessors of taxes.

Arbitrary taxes, ^under which ~~confidence~~ denomination ^are compresed all those, that
leave the <u>quantum</u> of the tax to be raised on each person, to the <u>discre-</u>
tion of certain ^officers, are as contrary to the genius of liberty as to the ~~prece~~
maxims of industry. In this light, they have been viewed, by the most
judicious observers on government; who have bestowed upon them
the severest ^epithets of reprobation; ~~upon~~ as constituting one of the worst features usually to be met with in the practice of despotic governments.
~~A government, which desires to promote manufacturing~~
It is certain, ^at least, that such taxes are ^particularly inimical to the success of manufacturing industry and ought carefully to be avoided by a govern-
ment, which desires to promote it.

The ^great copiousness of the subject of this report has insensibly led to
a more lengthy preliminary discussion than was ^originally contemplated or intended. It appeared proper to investigate principles, to ~~remove~~ consider objections, and to endeavor to establish the utility of the thing ^proposed

to be encouraged; previous to a specification of the objects which might occur, as meriting or requiring encouragement and of the measures, which might be proper, in respect to each. The first purpose

having been fulfilled ~~to~~ remains to pursue the second.

In the selection of objects, ~~four~~ five circumstances ~~deserve principal~~ seem intitled to particular attention—the capacity of the Country to furnish the raw material—the ~~great~~ degree in which the nature of the manufacture admits of a substitute for manual labour, in machinery—the facility of execution—the extensiveness of the uses, to which the article can be applied—its subserviency to other interests, particularly the great one of national defence. ~~These are however objects~~ There are however objects to which these circumstances are little applicable, which for some special reasons, may have a claim to encouragement.

A designation of the principal raw material of which each manufacture is composed will serve to introduce the remarks upon it. As, ~~first~~ in the first place—

## Iron.

*The manufactures of this article are entitled to preeminent rank. None are more essential in their kinds nor so extensive in their uses.*

[the imps. or Mats. or both] *They constitute the implements and the materials in whole or in part and comm part of almost every useful occupation. Nothing is more easy than to begin, nor would be more difficult than to end the enumeration of the cases, in which Their instrumentality is conspicuous. It is felt and seen every where.*

*It is fortunate for the United States that they have peculiar advantages for deriving the full benefit of this most valuable ~~article~~ material, and they have every motive to improve it with ~~the most~~ systematic care.*

*It is to be found in various parts of the United States in great abundance and of almost every quality; And fuel the chief instrument in manufacturing it is both cheap and plenty ~~it can in few parts of the world be obtained with equal cheapness and with equal plenty.~~ This particularly applies to* mines

*Charcoal;* but there are productive coal ~~faeto~~ already in operation and

in every

~~there are~~ strong indications that the material is to be found in abun-

other

dance in a variety of places. *~~the kind best adapted to certain opera-~~*

the metal

~~to the refining of some of~~ giving to it toughness and malleability

*~~tions; though a process has lately been discovered~~* [116] *~~which is said to~~*

under                                              equally good for that purpose

~~*obviate the objections to the fossil* Coal *in these cases.* But it is a ques-~~

~~tion whether this process does not too much, diminish the mass of the~~

the material

~~metal.~~ Its ~~operation is, by means of grooved rollers, to expell all~~

hetero

~~seperate and heterogeneous matter: while the effect of the plogiston~~

~~in the Charcoal is to restore to their metallic state the demetallized~~

~~parts.~~ *The inquiries to which the subject of this report has led have*

though generally understood to be extensive

*been answered with proofs that manufactories of Iron* are *~~not only~~*

~~very extensive but so~~  so extensive

*far more* ~~*extensive*~~ *than is commonly supposed. The kinds in which*

*the greatest progress has been made have been mentioned in another*

*place and need not be repeated; but there is little doubt that every*

*other kind with due cultivation will rapidly succeed. It is worthy of*

116. "Pig iron made by smelting with coke was found unsuitable for conversion into wrought iron because of the impurities introduced into the iron by the
coke; these made wrought iron so brittle that it crumbled under the ham-
mer. . . . Henry Cort (1740–1800) of Gosport . . . in 1784 obtained a patent
for the conversion of pig iron into malleable, that is wrought, iron by puddling. . . . The process of puddling used by Cort consisted essentially of stirring
molten pig iron on the bed of a reverberatory furnace. The puddler turned and
stirred the molten mass until, through the decarburizing action of air which circulated through the furnace, it became converted into malleable iron. In this
process contact between the metal and the raw coal that served as fuel was
avoided, and the need for blowing-machinery was dispensed with. . . . Cort is
also credited with the invention of grooved rollers . . . patented in 1783. . . .
Previously, bars had to be made either by hammering, or by cutting hot strips
from a rolled plate with a slitting-mill. With grooved rollers 15 tons of iron
could be dealt with in 12 hours, whereas it was difficult to produce one ton in
the same time with the forge-hammer.
"Cort's success was immediate, owing to the combination of the two processes
he introduced. He achieved a simplification that resulted in lower cost of production. Although puddled iron was inferior in quality to charcoal iron, it was
very much cheaper." (Charles Singer, E. J. Holmyard, A. R. Hall, and Trevor
I. Williams, eds., *A History of Technology* [Oxford, 1958], IV, 106–07).

*remark that several of the particular trades, of which it is the basis, are capable of being carried on without the aid of large capitals.*

*Iron works have very greatly increased in the United States and are prosecuted with much more advantage than formerly. The average price before the revolution was about 64 Dollars ℔ Ton; at present*

*it is about Eighty; arise~ ~~This rise ought partly~~ which to be attributed to ~~a~~ is chiefly ~~to be attributed~~*

*~~considerable export to the East Indies~~~ ~~but more~~ is in a very great degree owing to the increase of manufactures of the materials.*

*The still further extension and multiplication of such manufactures will have the double effect of promoting the extraction of the Metal itself and of converting it to a greater number of profitable purposes.*

*Those manufactures too unite in a greater degree than almost any others the several requisites, which have been mentioned, as proper to be consulted in the selection of objects.*

The only~ further ~encouragement of manufactures of this article, ~~beyond what the existing laws~~ the propriety of which may be considered as unquestionable, seems to be an increase of the duties on foreign rival ~~articles~~ commodities.

Steel is a branch, which has already made a considerable progress, and it is ascertained that some new enterprizes on a more extensive scale have been lately set on foot. The facility of carrying it to an extent, which will supply all internal demands and furnish a considerable surplus for exportation cannot be doubted. The duty upon the importation of this article, which is at present 75 Cents ℔ Cwt [117] ~~or about 7½ ℔ Cent on the value~~, may it is conceived be safely and advantageously extended to 100 Cents. It is desireable, by decisive

arrangements, to second the efforts, which are making in~ so ~~this~~ very valuable a branch.

The United States already~ in a great measure ~~~chiefly~ supply themselves with nails and spikes. They are able, and ought certainly, to do it intirely. The first and most labourous operation, in this manufacture, is performed by water mills and of the persons afterwards employed a great proportion are boys, whose early habits of industry are of importance to the

117. The tariff rates to which H is referring in this paragraph and in the remainder of this section of the Report are cited in note 49.

community to the present support of their families and to their own future ~~support~~ comfort. It is not less curious than true that in certain parts of the country the making of Nails is an occasional family manufacture.

The expediency of an additional duty on these articles is indicated by an important fact. About one ~~Upwards of~~ a million ~~and a half of~~ pounds of 800000 them were imported into the U States in the course of a year ending the 30th of September 1790.    1,789,000

A duty of two Cents ℔ lb would, it is presumeable, speedily put an end to so considerable an importation. And it is in every view proper that an end should be put to it.    Qr. if no bounties GB    Qr. if G B grants no bounty.

The manufacture of these articles like that of some others, suffers from the carelessness and dishonesty of a part of those who carry it ~~them~~ on. An inspection in certain cases might tend to correct the evil.    Qr. It will deserve consideration whether a regulation of this sort cannot be applied without inconvenience to the exportation of the articles ~~Nails~~, either to foreign countries, or from one state to another.

The implements of husbandry are made in several States in great abundance. In many places it is done by the common blacksmiths. And there is no doubt that an ample supply for the whole country can with great ease be procured among ourselves. Various kinds of edged tools for the use of Mechanics are also made; and ~~there are instances~~ a considerable quantity ~~of the manufactures~~ of hollow wares; though the business of castings    considerable has not ~~obtained~~ yet attained the perfection which might be wished. It is however improving, and as there are respectable capitals in good hands, ~~in~~ embarked in the prosecution of those branches of ~~in~~ iron manufactories, which are yet in their infancy, they may all be contemplated as ~~within the reach of an~~ objects of easy ~~acquisition not difficult~~ objects not difficult to be acquired.

To ensure the end ~~object~~ it seems equally safe and prudent to extend the duty ad valorem upon all manufactures of Iron or of ~~in~~ which iron is the ~~chief~~ article of chief value to ten per Cent.

Fire arms and other military weapons may it is conceived ~~without inconvenience~~

15 ⅌ Ct

without inconvenience   of articles rated at 15 ⅌ Cent.
be placed ˄in the ~~same~~ class ˄There are already manufactories of these articles, which only require the stimul~~ous~~ of a certain~~ty of~~ demand to render them adequate to the supply of the United States.

It would also be a material aid to manufactories of this nature, as well as a mean of public security, if provision should be made for ~~an~~ an annual purchase of ~~the~~ military weapons, of home manufacture, to a certain determinate extent, in order to the formation of Arsenals; and to replace from time to time such as should be withdrawn for
                    always
use, so as ˄~~constantly~~ to have in store the quantity of each kind which should be deemed ~~requisite~~ a competent supply.
                may hereafter deserve
Government
to make an-
nual pur-
chase to
form arsen-
als—
But it ˄~~well merits~~ legislative consideration whether manufactories of all the necessary weapons of war ought not to be established on account of the Government itself. Such establishments are agreeable to the usual practice of Nations; and that practice seems founded on sufficient reason. There appears to be an improvidence, in leaving these essential instruments of national defence to the casual specula-
                    adventure
tions of individual ˄~~industry;~~ a resource which can less be relied upon, in this case, than in most others; the articles in question not being ob-
                    consumption or
jects of ordinary and indispensable private ˄use. As a general rule,
            on the immediate account
manufactories ~~under the direction~~˄of the Government are to be
                                which        admits,
avoided; but this seems to be one of the few exceptions ˄~~to~~ that rule ˄depending on very special reasons.
                generally
~~All~~ Manufactures of steel, ˄or of which steel is the article of chief value, may with advantage be placed in the class of goods rated at 7½ per Cent. As manufactures of this kind have not yet made any ~~very~~ considerable progress, it is a reason for not rating them, as high as those of iron; but as this material is the basis of them and as ~~they may~~ their extension, ~~while it is of great importance, is not likely to be attended with any extraordinary difficulty~~ is not less practicable, than important, it is desireable to promote it by a somewhat higher duty than the present.

A question arises, how far is might be expedient to permit the importation of iron in pigs and barrs free from duty. It would certainly be favourable to manufactures of the article; but the doubt is whether it might not interfere with its production. ~~The~~ Two circumstances, however, abate if they do not remove apprehension, on this score; one is, the considerable increase of price, which has been already remarked, and which renders it probable that the free admission of foreign iron would not be inconsistent with an adequate profit ~~on the production~~ to the proprietors of Iron Works;

~~article~~ the other is, the augmentation of demand, which would be

likely to attend the increase of manufactures of ~~it,~~ the article in consequence of the additional encouragements proposed to be given. But ~~nevertheless~~

nevertheless                    is
caution in a matter of this kind ~~will be~~ most adviseable. The measure

~~is prop~~ ought, perhaps,
suggested ~~seems proper~~ rather to be contemplated, subject to the lights of ~~some~~ further experience, than immediately ~~acted upon~~ adopted.

Quare as to exemption of Coal from duty.

## Copper

of which this article is susceptible are ~~also~~ also of great
The manufactures ~~of this article are of considerable~~ extent and utility. Under this description, those of brass, of which it is the principal ingredient are intended to be included.

is supposed to be
The material is a natural ~~and from many symptoms~~ an abundant     Qr

of the Country                              with
production. Mines of copper have actually been wrought and ~~to the~~

to
profit ~~of~~ the undertakers, though it is not known that any are now

nothing is easier than
in this condition. And the introduction of it from other countries on ~~rea~~ moderate terms and in great plenty. ~~is not difficult.~~

particularly the former
Coppersmiths and brass founders are ~~pretty~~ numerous in the

many some
United States; ~~some~~ of whom carry on ~~their respective bussinesses with spirit and latitude~~ business to a respectable extent.

To multiply and ~~extends~~ manufactories of the materials in question
well
is ~~particularly~~ worthy of attention ~~of attention~~ and effort. In order to

[(the former very much so)]

[Reduction of price of copper Qu.]

a plentiful
this, it is desireable to facilitate an ~~abundant~~ supply of ~~those materials~~ the materials.

[sp copper]    The most effectual foundation, for this purpose, would be laid in an encouragement of the production of the material. This may be
per quantity
done in two ways; either by granting a liberal bounty on all which shall be produced within a ~~limited~~ certain term of years; or by granting premiums to take effect in a certain number of instances, on the
and for a given term,
omissions    production of a given quantity, within a given time and at any one mine; something in the nature of the premiums granted by Great
upon
Britain vessels employed in the ~~whale~~ fisheries.[118] If the first would be most effectual, it might also be most expensive. ~~In~~ The last mode would have the advantage of assigning a limit to the utmost possible expence: And if the premiums were liberal, the prospect would not be bad of their answering the end.

to this end
And a ~~A~~ proper mean ~~independent of a domestic production, to~~
is to place them
~~facilitate an abundant supply of the material, will be to place it~~ in the class of free articles. Copper in plates and brass are already in this predicament, but copper in pigs and bars is not—neither is lapis cala-
together
minaris, which with copper and charcoal, constitute the component ingredients of brass. ~~A~~ The exemption from duty, by parity of reason,
as such of
ought to embrace ~~all~~ these articles as are objects of importation.

An additional duty, on brass wares, will tend to the general end in view. These now stand at 5 ℔ Cent, ~~wh~~ while those of tin, pewter and copper are rated at 7½. There appears to be a propriety in every view
It ~~may even~~ in placing brass wares upon the same level with them; and it merits
~~be worth~~ consideration whether the duty upon all of them ought not to be raised
~~consid~~
~~to ℔ C~~ to 10 ℔ Cent.

## Lead

there are numerous proofs, that this
~~This~~ material ~~certainly~~ abounds in the United States, and requires little to ~~unforl~~ unfold it to an extent more than equal to every domes-

118. For example, see 11 Geo. III, C. 38 (1771) and 28 Geo. III, C. 20 (1788).

been
tic occasion. A prolific mine of it has ~~been~~ long open ~~at~~ in the ~~W S~~
Western parts of ~~the State of~~ Virginia, and under a public administration during the ~~war~~ late war, yielded a considerable supply for ~~the pur~~
military use. This is now in the hands of individuals, who not only
carry it on with spirits; but have established ~~a~~ manufactories of it at
Richmond in the same state.

the importation of this article either in its     ~~With~~
The ~~duty~~ duties already laid upon ~~this material both in its~~ ~~manu~~-
or manufactured
~~factured or~~ unmanufactured state ~~afford~~ ensure it a decisive advantage in the home market—which amounts to considerable encouragement. If the duty on Pewter wares should be raised, it would ~~collat~~-
else
~~erally~~ afford further encouragement. Nothing occurs as proper to
be added.

be
Nothing occurs as proper to be added; unless it should thought
~~eligible~~ eligible to ~~grant~~ apply the idea of premiums, which has been
suggested, in respect to copper, to future enterprises towards the
production of ~~this article~~. Lead.

Fossil Coal          [fossil coal]

This, as an important instrument of manufactures may without impropriety be mentioned among the subjects of this report. A copious
supply of it would be of great consequence to the Iron branch. As an
[~~to artificers & all others~~]
article of household fuel also it is an interesting production; the
utility of which must increase in proportion to the decrease of wood
by the progress of settlement and cultivation: And its importance to
navigation as an immense article of transportation coastwise is signally
exemplified in Great Britain.

several
It is known that there are ~~one or more~~ coal mines in Virginia now
worked; and appearances of their existence are familiar in a ~~great~~     [several]
number of places.

will well                              ~~will~~ may          [nil. sit?]
It ~~may~~ deserve consideration how far it ~~may~~ be expedient to stim-
metal
ulate ~~enter~~ attempts to explore and work mines of this very useful
article                              The expediency of
article by premiums of the kind already suggested. ~~It well deserves~~

~~examination whether~~ a bounty on all ~~eo~~ this species of coal, of home
production and of premiums on the opening of new mines, under certain qualifications, appears to be worthy of particular examination.
The <sub>∧</sub>great importance of this <sub>∧</sub>~~object~~ article will amply justify a reasonable expence in this way, if it shall appear to be necessary <sub>∧</sub>to & shall be ~~deemed~~ thought
likely to answer, the end.

## Wood

Several manufactures of this article flourish in the U States. Ships are
no where built in greater perfection, and cabinet wares, generally,
are made little if at all inferior to those of Europe. Their extent is
such as to have admitted of considerable exportation.

An exemption from duty ~~for~~ of the several kinds of wood ordinarily
used in those manufactures seems to be all, that is requisite, <sub>∧</sub>by way of ~~to their
full~~ encouragement. ~~The doing of this will seem to be of manifest
expediency~~. It is recommended by the consideration of a similar
policy being pursued in other countries, and by the expediency of
giving equal advantages to our own workmen in wood. The abundance of Timber proper for Ship building in the U States does not
appear to be any objection to it. The increasing scarcity and the
growing importance of that article, in the European Countries, admonish the U States to commence and systematically to pursue
measures for the preservation of their Stock. Whatever may promote
the regular establishment of Magazines of Ship Timber is in various
views desireable.

## ~~Leather~~ Skins

There are scarcely any manufactories of greater importance, than
of this article. Their direct and very happy influence upon Agriculture, by promoting the raising of Cattle of different kinds, is a very
material recommendation.

It is pleasing, too, to observe the extensive progress they have made
in their principal branches; which are so far matured as almost to defy
foreign competition. Tanneries in particular ~~hav~~ are not only carried

on as a regular business in numerous instances ∧and in various parts of the
Country; but they constitute in ~~many~~ some places a valuable item of incidental family manufactures.

Representations however have been made, ~~tending to recommend two species of encouragements~~ importing the expediency of further
encouragement ∧to ~~of~~ the Leather-Branch in two ways— ∧one by increasing
the duty on ~~imported~~ the manufactures of it, which are imported—the
other by prohibiting the exportation of bark. In support of the latter
it is alleged that the price ~~has~~ of bark, chiefly in consequence of large
exportations, has risen within a few years from        to

These suggestions are submitted rather as intimations, which merit
consideration than as matters, the propriety of which is manifest. It is
not clear that an increase of duty is necessary and in regard to the
prohibition desired, there is no evidence of any considerable exportation hitherto; and it is most ~~propert~~ probable that whatever ~~increase~~ ∧augmentation
of price may have taken place is ~~rather~~ to be attributed to an extension of the home demand from the increase of ~~Tanneries~~ manufactures, and to a decrease of the supply, in consequence of ~~from~~ the
progress of settlement; rather than to the quantities ∧which have been exported. ~~it is liable to the objection that it would pr interfere with an export of some, though not of very great value: and it may admit of question whether the internal demand is equal to the~~ supply ~~quantity which is natu-rally produced in a new and well wooded country settlements coun~~
~~continually~~ ∧advancing ~~going forward in settlement.~~

It is mentioned ∧however as an additional reason for the prohibition that one
species of the bark usually exported is in some sort peculiar to the
country and the material of a very valuable dye, of great use in some
other manufactures, in which the U States have begun a competition. ~~Qr.~~

There ∧may ~~is~~ also ∧be this argument in favour of an increase of duty. The
object is of importance enough to claim decisive encouragement and
the progress which has been made leaves no room to apprehend any ~~Qr. is it exempted.~~

such an increase
inconvenience on the score of supply from ₋an augmentation of duty.

## Leather

It would be of ~~some~~ benefit to this branch, if glue which is now

already
rated at 5 per Cent were made the object of an excluding duty. It is ₋

large
~~now~~ made in ₋~~considerable~~ quantities at various tanneries, and like
paper, is an entire œconomy of materials, which ~~would otherwise be
lost~~, if not manufactured would be left to perish. It may be placed

15
with advantage in the class of articles paying ~~12½~~ per Cent.

## ~~Fish~~

## Grain

Manufactures of the several species of this article have a title to
peculiar favour; not only because they are most of them immediately
connected with the subsistence of the citizens; but because they enlarge the demand for the most precious products of the soil.

Though flour may with propriety be noticed as a manufacture of
Grain, it were useless to do it, but for the ~~subsist~~ purpose of submitting ~~to consideration~~ the expediency of a general system of inspection, throughout the ports of the U States; which, ~~it is presumed~~ if
established upon proper principles, would ~~li~~ be likely to improve the
quality of our flour every where, and to raise its reputation in foreign
markets. ~~Ter These~~ There are however considerations which stand
in the way of such an arrangement.

Ardent spirits and malt liquors are next to flour the two principal
manufactures of Grain. The first has made a very extensive, ~~and~~ the
last a considerable progress in the U States. In respect to both, an

home
exclusive possession of the ₋market ~~of the United States~~ ought to be
secured to the domestic manufacturers; as fast as circumstances will
admit. ~~of it.~~ Nothing is more practicable and nothing more desireable.

The existing laws of the U States [119] have done much towards
attaining this valuable object; but some additions to the present duties

and perhaps an abatement of those on home made spirits,
on foreign distilled spirits and foreign malt liquors ₋would more effec-

119. See note 101.

very
tually secure it; and there does not occur any ^weighty objection to
~~some further increase of them either.~~

An augmentation of the duties on imported spirits would ~~not~~ favour
as well the distillation of spirits from molasses as that from Grain. And
to secure to the nation the benefit of the manufacture, even of foreign
materials, is always of great, though perhaps of secondary importance.

A strong impression prevails in the minds of those concerned in
distilleries (including too, the most candid and enlightened) ~~of them~~
that greater differences in the rates of duty on foreign and domestic
spirits are necessary, completely to secure the successful manufacture
of the latter and there are facts which intitle this impression to
attention.

^known
It is ~~agreed~~, that the price of molasses, for some years past, has been
successively rising in the West India Markets owing partly to a com-
and partly
petition which did not formerly exist ^to an extension of demand in
this Country; and it is evident that the late disturbances in those
Islands, ~~especially the insurrection of the blacks in Hispaniola~~, from
which we draw our principle supply ~~of the article~~ must so far inter-
the article
fere with the production of ^~~it~~ as to occasion a material enhancement
of ~~the~~ price. ~~And~~ The destruction and devastation ~~which are said
to have been made in Hispaniola~~ attendant on the insurrection in
Hispaniola, in particular, must not only contribute very much to ~~Competitors~~
that effect but may be expected to give it some duration. These
circumstances, and the duty of three cents per Gallon on molasses,
may render it difficult for the distillers of that Material to maintain
with adequate profit a competition with the rum brought from the
West Indies, the quality of which is so considerably superior.

The consumption of ~~Gin~~ Geneva or Gin in this country is ~~very~~
extensive. It is not long since distilleries of it have grown among us
to any importance. They are now becoming of consequence, but
being still in their infancy they ~~require~~ require protection. ~~and aid~~

It is represented that the price of of some of the materials is greater
place
here than in Holland, from which ^large quantities are brought, the
price of labour considerably greater, the capital engaged in the
business there much larger, than those which are employed here, the

rate of profits, at which the Undertaker cannot afford to carry it on, much less—and the prejudices in favour of imported Gin strong. These circumstances are alleged to outweigh the expen charges of which attend the bringing of the Article from Europe to the U States

and
und the present difference of duty—so as to obstruct the prosecution of the manufacture with due advantage.

Experiment could perhaps alone decide with certainty the justness

relation to
of the suggestions which are made; but in such important branches of

so important      seem
manufacture it would be inexpedient to hazard an unfavourable issue, and better to err on the side of too great than of too small a difference in the particular in question.

It is therefore submitted that an addition of two cents per Gallon be

Quare rate    made to the duty on imported spirits, of the first class of proof, with

a deduction
a proportionable increase on those of higher proof, and that an abate-

from the duty
ment of one Cent per Gallons be made on the spirits distilled within the U States, beginning with the first class of proof and making a

of the duty
proportionable abatement on the higher classes a proportionable deduction from the duty on those of higher proof. It is conceived, that this would be likely to answer the end in view, and would not be attended with inconveniences, otherwise.

decrease    There are materials for a tolerable conjecture (though not for
+ Cent on
domestic              It is ascertained that by far the greatest part of
spirits    exact computation) that about two thirds of the malt liquors con-
☞    sumed in the U States are the produce of domestic breweries. This conjecture has reference to the importation of a year ending the 30th of September 1790. It is desirable, and, in all likelihood, attainable, that the whole consumption should be supplied by ourselves.

are equal to a great part of
The malt liquors, made at home, though inferior to the best, of

have been usually
those which are imported. The progress already made is an earnest of what may be accomplished. The growing competition is an assurance of improvement. This will be accelerated by measures tending to invite a greater capital into this channel of employment.

To render the encouragement to domestic breweries decisive, it may be adviseable to substitute to the present rates of duty 8 Cents per

Gallon generally and it will deserve to be considered ˄as a guard against evasions, whether there
ought not be be a prohibition of their importation except in casks of
a defin considerable capacity. It is to be hoped that such a duty would
banish from the market foreign malt liquors of inferior quality; and
that the best kind only would continue to be imported till it should
be supplanted by the efforts of equal skill or care at home. 'Till that

period, the importation ˄so qualified, would be an useful stimulous to improvement. And in the mean time, the payment of the increased price, for
the enjoyment of a luxury, in order to the encouragement of a most

useful branch of domestic industry ˄could cannot reasonably be deemed a
hardship.

As a further aid to manufactures of Grain, though upon a smaller

scale, the ~~duties~~ articles of starch, hair powder and wafers may with great

propriety be ~~placed among in the desciption of articles~~ placed among those which are rated at

15
12½ ⅌ Cent. No manufactures are more simple, nor more completely
within the reach of a full supply from domestic ~~resources~~; and it is
a policy, as common as it is obvious, to make them the objects either
of prohibitory duties or of express prohibition.

## Provisions

Salted provisions may not improperly be placed on the list of manufactured commodities. It is certain, that the U States are not only
completely adequate to their own supply but to a most abundant

exportation. The expediency of making them ~~them~~ the ~~objects~~ subjects of    Quare?
prohibitory duties has occasionally presented itself under ambiguous
shapes, but ~~upon that~~ the ~~result~~ final result of mature reflection is, in

the judgment of the Secretary, ~~in favour of~~ favourable to the measure.

As far as an Inspection of commodities of this kind can be pro-

nounced to be useful, the comprehending ˄of them in a general system is
recommended by reasons similar to those which operate in ~~favour~~
relation to flour.

## Flax and Hemp

Manufactures of these article have so much affinity to each other ^and^ ^they are^ ^so^ often blend ~~themed~~
that they ^may^ with advantage be considered in conjunction. The importance of the ~~linnen~~ branch to agriculture—its precious effects
upon ~~the~~ ^domestic^ ~~ind household~~ household industry—the ease, with which the materials can be produced at home to any requisite extent—the
greater ~~advanta~~ advances, which ^have^ been already made, in ~~manufactures of~~ the coarser ~~kinds~~ fabrics of them, expecially in the ~~household~~ ^family^
way ^constitute claims,^ ~~are considerations of the greatest weight for~~ ^of peculiar force, to^ ^the^ patronage of government. ~~of perculiar force.~~

This patronage may be afforded in various ways ~~by promoting the growth of the materials by increasing the impediments to an advantageous competition of rival foreign articles by direct bounties or premiums upon the manufactured articles~~.

Stand
Stet

First ~~By~~ ^As to^ promoting the growth of the materials.
In respect to Hemp, something has been already done by the high duty upon foreign hemp. If the facilities for ~~the~~ ^domestic^ production ~~of Hemp were this article~~ were not unusually great, the policy of the duty on the foreign raw material would be highly questionable as interfering with ~~manu~~ the growth of manufactures ^of it.^ ~~of the article~~. But making the proper allowances for those facilities, and ~~for the increasing tendencies~~ with an eye to the future and natural progress of the country, the measure does not appear, upon the whole, exceptionable. A strong wish ~~has been entertained~~ naturally suggests itself that some method could be devised, of affording a more direct encouragement to the growth both of Flax & Hemp; ~~which~~ ^such as^ would be effectual, and ^at the same time,^ not attended with too great inconveniences. To this end bounties and premiums ⟨are⟩ themselves ⟨a⟩ consideration; but no ~~mode~~ ^modification of them^ has yet occurred which would not ^either^ ~~eithe~~ hazard too much expence ^or^ ~~nor~~ op-

erate unequally in ^reference ~~relation~~ to the circumstances of different parts of the Union; and which would not be attended with very ^considerable ~~numerous~~ great difficulties in the execution.

In aid of this, it may be considered, whether either bounties or premiums ought not to be added ^with an extension to Flax. The latter ~~may be so managed~~ may not prove less effectual than the former, and ^they ~~it is presumed~~ claims a preference, from the circumstance of their capacity to be so managed, as ~~that~~ the expence ~~may be~~ ^to render definite and ~~not great~~ ^both very moderate.

They may be regulated somewhat after the following manner. A certain sum and that the largest may be offered to the person who shall raise ^and send to market the greatest quantity and upon the whole of the best quality; another certain sum of less amount may be offered to the person who shall raise ^and send to market the greatest quantity, though of inferior quality, and a third sum still less in amount to the person who shall raise ~~the article~~ and send to market at least a given quantity to be specified, and of the best quality. These premiums may be ~~multiplied under~~ confined within as few or multiplied to as many discriptions of cases ~~as dee~~ including as many degrees of successful ^exertion ~~competition~~ as may be judged necessary to the end. A designation of the markets to ~~which~~ some one of which the article should be sent would seem to be a proper precaution to ^secure the ~~subserviency~~ insure the utility of the production ~~to the manu-facture~~.    Omitted

The effect of premiums in stimulating enterprises ~~and experiment~~ has been remarked. It ~~is proper~~ probable that any, which might ^be established in relation to the objects in question, if sufficiently liberal, would more than compensate for the ^that expence ~~which~~ might be occasioned. An experiment at least may be ^tried ~~made~~ without inconvenience and at little expence.

Secondly ~~The desired patronage may be afforded by~~

As to increasing the impediment to an advantageous competition of rival foreign articles—

To this, ~~an increase~~ perhaps an augmentation of the duties on importation is the obvious expedient; which, in regard to certain ~~articles of certain descriptions~~ articles appears to be recommended by sufficient reasons.

The principal of these articles is sail cloath; ~~of which a~~ one intimately connected with Navigation and defence; and of which a

~~Salem~~ flourishing manufactory is established at Boston and very promising ones at ~~some~~ several other places.

It is presumed to be both safe and ~~expedient~~ adviseable to place this in the class of articles ~~which are~~ rated at 10 per Cent ~~ad valorum~~. A strong reason for it results from the consideration that a bounty of

Qr.
[~~from 15 to 20~~]
[~~10 ⅌. Ct~~]

2d. Sterling per ell is allowed in Great Britain [120] upon the exportation of the Sail Cloth ~~which is~~ manufactured in that kingdom: ~~which is equal~~ to [~~of the several Qualities~~] ~~per Cent on the value~~. And a still greater bounty ~~is allowed~~ in Ireland.

It would likewise appear to be good policy to raise the duty to 7½ per Cent on the following ~~articles namely coarse linnens —~~ articles Ozna-

~~Dowlass Canvass Drilling Oil Cloth Sheetings~~ burghs, Ticklenburghs, Dowlas Canvass, ~~Drilling Oil Cloth~~ Brown Rolls bagging and upon all other linnens, ~~which~~ the ~~price~~ value full cost of which, at the place of exportation, does not exceed 35 Cents per yard. A bounty of 12½ ⅌ Cent, upon an average, on the exportation of such or similar linnens from Great Britain encourages the manufacture of them in that country and increases the obstacles to a successful competition in the countries to which they are sent.[121]

The quantities of tow and other household linnens manufactured in different parts of the U States, and the expectations, which are derived from some late experiments of being able to ~~apply~~ extend the use of labor saving machines, in the coarser fabrics of linnen ~~are induceme~~ obviate ~~lessen~~ the danger of inconvenience from an increase of the duty upon

120. See note 105.        121. See note 105.

authorise
~~them~~ such articles, and ~~encourage~~ a hope of speedy and complete
                                          used
success to the endeavours which may be ∧~~made~~ for ~~supplying our-~~
~~selves~~ ~~with~~ ~~them~~ procuring an internal supply.

Thirdly   As to direct bounties or premiums upon the manufactured articles.

            afford
~~But~~ To ~~give still~~ ∧more effectual encouragement to the manufacture, and, at the same time, to ~~counteract~~ ~~any detriment to Ship-~~
~~building~~ ~~navigation from a rise~~ promote the cheapness of the article,
for the benefit of navigation, it will be ~~useful~~ of great use to allow a   calculate
bounty of two Cents per yard on all sail Cloth, which is made in the   amt.
          of ~~their~~ our growth.
U S, from ∧~~native~~ materials. ~~An encoura~~ This would also assist the   ~~Qr. native~~
          materials.                    kind
culture of those∧. An encouragement of this∧~~nature ought~~ if adopted
ought to be established for a moderate term of years, to invite to new
                      to                              an
undertakings and∧an extension of the old. This is∧article of ~~so~~ importance enough to warrant the employment of extraordinary means
in its favour.

                                                          other
A bounty ~~too~~ likewise of 5 per Cent on the exportation of all∧lin-
nens, of the manufacture of the United States, from domestic materials, the value of which does not exceed 40 Cents per yard, would
                                    standard
have a beneficial influence in respect to them. This∧~~value~~, ~~in the U~~
of value in our markets
~~States~~, is is adopted as corresponding with ~~that~~ 35 Cents in the Markets of Europe, ~~wh~~ in reference to articles of a similar kind.

## Cotton

There is something, in the texture of this material, which adapts it
      ~~particular~~ peculiar ~~manner~~ degree
in a∧~~peculiar~~ ~~manner~~∧to the application of Machines. The signal
utility of the Mill for spinning of Cotton not long since invented in
                                              ~~various~~
England has been noticed in another place; but there are∧other
machines scarcely inferior in utility, which, in the different manufactories of this article ~~serve~~ ~~as a substitute for manuf~~ ~~manual labour~~ are

employed either exclusively, or with more than ordinary effect. This very important circumstance recommends the fabrics of Cotton in a more particular ~~meth~~ manner to a country in which a defect of hands constitutes the greatest obstacle to success.

The ~~great~~ variety ^and extent of the^ ~~of~~ uses to which the manufactures of this article are applicable is another powerful argument in their favour.

And the faculty of the United States to produce the ^raw^ material in abundance, and of a quality which though ~~perhaps~~ ^hitherto alleged to be^ inferior to some that is produced in other quarters, is ~~never~~ nevertheless capable of being used with advantage in many fabrics, and is probably susceptible, ~~especially in the two states farthest South~~ of being carried, by a more experienced culture, to much greater perfection—suggests an additional, and a very cogent inducement to the vigorous pursuit of the Cotton branch in its several subdivisions.

How much has been already done has been stated, in a preceding part of this report.

In addition to this it may be announced, that a Society is forming with a capital which ~~will probably not fall short~~, is expected to be extended to ^at least^ half a milion of Dollars; on behalf of which measures are already in train for prosecuting, on a large scale, the making and printing of Cotton Goods.

These circumstances conspire to indicate the expediency of removing any obstructions, which may happen to exist, to the advantageous prosecution of the manufactories in question, and of adding such encouragements, as may appear necessary and proper.

The present duty of 3 Cents ℔ lb on the foreign raw material, is undoubtedly a very serious ~~d~~ impediment to the progress of those manufactories.

~~Its~~ ^The^ injurious tendency of similar duties ^either prior to the establishment, or in the infancy,^ ~~prior to the complete estab-~~ ~~lishment~~ of the domestic manufacture of the article, ^as it regards the manufacture,^ and their worse than inutility, in ~~reference~~ ^relation^ to the home production of ~~it~~ the material ^itself^ have been ancipated; particularly in discussing the subject of pecuniary bounties.

Cotton has ~~th~~ not the same pretensions, with Hemp, to form an exception to the general rule.

that Hemp ~~only, not~~
Not being, like ~~It is not~~ an universal production of the Country ~~and consequently affords less assurance~~ it affords less assurance of an adequate internal supply; but the chief objection arises from the

[ve]
doubts which are entertained concerning the quality of the national
alleged                                                    and weaker
Cotton. It is ~~observed~~ that the fibre of it is considerably shorter than that of some other places; ~~particularly those nearest the Equator~~ and
the place of growth
it has been observed as a general rule, that the nearer to the Equator, the better the quality of the Cotton. That which comes from Cayenne   (-) Surrinam and Demarara is said to be preferable, even at a material difference of price, to the Cotton of the Islands.                Geo~

While ~~it ought not to be~~ a hope may reasonably be indulged, that
[ve]
with due care and attention the national cotton may be made to approach nearer than it now does to that of regions somewhat more
authorise an opinion
favoured by climate; and while facts ~~demonstrate~~ that very great use may be made of it, and that it is a resource which gives greater security to the Cotton fabrics of this ~~land~~ Country, than can be en-
which                                              will
joyed by any ~~that~~ depends wholly on ~~an~~ external supply—it ~~is~~ cer-
be                                                    full
tainly wise in every view to let our infant manufactures have the benefit of the best materials on the cheapest terms.

such
It is obvious that the necessity of having ~~the best~~ materials is pro-
employed,
portioned to the unskillfulness and inexperience of the workmen who
inexpert will                        the materials they are to work with,
~~will~~ if not fail to commit great waste where they are of an indifferent
~~And~~ To secure to the National Manufactures so essential an advantage,
kind. ~~In order to them~~ a repeal of the present duty on ~~foreign~~ e imported Cotton ~~appears~~ is indispensable.

A substitute for this, far more encouraging to domestic production,
to
will be grant a bounty ~~on all cotton goods manufactured from the native materials of the Country. Two Cents per Yard. defining the~~

width, ~~would be a strong motive of preference to the national Cotton~~
[ve]        when        ^wrought      a home
on the national Cotton^ ~~which is consumed~~ ^at ~~any~~ ^national manufac-
          which
tory; ~~and~~ to ~~this,~~ a bounty on the exportation of it ~~if deemed~~ may be
                        much
added. Either or both would do^ more towards promoting the growth
              merely
of the article than the ~~ex~~ ^nominal encouragement, which it is pro-
                also
posed to abolish. The first would^ have a direct influence in encouraging the manufacture.

The bounty which has been mentioned, as existing in G Britain,
upon the exportation of coarse linnens, not exceeding a certain value,
          certain descriptions of
applies also to^ Cotton goods of similar value.

This furnishes an additional argument for allowing to the national
manufacturers the species of encouragement just suggested, and indeed for ~~extending~~ adding some other aid. ~~and~~

One cent per yard, not less than of a given width, on all ~~cotton~~
                                        in
goods of Cotton or of Cotton and linnen mixed ~~not exceeding~~ ^value
~~40 cents per yard,~~ which are manufactured in the U States; with the
                weight              [ve]
addition of one Cent ℔ lb^ of the Material, if made of national Cotton;
            ^considerable
would amount to an aid of^ ~~very great~~ importance, both to the pro-
Computation   duction and to the manufacture of that valuable ~~material~~ article. And
it is conceived that the expence would be well justified by the magnitude of the object. ~~The limitation in point of respect to the value of~~
~~the goods ought not to apply to the bounty on the material.~~

The Printing and Staining of Cotton goods is known to be a distinct
business from the fabrication of them. It is one ~~material~~ easily ac-
              as it adds
complished, and which, ~~by adding~~ materially to the value of the
            and prepares it for a variety of new uses
article, in its white state^ is of importance to be promoted.

As imported Cottons, equally with those which are made at home,
may be the objects of this manufacture, it will merit consideration
whether the whole or a part of the duty, on the white goods, ought
not to be allowed to be drawn back in favour of those, who print or
stain them. This measure would certainly operate as a powerful en-

couragement to the business; and though it may in a ~~slight~~ degree
original ^articles
~~contrac~~ counteract the ^fabrication of the ^~~articles~~, it would probably
more than compensate for this disadvantage, in the rapid growth of
a collateral branch, which is of a nature sooner to attain to maturity.
When a sufficient progress shall have been made, the drawback may
be abrogated; and by that time the domestic supply of the articles to    ~~Oil of~~
be printed or stained will have been extended.                            ~~Vitriol~~
                                                                          ~~aqua fortis~~
   If the duty of 7½ ₱ Cent on certain kinds of Cotton goods were         ~~Madder~~
extended to all goods of Cotton, or of which it is the principal
                        ^probably
material, it would ^more than counterballance the effect of the draw-
                               the fabrication
back proposed, in relation to ~~the fabrication~~ ^of the article. And no
material objection occurs to such an extension. The duty, then,
considering all the circumstances which attend goods of this descrip-
                                                    it
tion, could not be deemed inconveniently high & ~~It~~ may be inferred
                                               would
from various causes that the prices of them ^still continue moderate.
        Manufactories                         not long since established at Beverly in
   ~~A manufactory~~ ^of Cotton goods ^conducted with a ~~persever~~ per-    7½ ₱ Ct.
Massachusettes and at Providence in the State of R Island & ~~not long since~~
                                                             them
severance corresponding with the patriotic motives which began ^it,
~~established at Beverly in the State of Massachusettes,~~
seems to have overcome the first obstacles to success; producing cor-
                            and other similar articles,
duroy velverets fustians ~~and~~ jeans ^of a ~~very good~~ quality, which will
   a                        the like
bear ^comparison with ~~similar~~ ^articles brought from Manchester. The
one
^~~Manufacto~~ at Providence has the merit of being the first ~~which~~ in
introducing the celebrated Cotton Mill; which not only furnishes ~~the~~
materials for that manufactory itself but for the supply of private
families for household manufactures.
   Other Manufactories of the same Material as ~~a res~~ regular business    [~~Provide~~]
have also been begun ~~at~~ at different places in the state of Connecticut
        all ~~most if not all of them~~              those abovementioned.
but, ~~in a general~~ ^upon a smaller scale ~~that~~ than ^the one ~~at Beverly.~~
~~It is~~
~~That at Providence having has in some respect a superiority of advan-~~
~~tages & its progress does great credit to the undertakers; who have~~

~~the merit of having been the first to introduce into the Country the
Cotton Mill, the most~~ valuab~~le of the machines employed in this
Manufactory.~~

                      are also making
Some essays ~~have also been commenced~~ in the printing and stain-
                              several
ing of Cotton Goods. There are a small establishments of this kind ~~at~~
already on foot.
~~German town in the State of Pensylvania in the neighbourhood of
Philadelphia.~~


## Wool

~~In a Climate        In a climate~~
In a country, the climate of which partakes of so considerable a
                          a great part of
portion of Winter, as that of the U States, the woollen branch can-
                              which
not be regarded as inferior to any, ~~that~~ relates to the cloathing of the
inhabitants.

Household manufactures of ~~various articles~~ this material are carried
on, in different parts of the United States, to a very interesting extent;

                              n
but ~~five branches~~ there is only one bra ch, which as a regular business,
can be said to have acquired maturity. This is the making of Hats.
                                                              large
Hats ~~intirely~~ of wool and of wool mixed with furr are made in
                          [~~in various parts of~~]
[~~in a great~~    ~~great~~ quantities, ~~at a number of places,~~ in different states; and nothing
Number of
Shops]       seems                                      manufacture
             ~~is~~ wanting but an adequate supply of ~~the~~ materials to render the
             ~~supply~~ commensurate with the demand.

A promising essay towards the fabrication of Clo~~a~~ths cazimirs and
                              goods
Qr.          other woollen ~~stuffs~~ is likewise going on at Hartford in Connecticut.
             Specimens of the different kinds which are made, in the possession of
             the Secretary, evince that these fabrics have attained a very consider-
             able degree of perfection. Their quality certainly surpasses any thing,
             that could have been looked for, in so short a time, and under so great
[~~compared~~   disadvantages; and conspires with the scantiness of the means, which
~~the prices~~]   have been at the command of the Directors, to form the eulogium of

that
~~their~~ public spirit perseverance and judgment which have been able
to accomplish so much.

To cherish and bring to maturity this precious embryo ~~engages~~
must engage the most ardent wishes—and proportionable regret, as
                              doing
far as the means of ^~~aiding~~ it may appear difficult or uncertain.

Measures, which should tend to promote an abundant supply of
wool, of good quality, would probably afford the most ~~effectual~~ effi-
                    present
cacious aid, that ^circumstances permit.

To encourage the raising and improving the breed of sheep at home
would certainly be the most desireable expedient for that purpose; but
it may not be alone sufficient, especially as it is yet a problem, ~~wether~~
                 be
whether our wool ~~is~~ capable of such a degree of improvement, as to
render it fit for the finer fabrics.

Premiums would probably be found the best means of promoting
                 bounties
~~both~~ the domestic and ^the foreign supply. The first may be within
                                                           would
the compass of the institution hereafter to be submitted—the last ^~~may~~
                                        bounties                              Refd
require a specific legislative provision. If any ^are granted they ought   bounties
               be adjusted with an eye
of course to ^~~be adjusted to quantity different degrees of quantity~~,
  have regard to
~~and~~ ^quality as well as quantity.

There is one article of woollen manufacture, which being of the
first necessity and of universal use, ~~and a~~ may justify some extraordi-
                                          The expediency of a
nary encouragement. This alludes to blankets. ~~A~~ ^liberal bounty on
each blanket, which is made in the U States, in proportion to its dimensions, appears to merit consideration. The simplicity of the manufacture, and the great expence of transportation, to which the bulk
of the commodity, in proportion to its value, subjects it, are additional
                             a fit
reasons, for selecting it as ^~~an~~ object of particular encouragement.

A fund for the purpose may be derived from the addition of 2½
per Cent, to the present rate of duty, on carpets and carpeting; an increase, to which the nature of the article suggests no objection, and

which may ~~conduce to the intern~~ furnish a motive to the fabrication of it at home; towards which some beginnings have been made.

## Silk

The production of this article is attended with ~~peculiar~~ great facility in ~~some~~ most parts of the U States. Some pleasing essays are making in Connecticut as well towards that, as towards the manufacture of what is produced. Stockings, handerkiefs ~~in imitation of the same~~ ribbands and buttons are made; though as yet in but small quantities. A manufactory of lace upon a scale not very extensive has been long memorable at Ipswich in the state of Massachusettes.

An exemption of the ~~duty~~ material from the duty, which it now pays on importation, and premiums upon the production, to be dispensed under the direction of the Institution before alluded to, seem to be the only species of encouragement adviseable at so early a stage of the thing.

## Glass

The materials for making Glass are found every where. In the United States, there is no deficiency of them. The sands and stones called Tarso, which include ~~all~~ flinty and chrystalline substances generally, and the salts of various ~~weeds~~ plants, particularly of the sea weed kali or kelp constitute the essential ingredients. ~~The~~ An extraordinary abundance of fuel is a particular advantage enjoyed by this ~~U States~~ country for such manufactures. They, however, require large Capitals and involve much manual labour.

[and a third in New Jersey]
[Quare Albany]
~~Two or more~~ if not Different manufactories of Glass are now on foot in the U States, ~~one in Maryland, another in Massachusettes~~. The present duty of 12½ per Cent on all imported articles of glass amount to a considerable encouragement to ~~domestic fabrication~~ those manufactories.

If any thing in addition ~~is~~ is judged eligible, the most proper would appear to be a direct bounty on window glass and black bottles. The

first recommends itself as an object of general convenience; the last
adds to that character, the circumstance of being an important item

in ~~distilleries and~~ breweries. A complaint is made of ~~some~~ deficiency
[great]
in this respect.

Qr. if not
well to lay
12½ ℔ ₵ to
take effect
some time
hence

### Gunpowder

has been of late    in
No small progress ^is already~~ made ~~on~~ the manufacture of this very
important article: It may indeed be considered as already established;
but its high importance renders its further extension very desireable.

The encouragements, which it already enjoys, are a duty of 10 ℔
Cent on the foreign rival article, and an exemption of salt petre one of
the principal ingredients, of which it is composed, from duty. A like
exemption of ~~a~~ Sulphur, another chief ingredient, ~~stands on similar
ground would appeal~~ would appear to be equally proper. No quantity
of this article has yet been produced, from internal ~~resources~~. The
use made of it in finishing the bottoms of ships, ~~a manufactory, not
secondary to that of~~ is an additional inducement to placing it in the
class of free goods.

A regulation exists between the British Government, and the British
East India Company, which lays an obligation on the latter, to ~~impor-
tion~~ annually from the Indies, a certain quantity of Salt petre rough
or refined, which is taken from them at a determinate price and is
encouragement of the
understood to have for object the ^manufacture of Gunpowder.[122]
it may be eligible to impose                          as
How far ^a similar obligation ~~may be made~~ ^the condition ~~which~~ of
any advantages which are or may be granted to the trade between the
U States and that quarter of the Globe may not be unworthy of reflection. The United States not having factories established in other
parts of the East Indies, such a requisition could reasonably only extend to the Port of Canton.

of 4/6 Sterling ℔ hundred pounds
^A bounty ^has ~~hitherto~~ heretofore been allowed in Great Britain
(though its continuance at present is not known) on all home made
powder exported from that country. A similar regulation here, if
judged otherwise expedient would certainly aid the manufacture.

~~The plan~~

Examine
[it is con-
tinued qu:
the principal
of this al-
lowance—]

122. See note 71.

having for object        for the     of the article
Regulations ~for subjecting the article to for~ a careful inspection

a favourable
would have ~the like~ tendency.

## Paper

Manufactories of paper are among those which are arrived at the greatest maturity in the United States and are most adequate to ~the requisite~ national supply. That of Paper Hangings is a branch in which ~a~ respectable progress has been made.

Nothing material seems wanting to the further success of this valuable branch; what is already ~proper~ protected by a competent duty on similar imported articles.

made
In the enumeration of the several kinds, ~which are~ subject to that duty, sheathing and cartrige paper have been omitted. These, being the most simple manufactures of the ~kind~ sort and necessary to military supply as well as shipbuilding, recommend themselves equally with those of other descriptions, to encouragement, and appear to be as fully within the compass of domestic exertions.

[Qu: what would be the effect of a premium on the Collection of Rags in spreading the habit of doing it—]

## Printed books

[Qu: is there yet sufficient demand?]

The great number of presses, dessiminated throughout the Union, seem to afford an assurance, that there is no need of being indebted to foreign countries for the printing of the books which are used in the U States. A duty of ten per Cent instead of five, which is now charged upon the article, would have a tendency to aid the ~in~ business internally.

Quaere?

It occurs, as an objection to this, that it may have an unfavourable aspect towards Literature, by raising the prices of books in universal use in private families ~and~ Schools and other seminaries of learning.

But the
~The~ difference it is conceived would be without effect. ~but the objec-
it
tion, as far as~ may ~be one, is capable of being obviated by a small
printed at home
bounty on all such~ books ~according to some specific enumeration.~

As to books, which usually fill the libraries of the wealthier classes and of professional men, such an augmentation of prices as might be occasioned by an additional duty of 5 ⅌ Cent would be too little felt to be an impediment to the acquisition. ~~and in this, as in other cases, the extension of the domestic manufacture would finally conduce to a greater cheapness of the article.~~

And ~~With~~ regard to books which may be specially imported for the
                                    ^particular
use of ^Seminaries of Learning and of Public libraries, a total exemp-
                     be                    go far towards
tion from duty would ^adviseable, which would ~~also~~ obviating the objection just mentioned. They are now subject to a duty of 5 ⅌ Cent.

                                              ^general
As to the ~~more ordinary kinds of~~ books in most ^~~universal~~ family use the constancy & universality of the demand would ensure exertions to furnish them at home and the means are completely adequate. It may also be expected ultimately in this as in other cases that the
                                          would
extension of the domestic manufacture ~~will~~ conduce to the cheapness of the article.

                                      to
It ought not to pass unremarked that encourage~~ment to~~ the print-
            is to encourage
ing of books ^~~must likewise favour~~ the manufacture of paper.

## Oils

These generally are now subject to a duty of 10 ⅌ Cent. Those of sea and land animals and of flax seed are among the most plentiful objects of internal supply. It is not perceived that any inconvenience could arise from such an increase of the duty upon them as would have a prohibitory operation: and it would have the advantage of pro-
                                      branches
moting some valuable ~~branches objects~~ ^of national industry.

Spirits of Turpentine may with propriety by placed under a similar
Regulation
~~Regime~~.

## Refined Sugars and Chocolate
                    number
Are among the ~~objects~~ of extensive and prosperous domestic manufactories.

exemption of books imported for seminaries of learning & public libraries

[Qu: do these three want the aid]

Drawbacks of the duties upon the materials, of which they are respectively made in cases of exportation, would have a beneficial influence upon the manufacture, and would conform to a precedent, which has been already furnished, in the instance of molasses, on the exportation of distilled spirits.

Cocoa the raw material now pays a duty of one Cent ℔ lb, while Chocolate, which is a prevailing and very simple manufacture is comprised in the mass of articles rated at 5℔ no more than five ℔ Cent.

There would appear to be a propriety in ~~placing~~ encouraging the manufacture, by a somewhat higher duty, on its foreign rival, than is paid on the raw material. Two Cents ℔ lb on ~~C~~ imported Chocolate would it is presumed be without inconvenience.

*The foregoing heads comprise the most important of the several kinds of manufactures, which have occured as requiring, and, at the same time, as most proper for public encouragement: and such measures for affording it, as have appeared best calculated to answer the end, have been suggested.*

*The observations, which have accompanied this delineation of objects, supercede the necessity of many suppementary remarks. One or two however may not be altogether superfluous.*

*Bounties are in various instances proposed as one species of encouragement.*

*It is a familiar objection to them, that they are difficult to be managed and liable to frauds. But neither that difficulty nor this danger seems sufficiently great to countervail the advantages of which they are productive, when rightly applied. And it is presumed to have been shewn that they are in some cases, particularly in the infancy of new enterprises* indispensable ~~inadmissible~~.

*It will however be necessary to guard with extraordinary circumspection the manner of dispensing them. The requisite precautions have been thought of, but to enter into the detail would swell this report, already voluminous, to* a size *too inconvenient* a ~~size~~.

*If the principle shall not be deemed inadmissible the means of avoiding an abuse of it will not be likely to present insurmountable obstacles. There are* useful ~~good~~ *guides from practice in other quarters.*

*It shall therefor only be remarked here in relation to this point,
that any bounty, which may be applied to the* manufacture *of an
article, cannot with safety extend beyond those Manufactures, at*
Trade
*which the making of the Article is a* regular *business.* ~~Besides other
objections~~ *It would be impossible to annex adequate precautions to a
benefit of that nature if extended to every private family, in which
the manufacture was incidentally carried on* and its being a merely
incidental occupation, which engages a portion of time that would
                                    be
~~be~~ otherwise ∧ lost, it can be advantageously carried on without ~~any
so such~~ special an aid.

*The Possibility of a diminution of the revenue may also present
itself as an objection to the arrangements which have been submitted.*

*But there is no truth which may be more firmly relied upon than
that the interests of the Revenue are promoted by whatever promotes
an increase of National Industry and Wealth.*

*In proportion to the degree of these, is the capacity of every county
to contribute to the Public Treasury; and where the capacity to pay*
                    even
*is encreased, or* ∧ ~~rather~~ *is not decreased, the only consequence of
measures, which diminish any particular resource is a change of the
object. If by encouraging the Manufacture of an article at home, the
revenue which has been wont to accrue from its importation should
be lessened, an indemnification can easily be found either out of the
manufacture itself, or from some other object which may be deemed
more convenient.*

*The measures however which have been submitted, taken aggre-
gately, will for a long time to come rather augment than decrease the
public Revenues. There is little room to hope that the progress of
manufactures will so equally keep pace with the progress of population as to present, even, a gradual augmentation of the product of the
duties on imported articles.*

*As, nevertheless, an abolition in some instances and a reduction in
others of* ~~the~~ *duties which have been pledged for the public debt is
proposed it is essential that it should be accompanied with a competent substitute. In order to this, it is requisite, that all the additional
duties which shall be laid be appropriated in the first instance, to replace all defalcations which may proceed from any such abolition or*

only
*diminution. It is evident at first glance that they will not˄ be ~~only~~ ade-
quate to this, but will yield a considerable surplus.*

*This surplus will serve—*

*First—To constitute a fund for paying the bounties which shall
have been decreed.*

Board
*Secondly—To constitute a fund for the operations of a ~~Society~~ to
be established, for promoting Arts, Agriculture, Manufactures and
Commerce. Of this institution, different intimations have been given,
in the course of this Report. An outline of a plan for it shall now be
submitted.*

*Let a certain annual sum, be set apart, and placed under the manage-
ment of Commissioners, not less than three, to consist of certain
Officers of the Government and their successors in Office.*

*Let these Commissioners be empowered to apply the fund confided
to them—to defray the expences of the emigration of Artists and
Manufacturers in particular branches of extraordinary importance—
to induce the prosecution and introduction of useful discoveries,
inventions & improvements by proportionate rewards judiciously
held out and applied—to encourage by premiums both Honorable and
lucrative the exertions of individuals and of classes in relation to the
several objects they are charged with promoting—and to afford such
other aids to those objects as may be generally designated by law.*

*The Commissioners to render an annual account of their trans-
actions and disbursements; and all such sums as shall not have been
applied to the purposes of their trust at the end of every three years to
revert to the Treasury. It may also be enjoined upon them, not to
draw out the money, but for the purpose of some specific dis-
bursement.*

*It may moreover be of use to authorise them to receive voluntary
contributions; making it their duty to apply them to the particular
objects for which they may have been made, if any shall have been
designated by the donors.*

*There is reason to believe that the progress of particular manufac-
tures has been much retarded by the want of skilful workmen. And it
often happens that the capitals employed are not equal to the purpose
of bringing from abroad workmen of a superior kind. Here, in cases*

*worthy of it, the auxiliary agency of Government would in all probability be useful. There are also valuable workmen, in every branch, who are prevented from emigrating solely by the want of means. Occasional aids to such persons properly administered might be a source of valuable aquisitions to the country.*

*The propriety of stimulating by rewards the invention and introduction of useful improvements is admitted without difficulty. But the success of attempts in this way must evidently depend much on the manner of conducting them. It ₍is₎ probable that the placing of the dispensation of those rewards under some proper discretionary direction, where they may be accompanied by <u>collateral expedients</u>, will serve to give them the surest efficacy. It seems impracticable to apportion by general rules specific compensations for discoveries of unknown and disproportionate utility.*

*The great use which may be made of a fund of this nature to procure and import foreign improvements is particularly obvious. Among these the article of machines would form a most important item.*

*The operation and utility of premiums have been adverted to; together with the advantages which have resulted from their dispensation under the direction of certain public and private societies. Of this some experience has been had in the instance of the Pennsylvania Society* <u>name</u> *but the funds of that association have been too contracted to produce more than a very small portion of the good to which the principles of it would have led. It may confidently be affirmed that there is scarcely any thing, which has been devised, better calculated to excite a general spirit of improvement than the institutions of this nature. They are truly invaluable.*

*In countries where there is great private wealth much may be effected by the voluntary contributions of patriotic individuals; but in a community situated like that of the United States, the public purse must supply the deficiency of private resource. In what can it be so useful as in prompting and improving the efforts of industry?*

<u>Ascertain if British G does not make grants to a similar society</u>

*All which is humbly submitted*

## ALEXANDER HAMILTON'S FINAL VERSION OF THE REPORT ON THE SUBJECT OF MANUFACTURES [123]

[Philadelphia, December 5, 1791
Communicated on December 5, 1791] [124]

[To the Speaker of the House of Representatives]

The Secretary of the Treasury in obedience to the order of ye House of Representatives, of the 15th day of January 1790,[125] has applied his attention, at as early a period as his other duties would permit, to the subject of Manufactures; and particularly to the means of promoting such as will tend to render the United States, independent on foreign nations, for military and other essential supplies. And he there[upon] respectfully submits the following Report.

The expediency of encouraging manufactures in the United States, which was not long since deemed very questionable, appears at this time to be pretty generally admitted. The embarrassments, which have obstructed the progress of our external trade, have led to serious reflections on the necessity of enlarging the sphere of our domestic commerce: the restrictive regulations, which in foreign markets abrige the vent of the increasing surplus of our Agricultural produce, serve to beget an earnest desire, that a more extensive demand for that surplus may be created at home: And the complete success, which has rewarded manufacturing enterprise, in some valuable branches, conspiring with the promising symptoms, which attend some less mature essays, in others, justify a hope, that the obstacles to the growth of this species of industry are less formidable than they were

123. DS, with additions in H's handwriting, RG 233, Original Reports of the Secretary of the Treasury, 1791–1792, National Archives.

This document is in the handwriting of four clerks. In addition, there are insertions and corrections in H's handwriting which are printed in brackets.

124. *Journal of the House*, I, 468. The communicating letter, which is dated December 5, 1791, may be found in RG 233, Original Reports of the Secretary of the Treasury, 1791–1792, National Archives.

125. On January 15, 1790, the House "*Ordered*, That it be referred to the Secretary of the Treasury to prepare and report to this House, a proper plan or plans, conformably to the recommendation of the President of the United States, in his speech to both Houses of Congress, for the encouragement and promotion of such manufactories as will tend to render the United States independent of other nations for essential, particularly for military supplies" (*Journal of the House*, I, 141–42).

apprehended to be; and that it is not difficult to find, in its further
extension; a full indemnification for any external disadvantages, which
are or may be experienced, as well as an accession of resources,
favourable to national independence and safety.[126]

There still are, nevertheless, respectable patrons of opinions, unfriendly to the encouragement of manufactures. The following are,
substantially, the arguments, by which these opinions are defended.

"In every country (say those who entertain them) Agriculture is
the most beneficial and *productive* object of human industry. This
position, generally, if not universally true, applies with peculiar
emphasis to the United States, on account of their immense tracts of
fertile territory, uninhabited and unimproved. Nothing can afford so
advantageous an employment for capital and labour, as the conversion
of this extensive wilderness into cultivated farms. Nothing equally
with this, can contribute to the population, strength and real riches of
the country." [127]

126. *The American Museum*, to which H was a charter subscriber, contains
many statements of the pre-Revolutionary idea that the establishment of American manufactures would be difficult, if not impossible. One writer commented:
"Previous to the late revolution, it was a favourite sentiment among Englishmen,
and an opinion imbibed by too many Americans, that it was contrary to the
interest of this country to carry on manufactures" (*The American Museum*,
II [September, 1787], 257–58).

On the other hand, post-Revolutionary writers in the same periodical maintained that the establishment of American manufactures was both practicable
and necessary. By 1791 innumerable examples of the growing interest of Americans in manufactures might be given. Among the examples with which H was
certainly familiar are William Barton's "Remarks on the state of American
manufactures and commerce" (*The American Museum*, VII [June, 1790], 285–
92), a copy of which is in the Hamilton Papers, Library of Congress; Tench
Coxe's *Brief Examination*, which appeared in *The American Museum* in serial
form during the spring and summer of 1791 while Coxe was Assistant Secretary
of the Treasury; and William Bingham's *A Letter from an American*, which
was published in 1784 together with *Mentor's Reply to Phocion's Letter* (*A
Letter from an American, Now resident in London, to a Member of Parliament,
On the Subject of the Restraining Proclamation: and Containing Strictures
on Lord Sheffield's Pamphlet, on the Commerce of the American States. Said
to be written by William Bingham, Esquire: late Agent for the Congress of the
United States of America, at Martinico. To which are Added, Mentor's Reply to
Phocion's Letter; with some Observations on Trade, addressed to the Citizens
of New York*) (Philadelphia: Printed and Sold by Robert Bell, in Third-Street,
1784). See also "Tench Coxe's Draft of the Report on the Subject of Manufactures."

127. The views expressed in this paragraph—like similar statements later in
the Report in which H outlines a Physiocratic approach to the subject under
discussion—had been expounded by Physiocratic economists not only on the
Continent but in England. H's notes, drafts, or finished writings do not indicate,

"To endeavor by the extraordinary patronage of Government, to accelerate the growth of manufactures, is in fact, to endeavor, by force and art, to transfer the natural current of industry, from a more, to a less beneficial channel. Whatever has such a tendency must necessarily be unwise. Indeed it can hardly ever be wise in a government, to attempt to give a direction to the industry of its citizens. This under the quicksighted guidance of private interest, will, if left to itself, infallibly find its own way to the most profitable employment: and 'tis by such employment, that the public prosperity will be most effectually promoted. To leave industry to itself, therefore, is, in almost every case, the soundest as well as the simplest policy." [128]

---

however, that he had read the works of any of the leading Physiocratic thinkers. There is little doubt that H made use of Adam Smith's discussion of Physiocratic views. Some excerpts from *The Wealth of Nations* which parallel this paragraph are:

"When the capital of any country is not sufficient for all those three purposes [agriculture, manufactures, and trade], in proportion as a greater share of it is employed in agriculture, the greater will be the quantity of productive labour which it puts into motion within the country; as will likewise be the value which its employment adds to the annual produce of the land and labour of the society." (Smith, *Wealth of Nations*, I, 364.)

"In North America . . . the purchase and improvement of uncultivated land, is . . . the most profitable employment of the smallest as well as of the greatest capitals. . . ." (Smith, *Wealth of Nations*, I, 414–15.)

"Compare the slow progress of those European countries of which the wealth depends very much upon their commerce and manufactures, with the rapid advances of our North American colonies, of which the wealth is founded altogether in agriculture. Through the greater part of Europe, the number of inhabitants is not supposed to double in less than five hundred years. In several of our North American colonies, it is found to double in twenty or five-and-twenty years." (Smith, *Wealth of Nations*, I, 413–14.)

"It has been the principle cause of the rapid progress of our American colonies towards wealth and greatness, that almost their whole capitals have hitherto been employed in agriculture." (Smith, *Wealth of Nations*, I, 365.)

Necker, like Smith, on occasion summarized the views of the Physiocrats. Thus, in an effort to refute Physiocratic critics of Colbert's policies, Necker paraphrased Physiocratic ideas as follows: "Mais, dit-on, il n'a pas permis dans tous les tems la sortie des bleds, sans mesure et sans limite. Il n'a donc pas senti que la liberté est l'ame du commerce; il n'a donc pas connu les effets invincibles de la concurrence; il n'a donc pas apperçu la puissance de l'intérêt personnel" (Necker, *Œuvres*, III, 204).

Clavière, who defined "the force of things" as the "political law which governs all, in politics, as in physics," wrote: "*Favouring*, in political œconomy, signifies for the most part, not to shackle industry with too many regulations; however favourable certain of these may be, they restrain it in some respect or other. It is never more encouraged than when left to itself" (Clavière, *Considerations on America*, 9, 7).

128. Smith summarizes the effect of mercantilist restriction as follows: "The industry of the country, therefore, is thus turned away from a more to a less advantageous employment, and the exchangeable value of its annual produce,

"This policy is not only recommended to the United States, by considerations which affect all nations, it is, in a manner, dictated to them by the imperious force of a very peculiar situation. The smallness of their population compared with their territory—the constant allurements to emigration from the settled to the unsettled parts of the country—the facility, with which the less independent condition of an artisan can be exchanged for the more independent condition of a farmer, these and similar causes conspire to produce, and for a length of time must continue to occasion, a scarcity of hands for manufacturing occupation, and dearness of labor generally. To these disadvantages for the prosecution of manufactures, a deficiency of pecuniary capital being added, the prospect of a successful competition with the manufactures of Europe must be regarded as little less than desperate. Extensive manufactures can only be the offspring of a redundant, at least of a full population. Till the latter shall characterise the situation of this country, 'tis vain to hope for the former." [129]

---

instead of being increased, according to the intention of the lawgiver, must necessarily be diminished by every such regulation" (Smith, *Wealth of Nations*, I, 449).

The similarity between the views summarized by H in this paragraph and those stated by Smith can be seen in the following quotations from *The Wealth of Nations:*

"To give the monopoly of the home-market to the produce of domestic industry, in any particular art or manufacture, is in some measure to direct private people in what manner they ought to employ their capitals, and must, in almost all cases, be either a useless or a hurtful regulation. . . . But though the industry of the society may be thus carried with advantage into a particular channel sooner than it could have been otherwise, it will by no means follow that the sum total, either of its industry, or of its revenue, can ever be augmented by any such regulation." (Smith, *Wealth of Nations*, I, 448–49.)

"The sovereign is completely discharged from a duty, in the attempting to perform which . . . no human wisdom or knowlege could ever be sufficient; the duty of superintending the industry of private people, and of directing it towards the employments most suitable to the interest of the society." (Smith, *Wealth of Nations*, II, 203.)

"What is the species of domestic industry which his capital can employ, and of which the produce is likely to be of the greatest value, every individual, it is evident, can, in his local situation, judge much better than any statesman or lawgiver can do for him." (Smith, *Wealth of Nations*, I, 447–48.)

"Every individual is continually exerting himself to find out the most advantageous employment for whatever capital he can command. . . . the study of his own advantage naturally, or rather necessarily leads him to prefer that employment which is most advantageous to the society." (Smith, *Wealth of Nations*, I, 445.)

129. The views summarized by H in this paragraph had been expressed by Smith as follows:

". . . the disproportion between the great extent of the land and the small number of the people [in America], which commonly takes place in new colo-

"If contrary to the natural course of things, an unseasonable and premature spring can be given to certain fabrics, by heavy duties, prohibitions, bounties, or by other forced expedients; this will only be to sacrifice the interests of the community to those of particular classes. Besides the misdirection of labour, a virtual monopoly will be given to the persons employed on such fabrics; and an enhancement of price, the inevitable consequence of every monopoly, must be defrayed at the expence of the other parts of the society. It is far

---

nies, makes it difficult for . . . [a proprietor] to get . . . labour." (Smith, *Wealth of Nations*, II, 68.)

"A new colony must always for some time be more under-stocked in proportion to the extent of its territory, and more under-peopled in proportion to the extent of its stock, than the greater part of other countries." (Smith, *Wealth of Nations*, I, 93.)

"In our North American colonies, where uncultivated land is still to be had upon easy terms, no manufactures for distant sale have ever yet been established in any of their towns. When an artificer has acquired a little more stock than is necessary for carrying on his own business in supplying the neighbouring country, he does not, in North America, attempt to establish with it a manufacture for more distant sale, but employs it in the purchase and improvement of uncultivated land. From artificer he becomes planter, and neither the large wages nor the easy subsistence which that country affords to artificers, can bribe him rather to work for other people than for himself." (Smith, *Wealth of Nations*, I, 378.)

Clavière, among others, had expressed ideas similar to those summarized by H in this paragraph. Clavière wrote:

". . . if they [the Americans] had raw materials in plenty, they ought to be advised not to establish manufactures; or, to speak more justly, *manufactures could not be established; the nature of things ordains it so.*" (Clavière, *Considerations on America*, 50.)

"As population must for many ages be disproportioned to the extent of the United States, land will be cheap there during the same length of time, and consequently the inhabitants will for a long time be cultivators.

"Those whom ambition, thirst of gain, or ignorance should incline to establish manufactures, will, from that moment be disbanded from it, by the dearness of workmanship. This dearness is already very considerable, and may become still more so, as the cause which occasions it must naturally become more extended." (Clavière, *Considerations on America*, 53–54.)

"These manufactures ought, according to natural order, to be the productions of an excess of population only, which cannot give its industry to agriculture or simple manufactures; but in general they are the result of the gathering together of the poor and wretched, in great cities." (Clavière, *Considerations on America*, 5–6.)

The argument that the scarcity of labor precluded manufactures was mentioned by most Americans who discussed the encouragement of manufactures. See *The American Museum*, I [January, 1787], 17; II [September, 1787], 258; II [October, 1787], 331; VI [July, 1789], 72, 74. Arguments similar to those advanced in *The American Museum* had also been used during the first session of Congress. See, for example, the remarks of Thomas Scott of Pennsylvania on April 16, 1789 (*Annals of Congress*, I, 160–61).

preferable, that those persons should be engaged in the cultivation of the earth, and that we should procure, in exchange for its productions, the commodities, with which foreigners are able to supply us in greater perfection, and upon better terms." [130]

This mode of reasoning is founded upon facts and principles, which have certainly respectable pretensions. If it had governed the conduct of nations, more generally than it has done, there is room to suppose, that it might have carried them faster to prosperity and greatness, than they have attained, by the pursuit of maxims too widely opposite. Most general theories, however, admit of numerous exceptions, and there are few, if any, of the political kind, which do not blend a considerable portion of error, with the truths they inculcate.

130. In this paragraph, as in the preceding paragraphs which H set off as a quotation, H was apparently relying upon similar statements made by Smith. Thus, Smith wrote:

"It is thus that through the greater part of Europe the commerce and manufactures of cities, instead of being the effect, have been the cause and occasion of the improvement and cultivation of the country.

"This order, however, being contrary to the natural course of things, is necessarily both slow and uncertain." (Smith, *Wealth of Nations*, I, 413.)

"Though, by this oppressive policy, a landed nation should be able to raise up artificers, manufacturers and merchants of its own, somewhat sooner than it could do by the freedom of trade; a matter, however, which is not a little doubtful; yet it would raise them up, if one may say so, prematurely, and before it was perfectly ripe for them." (Smith, *Wealth of Nations*, II, 187.)

"Were the Americans, either by combination or by any other sort of violence, to stop the importation of European manufactures, and, by thus giving a monopoly to such of their own countrymen as could manufacture the like goods, divert any considerable part of their capital into this employment, they would retard instead of accelerating the further increase in the value of their annual produce, and would obstruct instead of promoting the progress of their country towards real wealth and greatness." (Smith, *Wealth of Nations*, I, 365–66.)

"By restraining, either by high duties, or by absolute prohibitions, the importation of such goods from foreign countries as can be produced at home, the monopoly of the home-market is more or less secured to the domestic industry employed in producing them." (Smith, *Wealth of Nations*, I, 444.)

"In the restraints upon the importation . . . the interest of the home-consumer is evidently sacrificed to that of the producer. It is altogether for the benefit of the latter, that the former is obliged to pay that enhancement of price which this monopoly almost always occasions." (Smith, *Wealth of Nations*, II, 173.)

"If a foreign country can supply us with a commodity cheaper than we ourselves can make it, better buy it of them with some part of the produce of our own industry, employed in a way in which we have some advantage." (Smith, *Wealth of Nations*, I, 448.)

A number of American observers held opinions similar to those summarized by H in this paragraph. For example, see *The American Museum*, I (January, 1787), 16–17; II (September, 1787), 214–15; VI (July, 1789), 72–73.

In order to an accurate judgement how far that which has been just stated ought to be deemed liable to a similar imputation, it is necessary to advert carefully to the considerations, which plead in favour of manufactures, and which appear to recommend the special and positive encouragement of them; in certain cases, and under certain reasonable limitations.

It ought readily to be conceded, that the cultivation of the earth— as the primary and most certain source of national supply—as the immediate and chief source of subsistence to man—as the principal source of those materials which constitute the nutriment of other kinds of labor—as including a state most favourable to the freedom and independence of the human mind—one, perhaps, most conducive to the multiplication of the human species—has *intrinsically a strong claim to pre-eminence over every other kind of industry*.

But, that it has a title to any thing like an exclusive predilection, in any country, ought to be admitted with great caution. That it is even more productive than every other branch of Industry requires more evidence, than has yet been given in support of the position. That its real interests, precious and important as without the help of exaggeration, they truly are, will be advanced, rather than injured by the due encouragement of manufactures, may, it is believed, be satisfactorily demonstrated. And it is also believed that the expediency of such encouragement in a general view may be shewn to be recommended by the most cogent and persuasive motives of national policy.

It has been maintained, that Agriculture is, not only, the most productive, but the only productive species of industry. The reality of this suggestion in either aspect, has, however, not been verified by any accurate detail of facts and calculations; and the general arguments, which are adduced to prove it, are rather subtil and paradoxical, than solid or convincing.[131]

Those which maintain its exclusive productiveness are to this effect.

Labour, bestowed upon the cultivation of land produces enough,

131. Although Smith indicated his respect for the economic liberalism of Physiocratic thought, his criticism of the Physiocratic theory of manufactures as paradoxical is similar to H's statement. Smith wrote that the followers of the Physiocrats were "very numerous; and as men are fond of paradoxes, and of appearing to understand what surpasses the comprehension of ordinary people, the paradox which it maintains, concerning the unproductive nature of manufacturing labour, has not perhaps contributed a little to increase the number of its admirers" (Smith, *Wealth of Nations*, II, 194).

not only to replace all the necessary expences incurred in the business, and to maintain the persons who are employed in it, but to afford together with the *ordinary profit* on the stock or capital of the Farmer, a nett surplus, or *rent* for the landlord or proprietor of the soil. But the labor of Artificers does nothing more, than replace the Stock which employs them (or which furnishes materials tools and wages) and yield the *ordinary profit* upon that Stock. It yields nothing equivalent to the *rent* of land. Neither does it add any thing to the *total value* of the *whole annual produce* of the land and labour of the country. The additional value given to those parts of the produce of land, which are wrought into manufactures, is counterbalanced by the value of those other parts of that produce, which are consumed by the manufacturers. It can therefore only be by saving, or *parsimony* not by the positive *productiveness* of their labour, that the classes of Artificers can in any degree augment the revenue of the Society.[132]

To this it has been answered—

I  "That inasmuch as it is acknowleged, that manufacturing labour reproduces a value equal to that which is expended or consumed in carrying it on, and continues in existence the original Stock or capital employed—it ought on that account alone, to escape being considered as wholly unproductive: That though it should be admitted, as alleged, that the consumption of the produce of the soil,

132. Smith, in a section which H is paraphrasing in this paragraph, wrote: "The rent which properly belongs to the landlord, is no more than the neat produce which remains after paying in the compleatest manner all the necessary expences which must be previously laid out in order to raise the gross, or the whole produce. It is because the labour of the cultivators, over and above paying completely all those necessary expences, affords a neat produce of this kind, that this class of people are in this system peculiarly distinguished by the honourable appellation of the productive class. . . . Artificers and manufacturers . . . are in this system represented as . . . unproductive. Their labour, it is said, replaces only the stock which employs them, together with its ordinary profits. That stock consists in the materials, tools, and wages, advanced on them by their employer. . . . The profits of manufacturing stock, therefore, are not, like the rent of land, a neat produce which remains after completely repaying the whole expence which must be laid out in order to obtain them. . . . The labour of artificers and manufacturers never adds any thing to the value of the whole annual amount of the rude produce of the land. It adds indeed greatly to the value of some particular parts of it. But the consumption which in the mean time it occasions of other parts, is precisely equal to the value which it adds to those parts. . . . Artificers, manufacturers and merchants, can augment the revenue and wealth of their society by parsimony only . . ." (Smith, *Wealth of Nations*, II, 179–82).

by the classes of Artificers or Manufacturers, is exactly equal to the value added by their labour to the materials upon which it is exerted; yet it would not thence follow, that it added nothing to the Revenue of the Society, or to the aggregate value of the annual produce of its land and labour. If the consumption for any given period amounted to a *given sum* and the *increased* value of the produce manufactured, in the same period, to a *like sum*, the total amount of the consumption and production during that period, would be equal to the *two sums*, and consequently double the value of the agricultural produce consumed. And though the increment of value produced by the classes of Artificers should at no time exceed the value of the produce of the land consumed by them, yet there would be at every moment, in consequence of their labour, a greater value of goods in the market than would exist independent of it." [133]

II—"That the position, that Artificers can augment the revenue of a Society, only by parsimony, is true, in no other sense, than in one, which is equally applicable to Husbandmen or Cultivators. It may be alike affirmed of all these classes, that the fund acquired by their labor and destined for their support is not, in an ordinary way, more than equal to it. And hence it will follow, that augmentations of the wealth or capital of the community (except in the instances of some extraordinary dexterity or skill) can only proceed, with respect to any of them, from the savings of the more thrifty and parsimonious." [134]

133. This paragraph is a paraphrase of the following sections from *The Wealth of Nations:* "First, this class, it is acknowledged, reproduces annually the value of its own annual consumption, and continues, at least, the existence of the stock or capital which maintains and employs it. But upon this account alone the denomination of barren or unproductive should seem to be very improperly applied to it." (Smith, *Wealth of Nations*, II, 189.)

"Though we should suppose, for example, as it seems to be supposed in this system, that the value of the daily, monthly, and yearly consumption of this class was exactly equal to that of its daily, monthly, and yearly production, yet it would not from thence follow that its labour added nothing to the real revenue, to the real value of the annual produce of the land and labour of the society. . . . The value, therefore, of what has been consumed and produced during these six months is equal, not to ten, but to twenty pounds. . . . Though the value of what the artificer produces, therefore, should not at any one moment of time be supposed greater than the value he consumes, yet at every moment of time the actually existing value of goods in the market is, in consequence of what he produces, greater than it otherwise would be." (Smith, *Wealth of Nations*, II, 190–91.)

134. This paragraph is a paraphrase of the following section from *The Wealth*

III—"That the annual produce of the land and labour of a country can only be encreased, in two ways—by some improvement in the *productive powers* of the useful labour, which actually exists within it, or by some increase in the quantity of such labour: That with regard to the first, the labour of Artificers being capable of greater subdivision and simplicity of operation, than that of Cultivators, it is susceptible, in a proportionably greater degree, of improvement in its *productive powers*, whether to be derived from an accession of Skill, or from the application of ingenious machinery; in which particular, therefore, the labour employed in the culture of land can pretend to no advantage over that engaged in manufactures: That with regard to an augmentation of the quantity of useful labour, this, excluding adventitious circumstances, must depend essentially upon an increase of *capital*, which again must depend upon the savings made out of the revenues of those, who furnish or manage *that*, which is at any time employed, whether in Agriculture, or in Manufactures, or in any other way." [135]

But while the *exclusive* productiveness of Agricultural labour has

---

*of Nations:* "When the patrons of this system assert that the consumption of artificers, manufacturers and merchants, is equal to the value of what they produce, they probably mean no more than that their revenue, or the fund destined for their consumption, is equal to it. But if they had expressed themselves more accurately, and only asserted that the revenue of this class was equal to the value of what they produced, it might readily have occurred to the reader, that what would naturally be saved out of this revenue, must necessarily increase more or less the real wealth of the society. . . . farmers and country labourers can no more augment, without parsimony, the real revenue, the annual produce of the land and labour of their society, than artificers, manufacturers and merchants" (Smith, *Wealth of Nations*, II, 191–92).

135. This paragraph is a paraphrase of the following sections from *The Wealth of Nations:* "The annual produce of land and labour of any nation can be increased in its value by no other means, but by increasing either the number of its productive labourers, or the productive powers of those labourers who had before been employed." (Smith, *Wealth of Nations*, I, 342.)

"The improvement in the productive powers of useful labour depend[s], first, upon the improvement in the ability of the workmen; and, secondly, upon that of the machinery with which he works. But the labour of artificers and manufacturers, as it is capable of being more subdivided, and the labour of each workman reduced to a greater simplicity of operation, than that of farmers and country labourers, so it is likewise capable of both these sorts of improvement in a much higher degree. In this respect, therefore, the class of cultivators can have no sort of advantage over that of artificers and manufacturers.

"The increase in the quantity of useful labour actually employed within any society, must depend altogether upon the increase of the capital which employs it; and the increase of that capital again must be exactly equal to the amount of the savings from the revenue, either of the particular persons who manage and

been thus denied and refuted, the superiority of its productiveness has been conceded without hesitation.[136] As this concession involves a point of considerable magnitude, in relation to maxims of public administration, the grounds on which it rests are worthy of a distinct and particular examination.

One of the arguments made use of, in support of the idea may be pronounced both quaint and superficial. It amounts to this—That in the productions of the soil, nature co-operates with man; and that the effect of their joint labour must be greater than that of the labour of man alone.[137]

This however, is far from being a necessary inference. It is very conceivable, that the labor of man alone laid out upon a work, requiring great skill and art to bring it to perfection, may be more productive, *in value*, than the labour of nature and man combined, when directed towards more simple operations and objects: [138] And when

---

direct the employment of that capital, or of some other persons who lend it to them." (Smith, *Wealth of Nations*, II, 192.)

136. In this connection Smith wrote: "The capital employed in agriculture, therefore, not only puts into motion a greater quantity of productive labour than any equal capital employed in manufactures, but in proportion too to the quantity of productive labour which it employs, it adds a much greater value to the annual produce of the land and labour of the country, to the real wealth and revenue of its inhabitants" (Smith, *Wealth of Nations*, I, 362).

137. H is referring to the following section in *The Wealth of Nations*: "In agriculture too nature labours along with man; and though her labour costs no expence, its produce has its value, as well as that of the most expensive workmen. . . . No equal quantity of productive labour employed in manufactures can ever occasion so great a reproduction. In them nature does nothing; man does all; and the reproduction must always be in proportion to the strength of the agents that occasion it" (Smith, *Wealth of Nations*, I, 361–62).

138. Necker wrote: "Je sais bien que presque tous les objets d'industrie sont composés d'une production du sol; mais quand le prix de ces ouvrages dérive principalement du travail, la portion de terre, consacrée à la matiere premiere, est presqu'imperceptible" (Necker, *Œuvres*, IV, 99).

"Le prix du travail commun et grossier est composé de la valeur des diverses productions nécessaires aux ouvriers; mais le prix du talent ou d'une industrie rare ou particuliere, est encore composé d'une somme quelconque qu'on ne dépense pas, mais qu'on thésaurise. . . .

"Rendons cette vérité sensible. Un habile peintre fait dans le cours d'une année un nombre quelconque de tableaux qui sont vendus aux étrangers, et qui introduisent en France dix mille écus; ce peintre cependant n'en a voulu dépenser que cinq mille; ainsi lors même que toutes les productions que lui, sa famille et ses serviteurs ont consommées, auroient pu être vendues aux étrangers, il est sûr qu'elles n'auroient rapporté dans le Royaume que la moitié du prix du travail du peintre.

"Cet exemple frappant peut s'appliquer à tous les hommes industrieux, depuis

it is recollected to what an extent the Agency of nature, in the application of the mechanical powers, is made auxiliary to the prosecution of manufactures, the suggestion, which has been noticed, loses even the appearance of plausibility.

It might also be observed, with a contrary view, that the labour employed in Agriculture is in a great measure periodical and occasional, depending on seasons, liable to various and long intermissions;[139] while that occupied in many manufactures is constant and regular, extending through the year, embracing in some instances night as well as day.[140] It is also probable, that there are among the cultivators of land more examples of remissness, than among artificers. The farmer, from the peculiar fertility of his land, or some other favorable circumstance, may frequently obtain a livelihood, even with a considerable degree of carelessness in the mode of cultivation;[141]

---

l'artiste célebre ou le chef de manufacture qui thésaurisent peut-être dix mille francs chaque année, jusqu'à l'artisan grossier qui n'épargne qu'un écu." (Necker, *Œuvres*, IV, 102–03.)

Similar views had been expressed by Americans. For example, see Coxe, *Address*, 7; *The American Museum*, II (September, 1787), 256.

139. In this connection Smith wrote: "The occasions for those different sorts of labour returning with the different seasons of the year, it is impossible that one man should be constantly employed in any one of them" (Smith, *Wealth of Nations*, I, 7).

140. Emphasizing the difference between agriculture and manufactures, Clavière stated: "The most necessary conditions for manufacturing, at a cheap rate, articles complicated, or extremely fine and perfect, or which require the union of several kinds of workmanship, are a constant and assiduous application, and a numerous population; one half of which must be at a distance from the labours of the field, and applied to manufacture alone" (Clavière, *Considerations on America*, 5).

There are numerous references to the uninterrupted operation of mills. For example, a writer describing the silk mills at Derby, England, stated: "In these mills are 26,586 wheels, and 97,746 movements, continually working, except on Sundays" (*The American Museum*, II [September, 1787], 255). See also Thomas Marshall to H, July 24-31, 1791.

141. Hume had also made invidious comparisons between the industry of farmers and that inspired by commerce and manufactures. For example, he wrote: "It may seem an odd position, that the poverty of the common people in *France, Italy*, and *Spain* is, in some measure, owing to the superior riches of the soil and happiness of the climate; and yet there want not many reasons to justify this paradox. In such a fine mold or soil as that of those more southern regions, agriculture is an easy art. . . . All the art, which the farmer knows, is to leave his ground fallow for a year, as soon as it is exhausted; and the warmth of the sun alone and temperature of the climate enrich it, and restore its fertility" (Hume, *Political Discourses*, 20).

One writer, quoted in an article in an American periodical, stated: "A nation peopled only by farmers, must be a region of indolence and misery.—If the

but the artisan can with difficulty effect the same object, without exerting himself pretty equally with all those, who are engaged in the same pursuit.[142] And if it may likewise be assumed as a fact, that manufactures open a wider field to exertions of ingenuity than agriculture,[143] it would not be a strained conjecture, that the labour employed in the former, being at once more *constant*, more uniform and more ingenious, than that which is employed in the latter, will be found at the same time more productive.

But it is not meant to lay stress on observations of this nature—they ought only to serve as a counterbalance to those of a similar complexion. Circumstances so vague and general, as well as so abstract, can afford little instruction in a matter of this kind.

Another, and that which seems to be the principal argument offered for the superior productiveness of Agricultural labour, turns upon the allegation, that labour employed in manufactures yields nothing equivalent to the rent of land; or to that nett surplus, as it is called, which accrues to the proprietor of the soil.[144]

---

soil is naturally fertile, little labour will produce abundance; but, for want of exercise, even that little will be burthensome, and often neglected:—want will be felt in the midst of abundance, and the human mind be abased nearly to the same degree with the beasts that graze the field. If the region is more barren, the inhabitants will be obliged to become somewhat more industrious, and therefore more happy—But miserable at best must be the happiness of such a people" (*Columbian Magazine*, I [September, 1786], 27).

142. In this connection, Hume wrote: "In times, when industry and arts flourish, men are kept in perpetual occupation, and enjoy, as their reward, the occupation itself, as well as those pleasures, which are the fruits of their labour. . . . Banish those arts from society, you deprive men both of action and of pleasure; and leaving nothing but indolence in their place . . ." (Hume, *Political Discourses*, 25–26).

143. H's point of view had been shared by many earlier writers. Expressions of this view may be found in publications with which H was familiar. For example, Postlethwayt wrote: "In the management of the more estimable manufactures, there is required not only an extraordinary dexterity, care, and ingenuity, on the part of the common workmen, to execute their respective parts to the necessary perfection . . ." (Postlethwayt, *Universal Dictionary*, II, 134).

An article in *The American Museum* stated: "The labour and ingenuity bestowed upon the fabric, by the manufacturer, create, in most cases, the greater part of its value: and, therefore, the industry and genius of our mechanics and artisans may be considered as a valuable portion of the productive stock of our country" (*The American Museum*, VII [June, 1790], 286).

144. In the following statement Smith combines both arguments criticized by H: "Over and above the capital of the farmer and all its profits, they regularly occasion the reproduction of the rent of the landlord. This rent may be considered as the produce of those powers of nature, the use of which the landlord lends to the farmer" (Smith, *Wealth of Nations*, I, 362).

But this distinction, important as it has been deemed, appears rather *verbal* than *substantial*.

It is easily discernible, that what in the first instance is divided into two parts under the denominations of the *ordinary profit* of the Stock of the farmer and *rent* to the landlord, is in the second instance united under the general appellation of the *ordinary profit* on the Stock of the Undertaker; and that this formal or verbal distribution constitutes the whole difference in the two cases.[145] It seems to have been overlooked, that the land is itself a Stock or capital,[146] advanced or lent by its owner to the occupier or tenant, and that the rent he receives is only the ordinary profit of a certain Stock in land, not managed by the proprietor himself, but by another to whom he lends or lets it, and who on his part advances a second capital to stock & improve the land, upon which he also receives the usual profit. The rent of the landlord and the profit of the farmer are therefore nothing more than the *ordinary profits* of *two* capitals belonging to *two* different persons, and united in the cultivation of a farm: As in the other case, the surplus which arises upon any manufactory, after replacing the expences of carrying it on, answers to the ordinary profits of *one* or *more* capitals engaged in the prosecution of such manufactory. It is said *one* or *more* capitals; because in fact, the same thing which is contemplated, in the case of the farm, sometimes happens in that of a manufactory. There is one, who furnishes a part of the capital, or lends a part of the money, by which it is carried on, and another, who carries it on, with the addition of his own capital. Out of the surplus, which remains, after defraying expences,

145. In a passage from a chapter which Smith devotes to distinguishing wages of labor, profits of stock, and rent of land he states:

"When those three different sorts of revenue belong to different persons, they are readily distinguished; but when they belong to the same they are sometimes confounded with one another, at least in common language.

"A gentleman who farms a part of his own estate, after paying the expence of cultivation, should gain both the rent of the landlord and the profit of the farmer. He is apt to denominate, however, his whole gain, profit, and thus confounds rent with profit, at least in common language. The greater part of our North American and West Indian planters are in this situation. They farm, the greater part of them, their own estates, and accordingly we seldom hear of the rent of a plantation, but frequently of its profit." (Smith, *Wealth of Nations*, I, 53.)

146. Necker wrote: "Le bénéfice du propriétaire est toujours le résultat d'une comparaison faite entre le capital de la terre qu'il possede, et le revenu qu'il en tire" (Necker, *Œuvres*, IV, 82).

an interest is paid to the money lender for the portion of the capital furnished by him, which exactly agrees with the rent paid to the landlord; and the residue of that surplus constitutes the profit of the undertaker or manufacturer, and agrees with what is denominated the ordinary profits on the Stock of the farmer. Both together make the ordinary profits of two capitals [employed in a manufactory; as in the other case the rent of the landlord and the revenue of the farmer compose the ordinary profits of two Capitals] employed in the cultivation of a farm.

The rent therefore accruing to the proprietor of the land, far from being a criterion of *exclusive* productiveness, as has been argued, is no criterion even of superior productiveness. The question must still be, whether the surplus, after defraying expences, of a *given capital*, employed in the *purchase* and *improvement* of a piece of land, is greater or less, than that of a like capital employed in the prosecution of a manufactory: or whether the *whole value produced* from a *given capital* and a *given quantity of labour*, employed in one way, be greater or less, than the *whole value produced* from an *equal capital* and an *equal quantity of labour* employed in the other way: or rather, perhaps whether the business of Agriculture or that of Manufactures will yield the greatest product, according to a *compound ratio* of the quantity of the Capital and the quantity of labour, which are employed in the one or in the other.

The solution of either of these questions is not easy; it involves numerous and complicated details, depending on an accurate knowlege of the objects to be compared. It is not known that the comparison has ever yet been made upon sufficient data properly ascertained and analised. To be able to make it on the present occasion with satisfactory precision would demand more previous enquiry and investigation, than there has been hitherto either leisure or opportunity to accomplish.

Some essays however have been made towards acquiring the requisite information; [147] which have rather served to throw doubt upon,

147. See H to Benjamin Lincoln, January 25, 1790; circular letter of May 11, 1790, signed by Tench Coxe, quoted in H to Lincoln, January 25, 1790, note 4; "Treasury Department Circular to the Supervisors of the Revenue," June 22, 1791; and "Treasury Department Circular," August 13, 1791.
For examples of replies to H's requests for information from manufacturers, see Samuel Paterson to H, February 10, 1791; Nathaniel Hazard to H, March 9,

than to confirm the Hypothesis, under examination: But it ought to be acknowledged, that they have been too little diversified, and are too imperfect, to authorise a definitive conclusion either way; leading rather to probable conjecture than to certain deduction. They render it probable, that there are various branches of manufactures, in which a given Capital will yield a greater *total* product, and a considerably greater *nett* product, than an equal capital invested in the purchase and improvement of lands; [148] and that there are also *some* branches, in which both the *gross* and the *nett* produce will exceed that of Agricultural industry; according to a compound ratio of capital and labour: But it is on this last point, that there appears to be the greatest room for doubt. It is far less difficult to infer generally, that the *nett produce* of Capital engaged in manufacturing enterprises is greater than that of Capital engaged in Agriculture.

In stating these results, the purchase and improvement of lands, under previous cultivation are alone contemplated. The comparison is more in favour of Agriculture, when it is made with reference to the settlement of new and waste lands; but an argument drawn from so temporary a circumstance could have no weight in determining the general question concerning the permanent relative productiveness of the two species of industry. How far it ought to influence the policy of the United States, on the score of particular situation, will be adverted to in another place.

The foregoing suggestions are *not designed to inculcate an opinion that manufacturing industry is more productive than that of Agriculture.* They are intended rather to shew that the reverse of this proposition is not ascertained; that the general arguments which are brought to establish it are not satisfactory; and consequently that a supposition

---

1791; Samuel Breck to H, September 3, 1791; Daniel Stevens to H, September 3, 1791; George Cabot to H, September 6, 1791; Aaron Dunham to H, September 9, 1791; Edward Carrington to H, October 4, 8, 1791; John Chester to H, October 11, 1791; Nathaniel Gorham to H, October 13, 1791; and John Dexter to H, October, 1791.

For examples of replies concerning agriculture, see Richard Peters to H, August 27, 1791; Henry Wynkoop to H, August 29, 1791; Timothy Pickering to H, October 13, 1791; John Neville to H, October 27, 1791; and John Beale Bordley to H, November 11, 1791. See also *The Massachusetts Magazine,* II (July, 1790), 410–12; III (February, 1791), 110.

148. Richard Peters, in his answer to H's request for information, wrote: "Yet with all this I find Farming but a bad Trade when Capital is calculated upon. There are few Men of any Talents who cannot employ themselves in any other Business to greater advantage" (Peters to H, August 27, 1791).

of the superior productiveness of Tillage ought to be no obstacle to listening to any substantial inducements to the encouragement of manufactures, which may be otherwise perceived to exist, through an apprehension, that they may have a tendency to divert labour from a more to a less profitable employment.

It is extremely probable, that on a full and accurate devellopment of the matter, on the ground of fact and calculation, it would be discovered that there is no material difference between the aggregate productiveness of the one, and of the other kind of industry; and that the propriety of the encouragements, which may in any case be proposed to be given to either ought to be determined upon considerations irrelative to any comparison of that nature.

II   But without contending for the superior productiveness of Manufacturing Industry, it may conduce to a better judgment of the policy, which ought to be pursued respecting its encouragement, to contemplate the subject, under some additional aspects, tending not only to confirm the idea, that this kind of industry has been improperly represented as unproductive in itself; but [to] evince in addition that the establishment and diffusion of manufactures have the effect of rendering the total mass of useful and productive labor in a community, *greater than it would otherwise be*. In prosecuting this discussion, it may be necessary briefly to resume and review some of the topics, which have been already touched.

To affirm, that the labour of the Manufacturer is unproductive, because he consumes as much of the produce of land, as he adds value to the raw materials which he manufactures, is not better founded, than it would be to affirm, that the labour of the farmer, which furnishes materials to the manufacturer, is unproductive, *because he consumes an equal value of manufactured articles*. Each furnishes a certain portion of the produce of his labor to the other, and each destroys a correspondent portion of the produce of the labour of the other. In the mean time, the maintenance of two Citizens, instead of one, is going on; the State has two members instead of one; and they together consume twice the value of what is produced from the land.

If instead of a farmer and artificer, there were a farmer only, he would be under the necessity of devoting a part of his labour to the fabrication of cloathing and other articles, which he would procure of the artificer, in the case of there being such a person; and of course he would be able to devote less labor to the cultivation of his farm; and would draw from it a proportionably less product. The whole quantity of production, in this state of things, in provisions, raw materials and manufactures, would certainly not exceed in value the amount of what would be produced in provisions and raw materials only, if there were an artificer as well as a farmer.

Again—if there were both an artificer and a farmer, the latter would be left at liberty to pursue exclusively the cultivation of his farm. A greater quantity of provisions and raw materials would of course be produced—equal at least—as has been already observed, to the whole amount of the provisions, raw materials and manufactures, which would exist on a contrary supposition. The artificer, at the same time would be going on in the production of manufactured commodities; to an amount sufficient not only to repay the farmer, in those commodities, for the provisions and materials which were procured from him, but to furnish the Artificer himself with a supply of similar commodities for his own use. Thus then, there would be two quantities or values in existence, instead of one; and the revenue and consumption would be double in one case, what it would be in the other.[149]

If in place of both these suppositions, there were supposed to be two farmers, and no artificer, each of whom applied a part of his labour to the culture of land, and another part to the fabrication of Manufactures—in this case, the portion of the labour of both bestowed upon land would produce the same quantity of provisions

149. In the two preceding paragraphs H gives specific examples for a general Physiocratic view described by Smith as follows: "By means of the industry of merchants, artificers and manufacturers, the proprietors and cultivators can purchase both the foreign goods and the manufactured produce of their own country which they have occasion for, with the produce of a much smaller quantity of their own labour, than what they would be obliged to employ, if they were to attempt, in an aukward and unskilful manner, either to import the one, or to make the other for their own use. By means of the unproductive class, the cultivators are delivered from many cares which would otherwise distract their attention from the cultivation of land. The superiority of produce, which, in consequence of this undivided attention, they are enabled to raise, is fully sufficient to pay the whole expence which the maintenance and employment of the unproductive class costs either the proprietors, or themselves. The industry of merchants, artificers, and manufacturers, though in its own nature altogether unproductive, yet contributes in this manner indirectly to increase the produce of the land. It increases the productive powers of productive labour, by leaving it at liberty to confine itself to its proper employment, the cultivation of land . . ." (Smith, *Wealth of Nations*, II, 183).

and raw materials only, as would be produced by the intire sum of the labour of one applied in the same manner, and the portion of the labour of both bestowed upon manufactures, would produce the same quantity of manufactures only, as would be produced by the intire sum of the labour of one applied in the same manner. Hence the produce of the labour of the two farmers would not be greater than the produce of the labour of the farmer and artificer; and hence, it results, that the labour of the artificer is as possitively productive as that of the farmer, and, as positively, augments the revenue of the Society.

The labour of the Artificer replaces to the farmer that portion of his labour, with which he provides the materials of exchange with the Artificer, and which he would otherwise have been compelled to apply to manufactures: and while the Artificer thus enables the farmer to enlarge his stock of Agricultural industry, a portion of which he purchases for his own use, *he also supplies himself with the manufactured articles of which he stands in need.*

He does still more—Besides this equivalent which he gives for the portion of Agricultural labour consumed by him, and this supply of manufactured commodities for his own consumption—he furnishes still a surplus, which compensates for the use of the Capital advanced either by himself or some other person, for carrying on the business. This is the ordinary profit of the Stock employed in the manufactory, and is, in every sense, as effective an addition to the income of the Society, as the rent of land.

The produce of the labour of the Artificer consequently, may be regarded as composed of three parts; one by which the provisions for his subsistence and the materials for his work are purchased of the farmer, one by which he supplies himself with manufactured necessaries, and a third which constitutes the profit on the Stock employed. The two last portions seem to have been overlooked in the system, which represents manufacturing industry as barren and unproductive.

In the course of the preceding illustrations, the products of equal quantities of the labour of the farmer and artificer have been treated as if equal to each other. But this is not to be understood as intending to assert any such precise equality. It is merely a manner of expression adopted for the sake of simplicity and perspicuity. Whether the value of the produce of the labour of the farmer be somewhat more or less, than that of the artificer, is not material to the main scope of the argument, which hitherto has only aimed at shewing, that the one, as well as the other, occasions a possitive augmentation of the total produce and revenue of the Society.

It is now proper to proceed a step further, and to enumerate the principal circumstances, from which it may be inferred—That manufacturing establishments not only occasion a possitive augmentation of the Produce and Revenue of the Society, but that they contribute essentially to rendering them greater than they could possibly be, without such establishments.[150] These circumstances are—

1. The division of Labour.
2. An extension of the use of Machinery.
3. Additional employment to classes of the community not ordinarily engaged in the business.
4. The promoting of emigration from foreign Countries.
5. The furnishing greater scope for the diversity of talents and dispositions which discriminate men from each other.
6. The affording a more ample and various field for enterprize.
7. The creating in some instances a new, and securing in all, a more certain and steady demand for the surplus produce of the soil.

Each of these circumstances has a considerable influence upon the total mass of industrious effort in a community. Together, they add to it a degree of energy and effect, which are not easily conceived. Some comments upon each of them, in the order in which they have been stated, may serve to explain their importance.

I.   As to the Division of Labour.

It has justly been observed, that there is scarcely any thing of greater moment in the œconomy of a nation, than the proper division of labour. The seperation of occupations causes each to be carried to a much greater perfection, than it could possible acquire, if they were blended. This arises principally from three circumstances.

1st—The greater skill and dexterity naturally resulting from a constant and undivided application to a single object. It is evident, that these properties must increase, in proportion to the separation

150. In a criticism of Physiocratic theory Smith wrote: ". . . the revenue of a trading and manufacturing country must, other things being equal, always be much greater than that of one without trade or manufactures" (Smith, *Wealth of Nations*, II, 192).

and simplification of objects and the steadiness of the attention devoted to each; and must be less, in proportion to the complication of objects, and the number among which the attention is distracted.[151]

2nd. The œconomy of time—by avoiding the loss of it, incident to a frequent transition from one operation to another of a different nature. This depends on various circumstances—the transition itself— the orderly disposition of the impliments, machines and materials employed in the operation to be relinquished—the preparatory steps to the commencement of a new one—the interruption of the impulse, which the mind of the workman acquires, from being engaged in a particular operation—the distractions hesitations and reluctances, which attend the passage from one kind of business to another.[152]

3rd. An extension of the use of Machinery. A man occupied on a single object will have it more in his power, and will be more naturally led to exert his imagination in devising methods to facilitate and abrige labour, than if he were perplexed by a variety of independent and dissimilar operations. Besides this, the fabrication of Machines, in numerous instances, becoming itself a distinct trade, the Artist who follows it, has all the advantages which have been enumerated, for

151. In this section H is apparently paraphrasing the following statement by Smith:
"This great increase of the quantity of work, which, in consequence of the division of labour, the same number of people are capable of performing, is owing to three different circumstances; first, to the increase of dexterity in every particular workman; secondly, to the saving of the time which is commonly lost in passing from one species of work to another; and lastly, to the invention of a great number of machines which facilitate and abridge labour, and enable one man to do the work of many.
"First, the improvement of the dexterity of the workman necessarily increases the quantity of the work he can perform; and the division of labour, by reducing every man's business to some one simple operation, and by making this operation the sole employment of his life, necessarily increases very much the dexterity of the workman." (Smith, *Wealth of Nations*, I, 8–9.)
152. Compare H's remarks with the following statement by Smith: "Secondly, the advantage which is gained by saving the time commonly lost in passing from one sort of work to another, is much greater than we should at first view be apt to imagine it. It is impossible to pass very quickly from one kind of work to another, that is carried on in a different place, and with quite different tools. . . . A man commonly saunters a little in turning his hand from one sort of employment to another. . . . The habit of sauntering and of indolent careless application, which is naturally, or rather necessarily acquired by every country workman who is obliged to change his work and his tools every half hour, and to apply his hand in twenty different ways almost every day of his life; renders him almost always slothful and lazy, and incapable of any vigorous application even on the most pressing occasions" (Smith, *Wealth of Nations*, I, 9–10).

improvement in his particular art; and in both ways the invention and application of machinery are extended.[153]

And from these causes united, the mere separation of the occupation of the cultivator, from that of the Artificer, has the effect of augmenting the *productive powers* of labour, and with them, the total mass of the produce or revenue of a Country. In this single view of the subject, therefore, the utility of Artificers or Manufacturers, towards promoting an increase of productive industry, is apparent.[154]

II. As to an extension of the use of Machinery a point which though partly anticipated requires to be placed in one or two additional lights.

The employment of Machinery forms an item of great importance in the general mass of national industry. 'Tis an artificial force brought in aid of the natural force of man; and, to all the purposes of labour, is an increase of hands; an accession of strength, *unincumbered too by the expence of maintaining the laborer*.[155] May it not therefore be fairly inferred, that those occupations, which give greatest scope to the use of this auxiliary, contribute most to the general Stock of industrious effort, and, in consequence, to the general product of industry?

It shall be taken for granted, and the truth of the position referred

153. Smith wrote: "Thirdly, and lastly, every body must be sensible how much labour is facilitated and abridged by the application of proper machinery. . . . Men are much more likely to discover easier and readier methods of attaining any object, when the whole attention of their minds is directed towards that single object, than when it is dissipated among a great variety of things" (Smith, *Wealth of Nations*, I, 10).

Smith also wrote: "Many improvements have been made by the ingenuity of the makers of the machines, when to make them became the business of a peculiar trade . . ." (Smith, *Wealth of Nations*, I, 11).

154. Compare H's conclusion of this section devoted to the division of labor with the following statement by Smith: "The division of labour, however, so far as it can be introduced, occasions, in every art, a proportionable increase of the productive powers of labour. The separation of different trades and employments from one another, seems to have taken palce, in consequence of this advantage. . . . In every improved society, the farmer is generally nothing but a farmer; the manufacturer, nothing but a manufacturer" (Smith, *Wealth of Nations*, I, 7). See also note 149.

155. Among the works with which H had indicated an earlier acquaintance is Sir James Steuart's *Political Economy*. Steuart wrote: "As agriculture, exercised as a trade, purges the land of idle mouths, and pushes them to a new industry which the state may turn to her own advantage; so does a machine introduced into a manufacture, purge off hands which then become superfluous *in that branch*, and which may quickly be employed in another. . . . now the

to observation, that manufacturing pursuits are susceptible in a greater degree of the application of machinery, than those of Agriculture.[156] If so all the difference is lost to a community, which, instead of manufacturing for itself, procures the fabrics requisite to its supply from other Countries. The substitution of foreign for domestic manufactures is a transfer to foreign nations of the advantages accruing from the employment of Machinery, in the modes in which it is capable of being employed, with most utility and to the greatest extent.

The Cotton Mill invented in England, within the last twenty years, is a signal illustration of the general proposition, which has been just advanced. In consequence of it, all the different processes for spining Cotton are performed by means of Machines, which are put in motion by water, and attended chiefly by women and Children; [and by a smaller] number of [persons, in the whole, than are] requisite in the ordinary mode of spinning. And it is an advantage of great moment that the operations of this mill continue with convenience, during the night, as well as through the day. The prodigious affect of such a Machine is easily conceived. To this invention is to be attributed essentially the immense progress, which has been so suddenly made in Great Britain in the various fabrics of Cotton.[157]

III.   As to the additional employment of classes of the community, not ordinarily engaged in the particular business.

---

machine eats nothing, so does not diminish subsistence . . ." (Steuart, *Political Economy*, I, 122–23).

The interest shared by H and Tench Coxe in the utility of power-driven machines has been emphasized as one important point of similarity between the views of the two men. In a speech in 1787 Coxe said: "Factories, which can be carried on by watermills, windmills, fire, horses and machines ingeniously contrived, are not burdened with any heavy expence of boarding, lodging, cloathing and paying workmen, and they multiply the force of hands to a great extent without taking our people from agriculture" (Coxe, *Address*, 8).

156. See note 135.

157. The progress made by the British cotton textile industry despite the interruption of American demand had also been noted by Coxe. In the summer of 1791 Coxe wrote: "It is to be observed further, that the eight years which followed 1774, were those in which machinery was first rendered considerably profitable in Great Britain. Before the American war, the cotton branch was very inconsiderable in that country; but though it has increased wonderfully since the peace, it must have felt a very large advancement during the term in which our regular importations from thence were cut off. Other branches were aided during those years, by the introduction of machinery, manual flight, and new processes, so as to diminish the effects of the interruption of the American demand. . . . Such extraordinary *new* inventions of mechanical aid are not to be expected again . . ." (Coxe, *Brief Examination*, 108–09).

This is not among the least valuable of the means, by which manufacturing institutions contribute to augment the general stock of
industry and production. In places where those institutions prevail,
besides the persons regularly engaged in them, they afford occasional
and extra employment to industrious individuals and families, who
are willing to devote the leisure resulting from the intermissions of
their ordinary pursuits to collateral labours, as a resource of multiplying their acquisitions or [their] enjoyments. The husbandman
himself experiences a new source of profit and support from the encreased industry of his wife and daughters; invited and stimulated by
the demands of the neighboring manufactories.

Besides this advantage of occasional employment to classes having
different occupations, there is another of a nature allied to it [and] of
a similar tendency. This is—the employment of persons who would
otherwise be idle (and in many cases a burthen on the community),
either from the byass of temper, habit, infirmity of body, or some
other cause, indisposing, or disqualifying them for the toils of the
Country. It is worthy of particular remark, that, in general, women
and Children are rendered more useful and the latter more early useful by manufacturing establishments, than they would otherwise
be.[158] Of the number of persons employed in the Cotton Manufactories of Great Britain, it is computed that $\frac{4}{7}$ nearly are women and
children; of whom the greatest proportion are children and many of
them of a very tender age.

And thus it appears to be one of the attributes of manufactures, and
one of no small consequence, to give occasion to the exertion of a
greater quantity of Industry, even by the *same number* of persons,
where they happen to prevail, than would exist, if there were no such
establishments.

IV. As to the promoting of emigration from foreign Countries.
Men reluctantly quit one course of occupation and livelihood for

158. Advocacy of child labor and the industrial employment of women was,
of course, common in the eighteenth century in Europe and America. For
representative statements of Americans with which H was presumably familiar,
see *The American Museum*, II (September, 1787), 257; V (March, 1789), 256;
V (June, 1789), 584; VII (January, 1790), 25.
See also Moses Brown to John Dexter, July 22–October 15, 1791, and "Report
of a Committee Appointed to Obtain Information on Manufacturing in
Providence," October 10, 1791, both printed as enclosures to John Dexter to H,
October, 1791.

another, unless invited to it by very apparent and proximate advantages. Many, who would go from one country to another, if they had a prospect of continuing with more benefit the callings, to which they have been educated, will often not be tempted to change their situation, by the hope of doing better, in some other way. Manufacturers, who listening to the powerful invitations of a better price for their fabrics, or their labour, of greater cheapness of provisions and raw materials, of an exemption from the chief part of the taxes burthens and restraints, which they endure in the old world, of greater personal independence and consequence, under the operation of a more equal government, and of what is far more precious than mere religious toleration—a perfect equality of religious privileges; would probably flock from Europe to the United States to pursue their own trades or professions, if they were once made sensible of the advantages they would enjoy, and were inspired with an assurance of encouragement and employment, will, with difficulty, be induced to transplant themselves, with a view to becoming Cultivators of Land.

If it be true then, that it is the interest of the United States to open every possible [avenue to] emigration from abroad, it affords a weighty argument for the encouragement of manufactures; which for the reasons just assigned, will have the strongest tendency to multiply the inducements to it.

Here is perceived an important resource, not only for extending the population, and with it the useful and productive labour of the country, but likewise for the prosecution of manufactures, without deducting from the number of hands, which might otherwise be drawn to tillage; and even for the indemnification of Agriculture for such as might happen to be diverted from it. Many, whom Manufacturing views would induce to emigrate, would afterwards yield to the temptations, which the particular situation of this Country holds out to Agricultural pursuits. And while Agriculture would in other respects derive many signal and unmingled advantages, from the growth of manufactures, it is a problem whether it would gain or lose, as to the article of the number of persons employed in carrying it on.

V. As to the furnishing greater scope for the diversity of talents and dispositions, which discriminate men from each other.

This is a much more powerful mean of augmenting the fund of

national Industry than may at first sight appear. It is a just observation, that minds of the strongest and most active powers for their proper objects fall below mediocrity and labour without effect, if confined to uncongenial pursuits. And it is thence to be inferred, that the results of human exertion may be immensely increased by diversifying its objects.[159] When all the different kinds of industry obtain in a community, each individual can find his proper element, and can call into activity the whole vigour of his nature. And the community is benefitted by the services of its respective members, in the manner, in which each can serve it with most effect.[160]

159. In another connection Smith wrote: ". . . the understandings of the greater part of men are necessarily formed by their ordinary employments. The man whose whole life is spent in performing a few simple operations, of which the effects too are, perhaps, always the same, or very nearly the same, has no occasion to exert his understanding, or to exercise his invention in finding out expedients for removing difficulties which never occur. He naturally loses, therefore, the habit of such exertion, and generally becomes as stupid and ignorant as it is possible for a human creature to become" (Smith, *Wealth of Nations*, II, 298).

In "Of Luxury" Hume wrote: "In times, when industry and arts flourish, men are kept in perpetual occupation, and enjoy, as their reward, the occupation itself, as well as those pleasures, which are the fruits of their labour. The mind acquires new vigour; enlarges its powers and faculties; and by an assiduity in honest industry, both satisfies its natural appetites, and prevents the growth of unnatural ones, which commonly spring up, when nourish'd with ease and idleness" (Hume, *Political Discourses*, 25–26).

Observations similar to those made by H may be found in *The American Museum*, V (June, 1789), 584; *Columbian Magazine*, III (March, 1789), 177–78; III (May, 1789), 295; III (June, 1789), 349.

160. In connection with the division of labor Smith wrote: "And thus the certainty of being able to exchange all that surplus part of the produce of his own labour, which is over and above his own consumption, for such parts of the produce of other men's labour as he may have occasion for, encourages every man to apply himself to a particular occupation, and to cultivate and bring to perfection whatever talent or genius he may possess for that particular species of business. . . . The effects of those different geniuses and talents, for want of the power or disposition to barter and exchange, cannot be brought into a common stock, and do not in the least contribute to the better accommodation and conveniency of the species. . . . Among men, on the contrary, the most dissimilar geniuses are of use to one another; the different produces of their respective talents, by the general disposition to truck, barter, and exchange, being brought, as it were, into a common stock, where every man may purchase whatever part of the produce of other men's talents he has occasion for" (Smith, *Wealth of Nations*, I, 16–17).

Smith also wrote: "The difference of natural talents in different men is, in reality, much less than we are aware of; and the very different genius which appears to distinguish men of different professions, when grown up to maturity, is not upon many occasions so much the cause, as the effect of the division of labour" (Smith, *Wealth of Nations*, I, 16).

If there be anything in a remark often to be met with—namely that there is, in the genius of the people of this country, a peculiar aptitude for mechanic improvements, it would operate as a forcible reason for giving opportunities to the exercise of that species of talent, by the propagation of manufactures.

VI. As to the affording a more ample and various field for enterprise.

This also is of greater consequence in the general scale of national exertion, than might perhaps on a superficial view be supposed, and has effects not altogether dissimilar from those of the circumstance last noticed. To cherish and stimulate the activity of the human mind, by multiplying the objects of enterprise, is not among the least considerable of the expedients, by which the wealth of a nation may be promoted. Even things in themselves not positively advantageous, sometimes become so, by their tendency to provoke exertion. Every new scene, which is opened to the busy nature of man to rouse and exert itself, is the addition of a new energy to the general stock of effort.

The spirit of enterprise, useful and prolific as it is, must necessarily be contracted or expanded in proportion to the simplicity or variety of the occupations and productions, which are to be found in a Society. It must be less in a nation of mere cultivators, than in a nation of cultivators and merchants; less in a nation of cultivators and merchants, than in a nation of cultivators, artificers and merchants.

VII. As to the creating, in some instances, a new, and securing in all a more certain and steady demand, for the surplus produce of the soil.[161]

161. Steuart expressed a view similar to that of H when he wrote: "The proper and only right encouragement for agriculture, is a moderate and gradual increase of demand for the productions of the earth . . ." (Steuart, *Political Economy*, I, 54).

According to Smith, the first way in which towns contributed to the improvement and cultivation of land was "by affording a great and ready market for the rude produce of the country, they gave encouragement to its cultivation and further improvement" (Smith, *Wealth of Nations*, I, 405).

Hume discussed the effect of a limited market on agriculture in the following manner: "Where manufactures and mechanic arts are not cultivated, the bulk of the people must apply themselves to agriculture; and if their skill and industry increase, there must arise a great superfluity from their labour beyond what suffices to maintain them. They have no temptation, therefore, to increase their skill and industry; since they cannot exchange that superfluity for any commodities, which may serve either to their pleasure or vanity. A habit of indolence

This is among the most important of the circumstances which have been indicated. It is a principal mean, by which the establishment of manufactures contributes to an augmentation of the produce or revenue of a country, and has an immediate and direct relation to the prosperity of Agriculture.

It is evident, that the exertions of the husbandman will be steady or fluctuating, vigorous or feeble, in proportion to the steadiness or fluctuation, adequateness, or inadequateness of the markets on which he must depend, for the vent of the surplus, which may be produced by his labour; and that such surplus in the ordinary course of things will be greater or less in the same proportion.

For the purpose of this vent, a domestic market is greatly to be preferred to a foreign one; because it is in the nature of things, far more to be relied upon.

It is a primary object of the policy of nations, to be able to supply themselves with subsistence from their own soils; and manufacturing nations, as far as circumstances permit, endeavor to procure, from the same source, the raw materials necessary for their own fabrics. This disposition, urged by the spirit of monopoly, is sometimes even carried to an injudicious extreme. It seems not always to be recollected, that nations, who have neither mines nor manufactures, can only

---

naturally prevails. The greater part of the land lyes uncultivated. What is cultivated, yields not its utmost, for want of skill or assiduity in the farmers" (Hume, *Political Discourses*, 11). See also Hume, *Political Discourses*, 12, 209.

Necker gave preference to the home market for reasons similar to those expressed by H when he wrote:

"J'oppose à ce raisonnement, que l'échange des bleds contre l'industrie nationale, est beaucoup plus sûr et plus encourageant pour les propriétaires, que l'échange de ces mêmes denreés contre les productions des autres pays. . . .

"Cet échange des subsistances dans l'intérieur d'un État, est aussi beaucoup plus sûr; car la nourriture des hommes étant fixée par la nature, le besoin des bleds est nécessairement limité; ainsi, les propriétaires François ne pourroient convertir leurs grains superflus dans d'autres richesses, par la voie de l'exportation, qu'autant qu'il y auroit disette dans les pays étrangers, et dès-lors ce commerce seroit incertain; au lieu que l'échange de ces denrées est constamment assuré, lorsque le même Royaume qui les a produites, abonde en ouvriers, en fabriquans et en artistes de toute espece." (Necker, *Œuvres*, IV, 31-32.)

Examples of statements by Americans of a preference for a domestic market as a market less subject to the fluctuations introduced by foreign wars, foreign commercial policies, and irregular foreign harvests may be found in *The American Museum*, II (October, 1787), 361; *Columbian Magazine*, I (September, 1786), 27; VI (May, 1791), 295; [Philadelphia] *Gazette of the United States*, September 7, 1791; Barton, *The True Interest*, 26. See also H to Benjamin Goodhue, June 30, 1791.

obtain the manufactured articles, of which they stand in need, by
an exchange of the products of their soils; and that, if those who can
best furnish them with such articles are unwilling to give a due course
to this exchange, they must of necessity make every possible effort
to manufacture for themselves, the effect of which is that the manufacturing nations abrige the natural advantages of their situation,
through an unwillingness to permit the Agricultural countries to
enjoy the advantages of theirs, and sacrifice the interests of a mutually
beneficial intercourse to the vain project of *selling every thing* and
*buying nothing.* [162]

But it is also a consequence of the policy, which has been noted,
that the foreign demand for the products of Agricultural Countries, is,
in a great degree, rather casual and occasional, than certain or constant. To what extent injurious interruptions of the demand for some
of the staple commodities of the United States, may have been experienced, from that cause, must be referred to the judgment of those
who are engaged in carrying on the commerce of the country; but it
may be safely assumed, that such interruptions are at times very
inconveniently felt, and that cases not unfrequently occur, in which
markets are so confined and restricted, as to render the demand very
unequal to the supply.

Independently likewise of the artificial impediments, which are
created by the policy in question, there are natural causes tending to
render the external demand for the surplus of Agricultural nations a
precarious reliance. The differences of seasons, in the countries, which

---

162. ". . . nations, whose politicians now grudgingly perceive them take from
us the food they are unable to raise, and who treat as a favour the reception of
our precious raw materials, may discover, when it is too late, the evils induced
by an over-driven spirit of monopoly." (Coxe, *Brief Examination*, 85.)

"For each, led on by a blind ambition, has wished to embrace every thing, to
do every thing at home, and furnish every thing to others; each has taken for
principle to receive nothing from others, except it be gold; each has accustomed
itself to look upon every production, manufactured or unmanufactured, which
it sent abroad as a profit, and all those which it received, as so many losses.
Such is the false principle, according to which, all the European nations have
directed their exterior commerce." (Clavière, *Considerations on America*, 270.)

"Exportation, is that part of foreign commerce, which is distinguished by the
active, or selling part, in opposition to importation, which is called the passive,
or buying part. And, although mutual intercourses of trade cannot be supposed
to be carried on with other nations by selling, or exporting all, and buying or
importing no merchandizes from others; yet that nation is certainly the wisest,
that so conducts it's affairs, as to sell more to other nations than it buys of
them. . . ." (Postlethwayt, *Universal Dictionary*, I, 758.)

are the consumers make immense differences in the produce of their own soils, in different years; and consequently in the degrees of their necessity for foreign supply. Plentiful harvests with them, especially if similar ones occur at the same time in the countries, which are the furnishers, occasion of course a glut in the markets of the latter.

Considering how fast and how much the progress of new settlements in the United States must increase the surplus produce of the soil, and weighing seriously the tendency of the system, which prevails among most of the commercial nations of Europe; whatever dependence may be placed on the force of natural circumstances to counteract the effects of an artificial policy; there appear strong reasons to regard the foreign demand for that surplus as too uncertain a reliance, and to desire a substitute for it, in an extensive domestic market.

To secure such a market, there is no other expedient, than to promote manufacturing establishments. Manufacturers who constitute the most numerous class, after the Cultivators of land, are for that reason the principal consumers of the surplus of their labour.[163]

This idea of an extensive domestic market for the surplus produce of the soil is of the first consequence. It is of all things, that which most effectually conduces to a flourishing state of Agriculture. If the effect of manufactories should be to detatch a portion of the hands, which would otherwise be engaged in Tillage, it might possibly cause a smaller quantity of lands to be under cultivation but by their tendency to procure a more certain demand for the surplus produce of the soil, they would, at the same time, cause the lands which were in cultivation to be better improved and more productive. And while,

163. Similar views had been expressed by Necker when he wrote:
". . . la variété des établissemens d'industrie sera l'unique moyen d'exciter les possesseurs de vastes domaines à perfectionner la culture, et d'admettre la multitude au partage des fruits de la terre." (Necker, Œuvres, IV, 35.)

"C'est ici qu'on découvre le service important que rendent les métiers, les arts et les manufactures; ils augmentent la population, en arrêtant sans contrainte les excédens de subsistances que les propriétaires tiennent dans leurs mains, et dont ils ont le droit de disposer à leur gré." (Necker, Œuvres, III, 198.)

Many Americans interested in manufacturing agreed with H on this point. One writer commented: "If there be any among you, who suppose that the interests of agriculture will be injured by an attention to manufactures, they should recollect, that a constant demand for the productions of our lands, cannot be secured, without manufacturing towns to consume them . . ." (The American Museum, II [October, 1787], 361). See also Columbian Magazine, VII (October, 1791), 285.

by their influence, the condition of each individual farmer would be meliorated, the total mass of Agricultural production would probably be increased. For this must evidently depend as much, if not more, upon the degree of improvement; than upon the number of acres under culture.[164]

It merits particular observation, that the multiplication of manufactories not only furnishes a Market for those articles, which have been accustomed to be produced in abundance, in a country; but it likewise creates a demand for such as were either unknown or produced in inconsiderable quantities. The bowels as well as the surface of the earth are ransacked for articles which were before neglected. Animals, Plants and Minerals acquire an utility and value, which were before unexplored.[165]

The foregoing considerations seem sufficient to establish, as general propositions, That it is the interest of nations to diversify the industrious pursuits of the individuals, who compose them [166]—That the

164. Steuart and H agreed on this point. On one occasion Steuart wrote: ". . . when the earth is not improved it cannot produce so much nourishment for man as when it is. . . . if industry does not draw into the hands of the indigent, wherewith to purchase this additional nourishment, no body will be at a considerable first expence to break up grounds in order to produce it. The withdrawing therefore a number of hands from a trifling agriculture forces, in a manner, the husbandman to work the harder; and by hard labour upon a small spot, the same effect is produced as with slight labour upon a great extent" (Steuart, *Political Economy*, I, 105). Steuart also wrote: "The natural and necessary effect of industry, in trades and manufactures, is to promote the increase of relative husbandry; which, by augmenting the surplus, tends of course to increase the proportion of the free hands relatively to the farmers" (Steuart, *Political Economy*, I, 132).

165. Tench Coxe expressed a similar belief when he wrote: ". . . [Manufacturing] will consume our native productions now encreasing to super-abundance—it will improve our agriculture and teach us to explore the fossil and vegetable kingdoms, into which few researches have heretofore been made. . ." (Coxe, *Address*, 29).

The idea expressed by H in this paragraph had also been stated in American periodicals. For example, one writer stated: "The carrying on of manufactures increases the consumption, the demand, and the value of our produce in general; but especially of a great variety of our raw materials. . ." (*The American Museum*, VII [January, 1790], 24). See also *The American Museum*, VII (June, 1790), 286.

166. Necker stressed the importance of diversifying industry in several parts of his works. For example, he wrote:

"Il résulte de ces observations, que l'étendue et la variété de l'industrie nationale sont le premier des encouragemens qu'on puisse présenter à l'agriculture. . . ." (Necker, *Œuvres*, IV, 32.)

"Ainsi les progrès de l'agriculture rameneront toujours à l'augmentation de l'in-

establishment of manufactures is calculated not only to increase the general stock of useful and productive labour; but even to improve the state of Agriculture in particular; certainly to advance the interests of those who are engaged in it.[167] There are other views, that will be hereafter taken of the subject, which, it is conceived, will serve to confirm these inferences.

III Previously to a further discussion of the objections to the encouragement of manufactures which have been stated, it will be of use to see what can be said, in reference to the particular situation of the United States, against the conclusions appearing to result from what has been already offered.

It may be observed, and the idea is of no inconsiderable weight, that however true it might be, that a State, which possessing large tracts of vacant and fertile territory, was at the same time secluded from foreign commerce, would find its interest and the interest of Agriculture, in diverting a part of its population from Tillage to Manufactures; yet it will not follow, that the same is true of a State, which having such vacant and fertile territory, has at the same time ample opportunity of procuring from abroad, on good terms, all the fabrics of which it stands in need, for the supply of its inhabitants. The power of doing this at least secures the great advantage of a division of labour; leaving the farmer free to pursue exclusively the culture of his land, and enabling him to procure with its products the

---

dustrie, et la variété de celle-ci servira d'encouragement aux travaux de la terre." (Necker, Œuvres, IV, 34.)

". . . ainsi les institutions qui entretiennent à un taux modéré le prix de la main-d'œuvre, qui accroissent et diversifient l'industrie nationale, sont la meilleure et la moins dispendieuse de toutes les sauvegardes contre la concurrence étrangère." (Necker, Œuvres, IV, 89.)

Postlethwayt discussed the views of a promoter of the useful arts who made "the prosperity of a trading nation to consist in the multiplying of the number of new trades; that is to say, in the multiplying of the different species of mechanics, artificers, and manufacturers: for want of this it is, that all the old ways of gain become overstocked, as has been observed, and then people complain for want of trade, when the true cause is owing to the want of art, or to the want of the invention of a number of new trades and new arts, in proportion to the increase of people among ourselves, and in proportion as other rival states strike into the like trades and arts which we have been long used to" (Postlethwayt, Universal Dictionary, I, 118).

167. Coxe had made a particular point of the benefit which the landed interest would derive from the development of manufactures. In this connection he said: "I cannot conclude this address, gentlemen, without taking notice of *the very favorable and prodigious effects upon the landed interest*, which may result from manufactures" (Coxe, Address, 25).

manufactured supplies requisite either to his wants or to his enjoyments. And though it should be true, that in settled countries, the diversification of Industry is conducive to an increase in the productive powers of labour, and to an augmentation of revenue and capital; yet it is scarcely conceivable that there can be any [thing] of so solid and permanent advantage to an uncultivated and unpeopled country as to convert its wastes into cultivated and inhabited districts.[168] If the Revenue, in the mean time, should be less, the Capital, in the event, must be greater.

To these observations, the following appears to be a satisfactory answer—

1.   If the system of perfect liberty to industry and commerce were the prevailing system of nations—the arguments which dissuade a country in the predicament of the United States, from the zealous pursuits of manufactures would doubtless have great force. It will not be affirmed, that they might not be permitted, with few exceptions, to serve as a rule of national conduct. In such a state of things, each country would have the full benefit of its peculiar advantages to compensate for its deficiencies or disadvantages. If one nation were in condition to supply manufactured articles on better terms than another, that other might find an abundant indemnification in a superior capacity to furnish the produce of the soil. And a free exchange, mutually beneficial, of the commodities which each was able to supply, on the best terms, might be carried on between them, supporting in full vigour the industry of each. And though the circumstances which have been mentioned and others, which will be unfolded hereafter render it probable, that nations merely Agricultural would not enjoy the same degree of opulence, in proportion to their numbers, as those which united manufactures with agriculture; yet the progressive improvement of the lands of the former might, in the end, atone for an inferior degree of opulence in the mean time: and in a case in which opposite considerations are pretty equally balanced, the option ought perhaps always to be, in favour of leaving Industry to its own direction.

But the system which has been mentioned, is far from characterising the general policy of Nations. [The prevalent one has been regulated by an opposite spirit.]

168. See note 127.

The consequence of it is, that the United States are to a certain extent in the situation of a country precluded from foreign Commerce. They can indeed, without difficulty obtain from abroad the manufactured supplies, of which they are in want; but they experience numerous and very injurious impediments to the emission and vent of their own commodities. Nor is this the case in reference to a single foreign nation only. The regulations of several countries, with which we have the most extensive intercourse, throw serious obstructions in the way of the principal staples of the United States.

In such a position of things, the United States cannot exchange with Europe on equal terms; and the want of reciprocity would render them the victim of a system, which should induce them to confine their views to Agriculture and refrain from Manufactures. A constant and encreasing necessity, on their part, for the commodities of Europe, and only a partial and occasional demand for their own, in return, could not but expose them to a state of impoverishment, compared with the opulence to which their political and natural advantages authorise them to aspire.[169]

169. Impediments to the institution of free trade policies, which H discusses in this and the three preceding paragraphs, had been discused by several writers. Although Smith was critical of the corn laws, which he compared to laws of religion, he also wrote in their defense: "Were all nations to follow the liberal system of free exportation and free importation, the different states into which a great continent was divided would so far resemble the different provinces of a great empire. . . . But very few countries have entirely adopted this liberal system. . . . The very bad policy of one country may thus render it in some measure dangerous and imprudent to establish what would otherwise be the best policy in another" (Smith, *Wealth of Nations*, II, 38).

The following statements by Necker should also be noted:

"Une académie distinguée avoit proposé pour question, il y a quelque tems, d'examiner quel seroit l'effet de l'abolition des loix prohibitives à l'égard de la nation que les abrogeroit la premiere. . . .

"Une société qui laisseroit entrer toutes les productions de l'industrie étrangere, tandis que les autres nations continueroient à interdire l'introduction des siennes, seroit peu-à-peu obligée de payer, en subsistances ou en argent, ce qu'elle demanderoit aux étrangers; bientôt ses richesses et sa population diminueroient. Ce que nous venons de dire, dans une hypothese absolue, telle que l'interdiction totale des marchandises d'un pays, jointe à la libre introduction dans ce même pays de toutes les marchandises étrangeres, s'appliqueroit proportionnellement aux hypotheses mixtes et tempérées." (Necker, *Œuvres*, III, 260–61.)

"Un pays ne peut acheter qu'autant qu'on reçoit ses propres richesses en paiement; ainsi refuser d'acheter de lui, c'est refuser de lui vendre, c'est détruire le commerce." (Necker, *Œuvres*, III, 259.)

"Doubtless if all other nations, by a general compact, would agree to abolish all prohibitions, and all import duties, France ought not to refuse to accede; for it is probable that she would be a gainer by such a convention. However, she

Remarks of this kind are not made in the spirit of complaint. 'Tis for the nations, whose regulations are alluded to, to judge for themselves, whether, by aiming at too much they do not lose more than they gain.[170] 'Tis for the United States to consider by what means they can render themselves least dependent, on the combinations, right or wrong of foreign policy.

It is no small consolation, that already the measures which have embarrassed our Trade, have accelerated internal improvements, which upon the whole have bettered our affairs. To diversify and extend these improvements is the surest and safest method of indemnifying ourselves for any inconveniences, which those or similar measures have a tendency to beget. If Europe will not take from us the

---

would still have occasion to reflect upon it maturely, if either the increase of the public burthens should sensibly raise the price of labour, or if an industrious nation should spring up in the midst of a fertile country, free from those taxes which wars and the luxury of modern governments have introduced into Europe. But all those hypotheses which are founded upon a general freedom of commerce, are chimerical propositions; the powers who would lose by this freedom would never adopt it, and those who would gain by it, might in vain desire it; however, that power which should wish to introduce it, by setting the example, would imitate the folly of a private individual, who in the hope of establishing a community of effects, suffered all his neighbours to share his patrimony." (Necker, *Finances of France*, II, 192.)

This point of view did not disappear in France with Necker's resignation. See, for example, Gaspard Joseph Amand Ducher, *Analyse des Loix Commerciales, Avec le Tarif des Droits sur les Batiments & les Marchandises dans les Treize Etats Unis de l'Amerique* (n.p., n.d.).

The difficulties in the way of inaugurating free trade policies were also appreciated by many Americans. On April 9, 1789, Madison in a speech in Congress said:

"If my general principle is a good one, that commerce ought to be free, and labor and industry left at large to find its proper object, the only thing which remains will be to discover the exceptions that do not come within the rule I have laid down. . . . Although the freedom of commerce would be advantageous to the world, yet, in some particulars, one nation might suffer to benefit others, and this ought to be for the general good of society.

"If America was to leave her ports perfectly free, and make no discrimination between vessels owned by her citizens and those owned by foreigners, while other nations make this discrimination, it is obvious that such policy would go to exclude American shipping altogether from foreign ports, and she would be materially affected in one of her most important interests." (*Annals of Congress*, I, 117.)

For the viewpoint of many American merchants on this subject, see the article by Charles Pettit in *The American Museum*, VIII (July, 1790), 28.

170. On this problem Smith wrote:

"But if foreigners, either by prohibitions or high duties, are hindered from coming to sell, they cannot always afford to come to buy; because coming without a cargo, they must lose the freight from their own country to Great

products of our soil, upon terms consistent with our interest, the natural remedy is to contract as fast as possible our wants of her.

2. The conversion of their waste into cultivated lands is certainly a point of great moment in the political calculations of the United States. But the degree in which this may possibly be retarded by the encouragement of manufactories does not appear to countervail the powerful inducements to affording that encouragement.[171]

An observation made in another place is of a nature to have great influence upon this question. If it cannot be denied, that the interests even of Agriculture may be advanced more by having such of the lands of a state as are occupied under good cultivation, than by having a greater quantity occupied under a much inferior cultivation, and if Manufactories, for the reasons assigned, must be admitted to have a tendency to promote a more steady and vigorous cultivation of the lands occupied than would happen without them—it will follow, that they are capable of indemnifying a country for a diminution of the progress of new settlements; and may serve to increase both the capital [value] and the income of its lands, even though they should abrige the number of acres under Tillage.

But it does, by no means, follow, that the progress of new settlements would be retarded by the extension of Manufactures. The desire of being an independent proprietor of land is founded on such strong principles in the human breast, that where the opportunity of becoming so is as great as it is in the United States, the proportion will be small of those, whose situations would otherwise lead to it,

---

Britain. By diminishing the number of sellers, therefore, we necessarily diminish that of buyers, and are thus likely not only to buy foreign goods dearer, but to sell our own cheaper, than if there was a more perfect freedom of trade." (Smith, *Wealth of Nations*, I, 456.)

"Even the regulations by which each nation endeavours to secure to itself the exclusive trade of its own colonies, are frequently more hurtful to the countries in favour of which they are established than to those against which they are established. The unjust oppression of the industry of other countries falls back, if I may say so, upon the heads of the oppressors, and crushes their industry more than it does that of those other countries." (Smith, *Wealth of Nations*, II, 136.)

171. The importance of cultivating wasteland had been suggested by Smith, (see note 127) and also by many Americans. For example, one writer stated: ". . . the opposers of American manufactures may perhaps, object,—that, as we have large tracts of unsettled country, it would be more for the national benefit, that the people should be employed in cultivating the unimproved lands, than in manufacturing goods. . ." (*Columbian Magazine*, I [February, 1787], 282). See also *The American Museum*, II (October, 1787), 331.

who would be diverted from it towards Manufactures. And it is highly probable, as already intimated, that the accessions of foreigners, who originally drawn over by manufacturing views would afterwards abandon them for Agricultural, would be more than equivalent for those of our own Citizens, who might happen to be detached from them.

The remaining objections to a particular encouragement of manufactures in the United States now require to be examined.

One of these turns on the proposition, that Industry, if left to itself, will naturally find its way to the most useful and profitable employment: whence it is inferred, that manufactures without the aid of government will grow up as soon and as fast, as the natural state of things and the interest of the community may require.[172]

Against the solidity of this hypothesis, in the full latitude of the terms, very cogent reasons may be offered. These have relation to—the strong influence of habit and the spirit of imitation—the fear of want of success in untried enterprises—the intrinsic difficulties incident to first essays towards a competition with those who have previously attained to perfection in the business to be attempted—the bounties premiums and other artificial encouragements, with which foreign nations second the exertions of their own Citizens in the branches, in which they are to be rivalled.

Experience teaches, that men are often so much governed by what they are accustomed to see and practice, that the simplest and most obvious improvements, in the [most] ordinary occupations, are adopted with hesitation, reluctance and by slow gradations. The spontaneous transition to new pursuits, in a community long habituated to different ones, may be expected to be attended with proportionably greater difficulty. When former occupations ceased to yield a profit adequate to the subsistence of their followers, or when there was an

172. This objection to the encouragement of manufactures was, of course, stated most forcibly by Adam Smith, who wrote: "As every individual, therefore, endeavours as much as he can both to employ his capital in the support of domestic industry, and so to direct that industry that its produce may be of the greatest value; every individual necessarily labours to render the annual revenue of the society as great as he can. . . . By preferring the support of domestic to that of foreign industry he intends only his own security; and by directing that industry in such a manner as its produce may be of the greatest value, he intends only his own gain, and he is in this, as in many other cases, led by an invisible hand to promote an end which was no part of his intention" (Smith, *Wealth of Nations*, I, 447).

absolute deficiency of employment in them, owing to the superabundance of hands, changes would ensue; but these changes would be likely to be more tardy than might consist with the interest either of individuals or of the Society. In many cases they would not happen, while a bare support could be ensured by an adherence to ancient courses; though a resort to a more profitable employment might be practicable. To produce the desireable changes, as early as may be expedient, may therefore require the incitement and patronage of government.[173]

The apprehension of failing in new attempts is perhaps a more serious impediment. There are dispositions apt to be attracted by the mere novelty of an undertaking—but these are not always those best calculated to give it success. To this, it is of importance that the confidence of cautious sagacious capitalists both citizens and foreigners, should be excited. And to inspire this description of persons with confidence, it is essential, that they should be made to see in any project, which is new, and for that reason alone, if, for no other, precarious, the prospect of such a degree of countenance and support from government, as may be capable of overcoming the obstacles, inseperable from first experiments.[174]

173. In *A Treatise of Human Nature* Hume wrote: "By degrees the repetition produces a facility, which is another very powerful principle of the human mind, and an infallible source of pleasure, where the facility goes not beyond a certain degree. . . . But custom not only gives a facility to perform any action, but likewise an inclination and tendency towards it, where it is not entirely disagreeable, and can never be the object of inclination" (David Hume, *A Treatise of Human Nature: Being An Attempt to introduce the experimental Method of Reasoning Into Moral Subjects. Book II. Of The Passions* [London: Printed for John Noon, at the White-Hart, near Mercer's-Chapel, in Cheapside, 1739], 423–24).

In opposing free trade Necker emphasized the need for the central direction of a national economy in the following fashion: "Les hommes sont tellement gouvernés par l'habitude, qu'une nation industrieuse peut méconnoître long-tems ses forces, et faire un trafic continuel de ses grains contre les manufactures étrangeres, tandis qu'avec quelques efforts ou quelques privations momentanées, elle parviendroit à établir chez elle ces mêmes manufactures, et satisferoit ainsi le goût de ses propriétaires sans nuire à sa population" (Necker, *Œuvres*, IV, 36).

Again, in a discussion of Colbert's policies Necker wrote: "Nous voyons encore des nations agricoles échanger leurs bleds . . . contre des travaux qu'elles pourroient encourager chez elles . . . car l'habitude la plus déraisonnable et la plus stupide a souvent besoin d'être rompue par un administrateur éclairé . . ." (Necker, *Œuvres*, III, 205).

Steuart was also concerned with the role of habit and emphasized it as a limiting condition of economic growth (Steuart, *Political Economy*, I, 117–18).

174. The need for government encouragement of fledgling industries had been stressed by many Americans who were interested in domestic manufac-

The superiority antecedently enjoyed by nations, who have pre-occupied and perfected a branch of industry, constitutes a more formidable obstacle, than either of those, which have been mentioned, to the introduction of the same branch into a country, in which it did not before exist. To maintain between the recent establishments of one country and the long matured establishments of another country, a competition upon equal terms, both as to quality and price, is in most cases impracticable. The disparity in the one, or in the other, or in both, must necessarily be so considerable as to forbid a successful rivalship, without the extraordinary aid and protection of government.[175]

But the greatest obstacle of all to the successful prosecution of a new branch of industry in a country, in which it was before unknown, consists, as far as the instances apply, in the bounties premiums and other aids which are granted, in a variety of cases, by the nations, in which the establishments to be imitated are previously introduced. It is well known (and particular examples in the course of this report will be cited) that certain nations grant bounties on the exportation of particular commodities, to enable their own workmen to undersell and supplant all competitors, in the countries to which those commodities are sent. Hence the undertakers of a new manufacture have to contend not only with the natural disadvantages of a new undertaking, but with the gratuities and remunerations which other governments bestow. To be enabled to contend with success, it is evident, that the interference and aid of their own government are indispensible.

Combinations by those engaged in a particular branch of business in one country, to frustrate the first efforts to introduce it into another,

---

tures. For example, see [Philadelphia] *National Gazette,* November 24, 1791; *Annals of Congress,* I, 121. See also Moses Brown to John Dexter, July 22–October 15, 1791, printed as an enclosure to Dexter to H, October, 1791.

175. In opposing this view, Smith wrote: "Whether the advantages which one country has over another, be natural or acquired, is in this respect of no consequence. As long as the one country has those advantages, and the other wants them, it will always be more advantageous for the latter, rather to buy of the former than to make. It is an acquired advantage only, which one artificer has over his neighbour, who exercises another trade; and yet they both find it more advantageous to buy of one another, than to make what does not belong to their particular trades" (Smith, *Wealth of Nations,* I, 450).

Steuart considers the problem of new nations entering into foreign trade in Book II (Steuart, *Political Economy,* I, 285, 298–99, 301–05).

by temporary sacrifices, recompensed perhaps by extraordinary indemnifications of the government of such country, are believed to have existed, and are not to be regarded as destitute of probability.[176] The existence or assurance of aid from the government of the country, in which the business is to be introduced, may be essential to fortify adventurers against the dread of such combinations, to defeat their effects, if formed and to prevent their being formed, by demonstrating that they must in the end prove fruitless.

Whatever room there may be for an expectation that the industry of a people, under the direction of private interest, will upon equal terms find out the most beneficial employment for itself, there is none for a reliance, that it will struggle against the force of unequal terms, or will of itself surmount all the adventitious barriers to a successful competition, which may have been erected either by the advantages naturally acquired from practice and previous possession of the ground, or by those which may have sprung from positive regulations and an artificial policy. This general reflection might alone suffice as an answer to the objection under examination; exclusively of the weighty considerations which have been particularly urged.

The objections to the pursuit of manufactures in the United States, which next present themselves to discussion, represent an impracticability of success, arising from three causes—scarcity of hands—dearness of labour—want of capital.[177]

The two first circumstances are to a certain extent real, and, within due limits, ought to be admitted as obstacles to the success of manufacturing enterprize in the United States. But there are various considerations, which lessen their force, and tend to afford an assurance that they are not sufficient to prevent the advantageous prosecution of many very useful and extensive manufactories.

176. Interested Americans were aware of the attempts of industrial nations to frustrate the introduction of manufacturing in the United States. See, for example, *The American Museum*, III (January, 1788), 179; IV (October, 1788), 343–44; [Philadelphia] *National Gazette*, November 21, 1791. See also John Mix, Jr., to John Chester, September 30, 1791, printed as an enclosure to Chester to H, October 11, 1791, and Moses Brown to John Dexter, July 22–October 15, 1791, printed as an enclosure to Dexter to H, October, 1791.

177. During and after the American Revolution arguments similar to those mentioned by H concerning the impossibility of establishing manufactures in America were cited—in order to be refuted—by most of the publicists of American manufactures. See, for example, Barton, *The True Interest* 27; *The American Museum*, V (June, 1789), 583–84; Coxe, *Address*, 8.

With regard to scarcity of hands, the fact itself must be applied with no small qualification to certain parts of the United States. There are large districts, which may be considered as pretty fully peopled; and which notwithstanding a continual drain for distant settlement, are thickly interspersed with flourishing and increasing towns. If these districts have not already reached the point, at which the complaint of scarcity of hands ceases, they are not remote from it, and are approaching fast towards it: And having perhaps fewer attractions to agriculture, than some other parts of the Union, they exhibit a proportionably stronger tendency towards other kinds of industry. In these districts, may be discerned, no inconsiderable maturity for manufacturing establishments.

But there are circumstances, which have been already noticed with another view, that materially diminish every where the effect of a scarcity of hands. These circumstances are—the great use which can be made of women and children; on which point a very pregnant and instructive fact has been mentioned—the vast extension given by late improvements to the employment of Machines, which substituting the Agency of fire and water, has prodigiously lessened the necessity for manual labor—the employment of persons ordinarily engaged in other occupations, during the seasons, or hours of leisure; which, besides giving occasion to the exertion of a greater quantity of labour by the same number of persons, and thereby encreasing the general stock of labour, as has been elsewhere remarked, may also be taken into the calculation, as a resource for obviating the scarcity of hands—lastly the attraction of foreign emigrants. Whoever inspects, with a careful eye, the composition of our towns will be made sensible to what an extent this resource may be relied upon. This exhibits a large proportion of ingenious and valuable workmen, in different arts and trades, who, by expatriating from Europe, have improved their own condition, and added to the industry and wealth of the United States. It is a natural inference from the experience, we have already had, that as soon as the United States shall present the countenance of a serious prosecution of Manufactures—as soon as foreign artists shall be made sensible that the state of things here affords a moral certainty of employment and encouragement—competent numbers of European workmen will transplant themselves, effectually to ensure the success of the design. How indeed can it otherwise happen considering the various and powerful inducements, which the situation of this country offers; addressing themselves to so many strong passions and feelings, to so many general and particular interests?

It may be affirmed therefore, in respect to hands for carrying on manufactures, that we shall in a great measure trade upon a foreign Stock; reserving our own, for the cultivation of our lands and the manning of our Ships; as far as character and circumstances [shall] incline. It is not unworthy of remark, that the objection to the success of manufactures, deduced from the scarcity of hands, is alike applicable to Trade and Navigation; and yet these are perceived to flourish, without any sensible impediment from that cause.[178]

As to the dearness of labour (another of the obstacles alledged) this has relation principally to two circumstances, one that which has been just discussed, or the scarcity of hands, the other, the greatness of profits.

As far as it is a consequence of the scarcity of hands, it is mitigated by all the considerations which have been adduced as lessening that deficiency.

It is certain too, that the disparity in this respect, between some of the most manufacturing parts of Europe and a large proportion of the United States, is not nearly so great as is commonly imagined. It is also much less in regard to Artificers and manufacturers than in regard to country labourers; and while a careful comparison shews, that there is, in this particular, much exaggeration; it is also evident that the effect of the degree of disparity, which does truly exist, is diminished in proportion to the use which can be made of machinery.

---

178. Some members of Congress who had opposed government protection of manufactures had supported their position with arguments drawn from *The Wealth of Nations*. The same individuals had sometimes given support for the encouragement of American shipping. Smith had placed manufactures ahead of trade and navigation in a natural order of development. For example, Smith wrote:

"In seeking for employment to a capital, manufactures are, upon equal or nearly equal profits, naturally preferred to foreign commerce, for the same reason that agriculture is naturally preferred to manufactures. . . . If the society has not acquired sufficient capital both to cultivate all its lands, and to manufacture in the compleatest manner the whole of its rude produce, there is even a considerable advantage that that rude produce should be exported by a foreign capital, in order that the whole stock of the society may be employed in more useful purposes. . . .

"According to the natural course of things, therefore, the greater part of the capital of every growing society is, first, directed to agriculture, afterwards to manufactures, and last of all to foreign commerce. This order of things is so very natural, that in every society that had any territory, it has always, I believe, been in some degree observed." (Smith, *Wealth of Nations*, I, 379.)

To illustrate this last idea—Let it be supposed, that the difference of price, in two Countries, of a given quantity of manual labour requisite to the fabrication of a given article is as 10; and that some *mechanic power* is introduced into both countries, which performing half the necessary labour, leaves only half to be done by hand, it is evident, that the difference in the cost of the fabrication of the article in question, in the two countries, as far as it is connected with the price of labour, will be reduced from 10. to 5, in consequence of the introduction of that *power*.

This circumstance is worthy of the most particular attention. It diminishes immensely one of the objections most strenuously urged, against the success of manufactures in the United States.

To procure all such machines as are known in any part of Europe, can only require a proper provision and due pains. The knowledge of several of the most important of them is already possessed. The preparation of them here, is in most cases, practicable on nearly equal terms. As far as they depend on Water, some superiority of advantages may be claimed, from the uncommon variety and greater cheapness of situations adapted to Mill seats, with which different parts of the United States abound.

So far as the dearness of labour may be a consequence of the greatness of profits in any branch of business, it is no obstacle to its success. The Undertaker can afford to pay the price.

There are grounds to conclude that undertakers of Manufactures in this Country can at this time afford to pay higher wages to the workmen they may employ than are paid to similar workmen in Europe. The prices of foreign fabrics, in the markets of the United States, which will for a long time regulate the prices of the domestic ones, may be considered as compounded of the following ingredients—The first cost of materials, including the Taxes, if any, which are paid upon them where they are made: the expence of grounds, buildings machinery and tools: the wages of the persons employed in the manufactory: the profits on the capital or Stock employed: the commissions of Agents to purchase them where they are made; the expence of transportation to the United States [including insurance and other incidental charges;] the taxes or duties, if any [and fees of office] which are paid on their exportation: the taxes or duties [and fees of office] which are paid on their importation.

As to the first of these items, the cost of materials, the advantage upon the whole, is at present on the side of the United States, and the difference, in their favor, must increase, in proportion as a certain and extensive domestic demand shall induce the proprietors of land to devote more of their attention to the production of those materials. It ought not to escape observation, in a comparison on this point, that some of the principal manufacturing Countries of Europe are much more dependent on foreign supply for the materials of their manufactures, than would be the United States, who are capable of supplying themselves, with a greater abundance, as well as a greater variety of the requisite materials.

As to the second item, the expence of grounds buildings machinery and tools, an equality at least may be assumed; since advantages in some particulars will counterbalance temporary disadvantages in others.

As to the third item, or the article of wages, the comparison certainly turns against the United States, though as before observed not in so great a degree as is commonly supposed.

The fourth item is alike applicable to the foreign and to the domestic manufacture. It is indeed more properly a *result* than a particular, to be compared.

But with respect to all the remaining items, they are alone applicable to the foreign manufacture, and in the strictest sense extraordinaries; constituting a sum of extra charge on the foreign fabric, which cannot be estimated, at less than [from 15 to 30] [179] ℔ Cent. on the cost of it at the manufactory.[180]

179. In his final version of the Report H left blank spaces which he apparently intended to fill in later with the appropriate information. He also indicated points on which he had queries. In the Hamilton Papers, Library of Congress, is a list in H's handwriting which consists of a series of reminders to H of the omissions in the Report or queries concerning certain statements in the Report. This list, which corresponds to the blank spaces and queries, reads as follows:
"I   Amount of extra Charges          Page 57.  87.
II   Latitude of Virginia                      80
III  Examples of prohibitory duties           83
IV  Rise in price of bark                     114
V   Name of Pensylvania Society               147
     Cayenne."
The page numbers in the right-hand column of the list refer to the pagination of H's final version of the Report. Thus, the first item on H's list refers to material omitted on pages 57 and 87 of the final version of the Report, and H at a later time inserted the words "from 15 to 30" which are printed above in brackets.
180. In "Thoughts on the present situation of the united states" Coxe wrote:
". . . [British] manufacturers, by machines, placed at the distance of three

This sum of extra charge may confidently be regarded as more than a Counterpoise for the real difference in the price of labour; and is a satisfactory proof that manufactures may prosper in defiance of it in the United States. To the general allegation, connected with the circumstances of scarcity of hands and dearness of labour, that extensive manufactures can only grow out of a redundant or full population, it will be sufficient, to answer generally, that the fact has been otherwise—That the situation alleged to be an essential condition of success, has not been that of several nations, at periods when they had already attained to maturity in a variety of manufactures.

The supposed want of Capital for the prosecution of manufactures in the United States is the most indefinite of the objections which are usually opposed to it.

It is very difficult to pronounce any thing precise concerning the real extent of the monied capital of a Country, and still more concerning the proportion which it bears to the objects that invite the employment of Capital. It is not less difficult to pronounce how far the *effect* of any given quantity of money, as capital, or in other words, as a medium for circulating the industry and property of a nation, may be encreased by the very circumstance of the additional motion, which is given to it by new objects of employment. That effect, like the momentum of descending bodies, may not improperly be represented, as in a compound ratio to *mass* and *velocity*. It seems pretty certain, that a given sum of money, in a situation, in which the quick impulses of commercial activity were little felt, would appear inadequate to the circulation of as great a quantity of industry and property, as in one, in which their full influence was experienced.

It is not obvious, why the same objection might not as well be made to external commerce as to manufactures; since it is manifest that our immense tracts of land occupied and unoccupied are capable of giving employment to more capital than is actually bestowed upon them. It is certain, that the United States offer a vast field for the advantageous employment of Capital; but it does not follow, that there will not be found, in one way or another, a sufficient fund for the successful

thousand miles from all rivals, and enjoying a very great demand for low priced goods, will be long, very long protected in the profits of those machines by charges of 20 to 30 per cent. that will arise on the importation of foreign articles. . ." (*The American Museum*, IV [November, 1788], 403–04).

prosecution of any species of industry which is likely to prove truly beneficial.

The following considerations are of a nature to remove all inquietude on the score of want of Capital.

The introduction of Banks, as has been shewn on another occasion [181] has a powerful tendency to extend the active Capital of a Country. Experience of the Utility of these Institutions is multiplying them in the United States. It is probable that they will be established wherever they can exist with advantage; and wherever, they can be supported, if administered with prudence, they will add new energies to all pecuniary operations.

The aid of foreign Capital may safely, and, with considerable latitude be taken into calculation. Its instrumentality has been long experienced in our external commerce; and it has begun to be felt in various other modes. Not only our funds, but our Agriculture and other internal improvements have been animated by it. It has already in a few instances extended even to our manufactures.

It is a well known fact, that there are parts of Europe, which have more Capital, than profitable domestic objects of employment. Hence, among other proofs, the large loans continually furnished to foreign states. And it is equally certain that the capital of other parts may find more profitable employment in the United States, than at home. And notwithstanding there are weighty inducements to prefer the employment of capital at home even at less profit, to an investment of it abroad, though with greater gain, yet these inducements are over-ruled either by a deficiency of employment or by a very material difference in profit. Both these Causes operate to produce a transfer of foreign capital to the United States. 'Tis certain, that various objects in this country hold out advantages, which are with difficulty to be equalled elsewhere; and under the increasingly favorable impressions, which are entertained of our government, the attractions will become more and More strong. These impressions will prove a rich mine of prosperity to the Country, if they are confirmed and strengthened by the progress of our affairs. And to secure this advantage, little more is now necessary, than to foster industry, and cultivate order and tranquility, at home and abroad.

181. See "Second Report on the Further Provision Necessary for Establishing Public Credit (Report on a National Bank)," December 13, 1790.

It is not impossible, that there may be persons disposed to look with a jealous eye on the introduction of foreign Capital, as if it were an instrument to deprive our own citizens of the profits of our own industry: But perhaps there never could be a more unreasonable jealousy. Instead of being viewed as a rival, it ought to be Considered as a most valuable auxiliary; conducing to put in Motion a greater Quantity of productive labour, and a greater portion of useful enterprise than could exist without it. It is at least evident, that in a Country situated like the United States, with an infinite fund of resources yet to be unfolded, every farthing of foreign capital, which is laid out in internal ameliorations, and in industrious establishments of a permanent nature, is a precious acquisition.

And whatever be the objects which originally attract foreign Capital, when once introduced, it may be directed towards any purpose of beneficial exertion, which is desired. And to detain it among us, there can be no expedient so effectual as to enlarge the sphere, within which it may be usefully employed: Though induced merely with views to speculations in the funds, it may afterwards be rendered subservient to the Interests of Agriculture, Commerce & Manufactures.

But the attraction of foreign Capital for the direct purpose of Manufactures ought not to be deemed a chimerial expectation. There are already examples of it, as remarked in another place. And the examples, if the disposition be cultivated can hardly fail to multiply. There are also instances of another kind, which serve to strengthen the expectation. Enterprises for improving the Public Communications, by cutting canals, opening the obstructions in Rivers and erecting bridges, have received very material aid from the same source.

When the Manufacturing Capitalist of Europe shall advert to the many important advantages, which have been intimated, in the Course of this report, he cannot but perceive very powerful inducements to a transfer of himself and his Capital to the United States. Among the reflections, which a most interesting peculiarity of situation is calculated to suggest, it cannot escape his observation, as a circumstance of Moment in the calculation, that the progressive population and improvement of the United States, insure a continually increasing domestic demand for the fabrics which he shall produce, not to be affected by any external casualties or vicissitudes.

But while there are Circumstances sufficiently strong to authorise a considerable degree of reliance on the aid of foreign Capital towards the attainment of the object in view, it is satisfactory to have good grounds of assurance, that there are domestic resources of themselves adequate to it. It happens, that there is a species of Capital actually existing within the United States, which relieves from all inquietude on the score of want of Capital—This is the funded Debt.

The effect of a funded debt, as a species of Capital, has been Noticed upon a former Occasion; [182] but a more particular elucidation of the point seems to be required by the stress which is here laid upon it. This shall accordingly be attempted.

Public Funds answer the purpose of Capital, from the estimation in which they are usually held by Monied men; and consequently from the Ease and dispatch with which they can be turned into money. This capacity of prompt convertibility into money causes a transfer of stock to be in a great number of Cases equivalent to a payment in coin. And where it does not happen to suit the party who is to receive, to accept a transfer of Stock, the party who is to pay, is never at a loss to find elsewhere a purchaser of his Stock, who will furnish him in lieu of it, with the Coin of which he stands in need. Hence in a sound and settled state of the public funds, a man possessed of a sum in them can embrace any scheme of business, which offers, with as much confidence as if he were possessed of an equal sum in Coin.

This operation of public funds as capital is too obvious to be denied; but it is objected to the Idea of their operating as an *augmentation* of the Capital of the community, that they serve to occasion the *destruction* of some other capital to an equal amount.[183]

The Capital which alone they can be supposed to destroy must consist of—The annual revenue, which is applied to the payment of Interest on the debt, and to the gradual redemption of the principal— The amount of the Coin, which is employed in circulating the funds, or, in other words, in effecting the different alienations which they undergo.

But the following appears to be the true and accurate view of this matter.

182. See "Report Relative to a Provision for the Support of Public Credit," January 9, 1790.
183. H is apparently referring to the following statement by Smith: "This annuity, no doubt, replaced to them their capital, and enabled them to carry on

1st. As to the point of the Annual Revenue requisite for Payment of interest and redemption of principal.

As a determinate proportion will tend to perspicuity in the reasoning, let it be supposed that the annual revenue to be applied, corresponding with the modification of the 6 per Cent stock of the United States, is in the ratio of eight upon the hundred, that is in the first instance six on Account of interest, and two on account of Principal.

Thus far it is evident, that the Capital destroyed to the capital created, would bear no greater proportion, than 8 to 100. There would be withdrawn from the total mass of other capitals a sum of eight dollars to be paid to the public creditor; while he would be possessed of a sum of One Hundred dollars, ready to be applied to any purpose, to be embarked in any enterprize, which might appear to him eligible. Here then the *Augmentation* of Capital, or the excess of that which is produced, beyond that which is destroyed is equal to Ninety two dollars. To this conclusion, it may be objected, that the sum of Eight dollars is to be withdrawn annually, until the whole hundred is extinguished, and it may be inferred, that in process of time a capital will be destroyed equal to that which is at first created.

But it is nevertheless true, that during the whole of the interval, between the creation of the Capital of 100 dollars, and its reduction to a sum not greater than that of the annual revenue appropriated to its redemption—there will be a greater active capital in existence than if no debt had been Contracted. The sum drawn from other Capitals *in any one year* will not exceed eight dollars; but there will be *at*

---

their trade and business to the same or perhaps to a greater extent than before; that is, they were enabled either to borrow of other people a new capital upon the credit of this annuity, or by selling it to get from other people a new capital of their own, equal or superior to that which they had advanced to government. This new capital, however, which they in this manner either bought or borrowed of other people, must have existed in the country before, and must have been employed, as all capitals are, in maintaining productive labour. When it came into the hands of those who had advanced their money to government, though it was in some respects a new capital to them, it was not so to the country; but was only a capital withdrawn from certain employments in order to be turned towards others. Though it replaced to them what they had advanced to government, it did not replace it to the country. Had they not advanced this capital to government, there would have been in the country two capitals, two portions of the annual produce, instead of one, employed in maintaining productive labour. . . .

"When the public expence is defrayed by funding, it is defrayed by the annual destruction of some capital which had before existed in the country. . . ." (Smith, *Wealth of Nations*, II, 463–64.)

*every instant of time* during the whole period, in question a sum corresponding *with so much of the principal,* as remains *unredeemed,* in the hands of some person, or other, employed, or ready to be employed in some profitable undertaking. There will therefore constantly be more capital, in capacity to be employed, than capital taken from employment. The excess for the first year has been stated to be Ninety two dollars; it will diminish yearly, but there always will be an excess, until the principal of the debt is brought to a level with the *redeeming annuity,* that is, in the case which has been assumed by way of example, to *eight dollars.* The reality of this excess becomes palpable, if it be supposed, as often happens, that the citizen of a foreign Country imports into the United States 100 dollars for the purchase of an equal sum of public debt. Here is an absolute augmentation of the mass of Circulating Coin to the extent of 100 dollars. At the end of a year the foreigner is presumed to draw back eight dollars on account of his Principal and Interest, but he still leaves, Ninety two of his original Deposit in circulation, as he in like manner leaves Eighty four at the end of the second year, drawing back then also the annuity of Eight Dollars: And thus the Matter proceeds; The capital left in circulation diminishing each year, and coming nearer to the level of the annuity drawnback. There are however some differences in the ultimate operation of the part of the debt, which is purchased by foreigners, and that which remains in the hands of citizens. But the general effect in each case, though in different degrees, is to add to the active capital of the Country.

Hitherto the reasoning has proceeded on a concession of the position, that there is a destruction of some other capital, to the extent of the annuity appropriated to the payment of the Interest and the redemption of the principal of the deb⟨t⟩ [184] but in this, too much has been conceded. There is at most a temp⟨orary⟩ transfer of some other capital, to the amount of the Annuity, from those who pay to the Creditor who receives; which he again restor⟨es⟩ to the circulation to resume the offices of a capital. This he does ei⟨ther⟩ immediately by employing the money in some branch of Industry, or mediately by lending it to some other person, who does so employ ⟨it⟩ or by spending it on his own maintenance. In either sup⟨position⟩ there is no

184. All material within broken brackets in this MS has been taken from H's fourth draft of the Report.

destruction of capital, there is nothing more ⟨than a⟩ suspension of its motion for a time; that is, while it is ⟨passing⟩ from the hands of those who pay into the Public coffers, & thence ⟨through⟩ the public Creditor into some other Channel of circulation. ⟨When⟩ the payments of interest are periodical and quick and made by instrumentality of Banks the diversion or suspension of capita⟨l⟩ may almost be denominated momentary. Hence the deduction on this Account is far less, than it at first sight appears to be.

There is evidently, as far as regards the annuity no destruction nor transfer of any other Capital, than that por⟨tion⟩ of the income of each individual, which goes to make up the Annuity. The land which furnishes the Farmer with the s⟨um⟩ which he is to contribute remains the same; and the like m⟨ay⟩ be observed of other Capitals. Indeed as far as the Tax, w⟨hich⟩ is the object of contribution (as frequently happens, when it doe⟨s⟩ not oppress, by its weight) may have been a Motive to *greate⟨r⟩ exertion* in any occupation; [185] it may even serve to encrease the contributory Capital: This idea is not without importanc⟨e⟩ in the general view of the subject.

It remains to see, what further deduction ought to be mad⟨e⟩ from the capital which is created, by the existence of the Debt; on account of the coin, which is employed in its circulation. This is susceptible of much less precise calculation, than the Article which has been just discussed. It is impossible to say what proportion of coin is necessary to carry on the alienations which any species of property usually undergoes. The quantity indeed varies according to circumstances. But it may still without hesitation be pronounced, from the quickness of the rotation, or rather of the transitions, that the *medium* of circulation always bears but a small proportion to the amount of the *property* circulated. And it is thence satisfactorily deducible, that the coin employed in the Negociations of the funds and which serves to give them activity, as capital, is incomparably less than the sum of the debt negotiated for the purposes of business.

185. Hume expressed a similar view when he wrote: "But there is a third consequence, which very often follows upon taxes, *viz.* that the poor encrease their industry, perform more work, and live as well as before, without demanding more for their labour." But Hume qualified this statement, for he also wrote: "This doctrine, therefore, with regard to taxes, may be admitted in some degree: But beware of the abuse. Taxes, like necessity, when carry'd too far, destroy industry, by engendring despair . . ." (Hume, *Political Discourses*, 115, 118).

It ought not, however, to be omitted, that the negotiation of the funds becomes itself a distinct business; which employs, and by employing diverts a portion of the circulating coin from other pursuits. But making due allowance for this circumstance there is no reason to conclude, that the effect of the diversion of coin in the whole operation bears any considerable proportion to the amount of the Capital to which it gives activity. The sum of the debt in circulation is continually at the Command, of any useful enterprise—the coin itself which circulates it, is never more than momentarily suspended from its ordinary functions. It experiences an incessant and rapid flux and reflux to and from the Channels of industry to those of speculations in the funds.

There are strong circumstances in confirmation of this Theory. The force of Monied Capital which has been displayed in Great Britain, and the height to which every species of industry has grown up under it, defy a solution from the quantity of coin which that kingdom has ever possessed. Accordingly it has been Coeval with its funding system, the prevailing opinion of the men of business, and of the generality of the most sagacious theorists of that country, that the operation of the public funds as capital has contributed to the effect in question. Among ourselves appearances thus far favour the same Conclusion. Industry in general seems to have been reanimated. There are symptoms indicating an extension of our Commerce. Our navigation has certainly of late had a Considerable spring, and there appears to be in many parts of the Union a command of capital, which till lately, since the revolution at least, was unknown. But it is at the same time to be acknowledged, that other circumstances have concurred, (and in a great degree) in producing the present state of things, and that the appearances are not yet sufficiently decisive, to be intirely relied upon.

In the question under discussion, it is important to distinguish between an *absolute increase of Capital, or an accession of real wealth,* and *an artificial increase of Capital,* as an engine of business, or as an instrument of industry and Commerce. In the first sense, a funded debt has no pretensions to being deemed an increase of Capital; in the last, it has pretensions which are not easy to be controverted. Of a similar nature is bank credit and in an inferior degree, every species of private credit.

But though a funded debt is not in the first instance, an absolute increase of Capital, or an augmentation of real wealth; yet by serving as a New power in the operation of industry, it has within certain bounds a tendency to increase the real wealth of a Community, in like manner as money borrowed by a thrifty farmer, to be laid out in the improvement of his farm may, in the end, add to his Stock of real riches.

There are respectable individuals, who from a just aversion to an accumulation of Public debt, are unwilling to concede to it any kind of utility, who can discern no good to alleviate the ill with which they suppose it pregnant; who cannot be persuaded that it ought in any sense to be viewed as an increase of capital lest it should be inferred, that the more debt the more capital, the greater the burthens the greater the blessings of the community.

But it interests the public Councils to estimate every object as it truly is; to appreciate how far the good in any measure is compensated by the ill; or the ill by the good, Either of them is seldom unmixed.

Neither will it follow, that an accumulation of debt is desireable, because a certain degree of it operates as capital. There may be a plethora in the political, as in the Natural body; There may be a state of things in which any such artificial capital is unnecessary. The debt too may be swelled to such a size, as that the greatest part of it may cease to be useful as a Capital, serving only to pamper the dissipation of idle and dissolute individuals: as that the sums required to pay the Interest upon it may become oppressive, and beyond the means, which a government can employ, consistently with its tranquility, to raise them; as that the resources of taxation, to face the debt, may have been strained too far to admit of extensions adequate to exigencies, which regard the public safety.

Where this critical point is, cannot be pronounced, but it is impossible to believe, that there is not such a point.

And as the vicissitudes of Nations beget a perpetual tendency to the accumulation of debt, there ought to be in every government a perpetual, anxious and unceasing effort to reduce that, which at any time exists, as fast as shall be practicable consistently with integrity and good faith.

Reasonings on a subject comprehending ideas so abstract and complex, so little reducible to precise calculation as those which enter into the question just discussed, are always attended with a danger of runing into fallacies. Due allowance ought therefore to be made for this possibility. But as far as the Nature of the subject admits of it, there appears to be satisfactory ground for a belief, that the public funds operate as a resource of capital to the Citizens of the United States, and, if they are a resource at all, it is an extensive one.

To all the arguments which are brought to evince the impracticability of success in manufacturing establishments in the United States, it might have been a sufficient answer to have referred to the experience of what has been already done. It is certain that several important branches have grown up and flourished with a rapidity which surprises: affording an encouraging assurance of success in future attempts: of these it may not be improper to enumerate the most considerable.

| | |
|---|---|
| I of Skins. | Tanned and tawed leather dressed skins, shoes, boots and Slippers, harness and sadlery of all kinds. Portmanteau's and trunks, leather breeches, gloves, muffs and tippets, parchment and Glue. |
| II of Iron | Barr and Sheet Iron, Steel, Nail-rods & Nails, implem⟨ents⟩ of husbandry, Stoves, pots and other household utensils, the steel and Iron work of carriages and for Shipbuildin⟨g,⟩ Anchors, scale beams and Weights & Various tools of Artificers, arms of different kinds; though the manufacture of these last has of late diminished for want of demand. |
| III of Wood | Ships, Cabinet Wares and Turnery, Wool and Cotton ca⟨rds⟩ and other Machinery for manufactures and husband⟨ry,⟩ Mathematical instruments, Coopers wares of every kind. |
| IV of flax & Hemp. | Cables, sail-cloth, Cordage, twine and packthread. |
| V | Bricks and coarse tiles & Potters Wares. |
| VI | Ardent Spirits, and malt liquors. |
| VII | Writing and printing Paper, sheathing and wrapping Paper, pasteboards, fillers or press papers, paper hangings. |
| VIII | Hats of furr and Wool and of mixtures of both, Womens Stuff and Silk shoes. |

| IX | Refined Sugars. |
| X | Oils of Animals and seeds; Soap, Spermaceti and Tallow Candles. |
| XI | Copper and brass wares, particularly utensils for distillers, Sugar refiners and brewers, And—Irons and other Articles for household Use, philosophical apparatus |
| XII | Tin Wares, for most purposes of Ordinary use. |
| XIII | Carriages of all kinds |
| XIV | Snuff, chewing & smoking Tobacco. |
| XV | Starch and Hairpowder. |
| XVI | Lampblack and other painters colours, |
| XVII | Gunpowder |

Besides manufactories of these articles which are carried on as regular Trades, and have attained to a considerable degree of maturity, there is a vast scene of household manufacturing, which contributes more largely to the supply of the Community, than could be imagined; without having made it an object of particular enquiry. This observation is the pleasing result of the investigation, to which the subject of the report has led, and is applicable as well to the Southern as to the middle and Northern States; great quantities of coarse cloths, coatings, serges, and flannels, linsey Woolseys, hosiery of Wool, cotton & thread, coarse fustians, jeans and Muslins, check⟨ed⟩ and striped cotton and linen goods, bed ticks, Coverlets and Counterpanes, Tow linens, coarse shirtings, sheetings, toweling and table linen, and various mixtures of wool and cotton, and of Cotton & flax are made in the household way, and in many instances to an extent not only sufficient for the supply of the families in which they are made, but for sale, and (even in some cases) for exportation. It is computed in a number of districts that ⅔ ¾ and even ⅘ of all the clothing of the Inhabitants are made by themselves. The importance of so great a progress, as appears to have been made in family Manufactures, within a few years, both in a moral and political view, renders the fact highly interesting.[186]

Neither does the above enumeration comprehend all the articles, that are manufactured as regular Trades. Many others occur, which

186. See note 147.

are equally well established, but which not being of equal importance have been omitted. And there are many attempts still in their Infancy, which though attended with very favorable appearances, could not have been properly comprized in an enumeration of manufactories, already established. There are other articles also of great importance, which tho' strictly speaking manufactures are omitted, as being immediately connected with husbandry: such are flour, pot & pearl ash, Pitch, tar, turpentine and the like.

There remains to be noticed an objection to the encouragement of manufactures, of a nature different from those which question the probability of success. This is derived from its supposed tendency to give a monopoly of advantages to particula⟨r⟩ classes at the expence of the rest of the community, who, it is affirmed, would be able to procure the requisite supplies of manufactured articles on better terms from foreigners, than from our own Citizens, and who it is alledged, are reduced to a necessity of paying an enhanced price for whatever they want, by every measure, which obstructs the free competition of foreign commoditi⟨es.⟩ [187]

It is not an unreasonable supposition, that measures, which serve to abridge the free competition of foreign Articles, have a tendency to occasion an enhancement of prices and it is not to be denied that such is the effect in a number of Cases; but the fact does not uniformly correspond with the theory. A reduction of prices has in several instances immediately succeeded the establishment of a domestic manufacture. Whether it be that foreign Manufacturers endeavour to suppla⟨nt⟩ by underselling our own, or whatever else be the cause,

187. Smith mentioned the monopolistic effect of mercantile regulations in *The Wealth of Nations* when he wrote:

"In the restraints upon the importation . . . the interest of the home-consumer is evidently sacrificed to that of the producer. It is altogether for the benefit of the latter, that the former is obliged to pay that enhancement of price which this monopoly almost always occasions." (Smith, *Wealth of Nations*, II, 173.)

"Merchants and manufacturers are the people who derive the greatest advantage from this monopoly of the home market." (Smith, *Wealth of Nations*, I, 450.)

The argument to which H is referring was frequently used in debates in the First Congress. See, for example, the remarks of Thomas Tudor Tucker of South Carolina and Theodorick Bland of Virginia during the debate over the 1789 impost (*Annals of Congress*, I, 129, 307—08) and a speech by Andrew Moore of Virginia (*Annals of Congress*, I, 160). See also *The American Museum*, V (April, 1789), 422.

the effect has been such as is stated, and the reverse of what mig⟨ht⟩ have been expected.[188]

But though it were true, that the immedi⟨ate⟩ and certain effect of regulations controuling the competition of foreign with domestic fabrics was an increase of price, it is universally true, that the contrary is the ultimate effect with every successful manufacture. When a domestic manufacture has attained to perfection, and has engaged in the prosecution of it a competent number of Persons, it invariably becomes cheaper. Being free from the heavy charges, which attend the importation of foreign commodities, it can be afforded, and accordingly seldom or never fails to be sold Cheaper, in process of time, than was the foreign Article for which it is a substitute. The internal competition, which takes place, soon does away every thing like Monopoly, and by degrees reduces the price of the Article to the *minimum* of a reasonable profit on the Capital employed. This accords with the reason of the thing and with experience.

Whence it follows, that it is the interest of a community with a view to eventual and permanent oeconomy, to encourage the growth of manufactures. In a national view, a temporary enhancement of price must always be well compensated by a permanent reduction of it.

It is a reflection, which may with propriety be indulged here, that this eventual diminution of the prices of manufactured Articles; which is the result of internal manufacturing establishments, has a

188. After listing price increases caused by mercantile regulations, Smith wrote: "When a landed nation, on the contrary, oppresses either by high duties or by prohibitions the trade of foreign nations, it necessarily hurts its own interest in two different ways. First, by raising the price of all foreign goods and of all sorts of manufactures, it necessarily sinks the real value of the surplus produce of its own land, with which, or, what comes to the same thing, with the price of which, it purchases those foreign goods and manufactures. Secondly, by giving a sort of monopoly of the home market to its own merchants, artificers and manufacturers, it raises the rate of mercantile and manufacturing profit in proportion to that of agricultural profit . . ." (Smith, *Wealth of Nations*, II, 186–87).

On the other hand, in connection with the tendency of an increased demand for Indian goods in India and a consequent price increase he wrote: "The increase of demand, besides, though in the beginning it may sometimes raise the price of goods, never fails to lower it in the long run. It encourages production, and thereby increases the competition of the producers, who, in order to undersell one another, have recourse to new divisions of labour and new improvements of art, which might never otherwise have been thought of" (Smith, *Wealth of Nations*, II, 266).

direct and very important tendency to benefit agriculture. It enables
the farmer, to procure with a smaller quantity of his labour, the
manufactured produce of which he stan⟨ds⟩ in need, and consequently
increases the value of his income and property.[189]

The objections which are commonly made to the expediency of
encouraging, and to the probability of succeeding in manufacturing
pursuits, in the United states, having now been discussed; the Considerations which have appeared in the Course of the discussion, recommending that species of industry to the patronage of the Government, will be materially strengthened by a few general and some
particular topics, which have been naturally reserved for subsequent
Notice.

I   There seems to be a moral certainty, that the trade of a country
which is both manufacturing and Agricultural will be more lucrative
and prosperous, than that of a Country, which is, merely Agricultural.

One reason for this is found in that general effort of nations (which
has been already mentioned) to procure from their own soils, the
articles of prime necessity requisite to their own consumption and
use; and which serves to render their demand for a foreign supply of
such articles in a great degree occasional and contingent. Hence,
while the necessities of nations exclusively devoted to Agriculture, for
the fabrics of manufacturing st⟨ates⟩ are constant and regular, the
wants of the latter for the products of the former, are liable to very

189. Similarities between the preceding three paragraphs in the Report and
statements made by Smith may be found. Although Smith, of course, maintained
that the general revenue and industry of a country would not be increased by
mercantile regulations, he also wrote: "By means of such regulations, indeed, a
particular manufacture may sometimes be acquired sooner than it could have
been otherwise, and after a certain time may be made at home as cheap or
cheaper than in the foreign country" (Smith, *Wealth of Nations,* I, 449). In
addition, he advocated the use of restrictions which might force other nations to
remove trade barriers on the grounds that "the recovery of a great foreign
market will generally more than compensate the transitory inconveniency of
paying dearer during a short time for some sorts of goods" (Smith, *Wealth of
Nations,* I, 460).
In a description of Physiocratic views, Smith wrote: "But those artificers
and manufacturers, finding at home, both the materials of their work and the
fund of their subsistence, might immediately, even with much less art and skill,
be able to work as cheap as the like artificers and manufacturers of such mercantile states, who had both to bring from a great distance. Even though from want
of art and skill, they might not for some time be able to work as cheap, yet,
finding a market at home, they might be able to sell their work there as cheap
as that of the artificers and manufacturers of such mercantile states, which
could not be brought to that market but from so great a distance; and as their

considerable fluctuations and interruptions. The great inequalities resulting from difference of seasons, have been elsewhere remarked: This uniformity of deman⟨d⟩ on one side, and unsteadiness of it, on the other, must necessarily ha⟨ve⟩ a tendency to cause the general course of the exchange of commodit⟨ies⟩ between the parties to turn to the disadvantage of the merely agricultural States. Peculiarity of situation, a climate and soil ada⟨pted⟩ to the production of peculiar commodities, may, sometimes, contradi⟨ct⟩ the rule; but there is every reason to believe that it will be fou⟨nd⟩ in the Main, a just one.

Another circumstance which gives a superiority of commercial advantages to states, that manufact⟨ure⟩ as well as cultivate, consists in the more numerous attractions, which a more diversified market offers to foreign Customers, and greater scope, which it affords to mercantile enterprise. It is ⟨a⟩ position of indisputable truth in Commerce, depending too on very obvious reasons, that the greatest resort will ever be to those mar⟨ts⟩ where commodities, while equally abundant, are most various. Each difference of kind holds out an additional inducement. And it is a position not less clear, that the field of enterprise must be enlarged to the Merchants of a Country, in proportion ⟨to⟩ the variety as well as the abundance of commodities which they find at home for exportation to foreign Markets.

A third circumstance, perhaps not inferior to either of the other two, conferring the superiority which has been stated has relation to the stagnations of demand for certain commodities which at some time or other interfere more or less with the sale of all. The Nation which can bring to Market, but few articles is likely to be more quickly and sensibly affected by such stagnations, than one, which is

---

art and skill improved, they would soon be able to sell it cheaper" (Smith, *Wealth of Nations*, II, 185).

In a description of the advantages of towns, Smith wrote: "They work up the materials of manufacture which the land produces, and exchange their finished work, or what is the same thing the price of it, for more materials and provisions. They give a new value to the surplus part of the rude produce. by saving the expence of carrying it to the water side, or to some distant market; and they furnish the cultivators with something in exchange for it that is either useful or agreeable to them, upon easier terms than they could have obtained it before" (Smith, *Wealth of Nations*, I, 403).

A "natural effect" of the growth of industry, according to Smith, was "to diminish gradually the real price of almost all manufactures. That of the manufacturing workmanship diminishes, perhaps, in all of them without exception" (Smith, *Wealth of Nations*, I, 250).

always possessed of a great variety of commodities. The former frequently finds too great a proportion of its stock of materials, for sale or exchange, lying on hand—or is obliged to make injurious sacrifices to supply its wants of foreign articles, which are *Numerous* and *urgent*, in proportion to the smallness of the number of its own. The latter commonly finds itself indemnified, by the high prices of some articles, for the low prices of others—and the Prompt and advantageous sale of those articles which are in demand enables its merchant the better to wait for a favorable change, in respect to those which are not. There is ground to believe, that a difference of situation, in this particular, has immensely different effec⟨ts⟩ upon the wealth and prosperity of Nations.

From these circumstances collectively, two important inferences are to be drawn, one, that there is always a higher probability of a favorable balance of Trade, in regard to countries in which manufactures founded on the basis of a thriving Agriculture flourish, than in regard to those, which are confined wholly or almost wholly to Agriculture; the other (which is also a consequence of the first) that countries of the former description are likely to possess more pecuniary wealth, or money, than those of the latter.[190]

Facts appear to correspond with this conclusion. The importations of manufactured supplies seem invariably to drain the merely Agricultural people of their wealth. Let the situation of the manufacturing countries of Europe be compared in this particular, with that of Countries which only cultivate, and the disparity will be striking. Other causes, it is true, help to Account for this disparity between some of them; and among these causes, the relative state of Agriculture; but between others of them, the most prominent circumstance of dissimilitude arises from the Comparative state of Manufactures. In corroboration of the same idea, it ought not to escape remark, that

190. H, in this instance, agreed with Smith, who wrote: "A small quantity of manufactured produce purchases a great quantity of rude produce. A trading and manufacturing country, therefore, naturally purchases with a small part of its manufactured produce a great part of the rude produce of other countries; while, on the contrary, a country without trade and manufactures is generally obliged to purchase, at the expence of a great part of its rude produce, a very small part of the manufactured produce of other countries" (Smith, *Wealth of Nations*, II, 193).
Necker expressed a generally accepted tradition when he wrote: "Ainsi, moins une société achetera d'objets d'industrie étrangere, plus elle aura de moyens

the West India Islands, the soils of which are the most fertile, and the Nation, which in the greatest degree supplies the rest of the world, with the precious metals, exchange to a loss with almost every other Country.

As far as experience at home may guide, it will lead to the same conclusion. Previous to the revolution, the quantity of coin, possessed by the colonies, which now compose the United states, appeared, to be inadequate to their circulation; and their debt to Great-Britain was progressive. Since the Revolution, the States, in which manufactures have most increased, have recovered fastest from the injuries of the late War, and abound most in pecuniary resources.

It ought to be admitted, however in this as in the preceding case, that causes irrelative to the state of manufactures account, in a degree, for the Phœnomena remarked. The continual progress of new settlements has a natural tendency to occasion an unfavorable balance of Trade; though it indemnifies for the inconvenience, by that increase of the national capital which flows from the conversion of waste into improved lands: And the different degrees of external commerce, which are carried on by the different States, may make material differences in the comparative state of their wealth. The first circumstance has reference to the deficien⟨cy⟩ of coin and the increase of debt previous to the revolution; the last to the advantages which the most manufacturing states appear to have enjoyed, over the others, since the termination of the late War.

But the uniform appearance of an abundance of specie, as the con-

---

pour obtenir en échange de la sienne, ou des subsistances, ou de l'argent, seules fins de commerce qui augmentent la population et la richesse, tous les autres échanges n'étant qu'un troc de jouissances" (Necker, *Œuvres*, III, 260). Necker also wrote: "Il est donc manifeste que plus la valeur des marchandises qu'on vend aux étrangers est composée du prix la valeur du travail, plus on fait un commerce favorable à la population nationale. . . . Concluons donc, que de toutes les manieres de payer les biens étrangers, la plus avantageuse à un Royaume, c'est la vente du tems, c'est-à-dire, celle des productions de l'industrie . . ." (Necker, *Œuvres*, IV, 100–04).

H, himself, had previously emphasized the advantages of a diversified market. See, for example, essay 11 of *The Federalist* and "Prospectus of the Society for Establishing Useful Manufactures," August, 1791. In the latter he had stated: "⟨And⟩ both theory and experience conspire to prove that a nation (unless from a very peculiar coincidence of circumstances) cannot possess much *active* wealth but as the result of extensive manufactures."

Many Americans had also expressed views similar to those held by H. See, for example, Barton, *The True Interest*, 25; *The American Museum*, V, (June, 1789), 582–84.

comitant of a flourishing state of manufacture(s) and of the reverse, where they do not prevail, afford a strong presumption of their favourable operation upon the wealth of a Country.

Not only the wealth; but the independence and security of a Country, appear to be materially connected with the prosperity of manufactures. Every nation, with a view to those great objects, ought to endeavour to possess within itself all the essentials of national supply. These comprise the means of *Subsistence habitation clothing* and *defence*.

The possession of these is necessary to the perfection of the body politic, to the safety as well as to the welfare of the society; the want of either, is the want of an important organ of political life and Motion; and in the various crises which await a state, it must severely feel the effects of any such deficiency. The extreme embarrassments of the United States during the late War, from an incapacity of supplying themselves, are still matter of keen recollection: A future war might be expected again to exemplify the mischiefs and dangers of a situation, to which that incapacity is still in too great a degree applicable, unless changed by timely and vigorous exertion. To effect this change as fast as shall be prudent, merits all the attention and all the Zeal of our Public Councils; 'tis the next great work to be accomplished.

The want of a Navy to protect our external commerce, as long as it shall Continue, must render it a peculiarly precarious reliance, for the supply of essential articles, and must serve to strengthen prodigiously the arguments in favour of manufactures.

To these general Considerations are added some of a more particular nature.

Our distance from Europe, the great fountain of manufactured supply, subjects us in the existing state of things, to inconvenience and loss in two Ways.

The bulkiness of those commodities which are the chief productions of the soil, necessarily imposes very heavy charges on their transportation, to distant markets. These charges, in the Cases, in which the nations, to whom our products are sent, maintain a Competition in the supply of their own markets, principally fall upon us, and form material deductions from the primitive value of the articles furnished. The charges on manufactured supplies, brought from Europe are greatly enhanced by the same circumstance of distance. These charges, again, in the cases in which our own industry maintains no competition, in our own markets, also principally fall upon us; and are an additional cause of extraordinary deduction from the primitive value of our own products; these bei⟨ng⟩ the materials of exchange for the foreign fabrics, which we consume.

The equality and moderation of individual prope⟨rty⟩ and the growing settlements of new districts, occasion in this country an unusual demand for coarse manufactures; The charges of which being greater in proportion to their greater bulk augment the disadvantage, which has been just described.

As in most countries domestic supplie⟨s⟩ maintain a very considerable competition with such foreign productions of the soil, as are imported for sale; if the extensive establishment of Manufactories in the United states does not create a similar competition in respect to manufactured articles, it appears to be clearly deducible, from the Considerations which have been mentioned, that they must sustain a double loss in their exchanges with foreign Nations; strongly conducive to an unfavorable balance of Trade, and very prejudicial to their Interests.

These disadvantages press with no small weight, on the landed interest of the Country. In seasons of peace, they cause a serious deduction from the intrinsic value of the products of the soil. In the time of a War, which shou'd either involve ourselves, or another nation, possessing a Considerable share of our carrying trade, the charges on the transportation of our commodities, bulky as most of them are, could hardly fail to prove a grievous burthen to the farmer; while obliged to depend in so great degree as he now does, upon foreign markets for the vent of the surplus of his labour.

As far as the prosperity of the Fisheries of the United states is impeded by the want of an adequate market, there arises another special reason for desiring the extension of manufactures. Besides the fish, which in many places, would be likely to make a part of the subsistence of the persons employed; it is known that the oils, bones and skins of marine animals, are of extensive use in various manufactures. Hence the prospect of an additional demand for the produce of the Fisheries.

One more point of view only remains in which to Consider the expediency of encouraging manufactures in the United states.

It is not uncommon to meet with an opin⟨ion⟩ that though the promoting of manufactures may be the interest of a part of the Union, it is contrary to that of another part. The Northern & southern regions are sometimes represented as having adverse interests in this respect. Those are called Manufacturing, these Agricultural states; and a species of opposition is imagined to subsist between the Manufacturing a⟨nd⟩ Agricultural interests.

This idea of an opposition between those two interests is the common error of the early periods of every country, but experience gradually dissipates it. Indeed they are perceived so often to succour and to befriend each other, that they come at length to be considered as one: a supposition which has been frequently abused and is not universally true. Particular encouragements of particular manufactures may be of a Nature to sacrifice the interests of landholders to those of manufacturers; But it is nevertheless a maxim well established by experience, and generally acknowledged, where there has been sufficient experience, that the *aggregate* prosperity of manufactures, and the *aggregate* prosperity of Agriculture are intimately connected. In the Course of the discussion which has had place, various weighty considerations have been adduced operating in support of that maxim. Perhaps the superior steadiness of the demand of a domestic market for the surplus produce of the soil, is alone a convincing argument of its truth.

Ideas of a contrariety of interests between the Northern and southern regions of the Union, are in the Main as unfounded as they are mischievous. The diversity of Circumstances on which such contrariety is usually predicated, authorises a directly contrary conclusion. Mutual wants constitute one of the strongest links of political connection, and the extent of the⟨se⟩ bears a natural proportion to the diversity in the means of mutual supply.

Suggestions of an opposite complexion are ever to be deplored, as unfriendly to the steady pursuit of one great common cause, and to the perfect harmony of all the parts.

In proportion as the mind is accustomed to trace the intimate connexion of interest, which subsists between all the parts of a Society united under the *same* government—the infinite variety of channels which serve to Circulate the prosper⟨ity⟩ of each to and through the rest—in that proportion will it be little apt to be disturbed by solicitudes and Apprehensions which originate in local discriminations. It is a truth as important as it is agreeable, and one to which it is not easy to imagine exceptions, that every thing tending to establish *substantial* and *permanent order*, in the affairs of a Country, to increase the total mass of industry and opulence, is ultimately beneficial to every part of it. On the Credit of this great truth, an acquiescence may safely be accorded, from every quarter, to all institutions & arrangements, which promise a confirmation of public order, and an augmentation of National Resource.[191]

But there are more particular considerations which serve to fortify the idea, that the encouragement of manufactures is the interest of all parts of the Union. If the Northern and middle states should be the principal scenes of such establishments, they would immediately benefit the more southern, by creating a demand for productions; some of which they have in common with the other states, and others of which are either peculiar to them, or more abundant, or of better quality, than elsewhere.[192] These productions, principally are Timber, flax, Hemp, Cotton, Wool, raw silk, Indigo, iron, lead, furs, hides, skins and coals. Of these articles Cotton & Indigo are peculiar to the southern states; as are hitherto *Lead* & *Coal.* Flax and Hemp are or may be raised in greater abundance there, than in the More Northern

191. On the tendency of commerce and manufactures to promote "*substantial* and *permanent* order," Smith wrote: ". . . commerce and manufactures gradually introduced order and good government, and with them, the liberty and security of individuals, among the inhabitants of the country, who had before lived almost in a continual state of war with their neighbours, and of servile dependency upon their superiors. This, though it has been the least observed, is by far the most important of all their effects. Mr. Hume is the only writer who, so far as I know, has hitherto taken notice of it" (Smith, *Wealth of Nations,* I, 406).

192. The effect of internal commerce on the Union had often been discussed in the decade preceding 1791, and as early as 1775 H had written in *The Farmer Refuted:* "Nature has disseminated her blessings variously throughout this continent: Some parts of it are favourable to some things, others to others; some colonies are best calculated for grain; others for flax and hemp; others for cotton; and others for live stock of every kind: By this means, a mutually advantageous intercourse may be established between them all. If we were to turn our attention from external to internal commerce, we should give greater stability, and more lasting prosperity to our country, than she can possibly have otherwise" (*The Farmer Refuted, &c.,* February 23, 1775).

states; and the Wool of Virginia is said to be of better quality than that of any other state: a Circumstance rendered the more probable by the reflection that Virginia embraces the same latitudes with the finest Wool Countries of Europe.[193] The Climate of the south is also better adapted to the production of silk.

The extensive cultivation of Cotton can perhaps hardly be expected, but from the previous establishment of domestic Manufactories of the Article; and the surest encouragement and vent, for the others, would result from similar establishments in respect to them.

If then, it satifactorily appears, that it is the Interest of the United states, generally, to encourage manufactures, it merits particular attention, that there are circumstances, which Render the present a critical moment for entering with Zeal upon the important business. The effort cannot fail to be materially seconded by a considerable and encreasing influx of money, in consequence of foreign speculations in the funds—and by the disorders, which exist in different parts of Europe.

The first circumstance not only facilita⟨tes⟩ the execution of manufacturing enterprises; but it indicates them as a necessary mean to turn the thing itself to advantage, and to prevent its being eventually an evil. If useful employment be not found for the Money of foreigners brought to the country to be invested in purchase⟨s⟩ of the public debt, it will quickly be reexported to defray the expence of an extraordinary consumption of foreign luxuries; and distressing drains of our specie may hereafter be experienced to pay the interest and redeem the principal of the purchased debt.

This useful employment too ought to be of a Nature to produce solid and permanent improvements. If the money merely serves to give a temporary spring to foreign commerce; as it cannot procure new and lasting outlets for the products of the Country; there will be no real or durable advantage gained. As far as it shall find its way in Agricultural ameliorations, in opening canals, and in similar improvements, it will be productive of substantial utility. But there is reason to doubt, whether in such channels it is likely to find sufficient employment, and still more whether many of those who possess it, would be as readily attracted to objects of this nature, as to manufac-

193. See note 179.

turing pursuits; which bear greater analogy to those to which they are accustomed, and to the spirit generated by them.

To open the one field, as well as the other, will at least secure a better prospect of useful employment, for whatever accession of money, there has been or may be.

There is at the present juncture a certain fermentation of mind, a certain activity of speculation and enterprise which if properly directed may be made subservient to useful purposes; but which if left entirely to itself, may be attended with pernicious effects.

The disturbed state of Europe, inclining its citizens to emigration, the requisite workmen, will be more easily acquired, than at another time; and the effect of multiplying the opportunities of employment to those who emigrate, may be an increase of the number and extent of valuable acquisitions to the population arts and industry of the Country. To find pleasure in the calamities of other nations, would be criminal; but to benefit ourselves, by opening an asylum to those who suffer, in consequence of them, is as justifiable as it is pol⟨itic.⟩

A full view having now been taken of the inducements to the promotion of Manufactures in the United states, accompanied with an examination of the principal objections which are commonly urged *in opposition*, it is proper in the next place, to consider the means, by which it may be effected, as introductory to a Specification of the objects which in the present state of things appear the most fit to be encouraged, and of the particular measures which it may be adviseable to adopt, in respect to each.

In order to a better judgment of the Means proper to be resorted to by the United states, it will be of use to Advert to those which have been employed with success in other Countries. The principal of these are.

I   Protecting duties—or duties on those foreign articles which are the rivals of the domestic ones, intended to be encouraged.

Duties of this Nature evidently amount to a virtual bounty on the domestic fabrics since by enhancing the charges on foreign Articles, they enable the National Manufacturers to undersell all their foreign Competitors. The propriety of this species of encouragement need not be dwelt upon; as it is not only a clear result from the numerous topics which have been suggested, but is sanctioned by the laws of the United states in a variety of instances; it has the additional recommendat⟨ion⟩ of being a resource of revenue. Indeed all the duties imposed on imported articles, though with an exclusive view to Revenue, have the effect in Contemplation, and except where they fall on raw materials wear a beneficent aspect towards the manufactures of the Country.[194]

II. Prohibitions of rival articles or duties equivalent to prohibitions.

This is another and an efficacious mean of encouraging national manufactures, but in general it is only fit to be employed when a manufacture, has made such a progress and is in so many hands as to insure a due competition, and an adequate supply on reasonable terms. Of duties equivalent to prohibitions, there are examples in the Laws of the United States,[195] and there are other Cases to which the principle may be advantageously extended, but they are not numero⟨us.⟩

Considering a monopoly of the domestic market to its own manufacturers as the reigning policy of manufacturing Nations, a similar policy on the part of the United states in every proper instance, is dictated, it might almost be said, by the principles of distributive justice; certainly by the duty of endeavouring to secure to their own Citizens a reciprocity of advantages.

III Prohibitions of the exportation of the materials of manufactures.

The desire of securing a cheap and plentiful supply for the national workmen, and, where the article is either peculiar to the Country, or of peculiar quality there, the jealousy of enabling foreign workmen to rival those of the nation, with its ow⟨n⟩ Materials, are the leading motives to this species of regulation. ⟨It⟩ ought not to be affirmed, that it is in no instance proper, but it is certainly one which ought to be adopted with great circumspect⟨ion⟩ and only in very plain Cases.

194. Smith opposed protective duties on the following grounds: "All taxes upon consumable commodities, therefore, tend to reduce the quantity of productive labour below what it otherwise would be, either in preparing the commodities taxed, if they are home commodities; or in preparing those with which they are purchased, if they are foreign commodities; Such taxes too always alter, more or less, the natural direction of national industry, and turn it into a channel always different from, and generally less advantageous than that in which it would have run of its own accord" (Smith, *Wealth of Nations*, II, 431–32). See also "Tench Coxe's Draft of the Report on the Subject of Manufactures."

195. See note 179.

It is seen at once, that its immedi⟨ate⟩ operation, is to abridge the demand and keep down the price of the produce of some other branch of industry, generally speaking, of Agriculture, to the prejudice of those, who carry it on; and tho⟨ough⟩ if it be really essential to the prosperity of any very important nati⟨onal⟩ Manufacture, it may happen that those who are injured in the first instance, may be eventually indemnified, by the superior ⟨steadiness⟩ of an extensive domestic market, depending on that prosperity: yet in a matter, in which there is so much room for nice and difficult combinations, in which such opposite considerations combat each other, prudence seems to dictate, that the expedient in question, ought to be indulged with a sparing hand.[196]

IV                    Pecuniary bounties

This has been found one of the most efficacious means of encouraging manufactures, and it is in some views, the best. Though it has not

196. Necker, who also believed that in the United States, at least, prohibitions of export of grains would be too harsh upon farmers, wrote: "Chez les nations naissantes, telles que celles qui se forment aujourd'hui sur le continent de l'Amérique, l'exportation des grains doit être nécessairement libre. La culture s'étendant plus rapidement que les arts et les manufactures ne s'établissent, ce seroit la décourager, ce seroit interdire aux propriétaires la jouissance de leurs subsistances surabondantes, que de ne pas leur permettre de les échanger contre les commodités que fournissent les pays où l'industrie est plus avancée; car il faut du tems avant que le travail des nations naissantes puisse présenter d'autres objets d'échanges que les produits les plus simples de la terre" (Necker, Œuvres, III, 264).

In general, Necker agreed with H that there were few instances in which a prohibition of export would be sound policy. Necker said: "Une nation défend communément la sortie des outils de manufactures qui lui sont propres; et quand elle possede seule une matiere premiere susceptible d'être travaillée et qui excite l'envie générale, elle peut ordonner que l'exportation n'ait lieu qu'après que la matiere aura été fabriquée, afin d'augmenter le travail chez elle, et ses droits sur la puissance des autres nations: mais il est bien peu de circonstances où l'on puisse faire de pareilles loix, parce que, pour les objets d'un besoin indispensable, il y a presque toujours des concurrens, ou du moins des raisons qui empêchent de dicter la loi" (Necker, Œuvres, III, 262).

Adam Smith's objections to the prohibition of the export of raw materials were as follows:

"Our woollen manufacturers, in order to justify their demand of such extraordinary restrictions and regulations, confidently asserted, that English wool was of a peculiar quality, superior to that of any other country; that the wool of other countries could not, without some mixture of it, be wrought up into any tolerable manufacture; that fine cloth could not be made without it; that England, therefore, if the exportation of it could be totally prevented, could monopolize to herself almost the whole woollen trade of the world; and thus, having no rivals, could sell at what price she pleased, and in a short time acquire

yet been practiced upon by the Government of the United states (unless the allowance on the exportation of dried and pickled Fish and salted meat could be considered as a bounty) [197] and though it is less favored by public opinion than some other modes.

Its advantages, are these—

1  It is a species of encouragement more positive and direct than any other, and for that very reason, has a more immediate tendency to stimulate and uphold new enterprises, increasing the chances of profit, and diminishing the risks of loss, in the first attempts.

2.  It avoids the inconvenience of a temporary augmentation of price, which is incident to some other modes, or it produces it to a less degree; either by making no addition to the charges on the rival foreign article, as in the Case of protecting duties, or by making a smaller addition. The first happens when the fund for the bounty is derived from a different object (which may or may not increase the price of some other article, according to the nature of that object) the second, when the fund is derived from the same or a similar object of foreign manufacture. One per cent duty on the foreign article converted into a bounty on the domestic, will have an equal effect with a duty of two per Cent, exclusive of such bounty; and the price of the foreign commodity is liable to be raised, in the one Case, in the proportion of 1 ℔ Cent; in the other, in that of two ℔ Cent. Indeed the bounty when drawn from another source is calculated to promote a reduction of price, because without laying any new charge on the foreign article, it serves to introduce a competition with it, and to increase the total quantity of the article in the Market.

3  Bounties have not like high protecting duties, a tendency to produce scarcity. An increase of price is not always the immediate, though, where the progress of a domestic Manufacture does not

---

the most incredible degree of wealth by the most advantageous balance of trade. . . . It has been shown . . . that the effect of these regulations has been to depress the price of English wool. . . .

"To hurt in any degree the interest of any one order of citizens, for no other purpose but to promote that of some other, is evidently contrary to that justice and equality of treatment which the sovereign owes to all the different orders of his subjects. But the prohibition certainly hurts, in some degree, the interest of the growers of wool, for no other purpose but to promote that of the manufacturers." (Smith, *Wealth of Nations*, II, 162–66.)

197. See note 111.

counteract a rise, it is commonly the ultimate effect of an additional duty. In the interval, between the laying of the duty and a proportional increase of price, it may discourage importation, by interfering with the profits to be expected from the sale of the article.

4.  Bounties are sometimes not only the best, but the only proper expedient, for uniting the encouragement of a new object of agriculture, with that of a new object of manufacture. It is the Interest of the farmer to have the production of the raw material promoted, by counteracting the interference of the foreig⟨n⟩ material of the same kind. It is the interest of the manufactu⟨rer⟩ to have the material abundant and cheap. If prior to the domes⟨tic⟩ production of the Material, in sufficient quantity, to supply the manufacturer on good terms; a duty be laid upon the importation of it from abroad, with a view to promote the raising of it at home, the Interests both of the Farmer and Manufacturer will be disserved. By either destroying the requisite supply, or raising the price of the article, beyond what can be afforded to be given for it, by the Conductor of an infant manufacture, it is abandoned or fails; an⟨d⟩ there being no domestic manufactories to create a demand for t⟨he⟩ raw material, which is raised by the farmer, it is in vain, that the Competition of the like foreign article may have been destroy⟨ed.⟩

It cannot escape notice, that a duty upon the importation of ⟨an⟩ article can no otherwise aid the domestic production of it, than giving the latter greater advantages in the home market. It ca⟨n⟩ have no influence upon the advantageous sale of the article produced, in foreign markets; no tendency, there⟨fore⟩ to promote its exportation.

The true way to conciliate these two interests, is to lay a duty on foreign *manufactures* of the material, the growth of which is desired to be encouraged, and to apply the produce of that duty by way of bounty, either upon the production of the material itself or upon its manufacture at home or upon both. In this disposition of the thing, the Manufacturer commences his enterprise under every advantage, which is attainable, as to quantity or price, of the raw material: And the Farmer if the bounty be immediately to him, is enabled by it to enter into a successful competition with the foreign material; if the bounty be to the manufacturer on so much of the domestic material as he consumes, the operation is nearly the same; he has a motive of interest to prefer the domestic Commodity, if of equal quality, even at a higher price than the foreign, so long as the difference of price is any thing short of the bounty which is allowed upon the article.[198]

Except the simple and ordinary kinds of household Manufactures, or those for which there are very commanding local advantages, pecuniary bounties are in most cases indispensable to the introduction of a new branch. A stimulus and a support not less powerful and direct is generally speaking essential to the overcoming of the obstacles which arise from the Competitions of superior skill and maturity elsewhere. Bounties are especially essential, in regard to articles, upon which those foreigners, who have been accustomed to supply a Country, are in the practice of granting them.

The continuance of bounties on manufactures long established must almost always be of questionable policy: Because a presumption would arise in every such Case, that there were natural and inherent impediments to success. But in new undertakings, they are as justifiable, as they are oftentimes necessary.

There is a degree of prejudice against bounties from an appearance of giving away the public money, without an immediate consideration, and from a supposition, that they serve to enrich particular classes, at the expence of the Community.

But neither of these sources of dislike will bear a serious examination. There is no purpose, to which public money can be more beneficially applied, than to the acquisition of a new and useful branch of industry; no Consideration more valuable than a permanent addition to the general stock of productive labour.

198. Smith objected to bounties because they forced industry "not only into a channel that is less advantageous, but into one that is actually disadvantageous." On the other hand, he wrote: "To encourage the production of any commodity, a bounty upon production, one should imagine, would have a more direct operation, than one upon exportation. It would, besides, impose only one tax upon the people, that which they must contribute in order to pay the bounty. Instead of raising, it would tend to lower the price of the commodity in the home market; and thereby, instead of imposing a second tax upon the people, it might, at least, in part, repay them for what they had contributed to the first. Bounties upon production, however, have been very rarely granted. . . . But it is not the interest of merchants and manufacturers, the great inventors of all these expedients, that the home market should be overstocked with their goods, an event which a bounty upon production might sometimes occasion" (Smith, *Wealth of Nations*, II, 13–14).

H's suggestions on bounties had been recommended by other Americans. See, for example, Barton, *The True Interest*, 27–28; *The American Museum*, V (January, 1789), 50.

Necker, urging the use of "encouragements distributed to commerce, and

As to the second source of objection, it equally lies against other modes of encouragement, which are admitted to be eligible. As often as a duty upon a foreign article makes an addition to its price, it causes an extra expence to the Community, for the benefit of the domestic manufacturer. A bounty does no more: But it is the Interest of the society in each case, to submit to a temporary expence, which is more than compensated, by an increase of industry and Wealth, by an augmentation of resources and independence; & by the circumstance of eventual cheapness, which has been noticed in another place.

It would deserve attention, however, in the employment of this species of encouragement in the United states, as a reason for moderating the degree of it in the instances, in which it might be deemed eligible, that the great distance of this country from Europe imposes very heavy charges on all the fabrics which are brought from thence, amounting from [15 to 30] [199] ℁ Cent on their value, according to their bulk.[200]

A Question has been made concerning the Constitutional right of the Government of the United States to apply this species of encouragement, but there is certainly no good foundation for such a question. The National Legislature has express authority "To lay and Collect taxes, duties, imposts and excises, to pay the debts and provide for the *Common defence* and *general welfare*" with no other qualifi-

---

manufactories," wrote: "The diminution of this expence can never be reckoned in the number of prudent savings, but the intelligent distribution of such bounties is of a great importance: some principles must necessarily be adopted on that subject, if it is intended to produce an efficient benefit with a moderate sum.

"The most essential encouragements, are those that may contribute to introduce new branches of commerce and industry into the kingdom; then we are assured of reaping after having sown; because we shall then, either purchase less merchandize from other nations, or we shall have a greater quantity to dispose of.

". . . If a province, or a part of one, is by its situation, in the impossibility of carrying on any trade with the overplus of its produce, it becomes important to excite by bounties, the establishment of some branch of industry that may be an article of commerce, and that may, as it were, serve to convert the articles of consumption into works, the transport of which would be easier and less expensive. . . . Undoubtedly, the simple combinations of self-interest, may successively exhibit all these branches of industry: but when government has it in its power to forward that exhibition, and consequently the progress of public good; the pecuniary bounties destined thereto, are to be accounted some of the most profitable expences of the State." (Necker, *Finances of France*, II, 474–76.)

199. See note 179.

200. In 1787 Coxe wrote: "Here is a solid premium, operating like a bounty, while it happily costs the consumer nothing, for the charges of importation are

cations than that "all duties, imposts and excises, shall be *uniform* throughout the United states, that no capitation or other direct tax shall be laid unless in proportion to numbers ascertained by a census or enumeration taken on the principles prescribed in the Constitution, and that "no tax or duty shall be laid on articles exported from any state." These three qualifications excepted, the power to *raise money* is *plenary*, and *indefinite;* and the objects to which it may be *appropriated* are no less comprehensive, than the payment of the public debts and the providing for the common defence and *"general Welfare."* The terms *"general Welfare"* were doubtless intended to signify more than was expressed or imported in those which Preceded; otherwise numerous exigencies incident to the affairs of a Nation would have been left without a provision. The phrase is as comprehensive as any that could have been used; because it was not fit that the constitutional authority of the Union, to appropriate its revenues shou'd have been restricted within narrower limits than the "General Welfare" and because this necessarily embraces a vast variety of particulars, which are susceptible neither of specification nor of definition.

It is therefore of necessity left to the discretion of the National Legislature, to pronounce, upon the objects, which concern the general Welfare, and for which under that description, an appropriation of money is requisite and proper. And there seems to be no room for a doubt that whatever concerns the general Interests of *learning* of *Agriculture* of *Manufactures* and of *Commerce* are within the sphere of the national Councils *as far as regards an application of Money.*

The only qualification of the generallity of the Phrase in question, which seems to be admissible, is this—That the object to which an appropriation of money is to be made be *General* and not *local;* its operation extending in fact, or by possibility, throughout the Union, and not being confined to a particular spot.

No objection ought to arise to this construction from a supposition that it would imply a power to do whatever else should appear to

---

unavoidable and the duty being merely for the purpose of revenue, is applied to pay the public debts and expences . . ." (Coxe, *Enquiry*, 24–25). See also note 180. See also "Tench Coxe's Draft of the Report on the Subject of Manufactures."

Congress conducive to the General Welfare. A power to appropriate money with this latitude which is granted too in *express terms* would not carry a power to do any other thing, not authorised in the constitution, either expressly or by fair implication.[201]

V.                                    Premiums

These are of a Nature allied to bounties, though distinguishable from them, in some important features.

Bounties are applicable to the whole quantity of an article produced, or manufactured, or exported, and involve a correspondent expence. Premiums serve to reward some particular excellence or superiority, some extraordinary exertion or skill, and are dispensed on⟨ly⟩ in a small number of cases. But their effect is to stimulate gener⟨al⟩ effort. Contrived so as to be both honorary and lucrative, they address themselves to different passions; touching the chords as well of emulation as of Interest. They are accordingly a very economical mean of exciting the enterprise of a Whole Community.

There are various Societies in different countries, whose object is the dispensation of Premiums for the encouragemen⟨t⟩ of *Agriculture Arts manufactures* and *Commerce;* and though they are for the most part voluntary associations, with comparatively slender funds, their utility has been immense. Much has been done by this mean in great Britain: Scotland in particular owes materially to it a prodigious amelioration of Condition.[202] From a similar establishment in the

201. See "Opinion on the Constitutionality of an Act to Establish a Bank," February 23, 1791.

202. H's information concerning the encouragement to manufactures given in Scotland by a society established for that purpose may have been obtained from Postlethwayt or from a fragment of an undated document in the Hamilton Papers, Library of Congress (possibly written by Samuel Paterson), which describes the activities of "The Trustees for incouraging Fisheries & Manufactures in scotland."

Postlethwayt's description of the same organization and its early activities is as follows: "The wisdom of the legislature cannot be sufficiently admired, for annexing the Highland forfeited estates to the crown . . . and in appropriating the revenues thereof, for the improvement of the country in the manufactures, &c.: and farther for the same purpose, by an act of the last parliament, 3000 l. per ann. payable out of the customs, is granted and put under the management of the commissioners and trustees for improving fisheries and manufactures in Scotland; and they have already made a beginning, and published a plan for distributing the said sum for the first year. . . . For supporting and encouraging the manufacture in those places where it hath been already introduced, but hath not yet arrived to any considerable degree of perfection. . . . It is hoped that these wise and useful measures will have the desired effect" (Postlethwayt, *Universal Dictionary*, II, 672).

United states, supplied and supported by the Government of the Union, vast benefits might reasonably be expected.[203] Some further ideas on this head, shall accordingly be submitted, in the conclusion of this report.

VI The Exemption of the Materials of manufactures from duty.

The policy of that Exemption as a general rule, particularly in reference to new Establishments, is obvious. It can hardly ever be adviseable to add the obstructions of fiscal burthens to the difficulties which naturally embarrass a new manufacture; and where it is matured and in condition to become an object of revenue, it is generally speaking better that the fabric, than the Material should be the subject of Taxation. Ideas of proportion between the quantum of the tax and the value of the article, can be more easily adjusted, in the former, than in the latter case. An argument for exemptions of this kind in the United States, is to be derived from the practice, as far as

203. Postlethwayt, in supporting the distribution of premiums, wrote: "Nothing is more obvious than that the commerce and navigation of this nation principally depends on the daily improvements made by our artificers, in that infinite and amazing variety in our mechanic and manufactural arts. Wherefore artists of this kind, who strike out new inventions, or who improve the old mechanics and manufactures, are deserving of some public regard and encouragement more than what they acquire to themselves by dint of their peculiar profession only.

"Daily experience manifests the extraordinary effects of those small rewards which have been given in Scotland and Ireland, for the improvement of their manufactures; nor do the premiums, perhaps, operate so powerfully as the motive of emulation; for that credit and reputation which attends a man's excelling in his employment, has, sometimes, a far greater influence upon the industrious and ingenious mind, than pecuniary rewards only." (Postlethwayt, *Universal Dictionary*, I, 116.)

Smith, who also was in favor of premiums, wrote: "Premiums given by the public to artists and manufacturers who excel in their particular occupations, are not liable to the same objections as bounties. By encouraging extraordinary dexterity and ingenuity, they serve to keep up the emulation of the workmen actually employed in those respective occupations, and are not considerable enough to turn towards any one of them a greater share of the capital of the country than what would go to it of its own accord. Their tendency is not to overturn the natural balance of employments, but to render the work which is done in each as perfect and complete as possible. The expence of premiums, besides, is very trifling; that of bounties very great" (Smith, *Wealth of Nations*, II, 20).

In the first issue of the *Columbian Magazine* the author of an article on the encouragement of manufactures recommended "that a *Society* be instituted, *for the encouragement of arts, manufactures, and commerce*" (*Columbian Magazine*, I [September, 1786], 29). See also *Columbian Magazine*, IV (March, 1790), 156.

their necessities have permitted, of those nations whom we are to meet as competitors in our own and in foreign Markets.[204]

There are however exceptions to it; of which some examples will be given under the next head.

The Laws of the Union afford instances of the observance of the policy here recommended, but it will probably be found adviseable to extend it to some other Cases. Of a nature, bearing some affinity to that policy is the regulation which exempts from duty the tools and implements, as well as the books, cloths and household furniture of foreign artists, who come to reside in the United states; an advantage already secured to them by the Laws of the Union, and which, it is, in every view, proper to Continue.[205]

VII    Drawbacks of the duties which are imposed on the Materials of Manufactures.

It has already been observed as a general rule that duties on those materials, ought with certain exceptions to be foreborne. Of these exceptions, three cases occur, which may serve as examples—one— where the material is itself, an object of general or extensive consumption, and a fit and productive source of revenue: Another, where a manufacture of a simpler kind [the competition of which with a like domestic article is desired to be restrained,] partakes of the Nature of a raw material, from being capable, by a further process to be converted into a manufacture of a different kind, the introduction or growth of which is desired to be encouraged; a third where the Material itself is a production of the Country, and in sufficient abundance to furnish cheap and plentiful supply to the national Manufacturer.

204. In the following passage Smith described the familiar practices of mercantilism which H is recommending:

"Though the encouragement of exportation, and the discouragement of importation are the two great engines by which the mercantile system proposes to enrich every country, yet with regard to some particular commodities, it seems to follow an opposite plan: to discourage exportation and to encourage importation. . . . It encourages the importation of the materials of manufacture, in order that our own people may be enabled to work them up more cheaply, and thereby prevent a greater and more valuable importation of the manufactured commodities. . .

"The importation of the materials of manufacture has sometimes been encouraged by an exemption from the duties to which other goods are subject, and sometimes by bounties." (Smith, *Wealth of Nations*, II, 153–54). See also "Tench Coxe's Draft of the Report on the Subject of Manufactures."

205. See note 49 for the exemption to which H is referring.

Under the first description comes the article of Molasses. It is not only a fair object of revenue; but being a sweet, it is just that the consumers of it should pay a duty as well as the Consumer(s) of sugar.

Cottons and linens in their White state fall under the second description. A duty upon such as are imported is proper to promote the domestic Manufacture of similar articles in the same state. A drawback of that duty is proper to encourage the printing and staining at home of those which are brought from abroad: When the first of these manufac(tures) has attained sufficient maturity in a Country, to furnish a full supply for (the) second, the utility of the drawback ceases.

The article of Hemp either now does or may be expected soon to exemplify the third Case, in the United states.

Where duties on the materials of manufactures are not laid for the purpose of preventing a competition with some domestic production, the same reasons which recommend, as a general rule, the exemption of those materials from duties, would recommend as a like General rule, the allowance of draw backs, in favor of the manufacturer. Accordingly such drawbacks are familiar in countries which systematically pursue the business of manufactures; which furnishes an argument for the observance of a similar policy in the United states; [206] and the Idea has been adopted by the laws of the Union in the instances of salt and Molasses.[207] It is believed that it will be found advantageous to extend it to some other Articles.

VIII The encouragement of new inventions and discoveries, at home, and of the introduction into the United States of such as may have been made in other countries; particularly those, which relate to machinery.[208]

206. Smith's approval of drawbacks can be found in the following excerpt: "Of these encouragements what are called Drawbacks seem to be the most reasonable. To allow the merchant to draw back upon exportation, either the whole or a part of whatever excise or inland duty is imposed upon domestic industry, can never occasion the exportation of a greater quantity of goods than what would have been exported had no duty been imposed. . . . They tend not to destroy, but to preserve, what it is in most cases advantageous to preserve, the natural division and distribution of labour in the society" (Smith, *Wealth of Nations*, I, 493). See also "Tench Coxe's Draft of the Report on the Subject of Manufactures."

207. For the drawback allowed on salt and molasses, see notes 97 and 111.

208. In his first annual address to Congress, Washington stated: "The advancement of Agriculture, Commerce and Manufactures by all proper means,

This is among the most useful and unexceptionable of the aids, which can be given to manufactures. The usual means of that encouragement are pecuniary rewards, and, for a time, exclusive privileges. The first must be employed, according to the occasion, and the utility of the invention, or discovery: For the last, so far as respects "authors and inventors" provision has been made by Law.[209] But it is desireable in regard to improvements and secrets of extraordinary value, to be able to extend the same benefit to Introducers, as well as Authors and Inventors; a policy which has been practiced with advantage in other countries. Here, however, as in some other cases, there is cause to regret, that the competency of the authority of the National Government to the *good*, which might be done, is not without a question. Many aids might be given to industry; many internal improvements of primary magnitude might be promoted, by an authority operating throughout the Union, which cannot be effected, as well, if at all, by an authority confined within the limits of a single state.

But if the legislature of the Union cannot do all the good, that might be wished, it is at least desirable, that all may be done, which is practicable. Means for promoting the introduction of foreign improvements, though less efficaciously than might be accomplished with more adequate authority, will form a part of the plan intended to be submitted in the close of this report.

It is customary with manufacturing nations to prohibit, under severe penalties, the exportation of implements and machines, which they have either invented or improved. There are already objects for a similar regulation in the United States;[210] and others may be expected to occur from time to time. The adoption of it seems to be dictated by the principle of reciprocity. Greater liberality, in such respects, might better comport with the general spirit of the country;

---

will not I trust need recommendation. But I cannot forbear intimating to you the expediency of giving effectual encouragement as well to the introduction of new and useful inventions from abroad, as to the exertions of skill and genius in producing them at home . . ." (*GW*, XXX, 493).

209. See note 99.

210. "An Act to encourage and protect the Manufactures of this State," March 29, 1788 (*Laws Enacted in the Second Sitting of the Twelfth General Assembly of the Commonwealth of Pennsylvania, Which commenced at Philadelphia, on Tuesday the nineteenth Day of February, in the Year of our Lord, One thousand seven hundred and eighty-[eight]* [Philadelphia, n.d.]). See also "Tench Coxe's Draft of the Report on the Subject of Manufactures."

but a selfish and exclusive policy in other quarters will not always permit the free indulgence of a spirit, which would place us upon an unequal footing. As far as prohibitions tend to prevent foreign competitors from deriving the benefit of the improvements made at home, they tend to increase the advantages of those by whom they may have been introduced; and operate as an encouragement to exertion.

IX  Judicious regulations for the inspection of manufactured commodities.

This is not among the least important of the means, by which the prosperity of manufactures may be promoted. It is indeed in many cases one of the most essential. Contributing to prevent frauds upon consumers at home and exporters to foreign countries—to improve the quality & preserve the character of the national manufactures, it cannot fail to aid the expeditious and advantageous Sale of them, and to serve as a guard against successful competition from other quarters.[211] The reputation of the flour and lumber of some states, and of the Pot ash of others has been established by an attention to this point. And the like good name might be procured for those articles, wheresoever produced, by a judicious and uniform system of Inspection; throughout the ports of the United States.[212] A like system might also be extended with advantage to other commodities.

X  The facilitating of pecuniary remittances from place to place is a point of considerable moment to trade in general, and to manufactures in particular; by rendering more easy the purchase of raw materials and provisions and the payment for manufactured supplies. A general circulation of Bank paper, which is to be expected from the institution lately established [213] will be a most valuable mean to this

211. Necker discussed the question of inspection in "Compte Rendu au Roi," January, 1781. Concerning the removal of inspection, he wrote: "D'un autre côté, pour applanir tous ces obstacles, anéantir absolument, et par une loi positive, toute espece de reglemens, de marques ou d'examens, c'étoit risquer la réputation des fabriques françoises, c'étoit ôter aux consommateurs étrangers et nationaux la base de leur confiance, enfin c'étoit aller contre les idées des vieux fabricans qui avoient vu leurs manufactures et celles de leurs peres, prospérer à l'ombre des loix d'ordre" (Necker, Œuvres, III, 118).

212. According to Victor S. Clark, "Inspection laws guaranteeing the quality of flour, tar, nails, potash, and provisions were reënacted by State legislatures in terms almost identical with those employed by the colonial assemblies" (Victor S. Clark, History of Manufactures in the United States, 1607-1860 [Washington, 1916], 263).

213. The Bank of the United States.
For the encouragement to manufactures which would be rendered by a na-

end. But much good would also accrue from some additional provisions respecting inland bills of exchange. If those drawn in one state payable in another were made negotiable, everywhere, and interest and damages allowed in case of protest, it would greatly promote negotiations between the Citizens of different states, by rendering them more secure; and, with it the convenience and advantage of the Merchants and manufacturers of each.

XI   The facilitating of the transportation of commodities.

Improvements favoring this object intimately concern all the domestic interests of a community; but they may without impropriety be mentioned as having an important relation to manufactures. There is perhaps scarcely any thing, which has been better calculated to assist the manufactures of Great Britain, than the ameliorations of the public roads of that Kingdom, and the great progress which has been of late made in opening canals.[214] Of the former, the United States stand much in need; and for the latter they present uncommon facilities.

The symptoms of attention to the improvement of inland Navigation, which have lately appeared in some quarters, must fill with pleasure every breast warmed with a true Zeal for the prosperity of the Country. These examples, it is to be hoped, will stimulate the exertions of the Government and the Citizens of every state. There can certainly be no object, more worthy of the cares of the local administrations; and it were to be wished, that there was no doubt of the power of the national Government to lend its direct aid, on a comprehensive plan. This is one of those improvements, which could be prosecuted with more efficacy by the whole, than by any part or parts of the Union. There are cases in which the general interest will

---

tional bank and by Federal regulation of inland bills of exchange, see "Tench Coxe's Draft of a Report on the Subject of Manufactures."

214. The value of roads and canals had long been recognized by Europeans. For example, Steuart wrote: "Another advantage of cities is, the necessity arising from thence of having great roads, and these again prove a considerable encouragement to agriculture" (Steuart, *Political Economy*, I, 57).

Among the recommendations contained in Washington's first inaugural address is one concerning the desirability of "facilitating the intercourse between the distant parts of our Country by a due attention to the Post-Office and Post-Roads" (*GW*, XXX, 493). Other Americans in 1791 made similar statements. The following comment is typical: "Roads and Bridges, especially upon the great post road, through the union, are objects of national moment" ([Philadelphia] *Gazette of the United States*, June 29, 1791).

be in danger to be sacrificed to the collission of some supposed local interests. Jealousies, in matters of this kind, are as apt to exist, as they are apt to be erroneous.

The following remarks are sufficiently judicious and pertinent to deserve a literal quotation. "Good roads, canals, and navigable rivers, by diminishing the expence of carriage, put the *remote parts of a country* more nearly upon a level with those in the neighborhood of the town. They are *upon that account* the greatest of all improvements. They encourage the cultivation of the remote, which must always be the most extensive circle of the country. They are advantageous to the Town by breaking down the monopoly of the country in its neighborhood. They are advantageous *even to that part of the Country*. Though they introduce some rival commodities into the old Market, they open many new markets to its produce. Monopoly besides is a great enemy to good management, which can never be universally established, but in consequence of that free and universal competition, which forces every body to have recourse to it for the sake of self defence. It is not more than Fifty years ago that *some of the countries in the neighborhood of London petitioned the Parliament, against the extension of the turnpike roads, into the remoter counties. Those remoter counties, they pretended, from the cheapness of Labor, would be able to sell their grass and corn cheaper in the London Market, than themselves, and they would thereby reduce their rents and ruin their cultivation.* Their rents however have risen and their cultivation has been improved, since that time." [215]

Specimens of a spirit, similar to that which governed the counties here spoken of present themselves too frequently to the eye of an impartial observer, and render it a wish of patriotism, that the body in this Country, in whose councils a local or partial spirit is least likely to predominate, were at liberty to pursue and promote the general interest, in those instances, in which there might be danger of the interference of such a spirit.

The foregoing are the principal of the means, by which the growth of manufactures is ordinarily promoted. It is, however, not merely necessary, that the measures of government, which have a direct view to manufactures, should be calculated to assist and protect them, but that those which only collaterally affect them, in the

215. See note 100.

general course of the administration, should be gaurded from any peculiar tendency to injure them.

There are certain species of taxes, which are apt to be oppressive to different parts of the community, and among other ill effects have a very unfriendly aspect towards manufactures. All Poll or Capitation taxes are of this nature. They either proceed, according to a fixed rate, which operates unequally, and injuriously to the industrious poor; or they vest a discretion in certain officers, to make estimates and assessments which are necessarily vague, conjectural and liable to abuse. They ought therefore to be abstained from, in all but cases of distressing emergency.

All such taxes (including all taxes on occupations) which proceed according to the amount of capital *supposed* to be employed in a business, or of profits *supposed* to be made in it are unavoidably hurtful to industry. It is in vain, that the evil may be endeavoured to be mitigated by leaving it, in the first instance, in the option of the party to be taxed, to declare the amount of his capital or profits.

Men engaged in any trade of business have commonly weighty reasons to avoid disclosures, which would expose, with any thing like accuracy, the real state of their affairs. They most frequently find it better to risk oppression, than to avail themselves of so inconvenient a refuge. And the consequence is, that they often suffer oppression.

When the disclosure too, if made, is not definitive, but controulable by the discretion, or in other words, by the passions & prejudices of the revenue officers, it is not only an ineffectual protection, but the possibility of its being so is an additional reason for not resorting to it.

Allowing to the public officers the most equitable dispositions; yet where they are to exercise a discretion, without certain data, they cannot fail to be often misled by appearances. The quantity of business, which seems to be going on, is, in a vast number of cases, a very deceitful criterion of the profits which are made; yet it is perhaps the best they can have, and it is the one, on which they will most naturally rely. A business therefore which may rather require aid, from the government, than be in a capacity to be contributory to it, may find itself crushed by the mistaken conjectures of the Assessors of taxes.

Arbitrary taxes, under which denomination are comprised all those, that leave the *quantum* of the tax to be raised on each person, to the *discretion* of certain officers, are as contrary to the genius of liberty

as to the maxims of industry. In this light, they have been viewed by
the most judicious observers on government; [216] who have bestowed
upon them the severest epithets of reprobation; as constituting one
of the worst features usually to be met with in the practice of despotic governments.

It is certain at least, that such taxes are particularly inimical to the
success of manufacturing industry, and ought carefully to be avoided
by a government, which desires to promote it

The great copiousness of the subject of this Report has insensibly
led to a more lengthy preliminary discussion, than was originally
contemplated, or intended. It appeared proper to investigate principles, to consider objections, and to endeavour to establish the utility
of the thing proposed to be encouraged; previous to a specification of
the objects which might occur, as meriting or requiring encouragement, and of the measures, which might be proper, in respect to each.
The first purpose having been fulfilled, it remains to pursue the second. In the selection of objects, five circumstances seem intitled to
particular attention; the capacity of the Country to furnish the raw
material—the degree in which the nature of the manufacture admits
of a substitute for manual labour in machinery—the facility of execution—the extensiveness of the uses, to which the article can be applied
—its subserviency to other interests, particularly the great one of

216. In a similar vein, Smith wrote: "The tax which each individual is
bound to pay ought to be certain, and not arbitrary. The time of payment, the
manner of payment, the quantity to be paid, ought all to be clear and plain
to the contributor, and to every other person. Where it is otherwise, every
person subject to the tax is put more or less in the power of the tax-gatherer,
who can either aggravate the tax upon any obnoxious contributor, or extort, by
the terror of such aggravation, some present or perquisite to himself. The uncertainty of taxation encourages the insolence and favours the corruption of an
order of men who are naturally unpopular, even where they are neither insolent
nor corrupt. The certainty of what each individual ought to pay is, in taxation,
a matter of so great importance, that a very considerable degree of inequality,
it appears, I believe, from the experience of all nations, is not near so great an
evil as a very small degree of uncertainty" (Smith, *Wealth of Nations*, II, 349).
In the course of a discussion of Colbert's elimination of an arbitrary tax,
Necker wrote: "Convaincu que rien n'est plus insupportable à l'homme que le
caprice des autorités subalternes, il voulut y soustraire cet impôt par des reglemens uniformes, et il desira de le fixer d'une maniere invariable, en le propor-
tionnant à la terre, par un cadastre général" (Necker, *Œuvres*, III, 201).
Hume wrote: "But the most pernicious of all taxes are those which are
arbitrary. They are commonly converted, by their management, into punish-
ments on industry; and also, by their unavoidable inequality, are more grievous
than by the real burthen, which they impose" (Hume, *Political Discourses*, 119).

national defence.[217] There are however objects, to which these circumstances are little applicable, which for some special reasons, may have a claim to encouragement.

A designation of the principal raw material of which each manufacture is composed will serve to introduce the remarks upon it. As, in the first place—

## Iron

The manufactures of this article are entitled to preeminent rank. None are more essential in their kinds, nor so extensive in their uses. They constitute in whole or in part the implements or the materials or both of almost every useful occupation. Their instrumentality is everywhere conspicuous.

It is fortunate for the United States that they have peculiar advantages for deriving the full benefit of this most valuable material, and they have every motive to improve it, with systematic care. It is to be found in various parts of the United States, in great abundance and of almost every quality; and fuel the chief instrument in manufacturing it, is both cheap and plenty. This particularly applies to Charcoal; but there are productive coal mines already in operation, and strong indications, that the material is to be found in abundance, in a variety of other places.

The inquiries to which the subject of this report has led have been answered with proofs that manufactories of Iron, though generally understood to be extensive, are far more so than is commonly supposed.[218] The kinds, in which the greatest progress has been made,

217. Several Americans suggested similar criteria for deciding what manufactures should be encouraged. In 1791 Coxe wrote: "Should a considerable part of our capital be forced out of navigation and foreign trade, the government, without imposing *generally* heavy protecting duties, burdensome to the nation, may give employment for the money, by holding out effectual encouragement to *one branch of manufactures at a time*. If it be selected with judgment—if the use of manual labour be confined within as narrow limits as possible—if labour-saving machines be used—if the articles it works on, be made free of duty—if the growth of them be encouraged at home—if a convenient progressive duty be imposed, there can be little doubt of success" (Coxe, *Brief Examination*, 85).

For other examples, see *Columbian Magazine*, I (September, 1786), 28, and *The American Museum*, II (September, 1787), 258.

218. See Carrington to H, October 4, 1791; "Report of a Committee Appointed to Obtain Information on Manufacturing in Providence," October 10, 1791, printed as an enclosure to John Dexter to H, October, 1791; and Silas Condict to Aaron Dunham, August 25, 1791, printed as an enclosure to Dunham

have been mentioned in another place, and need not be repeated; but there is little doubt that every other kind, with due cultivation, will rapidly succeed. It is worthy of remark that several of the particular trades, of which it is the basis, are capable of being carried on without the aid of large capitals.

Iron works have very greatly increased in the United States and are prosecuted, with much more advantage than formerly. The average price before the revolution was about Sixty four Dollars ℔. Ton —at present it is about Eighty; a rise which is chiefly to be attributed to the increase of manufactures of the material.[219]

The still further extension and multiplication of such manufactures will have the double effect of promoting the extraction of the Metal itself, and of converting it to a greater number of profitable purposes.

Those manufactures too unite in a greater degree, than almost any others, the several requisities, which have been mentioned, as proper to be consulted in the selection of objects.

The only further encouragement of manufactories of this article, the propriety of which may be considered as unquestionable, seems to be an increase of the duties on foreign rival commodities.

Steel is a branch, which has already made a considerable progress, and it is ascertained that some new enterprizes, on a more extensive scale, have been lately set on foot. The facility of carrying it to an extent, which will supply all internal demands, and furnish a considerable surplus for exportation cannot be doubted.[220] The duty [221]

---

to H, September 9, 1791. Also see the following enclosures to John Chester to H, October 11, 1791: Peter Colt to Chester, July 21, 1791; Heman Swift to Chester, August 22, 1791; Joseph P. Cooke to Chester, September 12, 1791; Alexander King to Roger Newberry, September 12, 1791; Aaron Elliot to Hezekiah Lane, September 14, 1791.

219. Coxe, in replying to Lord Sheffield's remarks concerning the high price of American iron products, wrote: "Bar iron before the revolution, was usually sold for sixty four dollars. It fell, after the war, to the same price; and large quantities of iron in bars and pigs were exported. The progress of manufactures has raised these articles to the highest prices ever known in peace; and only 200 tons in bars, and 3555 tons in pigs were exported in thirteen months and a half of 1789, and 1790" (Coxe, Brief Examination, 14).

220. See Nathaniel Hazard to H, March 9, 1791. It should also be noted, however, that the belief that steel could be manufactured in sufficient quantity to meet the needs of the United States had been questiond in Congress. Richard Bland Lee of Virginia, for example, "did not believe that any gentleman would contend, that enough of this article to answer consumption could be fabricated in any part of the Union" (Annals of Congress, I, 153).

221. For the duties cited in this section, see note 49.

upon the importation of this article, which is at present seventy five cents ⅌ Cwt., may it is conceived be safely and advantageously extended to 100 Cents. It is desireable, by decisive arrangements, to second the efforts, which are making in so very valuable a branch.

The United States already in a great measure supply themselves with Nails & Spikes. They are able, and ought certainly, to do it intirely. The first and most laborious operation, in this manufacture is performed by water mills; and of the persons afterwards employed a great proportion are boys, whose early habits of industry are of importance to the community, to the present support of their families, and to their own future comfort. It is not less curious than true, that in certain parts of the country, the making of Nails is an occasional family manufacture.[222]

The expendiency of an additional duty on these articles is indicated by an important fact. About one million 800,000 pounds of them were imported into the United States in the course of a year ending the 30th. of September 1790. A duty of two Cents ⅌ lb [223] would, it is presumeable, speedily put an end to so considerable an importation. And it is in every view proper that an end should be put to it.

The manufacture of these articles, like that of some others, suffers from the carelessness and dishonesty of a part of those who carry it on. An inspection in certain cases might tend to correct the evil.[224] It will deserve consideration whether a regulation of this sort cannot be applied, without inconvenience, to the exportation of the articles either to foreign countries, or from one state to another.

The implements of husbandry are made in several States in great abundance. In many places it is done by the common blacksmiths. And there is no doubt that an ample supply for the whole country can with great ease be procured among ourselves.

Various kinds of edged tools for the use of Mechanics are also made; and a considerable quantity of hollow wares; though the business of castings has not yet attained the perfection which might be

222. See Nathaniel Gorham to H, October 13, 1791. Also see "Report of a Committee Appointed to Obtain Information on Manufacturing in Providence," October 10, 1791, printed as an enclosure to John Dexter to H, October, 1791.

223. See Chauncey Whittelsey to John Chester, September 27, 1791, printed as an enclosure to Chester to H, October 11, 1791.

224. Inspection had been recommended by Silas Condict (Condict to Aaron Dunham, August 25, 1791, printed as an enclosure to Dunham to H, September 9, 1791).

wished. It is however improving, and as there are respectable capitals in good hands, embarked in the prosecution of those branches of iron manufactories, which are yet in their infancy, they may all be contemplated as objects not difficult to be acquired.

To ensure the end, it seems equally safe and prudent to extend the duty ad valorem upon all manufactures of Iron, or of which iron is the article of chief value, to ten per Cent.

Fire arms and other military weapons may it is conceived, be placed without inconvenience in the class of articles rated at 15 ⅌. Cent. There are already manufactories of these articles, which only require the stimulus of a certain demand to render them adequate to the supply of the United States.

It would also be a material aid to manufactories of this nature, as well as a mean of public security, if provision should be made for an annual purchase of military weapons, of home manufacture to a certain determinate extent, in order to the formation of Arsenals; [225] and to replace from time to time such as should be withdrawn for use, so as always to have in store the quantity of each kind, which should be deemed a competent supply.

But it may hereafter deserve legislative consideration, whether manufactories of all the necessary weapons of war ought not to be established, on account of the Government itself. Such establishments are agreeable to the usual practice of Nations and that practice seems founded on sufficient reason.

There appears to be an improvidence, in leaving these essential instruments of national defence to the casual speculations of individual adventure; a resource which can less be relied upon, in this case than in most others; the articles in question not being objects of ordinary and indispensable private consumption or use. As a general rule, manufactories on the immediate account of Government are to be avoided; but this seems to be one of the few exceptions, which that rule admits, depending on very special reasons.

Manufactures of Steel, generally, or of which steel is the article of chief value, may with advantage be placed in the class of goods rated at 7½ per Cent. As manufactures of this kind have not yet made any considerable progress, it is a reason for not rating them as high as

225. Arsenals had been suggested by Washington in a letter to H of October 14, 1791.

those of iron; but as this material is the basis of them, and as their extension is not less practicable, than important, it is desireable to promote it by a somewhat higher duty than the present.

A question arises, how far it might be expedient to permit the importation of iron in pigs and bars free from duty. It would certainly be favourable to manufactures of the article; but the doubt is whether it might not interfere with its production.

Two circumstances, however, abate if they do not remove apprehension, on this score; one is, the considerable increase of price, which has been already remarked, and which renders it probable, that the free admission of foreign iron would not be inconsistent with an adequate profit to the proprietors of Iron Works; the other is, the augmentation of demand, which would be likely to attend the increase of manufactures of the article, in consequence of the additional encouragements proposed to be given. But caution nevertheless in a matter of this kind is most adviseable. The measure suggested ought perhaps rather to be contemplated, subject to the lights of further experience, than immediately adopted.

## Copper

The manufactures of which this article is susceptible are also of great extent and utility. Under this description, those of brass, of which it is the principal ingreedient, are intended to be included.

The material is a natural production of the Country. Mines of Copper have actually been wrought, and with profit to the undertakers, though it is not known, that any are now in this condition. And nothing is easier, than the introduction of it, from other countries, on moderate terms, and in great plenty.

Coppersmiths and brass founders, particularly the former, are numerous in the United States; some of whom carry on business to a respectable extent.

To multiply and extend manufactories of the materials in question is worthy of attention and effort. In order to this, it is desireable to facilitate a plentiful supply of the materials. And a proper mean to this end is to place them in the class of free articles. Copper in plates and brass are already in this predicament, but copper in pigs and bars is not—neither is *lapis calaminaris,* which together with *copper* and *charcoal,* constitute the component ingredients of brass. The exemption from duty, by parity of reason, ought to embrace all such of these articles, as are objects of importation. An additional duty, on brass wares, will tend to the general end in view. These now stand at 5 ꝑ. Cent, while those of tin, pewter and copper are rated at 7½. There appears to be a propriety in every view in placing brass wares upon the same level with them; and it merits consideration whether the duty upon all of them ought not to be raised to 10 ꝑ. Cent.[226]

## Lead

There are numerous proofs, that this material abounds in the United States, and requires little to unfold it to an extent, more than equal to every domestic occasion. A prolific mine of it has long been open in the South Western parts of Virginia, and under a public administration, during the late war, yielded a considerable supply for military use. This is now in the hands of individuals, who not only carry it on with spirit; but have established manufactories of it, at Richmond, in the same State.[227]

The duties, already laid upon the importation of this article, either in its unmanufactured, or manufactured state, ensure it a decisive advantage in the home market—which amounts to considerable encouragement. If the duty on pewter wares should be raised it would afford a further encouragement.[228] Nothing else occurs as proper to be added.

## Fossil Coal

This, as an important instrument of manufactures, may without impropriety be mentioned among the subjects of this Report.

A copious supply of it would be of great consequence to the iron branch: As an article of household fuel also it is an interesting production; the utility of which must increase in proportion to the de-

226. See "Report of a Committee Appointed to Obtain Information on Manufacturing in Providence," October 10, 1791, printed as an enclosure to John Dexter to H, October, 1791.
227. See Edward Carrington to H, October 4, 1791.
228. See "Report of a Committee Appointed to Obtain Information on Manufacturing in Providence," October 10, 1791, printed as an enclosure to John Dexter to H, October, 1791.

crease of wood, by the progress of settlement and cultivation. And its importance to navigation, as an immense article of transportation coastwise, is signally exemplified in Great Britain.[229]

It is known, that there are several coal mines in Virginia, now worked; and appearances of their existence are familiar in a number of places.

The expediency of a bounty on all the species of coal of home production, and of premiums, on the opening of new mines, under certain qualifications, appears to be worthy of particular examination. The great importance of the article will amply justify a reasonable expence in this way, if it shall appear to be necessary to and shall be thought it likely to answer the end.[230]

## Wood

Several manufactures of this article flourish in the United States. Ships are no where built in greater perfection, and cabinet wares, generally, are made little if at all inferior to those of Europe. Their extent is such as to have admitted of considerable exportation.

An exemption from duty of the several kinds of wood ordinarily used in these manufactures seems to be all, that is requisite, by way of encouragement. It is recommended by the consideration of a similar policy being pursued in other countries, and by the expediency of giving equal advantages to our own workmen in wood. The abundance of Timber proper for ship building in the United States does not appear to be any objection to it. The increasing scarcity and the growing importance of that article, in the European countries, ad-

229. Smith, in discussing the importance of coal to the coastal trade, wrote: "The coal-trade from Newcastle to London, for example, employs more shipping than all the carrying trade of England, though the ports are at no great distance" (Smith, *Wealth of Nations*, I, 370–71).

230. Coxe wrote: "All our coal has hitherto been accidently found on the surface of the earth, or discovered in the digging of common cellars or wells: so that when our wood-fuel shall become scarce, and the European methods of boring shall be skilfully pursued, there can be no doubt of our finding it in many other places. At present, the ballasting of ships from coal countries abroad, and the coal mines in Virginia, which lie convenient to ship-navigation, occasion a good deal of coal to be brought to the Philadelphia market. From this great abundance and variety of fuel, it results, that Pennsylvania, and the united states in general, are well suited to all manufactories which are effected by fire, such as furnaces, founderies, forges, glass-houses, breweries, distilleries, steel-works, smiths' shops, and all other manufactories in metal, soap-boiling, chandlers' shops, pot ash works, sugar and other rafineries, &c. &c." (*The American Museum*, VII [June, 1790], 299).

monish the United States to commence, and systematically to pursue, measures for the preservation of their stock. Whatever may promote the regular establishment of Magazines of Ship Timber is in various views desireable.

## Skins

There are scarcely any manufactories of greater importance, than of this article. Their direct and very happy influence upon Agriculture, by promoting the raising of Cattle of different kinds, is a very material recommendation.

It is pleasing too, to observe the extensive progress they have made in their principal branches; which are so far matured as almost to defy foreign competition. Tanneries in particular are not only carried on as a regular business, in numerous instances and in various parts of the Country; but they constitute in some places a valuable item of incidental family manufactures.

Representations however have been made, importing the expediency of further encouragement to the Leather-Branch in two ways— one by increasing the duty on the manufactures of it, which are imported—the other by prohibiting the exportation of bark. In support of the latter it is alleged that the price of bark, chiefly in consequence of large exportations, has risen within a few years from [about three Dollars to four dollars and a half per cord.] [231]

These suggestions are submitted rather as intimations, which merit consideration, than as matters, the propriety of which is manifest. It is not clear, that an increase of duty is necessary: and in regard to the prohibition desired, there is no evidence of any considerable exportation hitherto; and it is most probable, that whatever augmentation of price may have taken place, is to be attributed to an extension of the home demand from the increase of manufactures, and to a decrease of the supply in consequence of the progress of Settlement; rather than to the quantities which have been exported.

It is mentioned however, as an additional reason for the prohibition, that one species of the bark usually exported is in some sort peculiar to the country, and the material of a very valuable dye, of great use in some other manufactures, in which the United States have begun a competition.

231. See note 179.

There may also be this argument in favor of an increase of duty. The object is of importance enough to claim decisive encouragement and the progress, which has been made, leaves no room to apprehend any inconvenience on the score of supply from such an increase.

It would be of benefit to this branch, if glue which is now rated at 5 perCent, were made the object of an excluding duty. It is already made in large quantities at various tanneries; and like paper, is an entire œconomy of materials, which if not manufactured would be left to perish. It may be placed with advantage in the class of articles paying 15 perCent.

### Grain

Manufactures of the several species of this article have a title to peculiar favor; not only because they are most of them immediately connected with the subsistence of the citizens; but because they enlarge the demand for the most precious products of the soil.

Though flour may with propriety be noticed as a manufacture of Grain, it were useless to do it, but for the purpose of submitting the expediency of a general system of inspection, throughout the ports of the United states; which, if established upon proper principles, would be likely to improve the quality of our flour every where, and to raise its reputation in foreign markets. There are however considerations which stand in the way of such an arrangement.

Ardent spirits and malt liquors are, next to flour, the two principal manufactures of Grain. The first has made a very extensive, the last a considerable progress in the United States. In respect to both, an exclusive possession of the home market ought to be secured to the domestic manufacturers; as fast as circumstances will admit. Nothing is more practicable & nothing more desireable.

The existing laws of the United States [232] have done much towards attaining this valuable object; but some additions to the present duties, on foreign distilled spirits, and foreign malt liquors, and perhaps an abatement of those on home made spirits, would more effectually secure it; and there does not occur any very weighty objection to either.

232. "An Act repealing, after the last day of June next, the duties heretofore laid upon Distilled Spirits imported from abroad, and laying others in their stead; and also upon Spirits distilled within the United States, and for appropriating the same" (1 Stat. 199–214 [March 3, 1791]).

An augmentation of the duties on imported spirits would favour, as well the distillation of Spirits from molasses, as that from Grain. And to secure to the nation the benefit of the manufacture, even of foreign materials, is always of great, though perhaps of secondary importance.

A strong impression prevails in the minds of those concerned in distilleries [233] (including too the most candid and enlightened) that greater differences in the rates of duty on foreign and domestic spirits are necessary, completely to secure the successful manufacture of the latter; and there are facts which entitle this impression to attention.

It is known, that the price of molasses for some years past, has been successively rising in the West India Markets, owing partly to a competition, which did not formerly exist, and partly to an extension of demand in this country; and it is evident, that the late disturbances in those Islands,[234] from which we draw our principal supply, must so far interfere with the production of the article, as to occasion a material enhancement of price. The destruction and devastation attendant on the insurrection in Hispaniola, in particular, must not only contribute very much to that effect, but may be expected to give it some duration. These circumstances, and the duty of three cents per Gallon on molasses, may render it difficult for the distillers of that material to maintain with adequate profit a competition, with the rum brought from the West Indies, the quality of which is so considerably superior.

The consumption of Geneva or Gin in this country is extensive. It is not long since distilleries of it have grown up among us, to any importance. They are now becoming of consequence, but being still in their infancy, they require protection.

It is represented, that the price of some of the materials is greater here, than in Holland, from which place large quantities are brought,

233. On November 16, 1791, "A petition of the distillers of spirits in the town of Salem, in the State of Massachusetts, was presented to the House and read, praying a reduction of duties, and farther revision and amendment of the act, passed at the last session, for laying duties on spirits distilled within the United States. . . ." This petition was "referred to the Secretary of the Treasury, for his information" (*Journal of the House*, I, 455).

See also Fisher Ames to H, September 8, 1791.

234. A slave revolt on the plantations in Haiti began on August 23, 1791. It resulted in widespread property damage in most of the northern plain around Cap-Français.

the price of labour considerably greater, the capitals engaged in the business there much larger, than those which are employed here, the rate of profits, at which the Undertakers can afford to carry it on, much less—the prejudices, in favor of imported Gin, strong.[235] These circumstances are alleged to outweigh the charges, which attend the bringing of the Article, from Europe to the United states and the present difference of duty, so as to obstruct the prosecution of the manufacture, with due advantage.

Experiment could perhaps alone decide with certainty the justness of the suggestions, which are made; but in relation to branches of manufacture so important, it would seem inexpedient to hazard an unfavourable issue, and better to err on the side of too great, than of too small a difference, in the particular in question.

It is therefore submitted, that an addition of two cents per Gallon be made to the duty on imported spirits of the first class of proof, with a proportionable increase on those of higher proof; and that a deduction of one cent per Gallon be made from the duty on spirits distilled within the United states, beginning with the first class of proof, and a proportionable deduction from the duty on those of higher proof.

It is ascertained, that by far the greatest part of the malt liquors consumed in the United States are the produce of domestic breweries. It is desireable, and, in all likelihood, attainable, that the whole consumption should be supplied by ourselves.

The malt liquors, made at home, though inferior to the best are equal to a great part of those, which have been usually imported. The progress already made is an earnest of what may be accomplished. The growing competition is an assurance of improvement. This will be accelerated by measures, tending to invite a greater capital into this channel of employment.

To render the encouragement to domestic breweries decisive, it may be adviseable to substitute to the present rates of duty eight

235. On November 24, 1791, "A petition of Kendrick Doyer, Geneva distiller, in the city of New York, was presented to the House and read, praying that the act, passed at the last session, imposing a duty on distilled spirits, may be so modified and amended, that the duty on Geneva, imported from abroad, may be augmented, and the duty on the said article, distilled within the United States, reduced." This petition was "referred to the Secretary of the Treasury for his information" (*Journal of the House,* I, 461).

cents per gallon generally; and it will deserve to be considered as a gaurd against evasions, whether there ought not to be a prohibition of their importation, except in casks of considerable capacity. It is to be hoped, that such a duty would banish from the market, foreign malt liquors of inferior quality; and that the best kind only would continue to be imported till it should be supplanted, by the efforts of equal skill or care at home.

Till that period, the importation so qualified would be an useful stimulous to improvement: And in the mean time, the payment of the increased price, for the enjoyment of a luxury, in order to the encouragement of a most useful branch of domestic industry, could not reasonably be deemed a hardship.

As a further aid to the manufactures of grain, though upon a smaller scale, the articles of Starch, hair powder and wafers, may with great propriety be placed among those, which are rated at 15 perCent. No manufactures are more simple, nor more completely within the reach of a full supply, from domestic sources, and it is a policy, as common as it is obvious, to make them the objects either of prohibitory duties, or of express prohibition.

### Flax and Hemp

Manufactures of these articles have so much affinity to each other, and they are so often blended, that they may with advantage be considered in conjunction. The importance of the linnin branch to agriculture—its precious effects upon household industry—the ease, with which the materials can be produced at home to any requisite extent —the great advances, which have been already made, in the coarser fabricks of them, especially in the family way, constitute claims, of peculiar force, to the patronage of government.

This patronage may be afforded in various ways; by promoting the growth of the materials; by increasing the impediments to an advantageous competition of rival foreign articles; by direct bounties or premiums upon the home manufacture.

First.  As to promoting the growth of the materials.

In respect to hemp, something has been already done by the high duty upon foreign hemp. If the facilities for domestic production were not unusually great, the policy of the duty, on the foreign raw material, would be highly questionable, as interfering with the growth of manufactures of it. But making the proper allowances for those facilities, and with an eye to the future and natural progress, of the country, the measure does not appear, upon the whole, exceptionable. A strong wish naturally suggests itself, that some method could be devised of affording a more direct encouragement to the growth both of flax and hemp; such as would be effectual, and at the same time not attended with too great inconveniences. To this end, bounties and premiums offer themselves to *consideration;* but no modification of them has yet occurred, which would not either hazard too much expence, or operate unequally in reference to the circumstances of different parts of the Union; and which would not be attended with very great difficulties in the execution.

Secondly—

As to encreasing the impediments to an advantageous competition of rival foreign articles.

To this purpose, an augmentation of the duties on importation is the obvious expedient; which, in regard to certain articles, appears to be recommended by sufficient reasons.

The principal of these articles is Sail cloth; one intimately connected with navigation and defence; and of which a flourishing manufactory is established at Boston and very promising ones at several other places.[236]

It is presumed to be both safe and adviseable to place this in the class of articles rated at 10 Per cent. A strong reason for it results from the consideration that a bounty of two pence sterling per ell is allowed, in Great Britain, upon the exportation of the sail cloth manufactured in that Kingdom.[237]

It would likewise appear to be good policy to raise the duty to 7½ perCent on the following articles. Drillings, Osnaburghs, Ticklenburghs, Dowlas, Canvas, Brown Rolls, Bagging, and upon all other linnens the first cost of which at the place of exportation does not exceed 35 cents per yard. A bounty of 12½ ⊕ Cent, upon an average on the exportation of such or similar linens from Great-Britain encourages the manufacture of them in that country and increases the

236. See Nathaniel Gorham to H, October 13, 1791; Joseph Whipple to H, September 6, 1791.
237. See note 105.

obstacles to a successful competition in the countries to which they are sent.[238]

The quantities of tow and other household linnens manufactured in different parts of the United States and the expectations, which are derived from some late experiments, of being able to extend the use of labour-saving machines, in the coarser fabrics of linnen, obviate the danger of inconvenience, from an increase of the duty upon such articles, and authorize a hope of speedy and complete success to the endeavours, which may be used for procuring an internal supply.

Thirdly, As to direct bounties, or premiums upon the manufactured articles.

To afford more effectual encouragement to the manufacture, and at the same time to promote the cheapness of the article for the benefit of navigation, it will be of great use to allow a bounty of two Cents ℔ yard on all Sail Cloth, which is made in the United States from materials of their own growth. This would also assist the Culture of those materials. An encouragement of this kind if adopted ought to be established for a moderate term of years, to invite to new undertakings and to an extension of the old. This is an article of importance enough to warrant the employment of extraordinary means in its favor.

### Cotton

There is something in the texture of this material, which adapts it in a peculiar degree to the application of Machines. The signal Utility of the mill for spinning of cotton, not long since invented in England, has been noticed in another place; but there are other machines scarcely inferior in utility which, in the different manufactories of this article are employed either exclusively, or with more than ordinary effect. This very important circumstance recommends the fabricks of cotton, in a more particular manner, to a country in which a defect of hands constitutes the greatest obstacle to success.

The variety and extent of the uses to which the manufactures of this article are applicable is another powerful argument in their favor.

And the faculty of the United States to produce the raw material in abundance, & of a quality, which though alledged to be inferior to

238. See note 105.

some that is produced in other quarters, is nevertheles capable of being used with advantage, in many fabrics, and is probably susceptible of being carried, by a more experienced culture, to much greater perfection—suggests an additional and a very cogent inducement to the vigorous pursuit of the cotton branch, in its several subdivisions.

How much has been already done has been stated in a preceding part of this report.

In addition to this, it may be announced, that a society is forming with a capital which is expected to be extended to at least half a million of dollars; on behalf of which measures are already in train for prosecuting on a large scale, the making and printing of cotton goods.[239]

These circumstances conspire to indicate the expediency of removing any obstructions, which may happen to exist, to the advantageous prosecution of the manufactories in question, and of adding such encouragements, as may appear necessary and proper.

The present duty of three cents ℔ lb. on the foreign raw material, is undoubtedly a very serious impediment to the progress of those manufactories.[240]

The injurious tendency of similar duties either prior to the establishment, or in the infancy of the domestic manufacture of the article, as it regards the manufacture, and their worse than inutility, in relation to the home production of the material itself, have been anticipated particularly in discussing the subject of pecuniary bounties.

Cotton has not the same pretensions, with hemp, to form an exception to the general rule.

Not being, like hemp an universal production of the Country it affords less assurance of an adequate internal supply; but the chief objection arises from the doubts; which are entertained concerning the quality of the national cotton. It is alledged, that the fibre of it is considerably shorter and weaker, than that of some other places; and it has been observed as a general rule, that the nearer the place of growth to the Equator, the better the quality of the cotton. That which comes from Cayenne,[241] Surrinam and Demarara is said to

239. H is referring to the Society for Establishing Useful Manufactures.
240. See Moses Brown to John Dexter, July 22–October 15, 1791, printed as an enclosure to Dexter to H, October, 1791.
241. See note 179.

be preferable, even at a material difference of price, to the Cotton of the Islands.[242]

While a hope may reasonably be indulged, that with due care and attention the national cotton may be made to approach nearer than it now does to that of regions, somewhat more favored by climate; and while facts authorize an opinion, that very great use may be made of it, and that it is a resource which gives greater security to the cotton fabrics of this country, than can be enjoyed by any which depends wholly on external supply it will certainly be wise, in every view, to let our infant manufactures have the full benefit of the best materials on the cheapest terms.

It is obvious that the necessity of having such materials is proportioned to the unskilfulness and inexperience of the workmen employed, who if inexpert, will not fail to commit great waste, where the materials they are to work with are of an indifferent kind.[243]

To secure to the national manufactures so essential an advantage, a repeal of the present duty on imported cotton is indispensible.

A substitute for this, far more encouraging to domestic production, will be to grant a bounty on the national cotton, when wrought at a home manufactory;[244] to which a bounty on the exportation of it may be added. Either or both would do much more towards promoting the growth of the article, than the merely nominal encouragement, which it is proposed to abolish. The first would also have a direct influence in encouraging the manufacture.

The bounty which has been mentioned as existing in Great Britain, upon the exportation of coarse linnens not exceeding a certain value, applies also to certain discriptions of cotton goods of similar value.

This furnishes an additional argument for allowing to the national manufacturers the species of encouragement just suggested, and indeed for adding some other aid.

One cent per yard, not less than of a given width, on all goods of cotton, or of cotton and linnen mixed, which are manufactured in the United States; with the addition of one cent ℔ lb weight of the material; if made of national cotton; would amount to an aid of con-

242. See George Cabot to H, September 6, 1791.
243. See George Cabot to H, September 6, 1791.
244. See Moses Brown to John Dexter, July 22–October 15, 1791, printed as an enclosure to Dexter to H, October, 1791; Washington to H, October 14, 1791.

siderable importance, both to the production and to the manufacture of that valuable article. And it is conceived, that the expence would be well justified by the magnitude of the object.

The printing and staining of cotton goods is known to be a distinct business from the fabrication of them. It is one easily accomplished and which, as it adds materially to the value of the article in its white state, and prepares it for a variety of new uses, is of importance to be promoted.

As imported cottons, equally with those which are made at home, may be the objects of this manufacture, it will merit consideration, whether the whole, or a part of the duty, on the white goods, ought not to be allowed to be drawn back in favor of those, who print or stain them. This measure would certainly operate as a powerful encouragement to the business; and though it may in a degree counteract the original fabrication of the articles it would probably more than compensate for this disadvantage, in the rapid growth of a collateral branch, which is of a nature sooner to attain to maturity. When a sufficient progress shall have been made, the drawback may be abrogated; and by that time the domestic supply of the articles to be printed or stained will have been extended.

If the duty of 7½ ℔. Cent on certain kinds of cotton goods were extended to all goods of cotton, or of which it is the principal material, it would probably more than counterbalance the effect of the drawback proposed, in relation to the fabrication of the article. And no material objection occurs to such an extension. The duty then considering all the circumstances which attend goods of this description could not be deemed inconveniently high; and it may be inferred from various causes that the prices of them would still continue moderate.

Manufactories of cotton goods, not long since established at Beverly, in Massachusetts, and at Providence in the state of Rhode Island and conducted with a perseverence corresponding with the patriotic motives which began them, seem to have overcome the first obstacles to success; producing corduroys, velverets, fustians, jeans, and other similar articles of a quality, which will bear a comparison with the like articles brought from Manchester. The one at Providence has the merit of being the first in introducing [into the United States] the celebrated cotton mill; which not only furnishes materials for that manufactory itself, but for the supply of private families for household manufacture.[245]

Other manufactories of the same material; as regular businesses, have also been begun at different places in the state of Connecticut, but all upon a smaller scale, than those above mentioned. Some essays are also making in the printing and staining of cotton goods. There are several small establishments of this kind already on foot

## Wool.

In a country, the climate of which partakes of so considerable a proportion of winter, as that of a great part of the United States, the woolen branch cannot be regarded, as inferior to any, which relates to the cloathing of the inhabitants.

Household manufactures of this material are carried on, in different parts of the United States, to a very interesting extent; but there is only one branch, which, as a regular business, can be said to have acquired maturity. This is the making of hats.

Hats of wool, and of wool mixed with furr, are made in large quantities, in different States; & nothing seems wanting, but an adequate supply of materials, to render the manufacture commensurate with the demand.[246]

A promising essay, towards the fabrication of cloths, cassimires and other woolen goods, is likewise going on at *Hartford* in Connecticut.[247] Specimens of the different kinds which are made, in the possession of the Secretary, evince that these fabrics have attained a very considerable degree of perfection. Their quality certainly surpasses anything, that could have been looked for, in so short a time,[248] and

245. See Moses Brown to John Dexter, July 22–October 15, 1791, printed as an enclosure to Dexter to H, October, 1791. See also George Cabot to H, September 6, 1791.

246. See "Report of a Committe Appointed to Obtain Information on Manufacturing in Providence," October 10, 1791, printed as an enclosure to John Dexter to H, October, 1791; and O. Burr and Company to John Chester, September 12, 1791, printed as an enclosure to Chester to H, October 11, 1791.

247. See Peter Colt to John Chester, July 21, 1791, printed as an enclosure to Chester to H, October 11, 1791.

248. In writing to an agent of the Hartford Company, George Washington had noted: "The patterns of Cloth which I have seen, and particularly the price which I have lately received, exceed in fineness and goodness whatever the most sanguine expectation could have looked for at this period" (*GW*, XXX, 279).

under so great disadvantages; and conspires with the scantiness of the means, which have been at the command of the directors, to form the eulogium of that public spirit, perseverance and judgment, which have been able to accomplish so much.

To cherish and bring to maturity this precious embryo must engage the most ardent wishes—and proportionable regret, as far as the means of doing it may appear difficult or uncertain.

Measures, which should tend to promote an abundant supply of wool, of good quality, would probably afford the most efficacious aid, that present circumstances permit.

To encourage the raising and improving the breed of sheep, at home, would certainly be the most desireable expedient, for that purpose; but it may not be alone sufficient, especially as it is yet a problem, whether our wool be capable of such a degree of improvement, as to render it fit for the finer fabrics.

Premiums would probably be found the best means of promoting the domestic, and bounties the foreign supply. The first may be within the compass of the institution hereafter to be submitted—The last would require a specific legislative provision. If any bounties are granted they ought of course to be adjusted with an eye to quality, as well as quantity.

A fund for the purpose may be derived from the addition of 2½ per Cent, to the present rate of duty, on Carpets and Carpeting; an increase, to which the nature of the Articles suggests no objection, and which may at the same time furnish a motive the more to the fabrication of them at home; towards which some beginnings have been made.[249]

### Silk.

The production of this Article is attended with great facility in most parts of the United States, Some pleasing essays are making in Connecticut, as well towards that, as towards the Manufacture of what is produced. Stockings, Handkerchiefs Ribbons & Buttons are made though as yet but in small quantities.[250]

---

249. See "Report of a Committee Appointed to Obtain Information on Manufacturing in Providence," October 10, 1791, printed as an enclosure to John Dexter to H, October, 1791; and William Hillhouse to John Chester, September 6, 1791, printed as an enclosure to Chester to H, October 11, 1791.

250. See Constant Southworth to William Williams, September 1, 1791, printed as an enclosure to John Chester to H, October 11, 1791.

A Manufactory of Lace upon a scale not very extensive has been long memorable at Ipswich in the State of Massachusetts.[251]

An exemption of the material from the duty, which it now pays on importation, and premiums upon the production, to be dispensed under the direction of the Institution before alluded to, seem to be the only species of encouragement adviseable at so early a stage of the thing.[252]

## Glass

The Materials for making Glass are found every where. In the United States there is no deficiency of them. The sands and Stones called Tarso, which include flinty and chrystalline substances generally, and the Salts of various plants, particularly of the Sea Weed Kali or Kelp constitute the essential ingredients.[253] An extraordinary abundance of Fuel is a particular advantage enjoyed by this Country for such manufactures. They, however, require large Capitals and involve much manual labour.

Different manufactories of Glass are now on foot in the United States.[254] The present duty of 12½ per Cent on all imported articles of glass amount to a considerable encouragement to those Manufactories. If any thing in addition is judged eligible, the most proper would appear to be a direct bounty, on Window Glass and black Bottles.

The first recommends itself as an object of general convenience; the last adds to that character, the circumstance of being an important item in breweries. A Complaint is made of great deficiency in this respect.

251. Among the papers relating to manufactures in the Hamilton Papers, Library of Congress, is an undated letter from George Cabot to Tench Coxe enclosing specimens of lace and information concerning the lace factory in Ipswich, Massachusetts. Cabot's letter reads in part: "In various parts of Masss the Females make Lace & edging for their own use & some small parcels for sale, but I believe the manufacture has nowhere become of sufficient consequence to attract notice except at Ipswich. The papers & specimens herewith handed you will enable you to form a good idea of the business as it is carried on at that place. I understand that the work is performed altogether by Women & Girls & that it occupies only (or chiefly) such portions of time as can be well spared from the concerns of the family" (ALS, Hamilton Papers, Library of Congress).

252. See Silas Condict to Aaron Dunham, August 25, 1791, printed as an enclosure to Dunham to H, September 9, 1791.

253. In "Pay Book of the State Company of Artillery," 1777, H had made notes from the section on glass in Postlethwayt's *Universal Dictionary*.

254. See Samuel Breck to H, September 3, 1791.

## Gun Powder

No small progress has been of late made in the manufacture of this very important article: It may indeed be considered as already established; but its high importance renders its further extension very desireable.

The encouragements, which it already enjoys, are a duty of 10 per Cent on the foreign rival article, and an exemption of Salt petre one of the principal ingredients of which it is composed, from duty. A like exemption of Sulphur, another chief ingredient, would appear to be equally proper. No quantity of this Article has yet been produced, from internal sources. The use made of it in finishing the bottoms of Ships, is an additional inducement to placing it in the class of free goods. Regulations for the careful inspection of the article would have a favourable tendency.[255]

## Paper

Manufactories of paper are among those which are Arrived at the greatest maturity in the United States, and are most adequate to national supply. That of paper hangings is a branch, in which respectable progress has been made.

Nothing material seems wanting to the further success of this valuable branch which is already protected by a competent duty on similar imported Articles.

In the enumeration of the several kinds, made subject to that duty, Sheathing and Cartridge paper have been omitted. These, being the most simple manufactures of the sort, and necessary to military supply, as well as Ship building, recommend themselves equally with those of other descriptions, to encouragement, and appear to be as fully within the compass of domestic exertions.[256]

255. Tench Coxe had made a report on gunpowder and cannon to the board of the Pennsylvania Society for the Encouragement of Manufactures and the Useful Arts. See Coxe to H, March 5–9, 1790.

256. Tench Coxe and William Barton were among those who mentioned paper hangings and books as examples of American manufactures which were already well established. See also the mention of sheathing in "Report of a Committee Appointed to Obtain Information on Manufacturing in Providence," October 10, 1791, printed as an enclosure to John Dexter to H, October, 1791. The

### Printed books

The great number of presses disseminated throughout the Union, seem to afford an assurance, that there is no need of being indebted to foreign Countries for the printing of the Books, which are used in the United States. A duty of ten per Cent instead of five, which is now charged upon the Article, would have a tendency to aid the business internally.

It occurs, as an objection to this, that it may have an unfavourable aspect towards literature, by raising the prices of Books in universal use in private families Schools and other Seminaries of learning. But the difference it is conceived would be without effect.

As to Books which usually fill the Libraries of the wealthier classes and of professional Men, such an Augmentation of prices, as might be occasioned by an additional duty of five per Cent would be too little felt to be an impediment to the acquisition.

And with regard to books which may be specially imported for the use of particular seminaries of learning, and of public libraries, a total exemption from duty would be adviseable, which would go far towards obviating the objection just mentioned. They are now subject to a duty of 5 ⅌ Cent.

As to the books in most general family use, the constancy and universality of the demand would insure exertions to furnish them at home and the means are compleatly adequate. It may also be expected ultimately, in this as in other cases, that the extension of the domestic manufacture would conduce to the cheapness of the article.

It ought not to pass unremarked, that to encourage the printing of books is to encourage the manufacture of paper.

### Refined Sugars and Chocolate.

Are among the number of extensive and prosperous domestic manufactures.

Drawbacks of the duties upon the materials, of which they are respectively made, in cases of exportation, would have a beneficial influence upon the manufacture, and would conform to a precedent,

---

progress in the manufacture of paper hangings was mentioned in the *Columbian Magazine*, V (July, 1790), 60.

which has been already furnished, in the instance of molasses, on the exportation of distilled spirits.[257]

Cocoa the raw material now pays a duty of one cent ℔ lb., while chocolate which is a prevailing and very simple manufacture, is comprised in the mass of articles rated at no more than five ℔ Cent.

There would appear to be a propriety in encouraging the manufacture, by a somewhat higher duty, on its foreign rival, than is paid on the raw material. Two cents ℔ lb. on imported chocolate would, it is presumed, be without inconvenience.[258]

The foregoing heads comprise the most important of the several kinds of manufactures, which have occurred as requiring, and, at the same time, as most proper for public encouragement; and such measures for affording it, as have appeared best calculated to answer the end, have been suggested.

The observations, which have accompanied this delineation of objects, supercede the necessity of many supplementary remarks. One or two however may not be altogether superfluous.

Bounties are in various instances proposed as one species of encouragement.

It is a familiar objection to them, that they are difficult to be managed and liable to frauds. But neither that difficulty nor this danger seems sufficiently great to countervail the advantages of which they are productive, when rightly applied. And it is presumed to have been shewn, that they are in some cases, particularly in the infancy of new enterprises indispensable.

It will however be necessary to guard, with extraordinary circumspection, the manner of dispensing them. The requisite precautions have been thought of; but to enter into the detail would swell this report, already voluminous, to a size too inconvenient.

If the principle shall not be deemed inadmissible the means of avoiding an abuse of it will not be likely to present insurmountable obstacles. There are useful guides from practice in other quarters.

It shall therefore only be remarked here, in relation to this point,

257. "*Sugars refined in various degrees,* form a branch so perfectly established as to require little attention, but to the acquisition of the raw material." (Coxe, *Brief Examination,* 124.)

258. See "Report of a Committee Appointed to Obtain Information on Manufacturing in Providence," October 10, 1791, printed as an enclosure to John Dexter to H, October, 1791.

that any bounty, which may be applied to the *manufacture* of an article, cannot with safety extend beyond those manufactories, at which the making of the article is a *regular trade*.

It would be impossible to annex adequate precautions to a benefit of that nature, if extended to every private family, in which the manufacture was incidentally carried on, and its being a merely incidental occupation which engages a portion of time that would otherwise be lost, it can be advantageously carried on, without so special an aid.

The possibility of a diminution of the revenue may also present itself, as an objection to the arrangements, which have been submitted.

But there is no truth, which may be more firmly relied upon, than that the interests of the revennue are promoted, by whatever promotes an increase of National industry and wealth.

In proportion to the degree of these, is the capacity of every country to contribute to the public Treasury; and where the capacity to pay is increased, or even is not decreased, the only consequence of measures, which diminish any particular resource is a change of the object. If by encouraging the manufacture of an article at home, the revenue, which has been wont to accrue from its importation, should be lessened, an indemnification can easily be found, either out of the manufacture itself, or from some other object, which may be deemed more convenient.

The measures however, which have been submitted, taken aggregately, will for a long time to come rather augment than decrease the public revenue.

There is little room to hope, that the progress of manufactures, will so equally keep pace with the progress of population, as to prevent, even, a gradual augmentation of the product of the duties on imported articles.

As, nevertheless, an abolition in some instances, and a reduction in others of duties, which have been pledged for the public debt, is proposed, it is essential, that it should be accompanied with a competent substitute. In order to this, it is requisite, that all the additional duties which shall be laid, be appropriated in the first instance, to replace all defalcations, which may proceed from any such abolition or diminution. It is evident, at first glance, that they will not only be adequate to this, but will yield a considerable surplus.

This surplus will serve.

First. To constitute a fund for paying the bounties which shall have been decreed.

Secondly. To constitute a fund for the operations of a Board, to be established, for promoting Arts, Agriculture, Manufactures and Commerce. Of this institution, different intimations have been given, in the course of this report. An outline of a plan for it shall now be submitted.[259]

Let a certain annual sum, be set apart, and placed under the management of Commissioners, not less than three, to consist of certain Officers of the Government and their Successors in Office.

Let these Commissioners be empowered to apply the fund confided to them—to defray the expences of the emigration of Artists, and Manufacturers in particular branches of extraordinary importance— to induce the prosecution and introduction of useful discoveries, inventions and improvements, by proportionate rewards, judiciously held out and applied—to encourage by premiums both honorable and lucrative the exertions of individuals, And of classes, in relation to the several objects, they are charged with promoting—and to afford such other aids to those objects, as may be generally designated by law.

The Commissioners to render [to the Legislature] an annual ac-

259. Postlethwayt had offered suggestions for changes in the Royal Society of London which resemble H's suggestions in the six following paragraphs. Postlethwayt wrote: "This celebrated body may, in other respects also, become instrumental to a still further advancement of all arts that are subservient to the interest of our trade and navigation. And this is submitted to be done, by enabling the Royal Society to confer suitable rewards and honours on all working mechanics, artisans, and manufacturers, who shall make any capital improvements in their several branches, and the like on those who shall make any important advancement in the arts of agriculture, or any thing connected therewith, as farming, grazing, nurserying, minerology, metallurgy, &c" (Postlethwayt, *Universal Dictionary*, II, 638).

Concerning the encouragement of manufactures, Postlethwayt wrote:

"It is a maxim generally received, that one of the most effectual means to settle and improve commerce, or any other political interest, is the patronage of princes. Dispensing rewards, and exciting emulation, by investing with honours, and other marks of distinction, those persons who, by the force of genius or application, have made new discoveries, or improved upon any thing laudable, and conducive to the interest of the public; more especially such as, upon the strength of their own genius, and at their sole charge, have set up and maintained manufactures, and other works beneficial to the community; and when the introduction of them has been intirely owing to their industry and public spirit.

"This point we shall only treat in a general way, as it is not possible to prescribe rules for the conduct of it on particular occasions, since the honours, as well as rewards and encouragements, are always to be dispensed according to the station, and other circumstances of the claimants, and with an eye to the

count of their transactions and disbursments; and all such sums as shall not have been applied to the purposes of their trust, at the end of every three years, to revert to the Treasury. It may also be enjoined upon them, not to draw out the money, but for the purpose of some specific disbursment.

It may moreover be of use, to authorize them to receive voluntary contributions; making it their duty to apply them to the particular objects for which they may have been made, if any shall have been designated by the donors.

There is reason to believe, that the progress of particular manufactures has been much retarded by the want of skilful workmen.[260] And it often happens that the capitals employed are not equal to the purposes of bringing from abroad workmen of a superior kind. Here, in cases worthy of it, the auxiliary agency of Government would in all probability be useful. There are also valuable workmen, in every branch, who are prevented from emigrating solely by the want of means. Occasional aids to such persons properly administered might be a source of valuable acquisitions to the country.

The propriety of stimulating by rewards, the invention and introduction of useful improvements, is admitted without difficulty. But the success of attempts in this way must evidently depend much on the manner of conducting them. It is probable, that the placing of the dispensation of those rewards under some proper discretionary direction, where they may be accompanied by *collateral expedients*, will

---

charge they shall have been at, and the benefits that shall result to the public from them.

"It is good policy to give yearly pensions, in order to draw over, and engage to stay in any country, able masters in manufactures, fulling, dyeing, and other works, either to introduce these sorts of businesses, or to improve such as have been already established, by advancing them to a degree of perfection and goodness that is certain to make them esteemed, and procure them a market every where." (Postlethwayt, *Universal Dictionary*, II, 129.)

260. The need for skilled workmen and the laws of Great Britain that were intended to discourage the emigration of such workmen caused some discussion of this question. On July 6, 1790, "a Hosier" from Glasgow (possibly Samuel Paterson) had written to "The Manager or Partners of a Company for Weaving Cotton Cloth late got up or Erected in Philadelphia" and made a plea for stock weavers willing but unable to emigrate to America (ALS, Hamilton Papers, Library of Congress). See also Paterson to H, February 10, 1791.

Constant Southworth, among others, had complained of the lack of skilled workmen. See Southworth to William Williams, September 1, 1791, printed as an enclosure to John Chester to H, October 11, 1791, and George Cabot to H, September 6, 1791.

serve to give them the surest efficacy. It seems impracticable to apportion, by general rules, specific compensations for discoveries of unknown and disproportionate utility.

The great use which may be made of a fund of this nature to procure and import foreign improvements is particularly obvious. Among these, the article of machines would form a most important item.

The operation and utility of premiums have been adverted to; together with the advantages which have resulted from their dispensation, under the direction of certain public and private societies. Of this some experience has been had in the instance of the Pennsylvania society, [for the Promotion of Manufactures and useful Arts;] [261] but the funds of that association have been too contracted to produce more than a very small portion of the good to which the principles of it would have led. It may confidently be affirmed that there is scarcely any thing, which has been devised, better calculated to excite a general spirit of improvement than the institutions of this nature. They are truly invaluable.

In countries where there is great private wealth much may be effected by the voluntary contributions of patriotic individuals, but in a community situated like that of the United States, the public purse must supply the deficiency of private resource. In what can it be so useful as in prompting and improving the efforts of industry?

All which is humbly submitted            [Alexander Hamilton
                                          Secy of the Treasury]

261. See note 179.


## To Otho H. Williams

Treasury Department
December 5. 1791

Sir

If the Supervisor of the District of Maryland [1] should apply to you for four hundred Dollars, you will advance him that sum, which he will repay to you out of the duties on Spirits distilled within his district as soon as a sufficient sum shall be received. You will nevertheless take duplicate receipts and transmit one to the Treasury.

The state of the business does not permit that this sum should be brought into your account as Collector. It will appear therefore in your returns as a part of the Cash in hand; but the fact will be properly noted here and finally regulated so as either to end in a credit or reimbursement.[2]

I am, Sir,   Your Most Obed Servant              Alexander Hamilton

Otho H Williams Esqr.
Collector, Baltimore.

LS, Columbia University Libraries.
  1. The supervisor of the District of Maryland was George Gale.
  2. A note attached to MS reads: "Four hundred dollars were advanced to Mr. Gale, in consequence of this letter, and a duplicate receipt transmitted to the Secy of the Treasury: on the 30 July they were refunded by Mr. Gale, and his receipt given up to him. D. Delozier, D. Colr."

## From Oliver Wolcott, Junior [1]

T. D
C. Off Decr. 5th. 1791

Sir,

I have considered the application of Benjamin Bourne Esq.[2] for the renewal of certain Certificates and Warrants for transfering funded Stock alledged to have been lost and am of opinion that the following rules should be adopted.

That in case a transfer Certificate is lost, before the Treasury Warrant has been issued, the claimant or some person having knowledge thereof should in the first instance make an Affidavit before some proper authority, of the circumstances attending the loss, which Affidavit being produced to the Officer who issued said transfer Certificate, should require & justify him in issuing a special Certificate descriptive of the Certificate so alledged to have been lost.

That when, as in the case stated by Mr. Bourne, a transfer Certificate, with the Treasury Warrant annexed, is lost before a Credit is obtained at the Office to which the transfer was directed; an affidavit of the loss as in the preceding case, should be exhibited to the Register of the Treasury, who should thereon issue a special Certificate descriptive of the transfer Certificate & Warrant so alledged to have been lost. On which special Certificate of the Register of the Treasury, the Officer to whom the Warrant of transfer was directed should further certify, that no such Warrant had been presented for entry at his office.

These documents being filed at the Treasury with a suffient bond with sureties, to indemnify the United States against all claims on account of the first transfer Certificate and Warrant or either of them, would in my opinion render it safe & expedient for the Secretary of the Treasy. to issue a new Warrant for such transfers.

The Honble A. H.

ADf, Connecticut Historical Society, Hartford.
   1. Wolcott was comptroller of the Treasury.
   2. Bourne was a Federalist member of the House of Representatives from Rhode Island.

## From Abishai Thomas [1]

Philad. 6th Decemr. 1791

Sir

In submitting the following facts and observations to your consideration perhaps I may have exceeded the bounds of propriety in obtruding any thing like an opinion on the subject, but I have been involuntarily drawn into the measure, I hope it is done with due deference and I rely on your candour for an extenuation of the fault.

On the subject of the claim of Wm Courtney esqre refer'd to you to report on [2] I beg leave to observe, that by a resolution of Congress of the 3rd June 1784 it is recommended to the States individually *"to grant such relief to their Citizens who have been injured as aforesaid"* (which applies to Mr. Courtney's case) *"as they may think requisite and if it shall hereafter appear reasonable that the United States should make any allowance to any particular States who may be burthened much beyond others that the allowance ought to be determined by Congress."* [3]

As Mr. Courtney made repeated applications to the Legislature of North Carolina [4] without obtaining any redress it only remains with

Congress to make him such compensation as shall appear just & reasonable.

The tract of Land on which the Troops of the Southern Army encamped after the defeat near Cambden in South Carolina which happened on the 16th August 1780, had been immediately preceding, purchased by Mr. Courtney for the sum of 4000 dollars. The Huts which were then made were continued to be occupied during the Autumn & ensuing Winter until the Month of February 1781 when they were evacuated on the approach of the British Army under command of Lord Cornwallis, the depredations committed during this period were immense, the Timber cut down together with the fencing appropriated for the purposes of Hutting & Fuel, rendered the plantation, (from being in a high state of improvement and cultivation) a perfect waste or common and I verily believe that one half the sum which Mr. Courtney gave for the Land &c. could not then have been obtained for it.

With regard to the damage Mr. Courtney sustained on his Lots in the Town of Hillsborough the enclosed Certificate which he has just sent to me, and which I had given to him when I acted as Quarter Master at that post, is something descriptive of it, but there being no valuation affixed it is difficult at this remote period to ascertain what would be an adequate compensation, however I consider that I am within the bounds of moderation when I say that the sum of 750 dollars would not then have been commensurate to the object of placing him in as eligible a situation in respect to his Town property as he was at the time of the arrival of the Army as aforesaid.

The resolution of Congress before alluded to expresses *"That according to the Laws and usages of nations a State is not obliged to make compensation for damages done to its own Citizens by an Enemy, or Wantonly & unauthorized by its own Troops, yet humanity requires that some relief should be granted to persons who by such losses are reduced to indigence and want, and as the circumstances of such sufferers are best known to the States to which they belong"* to them it is recommended as before mentioned.

Now sir as Mr. Courtney notwithstanding the *"circumstances"* of his sufferings were well known to the State, never could obtain any relief from it, I trust there is good ground to hope that the justice and *"humanity"* of the U.S. will be extended to him. I consider that his case does not altogether come within the meaning of that part of the foregoing resolution which says *"wantonly and unauthorized by its own Troops."*

The encamping on his Land, making use of his Timber for Huts and fuel, Occupying his Town Lots for pasturage, Continental yards &c. were certainly *"authorized"* *and necessary.* Perhaps the burning of his fencing and the destruction of his buildings were not so. Be that as it may the suffering of an individual (whose fortune may not be considered large), to the amount of three thousand Dollars beyond his proportion for the common defence of the Union will certainly be considered an object worthy of deliberation.        A Thomas

ADfS, North Carolina Department of Archives and History, Raleigh.
    1. Thomas was the North Carolina agent for settling the state's claims arising from the American Revolution.
    2. No record of a petition made by Courtney before the date of this letter has been found in the *Journal of the House.* On December 14, 1795, however, "A petition of William Courtney, of the town of Hillsborough, in the State of North Carolina, was presented to the House and read, praying compensation for the loss of a dwelling-house and other property of the petitioner, which were taken and destroyed by a detachment of the Continental Army, during the late war" (*Journal of the House,* II, 373). The petition was not granted (*Journal of the House,* II, 429).
    3. *JCC,* XXVII, 543.
    4. Courtney petitioned the North Carolina legislature in 1783, 1784, and 1788 (Clark, *State Records of North Carolina,* XIX, 203, 507, 553; XX, 497).

# To Otho H. Williams

Treasury Department
December 6. 1791.

Sir

It is understood that a brig called the Dove formerly of Glocester in Massachusetts and commanded by Josiah Parsons has been sold in Europe, under circumstances that give rise to some apprehensions in regard to the misuse of her certificate of registry. I wish to be informed, if it has been returned to your office and when.

I am, Sir,   Your obedt. servant        Alex Hamilton

Otho H. Williams Esq.
Collector Baltimore.

LS, Columbia University Libraries.

## To the Directors of the Society for Establishing Useful Manufactures [1]

Philadelphia Decbr. 7. 1791.

Gentlemen

In consequence of powers vested in me by the Agents named in the instrument of Subscription towards the Society for establishing useful Manufactures,[2] I have made Contracts on behalf of the Society with William Hall, as Superintendent of the printing Business; [3] with Joseph Mort, as an Assistant in the Manufactory,[4] in such way as his Services may be thought most useful. This Gentleman I understand has had opportunities of being acquainted both with the making and printing of Cotton Goods; with Thomas Marshal to superintend the Cotton Mill.[5]

The Contracts with these different Persons are transmitted herewith.

There is a William Pearce who has been employed by me in preparing Machines for the use of the Society; and with whom I have advanced pretty far in an Agreement, but without having reduced it to a definitive form.[6] He pretends to a knowlege of the fabrication of most of the most valuable Machines now in use in the Cotton Manufactory; and his Execution hitherto, as far as he has gone, confirms his pretentions. Among other Machines he has prepared a double Loom, to be worked by one person. Of this he gives himself as the Inventor, and has applyed for a Patent, which he will probably obtain. It is certain that the Machine, if in use at all in Europe is quite new; and as far as without seeing it worked, it can be judged of, promises to answer the Expectations it gives—with (Geoe) Perkinson, as Foreman or Master of a room in the Cotton-Mill. This appears to be an ingenious Mechanic, who has obtained a Patent for a Flax-Mill, which he alleges his having improved.[7] How far these improvements may be of real Utility, or the Mill itself capable of answering it's End, ought to be considered as uncertain: since it is a question whether the spinning of Flax by Mills, which has been for sometime a desideratum in Great Britain, is practicable. The object of engaging this Man was to secure to the Society an ingenious Mechanic, and securing to them whatever advantage there may be in the Patent.

All the Contracts leave to the Society the power of dismissing at pleasure, if on experiment, they find it their interest.

I thought it adviseable in the first instance, to secure Persons of whose Usefulness there was reason to entertain a favorable Opinion, tho' upon terms which may appear high, that the Business might be early put in Motion.

It is a point understood between Mr. Mort and myself, that if desired by the Society, he is to go to Europe, to bring over Workmen, at his own Expence in the first instance; but with the assurance of re-imbursement and indemnification. To engage such a Person as Mr. Mort for this purpose appeared to me a Point of some consequence.[8]

I have the honor to be  with great consideration  Gentlemen Your Obedient servt                                      A Hamilton.

The Directors of the Society for establishg. useful Manufactures.

"Minutes of the S.U.M.," 3–5.
1. This letter was read and approved at the first meeting of the directors of the Society for Establishing Useful Manufactures at New Brunswick, New Jersey, on December 9, 1791.
2. See "Power of Attorney from the Society for Establishing Useful Manu-factures," August 9, 1791.
3. See "Contract with William Hall," August 20, 1791.
4. Contract not found. According to the "Minutes of the S.U.M.," this contract was dated August 22, 1791.
5. Contract not found. According to the "Minutes of the S.U.M.," this contract was dated August 17, 1791.
6. See "Receipt from William Pearce," August 20, 1791.
7. George Parkinson had come to the United States from Great Britain as early as August, 1790. He secured a patent on his machine, and from March 19 to April 16, 1791, advertised his services in the [Philadelphia] *Gazette of the United States*. A manuscript copy of this advertisement in the Hamilton Papers, Library of Congress, reads as follows:
      "*Machinery for spinning Flax, hemp & combed wool.*
"The subscriber hereby gives public Notice that he has obtained a Patent for a slivering wheel and table, a movement for wetting the thread by conical, clothcoated thrumblers and another for the same purpose by a cloth coated roller, a leathern belt moved by rollers for the purpose of the preparatory drawing of the slivers and another leathern belt moved in like manner by rollers for the purpose of drawing the roved flax, hemp and wool being im-provements upon the mill or machinery of Kindrew Porthouse of the Town of Darlington in Great Britain.
"This machinery, with the original mechanism on which it is grafted, being of the utmost value to the United States the subscriber hereby offers to make and erect a complete mill or mills, including both the original works and his

above improvements thereon for any individual or company on terms to be by them agreed on; and to conduct the manufactory either for a share of the profits or stipulated wages.

George Parkinson"

There is also in the Hamilton Papers, Library of Congress, an undated, unsigned document entitled "A flax and hemp spinning mill is applicable to manufacturing." This document consists of a list of goods that Parkinson's flax mill could manufacture.

8. Following the reading of this letter at the meeting of the directors of the society on December 9, 1791, "The several Agreements were also read and considered, upon which it was Unanimously Resolved that the said Agreements be adopted on behalf of this Society; and that this Board will carry the same into Effect on their part: and Ordered that the said several Agreements be filed" ("Minutes of the S.U.M.," 5).

## From Stephen Van Rensselaer [1]

Albany December 7 1791

Dear Sir

At the request of several officers of our late Army, I transmit you the enclosed Memorandum. If any provision is made for such cases you will oblige me by informing me. Mrs. Rensselaer joins in love to you & Mrs. Hamilton.

I am D Sir Your Hum Sert      Stephen Van Rensselaer

[ENCLOSURE]

*John Ostrander, Junior, to Stephen Van Rensselaer* [2]

Memorandum for Stephen Van Rensselaer Esquire

John Ostrander Late Leiutanant in Colo James Livingstons Regement of foot in the Service of the united states resigned the fourteenth day of april 1779 three months full pay due besides depreciation begs to know from the Secretary of The Treasury if any provission has been made by Congress for the payment of Arrearages of this kind, and if there has what Vouchers are necessary to procure the same.

Several Officers of the same Regt. Join in the request (To Witt) Timothy Hughes Capt Peter Ristan William Wallis Leiuts. and Wm Gates Ensign.

Obtaining will Sir Oblige   your most obedient and very Humble
Servent                                               John Ostrander Jnr

To Stephen Van Rensselaer Esqr

ALS, Hamilton Papers, Library of Congress.
   1. Van Rensselaer was a member of the New York Assembly in 1789 and
1790, and served in the state Senate from 1791 to 1795. In 1783 he had married
Margaret (or Margarita) Schuyler, Elizabeth Hamilton's sister.
   2. ALS, Hamilton Papers, Library of Congress.

## To Otho H. Williams

Treasury Department Decembr 7th 1791

sir

   I request that You will pay to Messrs Elliot and Williams [1] ten
thousand Dollars on the first of January next, on account of their
contract with the united States of the 27th September instant, taking
duplicate receipts, one of which to be transmitted to the Treasury.
You will of course retain money in Your hands for the purpose and
in case there should not be a probability of a Sufficient sum being
received in time, You will inform me of it.
   I am, sir,   Your obedt Servt                    Alexander Hamilton


Otho H. Williams Esquire
Collector Baltimore


LS, Hamilton Papers, Library of Congress.
   1. This was the firm of Robert Elliot and Elie Williams, which had contracted to supply the Army on the western frontier.


## From George Cabot [1]

1ober. 8th. 91.

Dear Sir

   I have understood that after the peace of 63 & 'till the late war
France gave direct assistance to her Cod fishery beside the monopoly
of her *home* & colonial markets—but notwithstanding these encouragements the supply from her own fishery was so scanty that her

prohibotory laws were evaded & very large supplies of foreign fish were continually smuggled into her Colonies & consumed there at prices 40 per cent higher to the Planters than English & American fish was worth at the free ports in the neighbouring Islands.

Since the peace of 83 fish of the U S has not been wholly prohibited but its admission has been generally confined to a single port in an Island (sometimes very distant from the Consumers); the duty demandable on each quintal has been from 3 to 8 livres & the amount actually paid from 2½ to 3, while the french fish has enjoyed a free access to every place & upon landing has been entituled to a very liberal bounty.[2] Yet under all these disadvantages the fishery of the U S *has* successfully rivalled that of France.

There facts at first view seem to indicate such a preponderance of natural advantages in the U S for carrying on the fishery as can hardly be balenced by France but it shou'd be noticed that about 5 years ago the french West India markets were surcharged to such a degree that the Exporters of fish from the U S suffered great losses upon all they shipped thither,[3] & the fishery exhibited such symptoms of decline in consequence of it that it may be doubted whether it coud possibly have been supported if that of France had not been interrupted by the Commotions at home. It shou'd be observed too that the equipments of armed fleets & appearances of war occur so frequently to the European nations & especially to France that no fair experiment can be tried to determine the extent to which their fishery wou'd be carried in a long period of uninterrupted pursuit. These & similar events however have great influence upon the fishery of the U S but their frequency & effect in future can neither be foreseen nor accurately estimated, & hence it is the more difficult to say what is the greatest *disparity* of duties the fish of the U S cou'd bear & meet the fish of France in the french market—but on the whole shou'd the Govt of the U S restore to their Cod fisheries in some direct form the full amount which they pay to it's treasury by the comsumption of dutied articles, & shou'd the fisheries of France be left without aid from their Govt, except like those of the U S a bare indemnity from contribution to the public revenue, & shou'd the markets of the french west Indies be open to the fish of both Countries, I think it may be safely relied on that the fish of the U S cou'd be afforded full 10 per Cent cheaper than that of France & consequently cou'd bear a duty of 10 per Cent on it's value at the place & time of sale & yet sustain the competition with french fish selling in the same market duty free.

I have thus my dear Sir given you the best opinion I can form at present on the subject of your enquiry. This I have done not with the expectation of adding to your information but solely to shew my readiness to obey your command & to convince you of the esteem & respect with which

   I am very sincerely your assured Friend   & mo. ob. Servt

George Cabot

ALS, Hamilton Papers, Library of Congress.
 1. There are two possibilities concerning the reasons why H asked Cabot, who was Senator from Massachusetts and chairman of the Senate Committee on Fisheries, for the information contained in this letter. The first is that H wished this information for the draft of a commercial treaty with France. The second is that H needed the material for a comparative study of the commercial systems of Britain and France.
 As to the first of these possibilities, deteriorating commercial relation between France and the United States after 1789 had led to efforts to negotiate a new trade agreement. On June 2, 1791, the French National Assembly had instructed the king to negotiate a new commercial treaty with the United States (*Archives Parlementaires*, XXVI, 710), but the French Ministry failed to act on the proposal. On November 24, 1791, Thomas Jefferson, who believed that France wished to encourage the United States to make the first proposals for a treaty, wrote to William Short: "M. [Jean Baptiste] de Ternant tells me he has no instructions to propose to us the negotiation of a commercial treaty, and that he does not expect any" (ALS, letterpress copy, Thomas Jefferson Papers, Library of Congress). H discussed the matter with the French Minister in October (see "Conversation with Jean Baptiste de Ternant," October 7, 1791). A debate in Washington's cabinet on the advisability of opening negotiations with France followed, and the President acceded to H's suggestion that a draft of a new treaty should be drawn up, even though Jefferson maintained that the United States should not take the initiative in the commercial negotiations. In November, 1791, Jefferson reluctantly drew up the draft of a commercial treaty (see Ford, *Writings of Jefferson*, V, 397–99). H opposed it on the ground that rates were too low, and the negotiations were finally dropped. For Ternant's reports to his government on his commercial discussions with United States officials, see Ternant to Comte de Montmorin, October 9, 1791, and Ternant to Claude Antoine de Valdec de Lessart, April 8, 1792 (Frederick J. Turner, ed., "Correspondence of the French Ministers to the United States, 1791–1797," *Annual Report of the American Historical Association for the Year 1903* [Washington, 1904], II, 57–65, 108–14). Jefferson's account of the negotiations for this abortive treaty is contained in an entry in the "Anas," dated March 11, 1792. He stated that he "prepared a plan of treaty for exchanging the privileges of native subjects and fixing all duties forever as they now stood. . . . [H] did not like this way of fixing the duties because he said that many articles here would bear to be raised and therefore he would prepare a tariff. He did so raising duties for the French from 25. to 50 per cent" (Ford,

*Writings of Jefferson,* I, 185). A copy of this tariff in Jefferson's handwriting, labeled "The above contains Hamilton's tariff of the duties which cannot be receded from in treaty with France, spoken of in my private note of March 11, 92," may be found in the Thomas Jefferson Papers, Library of Congress. It is printed in Ford, *Writings of Jefferson,* V, 398.

The possibility also exists that H may have requested this information for a comparative study of the French and British commercial systems which he was compiling in late 1791 and early 1792. George Hammond reported to Lord Grenville on December 19, 1791, that "Mr. Hamilton informed me he was preparing a report upon the actual state of the navigation and commerce of this country, whence it would appear that the present system of France was more favorable to the former, and that of Great Britain to the latter" (see "Conversation with George Hammond," December 15–16, 1791). On January 1, 1792, H stated in a letter to Jefferson that he was "engaged in making a comparative statement of the Trade between the U S & France & between the U S & G Britain" and asked Jefferson for information concerning French commercial regulations. Although no completed report has been found, there is a draft in H's handwriting in the Hamilton Papers, Library of Congress, of a comparative study of the British and French commercial systems in relation to the United States. This document is printed in these volumes as "View of the Commercial Regulations of France and Great Britain in Reference to the United States," 1792–1793.

2. Although French administrative ordinances permitted American vessels into French colonial ports after the French alliance of 1778, most of these concessions were withdrawn by a ministerial letter of May 24, 1783 (Moreau de Saint-Méry, *Loix et Constitutions des Colonies Françoises de l'Amérique sous le Vent,* VI, 314–15). Restrictions were again relaxed by the "Arrêt du conseil concernant le commerce étranger dans les îles françaises de l'Amérique" of August 30, 1784. The number of entrepôts in the French West Indies was increased from two to seven, and the list of products permitted to be imported into the islands was considerably liberalized. Under the terms of Article 5 of the *arrêt* of August 30, 1784, salt fish appeared on the permitted list but was charged a duty of three livres per quintal, the money to be collected from this duty to be applied for the encouragement of the French fisheries (Isambert, *Recueil Général des Anciennes Lois Françaises,* XXVII, 459–64). Vigorous protests on the part of the French fishing industry to this relaxed policy led to the passage of two *arrêts* of September 18 and 25, 1785, which gave a premium of ten livres per quintal on French cod shipped to the West Indies and imposed a duty of five livres per quintal on foreign codfish imported into the French islands (Moreau de Saint-Méry, *Loix et Constitutions des Colonies Françoises de l'Amérique sous le Vent,* VI, 847–51, 863–65). Concerning these *arrêts* Jefferson observed: "The late Arrets of the 18th. and 25th. of September, which increasing to excess the duty on foreign importations of fish into the West Indies, giving the double in bounty on those of the natives, and thereby rendering it impossible for the former to sell in competition with the latter, have in effect prohibited the importation of that article by the citizens of the United States" (Jefferson to Comte de Vergennes, November 20, 1785, Boyd, *Papers of Thomas Jefferson,* IX, 50).

3. Cabot is referring to an "Arrêt du Conseil D'État Du Roi, Qui porte à Huit livres le droit de Cinq livres par quintal, établi par l'Arrêt du 25 septembre 1785, sur la Morue sèche de pêche étrangère importée aux Isles du Vent & sous le Vent; & à Douze livres la Prime de Dix livres accordée par l'Arrêt du 18 même mois, par quintal de Morue sèche de pêche françoise, importée aux mêmes Isles" of February 11, 1787. A copy of this *arrêt* may be found in the Papers of the Continental Congress, National Archives.

## From Charles Lee [1]

Alexandria [Virginia] 8th. December 1791

Sir!

The Ship Washington and the Brandy that were seized here, have been delivered up to the Owners, they having given bond with security to abide the legal decision of the seizure.

I am Sir! respectfully   Your most Obedient Servant

Charles Lee
Collector at Alexandria.

Copy, RG 56, Letters to and from the Collector at Alexandria, National Archives.
  1. For background to this letter, see H to Lee, November 10, 1791.

## To Jeremiah Olney

Treasury Department
December 8 1791

Sir

The monies which shall be deposited by you in the Bank of Providence, pursuant to my direction,[1] will upon your forwarding to the Treasury a duplicate receipt of such deposits, be considered as payments made to the United States, and for which you will receive credit by regular warrants which will issue to cover such payments.

I am Sir   Your Obedt. Servant          Alex Hamilton

Jere. Olney Esq.
Collr. Providence

LS, Rhode Island Historical Society, Providence; copy, RG 56, Letters to the Collector at Providence, National Archives; copy, RG 56, Letters to Collectors at Small Ports, "Set G," National Archives.
  1. See H to Olney, November 10, 1791, and Olney to H, November 21, 1791.

## From Jeremiah Olney [1]

*Providence, December 8, 1791.* ". . . Having recd. a Letter from the Master of the Cutter Argus, informing me, that the Schooner

Alice was at Anchor about Four Miles from Rhode-Island Light-House when his Mate boarded her, I have this day requested the District Attorney [2] to commence a Prosecution against Captain Andrus."

ADfS, Rhode Island Historical Society, Providence.
1. For background to this letter, see Olney to H, October 31, November 24, 1791; H to Olney, November 11, 1791.
2. William Channing.

## To George Washington

[*Philadelphia, December 8, 1791.* On December 9, 1791, Washington wrote to Thomas Jefferson: [1] "Yesterday afternoon Colo. Hamilton was desired, as soon as the Tariff was ready, to let it be known. Enclosed is his answer." *Letter not found.*]

1. *GW*, XXXI, 442.

## To Benjamin Hawkins [1]

Philadelphia dec. 9. 1791

Dear Sir,

The ground upon which was founded the refusal to receive upon the subscription to the loan in State debt, the Certificates of North Carolina, on account of the *Government of that State* was simply this. The preamble to the clauses which relate to the assumption and various expressions in those clauses evidently contemplate "a provision for the *debts* of the respective states." [2] Now a bond or other *security* for a *debt* being once cancelled or discharged by, or surrendered to the *Debtor* without *fraud* or *accident*, there *ceases* to be a *debt*. The certificates therefore of the State of North Carolina, in this case the *debtor*, which were in the hands of its government, constituted no *existing* debt of the state; of course nothing upon which the assumption could operate.

If any thing was requisite to elucidate so clear a position, or make plainer the intent of the law, it might be found in that provision which directs, That interest on the difference between the sum in each case assumed and the sum actually subscribed shall be paid to each state, *in trust for the non subscribing creditors* of such state;[3] this clearly indicating that a state is in no event to receive any of the monies appropriated to the purpose of its own debt except as a trustee for *actual creditors* which necessarily supposes existing *debts*.

Here too is found an answer to the claim that a state should be permitted to subscribe, on its own account, such part of its debt as may have been extinguished subsequent to the act of assumption. As the state is to receive interest on all the *unsubscribed* part of its debt, within the limits of the sum assumed, untill a settlement of accounts shall determine the equity of a further continuance of the payment, there is no necessity *in point of equity*, that a State should be permitted to subscribe the part of its debt, so subsequently extinguished. If the idea of a settlement of accounts were excluded, an equity of that kind would doubtless arise

Not chusing in a matter of this kind to rely wholly on my own opinion, I suspended a definitive judgment, untill an opinion of the Attorney General had confirmed my own ideas.[4]

I have already incidentally answered the second object of your enquiry. It appears to me that both the letter and the spirit of the act require that the interest on the abovementioned *difference* between the sum *assumed* and the sum *subscribed* should be paid to each state *untill* there shall be a settlement of accounts and "a provision for the balance, if any, which may then appear in favour of the State," without enquiry in the mean time into the existance or number of non subscribing creditors. The Law appears to me to take there existance for granted, and to rely on the settlement of accounts to furnish a rule for the continuance or discontinuance of the payment of interest to a State. This construction is strengthened by the circumstance of the payment being directed to continue untill provision shall be made for any balance which may appear in favour of a State. That payment has therefore the further operation of a pledge for this provision.

I have the honor to be, with great   consideration, Dear Sir   your obedient servant                                        Alexander Hamilton

The honorable Benj Hawkins Esq.

Copy, North Carolina Department of Archives and History, Raleigh.
    1. Hawkins was United States Senator from North Carolina. This letter was written in reply to Hawkins to H, November 26, 1791.

2. See "An Act making provision for the (payment of the) Debt of the United States" (1 *Stat.* 138–44 [August 4, 1790]).

3. For Section 17 of the Funding Act to which H is referring, see Thomas Smith to H, June 6, 1791, note 1.

4. See Edmund Randolph to H, November 9, 1791.

## *To John Henry* [1]

[Philadelphia, December 9, 1791]

The Secretary of the Treasury not relying entirely on the accuracy of the data upon which the calculations in his Report on the subject of the Mint were founded,[2] as they respect the quantity of fine silver contained in the silver dollar, thought it advisable to embrace the opportunity of the interval between the last and the present sessions of Congress to endeavour to obtain from Europe more certain information on the point.[3]

The result has been—He first received from Amsterdam an account of the Standard of the new M. dollar which is almost the only one in circulation according to the regulations of the Spanish Mint.

This account States

1st as to weight, That there are 913 to 914 dollars in 100 marcs, or 791 ounces aveirdupois.

Consequently on the computation of 913 to                    dwt. grs
    100 marcs each dollar would weigh              $17 - 7 \ ^{785}\!/_{913}$
On computation of 914 to 100 Marcs                           $17 - 7 \ ^{370}\!/_{914}$

2nd As to the standard—That it is 258 parts fine to 30 alloy

             dwt. gr.

Consequently a dollar of $17 - 7 \ ^{785}\!/_{913}$ would contain
                         of fine silver    $372 \ ^{494}\!/_{913}$
    "        a dollar of $17 - 7 \ ^{370}\!/_{914}$ would contain
                         of ditto          $372 \ ^{370}\!/_{914}$

It is ascertained that it was formerly usual at the Spanish Mint to allow a remedy of weight and alloy of $^{2}\!/_{288}$ parts.

If the remedy continues, the quantity of fine silver in

  a dollar of the first description above would be          $369 \ ^{597}\!/_{913}$
In a dollar of the second description    "    "    $369 \ ^{228}\!/_{914}$

But he afterwards received a return of an actual assay at the Mint of Amsterdam which states the dollar at 258 parts fine to 30 parts alloy in exact conformity to the Standard of the Spanish Mint as before given and exclusive of all allowance for Remedy.

According to which a dollar would actually contain of
fine silver . . . . . . . . . . . . . . . $372 \ ^{494}\!/_{913}$

or, $372 \ ^{370}\!/_{914}$

Three conjectures arise—either that the Account given as conformable to the legal standard of the Spanish Mint was not just, but was predicted upon the result of assays at the Mint of Amsterdam, or that being so conformable the remedy formerly allowed at the Spanish Mint has ceased, Or that the Assay at the Mint of Amsterdam was not perfectly accurate.

There has been also received the result from assay at the Mint of London which makes the Standard of the Spanish Dollar 5172 parts fine to 588 parts alloy.

According to which a silver dollar weighing 17 7 $^{785}\!/_{913}$
would contain of fine Silver . . . . . . . . $373 \ ^{376}\!/_{913}$

a dollar weighing . . . . . . . . 17 7 $^{370}\!/_{914}$  $372 \ ^{913}\!/_{914}$

Here is a small difference which indicates a difference of accuracy in the assays, or a difference in the pieces assayed arising from errors in the Spanish Mint.

The two statements from Amsterdam seem entitled to most confidence not only because there is a correspondency between them, but because there are some marks of inaccuracy in the proceedings at the Mint of London. It is stated in the body of the certificate that the gross weight of the Dollar is presumed to be 17 dwt., 10 Grains and in the Margin it is mentioned as certain that the average is 17 dwt. 8 Grains.

The latter however is the truth or very near it, according to the trials in large masses made at the Banks of N. America & New York, but the cashier of the former bank [4] seems to be of opinion that for a time the dollar rather gains in weight from the dirt which adheres to it, though in the course of a long circulation it loses.[5]

Philadelphia, December 9, 1791
Alexander Hamilton
Secy. of the Treasy.

*Maryland Historical Magazine,* IV (September, 1909), 282–84.
   1. In the *Maryland Historical Magazine* this document is described as follows:
"An Official Paper, dated December 9th, 1791, of Alexander Hamilton, Secretary of the U.S. Treasury, given to Senator John Henry of Maryland, in reference to the quantity of fine silver contained in the silver dollar.
"The Original paper is in the handwriting of the Hon. Alexander Hamilton

and is now in the possession of J. Winfield Henry of Baltimore, a great grandson of Governor John Henry."

Henry was a member of the Senate committee to draft a bill on the mint. The committee was appointed on October 31, 1791, and reported a bill on December 21, 1791 (*Annals of Congress,* III, 20, 52).

2. See "Report on the Establishment of a Mint," January 28, 1791.

3. H requested this information from William Short. See H to Short, April 13, 1791; Short to H, June 5, August 23, 1791.

4. Tench Francis.

5. See Francis to H, December 7, 1790; William Seton to H, December 28, 1790.

# Report on the Petition of George Webb

Treasury Department.
December 9th. 1791.
[Communicated on December 12, 1791][1]

[To the Speaker of the House of Representatives]

The Secretary of the Treasury, to whom was referred the petition of George Webb, by an order of the House of Representatives, of the 24th. of February 1791,[2] respectfully submits the following report thereupon.

The prayer of the said petition has reference to two objects.

One, a farther compensation for services rendered, while the petitioner acted in the capacity of Receiver of Continental taxes for the State of Virginia.

The other, an allowance for a sum of nine hundred and fifty six pounds, Virginia Currency, being public money, which the petitioner alledges to have been stolen out of his possession.

In relation to the first point, the following facts appear.

That by a resolution of Congress, of the 30th October 1781, the respective States were required to furnish their quotas of eight millions of dollars, for the service of the year 1782, to be paid quarterly

Copy, RG 233, Reports of the Treasury Department, 1791–1792, Vol. II, National Archives.

1. *Journal of the House,* I, 471.

2. On February 24, 1791, "A petition of George Webb was presented to the House and read, praying farther compensation for his services, and also to be reimbursed for the loss of a sum of the public money, whilst receiver of continental taxes, for the state of Virginia.

"*Ordered,* That the said petition be referred to the Secretary of the Treasury,

in equal proportions, the first payment, on the first day of April then next ensuing.[3]

That by another resolution of the 2nd of November following, the respective quotas of the States of the said eight millions of dollars are fixed; and it is, among other things, recommended to the States, to cause their collectors to make payment to the Commissioners of Loans, or such other persons, as should be appointed by the Superintendant of Finance, to receive the same.[4]

That upon the strength of this resolution, the said Superintendant appointed Receivers of Continental Taxes for the respective States, and, among others, the petitioner for the State of Virginia.

That the letters from the said Superintendant, announcing these appointments, inform the Receivers, that they are severally to be allowed, in lieu of all salary and expenses whatever, a certain rate per centum; but without designating any term of time for which this allowance, or whether the rate per centum is to be computed upon the actual receipts of each Receiver, or upon the amount of the quota of each State.[5]

That subsequent explanations establish, that the percentage was to be computed on the amount of each quota, but nothing was said with regard to the term of time, for which the compensation was to be deemed applicable

That, previous to these appointments, it had been the practice of Congress, to assess, each year, quotas upon the several States; but no quotas were assessed, after the one for the year 1782, until the 27th of September 1775,[6] except by a requisition of the 10th of September 1782, for 1.200.00 dollars towards payment of interest on the domestic debt, the application of which seems to have been left to the States themselves; and by another requisition of the 16th of October in the same year, for 2.00.000 of dollars, for the service of the year 1783.[7]

---

with instructions to examine the same, and report his opinion thereupon to the House." (*Journal of the House*, I, 388.)

3. *JCC*, XXI, 1087–88.          4. *JCC*, XXI, 1089–91.

5. According to the report Robert Morris, Superintendent of Finance, made to Congress on March 10, 1783, on the "several officers employed in the Department of Finance and Marine," the percentage of the Virginia quota allowed Webb was one-eighth (DS, Papers of the Continental Congress, National Archives).

6. This date should read 1785.          7. *JCC*, XXIII, 564–71, 659–60.

That the Receivers, and, among the rest, the petitioner, continued to act as such until the first. of July 1785, when they were discontinued by virtue of a resolution of Congress of the 15th. of April preceding.[8]

That there is a letter from the Superintendant of Finance to the petitioner, dated 31st of August 1784, in the following terms: "I have received your favor of the 23d Instant. The Account, which was enclosed, is transmitted to the Treasury. In my circular letter of the 5th of May 1783,[9] I sent to the several Receivers a copy of my return to Congress of the tenth of March preceding,[10] in which was mentioned the percentage to be allowed to those officers, on the quotas assigned to the States. No alteration has taken place for or against them. They certainly are entitled to the benefit of their original engagement, and no new quotas having been assigned, I am not in capacity to stipulate compensation anew. The Grand Committee were disposed, more to abridge, than to extend the salary." That the account, referred to in the said letter, contains charges of percentage for the years 1783 and 1784, computed upon the sum which constituted the quota of 1782.

That in the settlements which have been made with these officers at the Treasury, they have been allowed nothing more than the stipulated percentage upon the quota of 1782, though the claims of all of them have extended to farther compensation; and some of them retain balances in their hands, as a security for those claims.

That there is ground to believe, that, in certain cases, the compensation allowed by this rule of settlement has been adequate to the services rended; but that this appears not to have been universally the case, and particularly not so, in regard to the petitioner; who, from the manner of conducting the business, by the laws of Virginia, was subjected to more various operations, than were usual elsewhere; and it appears, moreover, that the petitioner had to perform certain extra services, not applicable to other Receivers.

That it also appears satisfactorily, though not from official documents, that the rule of settlement, adopted at the Treasury, was

8. JCC, XXVIII, 267.
9. LC, Robert Morris Papers, Library of Congress.
10. JCC, XXIV, 180–81. This report may be found in the Papers of the Continental Congress, National Archives.

founded upon the supposition of a want of authority to make a farther allowance.

Upon these facts and circumstances, the following observations arise.

That it must have been in contemplation, as well of the Superintendant of Finance, who, on behalf of the government, made the appointments, as of the persons who were appointed, "That annual quotas would continue to be assessed upon the States, as had before been practised, and that the percentage, allowed to the Receivers, would operate, as a yearly compensation, regulated, as to quantum, by yearly requisitions."

That, the requisition for the year 1782 being payable within the year, 1782, the natural presumption is, that the percentage on the quotas of that requsition were to be a compensation to the Receivers for their services during that year.

That it neither appears reasonable in itself, nor consistent with the spirit of the contract, that the services of those officers, for more than three years, should be requited by no greater compensation, than was calculated with a view to one year.

And that it is therefore equitable, that some farther allowance should be made.

It remains to consider, whether the making of such farther allowance, at this time, would form an inconvenient precedent, or contravene any rule, the maintenance of which is necessary to the preservation of order.

Deviations from general rules, which have prevailed in settlements at the Treasury, in cases, in which there has been understood to be competent authority, can never take place, without extreme hazard of extensive inconveniences.

And a revision of the compensations, which have been, in any case allowed, under the former government, on the mere ground of insufficiency, would lead to much embarrassment, and might be productive of very great expense.

But the case of the petitioner does not appear liable to objection, from either of these considerations.

The refusal of the Treasury to admit a farther allowance, seems to have proceeded on the ground of want of authority, and probably, upon the supposition, that some farther legislative provision was necessary.

And the claim of the petitioner does not rest upon the mere insufficiency of the compensation, to which he was entitled. It is founded on the spirit of a contract, which is supposed to have authorised the expectation of a greater compensation, than has actually been allowed.

It is, therefore, not perceived, that any great inconvenience can attend a farther allowance.

Should an additional compensation to the petitioner and others in his situation be judged advisable, the Secretary submits an opinion, that the most equitable mode of doing it, and that, which, upon the whole, will best proportion the recompence to the service, will be, to allow a certain commission, or percentage, upon all the monies which were received by each Receiver, after the expiration of the year 1782.

In relation to the claim of the petitioner, for an allowance of the sum, which he alledges to have been stolen from him, the following observations occur.

It is a principle, which has been admitted in practice, at the Treasury, upon the strength of legal opinions officially given, that where a receiver of public money, as a *mere agent*, is robbed of such money, which may have been in his keeping, the loss is to be borne by the government.

But, from the very great danger of abuse, to which a principle of this nature is liable, it is conceived to be essential to the public safety, that the utmost strictness and exactness should be observed in the manner of proceeding.

Several circumstances appear necessary to be insisted upon, due caution and care on the part of the agent, full, precise and unexceptionable proof of the theft, and immediate notice of it to the proper superior or department.

In the last particular, the petitioner altogether failed. No notice was given, of the robbery, to the Treasury, 'till several months after it happened.

The proof of the theft, though satisfactory to the mind, is not entirely free from exception. The discovery of it did not immediately follow the fact. It is not even ascertained, in what month it happened. One deposition of the Clerk, in whose custody the money was, taken the first of September 1788, states that the theft was committed, in the month of April or May, and represents the money as having been taken from an iron chest, where it was deposited. A subsequent deposition of the same person, taken in May 1789, states, that the chest being full, a large sum of money, received from a certain sheriff, was placed in one of the drawers of a desk, and expresses a suspicion, that the money stolen was taken from the desk.

These circumstances mark less accuracy, than is desirable in a similar case.

But the greatest objection to the claim of the petitioner in this respect, is the delay of notice.

To this, he answers, that the omission arose from a hesitation in his mind, originating in motives of delicacy, whether to bear the loss himself, or to transfer it to the government; alledging, that if he had not sustained severe losses, in consequence of transactions connected with his official situation, he would have preferred the former to the latter. And he produces proof of his having expressed this hesitation, at, or about the time of the accident.

How far an excuse of this nature may be sufficient to obviate an objection arising from the omission of a precaution, the observance of which is of so much importance to the security of the public, is alone for legislative consideration.

All which is humbly submitted          Alexander Hamilton.
                                        Secretary of the Treasury.


## From Jeremiah Wadsworth [1]

[December 10, 1791]

Dear Sir

Inclosed you have the paper I promised You; if you wish for anything more or any explanation of that inclosed I will wait on you when You Please.

Your Hume Svt                                    J Wadsworth
                                                 Decr 10 1791

[ENCLOSURE]

*From Jeremiah Wadsworth* [2]

[December 10, 1791]

Dear Sir

A duty of ten per Cent on our Salted provisions imported into the French Islands would be too much unless we were relieved from other impositions which you will see by the paper herewith are more than ten ℔ Cent on our Cargoes. When our Vessels arrive in Hispaniola the Captain must find a Bondsman tho his whole Vessel and Cargo is in the Power of the Government; this Bondsman is the Merchant who charges five ℔ Ct on the Sales and the same on the return Cargo. We are happy if he will let our Captains do the business & not meddle in the Sales or purchase for in bothe we are in most instances sure to suffer, in the first from want of knowledge of the Value of our Horeses in the latter a carelessness of the quality of the goods, and often short weght & Short measure, sometimes delay of payment we are under the necssity of imploying a Captain or Merchant of our own who is paid five per Cent to save us from greater impositions

Our t[r]ade to the French Islands consists of a great Variety of Articles [on] many of which a small duty is charged, for Horses Oxen Sheep & Hogs alive Beans, Peas Hoops Staves, Boards, Scantling &c. What the legal duties are I do not know but We pay about one per Cent and the duty on Melasses outward is about the same.

It would be of consequence to have the Charges of every kind Mentioned in the treaty as their general regulations are not easily known; if it is agreed that we shall pay the same as the French Ships pay they will make us pay all the Charges which are made on their Ships & men for the purpose of establishing funds for their Various Cases, Beureaus &c.

a Brigantine of 130 Tons entered
Port au Prince in 1788
Paid duties on Cargo
duties 1 ℔ Ct                              344
on 50 Quintal Salted Beef
   @ 3 livres                               150

on Melasses exported 1 ⅌ct                        712

                                                                         1 206

Collectors fees. 8 dollars                         66
Expedition                                         66
Admiralty & Anchorage                             210
Harbour Master                                     60
Gratification Extra                                66
Commandant                                       49.10
Soldiers                                         49.10
interpreter                                        99

                                                                          666

Sales—40 Hor[s]es @ 390 livr                    14 600
Beef Lumber Beans Peas &c                        5 400
                                                ───────
                                                20.000
Commission 5 ⅌ C                                 1 000        1.000
                                                ───────    ───────
                                                18 000       2 866
                                                 2 866
                                                ───────
                                                15 134
Commission 5 ⅌ c                                   700
                                                ───────
                                                14 434

Thus a Cargo of 20-000 livres is reduced to 14434 livres without any
Commission to our own Merchant or Captn. In many instances the
French Merchant takes 10 ⅌ Cent at once out of the Grocce Sales.
The Melasses rising in price they latterly put water into it. On an
average the Melasses falls short on Gauge 5 ⅌ Ct. Our trade has so increased to the French Islands that American produce gradually falls
& that of the Islands has rapidly increased. We do not now get more
Gallons of Melasses or pounds sugar &c for £1000 than we used to get
in 1786. 7. & 8 for £750. I do not mean since the insurrection,[3] but
before.

    The Practise of Extorting a Commission under Pretence of Being
Bondsman is confined to Hispaniola. The Windward Islands do not
practice so but all the Other impositions are nearly the Same. Many
Vessels of the Burthen of 130 Tons Carry lumber only which does
not amount to the Sum Stated above. The Charges are the Same except the duties thus of a Cargo of Lumber in such a Vessel sells for
10.000 livr.

| | |
|---|---|
| Port Charges would be | 666 |
| leaving | 9 334 livres |
| from which a Commisn of 5 ℔ C on the | 500 |
| groce Sales | 8 834 |
| from which 5 ℔ C more as Commn. | 434 |
| | 8 400 |

which is 16 ℔ Ct in port Charges & Commissn. without any duties
which is at least one ℔ Ct.

ALS, Hamilton Papers, Library of Congress.

1. For background to this letter, see George Cabot to H, December 8, 1791, note 1.

Wadsworth, who during the American Revolution had served as commissary general of purchases and as a representative from Connecticut to the Continental Congress, had widespread business interests. He was a founder of the Bank of North America, the Hartford Bank, and the Hartford Manufacturing Company, and had engaged in a number of speculative enterprises. For several years he was a member of a Hartford firm which carried on an extensive trade with the West Indies. During the Confederation period H had handled legal affairs for Wadsworth and his wartime business partner, John B. Church.

2. AL, Hamilton Papers, Library of Congress.

3. This is a reference to the slave insurrection which began in Santo Domingo in August, 1791.

## From Joseph Whipple [1]

Portsmo New Hamp Decr. 10th. 1791

Sir

I have recd. your letter of the 22 Ulto.[2] & have communicated it to Capt. Yeaton.[3]

Conceiving that I can in no better way possess you of Cap. Yeatons reasons for deviating from your limits and my directions respecting the fitting of the Cutter, than by transmitting you his letter to me on that Subject I now inclose it.

I must observe that the last additional and reprehensive clause of your letter So far as it may be intended for me as such, could not be read unfelt, not from a conciousness of having in the Smallest degree deviated from the Strictest attention to œconomy in my transacting the business of the Scammell or from having ever in the most minute instance departed from that principle in transacting the public business committed to my charge, but from reflecting on the disagreeable

circumstance of being charged with unreasonable parsimony on one
Side, and on the other to receive an unmeritted reproof.

I have the honor to be &c.

Hon. Alex Hamilton Esqr.

ADf, RG 36, Collector of Customs at Portsmouth, Letters Sent, 1791–1792,
Vol. 3, National Archives; copy, RG 56, Letters from the Collector at Ports-
mouth, National Archives.
    1. Whipple was collector of customs at Portsmouth.
    2. Letter not found.
    3. Hopley Yeaton was the master of the New Hampshire revenue cutter
*Scammell.*

# *To Otho H. Williams*

Treasury Department
Dec. 10. 1791.

Sir

I have received a statement of the case of the Brig Trimmer from
the Judge of the District Court of Maryland,[1] and have determined
to remit the forfeitures and penalties incurred by the vessel, goods
and captain,[2] on the repayment of the disbursements of money actually made. As the season of the year is critical, and the vessel may,
if detained, be caught by the ice, I request that you will dismiss her
on the repayment of the abovementioned disbursements. A formal
act of remission will be sent to the Clerk of the District court in the
next week.

I am, Sir,   Your obedt. servant                    Alexander Hamilton

Otho H. Williams Esq.
Collector, Baltimore.

LS, Columbia University Libraries.
    1. William Paca.
    2. "An Act to provide for mitigating or remitting the forfeitures and penalties
accruing under the revenue laws, in certain cases therein mentioned" (1 *Stat.* 122–
23 [May 26, 1790]) provided in part that "whenever any person who now is,
or hereafter shall be liable to a fine, penalty or forfeiture . . . shall prefer his
petition to the judge of the district in which such fine, penalty or forfeiture
may have accrued . . . the said judge shall inquire in a summary manner into
the circumstances of the case . . . and shall cause the facts which shall appear

upon such inquiry, to be stated and annexed to the petition, and direct their transmission to the Secretary of the Treasury of the United States, who shall thereupon have power to mitigate or remit such fine, penalty or forfeiture, or any part thereof, if in his opinion the same was incurred without wilful negligence or any intention of fraud."

# To Otho H. Williams

Treasury Department
Dec. 10. 1791.

Sir

It has been represented to me by Mr. Kearney Wharton [1] of Philadelphia, that some hardship has fallen on him in consequence of the want of proper instruments to ascertain the strength of a parcel of Rum belonging to him and lately imported by Messrs. Oliver and Thompson [2] from Antigua. Though I have not yet decided how far it may be proper to make these revisions, I wish that measures may be taken by you in conjunction with the Surveyor [3] to have the whole invoice reexaminied, and such enquiries made as to the difference of price between it and Rum of Antigua as has been taken, or as it appears likely to be necessary for the owners to accept. You will be aware that particular care is necessary in examining goods, which have been so long unladen, and which may have passed through several hands.

I am, Sir, Your obedt. servant            Alexander Hamilton

Otho H. Williams Esq
Collector Baltimore.

LS, Columbia University Libraries.
 1. Wharton was a Philadelphia merchant.
 2. Presumably John Oliver and Henry Thompson, Baltimore merchants.
 3. The surveyor of the port of Baltimore was Robert Ballard.

# To William Ellery [1]

[*Philadelphia, December 12, 1791.* On December 26, 1791, Ellery wrote to Hamilton referring to "your last letter dated Decr. 12th." *Letter not found.*]

 1. Ellery was collector of customs at Newport, Rhode Island.

## From Caleb Gibbs [1]

*[Barre, Massachusetts, December 12, 1791.* On September 10, 1792, Gibbs wrote to Hamilton: "I wrote you On the 12th. of Decr. last." *Letter not found.]*

1. Gibbs, like H, had been an aide-de-camp to George Washington during the American Revolution.

## From Otho H. Williams

*Baltimore, December 12, 1791.* "I have no reason to doubt the probability of receiving a sufficient sum before the first of January next to pay 10,000 Dollars as you desire to Messrs. Elliot & Williams." [1]

ALS, Hamilton Papers, Library of Congress.
1. See H to Williams, December 7, 1791.

## From Otho H. Williams

Baltimore 12 December 1791

Sir

I have very lately received a letter which has a reference to your circular of the 5th. of August; and upon reperusing the latter I discover that I have been very remiss, but I hope not censurable, for not replying to some parts of it sooner. My attention to the previous parts, and a supposition that I was not immediately concerned in the latter, produced in my mind, a temperory suspension of the subjects, and other business, afterwards, detached them entirely from my memory. This is a bad appology; but it is true, and therefore the best I can offer.

The delay, which has unavoidably happened, in rendering the returns to the treasury from this Office has been occasioned partly by my own indisposition, which disqualifies me for the detail of the business and partly by the Nuptials of the Deputy Collector; [1] But more especially by the laborious task of calculating the duties on each

Copy, RG 53, "Old Correspondence," Baltimore Collector, National Archives.
1. Daniel Delozier was deputy collector at Baltimore.

particular specis of Merchandize, according to their several rates, which makes it some times necessary to make several calculations for the contents of a single package. They are however now in considerable forwardness and shall be transmitted as soon as possible.

In answer to the 4th paragraph of your letter it is proper for me to observe that if the oppinions upon which your instructions were founded are to be respected as law it ought not to be expected of me "to acertain in what instances there have been deviations in this district," because in this district I am myself the responsable person in the cases alluded to. I have, however, no hesitation to confess that I think the oppinions of Messrs J & H [2] were hastily assumed; and that the respectability of their judgments, uniting with the press of Important public business, might have a tendency to obtain the approbation of your own to their deccision.

Infallibility is the attribute of no man; and it cannot be imagined that I mean the least disrespect to any one when I say I think it entirely possible and even probable that a more deliberate consideration might have produced in the same persons different opinions, on the same subject. The first opinion delivered by Messrs. J & H is

"That Vessels of *less* than 20 tons, licenced as the act directs are exempt from *tonnage;* Because the act having declared that they shall be at liberty to trade without *entering* or *clearing*, the duty of tonnage, which is payable *only* on the *entry* of Vessels, can *never* arise." The latter part of the 23d section reads thus, "But *no* licence shall be granted for *any* vessel untill the owner or owners applying therefore shall have paid the *tonnage duty* thereon and shall enter into bond &c." [3] To reconcile this part of the law with the opinion of Messrs. J & H. is impossible without altering the language. In my apprehension it was the intention of Congress to subject Vessels of a certain discription to a duty on tonnage at *every entry*, and Vessels of another discription to a like duty only *once a year;* as was the custom formerly with several of the States. But my opinion is governed by instructions.

The 2nd. opinion of Messrs. J & H is

"That no fee is demandable for the *licence* directed to be given to

2. See Richard Harison and Samuel Jones to H, November 18, 1789; "Treasury Department Circular to the Collectors of the Customs," November 30, 1789.
3. See "An Act for Registering and Clearing Vessels, Regulating the Coasting Trade, and for other purposes" (1 *Stat.* 61 [September 1, 1789]).

such Vessels" because "the Legislature *seems* to have made a distinction &c." A provisional clause in the latter part of the 22d. section, which appears to have no relation to the previous part, requires "that the master or owner of every Vessel of less than 20 tons, and not less than 5 tons, which shall be employed *between any of the districts of the United States,* shall *annualy* procure a *licence* from the Collector of the district to which such Vessel belongs, who is thereby authorized to give the same, purporting that such Vessel is exempt from clearing and entering for the term of one year from the date thereof: And the master or owner shall give *bond* with sufficient security" &c.[4] What motive can be supposed to have induced the Legislature to have required of the Collector a certain service without compensation I cannot conceive; neither can I think that it was their intention, since they have been so very moderate in the compensations granted for other services; nor does any reason occur to me why the owner (of a Vessel of less than 20 tons) should be exempt from paying a fee for the *licence* any more than for the *bond;* Both are expresly provided for in the 31 section. "For *every* licence to trade *between the different districts of the United States*" (almost letter for letter with the clause requiring the licence to be procured) "and for taking every bond required by this act" &c.[5] But it is not pretended that the *bond* is not to be paid for.

The 3rd. opinion of Messrs. J. & H. is

That, by the 25 and 26 section, *only* the fee of 25 "Cents for a permitt to proceed to the place of destination is demandable." [6] By these sections it is required, in certain cases, that the Collector shall receive duplicate manifests of Cargoes intended to be transmitted from one district to another; He must necessarily compare them, and he is required to administer a long oath, a certificate whereof he must write on one of those manifests, to be delivered to the master: and the other manifest he must file in his Office; all which is much more labor and trouble than granting a permit. I think it unreasonable to conclude that Congress intended, in more instances than one, that the lesser service should be compensated and the greater performed for nothing. Yet the 5th. clause in the 31 section of the act, by connecting the compensation "for every entry of inward Cargo" with the compensation for "Receiving of and qualifying to every manifest of Vessels licenced to trade" (which last can be done according to section 25 & 26 at the place of export only) has so confounded the duties of two officers, in different situations, that according to Messrs. J & H neither of them can legally receive his just reward. The Gentlemen were "aware that their construction of the act would involve a consequence probably not intended by the Legislature". I perswade myself that a revision of their opinions would discover to themselves more than one consequence evidently inconsistant therewith. If I may be permited to abridge their conclusive remarks, (without altering a letter or transposing a syllable) they will read thus. "As it is expressly declared that no other or greater fees shall be taken by the several officers of the customes; we suppose that no *other* \* *construction* of the act is admissable, *except* \* the *one* which we have mentioned." To conceive the force of such reasoning I must be endowed with *other* than common sense. It is noticed merely to justify my conclusion that their opinions were hastily assumed, and I shall only add that I assure myself you will think my moity of the mite allowed, in either of the cases in question, too inconsiderable a motive to influence my Judgment. I am &c.

\* What a conclusion is here? They found the infallibility of their opinion of an act upon the act itself, and declare no *other* construction inadmissibly *except* the *ones* mentioned which is no *other*, and therefore can be no exception.[7]

7. This footnote is in Williams's handwriting.

## From Otho H. Williams

[*Baltimore, December 12, 1791*. According to its catalogue description, this letter relates to the "Registry of the Brig Dove, Josiah Parsons, master." [1] *Letter not found.*]

Sold by Harvard Trust Company, Cambridge, Massachusetts, 1962.
1. See H to Williams, December 6, 1791.

## To Jeremiah Olney [1]

Treasury Department Decemb 14 1791

Sir

I do not think you will be justifiable in making a deduction from the legal rate of duty on Coffee, on account of its being broken, nor on cocoa, because of an inferiority of quality, they being in each instance as I presume the unmixed article, on which the Legislature has imposed an uniform impost, without providing a variation of duty in case of differences of quality.[2]

The shells of Coffee cannot properly be considered as included in the duty on coffee, which was meant to apply, it is presumed, to the grain. It is however difficult to determine on the requisite deduction. If the Owners will permit a bag or cask of about one hundred weight to be impartially taken out, by one of the Officers of the Customs, and to be shelled, at their expence, by some person to be employed by you for the purpose, I would recommend your deducting from the whole in that proportion. The result I would wish to be communicated to me.

I am sir,   Your obedt Servt                    Alexander Hamilton

Jeremiah Olney Esquire
Collector Providence

LS, Rhode Island Historical Society, Providence; copy, RG 56, Letters to the Collector at Providence, National Archives; copy, RG 56, Letters to Collectors at Small Ports, "Set G," National Archives.
   1. For background to this letter, see Olney to H, November 28, 1791.
   2. See "An Act making further provision for the payment of the debts of the United States" (1 *Stat.* 180–82 [August 10, 1790]).

## From Otho H. Williams

Baltimore 14 December 1791

Sir

I have received your instructions respecting the Brige. Trimmer [1] and she shall be dispatched accordingly. What you say of disbursements of money actually made may make it necessary to inform you that in the case of the Brig Trimmer, and in others similar thereto (where the matter of illegality was duly reported without reserve, and manifestly without any intention of evading the law) the custom has been to detain the goods on board the Vessel *without seizure*, and to give the parties concerned, an opportunity of making representation; and prefering a petition to the Judge; which has always been done within the time limited by law for goods to be permitted to remain on board. The Judge has usually taken up the matter upon this ground and satisfied himself (by enquiry of the Custom House Officers) of the propriety of recommending the case. This mode of conducting the business has been adopted by the officers upon the following considerations. If any deception, or fraud, were intended it could not fail to be discovered, or strongly suspected, within fifteen days: the time allowed for vessels to unlade; and if no deception or fraud were intended it would be ungenerous, and, sometimes, cruel, to subject persons who are innocent, and, perhaps, unfortunate in the very circumstance which exposes them to a penalty, to expose them to unnecessary expences also.

I am, Sir, Your Most Obedient Humble Servant

A. Hamilton Esqr.

ADf, RG 53, "Old Correspondence," Baltimore Collector, National Archives.
1. See H to Williams, December 10, 1791.

## Conversation with George Hammond [1]

[Philadelphia, December 15–16, 1791]

Towards the end of last week, I had a very long and confidential conversation with Mr Hamilton, the Secretary of the Treasury, in the course of which the opinion, I had entertained, of that Gentleman's just and liberal way of thinking was fully confirmed. The late unfortunate expedition under General St Clair [2] naturally engrossed a great portion of our conversation, whence I was induced to express his Majesty's sincere desire to see tranquillity between the Indians and the United States permanently re-established. I took occasion distantly to intimate that if this government should think proper to solicit the King's interference for this purpose through his government in Canada, I had reason to believe that the application would not be ineffectual. [3] To this Mr Hamilton replied that the British Government might be assured that the United States, in the present war, were actuated by no motives of extending their territory, but simply by the desire of binding down the Indians to the stipulations of their last treaty, [4] and that if this object could not be attained by negociation, it was determined to prosecute the war with vigour—

that this government was however sincerely solicitous to effect a pacification, and if the *voluntary* interposition of the King's government in Canada could tend to accomplish it, such a measure would be received with the greatest gratitude.

In another part of our conversation, Mr Hamilton hinted to me, with as much caution, as the danger of committing himself too far rendered necessary, that in the affairs of this country the present is an important crisis, upon which may depend the future complexion as well of its political connexions as of its commercial arrangements with the nations of Europe. I farther collected from other incidental observations that the government of France seems inclined to hold out to this country, in their projected treaty, some additional circumstances of advantage, which will have a tendency still farther to favor and promote the navigation of the United States.[5]

Upon this last head, I must not omit mentioning to your Lordship that Mr Hamilton informed me he was preparing a report upon the actual state of the navigation and commerce of this country, whence it would appear that the present system of France was more favorable to the former, and that of Great Britain to the latter.[6] He however admitted, that upon balancing the general aggregate advantages resulting to the country from these respective systems, the scale had hitherto decidedly preponderated in favor of the *commercial* encouragements afforded by Great Britain.[7]

D, PRO: F.O., Series 4, Vol. 11 (Great Britain).

1. This conversation has been taken from Hammond to Lord Grenville, December 19, 1791, Dispatch No. 13.

Hammond, the first British Minister to the United States, was sent his general instructions on September 2, 1791, by Lord Grenville, who had been made Secretary of State for Foreign Affairs on June 8, 1791. His private instructions, which had been given by Lord Hawkesbury, president of the Board of Trade, had been written on July 4, 1791 (Mayo, *Instructions to British Ministers*, 1–13). Hammond, only twenty-eight years old at the time of his appointment, had already had extensive diplomatic experience. He had been secretary to David Hartley during the peace negotiations at Paris in 1783, chargé d'affaires at Vienna from 1788 to 1790, and for a short time Minister Plenipotentiary under Lord St. Helens, the British Ambassador to Spain.

Hammond arrived in the United States in October, 1791, but, wishing tangible proof that the United States intended to send an envoy to England, he waited several weeks before presenting his credentials. After assurances by Jefferson that negotiations were under way for the appointment of an American emissary, Hammond was presented to the President on November 11, 1791.

2. In the fall of 1791, Major General Arthur St. Clair, governor of the Northwest Territory, attempted to atone for the disastrous defeat suffered by

American troops under Brigadier General Josiah Harmar at the hands of the Indians the previous year. From his base at Fort Washington near Cincinnati he drew up plans for an invasion of the Indian country. The expedition had traveled no more than ninety miles before the Americans, on November 4, 1791, were surprised and decisively defeated by the Indians. Nine hundred of St. Clair's men were killed, and the larger part of the remaining American troops discarded their arms and fled. St. Clair's account of his defeat is printed in *ASP, Indian Affairs*, I, 137-38.

3. As early as the spring of 1791, George Beckwith, the unofficial British emissary to the United States, following instructions sent to him by Lord Dorchester, Governor General of Canada, had suggested to United States officials that Dorchester should intervene to bring peace between the Americans and the Indians (see "Conversation with George Beckwith," May 15, 1791). Although H had informed Beckwith that British mediation was inadmissible, neither Dorchester nor the British Ministry was willing to drop the idea. On September 16, 1791, Henry Dundas, Secretary for Home Affairs, wrote to Dorchester that "it is His Majesty's pleasure that every means which your prudence can suggest should be taken by you for healing the differences which at present exist, and for effecting, if possible, a speedy termination of the war" (Brymner, *Canadian Archives*, 1890, 173). Lord Grenville had instructed Hammond that "nothing would be more satisfactory to His Majesty" than to mediate between the Indians and Americans (Mayo, *Instructions to British Ministers*, 16).

4. This is a reference to the treaties of Fort Harmar, which were signed on January 9, 1789. For the texts of these treaties, see *ASP, Indian Affairs*, I, 5-7.

5. For the proposed commercial treaty with France, see George Cabot to H, December 8, 1791, note 1.

6. Although no evidence has been found that H completed such a report, the draft of a comparative study of the British and French commercial systems in relation to the United States may be found in the Hamilton Papers, Library of Congress. This may be a draft of the report referred to by Hammond or H may have compiled the information for the proposed commercial treaty with France. See Cabot to H, December 8, 1791, note 1. This document is printed in these volumes as "View of the Commercial Regulations of France and Great Britain in Reference to the United States," 1792-1793.

7. Another version of this conversation with Hammond reads as follows: "In some of my earliest conversations with Mr Hamilton, subsequently to the defeat of the 4th of November, that Gentleman resisted my insinuation of the good effect that would arise from requesting the Kings mediation, by stating that a part of the Indians, now engaged in war with the United States, lived within their territory and were considered in some measure as their subjects, and that upon that ground no external intervention could be allowed. But even admitting them not to be subjects, it was the opinion of himself and his colleagues, that the most advisable and feasible mode of procuring and preserving a lasting peace with the Indians would be—to inspire them with a confidence that the United States meditated no encroachment that would affect their right to inhabit the territory situated within the United States, and allotted to them by treaty—to redress any real grievances of which they may complain—and to conciliate their affections by acts of kindness and attention to their wants. But if these objects could not be accomplished by persuasion and gentle means it would be indispensably necessary to complete their subjection by the terror and success of the American arms. He added that the mediation or intervention of any foreign power would degrade the United States in the estimation of the Indians, and would sow the seeds of future dissension, as the latter would be tempted to aggression by the expectation of a

similar interference on any other occasion" (Hammond to Grenville, June 8, 1792, PRO: F.O., Series 4, Vol. 15, Dispatch No. 23).

## *From James Reynolds* [1]

Philadelphia, 15th December, 1791.

Sir

I am very sorry to find out that I have been so Cruelly treated by a person that I took to be my best friend instead of that my greatest Enimy. You have deprived me of every thing thats near and dear to me, I discovred whenever I Came into the house. after being out I found Mrs Reynolds weeping I ask'd her the Cause of being so unhappy. She always told me that she had bin Reding. and she could not help Crying when she Red any thing that was Afecting. but seing her Repeatedly in that Setevation gave me some suspicion to think that was not the Cause, as fortain would have it. before matters was Carred to two great a length. I discovered a letter directed to you which I copied of and put it in the place where I found it. without being discovered by Her. and then the evining after. I was Curious anough to watch her. and see give a letter to a Black man in Markett Street. which I followed Him to your door. after that I Returned home some time in the evening, and I broutched the Matter to her and Red the Coppy to her which she fell upon her knees and asked forgiveness and discovered every thing to me Respecting the matter And ses that she was unhappy. and not knowing what to do without some assistance. She Called on you for the lone of some money. which you toald her you would Call on her the Next Evening. which accordingly you did. and there Sir you took the advantage a poor Broken harted woman. instead of being a Friend. you have acted the part of the most Cruelist man in existance. you have made a whole family miserable. She ses there is no other man that she Care for in this world. now Sir you have bin the Cause of Cooling her affections for me. She was a woman. I should as soon sespect an angiel from heven. and one where all my happiness was depending. and I would Sacrefise almost my life to make her Happy. but now I am determed to have satisfation. it shant be onely one [f]amily thats miserable. for I am Robbed of all happiness in this world I am determed to leve her. and take my daughter with me that She shant see her poor mother Lot. now Sir if I Cant see you at your house call and see me. for there is no person that Knowes any thing as yet. And I am tiremd to see you, by some Means or other. for you have made me an unhappy man for eve. put it to your own case and Reflect one Moment. that you should know shush a thing of your wife. would not you have satisfaction yes. and so will I before one day passes me more.

I am yours                                              James Reynolds.

Mr. Alexander Hamilton.

"Reynolds Pamphlet," August 31, 1797.

1. Reynolds was the husband of Maria Reynolds, H's mistress in one of the most famous and sordid affairs in American history. Writing in 1797, H described the background of this affair as follows:

"Some time in the summer of the year 1791 a woman called at my house in the city of Philadelphia and asked to speak with me in private. I attended her into a room apart from the family. With a seeming air of affliction she informed that she was a daughter of a Mr. Lewis, sister to a Mr. G. Livingston of the State of New-York, and wife to a Mr. Reynolds whose father was in the Commissary Department during the war with Great Britain, that her husband, who for a long time had treated her very cruelly, had lately left her, to live with another woman, and in so destitute a condition, that though desirous of returning to her friends she had not the means—that knowing I was a citizen of New-York, she had taken the liberty to apply to my humanity for assistance.

"I replied, that her situation was a very interesting one—that I was disposed to afford her assistance to convey her to her friends, but this at the moment not being convenient to me (which was the fact) I must request the place of her residence, to which I should bring or send a small supply of money. She told me the street and the number of the house where she lodged. In the evening I put a bank-bill in my pocket and went to the house. I inquired for Mrs. Reynolds and was shewn up stairs, at the head of which she met me and conducted me into a bed room. I took the bill out of my pocket and gave it to her. Some conversation ensued from which it was quickly apparent that other than pecuniary consolation would be acceptable.

"After this, I had frequent meetings with her, most of them at my own house; Mrs. Hamilton with her children being absent on a visit to her father. In the course of a short time, she mentioned to me that her husband had solicited a reconciliation, and affected to consult me about it. I advised to it, and was soon after informed by her that it had taken place. . . ." ("Reynolds Pamphlet," August 31, 1797.)

After his announcement of the discovery of his wife's infidelity, Reynolds proceeded in the course of the following year to extort from H various sums of money under threat of making the affair public. In December, 1792, three Republican congressmen, Frederick A. C. Muhlenberg, Abraham B. Venable, and James Monroe, were informed by Jacob Clingman, Reynolds's confederate, that H had engaged with Reynolds in speculation in public funds, offering in evidence some of the letters which had passed between Reynolds and H. H reassured the congressmen on the charge of speculation by revealing to them his relationship with Mrs. Reynolds and Reynolds's subsequent venture into blackmail. Here the affair rested until the summer of 1797, when the earlier charges of speculation with Reynolds were revived in James T. Callender's *American Annual Register, or Historical Memoirs of the United States for the*

*Year 1796* (Philadelphia, 1797). H answered the charges in the pamphlet *Observations on Certain Documents Contained in No. V. and VI of "The History of the United States for the Year 1796," in which the Charge of Speculation against Alexander Hamilton, Late Secretary of the Treasury, is Fully Refuted. Written by Himself* (Philadelphia: Printed for John Fenno, by John Bioren, 1797). This pamphlet contains H's version of the affair and its aftermath and is subsequently referred to in these volumes as the "Reynolds Pamphlet." H's draft of the pamphlet, together with the published version and appendix containing letters and statements relative to the affair, is printed in these volumes under the date of August 31, 1797.

The letter above is printed as document No. II in the appendix of the "Reynolds Pamphlet," August 31, 1797.

## To James Reynolds

[*Philadelphia, December 15, 1791.* In the "Reynolds Pamphlet" Hamilton wrote: "The same day, being the 15th of December 1791, I received from Mr. Reynolds the letter . . . by which he informs me of the detection of his wife. . . . In answer to this I sent him a note, or message desiring him to call upon me at my office, which I think he did the same day. . . ." [1] *Hamilton's letter of December 15, 1791, not found.*]

"Reynolds Pamphlet," August 31, 1797.

1. The conversation between H and Reynolds is described by H as follows:
   "He in substance repeated the topics contained in his letter, and concluded as he had done there, that he was resolved to have satisfaction.

   "I replied that he knew best what evidence he had of the alleged connection between me and his wife, that I neither admitted nor denied it—that if he knew of any injury I had done him, intitling him to satisfaction, it lay with him to name it.

   "He travelled over the same ground as before, and again concluded with the same vague claim of satisfaction, but without specifying the kind, which would content him. It was easy to understand that he wanted money, and to prevent an explosion, I resolved to gratify him. But willing to manage his delicacy, if he had any, I reminded him that I had at our first interview made him a promise of service, that I was disposed to do it as far as might be proper, and in my power, and requested him to consider in what manner I could do it, and to write to me. He withdrew with a promise of compliance." ("Reynolds Pamphlet," August 31, 1797.)

## From Maria Reynolds [1]

[Philadelphia, December 15, 1791]

Col. Hamilton

Dear Sir

I have not tim to tell you the cause of my present troubles only that Mr. has rote to you this morning and I know not wether you

have got the letter or not and he has swore that If you do not answer
It or If he dose not se or hear from you to day he will write Mrs.
Hamilton he has just Gone oute and I am a Lone I think you had
better come here one moment that you May know the Cause then
you will the better know how to act Oh my God I feel more for you
than myself and wish I had never been born to give you so mutch
unhappisness do not rite to him no not a Line but come here soon
do not send or leave any thing in his power                Maria

"Reynolds Pamphlet," August 31, 1797.
    1. This letter is printed as document No. I in the appendix of the "Reynolds
Pamphlet," August 31, 1797.
    For background to this letter, see James Reynolds to H, December 15, 1791;
H to Reynolds, December 15, 1791.

## From William Short [1]

Amsterdam Dec. 15. 1791.

Sir

   I have now the honor of inclosing you a copy of the contract for
the loan opened at Antwerp,[2] which could not be had in time to go
with my last of the 1st. inst. The customary ratification has been
promised on it, which it is hoped will be obtained & forwarded to
Antwerp. A duplicate will be sent by another conveyance. The
translation is in French, the English language not having been understood by the Notary. The act is copied as nearly as possible from
those passed here & you will find the terms at least as barbarous, but
as it seems they compose the technical language of Antwerp I imagine
no objection will be made to them, they being clear and intelligible.
I recieved yesterday a letter from M. de Wolf [3] in which he informed
me that the loan continued going on with prosperity as well as the
remittances he was making therefrom to France. I have already mentioned to you that it would be remitted in proportion as it was

ALS, letterpress copy, William Short Papers, Library of Congress.
    1. After serving from 1783 to 1784 as a member of the Executive Council of
Virginia, Short in 1784 accompanied Thomas Jefferson to France to serve as
Jefferson's secretary, and later as secretary of the American legation in Paris.
In 1789 he became chargé d'affaires at Paris.
    2. For an English translation of this contract, see Short to H, November 8,
1791, note 4.
    3. Charles John Michael de Wolf to Short, December 12, 1791 (ALS, Short
Family Papers, Library of Congress).

recieved as I understand that to be your wish, the reservation for your purposes having extended only to f 2,500,000. to be taken out of the last six millions loaned here.[4]

I come now to speak of the business at this place which I have postponed writing to you about until now because nothing new has occurred since my last & because I hoped after arriving here I should be able to give you information of greater certainty respecting it.

I have already informed you that the bankers [5] here in reply to my letter authorizing them to make a loan at 4½. p. cent interest had told me that they postponed it in the hopes of being able to make one in a short time at 4 p cent interest on the charges being augmented.[6] I informed you also how unexpected a circumstance this was to me & at the same time that my earnest desire to see it realized could not prevent my entertaining certain doubts respecting it. I wrote to them however immediately approving their having postponed the loan at 4½ p. cent, & authorized their opening one at 4. p. cent at the charges they mention.[7] Lest this offer of the loan at 4. p. cent should be intended merely to defeat that at Antwerp, or at least to be made use of as a pretext for shewing the disadvantage of opening a loan out of Holland, whilst they should make use of the authorization for one at 4½. p. cent interest here, I thought it advisable at the same time that I mentioned to them that their having not used it in the hopes of reducing the interest still lower, was an additional proof of their zeal for the service of the U.S. to desire them to consider that authorization as no longer in force, but to act under that for the loan at 4. p. cent interest; if they found such an one practicable.

This was the best means I had of satisfying myself fully whether a loan at 4. p. cent here was really practicable, as now having no longer the power to make one at 4½. p. cent & the tax on loans approaching [8] it was certain every effort would be used to effect one at 4. p. cent, even if their original offer should have been made with the intentions abovementioned.

4. See Short to H, December 1, 1791.

5. Wilhem and Jan Willink, Nicholaas and Jacob Van Staphorst, and Nicholas Hubbard, the bankers of the United States in Amsterdam.

6. See Short to H, November 22, 1791.

7. Short to Willink, Van Staphorst, and Hubbard, December 1, 1791 (ALS, letterpress copy, William Short Papers, Library of Congress).

8. After January 1, 1792, the Dutch government proposed to levy a tax on loans made in the Netherlands. See Short to H, August 31, 1791.

I mentioned to you in my last their letter respecting the loan at Antwerp & their adding that it had rendered impracticable the expected loan at 4. p. cent. I afterwards recieved another from them saying that if that loan could be arrested in its present state & no more of the bonds given out they could still effect the loan here, but otherwise that it would be impossible.[9] As they had been informed however that it was contracted for they must have known that they were placing their offer on a contingency that could not take place. Since my arrival here they persist in saying that the loan at 4. p. cent cannot take place at present, though it may be hoped for soon, & that it has been prevented only by that at Antwerp. Thus the affair stands at present.

My conversations with these gentlemen however have given me full proofs of what I informed you I was myself already fully satisfied about—namely that it is not the loan at Antwerp which has prevented the one held out here at 4. p. cent. The various reasonings they have made use of carry a strong conviction with them of what I assert. They laid down for example that the bonds of the Antwerp loan being for sale here & the money lenders finding thus an opportunity of placing their money at 4½. would not give it at 4., & this would seem reasonable. Yet they told me among other things that the tax on loans would not diminish their number, as those in whom the money lenders had confidence, such as brokers undertakers &c. would always prevent their placing their monies in loans made elsewhere, of course that those powers who have need of Dutch money must come & take it at Amsterdam. This is probably the truth. I asked them how they reconciled it however with what they had told me of the loan at Antwerp being brought here & spoiling the market for the loan they had considered as certain without it. M. de Wolf had also given me every reason that can be given in such cases to believe, that no part of these obligations had been or would be placed on the Amsterdam market. He observed that it was his interest as well as that of the undertakers of Antwerp to prevent it & accordingly to his knowlege one of the brokers from Amsterdam interested in the American loans having written to an undertaker of Antwerp to know on what terms he could take an interest with him, had been answered

9. Willink, Van Staphorst, and Hubbard to Short, December 1, 1791 (LS, Short Family Papers, Library of Congress).

that he had no part to dispose of in that manner. He suspected the intention was to get possession of a certain number of the obligations either to sell them under par on the Amsterdam market, or to shew me, as a proof of the money's coming from Amsterdam although the loan was opened at Antwerp, & of course to prove that it was no new source of credit. This you will easily concieve Sir is an underground kind of business where it would be useless & improper to employ myself in digging for the truth between assertions on one hand & denials on the other. Of course I do nothing more than hear indifferently all parties & draw the inferences which seem to me the most probable that they may serve as a future guide.

The bankers here finding that I did not consent to renew the authorisation for the 4½. p. cent loan on being told that the one at 4. p. cent was impracticable for the present, have taken some pains to shew me that the step from 5 to 4. p. cent was too rapid for the money lenders, that nothing but the extraordinarily favorable moment at which they concieved the idea of it could have justified it &c. They press me to renew that authorisation & among other reasons say that it will hasten the moment of making a loan at 4. p. cent. I asked them how they reconciled that with what they had told me of the 4½. p. cent obligations from Antwerp on this market having procrastinated the 4. p. cent loan. I was left unsatisfied on this & other points of the same nature.

On the whole I cannot at present entertain a doubt that the loan at Antwerp was the cause of the expectations held out from hence as to one at 4. p. cent. On that ground many things are easily accounted for which are inexplicable on any other. I have taken much pains to convince myself on this subject, as well because I considered it a point of importance to the U.S. as on my own account personally. For although I am fully persuaded that you will consider the loan at Antwerp as a measure that admitted of no hesitation at the time it was adopted, yet I should not have been able to have divested myself of pain if by any posterior & unforeseen contingency, it had been really the means of preventing the U.S. from reducing the rate of their interest to 4. p. cent. The bankers themselves agree that at the time of the loan being authorized at Antwerp the possibility of one here at a lower rate of interest was not discoverable by any human foresight.

I gave the bankers no hopes that I shall consent to a loan at

4½. p. cent. I shall wait until the delay necessary for making one at 4. p. cent shall be ascertained as nearly as possible—if not too considerable I shall suppose it not advisable to wait for it. Since the U.S. was not to derive the expected benefit from the present rate of exchange with France, former reasons for despatch in the making of loans do not exist.

Nothing has been yet settled as to the manner in which the payments are to be rated. The several data are known viz. the rate of exchange & depreciation & there can be no inconvenience in delaying the settlement of the mode.

The contract for the late loan of six millions was signed immediately on my arrival here.[10] It will be soon forwarded for ratification as usual. The bonds are printing & I shall have finished signing them in a few days. Immediately after which & taking arrangements for a new loan here I shall return to Paris by the way of Antwerp. The present state of affairs in France will have rendered my absence of little consequence—no business but that of the most urgent & pressing nature being attended to there by the ministry.

I have been favored by the bankers here with the President's speech at the opening of Congress & other articles of American intelligence. The last letters which I have had the honor of recieving from the U.S. are yours of Sep. 2 & Oct 3. & one from the Sec. of State of July 28.[11] Your last acknowleges the reciept of mine of July 26. & 27. There were three of an older date unacknowleged which I hope will have been since recieved, they were July 8, 19 & 24.

I beg you to be fully persuaded of the sentiments of respect & attachment with which I have the honor to remain, Sir, your most obedient humble servant                                                              W Short

The Honble
Alexander Hamilton. secretary of the Treasury—Philadelphia

10. This was the Holland loan of September, 1791. For a description of this loan, see Short to H, August 31, 1791.
11. Thomas Jefferson to Short, July 28, 1791 (LS, letterpress copy, Thomas Jefferson Papers, Library of Congress).

## From Joseph Whipple

*Portsmouth, New Hampshire, December 15, 1791.* "Mr. Parrott [1] the 2nd Mate of the Scammel having an advantageous offer in the

Command of a Ship has risigned his place in the Scammel. . . . I was obliged to acquiesce in this resignation which is rendered the more inconvenient by the Scarcity of young men Suitable for the Station of 1st. Mate to which I recommended Mr Parrott. . . .[2] I would propose for your consideration & direction the temporary appointment of such persons as may appear the most suitable. . . ."

ADfS, RG 36, Collector of Customs at Portsmouth, Letters Sent, 1791–1792, Vol. 3, National Archives; copy, RG 56, Letters from the Collector at Portsmouth, National Archives.
1. John Parrott.
2. See Whipple to H, October 7, 1791.

## To Sharp Delaney

Treasury Department
December 16 1791

Sir
I wish you to ascertain who is the present owner of the Brig Lydia commanded by Captain Vancise, of what place he is a resident, whether he is a Citizen of the United States, when he became owner of that vessel, and where he purchased her.

Should application be made for a new register for that Vessel, I wish to receive immediate information, and that you suspend the issuing of it until you shall afterwards hear from this office.

I am, Sir,   Your Most Obed Servant.          Alexander Hamilton

Sharp Delany Esqr.
Collr. Philadelphia.

LS, Historical Society of Pennsylvania, Philadelphia.

## From Joseph Whipple

Portsmouth, New Hampshire, December 16, 1791. "I have received your Circular letter to the Agents of the Cutters of the 17th. Ultimo.[1] As the directions given In that letter supersedes the Necessity of a particular Statement . . . I will only observe that the cost of 232 days of the mens victualling amounted to 332%/100 Dollars being about 14⅓ cents pr. ration. Cap Yeaton [2] has however agreed to Supply the people at 12 cents pr. diem for the whole term of Victualling the Vessel when at allowance & when not, and untill the 30th. of June next Accounting for the Cost of all the Provisions hitherto purchased for her which to the 1st. instant averaged about that Sum. . . ."

ADf, RG 36, Collector of Customs at Portsmouth, Letters Sent, 1791–1792, Vol. 3, National Archives; copy, RG 56, Letters from the Collector at Portsmouth, National Archives.
    1. "Treasury Department Circular to the Collectors of the Customs," November 17, 1791.
    2. Hopley Yeaton was the master of the New Hampshire revenue cutter *Scammell*.

# From Otho H. Williams

Baltimore 16 December 1791.

Sir
    I cannot discover by the acts of the Legislature that Collectors have any legal jurisdiction, or controul, over the Officers of the revenue cutters; or that they have, necessarily, any agency in that establishment further than to receive the reports of the Officers and to respect them as authentic documents whereby to ascertain the Cargoes of inwardbound vessels. I therefore conclude that the several letters and instructions, addressed to me from the Treasury department are intended to supply some defect of the law in that respect; [1] and have consequently given the business all the attention I could. It has not, however, been practicable for me to make any effectual arrangement respecting the rations of the Officers and men. Captain Gross [2] has always declined entering into any contract; and the object is too inconsiderable to gain the attention of any one else in whom I could confide.
    Unwilling as I am to intimate any disapprobation of an establishment which the wisdom of the Legislature has adopted I think it my duty to suggest my opinion that the Revenue cutter for Maryland has hitherto been of no more advantage to the United States, and perhaps much less, than if She had been built and manned on the *lake Erie*. The very few papers that have been sent to the Customs House

by the officers of the cutter have been informal, incorrect, or out of time, some of them 2 or three weeks after the entry of the Vessel to which they related and it does not appear to me that any essential service has been, or could have been, performed by the Cutter in the Chesepeak, than merely the inspection of such papers as the masters of Vessels had to produce.

It will perhaps be remembered that my sentiments were not favorable to the plan of employing cutters in this district, and thence it may *possibly* be concluded that I have not been disposed to render all the assistance in my power; But I certainly have had no power in the business beyond what has been delegated by the secretary of the Treasury in the form of particular permissions, or 'special directions with very exact limitations, and cautions which it was improper for me to exceed and which have not been neglected. That it may not *seem* that I have been, at any time, unmindful of the public interest in this respect I think it expedient to mention to you at this time the foregoing particulars very lately communicated by Lieutenant Thomas [3] of the Cutter, and of whom I made very minute enquiry respecting the affairs. The first Lieutenant Mr. Porter [4] about the 11 November went as Master of the schooner Polly, cleared from this port for New Orleans: But supposed to be destined on a secret voyage to the Island of Cuba. He expected, I am informed, to return and take his command on board the Cutter in about two months after his departure. The 3d. Lieut. Mr. Forbes,[5] I understand, had waited a considerable time for his Commission without receiving it, and being an expert and necessitous seaman was induced to make a Voyage to Sea. When he returned his Commission was in the possession of the Captain; But as the Cutter was not then prepared for a cruise he went again to Sea. He sailed last in the schooner Polly, which cleared from this port about 3 weeks ago 26 Novmr. for St. Eustasia. Lt. Thomas further informs me that Captn Gross left the Cutter in his charge the 15 November, with instructions to hire *five* good hands; to fit out the cutter and sail as far as Annapolis; and there wait his orders. That he has not been able to procure the hands for the pay and subsistence allowed by Congress, *ten* to *twelve* Dollars ℔ mo. being given here for good Seamen to sail in merchant Ships. Captn Gross expected to return from the Eastern shore of Maryland in ten or twelve days after his departure. Mr. Thomas supposes that he has been detained by bad weather, head winds, and an apprehension that the late severe cold has closed this harbour, and that it is uncertain whether he will return this winter, as he left orders how the affairs of the cutter were to be managed in case he should not return. Yet Mr. Thomas thinks it may be that Captn. Gross is at this time returning. Two men only are all that have been on board the cutter for near two months, and these are supplied with provision and fuel by Mr. Thomas in port. This is a different account from that which would give me pleasure to communicate; But as I do not know how, or when, matters can be better arranged without your interposition I have thought it right to trouble you with this detail.

Simon Deagle master of a coasting Vessel from this port, last from Norfolk, brought 10 Musketts & 10 Bayonets 20 pistols 2 Lanthorns and 1 Chissell which he said he recd from the Collector at Norfolk [6] for the use of the Cutter belonging to this District and which he has delivered to Lieutenant Thomas.

I am, Sir, Your most obedient Humble Servant

ADf, RG 53, "Old Correspondence," Baltimore Collector, National Archives.
1. See "Treasury Department Circular to the Collectors of the Customs," June 1, September 21, November 17, 1791; H to Williams, November 11, 1791. See also "Treasury Department Circular to the Captains of the Revenue Cutters," June 1, 1791.
2. Simon Gross was master of the Maryland revenue cutter *Active*.
3. William Thomas.
4. David Porter.
5. James Forbes.
6. William Lindsay.

## From James Reynolds [1]

Saturday Evening 17th December 1791.

Sir,

I now have taken till tuesday morning to Consider on What Steps will be Best for me to take. I should not have let the matter Rested till then, if it had not been for the newes of the death of my Sister. which it Semes as if all my troubles are Comming on me in one moment. if it had been any other person except yourself. that treated me as you have done. I should not have taken the trouble to Call on them more than once. *but your being in the Station of life you are.* induses me to way every Surcomstance well Respecting the matter it will be imposible for me ever to think of liveing or Reconsiling myself to Stay with a woman that I no has plased her affections on you. and you know if you Reflect one moment. that you have been the sole Cause of it. I have all Reason in the world to believe its true. I am that man that will always have Satisfaction by some means or other when treated ill. Especially when I am treated in the mannor, as you have done. you may rest ashured that the matter as yet is Not known. If think proper to Call at the sighn of the George tuesday morning at 8 oclock I will be there. for your house or office is no place to converse about these matters. if that is not agreeable to you. let me no what plase I shall see you at. at that time, for I am determened to know what corse I shall take, more miserable I cant be than I am at present. let the consiquence be as it will. for when I come into the house. I find the wife always weeping and praying that I wont leve her. And its all on your account. for if you had not seekd for her Ruin it would not have happined. Could you not have Relieved the disstressed without. transgreessing in the mannor as you have done. Sertainly you did not show the man of honnor. in taking the advantage of the afflicted, when Calling on you as a father and protector in the time of disstress. put that home to yourself and tell me what you would do in such a Case. or what amend Could be made to you or wether it would be possible to make any. you will answer no. it be imposible after being Robbed of all your happiness and your whole family made misseable. I know you are a man thats not void of feeling. I am not a man that wishes to do any thing Rashly. or plunge myself into Ruin. now if you think proper to se me at the place I have mentioned. or any other. please to let me no before. for I wish to be by ourselfs where we Can converse together. for if you do not Call on me or let me no where I Can see. you at that time. I shant call on you after this.

I am yours                                          James Reynolds

Mr. Alexander Hamilton.

"Reynolds Pamphlet," August 31, 1797.
    1. This letter is printed as document No. III in the appendix of the "Reynolds Pamphlet," August 31, 1797.
    For background to this letter, see Reynolds to H, December 15, 1791; H to Reynolds, December 15, 1791; Maria Reynolds to H, December 15, 1791.

## From Jacob Sarly [1]

[*Calcutta, December 17, 1791*. The catalogue description of this letter reads as follows: "Long letter describing the military situation around Seringapatam, the British forces under Cornwallis and the strength of Tippoo Sahib: [2] '. . . The sensible part of the Officers view him by no means as a despicable enemy, and at present express doubts of success, the taking of Bangalore was merely accidental. . . .'" *Letter not found.*]

ALS, sold at Carnegie Book Shop, 1962, Catalogue No. 261, Lot 515.
 1. Sarly was a member of the New York merchant firm of Sarly and Barnewell.
 2. Tippo Sahib was Sultan of Mysore. The British had invaded Mysore in 1790 in retaliation for Tippo's raids on neighboring territory. At first Tippo was successful in repelling the British, but he was finally defeated by Lord Cornwallis near Seringapatam in early 1792 and compelled to surrender half of his dominions.

## From Joseph Whipple

*Portsmouth, New Hampshire, December 17, 1791*. "I received by the last post your letter of the 2nd Instant [1] directing me to Mention to Cap Yeaton [2] his omitting to notice in the abstract of his journal for October the receiving of manifests from Vessels which I shall mention to him on his return into port. . . ."

ADf, RG 36, Collector of Customs at Portsmouth, Letters Sent, 1791–1792, Vol. 3, National Archives; copy, RG 56, Letters from the Collector at Portsmouth, National Archives.
 1. Letter not found.
 2. Hopley Yeaton.

## To ─────── [1]

Philadelphia, December 18, 1791]

My Dear Sir
    I am this moment going to a rendezvous which I suspect may involve a most serious plot against me,[2] but various reasons, and among others a desire to ascertain the truth induce me to hazard the

consequence. As any disastrous event might interest my fame; I drop you this line, that from my impressions may be inferred the truth of the matter.

Yrs. sincerely                                                    A Hamilton

Sunday December 17th [3] 1791

ALS, Hamilton Papers, Library of Congress.
    1. For background to this document, see James Reynolds to H, December 15, 1791, note 1.
    2. This "rendezvous" was with James Reynolds.
    3. Sunday was on December 18.

## From George Cabot [1]

Dec. 18. 91

It is well stated by a Gentleman who has examined the subject [2] that in 1784 the British Govt having taken measures for drawing over to their service the whalefishermen of the U S, the Govt of France at once saw the danger of suffering her great maritime Rival to acquire the advantage of 4 or 5000 excellent Seamen & with them an Act of immense value in marine consideration (as the Nursery of Sailors) which they possessed almost exclusively. France therefore did not hesitate to arrest these proceedings by giving *informal* but strong assurances that if the Whalefishermen wou'd, but for a moment, resist the temptations held out by the English, their friends in France wou'd soon procure for them advantages superior to those they were required to refuse. Accordingly liberal bounties in money accompanied with other allurements were offered to those Persons who wou'd remove from the U S to Dunkirk & from thence carry on the whale fishery.[3]

This measure at first did not have all the effects expected from

AL, Hamilton Papers, Library of Congress.
    1. For background to this letter, see Cabot to H, December 8, 1791, note 1.
    2. See Thomas Jefferson's "Observations on the Whale Fisheries," Boyd, *Papers of Thomas Jefferson*, XIV, 242–54, and Jefferson's report on the fisheries transmitted to the House of Representatives on February 4, 1791, which is printed in *ASP, Commerce and Navigation*, I, 8–19.
    3. This is a reference to the migration of the New England whalemen, particularly those from Nantucket, to the English and French fisheries. Discouraged by the serious depression in the whaling industry in the United

it, & rather than hazard the emigration of the Fishermen to the dominions of Britain it was thought expedient to create in France a market for the produce of the whalefishery of the U S. This has been of much benefit to us, but partly from the fluctuating policy of France toward us & partly from the excessive premiums she gives to her own Vessels, it is to be feared that her whalefishery will be eventually established on the ruins of ours. Already this business has extended itself considerably at Dunkirk, & the enormous profits which have been made by the aid of public bounties cannot fail to draw from the U S many more Adventurers.

France is undoubtedly an important market for Tobacco Rice Lumber Oil & *occasionally* for some other articles but the Ordinance of the Natl Assembly requiring that after Octr 91 Tobacco in Amn~ Ships shoud pay 6¼ livres per quintal duty more than in french Ships (equal to near double freight)[4] & determining also that after that period Amn~ built Vessels can not be sold to the Citizens of France,[5] must render our trade to that Country in our own bottoms comparatively small.

In the course of the late war France opened the ports of her Colonies to foreign Ships. These very soon engrossed a large share of their trade, & soon after the peace an Arrêt of the Council of State was passed restricting the intercourse between those Colonies

States after the American Revolution and attracted by British concessions, a number of the whalemen moved with their families first to the vicinity of Halifax, Nova Scotia, and later to Milford Haven in England. A number of others migrated to France. In 1785 William Rotch, of the leading Nantucket whaling firm of William Rotch and Sons, traveled to England to seek the support of the British Ministry for the transfer of a large part of the Nantucket whale fishery to England. Although the British government was interested in such a transfer, Lord Hawkesbury, in 1785 an influential member of the Board of Trade, delayed in meeting Rotch's demands. Rotch thereupon left for France to open negotiations with the French government for a transfer of the Nantucket whalemen to France. The concessions offered by the French government were so attractive that a substantial number of whalemen emigrated to France and set up a whale fishery at Dunkirk. For a description of Rotch's negotiations and the transfer of the Nantucket whalemen, see Alexander Starbuck, *History of the American Whale Fishery from Its Earliest Inception to the Year 1876* (Reprinted: New York, 1964), I, 77–90; Boyd, *Papers of Thomas Jefferson*, XIV, 217–25.

4. See "Report on the Subject of Manufactures," December 5, 1791, note 82.

5. The decree "qui prohibe l'importation des navires et autres bâtimens de construction étrangère" was introduced on March 4, 1791, and sanctioned on May 13, 1791 (Duvergier, *Lois*, II, 287; see also *Archives Parlementaires*, XXIII, 658–59).

& Strangers.[6] The precise intent or effect of this first public regulation after the peace is not within my present recollection & I have no authority to which I can recur, but soon after it (in 1784) another Arrêt was published which established in each of the Windward Islands one port & in Hispaniola three ports [7] to which *foreign* vessels might have free access with Fish Lumber Live Stock Rice Indian Corn salted beef (but not Pork) vegetables of a certain kind, hides Peltry Pitch Tar & Turpentine, but no other commodities. The duty on fish to be 3 livres per quintal & on salted beef 3 livres per barrel, & on all these commodities such local duties as might be imposed in the Islands, besides an established one per cent on the value.

In return & as payment for these commodities Molasses & Rum of the Islands, & *Goods previously imported from France* are the only articles allowed to be brought away.

Several years after the 2d Arrêt a 3d passed which raised the duty on salted beef to a dollar per barrel & on fish to a dollar per quintal, & at all times a sum, equal to the duty per quintal imposed on foreign

6. The "Ordonnance des Administrateurs, concernant la cessation de l'introduction des Bâtimens Etrangers, appartenans à des Puissances neutres, dans les Ports d'Amirauté de la Colonie" of May 24, 1783, annulled many of the trading privileges in the French West Indies given to the United States during the American Revolution. It reads in part as follows: "Les circonstances de la guerre avoient déterminé nos Prédéceseurs à permettre, par leur Ordonnance du 20 Juillet 1778, l'introduction dans les Ports de cette Colonie, des Bâtimens étrangers appartenans à des Puissances noutres, et ce, jusqu'à ce qu'il en fût autrement ordonné: aujourd'hui que la paix, dont nous avons le bonheur de jouir, doit ramener l'exécution des Loix prohibitives, nous devons nous empresser, pour le bien du Commerce de la Métropole, à fixer le terme où cette introduction devra cesser. Nous, en vertu des pouvoirs à nous donnés par Sa Majesté, avons ordonné et ordonnons que ladite Ordonnance de 20 Juillet 1778 cessera d'avoir son exécution, à compter du 1er Juillet prochain, passé lequel temps l'introduction des Bâtimens dans cette Colonie reprendra le cours qu'elle avoit avant ladite Ordonnance; n'entendons apporter à cet égard aucune innovation, jusqu'à ce qu'il en soit autrement ordonné par Sa Majesté" (Moreau de Saint-Méry, *Loix et Constitutions des Colonies Françoises de l'Amérique sous le Vent*, VI, 314-15).

7. Article 1 of the French colonial *arrêt* of August 30, 1784, reads as follows: "L'entrepôt ci-devant assigné au carénage de Sainte-Lucie, sera maintenu pour ladite île seulement, et il en sera établi trois nouveaux aux îles du vent; savoir, un à Saint-Pierre pour la Martinique, un à la Pointe-à-Pitre pour la Guadeloupe et dépendances, un à Scarboroug pour Tabago. Il en sera pareillement ouvert trois pour Saint-Domingue, savoir, un au cap Français, un au Port-au-Prince, un aux cayes Saint-Louis: celui qui existe au mole Saint-Nicolas dans la même colonie, sera demeurera supprimé." According to Article 5, "Indépendamment du droit d'un pour cent, porté en l'article ci-dessus, les boeufs salés, la morue et

fish, was given as a bounty on each quintal of fish of the french fisheries.[8]

Altho some important products of the U S are excluded by the Arrêts or standing laws, yet the pressing wants of the Colonists have occasionally induced a suspension of those laws in relation to particular articles, but so versatile has been the conduct of the french Govt in this part of their administration that the People of the U S have sometimes suffered exceedingly, tho' perhaps oftener profited, by these temporary indulgencies. Since the commencement of the Revolution in France & partly in consequence of scarcity there, the Colonists have been obliged to take from the U S large supplies of Flour & some other items not usually admitted.

The importance of the french west india market for the fish of the U S will appear from observing that nearly one half of the whole fish is consumed there. Shou'd this advantage be taken the fishery wou'd be almost if not quite ruined.

The Molasses received from the french Islands is an excellent payment for what they buy of us but it may be noted that this article has been raised to its value and consequence as an object of commerce chiefly if not altogether by the People of the U. S—it was not thought to be worth saving by the french Planters until the Anglo Americans became its Purchasers & created a demand for it. At the commencement of the Molasses trade with the french it was bought by the Tierce supposed to measure 60 gallons or by the Hogshead supposed to contain 100; the New England People at that time used to receive upwards of 90 galons for a tierce & 150 for a Hhd. So little was it valued by the Planters that they for a long time submitted to this imposition in the measure. It has been much complained of that at Cape Francois bonds are required before a Vessel is allowed to trade with such Sureties as cannot be had unless the Captain pays an extravagant commission on his whole cargo to some Merchant of the place whether he needs any other aid of such Merchant or not. What share of this abuse or whether any is chargeable to the Govt

---

le poissons salés, paieront 3 liv. par quintal; et sera le produit dudit droit de 3 liv., converti en primes d'encouragement pour l'introduction de la morue et du poisson salés, provenant de la pêche française" (Isambert, *Recueil Général des Anciennes Lois Françaises*, XXVII, 460).

8. For the increases in the duties on foreign fish imported into the French West Indies, see Cabot to H, December 8, 1791, note 2.

I am unable to say—or whether it extends to the other ports of Hispaniola I am uncertain but I think it does.

I am not able to discern any essential difference of *principle* between the French & English Colonial systems. Both aim at a monopoly of their trade but neither can effect it perfectly without ruining the Colony, each therefore relaxes occasionally in some points & constantly in others according to the necessity of the case. Both nations admit *nearly* the same commodities except that France takes fish & refuses Flour while England takes flour & refuses fish.

England being more solicitous as well as more able to *carry* the supplies of her colonies than she is to furnish them insists only on being the Carrier.

France being unable to *carry* the requisite supplies of her Colonies insists only on furnishing them so far as she can, & permits others to supply whatever of prime necessity she cannot supply herself.

The English reserve the exclusive right of carrying the commodities their Colonists need from the U S but they impose no duty on the importation of the Commodities themselves.

The french *allow Foreigners* to *carry* certain commodities which their Colonies need but they impose a duty on the most valuable of those commodities greater than the whole freight or price of carriage is worth.

The french Colonies are I believe more extensive than the English, but if the french had not from necessity taken some things which they legally prohibit, it may be doubted whether the exports of the U S to the British West Indies would not equal the exports to the French West Indies.

Some unavoidable business & some unavoidable dissapations have prevented me 'till this moment from obeying your commands. Upon a review of what I have written 'tis some consolation in seeing how unimportant the information is, that you have lost nothing by the delay.

## To Melancton Smith [1]

[*Philadelphia, December 18, 1791.* On December 23, 1791, Smith wrote to Hamilton: "I am favored with yours of the 18th Instant." *Letter not found.*]

1. Smith was a New York City merchant who had a contract in partnership with Hendrick Wykoff with the United States Government for supplying West Point. He had been H's principal opponent at the New York Ratifying Convention in 1788.

# George Washington to Alexander Hamilton and Thomas Jefferson

[Philadelphia, December 18, 1791]

The President requests that Mr ———— would give the Letter & statement herewith sent, from the Secretary of War [1] a perusal and return it to him in the course of the day with his opinion as to the propriety of the manner of making the communication to Congress: and whether it ought not, at any rate, to be introduced in some such way as this, (if it is to pass through him to Congress) "Pursuant to directions I submit" &c. Or (if it is to go immediately from the War-Department to that Body) "I lay before Congress by direction of the Prest. of the U.S. the following Statement." &c.

18th. Decr. 1791.

Copy, RG 59, State Department Correspondence, 1791–1796, National Archives.
1. Both documents are printed in *ASP, Indian Affairs*, I, 139–40. The letter is from Henry Knox to Washington and it was eventually dated December 26, 1791. The statement is entitled "A summary statement of facts, relatively to the measures taken, in behalf of the United States, to induce the hostile Indians, northwest of the Ohio, to peace, previously to the exercise of coercion against them; and also a statement of the arrangements for the campaign of 1791."

# From Jeremiah Olney

*Providence, December 19, 1791.* "I have received your Letter of the 8th. Instant. I shall charge in my present quarter's and future Accounts, all Monies paid by me into the Providence Bank, as accounted for by the duplicate Receipts forwarded agreeable to your directions. . . ."

ADfS, Rhode Island Historical Society, Providence.

## From James Reynolds [1]

Philadelphia 19th December 1791.

Sir.

When we where last togeather you then would wis to know my Determination what I would do and. you exspess a wish to do any thing that was in your power to Serve me, its true its in your power to do a great deal for me, but its out of your power to do any thing that will Restore me to my Happiness again for if you should give me all you possess would not do it. god knowes I love the woman and wish every blessing may attend her, you have bin the Cause of Winning her love. and I Dont think I Can be Reconsiled to live with Her. when I know I hant her love. now Sir I have Considered on the matter Serously. I have This preposial to make to you. give me the Sum Of thousand dollars and I will leve the town and take my daughter with me and go where my Friends Shant here from me and leve her to Yourself to do for as you thin[k] proper. I hope you wont think my Request is in a vew of making Me Satisfaction for the injury done me. for there is nothing that you Can do will Compensate for it. your answer I shall expect This evening or in the morning early, as I am Determened to wate no longer till. I know my lot

yours                                            James Reynolds

Mr. Alexr. Hamilton

"Reynolds Pamphlet," August 31, 1797.
   1. This letter is printed as document No. IV in the appendix of the "Reynolds Pamphlet," August 31, 1797.
   For background to this letter, see Reynolds to H, December 15, 17, 1791; H to Reynolds, December 15, 1791; Maria Reynolds to H, December 15, 1791.
   The events which preceded this letter and followed H's receipt of Reynolds's letter of December 17, 1791, were described by H as follows: "I called upon Reynolds, and assuming a decisive tone, told him, that I was tired of his indecision, and insisted upon his declaring to me explicitly what it was he aimed at—He again promised to explain by letter. On the 19th, I received the promised letter . . ." ("Reynolds Pamphlet," August 31, 1797).

## From William Ellery

*Newport [Rhode Island] December 20, 1791.* ". . . I transmitted to the bank of Providence by water last friday seven thousand Dol-

lars under the care of an Inspector. The money arrived safe but he
has not had an opportunity to return with the Cashiers Receipts. I
expect him this day, and will send on a receipt by the first post."

LC, Newport Historical Society, Newport, Rhode Island.

## To Joseph Whipple

[*Philadelphia, December 20, 1791.* On January 12, 1792, Whipple
wrote to Hamilton: "I had the honor to receive your letter of the
20th. of last Month." *Letter not found.*]

## From Oliver Wolcott, Junior

Treasury Department
Comptrollers Office.
20th: December 1791.

Sir,
On examining the Accounts of Vincent Redman, Collector of the
Customs, for the District of Yeocomico River, in the State of Virginia, for the Quarter ending 31st: March 1791, it appears, that he
has charged duties on the Sloop Maria, an American Coasting Vessel,
under Twenty Tons burthen at the rate of six cents per Ton, per
Annum, to the amount of Ninety Cents.

As the Collection of those duties seems to have been made contrary
to the intent of your Circular Letter to the Collectors, dated 30th:
November 1789; I have taken the liberty to submit the circumstance
to your consideration.

I am &ca:                                         O: W: Jr:

LC, RG 217, First Comptroller's Office, Revenue Letters Sent (Customs), National Archives.

## From Royal Flint [1]

*New York, December 21, 1791.* "This letter will be presented you
by Dr. Hopkins [2] of Connecticut. He is on his way to Philadelphia,
and while he is in that City, I feel a desire that you become acquainted

with him. The literary talents of this gentleman, and the liberal way of thinking, he adopts on all public questions of importance, will render him not only a valuable, but a pleasing acquantance. . . ."

ALS, Hamilton Papers, Library of Congress.
    1. Originally a resident of Connecticut, Flint became a prominent New York businessman. In the seventeen-eighties he had been closely associated in several business ventures with William Duer and Jeremiah Wadsworth.
    2. Lemuel Hopkins was a Hartford physician and poet who collaborated with other "Hartford Wits" in the writing of political satire.

## To Nicholas Low [1]

Philadelphia December
21. 1791

My Dear Sir
    I have learnt with no small pain the animosities which seem to be kindling between the adherents to the Bank of New York and the Stockholders of the Bank of the United States; [2] though you will recollect it corresponds with what I expected. The little unpleasant incidents which have attended you personally are not you may be sure indifferent to me; at the same time that I have the consolation of believing they are not very material either to your interests or feelings.
    But permit me to observe that foreseeing much more important consequences in a public view from a rivalship between State banks and branches, I grow more and more anxious on that subject. And let me add that the more I contemplate the present scheme of branches, the more I am led to regard the operation as ticklish and hazardous and the less do I find a solid basis on which to rest my confidence. Indeed if the plan be persisted in, in every case in which I have an option left me concerning the disposition of the public funds, I shall be sadly perplexed between my attachment to an institution which has originated with myself and my judgment of what is due to the public safety.
    You recollect that when you was here I mentioned an idea of establishing branches on principles which would require a supplementary Act. The more I have reflected on those principles the more I am satisfied of their solidity and I have no doubt of the act being easily obtained.

Its object would be to enable the Bank of the United States to open subscriptions wherever the Directors thought fit to establish a branch; limiting the whole amount of those subscriptions every where to a *certain definite sum*. The Directors to have a preferable right to subscribe for as many shares of the Stock of each Branch as they should think fit and the rest to be subscribed by any others bodies politic or individuals.

Each branch to form a distinct Corporation but to be so organised as to be under the controul of the Directors of the Bank of the United States. The Directors of each branch, at the discretion of the Directors of the Bank of the United States, to be either wholly appointed by them or partly chosen by the Stockholders of the Branch & partly appointed by the Directors of the Bank of the United States.

The Directors of the Bank of the U States to have power to invest so much of the Capital of each branch as they may think fit in *public stock*.

The advantages of this plan will be the following—

1   Greater security and solidity; as the whole would not be liable for every part, each part being a distinct Corporation whose mismanagement could only affect its own funds and not involve the Main Institution.

2   *Greater acommodation* to the Community by uniting in one Center all the Banking Capital employed and removing the apprehensions which will naturally arise out of a state of competition & rivalship & which will be apt to check the operations of each Bank.

3   The avoiding the political parties which will naturally grow up in the monied interest from rival banks under Fœderal & State authorities; as an opportunity of uniting will be afforded to the State banks.

4   Appreciation of the intrinsic & permanent value of Bank Stock by giving greater security to the operation and inspiring more absolute confidence at home & abroad.

5   Additional profits, from the greater energy which will result from a more combined and extensive Capital, free from the restraints of an unfriendly competition.

The opposite of this last Idea, I am aware will be apt on a superficial view to prevail; but I plege myself the event will prove it is not well founded. In the first place I am persuaded that the present specie

Capital of the Bank of the U States will be found inadequate to the demand for loans. In the second place if state banks exist they will divide the business with the branches & neither will dare to act with as much vigour as if there was no enemy in the neighbourhood. In the third place if the capital is found to exceed the use for it, the surplus can be invested in public stock and while a future profit on the Capital may be derived from a judicious investment of it the interest of the Stock produced by the part of the Capital so invested will serve to increase the profits on the whole operation.

I could add a thousand things to prove the eligibility of the plan but I have not time to enlarge. I would you would turn it maturely in your mind, and I am sure that if you think it a good one, no little irritation from what has happened will prevent your affording your hearty cooperation. Adieu My Dear Sir

Believe me always truly    Yrs                                    A Hamilton

ALS, The Andre deCoppet Collection, Princeton University Library.
1. Low was a New York City merchant and a shareholder and director of the Bank of New York.
2. An authority on this subject has written: "The Bank of New York . . . after finally obtaining a State charter (March 21, 1791), had proceeded in August to enlarge its capital stock almost three-fold to $900,000, reserving 300 shares or $150,000 for ownership by the Bank of the United States. When the offer was formally made in November 1791, the directors of the National Bank declined to accept on the ground that such a purchase was prohibited by the terms of its charter. Inter-corporate stock-ownership being thus outlawed, there remained the possibility of interlocking directorates; but the practice, although not entirely unknown, does not seem to have become common" (James O. Wettereau, "The Branches of the First Bank of the United States," *The Journal of Economic History*, II [December, 1942], Supplement, 75).
See also William Seton to H, November 21, 1791, and H to Seton, November 25, 1791.

## To Thomas Mifflin [1]

*Treasury Department, December 21, 1791.* Writes to Mifflin concerning Pennsylvania creditors.[2]

Copy, Division of Public Records, Pennsylvania Historical and Museum Commission, Harrisburg; copy, Hamilton Papers, Library of Congress.
1. Mifflin was governor of Pennsylvania.
2. With the exception of the last paragraph and the insertion of the name of the state, this letter is exactly the same as H's letter to John Eager Howard, December 5, 1791. The last paragraph of H's letter to Howard is omitted in his letter to Mifflin.

## From Jeremiah Olney

*Providence, December 22, 1791.* "I yesterday received your favor of the 23rd. of Novemr. Your approbation of my Conduct in the Case of the Brigt. Betsey, affords me the sincerest Satisfaction; and in future, should similar breaches of the Law occur within this District, I shall proceed in the way you have now suggested, as a less expensive and more speedy Mode of Determination; and, in discharging the duties of my Office in general, I shall continue my endeavors to merit your support. . . ."

ADfS, Rhode Island Historical Society, Providence.

## From James Reynolds [1]

[Philadelphia, December 22, 1791]

Received December 22 of Alexander Hamilton six hundred dollars on account of a sum of one thousand dollars due to me.

James Reynolds

"Reynolds Pamphlet," August 31, 1797.
   1. This receipt is printed as document No. V in the appendix of the "Reynolds Pamphlet," August 31, 1797.
   This was the first of two payments of blackmail by H to Reynolds. The second payment was made on January 3, 1792. For background to this affair, see Reynolds to H, December 15, 17, 19, 1791; H to Reynolds, December 15, 1791; Maria Reynolds to H, December 15, 1791.

## From William Allibone [1]

*[Philadelphia] December 23, 1791.* "I have the Honor to call your attention to a Short report on the state of the establishments under my care as follows: The Light House in good order and well Supplied with every thing Necessary for the ensuing Season—the Publick Piers in good repair. The usual exhanges of Beacons & Buoys and those which were relieved brot. up and deposited in their usual places in safety. Enclosed is also a Certificate [2] by John Turner & Joshua Humphrys [3] Ship wrights who was required by me in aid of my own

Judgment, to examine the old Beacon Boat of the Brandywine, from which it will appear, that she may without much risque be employed another season. . . ."

ALS, RG 26, Lighthouse Letters Received, Vol. "A," Pennsylvania and Southern States, National Archives.

1. Allibone was superintendent of lighthouses, beacons, buoys, public piers, and stakage for Philadelphia, Cape Henlopen, and the Delaware River.

2. DS, RG 26, Lighthouse Letters Received, Vol. "A," Pennsylvania and Southern States, National Archives.

3. Joshua Humphreys, Jr.


# From Thomas Jefferson

[Philadelphia, December 23, 1791]

Th. Jefferson presents his respectful compliments to the Secretary of the treasury and incloses him the copy of a letter and table which he has addressed to the President of the United States,[1] and which being on a subject whereon the Secretary of the Treasury and Th: J. have differed in opinion,[2] he thinks it his duty to communicate to him.

Dec. 23. 1791.


AL, Hamilton Papers, Library of Congress.

1. Jefferson's letter to Washington is dated December 23, 1791. In this letter Jefferson submitted to the President a tabular exhibit of the English and French restrictions on American commerce entitled "Footing of the commerce of the United States with France & England, & with the French and English American colonies" (letterpress copy, Thomas Jefferson Papers, Library of Congress). The letter and table are both printed in Ford, *Writings of Jefferson*, V, 411-13. Jefferson explained his reasons for sending the table in the following section of his letter to Washington:

"As the conditions of our commerce with the French and British dominions, are important, and a moment seems to be approaching, when it may be useful that both should be accurately understood, I have thrown a representation of them into the form of a table, shewing at one view, how the principal articles, interesting to our agriculture and navigation, stand in the European and American Dominions of these two powers" (letterpress copy, Thomas Jefferson Papers, Library of Congress).

2. The difference of opinion between H and Jefferson arose over the question of the proposed commercial treaty with France. See George Cabot to H, December 8, 1791, note 1.

## From William Short

*Duplicate to go by the way of the Texel.* 1st & 3d. sent by way of England

Amsterdam Dec 23d 91

Sir

I had the honor of writing to you from hence on the 15th. inst. & of informing you of the posture of the American business here at that time. I am now happy in being able to announce to you the conclusion of a loan here for the U.S. at 4. p. cent interest.[1] The re-imbursements are to begin at the end of ten years & to be made in equal parts during the five succeeding. It has been found absolutely necessary to abandon the clause for re-imbursement at the will of the U.S. the lenders having lately become much dissatisfied with it, since the fall of interest in the other loans. In future however it will be found practicable for the U.S. to reserve this right after a given number of years. The sum of the loan is three millions of florins. The Undertakers have insisted on eight months, instead of five as allowed in the last loan. Although it will probably be furnished before the term, yet it will certainly not be done as expeditiously as the last, the market being at present excessively charged with loans. The charges will be between 5–6 p. cent, that point however is not finally settled, the bankers insisting now with some earnestness on 6. p. cent, notwithstanding in their first letter they stated them at less.[2] I shall settle with them the terms at which this loan may be considered as at your disposal, so that you may regulate your draughts for such parts as you may chuse to call for. No reservation having been made by you I shall continue to have it applied towards the French payments until I hear from you, in proportion as it is recieved.

The departure of the English post by which this letter will be sent precludes me from saying anything further to you at present. In my next I will inform you of the steps which have preceded this loan, & which have convinced me that that at Antwerp has not had an un-favorable influence as the bankers here pretended.

I inclose you the second copy of the Antwerp contract mentioned in my last. Immediately after signing the bonds for the new loan which will be in five or six days unless delayed in the press, I shall return to Paris. I beg you to be persuaded of the sentiments with which I have the honor to be Sir, your most obedient servant

W Short

The Honble. Alexander Hamilton Secretary of the Treasury Philadelphia

ALS, letterpress copy, William Short Papers, Library of Congress.

1. Rafael Bayley describes the Holland loan of December, 1791, as follows: "The information respecting this loan is very scanty. It was negotiated in Holland under the authorizing acts of August 4 and 12, 1790, by Mr. Short. Finding that money could be obtained cheaper in Holland, he withdrew a portion of the Antwerp loan from market and opened a loan of 3,000,000 guilders ($1,200,000) in Amsterdam. He obtained the money at a lower rate of interest but a higher commission. It appears to have been negotiated to run for twelve years, at 4 per cent. interest, then to be redeemable in five equal annual payments of 600,000 guilders each. The charges for commission, brokerage, &c., were 5½ per cent. W. & J. Willinks, N. & J. van Staphorst, and Hubbard were the bankers employed in the transaction. The redemption commenced in 1803 and was completed in 1807" (Bayley, *The National Loans of the United States from July 4, 1776, to June 30, 1880* [Washington, 1882], 26).

A copy of the contract for this loan may be found in RG 59, Records Relating to Foreign Accounts, 1782–1797, Letters, Accounts, and Contracts, National Archives.

2. Willink, Van Staphorst, and Hubbard had written to Short on November 17, 1791: "We forbear doing it [opening a loan at 4½ percent] in the flattering hope that towards the End of this Month or Commencement of the next, the great plenty of Money, that will be poured upon this Market, from the States of English Stocks, may enable us . . . to reduce the Interest for the United-States to Four per Cent. To obtain this, the Charges must probably exceed a Triffle Five per Cent, but lower than that they assuredly cannot be . . ." (LS, Short Family Papers, Library of Congress).

## From Melancton Smith

Newyork 23rd Dec. 1791

Sir I am favored with yours of the 18th Instant.[1] In a letter I wrote to Genl. Knox of the 5th instant I mentioned that that I had seen no Advertisement for a contract for West point and wished to know whether that post was to be supplied under his Orders, as the recruits were or whether a new Contract was to be formed if the latter I offered to furnish the Garrison at ten cents pr Ration. As I had not received any answer to this proposal, and there was every reason to expect the River would every day be Obstructed with Ice, I forwarded some provisions to be ready to supply them after my Contract had expired. I hope this has arrived. The lowest I would undertake to supply West Point is nine and an half Cents pr ration.

I am Sir    Your Ob ser                                            Meln Smith

Copy, RG 217, Miscellaneous Treasury Accounts, 1790–1894, Account No. 2052, National Archives.

1. Letter not found.

## From William Ellery

### Collector's Office [Newport, Rhode Island] Decr 26th 1791

Sir,

This will be accompanied by a duplicate of my letter to you of the 14th. of Octr. last. In your last letter dated Decr. 12th.,[1] which I recd. on the 23d., you mention that "No letter of the 14th. of October has been received from you at this office a Duplicate will therefore be requisite." In your letter of the 17th. of Novr. last [2] you say "your letter *of the 14th. ulto.* remains to be answered" and answer that part of it, which respects the prolongation of the term of payment for duties on teas.

In my last I wrote that I had transmitted Seven Thousand Dollars, under the care of an Inspector to the Bank in Providence &c. Inclosed is the Cashier's receipt for that Sum.[3] I shall continue to transmit the monies which can be spared from the Office to the bank in Providence in the safest & cheapest manner I can devise; and shall exchange Specie for the Notes of that bank as well as of the banks of North America & New York. The necessity of an iron chest is indeed lessend,[4] but not removed by depositing cash in the Providence Bank. The Cash on hand at the expiration of each week, and monies received should be safely and conveniently lodged until they can be sent to Providence or shall be paid out or exchanged. Thinking that the publick money woud be safer in my dwelling house than in the Dwelling house in which my office is kept I have never suffered any part of it to remain a night in the Office, and great inconvenience has attended the moving it backwards & forwards. As Exchanges of Specie for Bank Notes will be multiplied, it will be necessary that

Specie should be kept in the Office for that purpose, and a wooden can be more easily opened or broken than an iron chest. It is not my wish to put the public to any unnecessary expence. My only wish in this repect is, that the monies of the public should be safely and conveniently placed.

Inclosed is a weekly return of monies received and paid, a Certife. of Regy. No. 67. granted at this port Decr. 13th. 1790 and delivered up on a transfer of property, and by a copy of endorsmt. of change of master on Certife. of Regy. No. 22. granted at this Port Apl. 23d. 1791.[5]

I am Sir yr. most obedt servt.                        Wm Ellery Collr.

A Hamiton Esqr. Secry Treasy

LC, Newport Historical Society, Newport, Rhode Island.
    1. Letter not found.
    2. Letter not found.
    3. See Ellery to H, December 20, 1791.
    4. See Ellery to H, September 6, 1791.
    5. Ellery endorsed the letter book copy of this letter "Answered Jany. 13th."
H's reply has not been found.

## From Jeremiah Olney

*Providence, December 26, 1791.* "I have received your Letter of the 14th. Instant: The contents shall be attended to; and the result of the first Instance that occurs, respecting unshelled Coffee, shall be communicated to you. . . ."

ADfS, Rhode Island Historical Society, Providence.

## Report on the Petition of Catharine Greene

[Philadelphia, December 26, 1791
Communicated on December 26, 1791][1]

[To the Speaker of the House of Representatives]
The Secretary of the Treasury, to whom was referred a petition of

Copy, RG 233, Reports of the Treasury Department, 1791–1792, Vol. II, National Archives.
    1. *Journal of the House,* I, 481. The communicating letter may be found in RG 233, Reports of the Treasury Department, 1791–1792, Vol. II, National Archives.

Catharine Greene, of the 4th of March 1790,[2] respectfully submits the following report thereupon.

The said petition [3] seeks to obtain an indemnification from the United States, against the effects of certain engagements which were entered into by the now deceased husband of the petitioner, the late

2. On March 5, 1790, "A petition of Catharine Green, relict of the late General [Nathanael] Greene, was presented to the House and read, praying that an inquiry may be had on the claims and petition of her late husband, as exhibited to the late Congress, on the twenty-second of August, one thousand seven hundred and eighty-five.

"*Ordered*, That the said petition be referred to Mr. [Elbridge] Gerry, Mr. [Elias] Boudinot, Mr. [Josiah] Parker, Mr. Peter Muhlenberg, and Mr. [William L.] Smith, (of South Carolina;) that they do examine the matter thereof, and report the same, with their opinion thereupon, to the House." (*Journal of the House*, I, 168.)

An entry in the *Journal of the House* for July 29, 1790, reads: "Mr. Gerry, from the committee to whom was referred the petition of Catharine Greene, made a report; which was read, and ordered to lie on the table" (*Journal of the House*, I, 285).

On July 30, 1790, "The House proceeded to consider the report of the committee to whom was referred the petition of Catharine Greene: Whereupon,

"*Ordered*, That the said petition be referred to the Secretary of the Treasury, with instruction to examine the same, and report his opinion thereupon to the House forthwith." (*Journal of the House*, I, 285.)

3. Catharine Greene's petition reads as follows: "To the Honorable the Senate, and the Honorable the House of Representatives, of the United States in Congress assembled. The Petition of Catharine Greene, relict of the late General Greene, Humbly sheweth:

"That the object, on which her petition is founded, is generally stated in the representation hereunto annexed, made by her late husband, to the United States in Congress assembled, on the 22d. day of August 1785.

"That it will appear by the said Representation, that it was the intention of her late husband, to have ascertained the loss on the transaction therein stated, previously to his making application to the United States for indemnification; and, in pursuit of this intention, he instituted suits for the recovery of the bonds and mortgages by him received of Messrs. Banks and Company, as collateral securities; but his designs in this and all other earthly respects were frustrated by his untimely death.

"That the Suits for the recovery of the said bonds and other collateral securities have been protracted by the death of the debtors, and various other circumstances entirely without the controul of your petitioner.

"That while the recovery of the said bonds and other collateral securities is placed at a future distant period, and their amount uncertain, not only the estates conferred on her late husband, by the munificent gratitude of the States of South Carolina and Georgia, but his paternal estate will be legally wrested from your petitioner and her children, in order to satisfy those obligations, which her late husband was constrained to enter into, for the public service, whereby your petitioner and her helpless children will be exposed to all the bitter effects of poverty.

"That your petitioner thus brings forward her situation and that of her children, with the firmest hope and expectation, that the United States will, after a full examination into the transaction stated in her late husband's representation, grant her effectual relief, by assuming the payment of the said

Major General Nathaniel Greene, while commanding officer in the southern department; and, for the circumstances, on which it is founded, refers to a representation of the 22d: of August 1785, which was made by the said General Greene, to the United States in Congress assembled;[4] a copy of which representation, marked A, is herewith transmitted.

The following are the principal facts, which appear in relation to this application.

1. The department of War, in the fall of the year 1782, authorised the said Major General Greene, to obtain supplies of clothing for the troops under his command.[5]

2. In consequence of this authority, in November or December of the same year, he entered into a contract, for the supply of clothing to the Army, with John Banks, a partner in the house of Hunter,[6] Banks and Company, who contracted on behalf of the Company; and, upon account of the contract, advanced him eleven hundred guineas in money, and drew Bills upon the Superintendant of Finance for the residue. This transaction was duly notified to the department of War, and received the approbation of that department.

3. The goods for completing this contract were purchased on credit, by the contractors, from certain British merchants then in Charleston.

4. About the same period, the Superintendant of Finance empowered General Greene to contract for the supply of all such provisions as might be wanted for the use of the army in the States of

---

obligations, entered into for the benefit of the United States, or, in such other manner, save her and her children's estate from impending ruin, as, in the judgment of Congress, shall appear meet and proper.

"And Your Petitioner, as in duty bound, shall continue to pray.

Catharine Greene.

New York, 4th March 1790." (Copy, RG 233, Reports of the Treasury Department, 1791–1792, Vol. II, National Archives.)

4. The original of this letter may be found in Letters from Major General Nathanael Greene, 1776–1785, Papers of the Continental Congress, National Archives. According to the endorsement, it was read in Congress on August 25, 1785. The *Journals* incorrectly give the date of the letter as August 25 (*JCC*, XXIX, 660).

5. Extracts of letters between Benjamin Lincoln, who was Secretary at War from 1781 to 1783, and Greene concerning the purchase of supplies for the Army are printed below as Sections B and C of this Report.

6. John Banks's partner in Hunter, Banks, and Company was James Hunter of Fredericksburg, Virginia.

North and South Carolina and Georgia, with permission, if more convenient to him, to commit the execution of the business to Edward Carrington, esquire, to whom it was accordingly committed.[7]

5. An engagement, which had been taken by the State of South Carolina, for the supply of the army, was to expire at the end of the year 1782. It became urgent to complete a contract for the supply after that period. Advertisements for receiving proposals were published; and particular applications were made by General Greene, to sundry characters of property and influence, who had been formerly men of business, to endeavor to engage them to enter into a competition for the contract. But these efforts did not produce the desired effect; owing, partly to the distressed and deranged situation of the country, and partly to the then state of public credit. No offer was made, except by the same John Banks, who was the contractor for supplying the troops with clothing, acting on behalf of the same copartnership of Hunter, Banks and Company. The terms, proposed by him, being thought too disadvantageous, were not accepted, in the first instance. The State of South Carolina having consented to extend it's measures for supplying the army, to the 20th of February following, advantage was taken of the extension, to endeavor to procure better terms. A conclusion was delayed, to give a farther opportunity for other offers, and negociations were carried on with Mr. Banks, to induce him to moderate his terms. He fell somewhat in his demands, but as they still continued to be thought too high, General Greene would not suffer a contract to be concluded, till every possible effort to obtain more favorable terms had failed. As a last expedient for this purpose, a letter was written by the said Ed-

7. On October 17, 1782, Robert Morris wrote to Greene as follows: "You will find enclosed an Advertisement for Contracts in which I have taken the Liberty to direct the Proposals for those of North and South Carolina and Georgia to be made to you. I did this because it was possible you might be on the Spot until that Period but if you find the Business at all inconvenient I will be glad that you in the Republications of the Advertisement point out some other Person, if Colo. Carrington is in that Quarter he will, I dare say, undertake it. I will in due Season send forward the Form of a Contract and the Modes of Issues and other proper Materials for the Information of yourself or of such other Person as you may direct to the Management of it" (LC, Robert Morris Papers, Library of Congress).

Greene's instructions to Carrington are printed below as Section D of this Report. Carrington, a native of Virginia, had served as lieutenant colonel in the Continental Army after 1776. In 1782 he was acting as deputy quartermaster general with Greene's army.

ward Carrington, to the Speaker of the House of Representatives of South Carolina,[8] stating the then situation of the business, and asking, through him, the opinion of the House, whether there was a probability of obtaining, from any part of the country, more advantageous terms, and whether it would be advisable, in the expectation of such an event, to keep open the contract, for any longer period. It appears to have been an object of this letter, through the medium of that body, to excite, if possible, some farther competition. But the end was not answered. The Speaker, in his reply, states, that no competition had been excited, in consequence of it, and that, though the terms, proposed by Banks, were thought too high, yet, as no other proposals had been made, and as the pressing necessities of the army called for immediate relief, it was deemed needless to keep open the contract any longer, under an idea, that more advantageous propositions might be made. Under these circumstances, on the 18th of the same month of February, a contract with Hunter, Banks and Company was concluded, and was, immediately after, notified to the Superintendant of Finance.

6. It is stated by General Greene, in his representation to Congress [9]—That the Company's funds were inadequate to the execution of what they had undertaken—That bills sold greatly under par, and few could be sold at any rate—That the funds, of which the Company were possessed, were tied up be prior engagements—That the creditors insisted in farther security, before they would consent to an application of those funds for the support of the army—That he was reduced to a choice of difficulties, either to turn the army loose upon the country, or take upon himself, the risk of supporting the contractors; that he chose the latter, as the least evil, and became bound, for them, to their creditors, for a sum of upwards of thirty thousand pounds sterling—That to render the hazard as small, as possible, he made the Company give an order on their agent in Philadelphia, Mr. Pettit,[10] for all the contract money, and sums due upon the clothing

8. Carrington's letter to Hugh Rutledge, speaker of the South Carolina House of Representatives, and Rutledge's reply are printed below as Section H of this Report.

9. See note 4.

10. Charles Pettit, a Philadelphia merchant, had served as deputy quartermaster general from 1779 to 1781. In 1782 he was agent for Hunter, Banks, and Company in Philadelphia.

department, to be paid into the hands of the persons, whose debts he had guaranteed, and that one of the Creditors was sent forward to receive them; but that these funds were diverted into other channels.

And it appears in proof, that public bills, as alledged, were of very difficult sale, being subject to a discount of fifteen per cent for prompt payment, (as much as twenty five being sometimes demanded) that the army, at the time when this engagement was entered into by General Greene, was in a very critical situation; that discontents, from various causes had produced several instances of actual mutiny; that if the contractors had failed, there was no ground to count on any other resource, as a substitute, and if a want of provisions had been added to other causes of dissatisfaction, there was reason to apprehend a disbanding or dissolution of the army—That General Greene, on or about the 8th of April 1783, did become surety for the contractors, to different persons, in very considerable sums; and it is to be inferred, as well from the fact itself, as from the evidence, that the doing of it was necessary, by quieting their creditors, to enable them to proceed in the supply of the army.

It further appears in proof, that Mr. Burnet,[11] one of the Company, had informed Mr. Pettit, their agent, that they had purchased a quantity of goods from British merchants in Charleston—That these goods had enabled them to undertake for the supply of the army in clothing and provisions, and that they had stipulated with those merchants, "that the monies arising from the contract should be appropriated to the payment of the debt contracted by that purchase;" that repeated instructions, by letter, in the name of the Company, sometimes in the handwriting of Banks, and sometimes of Burnet, uniformly held up to him, Mr. Pettit, the idea of paying the produce of the contract to the same merchants, in proportion to their respective claims, of which they sent a list, amounting to upwards of thirty two thousand pounds sterling, due to three Houses—That two payments, one for twenty two thousand eight hundred and seventy five dollars, and the other for four thousand two hundred and twenty two dollars, were made by him to the British merchants; that a Mr

11. Major Ichabod Burnet had served as Greene's aide-de-camp after 1778. In 1782, before the evacuation of Charleston, Burnet and another of Greene's officers, Major Robert Forsyth, commissary of purchases, had entered into secret partnership with Hunter, Banks, and Company, apparently without Greene's knowledge.

Warrington,[12] one of them, had come forward to Philadelphia, to receive the money, both on his own account, and as an agent for others; but that, in consequence of subsequent arrangements and instructions, the residue of the contract money was diverted to other purposes.

7. Precautions were taken by General Greene, when he became apprised of his danger, to obtain counter-security. This was actually effected, to a considerable extent; but it seems now reduced to a certainty, that a loss, of not less than eight thousand pounds sterling, will be sustained by his estate, in consequence of the transaction, unless indemnified by the government; and that the probable result will be the entire ruin of the estate.

8. No document appears, shewing that the notice of his having become surety for the Company was ever given by General Greene to Congress, or any of the public departments, prior to his representations of the 22nd of August 1785, claiming an indemnity, in case of such eventual loss. The omission of such notice is, indeed, to be inferred from the silence of that representation on the point. The evidence of the foregoing facts is to be found with the documents herewith transmitted, marked from A to Z inclusively.

Under this state of facts, it remains to be considered, whether it be incumbent upon the government of the United States, to grant the indemnification to the estate of Major General Greene, which is sought by the petition.

Objections to such an indemnification might arise from three sources.

1. Want of authority from the government to enter into the suretyship in question.

But this, it is conceived, would not be a valid objection. There certainly are numerous cases, in which a commanding officer of an army is justifiable in doing more, than he has a regular authority to do; from the exigency of particular conjunctures. And where it appears, that the unauthorized procedure was prudent and necessary, in itself, and was warranted by motives sufficiently important and emergent, it is just and proper in the government to ratify what has been done, and to indemnify the officer from injury on account of

12. James Warrington.

it. That an emergency of this kind did exist, to justify the measure, which was adopted by General Greene, appears to be satisfactorily established. The keeping of an army from disbanding may be presumed, upon strong grounds of evidence, to have materially depended upon it. And there does not seem to have been a deficiency of precaution in guarding, as far as was practicable, against eventual loss.

2. A personal or private interest in doing what was done foreign to the duties and relations of a commanding officer.

This, if it did exist, would be a decisive objection. The existence of it having been alledged,[13] it remains to examine, what probability there is of the allegation being well founded. It's source is traced to a letter of John Banks, containing a suggestion or conjecture, that General Greene was, or probably would be, concerned in the Copartnership of Hunter, Banks and Company.

But this circumstance loses all force from the following considerations.

1. From a letter which General Greene wrote to John Banks, dated

---

13. Concerning the charges against Greene of speculation in Army supplies during the American Revolution, one of Greene's biographers has written: "Robert Forsyth, Commissary of Purchases . . . had met Banks at Georgetown. Like Burnet, he agreed to become a partner in the firm and also took one-fourth interest in the clothing contract. When Greene gave the bills for $8,000 to Banks, the latter had Forsyth send them through the army mails with a letter to James Hunter, Banks's partner in Virginia. . . . General Charles Scott . . . thought it his duty to open and examine the contents. Banks's letter disclosed that Forsyth and Burnet were partners. But most astonishing was the statement: 'I find General Greene an exceedingly agreeable man; and from hints dropt already, expect his proposals for an interest in a house we may establish in Charleston.' Believing it his duty to disclose what he had learned, Scott sent the papers to Governor [Benjamin] Harrison of Virginia. . . . the story was spreading like wildfire that the American general was using public funds in a lucrative trade with Charleston. Soon the rumor was heightened by others. As Greene's officers were in desperate straits having had no pay for a long time, he decided to relieve their wants by drawing bills for $4,000 on Robert Morris. As Banks and Company was the only party which would cash the bills for merchandise, Greene considered it really generous of them. Although Banks upped the prices, the bills which he took had a very uncertain value. . . . Then the gossip arose that Greene had not only speculated with government funds but had profited on 'the necessities of his own officers. . . .' All this was damaging enough, but when it became known that Greene had signed notes for Banks guaranteeing payment to his creditors, it seemed undeniable proof to many that he was a partner of John Banks and Company" (Theodore Thayer, *Nathanael Greene, Strategist of the American Revolution* [New York, 1960], 415-17). Quoted by permission of Twayne Publishers, Inc.

the 25th of December 1782, in which the General makes his acknowledgments to Mr. Banks, for the services he had rendered to the army, in respect to clothing, and invites him to become a competitor for supplying it with provisions. The scope and language of this letter strongly indicate, that General Greene had then no interested connection with Mr. Banks, in relation to any of the matters, which are the subjects of it. As this conclusion results rather from the general tenor of the letter than from particular expressions, it's justness will best appear by an insertion of the entire letter. It is in these words.

Head Quarters, December 25th 1782.

Dear Sir,

The comfortable situation, in which you have put the Army, from the large supply of blankets and clothing furnished it, claims my particular acknowledgments; for, although I expect the public will make you a reasonable compensation, yet, as you were the only person, who had the will and the means to serve us, our obligation is equally great. I am happy to find also, that most, if not all our officers are likely to get supplies of clothing, through your agency. Colo. Carrington, who is appointed to make the contracts for the subsistence of the southern army, also informs me, your House have it [in] contemplation to engage in this business. Great, as our other obligations are, if you contract for the supplies of the army, this will be greater than all the rest. For the present mode, in which we are supplied, is truly distressing, both to the people and to the army. The manner of collecting by military parties renders it distressing to the citizens, and, from the uncertain collections, the army is often without any thing to eat. This is hard upon troops who have bled so freely for an oppressed people. I must beg you to hasten your proposals; and, I flatter myself, you will, from your attachment to the cause, as well as a regard for the army, serve the public, on the lowest terms.

I am, dear Sir,   Your most obedient humble Servant,

Nath. Greene.

Mr. John Banks.

2. From the pains taken by that officer to induce competition from other quarters; the delays which, with his participation and direction,

attended an acceptance of the proposals made by Hunter, Banks and Company, after the time for receiving proposals had expired, in order to afford a still farther opportunity, for other proposals, and to bring that company to more moderate terms—the reference, which, in the last resort, was had to the Assembly of South Carolina, as the only remaining expedient for exciting a competition, which had in vain been sought by other means; and, respecting which Colo. Carrington, in his affidavit (document R) expresses himself in these strong terms: "General Greene would not suffer a contract to be closed, without making every possible effort to excite a competition, and, as a last resort, a letter was written to the Assembly of South Carolina, &c." [14] —circumstances, which satisfactorily prove, that General Greene had, in the first instance, no common interest with Hunter, Banks and Company, in the contract for supplying the army with provisions.

3. From a letter of Major Forsythe, one of the partners, to General Greene, December 29th 1782, (document F) in which he thanks General Greene for a letter of approbation of his public conduct, and expresses a hope of that countenance and aid from the General, in private life, which he had enjoyed, while serving under his command; and then proceeds to mention the case of a Brig, belonging to the Company, which had been siezed at Savannah, and asks, as a favor, a letter from the General to the judge, before whom the cause of the vessel was expected to be tried, to remove a prejudice against Mr. Banks (as being a person inimical to the American cause) which, it was feared, might occasion her condemnation. The style of this letter is the reverse of that of one partner writing to another, on a subject of mutual interest. It is that of a person, who had received favors from a patron, asking a farther favor.

4. From the counter-securities, which General Greene took in consequence of his having become surety for the Company, to their creditors; one, being a bond from Banks, Patton and Hunter, three of the partners, bearing the date the 7th of May 1783 (document M) in which it is acknowledged, as is usual in such cases, that General Greene had no concern in the debts for which he had become bound; and the parties, accordingly engage to exonerate him from those debts, or any damages which might arise from becoming security for

14. Carrington's letter to Hugh Rutledge, speaker of the South Carolina House of Representatives, is printed below in Section H of this Report.

them; another, being an assignment from Robert Forsythe, another of the partners, to General Greene, bearing date the second of September 1784, (document N) of debts due to the partnership, as a counter security to him, in which it is stated, that General Greene, at the special instance and request of the Company, had become their security to certain persons, to whom they were indebted. The latter, however, being a considerable time after the transaction, is far less conclusive than the former.

5. From the affidavits of John Banks, and James Hunter, two of the partners, one dated the third of January 1783, (document O) the other, the twenty sixth of September 1785 (document P); the first, denying explicitly all connection of General Greene, in the affairs of the Company, the last, declaring that the deponent never considered General Greene as directly or indirectly interested in the purchase of the goods, upon which the debts, for which he had become bound, appear to have been founded; that this purchase was on the proper account of John Banks, Robert Forsyth, Ichabod Burnet, John Ferrie, Robert Patton and the deponent; and that he never heard nor understood from either of the other partners, that General Greene was any way concerned or interested in that purchase. There is also, a certificate from Robert Forsyth, of the third of March 1785, (document Q) declaring that the General was not interested, either in that purchase, or in the contract for the army.

6. From a suit in Chancery, which was brought by General Greene, and, after his death, prosecuted by his executors to a recovery, against John Ferrie, one of the partners of the House of Hunter, Banks and Company; which suit, it appears, might have been defeated by proof of interest in the partnership, on the part of General Greene; but not only, no such proof was made, but it is asserted, on oath, by Charles C. Pinckney (document Y) who was solicitor and counsel for Ferrie, and who professes to have obtained, in a professional capacity, considerable knowledge of their affairs, that Ferrie had assisted Banks in the purchase of the goods in question, had been instrumental in his obtaining credit—had kept the books of the Company, and appeared to have known all the concerns of the Company most intimately and minutely; that if General Greene had been concerned in the speculation, he (Ferrie) must have known it,

and that knowing it, he would have made it known—that he was under no obligation to conceal it, having been put at defiance by the suit, and could he have proved the fact, he would have been successful in his defence; but he neither produced one tittle of evidence, nor deduced a single circumstance to shew, that the General had, in any manner, been concerned in the purchase; the consequence of which was, that the Bill was sustained, the lands were decreed to be sold, and, after defraying the expenses of the suit, and discharging the money due on a mortgage, which had been given by a prior owner, the balance of the sale was directed to be paid over, into the hands of the Complainant, towards an indemnification of the General. This statement has peculiar force, especially, as the General, by commencing the suit, exposed himself to the hazard, if any connection of interest had subsisted, either of being defeated, by a discovery of that connection on oath upon a cross bill, or by perjury in the concealment and denial of it.

7. From a certificate (document X) of the two Chancellors of South Carolina which, after stating the insinuations that had been made of General Greene's connection with Hunter, Banks and Company, proceeds thus: "We think ourselves authorised to say, that we are as competent to his vindication, from any aspersion of that nature, as any two persons in the State of South Carolina; as we were both in the executive department, at the time of the evacuation of this Capitol, the one, Governor, and the other Lieutenant Governor, and a suit in Chancery has been since brought to issue before us, as Chancellors, in the prosecution of which, the several grounds, principles and obligations of the various connections or copartnerships, by whom the respective speculations, alluded to, were entered into, were very fully, ably, and minutely discussed, by some of the most eminent solicitors in the Court. And we have no hesitation, in the most inevasive, unreserved and unequivocal manner, to declare, that we never had, from our own observation, or from the strictest and most scrutinizing investigation, on the Chancery-bench, the most distant reason to conceive, that the honorable General Greene was ever, either directly or indirectly engaged in any of the aforesaid speculations, any further than as surety for Mr. Banks. We think ourselves warranted, also, in asserting, that the contract with Mr. Banks for

the supply of the army, was the most advantageous he could obtain, at a time when the want of provisions threatened a mutiny."

"John Mathews"
"Richd Hutson."

Charleston, October 30th. 1790.

8. From the concurrent opinions of other respectable characters, who had the best opportunities of judging of circumstances, that Genl. Greene was totally unconnected in interest with that Company. On this point, the documents S,T,U,V,W,Z, are interesting; that, marked V, states several particulars, as argumentative of the opinion expressed, which merit particular attention.

From the foregoing circumstances combined, there is conceived to be conclusive evidence, that General Greene was not interested, either in the purchase of the goods, which had created the debts afterwards guaranteed by him, nor in either of the contracts for clothing or provisions, was not a partner in the House of Hunter, Banks and Company, nor had any concern whatever in the affairs of that Company, further than as surety.

There is nothing to oppose these conclusions, but the suggestion in Banks's letter, and the fact of the suretyship. The former is obviated by the contradiction, on oath, of the party himself: and the circumstances of this contradiction, as represented by General Wayne [15] and Colonel Carrington, in their affidavits, (documents T and S) give it every possible appearance of genuineness. A question naturally arises —What could have been the inducement to the suggestion made by Banks? This is answered by Colonel Carrington, who represents him, as a man of "excessive vanity, much disposed to make a shew of connections with high characters." It is also possible, that he may have expected to derive advantage from the reputation of such a connection. The observation, moreover, is of great force, that if General Greene had been a secret partner, unknown to the partners in general, Banks's character precludes the supposition, that he would have been the selected depositary of the secret.

The fact of the suretyship is accounted for by the necessity of the measure, as it related to the situation of the army. And relying on the

15. Brigadier General Anthony Wayne had served under Greene during the southern campaign from 1781 to 1783.

appropriation of the funds, which should arise out of the contracts with the public, to the payment of the persons, to whom he had become bound, it was natural that he should have considered the risk as not very great.

This full statement of the circumstances, which are conceived to exculpate General Greene from the imputation of being concerned in the transaction, has appeared not only essential to placing the merits of the subject properly before the House, but a debt due to the memory of an Officer, who had rendered essential services to his country; and of a man who, by a life of probity, had secured to himself the strongest of all titles to a candid construction of his conduct.

It remains to advert to the third source of objection, which has been intimated, as capable of bringing into question the propriety of an indemnification, namely, the omission of notice to the government, at, or about the time of the transaction, that the suretyship in question had been entered into.

Here, in the judgment of the Secretary, lies the only difficulty, which attends the question of indemnification.

It appears to have been incumbent upon General Greene, if he meant to look to the government for indemnification, in case of eventual loss, to have given early notice of the step he had taken. In proportion, as that step was unauthorised or unusual, the necessity for the communication was encreased. It seems to be a matter of obvious propriety, that a public officer, who expects the sanction of the government to an unauthorised proceeding, especially an indemnification against pecuniary loss, on account of it, ought to embrace the first convenient opportunity to make known the object, for which such sanction and indemnification are desired. And the motives, on the part of the government, to require a due observance of that precaution, are of great force in regard to the security of the public. It is necessary, to enable the government to investigate the circumstances, at the time, when the truth can best be discovered, and unfounded pretensions best be detected. And where an indemnification against pecuniary loss is expected, a prompt disclosure is necessary, to put the government in a condition to take care of it's own interests, in the manner, which shall appear to itself most efficacious.

It is, indeed, to be observed, that General Greene was naturally led to imagine, that all hazard in the affair was obviated by the measures which had been taken to secure, as he supposed, an application of the monies to be received from the public, on account of the contract, to the payment of the debts, for which he had become surety; and, therefore, omitted a communication to the government, as not necessary to his safety.

But whether this, which appears to be a satisfactory explanation of the motive for the omission, which did take place, be, also, a sufficient ground for dispensing with the observance of a precaution, which, as a general rule, would be proper to be made a condition of indemnification; or how far, the peculiar merit of the officer, or the peculiar hardship and misfortune of the case, may render advisable a deviation from that rule, are points, which the Secretary begs leave to submit, without observation, to the contemplation of legislative discretion.

If a direct indemnification should be conceived inadmissible, as a public precedent, a question would still present itself, whether, under all the circumstances of the case, the family of General Greene ought to be left to the ruinous consequences of an act, which was dictated by a well advised zeal for the public service because he omitted a precaution, which the rules of public policy may require to have been observed.

The Secretary is not certain, whether an opinion on this point be within the province assigned him by the reference, which is the subject of this report, and he, therefore, forbears an explicit sentiment. He hopes, however, to be thought justified by the occasion, when he permits himself to observe, That strong and extraordinary motives of national gratitude for the very signal and very important services, rendered by General Greene to his country, must serve to give a keener sting to the regret, which ought ever to attend the necessity of a strict adherence to maxims of public policy, in opposition to claims, founded on useful acts of zeal for the public service, if no means of protecting from indigence and penury, the family of that most meritorious officer, shall, upon examination, be found inadmissible.

All which is humbly submitted,          Alexander Hamilton
                                          Secretary of the Treasury.

Documents referred to in the preceding report.

A.

Newport, 22d August, 1785.

Sir,

Misfortunes are more or less painful, as they have been brought upon us by folly, extravagance, or imposed by public necessity. Those of the latter kind may be distressing, but cannot be dishonorable. I have long struggled with difficulties, in which I was involved, while in command to the southward, and which I should have laid before Congress, at an earlier period, but from a hope, that I should extricate myself without their intervention. But, as life is uncertain, I should do great injustice to my family, not to lay the matter before them and claim their indemnity, should the precautions, which I have taken, prove insufficient for this purpose. I will gve them a history of the matter, and leave the rest to their justice and the event of things.

The sufferings of the southern army in the campaigns of eighty one and eighty two, for want of supplies of all kinds, are known to all America. The inability of Congress to give effectual support, at those periods, needs no explanation. In this situation, without funds or public credit, necessity compelled us to have recourse to many expedients, to prevent a dissolution of the army. In the spring of eighty two, the troops would have disbanded, but from a seasonable supply of clothing from Charleston, by the Governor and Council of South Carolina. Several hundred men had been as naked as they were born, except a clout about their middle, for more than four months, and the enemy in force within four hours march of us, all the time. Soon after this, I got instructions from the War-Office, to get supplies of clothing in the best manner I could, as there could be none sent from the northward. Mr. John Banks, one of the House of Hunter, Banks and Company, contracted to supply us. I advanced him a sum of money, and gave him bills on Mr. Morris for forty thousand dollars, to secure the clothing. The whole of which was reported to the Secretary of War at the time. Mr. Banks's prospects for securing the clothing was with a set of merchants in Charleston, then in treaty with the Governor and Council of South Carolina, for permission to remain with their goods, after the place should be evacuated; and if the place should not be evacuated, those merchants were to contrive a plan for sending out the clothing for the army. Mr. Banks, in writing of this transaction to his partners in Virginia, and enclosing a number of the public bills, his letters being opened and the circumstances not known, it gave birth to a report, that I held a commercial connection with him.[16] And this interpretation was more readily given to the affair, from Mr. Bank's hazarding a conjecture, that it was probable I might. On this being communicated to me by the Governor of Virginia, I took Mr. Banks before the Chief Justice of South Carolina, to make oath on the subject.[17] A copy of his affidavit, I enclose, and have the original in keeping. There are no transactions in life, which are more vexatious than those, where our zeal to serve the publc is made the subject of private accusation. It is no elss mortifying to our pride, than unfriendly to our character. I despise popular prejudices, and disdain vulgar suspicions. But lest the army might be tinctured with the rumors on the subject, and sap their confidence so essential to military operations, and the propsects of peace uncertain, I got General Wayne and Colonel Carrington to look over the original papers, that the army might be convinced it was a public, and not a private transaction. And such they found it. Their report has been made public.[18] Soon after the enemy left

16. See note 13.
17. This document is printed below as document No. 5 of Section C of this Report.
18. The statement by Wayne and Carrington, dated February 15, 1783, reads in part as follows: "It cannot be supposed that a character, stamped with so many marks of public integrity as General Greene's, will receive an injury in the minds of generous men, from the incautious expressions of a private letter, communicating to a friend the surmises of the writer; nor would it be thought necessary to regard the opinions of those of another cast, did the general stand in a private capacity alone; but as it is the duty of public characters to preserve the full confidence of all orders of people, so it is requisite that, whenever any circumstance shall happen, admitting of constructions and interpretations, which may tend to impair the general confidence, such explanations be immediately made as to remove every possible ground for suspicion. Upon these considerations, General Greene, having received from Governor Harrison, copies of letters wrote by Mr. John Banks to Mr. James Hunter, which had been opened by General Scott, wherein the writer had mentioned, that he had reason to think the general had some thoughts of proposing a connexion with him in a house to be set up in Charleston, after the evacuation of that place, immediately called on Mr. Banks, and laying the letters before him, in our

Charleston, the inhabitants, who had been much harrassed, from the mode of subsisting the troops, began to clamor against it. The discontent was so great, as to give opposition, in some cases, and to threaten it, in all. This rendered our collections difficult and precarious. Our soldiers were soon reduced to the utmost distress, and, at times, compelled, from hunger, to plunder the market in Charleston for support. I believe, these are facts, known to some of the members on your floor. The universal cry was, a contract for the subsistence of the army; but such was the critical situation of our Financier, the difficulty lay in finding persons of property to engage in the business. Applications were made to almost every man of property and influence in the State. No one could be found, and so scrupulous were the people, at one period, that no body would take bills on the Financier, except Mr. Banks and Company, and they were the only persons, that made any propositions for contracting, and their conditions were high, and their funds inadequate. The matter was referred to the General Assembly, and their advice and assistance solicited upon the occasion. The General Assembly, after making the necessary enquiry on the subject, discovered such a backwardness in the people to engage in a contract, that they recommended our closing with the offer made by Banks and Company, even under all the disadvantages,

---

presence, requested we would hear his explanation of the grounds on which he had taken up such an opinion; from which it fully appeared to have arisen in mere conjecture, from the general's having taken an opportunity to recommend Major Burnet, who had long been in his family, and had some views of quitting the service to go into business. . . . As to the advancement of moneys, and the bills on the superintendant of finance, the general, for our information, laid before us the whole papers relative to them; from which we find that the secretary at war, early in the fall, apprehending the evacuation of Charleston to be near at hand, requested him to take measures for procuring from thence clothing for the army, by drafts on the superintendant of finance; that those advancements of eleven hundred guineas, and eight thousand dollars in bills, were made to Mr. Banks for that purpose, at an early period, on account, for procuring the clothing on the most advantageous terms; that due notice of the bills was given to the secretary at war, with a full state of the steps taken for accomplishing that object—that he fully approved of them, and thanked the general, in the warmest terms, for his prudent attention to the business, informing him, at the same time, that the superintendant of finance was perfectly satisfied with the drafts, and was ready to take them up. We are happy in being able to add to this state of the affair, that, in consequence of these measures, the southern army is now better clothed than we have ever seen any American troops since the beginning of the war . . ." (Johnson, *Greene*, II, 381–82).

in which it presented itself.[19] The difficulties, which were foreseen, were soon felt. The Company's funds were inadequate, bills sold greatly under par, and but few could be sold at any rate. Those funds, which were in the hands of the Company, were tied up by prior engagements, and the creditors insisted on farther security, before they would consent to their application for the support of the army. The repeal of the impost law in South Carolina added another difficulty. My Address on this subject gave offence to the Assembly.[20] In this critical situation, I had but a choice of difficulties; to turn the

19. See the exchange of letters between Carrington and Rutledge printed below as Section H of this Report.

20. On February 3, 1781, Congress had recommended to the states "as indispensably necessary, that they vest a power in Congress, to levy for the use of the United States, a duty of five per cent. *ad valorem* . . . upon all goods, wares and merchandises of foreign growth and manufactures, which may be imported into any of the said states from any foreign port, island or plantation, after the first day of May, 1781; except arms, ammunition, cloathing and other articles imported on account of the United States, or any one of them; and except wool-cards and cotton-cards, and wire for making them; and also, except salt, during the war:

"Also, a like duty of five per cent. on all prizes and prize goods condemned in the court of admiralty of any of these states as lawful prize:

"That the monies arising from the said duties be appropriated to the discharge of the principal and interest of the debts already contracted, or which may be contracted, on the faith of the United States, for supporting the present war:

"That the said duties be continued until the said debts shall be fully and finally discharged." (*JCC*, XIX, 112–13.)

The states, however, were reluctant to accede, and by January, 1783, only ten had agreed, with Rhode Island and Georgia still withholding assent and Virginia repealing her earlier agreement to the impost (*JCC*, XXIV, 101–02). Greene had been depending upon the South Carolina impost to provide funds for his contracts for Army supplies. When it became apparent that South Carolina intended to repeal the impost, Greene wrote to the governor, Benjamin Guerard, with a request that his letter be read in the South Carolina legislature. This letter, dated March 8, 1783, reads as follows:

"Persuaded that public happiness is the great object of every Legislature, and that they would wish for full information upon every political question, I take the liberty to inform your Excellency upon two points, which may have some weight in determining the great question before the Assembly respecting an impost upon trade. I should not presume to offer my sentiments upon the present occasion, or take the liberty to lay matters of information before them, did I not conceive I stand connected with the consequences, and should be justly chargeable with every public misfortune, which may result from having concealed the temper of the Army, and the situation of the Financier—a knowledge of which may influence the decision. These reasons, I hope will apologize for this address, however unpleasing the subject.

"Before a measure is adopted that may disturb the tranquillity of Government, unhinge the present Constitution of things, and bring on convulsions, which we know not the end of, it may be well to weigh the reasons for, and against it.

"I confess I am one of those, who think our Independence can only prove a blessing under congressional influence. Every Government has the seeds of commotion in it, and there will never be wanting occasion to kindle them into life, while public prejudice and private resentments operate so powerfully on man and measures. The situation of the several States, the various interests prevailing in them, and a thousand other sources of discontent, either real or imaginary, may give birth to civil discord, unless there is some controuling power to Check it in its infancy. Several instances have already happened that have nearly produced an appeal to the sword, which have been happily accomodated by the intervention of Congress; But the weight and influence of this body in future, will depend upon the estimation and support they receive from the States. There are principles in human nature, which influence Society, at a particular point through all their turnings and windings, with as much certainty as the streams direct thier motions, from their sources to the Sea. Congress can have neither weight or influence without revenue, and where is the danger of granting it? There is no plan of policy free from possible evils. That which promises the greatest share of private security, and public tranquillity must be the most eligible. To decide fairly what may be expected from this body you should examine its component parts. Are not the members of Congress citizens of each State, annually elected? And has not every member a much greater, interest in the State to which he belongs, than he can have in that collective body. This being the case what temptation have they to betray the interest they represent, and more especially as they may be called to a severe account for their Conduct, in the State to which they severally belong, for any breach of trust, or neglect of duty? If this body was independant of the united States, and had a permanent Standing, there might be something to apprehend, both from extensive powers, and extensive revenue, but upon their present constitution there is as little reason to suppose they will betray their trust, as that the representatives of the people in each State will do it. If we have any thing to apprehend it is, that the members of Congress will sacrifice the general interest to their particular interest, in the State to which they belong. This has been the Case, and from the very nature and constitution of that body, more is to be dreaded from their exercising too little, than too much power.

"The Financier says the affairs of his Department are tottering on the brink of ruin; The Army to the Northward are in the highest State of discontent; and the same may be expected to the Southward. It must be confessed the soldiers have given noble proofs of virtue and patriotism, under almost every species of distress and suffering; But this has been in full persuasion that Justice would be done them in due time. The distresses of a suffering Country has been urged with Success, to silence their present Demands, but these arguments will have no weight in future. The present repose affords a prospect for permanent revenue. The eyes of the Army are turned upon the States in full expectation of it. It is well known that Congress have no revenue, and the measures of the States will determine the conduct of the Army. I need not tell your Excellency the moment they are convinced they have nothing to hope for from that quarter, they will disband; nor will they be satisfied with General promises. Nothing short of parmanent and certain revenue can or will keep them subject to authority. I think it my duty to be explicit, because I know the sentiments of the army. Men will suffer to a certain degree, beyond which it is dangerous to push them. My influence shall never be wanting to promote the tranquillity of Government, but this will have little weight when opposed to the Demands of an injured soldiery. My heart is warm with good wishes for this Country, and I cannot contemplate future dangers that threaten it, but with pain and anxiety. I am sure I shall never turn my back when troubles overtake her, but it is much easier to prevent evils than correct them. This Country is much better calculated for revenue, than for War. It may loose by every new

army loose upon the country, or take the risk upon me of supporting the contractors. I chose the latter, as the least evil. The sum, I first engaged for, was upwards of thirty thousand pounds sterling; but afterwards, when public bills got into better credit, I was obliged to give occasional support, by lodging bills to raise money upon; and this was attended with no small risk, but, happily, with no loss. And, that as little hazard might be run, as possible, in my engagements, I made the Company give an order for all the contract money, and sums due on the clothing department, to be paid into the hands of those persons, whose debts I had guaranteed. The order was given on Mr. Pettit, the Company's agent, in Philadelphia, and one of the Creditors, commissioned by the whole, sent forward to receive it; and had it been complied with, it would have discharged all my engagements. From this until my return to the northward, I was ignorant that those funds were diverted into other channels. My indignation at the vulgar suspicions of my holding a concern with Banks and Company, imposed a sort of silence on me, which kept me ignorant of Mr. Banks's villainy,[21] until my arrival at Philadelphia. Mr. Pettit

---

convulsion; but can never gain where liberty is not the object. Your wealth and weakness are a double temptation to invite an invasion, and are the strongest arguments for uniting in the closest terms your interest with others. View but for a moment the vast property you have exposed, and the little permanent force for its Defence. Again Consider how unhealthy your Climate, and the prejudices prevailing against it. Should you add new difficulties in matters of Finance, the War continue, and the Army disband, your ruin will be inevitable. There is a great difference between personal consequence and national strength; nor will the feelings of one always dictate a just policy for the other.

"I have only to add, if in the present plan there are insuperable difficulties, and such as should induce you to hazard every consequence, rather than adopt the plan under its present form, change the mode but let the revenue be applied to the same purposes. This may serve to rest the hopes of the Army upon, and lay a foundation for public credit abroad. It will carry the fullest conviction that your objections are not to the thing, but the mode, without which, it will be thought the mode is only the ostenssible objection, while the thing is the real one." (LS, William L. Clements Library of the University of Michigan.) The South Carolina legislature considered Greene's letter an unwarranted interference by the military and promptly repealed the impost.

21. One of Greene's biographers describes this affair as follows: "Banks . . . was speculating in various directions in anticipation of the change in prices that would result from a declaration of peace, and he soon became deeply involved. Distrust of the value of the bills on Morris also began to spread, and Banks's creditors refused to advance him anything further. . . . At this juncture the merchants proposed that if Greene would guarantee Banks's debts they would furnish the latter further credit, and would surrender the interest which Banks had assigned to them in the bills on Morris. For the purpose of keeping his men from starvation Greene agreed to this, and executed a bond of surety guaran-

then told me what had been done. Alarmed at the situation of the business, I got Doctor Burnet, whose son had been one of the Company, and was then deceased, to send another of his sons to Charleston, to have deposits made from the Company's funds, for the security of those debts, for which I stood engaged.[22] He went, and the greater part was settled, and I should have been discharged from the whole, but from new acts of villainy in Mr. Banks. Part of what now remains due is in dispute, and I have a bond of indemnity and some mortgages for the rest. But after every precaution I have taken, if I should suffer, I hope, Congress will indemnify. I have been much perplexed with the business, distressed, to the greatest degree, in my private affairs, and have already travelled some thousand miles upon it, and am still involved in a law-suit, and sundry other difficulties, concerning the payments which have been made. Thus have I given your Excellency a short narration of the origin and situation of this matter, and have only to add, on this subject, that I never held any commercial connection with this Company, other than what concerned the public, either directly or indirectly, or ever received one farthing profit or emolument, or the promise of any from them; and my bond of indemnity expressly declares, that I have no interest, connection or concern in the debts, for which I became bound: all which, I am willing to verify on oath.

Another instance of private loss has attended my command, which, in many instances, has been rendered more difficult and distressing, than can be readily conceived. Baron Glusbeck,[23] an officer created

teeing the debts of Banks. For his security Banks pledged all the bills he had received, both for the clothing and the feeding contracts; the merchants executed a release of their interest in them, and an agent was sent on to Philadelphia during the latter part of May with an order for them on Mr. Pettit . . . in whose hands they were reported to be. Before he could return, Greene started North, and, traveling leisurely, did not reach Philadelphia until the autumn. Then, to his dismay, he learned that Banks had previously disposed of the bills in Pettit's hands, and that his security was lost. Banks meantime had gone into bankruptcy, with liabilities of over thirty thousand pounds" (Francis Vinton Greene, *General Greene* [New York, 1897], 297-98).

22. Dr. William Burnet, a resident of Newark, New Jersey, had served in the Continental Congress from 1780 to 1781 and with the Continental Army as surgeon-general for the Eastern District. His son, Ichabod Burnet, Greene's aide, had died in Havana. For Ichabod Burnet's connection with Banks, see notes 11 and 13.

23. Baron Glaubeck served during the American Revolution as volunteer aide-de-camp to Brigadier General Daniel Morgan. He was brevetted a captain in the Continental Army on March 9, 1781, in consideration of his services at the Battle of Cowpens.

for special merit in the action at the Cowpens, was in Charleston, without money or means to get to the northward, and a foreigner and without credit. I had no money to advance him, and endorsed his bills, which were returned upon my hands with damages and interest, to the amount of near a thousand dollars, which I have been obliged to borrow the money to settle, and still owe it. My public station imposed this business upon me, and, although I would not have done it, if I had known the fellow to have been as great an impostor, as I have reason to believe him since, yet, at the same time, being commanding officer, I could not well refuse it.

I have the honor to be with great respect and esteem, Your Excellency's most Obedient   Humble Servant,     Nathaniel Greene.

His Excellency The President of Congress.[24]

## B.
### Extracts from the Secretary of War's letters to the late Major General Greene.

July 10th. 1782.

"The sufferings of your troops have impressed me with the deepest concern, and the very painful sensations, which your relation of them excites, are powerfully enhanced, that these distresses should have been the lot of an army, not only entitled, by special contract, to better fare, but whose meritorious and gallant exertions under the most extreme difficulties, merited a very different fate; mine is the unhappy station, in which I must hear complaints, without having it in my power to redress the grievances."

"September 30th 1782.

"The moment you have taken your determinations, what troops you will retain, I wish to be informed, whether they can, or cannot be supplied with clothing, with you; of this, I suppose, there will be

24. Richard Henry Lee was elected President of the Continental Congress on November 30, 1784.

no doubt, in case Charleston should be evacuated—indeed, we had almost better give any price, than think of sending it from here. We have met with so many losses and delays, that we have little hope of success, should it be again attempted; however, if the clothing cannot be had with you, it must go from hence."

November 5th 1782.

"If the whole (the army) are to remain, and Charleston is not left by the British, large supplies must be immediately forwarded—if it should be evacuated, I hope, we shall have it in our power to procure the necessary articles of clothing in that town. On these matters, I wish for the earliest information."

"December 1st 1782.

"I trust, you will be enabled to furnish an ample supply of clothing for the troops, from the Warehouses in Charleston, as I mentioned to you in a former letter."

"If clothing cannot be supplied there, I hope, we shall be in a capacity to afford you a considerable supply from Virginia, which, I think, might be speedily forwarded, in coasting craft, to Charleston."

"December 16th 1782.

"I am exceedingly obliged by your attention to the arrangement, and by the manner, in which you have conducted it—I am equally so, by your care in procuring clothing for the troops, which has happily relieved me from an anxiety, that has long oppressed me. Mr. Morris will honor your draughts—he appears to be well satisfied with the steps, which you have taken."

"April 2nd 1783.

"The idle surmise, you mention, has not reached us—nor do I suppose it ever will; but should any one presume to echo the malicious whisper, you may be assured, that the most pointed contradiction shall suppress it."

Extract of a letter from the Secretary at War to the
Commander in Chief.

"January 22d. 1783.

"Clothing has been purchased for the Southern Army, by General Greene, who advises the Superintendant of Finance, that he has drawn bills on him for the amount. This circumstance will enable us to order a quantity of clothing, which had been purchased in Virginia, to the main Army."

Extracts from the Records in the War Office.
January 20th 1791.                                H. Knox, Secry at War.

## C.

Extract of a letter from Major General Greene, to Major General Lincoln, Secretary at War, dated

"Head Quarters, November 11th 1782."

"I am taking measures to obtain clothing for the troops. We have on hand but a small part of our winter clothing, and after what we shall be obliged to issue to those troops going northwardly, we shall have but a small pittance left. I imagine, our purchases will amount to not less than forty thousand dollars, for which I shall draw bills on the Financier; and, as I provide the clothing, at your instance, and by your order, I hope, you will prepare the Financier for the draughts, that the bills may be punctually paid: I have already drawn in favor of a Messrs. Banks and Company, for eight thousand dollars, in bills of different values, to secure the clothing, and by this step, I am in hopes to save twenty per cent on the goods. I am to advance twelve hundred guineas, which I am in hopes to get from Mr. Hall,[25] the Continental Receiver. You will please to inform Mr. Morris, that I have applied, and propose to appropriate this sum to the payment of the clothing. If, in any thing, I have exceeded your intentions, you will please to inform me: My estimates are barely sufficient for covering the troops, and, as I am informed, the northern army is completely

25. George Abbott Hall had been appointed receiver of Continental taxes for South Carolina on January 18, 1782. Over Hall's protests Greene eventually obtained the twelve hundred guineas from him to meet the expenses for clothing.

clad, and, as you mention a desire, that this should, I have laid out, accordingly, as far as the articles, necessary for the purpose, could be had; many things cannot."

## No. 2.

Extract of a letter from Major General Greene to Major General Lincoln, Secretary at War, dated,

"Head Quarters, South Carolina,"
"December 19th 1782."

"You will see by some of my former letters, that, in consequence of your orders, I had taken measures, to provide such articles of clothing, as were necessary to complete the troops with their winter clothing. Messrs. Banks and Company have furnished most of the articles we shall want, and will provide the rest. Mr. Hamilton, the clothier,[26] had instructions to contract with such as would supply on the best terms, notwithstanding this agreement; but none offer their goods equally reasonable, and yet I think they are high: however, the demand among the planters is so great, that they would meet with a ready sale among them, and at an advanced price. Under these circumstances, contracts cannot be made on the best terms. The soldiers' clothing will amount to about fifty thousand dollars. I have advanced to the officers two months pay, by drawing bills on the Financier, which they will negociate for clothing or other things, as their necessities may urge.

"This will swell our drafts; but the peculiar situation of the officers, their long sufferings and distance from home, seem to render it absolutely necessary; some of the officers talk of sending their bills to Philadelphia, but I imagine, most of them will be negociated here with the merchants. I wish not to distress the Financier, but I am distressed myself, and know not, which way to turn, to feed, clothe, and satisfy the army on the article of pay. I would much rather, that clothing could have been sent from Philadelphia: but it was too late to expect any for this season: nor would I wish to negociate pay to the officers, in this way, but from absolute necessity. Troops will meet their sufferings with dignity and patience, when it appears unavoidable; but when their distresses continue longer, they grow

26. John Hamilton, deputy clothier general for the Southern Army.

impatient and clamorous. I have drawn only for such officers, as are continued in service, however urgent their necessity; many are discontented, but this I disregard, knowing the state of the Treasury."

## No. 3.
### Extract of a letter from Major General Greene to Major General Lincoln, Secretary at War, dated,

"Charleston, February 2nd. 1783"

"Lieutenant Colonel Carrington has closed a contract with Mr. Banks for the subsistence of the army, at something [less] than eleven pence sterling. It is high, but it could not be had lower. There was not an offer made but by Mr. Banks, although I wrote to all the principal men in the country. People have not that spirit for engaging in business, here, as with us.

"I shall get the troops pretty well clothed, and leave little room for complaint on this head; but, I fear, the expense will run high, most of the goods being in the hands of British Merchants, who were permitted by government to remain here, and those not willing to take bills, have confined the purchase to very few houses. Mr. Banks and Mr. Simmons,[27] I believe, are all, who have supplied—I gave the officers bills for two months pay; but they could negociate but few, except with Mr. Banks, who has offered us our greatest supplies; but, as every merchant will make an advantage of this opportunity, his goods have been higher, than if there had been many competitors for the business. I gave Mr. Hamilton, the clothier, a letter of general credit; but none would go largely into the business, except those mentioned, from a dislike to the bills."

## No. 4.
### Copy of a letter from Major General Greene; to Major General Lincoln, Secretary at War

dated "Head Quarters, South Carolina, "February 5th 1783."

"Dear Sir,

An idle surmise of Mr. Banks, and an improper curiosity of General Scott in the State of Virginia, may give an unjust complexion to the

27. James Simons, a Charleston, South Carolina, merchant.

late transaction respecting the measures taken to obtain clothing, as the Governor of Virginia writes, that it was considered a mere speculation for private emolument.[28] For fear, such rumors should spread to my disadvantage, I take the liberty to enclose you a copy of a Certificate from Mr. Banks; and my letter the 11th of November will give you a full knowledge of the transaction. I do not conceive this necessary for your information; but should any insinuations originate from the affair in Virginia, I wish to put it in your power to silence them, at once, and I flatter myself, I may hope for this piece of justice from your friendship. Reports are circulated here, that Mr. Morris and Mr. Banks are concerned together, otherwise he would not have taken my bills. These are done for malicious purposes; but, as I bid defiance to all the world, to tax me with improper connection, so I will not suffer even suspicions to circulate without control.

I am, dear Sir   Your most obedient   humble Servant

Nathaniel Greene.

Major General Lincoln.

## No. 5.
### John Banks's Certificate.

It having been suggested from an interpretation of my letter of October 1782, to Mr. James Hunter, that the honorable Major-General Greene was interested, or intimated a desire of holding a commercial connection with me in Charleston; I do, therefore, as well for the sake of removing such an idea, as to avert from myself any mischief, that a heedless surmise, expressed in a confidential letter to a partner, might inherit or deserve, hereby certify and declare upon the Holy Evangelists, that he never has or does hold any connection with me, either directly or indirectly, and that he never intimated, suggested, or expressed a wish or desire to this effect.

John Banks.

Sworn to before me this 3d. January 1783.
Hy. Pendleton.

I do certify, that the foregoing extracts of letters &c. from Major-General Greene, to Major-General Lincoln, Secretary at War, from

28. See note 13.

No. 1, to No. 5 inclusive, are true extracts and copies, taken from the files of the War Office of the United States.

John Stagg, jun. Ch. Clk.

War Department, December 23d. 1791.

## D.

Dear Sir,

Robert Morris, Esquire, Financier for the United States, has in his advertisements for receiving proposals for contracts for supplying the army with rations, directed them to be made to me, in the States of North and South Carolina and Georgia; but in his letter of the 17th of October, 1782, he desires me to commit the business to your care and management, should I find it more convenient for you to execute, than for me.[29] I am persuaded of your good disposition, and of your capacity to manage this important trust, and as I can give it every aid under your direction, as much as if under my own, and as you have more liesure to attend to it, than I have, I wish you to embark in the business. I have already written to all the principal characters in South Carolina, and to some in North Carolina, who are likely to enter into contracts, to make their proposals. As soon as I get their answers, I will lay them before you, and give you such farther information on the subject, as may enable you to close your contracts. I shall be always happy to communicate with you, on every matter necessary for the promotion and security of the public interest. Let me have your answer on the subject, as soon as possible, that I may inform the Financier, how the matter rests.

I am, dear Sir,    Your most obedient Servant,    Nathaniel Greene.

Lieut: Colo. Carrington.

## E.

Head Quarters, December 25th. 1782.

Dear Sir,

The comfortable condition, in which you have put the army, from the large supply of blankets and clothing furnished it, claims my

29. See note 7.

particular acknowledgments; for, although I expect the public will make you a reasonable compensation, yet, as you were the only person, who had the will and the means to serve us, our obligation is equally great. I am happy to find, that most, if not all our officers, are likely to get supplies of clothing through your agency. Colonel Carrington, who is appointed to make the contracts for the subsistence of the southern army, also informs me, your House have it in contemplation to engage in this business. Great as all our obligations are, if you contract for the supplies of the army, this will be greater than all the rest. For the present mode, in which we are supplied, is truly distressing, both to the people and the Army. The manner of collecting by military parties renders it distressing to the citizens, and, from the uncertain collections, the army is often without any thing to eat. This is hard upon troops, who have bled so freely for an oppressed people. I must beg you to hasten your proposals; and, I flatter myself, you will, from your attachment to the cause, as well as a regard for the army, serve the public, on the lowest terms.

I am, dear Sir,   Your most obedient   Humble Servant,

Nathaniel Greene

Mr. John Banks.


F.


Charleston, December 29th. 1782.

Dear Sir,

Some days ago, I was honored with your answer to my letter of resignation; the very warm approbation, given of my conduct in public service, gives me most singular pleasure and satisfaction, and makes me hope for that countenance and aid in private life, which I enjoyed, while I had the pleasure to serve under your command.

I must beg your attention to a brig of Mr. Banks's,[30] which he

---

30. For Forsyth's connection with Banks, see notes 11 and 13. After the evacuation of Charleston, Forsyth formed a company for speculation in supplies under the name of Robert Forsyth and Company. Banks, who was a partner in Forsyth's firm, was now operating under the name of John Banks and Company. Ichabod Burnet was apparently a partner in each firm.

loaded at George Town, cleared her out for Saint Thomas's, and she was taken into Savannah, and I find by letters from thence on the subject, that the proceedings of the people, interested in her condemnation, will go, a great way, to affect her, notwithstanding there are no papers, which can possibly make against her; but they have most industriously prejudiced the people against Mr. Banks, setting forth, that he is a person, very unfriendly to our cause. I find, Mr. Clay [31] is the judge of the Court, and he possibly may entertain the same opinion, which Mr. Banks wishes to remove, and if he could be favored with a line from you to Mr. Clay, to that effect, he has no doubt but the brig will escape. Her loss, (should it so turn out) will prove a very great inconvenience, especially, should we engage in the contract for the army. Money will be much wanted, and Mr. Banks purposes selling her, to reinforce us here with five thousand guineas.

I have the honor, to be, with great respect,   Your Humble Servant

Rob. Forsyth.

The Honble. Major General Greene.

## G.

Charleston, February 2d. 1783.

Sir,

Your letter of the 18th of September, by Mr. Hayward,[32] with the Bills enclosed, I forgot to acknowledge in my last. He promises me the money very soon; Mr. Drayton [33] also promises to pay me very shortly.

31. Joseph Clay of Savannah, who had served as lieutenant colonel and as paymaster general of the Continental Army for the Southern Department in 1777. From 1778 to 1780 he was a member of the Continental Congress and after his retirement from Congress returned to his business interests in Savannah. In 1785 he became a justice of Chatham County.

32. Thomas Heyward, a South Carolina lawyer and a signer of the Declaration of Independence, had served in the South Carolina legislature in 1772 and in the Continental Congress from 1776 to 1778. During the American Revolution he was appointed a captain in the Continental Army and was taken prisoner by the British at Charleston in 1780. After the Revolution he served as judge of the South Carolina Circuit Court until 1789 and was a member of the state constitutional convention in 1790.

33. William Drayton, a South Carolina lawyer, had served as chief justice of the province from 1763 to 1777. After the American Revolution he became judge of the Admiralty Court and in 1789 was appointed Federal judge of the District of South Carolina.

The clothier's, quarter master's and medical departments, together with the bills drawn for two months pay for the officers, give me no small uneasiness, for fear the amount should exceed your ability, and interfere with other engagements. I have contracted for every thing, upon as moderate a scale, as possible.

Even, since the enemy have been gone, we have been obliged to subsist ourselves with the point of the bayonet. All the State-agents quitted the business, the moment the enemy left Charleston. Our sufferings have been great, so much so, that the troops have taken meat out of the market, by force, in contempt of authority. This, you may well suppose, was no less alarming to the officers, than the citizens. Colo. Carrington has closed a contract with Mr. Banks, for the subsistence of the troops, at something less than eleven pence sterling per ration. This is the lowest, it could be had at. Not another man or set of men made an offer to enter into contract, but Mr. Banks. Colo. Carrington took great pains to reduce the contract as low as possible; but there being no competitors, and the army in a starving condition, Mr. Banks knew his advantages too well, not to avail himself of it; however, he rather wishes to be off, even on the terms agreed.

I have been to Georgia, to impress, upon the Legislature of that State, the necessity for their adopting the Impost-Act,[34] and for levying a tax, both of which will, I am in hopes, be agreed to. Their poverty and distress are great, but they must do something. I shall impress the same matters on this State. I have told both, that unless they took measures for the support of the army here, they would be ordered to the northward; and also, that the army could not be kept together, a moment longer, than the officers were satisfied, that the States would take no measures to support the servants of Congress, in their engagements; and this, you may be assured, is a serious truth.

I will transmit you a list of all the Bills drawn on you, and wish you to communicate your sentiments and propects, freely and fully, and, be assured, I will aid the business of your department, as much

34. See note 20. Georgia and Rhode Island had not yet agreed to the impost. On October 10, 1782, Congress had agreed to "call upon the states of Rhode Island and Georgia for an immediate definitive answer whether they will comply with the recommendation of Congress to vest them with power to levy a duty of five per cent. on all goods imported, and on prizes and prize goods" (JCC, XXIII, 643).

as in my power; but I am not a little alarmed at the political state of affairs in the southern world.

As I did not know of the opportunity, until the express was ready to go, I cannot write you so fully as I intended.

I am, with great respect,    Your most obedt. Hble Servant

Nathaniel Greene.

The Honble. Robert Morris Esqr.

I certify, that the foregoing is a true Copy, compared with the Original remaining on file in this Office.

Treasury Department. November 30th 1791.

### H.

Charleston, February 4th 1783.

Sir,

The pressing necessities of the army, the late season of the year, and the difficulty of conveying information through the country, in it's present situation, have prevented that extensive notice of contracts for the subsistence of the troops, which could be wished. General Greene, very early after the contracts were directed to be made,[35] wrote to every character, whose circumstances and views afforded him any prospects of being induced to undertake the business; but none offered any terms whatever, except Messieurs John Banks and Company, whose terms, I do myself the honor to enclose; payments being made, agreeably to the Financier's advertisement. These terms have remained open, for a considerable time, without a single competitor for the contracts. They are, in the opinion, both of the General and myself, much too high; but the distressed situation of the army, and the inadequacy of the measure pursued by impressment under the authority of the State, leaves us no relief, but in contracts, which must be closed on the above terms, if some competition cannot be excited. Wishing to embrace every means of giving information, and receiving terms on this subject, I do myself the honor to address myself to the General Assembly, through you. From the diffusive situations of the members of that honorable body, and the extensive knowledge, they naturally have of the resources,

35. See note 7.

interests and views of the people, it is probable, more advantageous terms may be advanced through that channel: it is with this view, that I have done myself the honor to address you on this business, and am well assured, your zeal in the interests of the army of the United States, and of this State in particular, will procure my Address, a generous and liberal reception.

You will confer on me a singular obligation, if you will be pleased to communicate to the House the contents of this letter, and give an early answer, whether more advantageous terms may be expected from any part of the country, and whether it will be prudent to keep open the contract any longer.

I have the honor to be,  with the most perfect respect,  Your most humble Servant                    Edwd. Carrington, D Q M G.

Sir,

I have laid your very polite letter to me, before the House of Representatives, agreeable to your desire, where it has received that attention, which the importance of it's subject demanded; however, no competition with Messrs. Banks and Company has been excited, in consequence thereof. Their terms are thought too high, but as no others have been offered, and the pressing necessities of the army call for immediate relief, it is thought, that it will be needless to keep open the contract, any longer, under the idea, that more advantageous propositions will be made.

I have the honor to be,  Sir,  with due esteem,  Your most obedt. Servant                                        Hugh Rutledge.

Friday morning.


## K.

Charleston, February 18th 1783.

Sir,

I do myself the honor to hand you herewith, a Contract entered into by Mr. John Banks, for the subsistence of the troops in the service of the United States, in the States of North Carolina, South Carolina and Georgia, for the present year. I am really concerned, that we have been obliged to close this contract, on the execessive high terms agreed to, but the circumstances, under which we had to treat, must justify the measure. For upwards of two months past, the army has been in a situation, little better than starving, rarely served with above rations, and frequently, five or six days without any meat at all, the measures of Government for supplies confessed to be ineffectual, and no longer to be depended on. In this situation, and under these prospects, the public could have no principles, on which, terms, mutually due, could be exacted, unless in a competition amongst persons willing to contract: this could not, by every notice and application, be excited, although the contract was kept open, near three months. The gentleman, who has undertaken it, is the only one who has made an offer at all. His first proposals amounted to thirteen pence farthing sterling per ration, the excess of which was so great, that we could not, at every hazard and inconvenience, accept them. After a long time, he fell, by several steps, to something less than eleven pence, equal to seventeen pence halfpenny Pennsylvania Currency per ration, and the difference, between that, and what would have been a due price, was not an object, so great as to lose a contract for, under the pressing distresses of the army, without another resort for relief. This, Mr. Banks knew too well, to be reduced lower, while he stood alone for the business. Still willing to take every opportunity for exciting a competition, the General Assembly having convened, I, on the 4th instant, addressed to them a letter, the copy whereof, with the answer thereto, is here also inclosed, from which you will see their opinion, as to the price of the ration, the probability of getting other proposals, and the necessity of closing on those we already had. In dividing the ration you will observe, that the greatest excess of the profits are thrown on the small articles, because they will, on issues to prisoners of war, be retained, and because, also, the contractors will find it more convenient to issue them, than pay money; or, if they should pay money, the same will be most valuable to the drawers: and further, should the army, by any means, become active, so as to go into the interior country, those articles will be entirely out of the reach of the officers and soldiers, at any price, and the contractors will find them at very high rates. The substitutions of rice and Indian meal for wheat flour is admitted, from the circumstance of flour being a foreign article, as to this quarter, and mostly depending on water-carriage by sea, and, I am persuaded, the substitutions will, in the arrangement of the issues, render the army equally well accommodated.

The condition of giving a month's previous notice of the removal of the army, in case that should happen, or else, for the public to take the stock on hand, not exceeding a month's rations, was insisted on by the contractor, because such a circumstance was more probable with this, than the northern army, and he wished, at least, to be secure against suffering by any unreasonable stocks that might be on hand.

Mr. Banks proposes, for his securities, Robert Forsyth, and Hunter, Banks and Company, the firm to which he belongs, which will, I think, be sufficient. He and Mr. Forsyth have signed the bond here, and one of the partners will sign it, as you send the bond through Virginia to Philadelphia. Mr. Forsyth, who is going to Virginia, will take charge of it, and enclose it for you to Mr. Morris, after he has got that signature.

I hope, the whole business will meet the approbation of Mr Morris, who will be very able to estimate the difficulties, under which it has been done, and will, from thence, conclude the impossiblity of procuring better terms. I must own, that I feel not a little mortified, that such excessive sums should be paid, but no alternative was left for subsisting the army. However, the exhausted state of this country in beeves, and it not being a flour-country, at all, occasion the supplies of both articles to be remote, and, of course, dearer than for the northern army, and this is also the case with most of the other articles, nor do I think the difference of flour more than made up, in the substitutions of Indian meal and rice, so that the rations must be, at any rate, higher than in New York and Jersey.

Mr. Banks has made some proposals for supplying hospital stores, which are high, and, as we are not so much distressed for them, as we were for rations, I shall not close with him, but on good terms. You shall hear from me, in a few days, with respect to them.

I have the honor to be, Sir,   Your most obedient,

Edw. Carrington. D.Q.M.G.

General Greene.

## L.

Know all men by these presents, That We, John Banks, for Hunter, Banks and Company, merchants, Richmond, Virginia, and Nathaniel Greene, are held and firmly bound unto Neucomen and Collett, merchants, Charleston, in the sum of seventeen thousand four hundred and eighty seven pounds, eleven shillings, sterling money of Great Britain, for the faithful payment of which, we bind ourselves, our heirs, executors and administrators, jointly and severally, firmly by these presents.

The nature and condition of the above obligation is such, That Whereas the said John Banks did purchase from the said Neucomen and Collett, in the month of September last past, their stock of merchandize, at seventy five pounds per Cent advance, sterling, upon the prime cost, amounting, in the whole, as per their Invoice, to the sum of eight thousand seven hundred and forty three pounds, fifteen shillings and six pence, sterling money. It is hereby understood and agreed, that if the said John Banks shall cause to be lodged at the house of Robert Patton, or Ball, Jennings and Wardrop, in the island of Saint Thomas, on or before the tenth day of November next, James river merchantable Tobacco, deliverable to the order of the said Neucomen and Collett, at six pence sterling money, each averdupoise pound, sufficient to cancel the said debt, (the said Neucomen and Collett have it, nevertheless, in their option, to take tobacco in Virginia at the market price, on notifying their application to James Hunter at Richmond, for such part of the tobacco, as may not actually be shipped at the time of such notification being received in Virginia.) Or should the said John Banks cause the said debt to be paid in specie or good bills of exchange, on or before the tenth day of November next, at the house of J. and M. Nesbitt and Company, Philadelphia, to the order of the said Neucomen and Collett, then, in either case, this obligation is void, and the said John Banks is hereby at liberty to pay in either of the above modes, as he may find convenient. In Testimony of the above, we have hereto affixed our hands and seals, at Charleston the eighth day of April, one thousand seven hundred and eighty three.

Signed, Sealed and ⎫  
delivered in presence of ⎰  
Edmd. Md: Hyrne [36]  
Thad. Koschiusko.[37]

John Banks,  
for self and Company.  
Nath. Greene.

36. Edmund Hyrne, a native of South Carolina, was a major in the Continental Army and served as aide-de-camp to Greene in 1781.

37. Thaddeus Kosciuszko, who had come from Poland during the American Revolution, served in the Continental Army as a colonel of engineers. In the campaign of 1781 he had been in charge of transportation for Greene's army.

Genl. Nath: Greene, to Neucomen & Collect . . . . Dr
1783. April 8th. To amount of your bond dated this
day . . . . . . . . . . . . 8.743.15. 6.
Cr. By Cash received from Hunter Banks & Co. ⎱
in Charleston . . . . . . . . . .⎰ 52. 6. 8.
                                                              8.691. 8.10.
1783. Octor. 23. To interest onto this day, is
6½ months at 7 pr. Cent . . . . . 329.10. 2.
                                                              £9 020.19
1783. Octor. 23. Cr. By Cash recd. this day from
Mr. Pettit . . . . . . . . . 1.400.18.
                                                              7 620. 1.
1784. Janry 1st. To Interest on do from 23d. ⎱
October to this day, is 69 days . . .⎰ 100.16. 8.
                                                              7.720.17. 8.
1784. Janry. 1. Cr. By Cash recd ∼ this day from
Mr. Pettit . . . . . . . . 252. 9
                                                              7.468. 8. 8.
1785. Janry 1st. To 12 months interest on ditto . 522.16
1786. Janry 1st. To 12 months do . . on ditto . 522.16
1786. May 1st. To 4 months do . . . on ditto . 174. 5. 4.
                                    Sterling, £8.688. 6.

Errors Excepted, Charleston, 1st May 1786.

Neucomen and Collett.

Savannah 12th June 1786. Received from General Nathaniel Greene, eight thousand six hundred eighty eight pounds six shillings, agreeable to the above Account, being the balance due upon the within bond, on the first of May last past, agreeable to an award signed by William Pierce and Donald Campbell, arbitrators chosen by Robert Forsyth and myself, in order to ascertain the amount then due.

John Collett.

£8688. 6.0 Sterling.

Witness, Nath. Pendleton.[38]

38. Nathaniel Pendleton, a native of Virginia, had served as Greene's aide-de-camp from November, 1780, to the close of the war.

## M.

Whereas the honorable General Greene did, in the month of April last past, become security for us, John Banks, James Hunter and Robert Forsyth, as for themselves as others concerned, in the sum of thirty two thousand one hundred and twenty five pounds, sterling money, unto Messrs Neucomen and Collett, Harris and Blackford, and James Warington, merchants, Charleston. We, the after-named, Do, by these presents, acknowledge, that the honorable General Greene was not, nor is not concerned or interested in said amount of monies, being purchase monies of goods, on account of the after-named parties; And we further do hereby agree and bind ourselves, our heirs and assigns, to release and exonerate the said General Greene, from the principal or damages, should any arise, of or from the being security for us to the above-named merchants, for the sums aforesaid. Sealed with our seals, and signed this seventh day of May 1783.
Witness, John Ferrie.

John Banks, for self and all parties concerned.
Robert Patton,
James Hunter.

## N.

To all to whom these presents shall come, be seen, or made known,—
Greeting.

Whereas Benjamin Johnston of the County of Culpeper, in the State of Virginia, in and by his bond or obligation, bearing date, the twenty eighth day of April, in the year of our Lord, one thousand seven hundred and eighty, became bound to Robert Forsyth, then of the Town of Fredericksburg, in the penal sum of ten thousand pounds Current money of the State of Virginia, conditioned, that the said Benjamin Johnston should convey to the said Robert Forsyth, certain lands in said bond mentioned; And Whereas Burgess Ball, of the County of King George, in the said State of Virginia, in and by his bond or obligation, bearing date the fourteenth day of June, one thousand seven hundred and eighty two, became bound to the said Robert Forsyth, in the penal sum of three hundred pounds, lawful money of said State; conditioned, that the said Burgess Ball should make good and sufficient deeds of conveyance to the said Robert Forsyth, his heirs and assigns, of certain lots of land in said bond mentioned, as by the said bonds, reference being thereunto had, may more fully appear. And Whereas, the honorable Major General Nathaniel Greene, at the special instance and request of Robert Forsyth and Company, did become surety for them, to Messrs. Harris and Blackford, and Neucomen and Collett, for the payment of very considerable debts, and which have not, as yet been satisfied. And Whereas the said Robert Forsyth is willing and desirous of saving harmless the said Nathaniel Greene, his heirs, executors and administrators, and his and their goods and chattels, lands and tenements, from all damages, which might otherwise arise to him or them, by reason of his said securityship. Now this Indenture Witnesseth, That the said Robert Forsyth, for the express purpose of indemnifying the said Nathaniel Greene, as aforesaid, and for no other purpose whatsoever, and in consideration of the sum of five shillings, Hath granted, assigned and set over, and by these presents Doth grant, assign and set over, unto the said Nathaniel Greene, the said recited Bonds or Obligations, and the monies thereupon due, or which may become due, for a breach of the said conditions, and all his right, title and interest, of, in and to the same; To Have, hold, receive, take and enjoy the said bonds, monies and all and singular the hereby assigned premises, unto, and to and for the only use and benefit of the said Nathaniel Greene, his executors, administrators and assigns from henceforth forever. But to, for and upon the special trust herein before mentioned, and none other. And the said Robert Forsyth, for the consideration aforesaid, Hath made, ordained, constituted and appointed, and by these presents, Doth make, ordain, constitute and appoint the said Nathaniel Greene, his executors and administrators, his true and lawful attorney and attornies, irrevocable, for him, and in his name, and in the name of his executors and administrators: But to, for, and upon the confidence and trust above-mentioned, to ask, require, demand and receive of the said Benjamin Johnston, and Burgess Ball, and either of them, their, and either of their heirs, executors and administrators, the monies thereupon due, or which may become due for a breach of the conditions of the aforementioned bonds. And also to accept and take from the said obligors, good and sufficient titles, in fee simple, in his the said Nathaniel Greene's name, for all and singular the premisses mentioned in the conditions of the said bonds. In witness whereof, the said Robert Forsyth hath hereunto set his hand and seal, this second day of September, in the year of our Lord, one thousand seven hundred, and eighty four.

Robert Forsyth.

Sealed and delivered⎱
In presence of    ⎰
Wm. Allen Deaz.

## O.

It having been suggested, from a misinterpretation of my letter of October 1782, to Mr. James Hunter, that the honorable Major General Greene was interested, or intimated a desire of holding a commercial connection with me in Charleston—I do, therefore, as well for the sake of removing such an idea, as to avert from myself any mischief, that a heedless surmise, expressed in a confidential letter to a partner, might inherit or deserve, hereby certify and declare upon the holy evangelists, that he never has, or does hold any connection with me, either directly or indirectly, and that he never intimated, suggested, or expressed a wish or desire to this effect.

John Banks.

Sworn to before me, this third day of January 1783.

N. Pendleton.

## P.

Norfolk Is.

James Hunter, of Portsmouth in Virginia, came personally before me, and made oath on the holy Evangelists, That he never considered the honorable Major General Greene, either directly or indirectly concerned or interested in a purchase of goods, made by John Banks in Charleston, on the proper account and benefit of the following persons only, viz: John Banks, Robert Forsyth, Ichabod Burnet, John Ferrie, Robert Patton, and said James Hunter; who further deposeth and saith, that he never heard, or ever understood, from either the

abovementioned persons, either by letter or words, that General
Greene was, any means concerned or interested in said purchase.

James Taylor.

## Q.

Savannah, 3d March 1785.

It having been insinuated by some, and propagated by others, that
the honorable General Greene was concerned in the Charleston speculation, with John Banks and Company, and with the contract for
the army, I do hereby certify, that the General was in no ways interested in either, with the said Copartnership.

Robert Forsyth.

## R.

Towards the latter end of the year 1782, when the engagement of
the State of South Carolina, to supply the southern army with provisions, was to expire, the honorable Robert Morris, Superintendant
of Finance, wrote to General Greene, to have a contract formed for
supporting the army, from the first of January 1783.[39] General
Greene requested my assistance in the business, and public notice, as
far as the circumstances of the country would admit, was immediately given, offering such a contract. General Greene, moreover,
wrote to sundry characters of property and influence in the country,
who had formerly been men of business, requesting them to come
forward, on their own accounts, or lend their aid in bringing others
into a Contract: the uniform reply was, that the war had so effectually deranged their capitals, that they could not venture upon so
extensive an undertaking. Indeed, such was the exhausted state of the
country, as to provisions of every kind, that none could calculate
upon complying with such an engagement, without large importations from the more northern States, which must have been made
through great hazards by sea, or with immense expense by land; and
could have been attempted by none, but men of capitals, in a current
of commercial business. Until the evacuation of Charleston, no person

39. See note 7.

whatever could be induced to listen to propositions for a Contract, nor could any one be led to overtures of the kind, afterwards, but Mr. John Banks, who established a House in Charleston, under the firm of Hunter, Banks and Company. Mr. Banks, at length, came forward, with propositions excessively high: these were rejected, and advantage was taken of the consent of the State, to extend it's measures for supporting the army, somewhat into the year 1783, in order that better terms might be obtained for the United States. Negociations were still carried on with Mr. Banks, with whom no competitor could be found, until the approach of the 20th of February, the period, beyond which the supplies of the State were not to extend; and, indeed, under such difficulties, were these supplies obtained from a country already exhausted, that the army was seldom served with more than half rations, and frequently, for five or six days, had no meat at all, unless by plunder, which had become exceedingly distressing to the neigboring inhabitants. In this time, Mr. Banks had somewhat abated in his demands; but it being thought, that they were still too high, General Greene would not suffer a contract to be closed, without making every possible effort to excite a competition, and, as a last resort, a letter was written to the Assembly of South Carolina, then in Session, stating the difficulties of obtaining a satisfactory contract, and requesting the advice of Government, as the members, then assembled, were from various parts of the country, and acquainted with the resources and views of such individuals, as might probably be disposed to such an undertaking, whether any competition might still be expected, or whether it would be prudent to keep open the contract longer. The reply was, that the terms of Mr. Banks were thought too high; but as no others had been offered, and the pressing necessities of the army called for immediate relief, it was thought, it would be needless to keep open the contract any longer, under the idea that more advantageous propositions would be made.[40] Upon this, a contract was closed with Mr. Banks, on account of Hunter, Banks and Company, to commence on the 20th of February 1783. I am satisfied, nay, absolutely certain, that, had Mr. Banks failed in this contract, at the time General Greene became his security in the several instances, in consequence whereof the estate of that officer

40. For the exchange of letters between Carrington and Hugh Rutledge, speaker of the South Carolina House of Representatives, see Section H of this Report.

hath since suffered; nothing less than the dissolution of the army must have followed, as no other possible means of supporting it could have been adopted: no other contract could have been obtained—nor was it in the power of the State, in any event, to renew her supplies. The army was, by this time, repeatedly upon the point of mutinying, from discontents, at being in an unhealthy climate, in an inactive state, and conceiving that there was a certainty of peace being established. A considerable body of the Cavalry actually went away from a station in the country, distant from Headquarters, in defiance of their officers, and several Corps of Virginia and Maryland troops made efforts of the same kind, but were stopped by the personal address of the General. Had a want of provisions been added to this other cause of discontent, I am well assured, that an entire dissolution of the army could, by no means, have been prevented.

From the first of General Greene's command of the southern army, there were scarcely any pecuniary aids for it's support, in any respect, until far advanced in the year 1782; and even, from thence to the disbanding of the army, the general diffidence, as to public credit, was such, that the supplies of the Superintendant of Finance could not be drawn, to our use, without excessive discounts, or negociations, which exposed the public agents to great hazards. Of this, I can give the most decided evidence, being in that predicament, as Deputy Quartermaster General. For the purposes of that department, I never could negociate a bill for direct payment, under a discount of 15 per cent, and, frequently, as high as twenty five was demanded. To avoid this loss, my practice was, to negociate bills at par, upon credit for thirty or sixty days, according to the sight of the bills, within which, the purchaser was to ascertain the fate of them. In these transactions, I risked the sufficiency of the purchasers, and, in case of failure in any instance, my dependance for indemnification was solely on the will of the government.

All the foregoing, I certify on Oath.                 Edwd. Carrington.

Henrico Is:

Edward Carrington personally appeared before me, a magistrate for this County, and made oath to the above, according to the best of his knowledge and belief.                                        John Harvie.

March 2nd. 1790.

## S.

Sometime in the early part of the year 1783, during General Greene's residence in Charleston, I received a message from him, requesting my attendance at his quarters. Upon my coming there, I met with General Wayne. General Greene told us, he had desired our attendance, in order that we might be present at an interview, he was about to have with Mr. John Banks, whom he had sent for—that he had just received a communication from Governor Harrison of Virginia, covering a letter (or a copy of it) which had been opened there, from Mr. Banks to his partners, enclosing some bills on the Superintendant of Finance, drawn by him, in favor of Mr. Banks, and containing some expressions, intimating a connection of the General with that Company in trade. After some short time, Mr. Banks came in, when the General put into his hands, the paper above alluded to, and asked him, if he had written to his partners in Virginia, what it contained? Mr. Banks, with confusion and agitation, after some pause, answered in the affirmative. The General then asked him, upon what foundation, he had undertaken to do it? Mr. Banks answered, none but a conjecture of his own, adding, as well as I recollect, that the conjecture arose from his conceiving that the war was drawing to a close, and as he, the General, had formerly been a man of business, he might be inclined to engage in the concern. The General told Mr. Banks that it was impertinent conduct, and that, for the public satisfaction, he must take effectual steps to shew, that the suggestion was a falsehood. To which, Mr. Banks replied, that he would make oath to that effect, which was accordingly done. During this interview General Greene desired Mr. Banks, to declare before General Wayne and myself, for what purpose, the bills mentioned had been paid him—his reply was, on account of the clothing, which he had procured from Charleston, for the army.

After this business was over, General Greene requested, General Wayne and myself would investigate the transaction, he had with Mr. Banks, in procuring the clothing for the army, and, for this purpose, laid before us the papers, which were connected with it; we gave them a very thorough investigation, and were fully satisfied, as appeared by a publication,[41] made upon the occasion, not only, that the transaction was a disinterested one, on the part of General Greene, but, that it was made, on as good terms for the public, as the circumstances, under which he acted, could have admitted. The effects of it were well felt by the army, too, which, from having been accustomed to nakedness, were, that winter, as well, and perhaps, better clothed, than I ever before saw American troops.

It would be presumptuous in any one, to make oath that General Greene was not concerned in trade with the House of Hunter, Banks, and Company, or with any other person, during his command of the Southern Army; but I can decidedly swear, that I am well assured, he was not, directly or indirectly. I will add, that John Banks, with whom I was well acquainted, was a man of excessive vanity, and was much disposed to make a shew of connections with high characters. All the foregoing, to the best recollection and belief, I certify on oath.                                              Edwd. Carrington.

Henrico Is:

Edward Carrington personally appeared before me, John Harvie, a Magistrate for the County aforesaid, and made oath, that the facts and circumstances, stated in this affidavit, are true, according to the best of his knowledge and belief. Given under my hand this second day of March, 1790.                                      John Harvie.

## T.

Georgia, 31st May, 1790.

Being called upon by the widow and the executors of the late Major General Nathaniel Greene, to relate such circumstances with regard to the situation of the army, and of the transactions between a certain Mr. John Banks and the General, as came within my knowledge, as second in command in the Southern District;

I think it unnecessary to go into a minute detail of every circumstance respecting those transactions, but I well recollect, that, some time after the evacuation of Charleston, which was on the [42] day of December 1782, orders were received by the General, either

41. See note 18.
42. Space left blank in MS. Charleston was evacuated on December 14, 1782.

from Congress, or the then Financier, to contract with some person or persons, for the necessary supplies for the southern army: and that it was, with the utmost difficulty, that any person could be found to undertake the business, on the terms in the power of the General to offer: and not until the troops had experienced, almost, every possible distress, for want of provision and clothing, a short time after making the contract, from some accidents, such as capturing of one or two vessels by the enemy, that were on their way from North Carolina, with flour and other provisions—the distresses became extreme, and a general mutiny and dereliction from the service began to present—nor could this evil possibly be prevented, but by an instantaneous relief, as the army was, for a long time, at short allowance, and had then been, for forty eight hours, without any kind of sustenance whatever—Under those pressing circumstances, the contractor, (Banks) not being in funds, and without credit, General Greene became his security, to a very considerable amount, for the purpose of procuring such articles of clothing, provision and other necessaries, as were wanted for the use of the army; by which means, a calamity was avoided, that appeared to us dreadful, and order, discipline and content restored among the respective corps. Sometime after this disagreeable business was accommodated, I believe, early in the spring of 1783, as I was about to proceed to reassume the command in Georgia, and to hold a treaty with the Indians, General Greene sent for me, and put into my hands a letter from the said Banks, addressed to his Copartners in Virginia, in which, he mentions "that General Greene was to be concerned with them in trade, and not to be uneasy, but, by all means, to keep that circumstance a secret." This letter had been intercepted, and sent to the General, the preceding evening—he appeared to be much agitated, whilst I was perusing it—upon returning it to him, I well recollect, that he asked me, what I thought of that infamous scoundrel; adding, "shall I put him to instantaneous death?—my feelings prompt me to it." He also solemnly declared, that he never had the most distant idea of being concerned with Banks in any kind of trade, either directly or indirectly: at this moment Colonel Carrington came to Head Quarters; he either had been previously, or was then made acquainted with the contents of that letter—the General requested our opinion upon the subject: we proposed to send for, and interrogate Banks upon oath; this advice was adopted, and his deposition [43] was taken before a Mr. Troop, a Notary-public, of Charleston, in which he most solemnly swears, that General Greene never was, at any time, either directly or indirectly, concerned with him in trade, or merchandize of any kind, or nature whatever, and that he was induced to write that letter, from some doubts entertained by his Copartners in Virginia, of his entering too deeply into speculation—in expectation, that they would be easy, under the idea of the support of General

43. Banks's deposition reads as follows:

"Whatever opinions prevail with the public, either from misconstruction or misrepresentation, operating to the prejudice of an individual, have ever been thought a sufficient apology for giving a state of facts, as an appeal to the people. I should feel less solicitude if I stood alone in this matter; but as my letter, lately opened by General [Charles] Scott in Virginia, has given grounds of suspicion to the prejudice of others, I feel an obligation to give a full history of the transactions mentioned in that letter.

"Some few weeks before the evacuation of Charleston took place, (but then hourly expected,) I was at Georgetown on business, when I was informed the governor and council of South Carolina, from the deplorable situation that the inhabitants and their negroes were in for want of clothing, and the impossibility of getting any before winter came on, but in this way, had granted permission to a number of the British merchants, with their property, to remain six months in Charleston after the evacuation. Persuaded that goods would immediately rise after this event, from the increasing demand, and that any contracts made before, to take place after the evacuation, was not counteracting either the views or wishes of the state, I determined to become a purchaser: for this purpose I obtained a flag from Colonel [Richard] Lushington, who commanded the militia at the post of Georgetown; and with this flag I went into Charleston and made some purchases, to take effect after the enemy were gone. While there, I was taken very sick, and detained much longer than I expected. After I recovered, in some measure, from my indisposition, I obtained a flag from General [Alexander] Leslie, through the interest of the British merchants, to visit some of my friends in our army, which lay between sixteen and eighteen miles from town, and to return into the garrison again, a privilege at that time granted to no others, and is the same expressed in my letter opened by General Scott.

"On my arrival at camp I was introduced to General Greene, who asked me many questions respecting the garrison, and, among other things, the practicability of purchasing clothing for the army. I told him, that it was not only practicable, but that if the goods were engaged before the enemy were gone, and before the country demands came on, they might be had on much better terms, of the same people, than they would afterwards, and offered my services in the business. The general closed with my offers, and advanced me eleven hundred guineas, and gave me a set of bills on the honourable Robert Morris, Esq. for eight thousand dollars, to secure the clothing; and those are the bills forwarded by Captain [Clough] Shelton. I procured the clothing, and have negotiated the whole business with Captain [John] Hamilton, clothier to the army.

"That I proposed a profit in this business, I readily agree; but I flatter myself, when the risk and mode of payment I am to make for the goods purchased, are

Greene, and that, as he had enjoined secrecy, he never expected, that what he had wrote, would come to the knowledge of the General. I think, that this was nearly the purport of Mr. Banks's deposition, but believe that the original is to be found upon the files of Congress.

I have thus given a relation of this business, as well as I can recollect from memory—and I do solemnly swear, that the circumstances and facts herein mentioned, are true, to the best of my knowledge and belief; and I am also confident, that General Greene was drawn into the security, I have mentioned, from the situation, in which he was placed by Congress, as Commander of the southern army, at a trying crisis, when destitute of public funds; a fact, which I have the best ground to believe, from the habits of friendship, in which we lived,

---

compared with those I am to receive, it will be found that I have not only dealt justly, but generously with the public, in the supplies of the army.

"Before my return to Charleston, in conversation with the general, on the commerce of this country, he told me Major [Ichabod] Burnet had thoughts of leaving the army, and going into trade after the evacuation; and that if he should, as he had been long in his family, and as he felt a friendship for him, should be much obliged to me for such services as I might have it in my power to afford him. It was from this conversation, I took the liberty of hinting to my partner the probability of the general's taking a concern with us, not considering his peculiar situation, and how dangerous a measure of this kind would prove to public confidence.

"During my stay in camp I had several conversations with Major Burnet, relative to his future plans and prospects; and finding his genius formed for business, I offered him a concern in the house I proposed to establish in Charleston after the enemy were gone, which he consented to engage in, provided his friends to the northward concurred in the measure, and approved of his leaving the army; and it was on this principle, I understood, he wished his name kept secret, until he had succeeded, and settled the matter with his friends, as well as the conditions of retiring, with the secretary at war.

"My conduct was known to the governor and council of this state; and if I had exceeded the limits of propriety, or taken an improper latitude, I should not have escaped their censure or punishment. My views were mercantile—upon just principles—and have contributed not to my own emolument alone, but also to the convenience of the inhabitants, as well as accommodation of the army.

"I am only sorry in this whole business, that I took an improper liberty with General Greene's name, but cannot suppose that an idle surmise can affect a reputation so permanently established; especially, as I have already published to the world, under the solemnity of an oath, that he neither has, or ever had, any commercial connexion with me, of a private nature, or intimated a wish or desire of the kind; and also, that he never granted me a flag in his life, or any other privilege or indulgence, for commercial purposes; I say, when these facts are known, I flatter myself every imputation, both with respect to the general and myself, will be removed." (Johnson, *Greene*, II, 379–81.)

and the confidence, with which I was always honored by that great
and good officer.                                    Anthony Wayne.

Brigadier General Wayne, being duly sworn, maketh oath, that
the contents of the above narrative are true.               J: Rutledge.

Savannah, 1st June 1791.


## U.

Philadelphia, 16th March, 1788.

Dear Sir,

Your favor of the 11th instant was handed to me yesterday-
afternoon, desiring my evidence respecting General Greene's disap-
pointment of monies, he expected from Banks and Company, which
were to have been paid in Philadelphia. How far the facts, within my
knowledge, and the circumstances arising from my transactions, will
tend to establish the material points, I am not ascertained; but I shall
give you a narrative of such facts and circumstances, as I suppose
likely to have an aspect, to the object you have in view, and which
may tend to explain the information you may derive from other
sources.

The latter end of March 1783, Major Burnet intimated to me, that
he had formed, or was about forming a connection in [trade] with
a view to settle in Charleston. On his way thither he wrote to me from
Virginia, making overtures, in behalf of the House, to become their
commercial agent in Philadelphia. Early in May, I received a letter,
signed Banks, Burnet and Company, enclosing some drafts on the
paymaster General, and containing advice of their drafts to me, in
consequence of such remittance; suggesting also, that Major Burnet
was on his way from Charleston to Philadelphia, and would make
arrangements with me, for farther business. On Major Burnet's
arrival, he mentioned to me, the plan of business formed by their
House: That they were possessed of a large quantity of goods, which
Mr. Banks had purchased from British merchants in Charleston, which
enabled them to furnish clothing and other supplies for the army,
as well as the country; that they had undertaken to supply the army

with provisions, at a rate below what any other person could furnish them, in consequence of their being possessed of these goods; and, although they did not expect a profit on the contract, but might, more probably lose by it, they should, by these means, enlarge their trade, turn their goods into cash, and, at the same time, benefit the public, by supplying the army, in a time of difficulty, when no other house or person, in that quarter, could do it, with equal certainty. That they should rely on me, to receive their accounts of issues, and draw the money from the treasury, at the periods stipulated for payment, which, I think, was four months after delivery of the rations; but that they had stipulated with the persons, to whom they were indebted for the goods, that the monies, arising from the contract, should be appropriated to the payment of the debt contracted by that purchase.

Some time afterwards, I received from Mr. Banks a copy of his contract for supplying the troops, which, it seems, was made in his own name, separately, together with a power of Attorney from him to me, to receive the money, as it became due, from the treasury. Still, however, the instructions concerning the business were under the signature of the Company, sometimes in the hand-writing of Banks, and sometimes of Burnet, but uniformly holding up the idea of paying the produce to the British merchants, in proportion to their respective claims, of which they sent me a list, amounting to upwards of thirty two thousand pounds sterling due to three houses.

Their remittances to me, by other means, were considerable; but their drafts upon me greatly exceeded them; insomuch that I held some of their bills in suspense, after having accepted more than their funds in my hands, exclusive of the contract-money, would warrant. They urged me very pressingly to give a prompt acceptance to all their bills, promising ample resources to support them, and intimating, that the contract-money would be a security in my hands, if other resources should fail. It so happened, that I took up all their bills, which became due, in June and July, without breaking in upon the contract-money; and early in August, I paid to the British merchants, on account of their claims, twenty two thousand eight hundred and seventy five dollars, being all the contract money which had then come to my hands. Their drafts on me continued to increase, beyond their provision for the payment of them; and, in order to induce me to accept them, they gave me direct instructions, to apply the contract money to the payment of them, if I should find it necessary, intimating, that their contracts with the British merchants were not strictly payable till the first of November, and that, before that time, they should turn into my hands, six thousand pounds sterling from the Havannah, and ten thousand pounds sterling from Virginia, besides other remittances. Mr. Warington, one of the British merchants, who was also authorised to receive for Messrs. Harris and Blackford, was frequent in his applications for farther payments. When I found it necessary to apply some of the contract-money to other purposes, I thought it right to mention it to Mr. Warington. He became enraged at Mr. Banks, and then mentioned to me, that it would injure General Greene, who was Banks's security for the money, without which, he said, they would not have trusted him. This, I believe, was the first direct information I received of General Greene's responsibility in that business. Out of the next instalment of the contract-money, I paid to the British merchants four thousand two hundred and twenty two dollars; the rest, I was obliged to apply to the payment of drafts which I had accepted. This last payment to the British merchants (which was the last they received from me) was in October 1783. Some time after which I understood, from several of Mr. Banks's letters to me, that they had obtained other payments and securities, for the residue of their respective claims; but, in what manner, I was never particularly informed. I rested satisfied, however, that it was done, and that General Greene was made safe in the business, till some time after Mr. Banks had drawn the whole money out of my hands. He had drawn, indeed, for abundantly more, than he had any pretensions to, though I was lucky enough to decline acceptances, in time to save myself from going beyond my resources.

I do not recollect any other circumstance within my knowledge, likely to throw light on the subject of your enquiry; but, possibly, pointed questions may bring to my recollection some matters, which do not now occur, or do not strike me, as material. If a more solemn attestation, than my signature, should be required, as to the facts, which I have related, it shall not be wanting; but, considering the nature and purport of the enquiry, it may not, perhaps, be demanded.

With great esteem, I am, dear Sir,   Your most obedient Servant

Charles Pettit.

Colo. Wadsworth.[44]

On this twenty sixth day of December, in the year of our Lord one thousand seven hundred and ninety one, before me, Clement Biddle, Esquire, Notary public for the Commonwealth of Pennsylvania, duly commissioned and authorised by law, to administer oaths and affirmations, dwelling in the City of Philadelphia, personally came Charles Pettit, of said City, Merchant, who, being duly sworn, according to law, on his solemn oath, deposes and says, that the annexed letter was written and subscribed by him, the deponent, at, or about the time of it's date, and that the contents thereof are, in all things, just and true, according to the best of his memory and belief. And the said Deponent doth further, on his oath, declare, that although he was much conversant in the affairs of General Greene, and had a general, and, in many respects, a confidential knowledge of them, and also of the affairs of Banks, Burnet and Company, he never perceived the smallest reason to believe, or suspect, that General Greene had any interest or concern, whatever, as partner in trade with the said Banks and Burnet, or with any other person or persons in Carolina. And further saith not.                    Charles Pettit.

(L:S) Sworne as above before me,
Quod attestor.

Clement Biddle,
Notary public.

## V.

In consequence of an application from the executors of the late General Greene, to relate what I know, concerning his securityship, for the payment of certain monies for John Banks and others, I have written the following statement of facts, which is all, I can remember;

44. Jeremiah Wadsworth had served as commissary general of purchases for the Continental Army until December, 1779, and from that time until the close of the war he was engaged in supplying the French forces in America and in other speculative enterprises. For a discussion of Greene's connection with Wadsworth's speculations, see Freeman, *Washington*, V, Appendix V-2, "The Wartime Speculations of Nathanael Greene," 505–09.

and many of them happening so long since, and having no written memorials to refer to, I cannot exactly ascertain or particularise.

I was an Aid-de-camp to General Greene, from February 1781, until the disbanding of the army in 1783; was usually with him, and, at the time of his entering into the securityship alluded to, had as much of his confidence, at least, as a person in such a situation usually has of his General; which gave me access to his papers, and an opportunity to know, almost, every matter of importance, that happened to him, or the army under his command.

The evacuation of Charleston happened in December, 1782; previous to which, and for some time after, the troops were supplied with provisions, by the State of South Carolina, and the mode was, by warrants of impressment, from the governor of that State. Soon after the evacuation of that place, powers arrived, either to General Greene, or Colonel Carrington, Quarter Master General, to make a contract for supplying the army, according to the mode then lately adopted with the northern army. It was difficult to find persons willing to contract, on the terms proposed, and the supplies from the State were so precarious and uncertain, that the troops began to complain and murmur. At length the contract was formed with John Banks. Mr. Banks had gone into Charleston, previous to the evacuation, and had contracted with some British merchants, for upwards of thirty thousand pounds sterling worth of goods—he had entered into partnership with several persons, in this speculation, who, under the firm of Robert Forsyth and Company, were retailing those goods, by a rapid sale, and at a high advance. As soon as the contract was made, the supplies, furnished by the State, were refused to be continued, and the army was reduced to great distress, for want of provisions. John Banks had failed to comply with the contract; a vessel of his, coming from North Carolina, was lost near the bar, with a quantity of pork, which, I remember well; and, I think, he had another taken by the enemy, but am not certain as to this, by which the army was, three or four days, with very little, or no provision at all. Several alarming circumstances of discontent appeared, and seemed to threaten a revolt. It was expected that the funds of Robert Forsyth and Company, of which Banks was a principal, would have enabled him to have complied with the contract; but it was found, that the partners of that House, who were not interested in the contract for supplies, refused to let Banks have any of their cash, to apply to that purpose, until the merchants, from whom the goods were purchased, were paid, or sufficient security given them for that purpose. Under these circumstances, I have been often told by the parties interested, but was not present, that Banks applied to General Greene, to become security for the payment of the debts due for those goods, that he might have the money, intended to pay for them, to supply the troops. Not being present, I cannot say, what inducements, Banks might have held out to the General. But I have heard from Banks and the General, what, from every circumstance, that has come to my knowledge, I believe to be true—which was, first, that the army would, by that means, be supplied with provision, and the dangerous consequences, that were apprehended, be prevented, and that there could be no risk in so doing, as their affairs were in a prosperous way; considerable remittances made to Virginia, to purchase tobacco to be remitted to their creditors, and that the monies, arising from the contract should be applied to the same purpose. The General became guarantee for those debts, or the greater part of them, the exact amount I dont know. Banks, in consequence, had the funds, he wanted, to supply the troops, and, I believe, there were no more complaints. But the General, soon after, began to find, that the money, sent to Virginia to purchase tobacco, to be remitted to pay these British creditors, as well as the money due, and received by Banks on the contract, had been applied to entirely different persons, and purposes, than that, to which they had been promised; and, although some payments had been made, after the General became security, considerable sums still remained due, when the affairs of Banks and his partners became desperate. He became exceedingly uneasy, and did all, he could, to get assignments of debts, and other payments made.

The House of Robert Forsyth and Company made an assignment of debts to a very considerable amount, (I cannot recollect, how much) to Harris and Blackford, which I drew, and they were, then, generally considered, as good debts. These, I believe, were afterwards, relinquished by Harris and Blackford, for some bonds, which bonds, I understood, are disputed; and I am informed, a suit in Chancery is still depending concerning that affair. In the latter end of 1784, I came to live in Georgia, where General Greene came, also, to reside, I think, in November 1785. The General informed me, he was about to settle the amount of the debt, he had guaranteed to Messrs. Newcomen and Collet, and asked my opinion, whether he could legally pay them, unless by compulsion, without weakening his claim to compensation, from the persons, for whom he was security. I was of opinion he could; and advised him to consult Mr. Edward Rutledge,[45] on the occasion, who being of the same opinion, Mr. Collet came to Savannah, and, on the Tuesday before the death of General Greene, in June 1786, in my house, they came to a settlement; and General Greene executed bonds for, I think, about six thousand pounds sterling, payable at different periods, and delivered them, in my presence, to Collet, who gave him, also, in my presence, the bond, the General had signed, as guarantee. There was a dispute between them concerning a sum, I think, about sixteen hundred pounds, which, Collet admitted, he had received from Banks, or some of his partners in Virginia, which Collet had retained on a private account with Banks, which, the General insisted, ought to be credited on the guarantee-bond. It was deducted, accordingly, upon the General's giving a special bond, which I drew, and he executed, with condition, that if ever he recovered from Banks, or his partners, as much as would indemnify him, for all his losses and expenses in consequence of his securityship, that then he would pay it—otherwise not. The motive, that induced the General to make this arrangement, was, that he might have the use of this bond, in suing the principals for indemnification; and to have time allowed him for payment. I know not, what the General might have done with it, but I saw it delivered to him, and suppose it must be among his papers, as he died on the Monday following.

It may be justly expected, I should say something of a report, that went abroad, at or about the time, Banks was opening his House in Charleston, that General Greene was a partner, and had an interest in Banks's speculations, which induced him to guarantee those debts. It arose from a letter from John Banks to his partners, or some friend

45. Rutledge, a prominent South Carolina landowner and politician, represented Charleston in the state legislature. After Greene's death he acted as executor of his estate.

in Virginia, which was opened, and made public; wherein it was insinuated, that the General was concerned.[46] I do not remember the exact expressions, it contained. As soon as the General knew of it, he sent for Banks, and insisted on his making an affidavit, which he readily agreed to, that the General was not, either directly or indirectly, concerned in any of his transactions. I was not present, at that time, (being, I believe, out of town, for a few days) so that I do not know, particularly, what passed; but the reason, I understood, Banks gave for writing such a letter, was, that it would give credit to his plans, and would never get to the General's knowledge. This affidavit was published in the newspapers in Charleston, I think, in May or June 1783. This report was strengthened by Major Burnet, one of General Greene's Aids-de camp, becoming concerned in a new partnership, with Banks and others, in consequence of which he went to the Havannah, where he died. I have often conversed in the most free and confidential manner, with General Greene, and with Major Forsyth, one of Banks's partners (who, having been one of General Greene's deputies, while he was Quarter Master General, and appointed by him Deputy Commissary General of purchases, for the army under his command, in the southern States; and continuing in his friendship and confidence, even till his death, had the best opportunity to know) and I do, from every circumstance within my knowledge, firmly believe, and can almost positively affirm, that General Greene had no pecuniary concern, or interest in Banks's speculation. The supposition of such an interest is irreconcilable to several circumstances, which, as they fully convince my own mind, I ought not to omit, though they are rather arguments than facts. First, having the opportunities I had to know it, I think it impossible, almost, it should have been kept so entirely a secret, as to have given me, not even the slightest suspicion. Secondly, General Greene has often expressed his doubts of Banks's capacity for carrying on the great plan he had in view—particularly, about the time, or some time after the contract, I heard him say, Banks wanted steadiness and judgment, and, though he might succeed at first, he would fall thro', in the end. This being the case, had General Greene been concerned in interest, in those speculations, being present on the spot, he would

46. See note 13.

have controuled the application of the funds—would have completed the Charleston speculation, which would have been done in a short time, and with an immense profit. Instead of this, Banks, having the sole management of the funds, as I have understood, applied them in payment to the debts of the copartnership of Virginia, and engaged also in several wild schemes, which, the influence, the prudence and judgment of the General would have prevented, if he had had an interest, and, of course, an authority to interpose. Thirdly, General Greene was long and intimately acquainted with Major Forsyth, and always had great confidence in him. If such a secret was to be entrusted to one of the partners only, it would have been, most probably, to him—Yet so far from this, that Major Forsyth has given some mortgages, though I do not know the amount, to indemnify the General, which he never would have done, had the General been interested as a partner. Hunter did the same thing, who was another partner. Major Burnet, one of the General's Aids-de-camp, was taken into the partnership of Banks and Company, but when, I do not know. I remember, when the circumstance was made known, the General censured Major Burnet, for entering into any mercantile connections, without communicating to him, his intentions, and previously withdrawing from his family. No paper, or any other proof, has, as yet, I believe, been produced, that could give the slightest foundation for any suspicion of this interest; though a Mr. Ferrie, who was one of the partners has done all, he could, to prove it, and whose interest is most materially affected, by a suit brought against him, by the executors of the late General Greene, for indemnification for being security, as above stated. Lastly, I know what were General Greene's principles, in matters of this kind, from a long and intimate confidence, which began, a little before the circumstances of his securityship for Banks, and continued to the time of his death. From this knowledge, I affirm, upon my oath, I do not believe, he would have suffered himself, from any motive of gain, to have been drawn into any commercial connections, while he remained at the head of the southern army.

I have not, nor can I be exact, as to particular times, and, no doubt, many circumstances have entirely escaped my memory, relative to the subject of this narrative. But, to the best of my remembrance and belief, what I have above related, is true; nor have I omitted any thing,

I thought material to the forming a right judgment of General Greene's conduct, in that unfortunate affair, so far as the same came to my knowledge.                                                 Nath: Pendleton.

Savannah June 4th 1790.

Sworne to before me, at Savannah, the 21st day of June 1790.
                                                                    Joseph Clay, J.P.


## W.

                                                            Newark, July 21st 1790.

Dear Sir,

I have received your favor of the 19th instant, informing me, that it had been suggested, that General Greene was a partner with the House of John Banks and Company—that the evidence of their partnership had been in my possession, I having received it among my sons papers; and that General Greene, in his life-time, induced me, by some means or other, to relinquish the said evidence to him; and desiring me to inform you, whether those suggestions are true or false.

Agreeably to your request, I must, therefore, freely declare, that those suggestions are not true—that no evidence of General Greene's having been a partner with John Banks, or John Banks and Company, had ever been in my possession—that I never saw any thing in my son's papers, that gave the least room for a suspicion of that kind— and that I do not know, or believe, that General Greene was ever in partnership with John Banks, or John Banks and Company.

I am, dear Sir, with due respect,   Your most obedient Humble Servant.                                                             Wm. Burnet.

General Knox.


## X.

We feel ourselves happy, in this opportunity, afforded us, of attempting to do justice to the injured reputation of the late Major General Greene, whose eminent services to this Continent in general,

must have greatly endeared his memory to every true friend to the American revolution; and whose distinguished and effectual exertions, for the recovery of this State, from the possession of the enemy, have erected an indelible monument in the breast of every good citizen of this State. We have, with sensible concern, heard some insinuations, of his having, in derogation to the high command, which he held here, entered into extensive speculations, for his own private emolument, soon after the relinquishment of this City by the British. We think ourselves authorised to say, that we are as competent to his vindication, from any aspersion of that nature, as any two persons in the State of South Carolina, as we were both in the Executive department, at the time of the evacuation of this Capitol, the one, Governor, and the other, Lieutenant Governor; and a suit in Chancery has been since brought to issue before us, as Chancellors, in the prosecution of which, the several grounds, principles and obligations of the various connections or copartnerships, by whom the respective speculations, alluded to, were entered into, were very fully, ably and minutely discussed by some of the most eminent solicitors in the Court—And we have no hesitation, in the most inevasive, unreserved, and un-equivocal manner, to declare, that we never had, from our own observation, or from the strictest and most scrutinising investigation, on the Chancery-bench, the most distant reason to conceive, that the honorable General Greene was ever, either directly or indirectly, engaged in any of the aforesaid speculations, any further, than as surety for Mr. Banks. We think ourselves warranted, also, in asserting, that the contract with Mr. Banks, for the supply of the army, was the most advantageous, he could obtain, at a time, when the want of provisions threatened a mutiny.　　　　　　　　　Jno. Mathews.
　　　　　　　　　　　　　　　　　　　　　　　Rd. Hutson.
Charleston, 30th October, 1790.

## Y.

Having been requested to relate all that I know of General Greene's connection with the late John Banks and Company and to declare, how far interested he was in their speculations, and having acquired, in my professional line, a considerable knowledge of their affairs, I think myself bound to give the following information.

In the summer or autumn of the year 1782, John Banks, and some other merchants purchased of Messrs Neucomen and Collet, Harris and Blackford, and Mr. McWhan, a very considerable quantity of goods, on speculation. The British troops evacuated this State, in the month of December 1782, and Mr. Banks, very soon after the evacuation, became contractor to the American troops. Subsequent to this period, Mr. Banks and his partners, being unable, (as I have been informed, and believe) both to continue their supplies to the army, and to discharge their engagements with the merchants, from whom they had purchased the goods abovementioned; and, being pressed by them, either to comply with their engagements, or to give security if they were indulged with a farther credit, had recourse to General Greene, and prevailed on him to guarantee the payment of some of their debts, particularly, those to Neucomen and Collet, and Harris and Blackford.

John Banks and Company having failed to discharge their debts, the General was called on to fulfil his guarantee. On the course of his enquiry into the affairs of the debtors, he was informed, that Mr. Ferrie had an interest therein—That he had been concerned in the purchases, and that he had drawn out of the stock, as his proportion of profits, a large debt due to the concern, from Messrs. Pierce, White, and Call, which debts he had negociated for lands on Savannah river.

On this information, the General, in his life-time, filed his Bill in Equity against Mr. Ferrie; but, the suit abating by his death, his executrix and executors revived it. To this Bill, Mr. Ferrie put in his answers; I was his solicitor, and united with the late Mr. Drayton[47] as his counsellor. Mr. Ferrie, in his defence, availed himself of every possible advantage. He obtained from the Court of Chancery, commissions for the examination of witnesses, in various parts of America. He produced a number of extracts from the books of John Banks and Company; and a number of extracts of letters to and from them. He had assisted Banks, in the purchase of the goods, and had been instrumental in his obtaining credit. He had kept the books of the Company. He appeared to me, to have known all the concerns of the Company, most intimately and minutely. And had General Greene

47. William Drayton had died on May 18, 1790.

been concerned in the speculation, I think he must have known it, and knowing it, I am sure, he would have made it known. He was under no obligation whatever, to conceal it. He was put at defiance, by the suit, and, could he have proved it, he would have been success-ful in his defence. But he neither produced one tittle of evidence, or deduced a single circumstance to shew, that the General had, in any manner, been concerned in the purchase. The consequence of which was, that the Bill was sustained, the lands were decreed to be sold, and, after defraying the expenses of the suit, and discharging the money due on a mortgage, which had been given by a prior owner, the balance of the sale was directed to be paid over into the hands of the complainants, towards an indemnification of the General.

Given under my hand, this second day of November 1790.

Charles Cotesworth Pinckney.

## Z.

Sir,

It gives me much pleasure, that I have it in my power, to state an occurrence, which cannot fail, with an unprejudiced mind, to remove every suspicion relative to an improper connection in speculation in trade, between the late General Greene, and John Banks and Com-pany, in the spring of 1783. Several days after a report had prevailed in Charleston, and it was generally believed, that an express had arrived from the northward, bringing certain information, to those most interested, that the preliminary articles, between the United States and Great Britain, had been agreed on, I met with Mr. John Banks, on the Bay; after expressing the confidence, he had in my keeping a profound secret, the intelligence, which he was about to communicate, he informed me, that he had received information from a confidential friend of his, to the northward, that the preliminary articles were certainly signed, and gave me a letter to read, which contained the information; which letter, he had received, several days before. I was with him, but a few minutes, before he received a message from General Greene, by a servant from his store, in Broad-street, informing him, that he wished to see him at his store im-mediately. Mr. Banks asked me to walk with him—on our way, Mr. Banks said, that he supposed that the General wanted to interrogate him, with respect to the intelligence which he had received, but that he was resolved not to give him any satisfaction. So soon as we got to the store, General Greene, addressing himself to Banks, requested to be informed, whether he had received any information, which could be relied on, relative to the preliminary articles having been signed. Mr. Banks, in the most positive manner, denied, that he had received any information to that purport. The artless and undisguised manner, in which the question was asked, produced the strongest conviction, in my mind, that General Greene was, at that time, ignorant of the intelligence, which Mr. Banks had received: and it can hardly be presumed, that a piece of intelligence, so important and interesting to Mr. Banks, at that crisis, would have been withheld from any person, who was, in the smallest degree, connected with him.

W: Washington.[48]

Charleston, November 6th: 1790.

48. William Washington of Stafford County, Virginia, had served as a lieutenant colonel in the Continental Army under Greene in the southern campaign. After the war he settled in South Carolina on a plantation near Charleston.


## From John Davidson [1]

[*Annapolis, December 27, 1791.* On January 9, 1792, Hamilton wrote to Davidson: "I have recieved your letter of the 27th ultimo." *Letter not found.*]

1. Davidson was collector of customs at Annapolis.


## From Thomas Mifflin

[Philadelphia, December 27, 1791]

Sir.

In order to enable me to answer your letter of the 21st instant, I directed the Comptroller general to furnish me with the necessary information upon the subject of your inquiry; and you will now receive an extract from his report.[1] But as this may not be deemed satisfactory, I have given that Officer instructions to confer with you upon the subject; [2] and, I hope, that after a full and candid communication, the inconveniency that you suggest, may be prevented, without claiming the interposition of the Legislature. Should you still think, however, that this step is requisite, it shall be pursued.

I am, with due consideration   Sir Your most obed Hble Servt

Thomas Mifflin

Phila. 27 Decr. 1791
To Alexr Hamilton Esqr
Secretary of the Treasury &c.

DfS, in the writing of Alexander Dallas, Division of Public Records, Pennsylvania Historical and Museum Commission, Harrisburg; LC, Division of Public Records, Pennsylvania Historical and Museum Commission.

1. John Nicholson's letter to Mifflin, governor of Pennsylvania, dated December 24, 1791, reads as follows:

"In compliance with your Excellencys desire communicated by letter from the secretary of The Commonwealth of yesterday evening covering a letter addressed to your Excellency by The secretary of The Treasury of the United states dated the 21st Instant I report

"That The whole of The Certificates of
this state granted for a like sum of Certificates
of debt of the United states amounts to . . . . . . £ 1.937.885.15.3.
Of Which there was redeemed £ 118.470.6.6.
Balance . . . . . . . . 1.819.415.8.9.

1 937.885.15.3.

"By an act passed in March 1789. The holders of this balance are intitled on presenting their Certificates of this state and liquidating the interest recd thereon to receive back their former ones or an equivalent. This hath taken place to a great amount insomuch that there does not at present remain much unexchanged on a comparison of the whole. The exact amount at present unexchanged I cannot tell, a number of exchanges to the Amount of 40 or 50 presented are pending for want of the partys paying the indents due, the remainder I estimate from 40. to 50 thousand pounds if absolute precision be necessary, I will have the additions and selections made so as to give the sum exactly.

"When I read the letter of The secretary of the Treasury refered to aforesd. I was doubtful until I consulted it again whether it really imported that the interest payable quarterly on the Certificates granted on the assumed debt of this state, would be suspended until the Certificates of the Federal debt not yet exchanged for the new Loans as aforesaid should be surrendered or an equivalent in stock under the funding system, as such a case would prostrate the faith of the united states to the will of the Legislature of this state. If they should refuse to surrender them, then the united states (without any fault on the part of the original subscribers or the present holders) would not pay the interest they had issued their obligation for in which they promised payment. It appeared to me that if such were the law the public credit of the united states might be shaken by it and rendered precarious; but on turning to the law it will appear that the provision for returning the Certificates of The united states was to prevent the united states from paying the interest twice on the same debt and that in conformity thereto if any of the Certificates of this state commonly called new Loan debt had been be⟨fore⟩ the 1st of October last, when the Loan closed, subscribed to the sd Loan, it w⟨ould⟩ have been requisite before the stock had issued therefor that an equal ⟨sum⟩ should have been surrendered by the state as aforesaid. The state wo⟨uld⟩ thus have redeemed her Certificates thro the united states in the same manner at present practised for individuals. But no such certifi⟨cates⟩ of this state were subscribed—consequently the united states are intitled to none Of the Continental Certificates, which are demandable by the persons holding the new Loan. If they should be delivered to ⟨the⟩ united states this state might have to pay the new Loan Certificates without having this resource to do it with. I think too highly of the faith of the public to suppose, that the holders of new Loans are compellable either to subscribe them to the United states to re-exchange them for the Continental Certificates, or that to such as do not, the state are absolved from payment both of principal and interest, but the market value and the irredeemable quality of the Continental stock and the present funds of the United states are generally sufficient to induce the change as is evinced from the great quantity already so exchanged of the remainder some part is exchanged almost every day and if the Loan should be opened by Congress the exchanges would be encreased thereby." (ALS, Division of Public Records, Pennsylvania Historical and Museum Commission.)

2. On December 27, 1791, Alexander Dallas, secretary of the Commonwealth of Pennsylvania, wrote to Nicholson: "The Governor has written to the Secretary of the Treasury of the U. S. upon the subject of his letter of the 21st inst. which was communicated to you; and having enclosed that part of your report, which states the amount of the New-Loan certificates issued, and redeemed, and the probable balance of the unexchanged certificates, he mentions, that he has given you instructions to confer with the Secretary of the Treasury in hopes that the difficulty suggested may be removed, without claiming the interposition of the Legislature. I am directed, therefore, to request your attention to the subject, and that you will communicate to the Governor, the result of the proposed conference" (Hogan, *Pennsylvania State Trials*, 227).

# To Melancton Smith

Treasury Department December 27th. 1791

Sir.

I accept your proposals for Supplying the post of West point for the ensuing Year, at nine and one half cents per ration, pursuant to your letter of the 23rd. instant.

I am Sir   Your Obt. Sert.                                    Alexr. Hamilton

Melancton Smith Esqr.
New York.

Copy, RG 217, Miscellaneous Treasury Accounts, 1790–1894, Account No. 2052, National Archives; LS, sold at Swann Galleries, November 3, 1949, Lot 52.

## From Oliver Wolcott, Junior

*Treasury Department, December 27, 1791.* "I have examined the memorial of Wm. W. Smith for himself and as Administrator to Gilbert Tennent deceased and of Joseph Eaker by his Attorney George Hunter,[1] and report the following state of facts and opinion thereon. That it appears from the books and documents appertaining to the late Hospital Department, that Wm. W. Smith continued in the service of the United States in the capacity of Junior Surgeon from the 22d. of April 1777 to the 18th. day of February 1780 at which time he resigned. That he has recd. at sundry payments the whole of the pay rations and subsistance to which he was intittled, in bills of old Emissions. . . . That it also appears from the books & documents of said department, that Gilbert Tennent served as a Mate in the General Hospital, from the 22d. of April 1777. and that no document exists in the Offices of the Treasury shewing that he continued in the service after the 10th. of Decr. 1779. . . . That even admitting the stating in the memorial to be accurate, to wit, that said Tennent served till some time in February 1780, still he would not be intittled to receive compensation for depreciation but only the value of the nominal pay due to him after Decr. 18th. 1779. for the period he continued in service, for the allowance of which at the Treasury no legislative Act is necessary, provided the claim shall appear to have been made in season. That it appears from the files of the Treasury that the account of Joseph Eaker was in February 1782. adjusted by the Clerks of the Treasury, when a balance in bills of old Emissions for pay & subsistance to the 17th. of February 1780. was found due amounting to Fourteen hundred and ninety eight dollars and fifteen ninetieths, Twelve hundred Dollars of which balance was for subsistance at the rate of two hundred Dollars ⅌ month, that said balance was liquidated to specie, at the exchange of seventy five for one. . . . That the claim exhibited in behalf of said Joseph Eaker, to have the balance of nominal pay due to him considered as Specie, cannot be admitted without invalidating a settlment which has been made by Officers who possessed competent authority to made such settlment & that said claim is also opposed by the rules which have hitherto governed the settlment of claims under similar circumstances, with respect to the late Army of the United States."

ADfS, Connecticut Historical Society, Hartford.

1. An entry in the *Journal of the House* for November 22, 1791, reads as follows: "A petition of William W. Smith, for himself, and as administrator to Gilbert Tennent, deceased, and Joseph Eaker, by his attorney, George Hunter, was presented to the House and read, praying compensation for services rendered as Surgeons in the General Hospital of the United States, during the late war" (*Journal of the House*, I, 458–59).

The petition was referred to H on December 28, 1791, with "instruction to examine the same, and report his opinion thereupon to the House" (*Journal of the House*, I, 482). H, however, did not report upon Smith's petition until February 27, 1794.

## From William Short

Amsterdam Dec. 28. 1791

Sir

In my last of the 23d. inst. I had the honor of simply announcing to you a loan being contracted for here on account of the U.S. for f 3,000,000 at 4. p. cent. The departure of the English post by which my letter was sent did not allow me to enter into details, except as to the terms of the loan. An alteration has since been made as to the times of payment from eight to six months. You may accordingly count on f 500,000. being recieved by the bankers monthly, the next month being considered as the first, so that the whole must be paid by the end of June, & will unquestionably be paid sooner, the undertakers having as you know always the facility of shortening the terms.

Until I shall hear from you, the monies arising on this loan will be applied towards the French debt, reserving what may be necessary to complete the two millions & an half of florins you had excepted out of the six million loan & which I had intended should have been kept out of it, having only given orders for 3½ millions.[1] I find here however that other dispositions have been made by other orders of two or three hundred thousand florins, so as to leave that deficit on the 2½ millions intended to be kept to answer your draughts. The sums

ALS, letterpress copy, William Short Papers, Library of Congress.

1. See H to Short, May 24, November 1, 1791. For a description of the Holland loan of September, 1791, for six million florins, see Short to H, August 31, 1791.

which become due here for interest in february & march will be also paid out of the present loan.

A vessel now lying at the Texel waiting for a wind gives me an opportunity of writing to you by that chanel to inform you of the steps which immediately preceded this loan; which in addition to what I have said in my former letters from Antwerp & this place, will I think stamp the proper value on the offers made from hence with respect to a loan at 4. p. cent.

As soon as I arrived here & found from the conversations of the bankers themselves that the Antwerp obligations of 4½. p. cent were not sold on this market, & also that a loan at 4. p. cent was then impracticable, as it certainly was at that time, I was persuaded that the impracticability could not arise from the Antwerp loan, & as that was the only circumstance which had intervened & the only reason for a change of circumstances I concluded naturally that no change had taken place & of course that the same impractibility which I was satisfied existed then must have existed at the time of their letters. It may be asked why they should have held out the hopes of the 4. p cent loan if they did not think they could be realized? They could not but have known or at least have had the strongest presumptions of the loan being intended at Antwerp, for although they did not recieve the printed prospectus of it until two days after their letter to me, yet the business had been settled between M. de Wolf [2] & the undertakers at Antwerp some time before & had been talked of there in a manner not to admit a doubt of its being known at Amsterdam. Supposing therefore a strong desire in the bankers here to prevent such a loan, which they do not deny, the most probable means were certainly to give assurances of a loan here at a lower rate of interest. They know well enough the nature of the loan business to be sure that a check given to it in this stage at Antwerp, would be for some time an obstacle to renewing the loan there in the case of our wishing to do it on finding that the 4. p. cent loan could not be made here. The imputation could be made them, as they could easily have said they held out the hopes of the 4. p. cent loan, from their zeal to the U.S. having reason to believe it could be made, but that circumstances which change here daily & of which no one can

2. For a description of the role of Charles John Michael de Wolf in the negotiation of the Antwerp loan, see Short to H, November 8, 12, 1791.

be master &c. &c. (according to their constant language) had changed the prospect.

If on the contrary, as took place, the loan was not stopped at Antwerp, they by the hopes thus held out remained on the most advantageous ground, as whilst they could thus demonstrate the impolicy of the loan at Antwerp, they supposed they should proceed equally in making the one that I had authorized them for at 4½. p. cent.

Apprehending however that something of this kind might be possible I immediately withdrew the authority as to the 4½. p. cent & I found on my arrival here full proofs that if I had not done this expressly a loan would have been made without delay at that rate. It was evident that they had had no apprehension that I should put a stop to such a loan here whilst I consented to that at Antwerp. They made use of all kinds of arguments daily to prove to me the propriety, the policy & advantage of renewing the powers I had withdrawn. I refused it constantly, & as they could not concieve that a loan at that rate of interest would be refused by the U.S. without a prospect of some advantageous arrangement of the French debt, & as their correspondents at Paris gave them some intimation of a plan in agitation in the French ministry, they began evidently to be some what alarmed. Agreeably to their example in such cases I did not seek to diminish it—on the contrary it was augmented by my silence and reserve on the subject. In this situation of the business no opportunity was lost by them of exalting their zeal for the service of the U.S: their attachment to their interests &c. of which they always quoted in proof their having not made the loan at 4½ p. cent. whilst they had the power to do it; but in such a manner as left me no doubt of their regret at having lost such an opportunity, at present that they were uncertain of what would be done with the French debt, & of course with future loans.

Under these circumstances I could have no doubt that every effort would be made to effect a loan at 4. p. cent, as well from the hopes of preventing any arrangement of the debt in France, which might derange the business in their hands as because they had every reason to believe I would consent to one on no other condition. The brokers were consulted who were unanimously of opinion in their meeting that it would be improper to propose such a loan at that time. On this

their instances became still more pressing for the loan at 4½. p. cent
& by way of securing it they urged my consenting to write two loans
together that they might propose them to the undertakers coupled,
one at 4½ & the other at 4. As this was however nothing more than
another way of making a loan at 4½ p. cent. wch I had refused, I
refused it also. They had assured me that no hopes could be entertained of doing better. I was closeted with one of the Willinks [3] listening to his arguments on this subject & refuting them when one of the
other houses came in unexpectedly & with much real joy announced
to us, that having got information that Russia was about to propose
a loan at 4. p. cent, he had gone immediately to the other Willink
to consult on it & that they were both of opinion that it might be
made a step to effect one for America. Accordingly the subject was
immediately discussed by the partners of both houses, & it was agreed
that if I consented to it they would *order* the brokers to propose the
loan the next morning to the undertakers & support it. I observed to
them that I consented willingly to the loan at 4. p. cent, provided
there was a certainty of its being carried through with éclat, but
that I was somewhat surprized to hear their talk of ordering now
those whom they had always represented to me as dictators in such
cases & would by no means wish that any risk should be run of a
defeat by precipitating the business. They said they would be responsible for that, & that there were occasions in which the brokers
must not be consulted but ordered.

The next day the loan of Russia was brought on & that of America
followed it, & was effected in the manner I have already mentioned
to you. The loan of Russia is for f 6,000,000. at 4. p. cent, payable in
the obligations of the same power on an old loan at 4½. p. cent,
which become re-imbursable in the next year. The interest is calculated at 4½. p. cent to the time of re-imbursement, & recieved for
that value in the present loan. Notwithstanding this mode of ful-
filling the loan, without which it would not have been attempted I
am assured by an authority which cannot be mistaken, that only four
millions were undertaken & that Hope [4] took the other two millions

3. Wilhem and Jan Willink had joined with the banking house of Nicholaas
and Jacob Van Staphorst and Nicholas Hubbard as the bankers of the United
States in Amsterdam.
4. Henry Hope. See Short to H, December 2, 1790.

for his house, without doubt in concert with the Russian government, so that he will risk nothing. The proof that Russia would not have attempted an original loan at 4. p. cent. at present & which I consider as sufficiently satisfactory is that her last at 5. p. cent was made in the month of November, since when nothing of any kind has taken place either here or in Russia to authorize such a diminution.

The inferences which I draw from what has been said above, are that the market here was not ripe for loans at 4. p. cent at the time these hopes were held out by the bankers, that they would not have been held out but for the Antwerp loan, & that my powers to them for making one at 4½. p. cent would have been executed, that the loan at 4. p. cent would not now have been effected if that for Russia had not been brought on the market, & that it would not have been brought on the market, but for the favorable circumstance of the approaching re-imbursement abovementioned & the influence & power of Hope's house.

The bankers whilst I was at Antwerp & after I had informed them that the loan there could not be stopped, wrote me that they would give me on my arrival here an unequivocal demonstration of the practicability there had been of their making a loan for the U.S. at 4. p. cent.[5] It has been reduced simply to an assertion that the abundance of money on the market arising from the sales of English funds, rendered it practicable, & that their having made a loan on the liquidated debt at 4½. p. cent proved it. As to the abundance of money which is a fact, it operated with equal force on the Russian as on the American credit, their obligations, since the presumed peace between Russia & the Porte,[6] having been at the same price, & yet this did not enable Russia to make a loan then at 4. p. cent although she had not made one at Antwerp as we had done, which was stated as the only obstacle to ours. With respect to the loan on the liquidated debt, it is certain that heretofore there was a greater difference in favor of the loans of Congress than ½. p. cent interest. But it is certain also that the loans on the liquidated debt have been so successful, so much has been gained by the lenders, & the obligations have always taken &

5. Willink, Van Staphorst, and Hubbard to Short, December 8, 1791 (LS, Short Family Papers, Library of Congress).

6. The second Russo-Turkish War was concluded by the Treaty of Jassy, which was signed on January 9, 1792.

kept such a rise, that these loans had acquired a degree of favor which enabled those who made them to propose them on almost any terms. It is known here with what enthusiasm & ardor the undertakers run into a business which has acquired that kind of favor, & of course it cannot be adopted as a point of comparison much less a conclusive proof. The bankers themselves have been obliged to acknowlege the justice & weight of this observation in general. Still they adhere to their former assertion on this particular instance, in opposition to it.

I have been thus diffuse Sir & wearied you with these irksome & lengthy details because I think it important that you should be able to form a true judgment on the subject of having the faculty, whether exercised or not, of making loans in more than one place. The best guide I can give you is thus furnishing the greatest number of facts possible, so that you may form your own opinion from them, instead of being informed of mine simply which always subject to error, is particularly exposed to be influenced in this instance. The rising credit of America & the increasing confidence which her present administration is acquiring in the monied parts of Europe, will necessarily present such a variety of choice to the U. S. that it is much to be desired that those who act for you should be kept acquainted with your sentiments on the subject.

My letter thus extended does not permit me to say any thing respecting the attempt of the bankers to increase the charges on this loan to six p. cent, but simply to mention that it was by leaving the question without being finally decided until after the loan was made & then to argue from the advantage of giving such an increase of charges for such a diminution of interest. They affirmed & I am persuaded with truth, that besides the usual bankers & undertakers they are obliged to employ others also with extra expences, to push the loan. As I did not suppose they had in doing this gone farther than would have been warranted by the charges of 5½. p. cent mentioned in their former letter,[7] I insisted on them & after some days they consented though with reluctance, & are to write me a letter to fix them at that rate.

After all that has been said above I should leave you perhaps an impression with respect to the bankers that is not in my intention, if I

7. See Short to H, December 23, 1791, note 2.

were to say nothing further. It is but justice to them that I should add that notwithstanding I am convinced their aversion to our opening loans out of Holland would induce them to use every means in their power for preventing it & that of themselves they would fix their profits on making the loans, probably somewhat above what we should think just, yet I am convinced also fully from what I have seen of them & of the other houses employed here in similar business that none have more zeal for the service of the countries by which they are employed, or act with more propriety & delicacy towards them.

All these houses make a common cause of a power accustomed to borrow here opening a loan in Antwerp, which they consider in this respect as a dependence on Amsterdam. Hope whose partiality for the interests of America nobody will presume has taken uncommon pains repeatedly since my arrival here to demonstrate to me the impolicy of the measure, & that by the most sophistical arguments imaginable. I listened to them with much attention because I was really desirous to be fully enlightened on the subject & particularly to hear what could be said on it by the most able & perhaps best informed man in Europe in that business. I have heard as well from him as others many good reasons for exercising the faculty (of making loans in more than one place) with more reserve than I should have perhaps thought necessary before, but nothing to diminish the advantages which may be expected from shewing that the faculty is in our power if we chuse to exercise it. It is certain that this is a vantage ground from which the borrower is much more enabled to command the lender. What has happened in the present instance is, unless I am very much mistaken, strong proof of its influence.

Mr. Hope as it appears, has stronger arguments to use with Russia. I mentioned to you formerly that he had in undertaking the re-establishment of Russian credit contracted for the monopoly of the loans of that country & lately that M. de Wolf had postponed the American loan he had been treating for because he was authorized to open one for Russia on much more advantageous terms.[8] I supposed then either that the monopoly had ceased or that Hope had consented to the loan. The contrary however was the case. The loan projeced for Russia was on a footing which it was thought would evade the engagement

8. See Short to H, July 27, 1791.

wih Hope; that is to say by being opened at Petersburg, & the bonds given there expressed in roubles, which bonds were to be sold at Antwerp & the interest on them paid there. A considerable part of the loan was effected, a part of it remitted to Petersburg, & notwithstanding it has been stopped (supposed to be by the influence of Hope) & the money returned to the lenders.

Previous to my leaving Paris, several of the sufferers by the revolt in S. Domingo had concieved the plan of the French Government coming to their aid by loans of money in order to enable them to rebuild & re-establish their cultivation.[9] As they knew the U.S. were paying off their debt they cast their eyes on that supply, & determined to collect it through the ministry of the assembly. It was an affair then in embryo & as it had to pass from the ministry to the assembly & was placing such a sum of money at the disposition of government it was much to be feared, under present circumstances, that it would not be brought to consistence and particularly as it was desired by the ministry of whom a great part of the assembly have really much more apprehension & fear than of the most declared & bitter enemies of the country, regarding them as the fosterers of what they call a counter-revolution, & by which they understand the destroying of the nation by war, plunder, & famine.

Some days ago the minister of the marine brought forward this business in the manner the most favorable to its success.[10] He made a general report on the troubles of S. Domingo & the losses which he estimates at a capital of 600,000,000₶. He considered the colony as a large manufacture belonging to the nation & placed at a distance, in which every member of the society in France was an *actionaire*, & of course interested in its support. This is the most popular way of considering the subject for the assembly; for the most exagerated lovers of liberty & individual independence among them, are much flattered with the idea of the inhabitants of the islands of all colours being their property & really regard them as such. The minister shewed the profits arising from this great manufacture for all its owners & the advantages to be derived from an immediate re-establishment of it, by

9. See Jean Baptiste de Ternant to H and H to Ternant, September 21, 1791.

10. Antoine François, Marquis de Bertrand de Molleville, who had been appointed Minister of Marine and Colonies on October 7, 1791, addressed the Legislative Assembly on Santo Domingo on December 19, 1791 (*Archives Parlementaires*, XXXVI, 253–56).

advances of money which would be thus placed on the most advantageous terms. He observed that the debt of America was the most immediate succour that could be given & proposed its being thus applied, adding an expression in favour of liberty which was much applauded. They did not however employ their usual mode of acceleration by a *décret d'urgence*. It was referred to a committee.[11] They are to report on it about this time but it is highly probable it will be still delayed. The minister thinks however it will be finally adopted. In that case he will come forward probably with proposals to me for carrying his plan into the earliest execution. Considering my powers as co-extensive with the whole debt at the present rate of interest here,[12] I shall co-operate with him most heartily, as it is evident that it must be highly advantageous for the U.S. to have their debt to France vested in their own productions, which is the object the minister has in view.[13] You will recieve from Paris in the papers which will have been regularly sent to the Secretary of State during my absence, the report of the minister abovementioned. I shall not fail to keep you acquainted with the progress of the business after my arrival there, & have the honor at present to be, with the highest respect,

Sir   Your most obedient humble servant          W Short

The Honble. Alexander Hamilton Secretary of the Treasury, Philadelphia

11. With a *décret d'urgence* the Assembly dispensed with the usual parliamentary procedure by approving a decree without bothering with either committee hearings or a report. Bertrand's proposal was referred to the Assembly's Committee on Commerce and Colonies (*Archives Parlementaires*, XXXVI, 256).

12. See H to Short, September 2, 1791.

13. Bertrand proposed that the needed goods and commodities be purchased in the United States.

## From Oliver Wolcott, Junior

T D
C. Off Decr. 28th. 1791

Sir,

For the purpose of obviating the difficulties which have been experienced in respect to the Act providing compensations for the

Officers of the judicial Courts of the United States & for jurors & Witnesses;[1] and for the more regular collection & payment of the monies accruing from fines & forfeitures; I take the liberty to submit the following sentiments to your consideration.

That all fees & compensations should as far as possible be accurately defined by Law; and that with respect to such services as may be omitted to be designated, or for which it may be judged inexpedient at present specially to provide, authority be reposed in the Judges of the Supreme Court to establish general rules of compensation from time to time to be certified to the officers of the Treasury to enable them to adjust the accounts for such services according to the rules so established.

That the whole expences of all suits commenced at the instance of any Revenue Officer, be paid by such Officer out of the product of the revenue in his hands and charged in his accounts as an expence attending the collection of the revenue.

That the expences of all suits commenced by the direction of the Secretary or Comptroller of the Treasury, be adjusted & paid at the Treasury.

That for the expences of all other suits and for discharging the compensations of Attornies, Clerks Jurors & Witnesses & generally for all contingcies of the judicial department, monies be advanced from time to time to the Marshals of Districts, to be by them accounted for at the Treasury according to such rules & forms as shall be prescribed.

The monies accruing from fines & forfeitures for breaches of the revenue Laws, ought to be paid by the Marshals to the revenue Officers who directed the prosecutions. The fines & forfeitures incurred for crimes & delinquencies, should be accounted for to the Treasury.

I am &c

The Hon A H

ADf, Connecticut Historical Society, Hartford.
1. 1 *Stat.* 216–17 (March 3, 1791).

## From Roger Alden, Brockholst Livingston, Carlile Pollock, Gulian Verplanck, and Joshua Waddington [1]

New York 29 Decr: 1791

Sir

A number of your fellow Citizens desirous of expressing the sense they entertain of the important Services you have rendered your Country, have raised by Subscription a Sum of money to defray the expence of a Portrait of you, ⟨to⟩ be executed by Mr Trumbull, and placed in one of our public Buildings.[2]

We have therefore to request that you will b⟨e⟩ so condescending as to allow Mr Trumbull to wait upon y⟨ou⟩ for the above purpose, at such time as will suit your convenie⟨nce⟩ and will also be pleased to permit the representation to exhib⟨it⟩ such part of your Political Life as may be most agreeable to yourself.

We have the honor to be,   with perfect sentiments of esteem  & respect; Your most humble sert.

> Gulian Verplanck
> Roger Alden
> Brockholst Livingston ⎬ Committ⟨ee⟩
> J Waddington
> Carlile Pollock

To Alexander Hamilton Esqr
Secretary of the Treasury of the United States

LS, Hamilton Papers, Library of Congress.

1. Alden, Pollock, and Waddington were New York City merchants; Livingston, the son of William Livingston, was a leading New York City attorney; and Verplanck was the president of the Bank of New York. H, with the assistance of Livingston, had served as Waddington's counsel in the famous case of *Rutgers* v *Waddington* in New York in 1784.

2. This full-length portrait of H by John Trumbull was completed in 1792 and now hangs in the Assembly Room of the Chamber of Commerce of the State of New York in New York City. H did not sit for the portrait; it was executed from Trumbull's earlier bust portrait of H which the artist had painted at the request of John Jay (Harry MacNeill Bland and Virginia W. Northcott, "The Life Portraits of Alexander Hamilton," *The William and Mary Quarterly*, 3d ser., XII [April, 1955], 190–91). See frontispiece of this volume.

## From John Nicholson

Compr. Genl. Office [Philadelphia]
Decr. 29th. 1791

sir

I have recd. instructions from his Excelly. the Governor [1] to confer with you on the subject contained in your letter to him of the 21 Inst. If the difficulty suggested should arise in a doubt, whether part of the assumed debt of Pennsa. by the United States might not consist of Certificates given for a like sum of others of the United States not exchanged and to be surrendered, it will be easily proven that it does not. At any rate I would propose a conference with you on the business at any time you may appoint provided you approve thereof.

I am   Yours &c                                   Jno: Nicholson

The Honble Alexr. Hamilton
Esqr secty Treasy. Ustates

Copy, Division of Public Records, Pennsylvania Historical and Museum Commission, Harrisburg; LC, Division of Public Records, Pennsylvania Historical and Museum Commission.
    1. See Thomas Mifflin to H, December 27, 1791, note 2.

## From Jeremiah Olney

Custom House
Providence 29th. Decer. 1791.

Sir

The Brigantine Polly James Munro Jur. Master, the Property of Messrs. Clark & Nightingale [1] Entered here the 27th Inst. from Charleston South Carolina. This Vessel Cleared at my office on the 24th August last for Port au Prince, but it appears from the Master that she arrived at the Cape, having on Board, when she cleared, Three hundred & Fourteen Barrels of salted Provisions One hundred & Twenty Barrels of Pickled Fish and Eleven Hhds. of Dryed Fish weighing Eighty Quintals one Quarter and 23 oz all duty entered for Exportation, but the Troubles at the Cape were such as entirely to prevent Trade, in consequence of which, the Master, after much Trouble and Solicitation obtained permission to Depart with Vessel and Cargo, and arrived on the latter Part of Octr. at Charles Ton where he says he landed and disposed of the Dryed Fish, Twenty & half Barrels salted Provisions and Forty five Barrels of Pickled Fish, having now on Board the Remainder of Said pickled Fish & Provisions: And as they cannot be Relanded by the 62nd Section of the Collection law,[2] I am induced Sir, from the peculiar Circumstance of the Case and a fixed belief that no Fraud was intended against the Revenue, to ask your opinion whether said articles may not be relanded (and the Bond Cancelled) or at least untill the Vessel, which is now unfit to proceed on a Forreign Voyage, can be repaired and put in order to take them again onbd? Should this expedient be inadmissable with your Ideas of the law, I request Sir your Speedy Instructions as to the Stepts it may be proper for me Further, to persue in the present Case.

I am very Respectfully   Sir   your Most Obed. Hum. Servt.

Jereh. Olney Collr.

Alexander Hamilton Esqr.
Secretary of the Treasury

ADfS, Rhode Island Historical Society, Providence.
    1. The Providence merchant and trading firm of John Clark and Joseph Nightingale.
    2. Olney is mistaken; he is actually referring to Section 60 of "An Act to provide more effectually for the collection of the duties imposed by law on goods, wares and merchandise imported into the United States, and on the tonnage of ships or vessels," which reads: "*And be it further enacted*, That if any goods, wares or merchandise, entered for exportation, with intent to draw back the duties, or to obtain any allowance given by law on the exportation thereof, shall be landed in any port or place within the limits of the United States as aforesaid, all such goods, wares and merchandise, shall be subject to seizure and forfeiture, together with the ship or vessel from which such goods shall be landed, and the vessels or boats used in landing the same; and all persons concerned therein, shall on indictment and conviction thereof, suffer imprisonment for a term not exceeding six months. And for discovery of frauds, and seizure of goods, wares and merchandise, relanded contrary to law, the several officers established by this act, shall have the same powers, and in case of seizure the same proceedings shall be had, as in the case of goods, wares and merchandise imported contrary to law: And for measuring, weighing or gauging goods for exportation, the same fees shall be allowed as in like cases upon the importation thereof" (1 *Stat.* 174 [August 4, 1790]).

## From William Short

Amsterdam Dec. 30. 1791.

Sir

My letter of the 23d. inst. which I sent by three separate conveyances will have informed you of a loan of 3,000,000 florins being contracted for at 4. p. cent interest. That of the day before yesterday sent by the way of the Texel contained the steps which preceded & led to this loan & the circumstances respecting the charges on it. The present which goes by the English packet of the next week will inform you that these charges are definitively settled at 5½. p. cent, which seems now perfectly agreeable to the commissioners, notwithstanding the effort they made to fix them higher. I have full confidence they may be reduced without difficulty on future loans. Instead of the eight months mentioned in my letter of the 23d. the undertakers have been brought to contract for the completion of the loan in six months, in equal portions monthly, the time to count from the 1st. of Jany. The commissioners are fully persuaded that the epochs will be anticipated.

The reservation which you formerly made will be kept to answer your draughts,[1] & the sums which fall due, here in february & march will be made from the monies arising on this loan; the surplus will be remitted to France until I hear from you. Not knowing the terms at which your draughts may arrive & they being as I learn here at ten days sight, I have found it necessary to inform the bankers of the amount to which they may go, in order that in making remittances they may take care to remain provided to answer your orders. Had I known the terms at which you would probably have sent your draughts in succession, as some of them will in all likelihood not arrive immediately, I should have thought it most advisable to have applied the monies now in hand to the French payments, & have counted on the successive entry of the present loan to anwer your successive

ALS, letterpress copy, William Short Papers, Library of Congress.
1. See H to Short, May 24, 1791.

draughts; at least as far as they should be found to correspond with each other.

I have formerly had the honor of mentioning to you Sir, a tax intended to be laid by this government on foreign loans made here.[2] It was represented to me by the commissioners as a thing beyond all doubt to take place from the 1st. of Jany. It is now under discussion in the States of Holland & if adopted in this province the example will be followed in the others. The commissioners proposed to me, in order to avoid this tax in the case of its taking place, to sign the original contract for a loan of six millions at 4. p. cent, & to leave it here in the hands of the notary, so as to be absolutely at my disposal, & to have no force until I shall call it into existence. I have done it accordingly because the measure can have no inconvenience & may be attended with the advantage of avoiding a tax of which the borrower will certainly be obliged to pay the whole or much the greatest part.

Should peace continue in Europe they think they shall ere long be enabled to bring it on the market. They understand that the charges are then to be fixed at what may be agreed on between us. The natural guide for this would seem to be those which they are obliged to pay the undertakers & others employed. They however will not consent to state them & say that you are perfectly satisfied with it, since in giving you formerly the analysis of a particular loan they informed you it was merely to satisfy curiosity & could not consent to its being taken as a precedent, to which you have not objected. They say it is contrary to usage here, contrary to their fixed principles &c. &c. The true objection however to give This analysis can only arise from its throwing too much light on the subject, to which all people in business here have an insuperable aversion.

About one fourth of the Antwerp loan was recieved at the date of my last letters from thence [3] & it was supposed a third would be, by the end of the month. A part has been remitted to Paris & the rest will be remitted also as fast as good bills can be found. M. de Wolf informs me that he is sure of obtaining money there for the U.S. at 4 p. cent, & hopes I shall allow him to give me proofs of it.[4] I observe

2. See Short to H, August 31, 1791.

3. Charles John Michael de Wolf to Short, December 22, 1791 (ALS, Short Family Papers, Library of Congress).

4. Wolf to Short, December 26, 1791 (ALS, Short Family Papers, Library of Congress).

however by your late letters that you prefer loans on equal terms at Amsterdam.[5] Until I hear from you therefore I shall probably postpone doing any thing further there unless some arrangement for the French debt not yet due shd. render it advisable. I should be happy to have your ideas as to the two places examined comparatively in the case of the tax being laid here. It is only by knowing how far your preference to Amsterdam extends that I shall be enabled to decide fully in some cases which may present themselves. I hope your answer to my letter announcing the loan at Antwerp will give me lights on this subject.[6]

In the statement which you formerly sent me of the arrears due on the debt of the U.S. to France, they are expressed in dollars & no notice is taken of the arrears of principal on the loan of six millions of livres nor of any payments which may have been made to France on account of the interest of the debt, previous to the orders you gave me.[7] It appears that several sums have been paid to the Royal Treasury by Mr: Grand [8] but I have not been able to learn from him, & much less from the commissaries of the treasury, who were not able to find on their books that any payments had been made at all, how the account stood at the time of my commencing the payments. I will ask the favor of you therefore to have the account up to that time stated in livres, that I may see what was then due & consequently know how much remains exigible at present. You will be furnished by the bankers here of course with the payments as made.

I hope also to learn from you in consequence of a former letter what measures you wish to be taken with respect to the debt to the farmers general & to Spain.[9]

I have already had the honor of mentioning to you that the depreciation of assignats & the fall of exchange in France although clearly connected with each other, were not uniform in their progression.[10]

5. See H to Short, August 1–2, September 2, 1791.
6. See Short to H, November 12, 22, December 1, 1791.
7. See H to Short, September 1, 1790. For a description of the 1783 French loan of six million livres, see Short to H, November 30, 1789, note 3.
8. Ferdinand Le Grand, Paris banker.
9. See Short to H, November 12, 1791. For a description of the loan from the Farmers-General, see H to Short, September 1, 1790, note 26. The Spanish loan is described in H to Short, September 1, 1790, note 19.
10. See Short to H, October 10, November 22, December 1, 1791.

In the late unprecedented fluctuation the assignats were even lower than the exchange, having depreciated 50. p. cent. They have now risen & were quoted by the last post 32. p. cent, but sooner or later they must inevitably experience the fate of all forced paper unsupported by regular taxes.

I mentioned to you in my last the proposal made by the minister of the marine to the national assembly respecting the application of the American loan to the relief of the sufferers in S. Domingo.[11] As yet the decision is not known here.

You will recieve from the bankers the contracts for the two last loans which they will forward to obtain the certification thereof. They will also probably mention a difficulty which arose respecting the re-imbursement of the six million loan.[12] Until then no objection was made to the loans opened here, to the clause for re-imbursement at the will of the U.S. In that it seems the brokers had concieved themselves authorized to promise that this clause should be suspended for ten years as in the first loan made here by Mr. Adams.[13] This was however contrary to my authorisation & their intention. The bonds have consequently been passed conformably thereto. The brokers & undertakers insisted on their proposing to me to change the clause which they refused to do. They have mentioned the circumstance to me incidentally.

You will probably find it advisable to take into consideration the means you may judge proper for exchanging the five p. cent obligations of the U.S. for others at a lower rate of interest. The peace which at present prevails in Europe & which can not be counted on as of certain duration, & the favorable point of view in which the U.S. are now regarded by the money lenders, would seem to recommend that no time should be lost. War would necessarily oblige the belligerent power to give an higher interest than one at peace, but it would oblige both to give an higher rate than the present of 4. p. cent, unless it should be for very small sums.

The East-India company continue their loans here. On their own

11. See Short to H, December 28, 1791.
12. For a description of the Holland loan of September, 1791, for six million florins, see Short to H, August 31, 1791.
13. See H to Short, November 30, 1791. The first loan negotiated by John Adams in Amsterdam was the Holland loan of 1782. For a description of this

credit they could borrow nothing. They are guaranteed therefore by the States of Holland, & yet they are obliged to pay 4. p. cent interest with a premium of 5. p. cent at the time of re-imbursement. These are the terms of one opened here within a few days for five millions of florins. It is generally supposed their affairs are in bad condition. Their partisans say that the loans they have made here (which I am told pass 50. millions since the peace) are to make up the losses sustained during the war & to extend their commerce. They have lately introduced a change in the mode of making their sales, which is found so injurious to the commerce of individuals that the merchants of Amsterdam are now in contestation with them before the States-general. It is supposed the Company will succeed, the apprehension of which displeases a good deal here. Their charter expires I think four years hence. No doubt however is entertained of its being renewed.

I have learned nothing here respecting the mint which seems worthy of your attention. M. Brantsen whom I formerly mentioned to you [14] as most likely to give lights on this subject returned to Paris a few days before my arrival here. I hope you will long before this have recieved my letters respecting Mr. Drosts change of mind,[15] which I am sorry not to have been able to have informed you of previous to the opening of Congress, as I observe by the Presidents speech that he was counted on.[16]

I shall be detained a few days longer than I expected by the Printer's not having furnished the bonds of the three million loan agreeably to promise. I am now signing them & shall leave this place for Antwerp on the 4th. of the next month, where I shall stop a day or two & then proceed to Paris.

This letter will accompany one to the Secretary of State [17] &

---

loan, see Willink, Van Staphorst, and Hubbard to H, January 25, 1790, note 15.

14. Gerard Brantsen. See Short to H, September 23, 1791.

15. Short wrote to H concerning Jean Pierre Droz on August 23 and September 23, 1791, but in neither letter did he state that Droz had changed his mind. Short had written to Thomas Jefferson on October 14, 1791, that Droz would not go to America (LC, RG 59, Despatches from United States Ministers to France, 1789–1869, January 16, 1791–August 6, 1792, National Archives).

16. See Washington's third annual address to Congress of October 25, 1791 (GW, XXXI, 403).

17. Short to Jefferson, December 30, 1791 (LC, RG 59, Despatches from United States Ministers to France, 1789–1869, January 16, 1791–August 6, 1792, National Archives).

carries with it assurances of the sentiments of respect & attachment with which I have the honor to be

Sir    Your most obedient humble servant                    W: Short

⟨I enclo⟩se you a state of the exportations ⟨from Pe⟩tersburg to America for the present ⟨– –⟩ the number of vessels as you will ⟨see is o⟩nly a third less than that of the last ⟨– – w⟩hich must prove the increase of the ⟨consumptio⟩n of those valuable articles in the U.S.

The Honble Alexander Hamilton Secretary of the Treasury, Philadelphia

## *From Thomas Smith* [1]

Pennsa Loan Office [Philadelphia] Decr 30. 1791

Sr.

The ballances of stock remaining on the Books of this Office for the quarter ending the 31st Decer. 1791 subject to the Payment of Interest on the 1st January 1792 are as follows Viz

| Dolls  Cts. | | | |
|---|---|---|---|
| 122,564.70. | of 6 ₩ Ct. Stock | Intst from Jany. | 7 353.88 |
| 1,348,379.47. | of ditto | Int. from Oct | 20.225.69 |
| 69,963.57 | 3 ₩ Ct. | do    do    Jany. | 2 098.90 |
| 541,252.78 | do | do    Oct. | 4 059.39 |
| 4.707.– | 4 ₩ Ct nonsubscrition stock | | 47. 7 |
| 847.16. | 3 ₩ Ct        do | | 6.35 |
| | | | 33.791.28 |

I have the honor to be &c.

Honbl Alexr Hamilton
secy. Treasy US.

LC, RG 53, Pennsylvania State Loan Office, Letter Book, 1790–1794, Vol. "615-P," National Archives.

1. Smith was commissioner of loans for Pennsylvania. For background to the loan office procedures to which Smith is referring, see Nathaniel Appleton to H, February 5, 1791, note 1.

## From William Barton [1]

[Philadelphia, December 31, 1791]

Sir,

The sheets which compose the pamphlet,[2] herewith inclosed, will be comprized in the third Volume of the Philosophical Society's Transactions, now in the press.[3] Being favored by the printer with a few Copies of this part, (with the addition of a Title page), I beg, Sir, Your Acceptance of One.

If some additional Observations on the same subject, resulting from the Census, which have been read in the Society, should be deemed worthy of a place in their Transactions, I shall take the liberty of sending You a Copy, when printed.

I have the Honor to be,   With great Respect,   Sir,   Your Most Obedt. And Most Hble. Servt.                                        W. Barton

Market street,  ⎱
Dec. 31st. 1791. ⎰
The Honble. A. Hamilton, Esq;
Secry. of the Treasury

ALS, Hamilton Papers, Library of Congress.
  1. Barton, a Philadelphia attorney, was the nephew of two distinguished scientists, David Rittenhouse and Benjamin Barton, the botanist. Both men were members of the American Philosophical Society. Barton was also a counselor of the society.
  2. William Barton, Observations on the Progress of Population, and the Probabilities of the Duration of Human Life, in the United States of America. Read before the American Philosophical Society held at Philadelphia, for Promoting Useful Knowledge (Philadelphia, 1791).
  3. Barton's paper was read before the society on March 18, 1791, and is printed in Transactions of the American Philosophical Society, Held at Philadelphia, for Promoting Useful Knowledge (Philadelphia, 1793), III, 25–62.

## From John Daves [1]

Collectors Office Port
of New Bern [North Carolina, December, 1791]

Sir,

I herewith enclose the description and dimensions of the Revenue

Cutter built at Washington taken by the examining Officer at Washington and sent me by Capt. Cooke.[2] I expect the Cutter round here shortly and would be thankful to be informed whether the articles for the Revenue Cutter mentioned in my letter of the 12th. November last, have yet been ordered for this Port or Washington.

I have the honour to be with much respect &c.
The Honble. Alexr. Hamilton Esqr.

Copy, RG 56, Letters from the Collector at New Bern, National Archives.
1. Daves was collector of the customs at New Bern.
2. William Cooke was the master of the *Diligence,* the revenue cutter from the District of North Carolina.

# 1792

## Conversation with George Hammond [1]

[Philadelphia, January 1–8, 1792]

Since my conversation with the Secretary of the Treasury, of which I had the honor of giving your Lordship an account in my dispatch No 13,[2] I have lately had another interview with that Gentleman, in the course of which we entered into a loose and general discussion of some of the questions that are likely to become subjects of negociation between our two countries.

After some comments upon the different facts which Mr Jefferson had adduced as specific infractions of the definitive treaty on the part of Great Britain,[3] Mr Hamilton expressed his conviction that the surrender of the posts was the only one which could produce any lengthy or difficult investigation. Upon this head he intimated that although he did not imagine this country would be easily induced to consent to a dereliction of any part of its territory acquired by the Treaty, it might perhaps still be possible to grant to his Majesty's subjects such privileges and immunities in the respective posts as would protect and secure them in the undisturbed prosecution of the Fur Trade.[4] Being in daily expectation of receiving your Lordship's

D, PRO: F.O. (Great Britain), Series 4, Vol. 14, Part I.

1. This conversation has been taken from Hammond to Lord Grenville, January 9, 1792, Dispatch No. 3.

2. See "Conversation with George Hammond," December 15–16, 1791.

3. After the exchange of several letters between Hammond and Jefferson following the presentation of the British minister's credentials on November 11, 1791, Jefferson proposed to Hammond in a letter of December 15, 1791, that they begin negotiations "by specifying, on each side, the particular acts which each considers to have been done by the other, in contravention of the treaty." In the same letter Jefferson discussed such British violations of the treaty as the retention of the western posts and the carrying off of American slaves at the end of the war. He also referred to the "difference of opinion" respecting the boundary between the United States and Canada in the area of the St. Croix River (*ASP, Foreign Relations*, I, 190).

4. On July 3, 1792, Hammond wrote to Lord Grenville further elaborating on this point: "In my informal conversations upon this matter, as well with the two ministers [Jefferson and Knox] mentioned in the former part of this letter as with Mr Hamilton, all those Gentlemen have uniformly expressed the utmost

instructions upon this point, I did not venture to throw out any opinions for his consideration, and therefore thought it most prudent not to dwell upon the Subject. With respect to the Negroes,[5] Mr Hamilton seemed partly to acquiesce in my reasoning upon this point,[6] and added that this matter did not strike him as an object of such importance as it had appeared to other members of this government. As to the river St. Croix, he acknowledged his personal belief that our statement of its position would, upon inquiry, be found accurate.[7]

---

readiness, on the part of this government to consent to any conditions with respect to the Posts on the Lakes, which Great Britain may deem essential to the security of any interests commercial or political, which might be considered as likely to be affected by the cession of those posts. For this purpose they would enter into any precise stipulations, by which the number of the troops to be stationed in the forts (if they were suffered to exist) might be limited. They would also enter into any engagements with Great Britain for fixing and ascertaining the nature and extent of the military force to be mutually maintained on the respective shores of the Lakes, and of the naval force on the Lakes themselves. And farther they would consent to any measures which the government of Canada might think necessary to the security and protection, of the persons and property of British Subjects engaged in the fur-trade, in the prosecution of their commerce either on the lakes, or in the communications between the different lakes" (PRO: F.O., Series 4, Vol. 16, Part I).

5. The American slaves carried off at the conclusion of the war by the British army.

6. Hammond's "reasoning upon this point" is described in a letter which he wrote to Lord Grenville on December 19, 1791: "I shall state that the letter (and I firmly believe the spirit) of the treaty of peace cannot be supposed to apply to any other description of Negroes than such as were the actual property of the inhabitants of the United States, at the period of the cessation of hostilities—that, of the Negroes, carried away from New York, under the permission and protection of Lord Dorchester, part may be presumed to have been captured during the war, and were consequently booty acquired by the rights of war: But that the principal part of them had fled to the British lines, in consequence of proclamations issued by the British Commanders in Chief (who were at the time in the exercise of legal authority in the Country) which promised to them freedom upon their joining the British army—and that this description of Negroes, thus emancipated, had acquired indefeasible rights of personal liberty, of which the British government was not competent to deprive them, by reducing them again to a state of slavery, and to the domination of their ancient masters" (PRO: F.O., Series 4, Vol. 11).

7. Concerning the boundary question, Samuel Flagg Bemis states: "The famous northeastern boundary dispute, arising over the doubtful identity of the River St. Croix,—stipulated as the boundary between the United States and New Brunswick, and from the source of which the line was to run north to the 'highlands of Nova Scotia,'—arose soon after the treaty had been ratified. The river is indicated on Mitchell's Map, used by the negotiators, but there proved to be no stream in that vicinity commonly called the St. Croix. The United States maintained that the Magaguadavic was the river really meant by the treaty. Great Britain asserted that it was the Schoodiac, nine miles west of the

On communicating to him the nature of the abstract, which I am preparing, of the several contraventions of the treaty by this country,[8] Mr Hamilton admitted their magnitude, and owned that they could not be vindicated upon any other principle than the inefficiency of the former Congress to enforce respect to its own regulations. Upon the subject of the British Creditors, which he considered as the chief ground of complaint on the part of Great Britain, he assured me that in all cases of this kind, which had been brought before the federal Courts, their determinations had been uniformly founded upon the treaty of peace, and had been consequently favorable to the British Creditors. He added that this principle would invariably guide all the future decisions of the federal Courts, and in proportion as their proceedings became more known and extended, the means of soliciting, and the certainty of obtaining, redress would be more obvious to the British Creditors in the presecution of their just demands. He thence inferred that this cause of complaint would be completely removed by the operation of the judiciary system.

In regard to other contraventions, in which from lapse of time and various causes, it might be impossible for this country to render substantial and individual justice, he concluded by saying that there appeared to him insurmountable difficulties in devising a mode of equivalent compensation either to the individual who had sustained the injury or to the nation at large, but he doubted not that this government would consent to any reasonable and practicable method of settling this point, if any such could be proposed.

In treating of the commercial arrangements between the two countries, Mr Hamilton readily admitted the importance of the British Commerce to the United States, and expressed his sanguine hopes that some system might be established mutually satisfactory to both countries. He did not fail to urge with much force and emphasis the anxiety of this country to obtain a small participation in the carrying

---

Magaguadavic. The disputed area comprised between 7,000 and 8,000 square miles at this time" (*Jay's Treaty, a Study in Commerce and Diplomacy* [New York, 1923], 96, note 11).

8. See note 3. On December 19, 1791, Hammond wrote to Jefferson that he was preparing "an abstract of the circumstances that appear to me contraventions, on the part of the United States, of the fourth, fifth, and sixth articles" of the treaty of peace (*ASP, Foreign Relations*, I, 193). Hammond's abstract was not sent to Jefferson until March 5, 1792. It is printed in *ASP, Foreign Relations*, I, 193–200.

trade with the West Indies, and the expediency of granting it; subject
nevertheless to such restrictions and regulations as Great Britain
might require to limit the size and tonnage of the vessels employed
in the trade, and to prevent the ships of the United States from interfering in the exportation to Europe of the productions of the British
West India Islands. I listened to him with attention, but studiously
avoided dropping any hint which might incline him to entertain the
belief that Great Britain would ever consent to any modification of
the system which she has so steadily and advantageously pursued in
relation to the carrying trade, and to the intercourse of other nations
with her colonies.[9]

These were the principal topics of our conversation. In one part
of it I took the liberty of inquiring of Mr Hamilton, when Mr Jefferson's report, on the relative situation of the commerce of the United
States with other powers, might be expected to appear.[10] He answered
that he believed, Mr Jefferson had, since my arrival in this country,
abandoned his intention of making any such report.

9. In Hammond's "Particular Instructions" he had been informed that the
anticipated request of the Americans to trade with the British West Indies on
the same basis as before the American Revolution should not "be admitted even
as a Subject of Negociation" (Mayo, *Instructions to British Ministers*, 12).

10. On February 23, 1791, the House of Representatives requested Jefferson
to report to Congress on "the nature and extent of the privileges and restrictions
of the commercial intercourse of the United States with foreign nations, and
such measures as he shall think proper to be adopted for the improvement of
the commerce and navigation of the same" (*Journal of the House*, I, 388).
In a letter to the Speaker of the House of Representatives, dated February 23,
1793, Jefferson explained the delay in presenting his report: "The report was
accordingly prepared during the ensuing recess ready to be delivered at their
next session. . . . It was thought possible at that time, however, that some
changes might take place in the existing state of Things, which might call for
corresponding changes in measures. I took the liberty of mentioning this in a
letter to the Speaker of the House of Representatives, to express an opinion that
a suspension of proceedings thereon for a time, might be expedient, and to
propose retaining the Report 'till the present session . . ." (letterpress copy,
Thomas Jefferson Papers, Library of Congress). Jefferson then requested a
second postponement, to which the House agreed (*Journal of the House*, I, 718).
The report in final form was not delivered to Congress until December 16, 1793
(*ASP, Foreign Relations*, I, 300–04).

## To Thomas Jefferson [1]

[Philadelphia, January 1, 1792]

Mr. Hamilton presents his Compliments to Mr. Jefferson. Being
engaged in making a comparative statement of the Trade between the

U S & France & between the U S & G Britain; [2] and being desirous of rendering it as candid as possible Mr. H will be obliged to Mr. Jefferson to point out to him the instances, in which the Regulations of France have made discriminations in favour of the U States, as compared with other foreign Powers. Those of Great Britain appear by its statutes which are in the hands of Mr. H; but he is not possessed of the General Commercial Regulations of France.

Mr. H also wishes to be informed whether the Arret of the 9th of May 1789 mentioned by Mr. J in the Notes to his Table [3] be the same with the Ordinance of the Governor General of St Domingo [4] which is at the end of the Collection of Arrets which Mr. J was so obliging as to lend to Mr. H—which is *of that Date.*

## Sunday January 1st 1792

AL, Thomas Jefferson Papers, Library of Congress.

1. On December 23, 1791, Jefferson sent to George Washington a comparative table of commercial restrictions imposed by England and France both in Europe and in the western hemisphere. On the same date Jefferson sent a copy of the table to H (Jefferson to Washington, December 23, 1791, letterpress copy, Thomas Jefferson Papers, Library of Congress; Jefferson to H, December 23, 1791).

2. H may be referring to his "View of the Commercial Regulations of France and Great Britain in Reference to the United States," 1792–1793.

3. In Jefferson's table, which is entitled "Footing of the commerce of the United States with France & England, & with French and English American colonies," note "g" reads as follows: "There is a general law of France prohibiting foreign flour in their Islands, with a suspending power to their governors, in cases of necessity. An Arret of May. 9. 1789. by their governor makes it free 'till 1794. Aug. 1. and in fact is generally free there" (Jefferson to Washington, December 23, 1791, letterpress copy, Thomas Jefferson Papers, Library of Congress).

On January 4, 1792, Jefferson wrote to Washington that on inquiry he had learned that "the colonial Arret of 1789, permitting a free importation of our Flour till 1793 . . . was revoked in France . . . and that the permission to carry Flour to the three usual ports . . . was immediately renewed by the Governor [of Santo Domingo]. Whether this has been regularly kept up by renewed Arrets during the present troubles he cannot say, but is sure that in practice it has never been discontinued, and that not by contraband, but openly and legally, as is understood. . . . This correction of the notes I took the liberty of laying before you, with the table containing a comparitive view of our commerce with France and England, I have thought it my duty to make" (letterpress copy, Thomas Jefferson Papers, Library of Congress).

4. "Ordonnance concernant la liberté du commerce pour la partie du Sud de Saint-Domingue," May 9, 1789, as well as the *arrêt* revoking this *ordonnance,* may be found in Saintoyant, *La Colonisation Française pendant la Revolution,* I, 452–53.

## Conversation with George Hammond [1]

[Philadelphia, January 2–9, 1792]

I have received a letter from Lieutenant Governor Clarke,[2] in which he intimates to me his apprehensions that much inconvenience might arise, if any attempt should be made to enforce an act of the last sessions of Congress for "giving effect to the laws of the United States within the State of Vermont." [3] By this act the residence of a Collector of the customs is established at Alburgh, within the district now occupied by his Majesty's forces.

In compliance with Lieutenant Governor Clarke's request, I have represented this matter to Mr Hamilton, who assured me that, at the time of fixing upon this particular place for the residence of the Collector of the customs, this government was ignorant of its being within the district then in possession of the King's troops; but, as soon as the mistake had been explained, it had been determined to suspend the operation of that part of the act, to which I alluded.[4]

From this circumstance I took occasion to suggest to the Secretary of the Treasury that, since the important points, relative to the Treaty of Peace, were likely to come into discussion in the way of negociation, it was not expedient to incur the risque of the two Governments being committed either by measures of this nature or by the enterprizes of individuals. In the propriety of this sentiment Mr Hamilton perfectly concurred.

D, PRO: F.O., Series 4, Vol. 14, Part I.
1. This conversation has been taken from Hammond to Lord Grenville, January 9, 1792, Dispatch No. 4.
2. Major General Alured Clarke was lieutenant governor of Lower Canada.
3. "An Act giving effect to the laws of the United States within the state of Vermont" (1 *Stat.* 197–98 [March 2, 1791]).
4. On May 2, 1792, Congress in Section 19 of "An Act for raising a farther sum of money for the protection of the frontiers, and for other purposes therein mentioned" settled this matter as follows:
"*And be it further enacted,* That the President of the United States be, and hereby is authorized to appoint such place within the district of Vermont to be the port of entry and delivery within the said district, as he may deem expedient, any thing in the act, intituled 'An act giving effect to the laws of the United States within the state of Vermont,' to the contrary notwithstanding." (1 *Stat.* 263.)
On July 17, 1792, Dispatch No. 31, Hammond again wrote to Grenville on this subject:

"Having received information from Lieutenant Governor Clarke of some attempts that had been made by the government of Vermont to exercise legal jurisdiction within the territory of the Posts now occupied by his Majesty's troops, and of consequent acts of violence which had been committed therein under the authority of that state, I lost no time in communicating to Mr Jefferson the circumstances that had occurred, in a letter, of which, and of his answer, I have the honor of inclosing copies.

"As I doubt not that a particular account of these transactions has been already transmitted to his Majesty's Ministers, it is needless for me to repeat them to your Lordship. It is however proper to observe, in addition to the assurances contained in Mr Jefferson's letter, that both Mr Hamilton and General Knox have expressed to me the most pointed, unequivocal disapprobation of the violent conduct of the state of Vermont, and their conviction that it is the duty and interest of the United States to use every effort to prevent a repetition of it. I could farther collect from my conversations with these Gentlemen—that the general government retains a considerable degree of resentment at the artifice which was practised upon it last year, by the State of Vermont, in pointing out the town of Alburgh as a proper port of entry for the United States within the district of Vermont—and that the present violence of that state is considered as a continuance of the same system of deception, which, having been baffled in the attempt before alluded to, is now employed to involve the United States in a more direct and hostile opposition to Great Britain. I learn from Mr Hamilton that the port of entry for the district of Vermont is at present fixed at the Southern extremity of *Isle Hero* in Lake Champlain, to the Southward of any of the posts now in the possession of his Majesty's arms."
(PRO: F.O., Series 4, Vol. 16, Part 1.)

## From Baron von Steuben [1]

N:Y: ce 2 de janv: 1792.

Agrees mon Cher Ami, Les voeux sincere d'un Coeur qui vous aime et vous Estime. Le success de tout vos Operations fait ma Consolation dans ma Sollitude. Mais mon cher Hamilton que Vous dirai-je sur la Sensibilite que je ne Scauroit Etouffer quand je voi les Armes des Etats Unis, si respecté dans la Guerre contre une puissance formidable, Aujourdhui disgracie par des Cohortes des sauvages. Je plains le digne Sinclair de tout mon Coeur, S'il a commis une faute c'est celle, d'entreprendre une Operation militaire quelconque avec de tells Utensiles.[2]

J'ecrivis une lettre tres longue que je comptait de Vous Envoyer, elle est devant moi—mais reflexion fait je croie quil vaut mieux de me taire, j'usqu'a ce qu'on me demande mon Avis, et je vous fait grâce de la lecture de mes reverie.

J'apprehende Cependant qu'on Envisage ce desastre avec plus d'indiference quil merite. Sans m'arretté sur le boucherie de tant des hommes, Sur les depense considerables, sans les consequences fasheuses que nous avons a apréhender, pour nos etablissement sur les frontiers je crains les impression que ces malheureuses afaires ont fait sur l'esprit des parties Belligerante. Les Cohortes des sauvages deviendront des héros rédoutable pour nous, et nos trouppes Continental actuel a moins quil ne sont entierement regenerer, ne seront plus fait pour la resistence.

Si nous voulons réparer le mal par L'Augmentation du nombre de tell troupes, nous accelleront notre perte, J'en suis aussi sure que de mon Existence. Plus que la masse serat grande, plus inevitable serat la confusion et plus Considerable la boucherie.

Croyez moi mon cher Ami, notre Présent Systheme Militaire est faux dans tout ses Principes—vos troupes ne sont que des hommes deguisé en Soldat. Il n'y a ni ordre, ni discipline, Enfin ils sont si peut exercé dans leurs metier, que la plus part n'ont jamais apris a Ammorier Leurs fusils, et les Officiers de ces mêmes Corps m'ont assuré, que de tout ces hommes qui ont été massacré dans les deux derniere defaites,[3] il n'y avait pas dix qui avait jamais tire deux Coup de fusil a Cartouches. Enfin ils n'ont ni articles de Guerre, ni reglement en Ordonence. Car ceux qui existe ne vaille rien ni L'un ni L'autre, Les premieres etoit une mauvaise imitation de la milice Anglaise,[4] et le second n'etoit pas du tout Calcules pour le Genre de Guerre dans lequel nous sommes engagé maintenant.[5] Il y faut changer J'usqu'a la formation, meme J'us[qu'a] L'armement des trouppes tant a pied qu'a cheval pour mettre notre militaire en Etat de combattre Les indiens avec avantage.

Mais comme il faut du tems pour de tell arrangement, et quil s'agit d'arreter le torrent pour le présent, il faut remettre le salut de la Patrie entre les mains de la milice de nos frontieres. Aussi peut que je me promet de Leur discipline, il en ont certainement autant que nos trouppe continentale. Elle sont plus fait aux faitiques, comme chasseur il connoissent au moins de faire Usage de Leurs fusil, ceque les trouppes continentales n'ont point du tout apris.

Detromper de cette ilusion que les trouppes (qu'on Apelloit sans aucune Raison) reglé, leur serviroit de secour et dans le besoin de point d'appui, il combatterons mieux quand ils ne peuvent compter que sur Leurs propre Courrages.

Quoi qu'il en faut bien que J'ai dit tout ceque je pense sur ce miserable Etablissement militaire je suis aller plus loin quil n'etoit mon intention.

Une Entrevue avec vous entrainerat plus de detaille sur cette matiere; ma santé ne me permet pas de L'Esperer sitot: Dailleur comme Vous n'etez pas Ministre de Guerre, ces arrangement ne sont pas de Votre Province, et quand a moi j'ai bien tort de donner mon Avis que personne ne Se Soucie de Scavoir.

Mes Respect a Mad: Hamilton et une heureuse anné a tout Votre famille.

Je suis avec les sentimens que Vous me Connoissez   sincerement
Le Votre                                                          Steuben [6]

ALS, Hamilton Papers, Library of Congress.
1. H had become friendly with von Steuben during the American Revolution when the baron was inspector general of the Continental Army. At the close of the war von Steuben settled in New York and engaged in the development of a large tract of land north of Utica which the New York legislature granted to him in 1786.
2. Von Steuben is referring to the defeat of troops under the command of Major General Arthur St. Clair by the Indians in November, 1791. See "Conversation with George Hammond," December 15–16, 1791, note 2.
3. Von Steuben is referring to Brigadier General Josiah Harmar's disastrous campaign against the Miami (Maumee) Indians in November, 1790, and St. Clair's defeat in 1791.
4. See Rules and Articles for the better Government of the Troops Raised, or to be raised and kept in pay by and at the expence of the United States of America (Philadelphia: John Dunlap, 1776). See also JCC, V, 670, 788–87.
5. Von Steuben is presumably referring to the Regulations for the Order and Discipline of the Troops of the United States (Philadelphia: Styner and Cist, 1779), which he had drawn up in 1779. The Continental Congress had adopted these regulations, familiarly known as "The Blue Book," on March 29, 1779. They remained the official regulations until 1812.
6. On the back of this letter H wrote "acknowleged;" the acknowledgment, however, has not been found.

## Treasury Department Circular to the Collectors of the Customs

Treasury Department,
January 2, 1792.

Sir,
It will prevent injury from accidents if the Collectors of the Customs, in all cases of the delivery of a Register to be cancelled, shall cut a hole in the like manner as is directed in the circular letter

of the 21st of September last, in regard to the Registers therein mentioned.

All certificates of Registry delivered up at any office, wherever issued, are hereafter to be transmitted to the Treasury, with an endorsement of the time and place of delivery and the cause of surrender, whether it be a transfer of property or any other.

Having in consequence of enquiry, instructed several of the Collectors that the annual compensations allowed in the 54th section of the last Collection Law [1] to themselves or the Surveyors might be paid out of the monies in their hands, I think it best to make the instruction circular. The officer entitled to the compensation will make out an account for the compensation due up to the first instant, which may be discharged out of the monies arising from Impost and Tonnage; and thereafter may be so paid quarterly. The commencement of the allowance is on the first day of October 1790.

The Bank of the United States being now in operation I have to desire that you will extend my instructions of the 22d of September 1789,[2] in regard to receiving the Cash Notes and Post Notes of the Bank of North America, to the Cash Notes and Post Notes of the Bank of the United States, which are to be received and exchanged in like manner. The Directors have been requested by me to transmit you the signatures of the President and Cashier, as was done in the case of the Bank of North America.

Circumstances of the utmost importance render it necessary that the quarterly returns up to the 31st of December 1791, be made with all possible expedition, particularly those relative to Impost and Tonnage.

I am, Sir,   Your obedient servant,                A Hamilton

The Collectors of the Customs.

LS, to Jedediah Huntington, MS Division, New York Public Library; LS, to Charles Lee, Charles Lee Papers, Library of Congress; L[S], to Benjamin Lincoln, RG 36, Collector of Customs at Boston, Letters from the Treasury, 1772–1818, Vol. 6, National Archives; LS, to Jeremiah Olney, Rhode Island Historical Society, Providence; LS, to William Webb, United States Finance Miscellany, Treasury Circulars, Library of Congress; LS, Office of the Secretary, United States Treasury Department; copy, RG 56, Circulars of the Office of the Secretary, "Set T," National Archives; copy, United States Finance Miscellany, Treasury Circulars, Library of Congress.
    1. This is a mistake, for H is referring to Section 53 of "An Act to provide

more effectually for the collection of the duties imposed by law on goods, wares and merchandise imported into the United States, and on the tonnage of ships or vessels" (1 *Stat.* 171–72 [August 4, 1790]). For an explanation of the confusion in the section numbers, see H to Richard Harison, April 26, 1791, note 2.

2. See "Treasury Department Circular to the Collectors of the Customs," September 22, 1789.

## From William Ellery

*Newport [Rhode Island] January 3, 1792.* "The Light House has been repaired. . . .[1] I wish for your opinion on this Question. Is a master of a vessel who is convicted of swearing falsly thereby disqualified from acting in future in that capacity?"

LC, Newport Historical Society, Newport, Rhode Island.
  1. See Ellery to H, July 18, November 11, 1791.

## From James Reynolds [1]

[Philadelphia, January 3, 1792]

Received Philadelphia January 3. 179[2] [2] of Alexander Hamilton four hundred dollars in full of all demands

James Reynolds

"Reynolds Pamphlet," August 31, 1797.
  1. This receipt is printed as document No. VI in the appendix of the "Reynolds Pamphlet," August 31, 1797.
  This was the second of two payments of blackmail made by H to Reynolds. The first payment was made on December 22, 1791. For background to this affair, see Reynolds to H, December 15, 17, 19, 1791; H to Reynolds, December 15, 1791; Maria Reynolds to H, December 15, 1791.
  2. In the pamphlet this date is incorrectly given as 1791.

## From Otho H. Williams

[*Baltimore, January 3, 1792*] Sends "a small account of expences incidental to the receipt and delivery of twelve Bolts of Canvass, which by your order were sent from Boston to this place, and from hence to Norfolk." Suggests that official papers be sent by water rather than by the post.

ADf, RG 53, "Old Correspondence," Baltimore Collector, National Archives.

# To Tench Coxe [1]

Treasury Department
Jany. 4 1792

sir

It is the intention of the President of the United States, verbally communicated to me that the salary [of the keeper of the Light House Cape Henry] [2] shall be equal to the keeper of the light House on the Delaware. [3]

In communicating this you will explain that the first salary proceeded from mistake.

I am with much Consideration    sir    Your Obed Servt

A Hamilton

[PS    Inclosed are the papers concerning the additions made to the Light House Establishment Cape Henry with the Presidents approbation.]

Tench Coxe Esq

LS, RG 26, Lighthouse Letters Received, "Segregated" Lighthouse Records, Hamilton, National Archives.
1. Coxe was Assistant Secretary of the Treasury.
2. The bracketed portions of this letter are in the handwriting of H.
3. Abraham Hargis.

# Report on Dried and Pickled Fish Exported and Entitled to Drawback

Treasury Department Jany. 5. 1792.
[Communicated on January 6, 1792] [1]

[To the President of the Senate]

The Secretary of the Treasury in obedience to the order of the Senate of the 28th. Ultimo. [2]

Respectfully Reports.

That it appears, as in the statement No. 1 herewith transmitted, [3] that the allowance in lieu of a drawback on dried and pickled fish, which was exported prior to the 31st. December 1790, amounts to 10,582 dollars, that the quantum of bounty actually paid on the exportation of dried and pickled fish from the 1st. of January 1791 to the 30th September last so far as the returns from the Collectors have been received appears as in the statement No. 2,[4] to be 3,934 dollars and 55 cents, but that the deficiencies of the Custom House returns render it impossible at this time correctly to exhibit either the amount of what has accrued prior to the 30th September last, or in the course of the year 1791.

The Secretary conceiving it may tend to elucidate the subject under consideration, also transmits the statement No. 3,[5] of the drawback on the foreign fish exported since the commencement of the impost Act of 1789 [6] and the statement No. 4 [7] of the bounty on dried and pickled fish of the United States which is known to have accrued, but which is not yet payable, together with a Note [8] of the expences incidental to the exportation of the fish comprehended in the four statements, and he begs leave to remark that the return of exports for 13½ Months ending on the 30th September 1790 contains 378,721 quintals of dried fish and 36,804 barrels of pickled fish, including as well the produce of foreign fisheries, as of the bank, bay and river fisheries of the United States.

Alexander Hamilton
Secy of the Treasury.

Copy, RG 46, Reports from Heads of Departments, Vol. 1, National Archives.
1. *Annals of Congress,* III, 56. The communicating letter may be found in RG 46, Second Congress, 1791–1793, Reports of the Secretary of the Treasury, National Archives.
2. The Senate *"Ordered,* That the Secretary of the Treasury be requested to certify the quantum of allowance in lieu of drawback on exported, dried, and pickled fish, which hath been paid under 'the act for laying a duty on goods, wares, and merchandises, imported into the United States,' of the 4th of July, 1789. And also the quantum of bounty paid on the exportation of dried or pickled fish, under 'the act for making further provision for the payment of the debts of the United States,' of the 10th of August, 1790" (*Annals of Congress,* III, 53).
3. Statement No. 1 is entitled "Statement of the Quantum of allowance in lieu of a Drawback on exported Dried and Pickled Fish from the commencement of the Act to 31st. December 1790." This enclosure, dated January 3, 1792, and signed by Joseph Nourse, may be found in RG 46, Second Congress, 1791–1793, Reports of the Secretary of the Treasury, National Archives. It is printed in *ASP, Commerce and Navigation,* I, 48.
4. Statement No. 2 is entitled "Statement of the Quantum of Bounty paid on the exportation of Dried and Pickled Fish under the Act of 4th. August 1790 from the 1st. January 1791 to the 30th September following (so far as Ac-

counts have been rendered)." This enclosure, dated January 3, 1792, and signed
by Joseph Nourse, may be found in RG 46, Second Congress, 1791–1793, Reports of the Secretary of the Treasury, National Archives. It is printed in *ASP,
Commerce and Navigation*, I, 49.

5. Statement No. 3 is entitled "Statement shewing the number of Quintals
and Barrels of Dried and Pickled Foreign Fish exported from the United States
with the amount of the Drawback allowed thereon." This enclosure, dated
January 3, 1792, and signed by Joseph Nourse, may be found in RG 46, Second
Congress, 1791–1793, Reports of the Secretary of the Treasury, National
Archives. It is printed in *ASP, Commerce and Navigation*, I, 49.

6. See Section 3 of "An Act for laying a Duty on Goods, Wares, and Merchandises imported into the United States" (1 *Stat.* 24–27 [July 4, 1789]).

7. Statement No. 4 is entitled "Statement shewing the number of Quintals
and barrells of dried and pickled Fish exported from the United States, on which
no bounty is payable until six months after exportation." This enclosure, which
is misdated "Jany 3. 1791," may be found in RG 46, Second Congress, 1791–
1793, Reports of the Secretary of the Treasury, National Archives. It is printed
in *ASP, Commerce and Navigation*, I, 49.

8. A note at the end of this letter reads as follows:
"Note. The following expences incidental to the exportation of dried and
pickled fish appear by calculation to be as near the amount as can be ascertained. Vizt.

|  |  |  |  |  | Dolls. | Cents. |
|---|---|---|---|---|---|---|
| For weighing | 291,721½ quintals at 2 cents ℔ Cwt. | | | | 5,834. | 43 |
| Inspection of | Do. | Do. | 1½ Do | | 4,375. | 82. |
| Do | | 17.672½ barrels at 1½ Cent ℔ Bbl. | | | 265. | 08. |
|  |  |  |  | Dollars | 10,475. | 33." |

## *From Charles Lee*

[*Alexandria, Virginia, January 7, 1792.* On January 17, 1792,
Hamilton wrote to George Washington: "The Secretary of the
Treasury has the honor to communicate to the President a letter of
the 7th. of January 1792. from the Collector of Alexandria." *Letter
not found.*]

## *To Jeremiah Olney*

Treasury Department Jany 8th 1792

Sir,

I have received your letter relative to the case of the Brig Polly
from Cape Francois and Charleston.[1] There is no doubt that under
the existing collection law, goods of the growth and manufacture of
the United States can be relanded after exportation and they are not
chargeable with duty on their importation into the United States as

you will perceive by the 24th Section of the Act.[2] I apprehend it is the 60th Section of the *late* Collection law [3] to which you must have recured, which however was only intended to prevent a fraudulent relanding which should enable the owner to procure the drawback tho' the Articles were brought back and consumed in the United States.

I am Sir   Your obedt Servt                    Alex Hamilton

P.S. The prohibition to reland does not appear to me to apply to a case in which a vessel has *bona fide* performed her voyage to a *foreign port* and returned from thence. This fact however ought to be well ascertained.[4]

Jereh. Olney Esqr
Providence Rhode Island

LS, Rhode Island Historical Society, Providence; LS, Rhode Island Historical Society; copy, RG 56, Letters to the Collector at Providence, National Archives; copy, RG 56, Letters to Collectors at Small Ports, "Set G," National Archives.
    1. See Olney to H, December 29, 1791.
    2. H is referring to "An Act to provide more effectually for the collection of the duties imposed by law on goods, wares and merchandise imported into the United States, and on the tonnage of ships or vessels." Section 24 reads:
    "*Be it further enacted,* That report and entry thereof shall be made as in other cases of goods, wares and merchandise imported from a foreign port or place, and proof by oath of the person or persons having knowledge of the facts, shall be made to the satisfaction of the collector of the district, with whom such entry shall be, jointly with the naval officer, if there be a naval officer, or alone if there be no naval officer, that the said articles had been exported from the United States, as of their growth, product or manufacture, and of the time when, by whom, in what ship or vessel, and or what port or place they were so exported; and if the said collector shall be other than the collector of the district from which the said articles shall have been exported, a certificate of the latter shall be produced to the former, testifying the exportation thereof in conformity to the proof aforesaid; whereupon a permit shall and may be granted for landing the same: *Provided,* That if the said certificate cannot be immediately produced, and if the proof otherwise required shall be made, and if bond shall be given, with one or more sureties to the satisfaction of the collector of the district within which the said articles are intended to be landed, in a sum equal to what the duties would be on the said articles, if they were not of the growth, produce or manufacture of the United States; with condition that the said certificate shall be produced within the term of four months, it shall be lawful for the said collector to grant a permit for the landing of the said articles, in like manner as if the said certificate had been produced." (1 *Stat.* 162–63 [August 4, 1790].)
    3. For Section 60 of "An Act to provide more effectually for the collection of the duties imposed by law on goods, wares and merchandise imported into

the United States, and on the tonnage of ships or vessels" (1 *Stat.* 174–75 [August 4, 1790]), see Olney to H, December 29, 1791.
4. The postscript is in H's handwriting.

## To John Davidson

Treasury Department
January 9th 1792

Sir

I have recieved your letter of the 27th ultimo [1] inclosing four paid draughts of the Treasurer No 1662 1663, 1664 and 1665, amounting together one thousand eight hundred Dollars. These draughts being directed to Tench Francis Cashier of the Bank of North America, they been taken up by you in an informal way, which being a deviation from the rules of the Treasury must be avoided in future.

My Circular letter of the 2d. instant authorizes you to change the compensation agreeable to the Collection Law [2] in your quarterly account.

I am Sir   Your Obedt Servant                      A Hamilton

John Davidson Esqr
Collector Annapolis.

Copy, RG 56, Letters to and from the Collectors at Bridgetown and Annapolis, National Archives; copy, RG 56, Letters to Collectors at Small Ports, "Set G," National Archives.
1. Letter not found.
2. "An Act to provide more effectually for the collection of the duties imposed by law on goods, wares and merchandise imported into the United States, and on the tonnage of ships or vessels" (1 *Stat.* 145–78 [August 4, 1790]).

## From William Ellery

*Newport* [*Rhode Island*] *January 9, 1792.* "This will be accompd. by a Statement of the case of Josh. Elliott master of the Sloop Industry from St Martins and destined for the district of New Haven. . . . It appears to me . . . that it was the intention of the Legislature that the manifest should be made out before the vessels departure from a foreign port for the United States, but as this is not expressly required by Law,[1] permit me to raise a question, and to ask of you a solution of it. Suppose that I should have sufficient evidence that a manifest produced to me was on board a vessel before She arrived within four leagues of the coast of the United States; but was not on board at the time of her departure from a foreign port or place for the United States, would it be proper that a prosecution should be commenced against the master of such vessel? . . ." [2]

LC, Newport Historical Society, Newport, Rhode Island.
   1. Legislative requirements for ships' manifests appear in Sections 9, 11, and 16 of "An Act to provide more effectually for the collection of the duties imposed by law on goods, wares and merchandise imported into the United States, and on the tonnage of ships or vessels" (1 Stat. 145–78 [August 4, 1790]).
   2. Ellery endorsed this letter "Answered." H's reply has not been found.

## To Sharp Delany [1]

*Treasury Department, January 11, 1792.* "I think it proper that you make an immediate demand of the difference between foreign Tonnage and foreign Impost and those duties of Tonnage & impost which have been paid at the several entries of the Brig Lydia, which have taken place since the 8th of October 1790. . . . It is my intention to write to Richd. Carrington Esquire of Richmond in Virginia upon the subject of Mr Gernon's citizenship. . . ." [2]

LS, Bureau of Customs, Philadelphia; copy, RG 56, Letters to Collectors at Small Ports, "Set G," National Archives; copy, RG 56, Letters to the Collector at Philadelphia, National Archives.
   1. Delany was collector of customs at Philadelphia.
   2. No letter to Richard Carrington on the question of Richard Gernon's citizenship has been found. Gernon subsequently became a procurement agent for the French government.

## From Charles Lee

Alexandria [Virginia] 11th. Janry. 1792

Sir!
   Due pains were taken by me in causing to be published the several parts of the last Collection Law,[1] which were necessary to be known to the Merchants, for regulating their conduct. The 9th. and 10th. Sections [2] are not accurately observed in scarcely any one instance; for the Manifest thereby required is generally made after the vessels

arrival to its port of destination. The account of the Cargo which the master brings from the place of shipment is always very imperfect, and so different from the Manifest required by Law as to most matters, that it deserves not be called a manifest. I have conceived that where there was no reason to suspect fraud the forfeiture ought not to be sought, as the manifest being produced conformable to the several particulars, the Revenue would sustain no damage. If however, more rigor ought to be observed in future, I should be glad to have your instruction.

The Coasting Law, being now under the consideration of Congress,[3] I take the liberty of suggesting that the doubts concerning fees may be all removed by attending to this principle, that each service in its self distinct should have its own compensation annexed to it. As the Law [4] now stands the Surveyor is entitled to an equal share of the fees under the Coasting Law. This I think ought to be altered, because the whole burden of the services in this Law mentioned is imposed upon the collector. The Surveyor performs no part of the duties, for which the fees are paid, is at no expense concerning them, and in this district the Surveyor refuses to pay any portion of the Stationary used in this branch of the business.

I hope that upon principles of Justice the Law will be altered, either by not allowing any part of these fees to the Surveyor, or by compelling him to perform his share of the duties and contributing his share of the expense.

When I consider the little service and the little responsibility of a Surveyor, I have been led to believe that their compensation would be very adequate, without recurring to an equal share of the coasting fees.

I am Sir!   with the greatest respect   Your most Obedt. Servt.

Charles Lee, Collector.

Copy, RG 56, Letters to and from the Collector at Alexandria, National Archives.

1. "An Act to provide more effectually for the collection of the duties imposed by law on goods, wares and merchandise imported into the United States, and on the tonnage of ships or vessels" (1 Stat. 145–78 [August 4, 1790]).

2. Sections 9 and 10 of the Collection Law read as follows:

"Sec. 9. And be it further enacted, That from and after the first day of October next, no goods, wares or merchandise shall be brought into the United States from any foreign port or place, in any ship or vessel belonging in the whole or in part to a citizen or citizens, inhabitant or inhabitants of the United States, unless the master or person having the charge or command of such ship or vessel shall have on board a manifest or manifests in writing, signed by such master or other person, containing the name or names of the port or ports, place or places where the goods in such manifest or manifests mentioned, shall have been respectively taken on board, and the port or ports, place or places within the United States for which the same are respectively consigned or destined, and the name and built of such ship or vessel, and the true admeasurement or tonnage thereof according to the register of the same, together with the name of the master or other person having the command or charge of such ship or vessel, and the port or place to which such ship or vessel truly belongs, and a just and particular account of all the cargo so laden or taken on board, whether in packages or stowed loose, together with the marks and numbers, in words at length, of the said packages respectively, with a description of each, as whether leaguer, pipe, butt, puncheon, hogshead, barrel, case, bale, pack, truss, chest, box, bundle, or other cask or package, describing the same by its usual name or denomination.

"Sec. 10. *And be it further enacted,* That if any goods, wares or merchandise shall, after the said first day of October next, be imported or brought into the United States, in any ship or vessel whatever, belonging in the whole or in part to a citizen or citizens, inhabitant or inhabitants of the United States, from any foreign port or place, without such manifest or manifests in writing, or shall not be included and described therein, or shall not agree therewith, in every such case the master or other person having the command or charge of such ship or vessel, shall forfeit a sum of money equal to the value of such goods, not included in such manifest or manifests: *Provided always,* That if it shall be made appear to the satisfaction of the collector, naval officer and surveyor, or the major part of them, where those offices are established at any port, or to the satisfaction of the collector alone, where either of the other of the said offices is not established, or to the satisfaction of the court in which a trial shall be had concerning such forfeiture, that no part of the cargo of such ship or vessel had been unshipped, after it was taken on board, except such as shall have been specified and accounted for in the report of the master or other person having the charge or command of such ship or vessel, and that the manifest or manifests had been lost or mislaid, without fraud or collusion, or that the same was or were defaced by accident, or incorrect by mistake, in every such case the forfeiture aforesaid shall not be incurred." (1 *Stat.* 155–56.)

3. On November 30, 1791, "Mr. [Benjamin] Goodhue, from the committee appointed, presented, according to order, a bill concerning the registering or recording of ships or vessels; which was received, and read the first time. On motion, The said bill was read the second time, and ordered to be committed to a Committee of the Whole House . . ." (*Journal of the House,* I, 465).

4. "An Act for Registering and Clearing Vessels, Regulating the Coasting Trade, and for other purposes" (1 *Stat.* 55–65 [September 1, 1789]). Section 31 of this act reads in part as follows:

"The whole amount of which fees shall be accounted for by the collector, and where there is a collector, naval officer and surveyor, shall be equally divided between the said officers, and where there is no naval officer, between the collector and surveyor, and where there is only a collector, he shall receive the whole amount thereof, and where there is more than one surveyor in any district, each of them shall receive his proportionable part of such fees as shall arise in the port for which he is appointed. *Provided always,* That in all cases where the tonnage of any ship or vessel shall be ascertained by any person specially appointed for that purpose, as is herein before directed, that such person shall be allowed and paid by the collector a reasonable compensation for the same, out of the fees aforesaid, before any distribution thereof as aforesaid."

# From Joseph Whipple

*Portsmouth, New Hampshire, January 12, 1792.* "I had the honor to receive your letter of the 20th. of last Month [1] together with three Commissions for the Mates of the Revenue Cutter. That for Mr. Flagg the first mate I now return he having left the Service of which information was given in my letter of the 15th. Ulto. . . ." [2]

LC, RG 36, Collector of Customs at Portsmouth, Letters Sent, 1791–1792, Vol. 3, National Archives.
  1. Letter not found.
  2. See also Whipple to H, October 7, 1791.

# To Otho H. Williams

Treasury Department
January 12. 1792.

Sir

The charges on the canvas intended for the Maryland Cutter [1] appear to be proper objects of debit to that vessel. The sum of one dollar and fourteen Cents may therefore be charged in her disbursements.

You will perceive that my Circular letter of the 2d instant will prevent future expence of postage to the Collectors in receiving Registers from one another.

I am, Sir,   Your Most Obed Servant.          Alex Hamilton

Otho H Williams Esqr.
Collr. Baltimore.

LS, Columbia University Libraries.
  1. See Williams to H, January 3, 1792.

# To William Ellery

[*Philadelphia, January 13, 1792.* On January 30, 1792, Ellery wrote to Hamilton and referred to "your letter of the 13th. of this month." *Letter not found.*]

# To Thomas Jefferson

Treasury Department
January 13. 1792

Sir

In a conference with you, some time ago, I took occasion to mention the detention of the certificate of registry of a vessel of the United States in one of the French offices on occasion of a sale of the vessel.[1] Several new instances having since occurred, I find it necessary to trouble you more particularly upon the subject. As the detention of these papers has taken place, as well in a port of France as in those of the colonies, it will require notice both in the home and in the colonial department.

The instrument in contemplation is of manifest importance to the navigation of the United States, and the legislature has therefore ordained that a heavy penalty shall follow the return of a master of a vessel to th⟨is coun⟩try, who shall fail within eight days to surrender the certificate of registry belonging to a vessel lately under his command, which shall have been shipwrecked or sold abroad. The payment of this penalty, in the event of its being incurred, is secured by an obligation taken at the granting of the certificate, and some of those bonds are now in a situation, wherein the la⟨w⟩ requires them to be put in suit.[2] The plea of detention by a foreign power, whenever it can be truly made, renders the penalty a hardship, and I am persuaded will recommend the measures necessary to prevent such inconveniences to your early attention.

I have the honor to be   Sir   Your obedt s⟨ervant⟩

Alexander ⟨Hamilton⟩

The honorable
The Secretary of State

LS, RG 59, Miscellaneous Letters, 1790–1799, National Archives.

1. See H to Jefferson, April 20, 1790.

2. Section 9 of "An Act for Registering and Clearing Vessels, Regulating the Coasting Trade, and for other purposes" reads in part as follows: ". . . That when the certificate of registry aforesaid shall be granted, sufficient security by bond, shall be given to the collector in behalf of the United States, by the

master and owner or owners, or by some other person or persons on his, her, or their behalf, such security to be approved of by the collector, in the penalties following, that is to say: if such ship or vessel shall be above the burthen of fifteen, and not exceeding fifty tons, in the penalty of four hundred dollars, if exceeding the burthen of fifty tons, and not exceeding one hundred tons, in the penalty of eight hundred dollars, if exceeding the burthen of one hundred tons, and not exceeding two hundred tons, in the penalty of twelve hundred dollars, if exceeding the burthen of two hundred tons, and not exceeding three hundred tons, in the penalty of sixteen hundred dollars, and if exceeding the burthen of three hundred tons, in the penalty of two thousand dollars. And the condition of every such bond shall be, that such certificate shall not be sold, lent or otherwise disposed of to any person or persons whomsoever, . . . and in case such ship or vessel shall be in any foreign port or place, or at sea, when such transfer of interest or property shall take place, the said master shall, within eight days after his arrival in any port or place within the United States, deliver up the said certificate to the collector of the district where he shall arrive . . ." (1 *Stat.* 57 [September 1, 1789]).

## From Oliver Wolcott, Junior

*Treasury Department, Comptroller's Office, January 13, 1792.* Submits "forms for regulating the payment of Drawbacks arising on the exportation of spirits distilled within the United States."

ADf, Connecticut Historical Society, Hartford.

## To Thomas Arnold [1]

[*Philadelphia, January 14, 1792.* The dealer's catalogue description of this letter reads: "Arnold's annual allowance as Surveyor." *Letter not found.*]

LS, sold by Stan V. Henkels, Jr., May 17, 1932, Lot 166.
   1. Arnold was the surveyor of the customs at East Greenwich, Rhode Island.

## To Otho H. Williams

Treasury Department
January 14 1792.

Sir

I am informed that a Brig which frequents Your port, and was, or is now the Hope, of Baltimore, is owned by a Mr Gernon. It is my wish to be informed whether it appears, and how, that Mr Gernon is a Citizen of the United States, how long he appears, by the

Register, to have owned the Hope, and whether she goes and comes between Your District and any one particular foreign port or island. There are some circumstances in the case of another vessel, said to belong to Mr Gernon,[1] which have attracted observation, and which induce me to wish for a particular knowledge of all circumstances that relate to the Brig Hope.

I am, Sir,   Your Most Obed Servant.                Alex Hamilton

Otho H Williams Esqr.
Baltimore.

LS, Columbia University Libraries.
    1. See H to Sharp Delany, January 11, 1792.


# To Roger Alden, Brockholst Livingston, Carlile Pollock, Guilian Verplanck, and Joshua Waddington

Philadelphia January 15
1792

Gentlemen

The mark of esteem, on the part of fellow Citizens, to whom I am attached by so many ties, which is announced in your letter of the 29 of December, is intitled to my affectionate acknowlegements.

I shall chearfully obey their wish as far as respects the taking of my Portrait; but I ask that they will permit it to appear unconnected with any incident of my political life. The simple representation of their fellow Citizen and friend will best accord with my feelings.

With true esteem & consideration   I have the honor to be   Gentlemen   Your Obed serv

ADf, Hamilton Papers, Library of Congress.


# From Thomas Jefferson

Philadelphia Jan. 15. 1792.

Sir

In answer to your favor of the 13th. I have the honor to inform you that the papers delivered to me on the subject of the Register of the sloop Polly [1] detained on her being sold at Port au-prince, were put into the hands of mr Bourne the Consul for the U.S. in St Domingo, & that he, being now returned from thence,[2] says that he applied several times on the subject to the Governor of the island,[3] who assured him that in the state of trouble in which the island then was, nothing could be done and mr. Bourne has returned me the papers. If a like detention of a register has taken place in France, I am of opinion it will be better to make that, & the colonial one, a subject of explanation at Paris, and will undertake to give the necessary instructions to our Minister there,[4] if you will favor me with the necessary documents relative to the case in France.

I have the honor to be with great respect Sir   Your most obedt. and most humble servt                                        Th: Jefferson

The Secretary of the Treasury.

ALS, letterpress copy, Thomas Jefferson Papers, Library of Congress; LC, Papers of the Continental Congress, National Archives.
    1. See William Lindsay to H, February 19, 1790, and H to Jefferson, April 20, 1790.
    2. Sylvanus Bourne of Massachusetts had resigned as consul in December, 1791. See Tobias Lear to Jefferson, December 30, 1791 (ALS, Thomas Jefferson Papers, Library of Congress).
    3. Philibert-François Rouxel de Blanchelande.
    4. Gouverneur Morris was appointed United States Minister Plenipotentiary to France on January 12, 1792.

## From William Ellery

[Newport, Rhode Island] January 16, 1792. States that expenses for the customs office and officers as well as the allowance on exported domestic spirits will exceed expected receipts. Wishes "to know whether under the above circumstances any further deposits should be made in the Bank of Providence until those allowances shall be discharged." [1]

LC, Newport Historical Society, Newport, Rhode Island.
    1. Ellery endorsed this letter "Answered." H's reply has not been found.

## *To John Nicholson* [1]

[Philadelphia, January 16, 1792]

The Secretary of the Treasury presents his Compliments to the Comptroller of the State of Pensylvania, & requests to see him at the Treasury Office tomorrow Morning at Nine oClock on a subject which the Governor has referred to a conference with the Comptroller.

Monday January 16th

AL, Glassboro State Teachers College, Glassboro, New Jersey.
1. For background to this letter, see H to Thomas Mifflin, December 21, 1791; Mifflin to H, December 27, 1791; and Nicholson to H, December 29, 1791.

## *From John Nicholson*

[Philadelphia, January 16, 1792]

The Comptr Gennl. of Pennsya. presents his Compls. to the Secretary of the Treasury of the U states will do himself the pleasure to attend at the time & place mentioned in his note of this morning.

Jany 16th 1792

LC, Division of Public Records, Pennsylvania Historical and Museum Commission, Harrisburg.

## *To the Directors of the Society for Establishing Useful Manufactures*

[Philadelphia, January 16, 1792]

I certify that Mr. Mort and Mr. Hall [1] who have been engaged on behalf of the Society for establishing useful Manufactures, informed me, while the Subscriptions were pending, that they wished to become Subscribers, the One in the sum of Eight, the other of six thousand Dollars; but that it would probably not be convenient to advance the first payment, at the time required: To which I answered, that I did not doubt the Directors of the Society would, if they should respectively subscribe the sums, be perfectly disposed to accommodate them on the subject of the payment in question, and that I was persuaded they might freely subscribe on that supposition. I was willing to encourage their Subscription, concerning it for the interest of the Society, that they should be concerned in it's success as Proprietors.[2]

Philadelphia   January 16. 1792
Alexander Hamilton

"Minutes of the S.U.M.," 8–9.
    1. For information on Joseph Mort and William Hall and their connection with the Society for Establishing Useful Manufactures, see H to the Directors of the Society for Establishing Useful Manufactures, December 7, 1791.
    2. After the certificate from H had been read, the board of directors "Resolved, That the said Messrs. Mort & Hall hold their Subscriptions agreeably to the said Certificate; and that they be charged in the Books of the Board with the amount of their Shares without paying the same for one Year" ("Minutes of the S.U.M.," 9).

## From Joseph Whipple

*Portsmouth [New Hampshire] January 16, 1792.* Acknowledges receipt of unsigned letter from Treasury Department.

LC, RG 36, Collector of Customs at Portsmouth, Letters Sent, 1791–1792, Vol. 3, National Archives.

## From Benjamin Lincoln [1]

Boston Jany 17th 1792

Sir

By the inclosed memorandum you will see the state of the imports into this district from Island of Hispaniole from the first of august 1790 to the end of that year and the state of the imports from the same Island from the first day of August 1791 to first Jany 1792 have not yet felt so sensibly as I expected we had the consequences of the disorders in that Island.[2]

From a suggestion given, when last in your office, that as there would be in April a large demand for interest due on monies loaned to the United States by the inhabitants of this you should not at present draw on me I think it therefore my duty thus early to mention to you that there is not the least prospect that the ballance in my hands will be augmented in any other way than by the receipt of the Bank notes of the United States. There are such a flood of them now here that they are bought up at a depreciated value by the Gentlemen indebted to us for the payment of their bonds.

Emptied rum hogs~, when the certificate can be had with them, are in great demand.

Secy of the Treasury

LC, Massachusetts Historical Society, Boston; LC, RG 36, Collector of Customs at Boston, Letter Book, 1790–1797, National Archives; two copies, RG 56, Letters from the Collector at Boston, National Archives.

1. Lincoln was collector of customs at Boston.
2. Lincoln is referring to the slave revolt on the plantations in Santo Domingo which began in August, 1791, and caused extensive property damage in most of the northern plain around Cap-Français.

## From John Nicholson

[Philadelphia, January 17, 1792][1]

Mr. Nicholson will do himself the Pleasure to attend about 10 OClock this day.

Tuesday January 18th. 1792.
Alexander Hamilton Esquire

LC, Division of Public Records, Pennsylvania Historical and Museum Commission, Harrisburg.

1. Nicholson dated this letter Tuesday, January 18, 1792, but this date fell on Wednesday. See the exchange of letters between H and Nicholson on January 16, 1792.

## From James Reynolds [1]

Philadelphia 17th January 1792.

Sir

I Suppose you will be surprised in my writing to you Repeatedly as I do. but dont be Alarmed for its Mrs. R. wish to See you. and for

My own happiness and hers. I have not the Least Objections to your
Calling. as a friend to Boath of us. and must Rely intirely on your
and her honnor. when I conversed with you last. I told you it would
be disagreeable to me for you to Call, but Sence, I am pritty well
Convinsed, She would onely wish to See you as a friend. and sence
I am Reconsiled to live with her, I would wish to do [e]very thing for
her happiness and my own, and Time may ware of every thing, So
dont fail in Calling as Soon as you Can make it Conveanant. and I
Rely on your befriending me if there should any thing Offer that
would be to my advantage. as you Express a wish to befrind me. So
I am

  yours to Serve          James Reynolds

Mr. Alexr. Hamilton

"Reynolds Pamphlet," August 31, 1797.
 1. This letter is printed as document No. VII in the appendix of the "Reynolds
Pamphlet," August 31, 1797.
 For background to this letter, see James Reynolds to H, December 15, 17, 19,
22, 1791, January 3, 1792; H to Reynolds, December 15, 1791; Maria Reynolds
to H, December 15, 1791.

## To George Washington

[Philadelphia, January 17, 1792]

 The Secretary of the Treasury has the honor to communicate to
the President a letter of the 7th. of January 1792. from the Collector
of Alexandria,[1] in answer to one written at the direction of the President;[2] and also the Answer of the Collector of Boston to an enquiry
in relation to the Keeper of the Lighthouse at Portland.[3]

January 17th. 1792.

LC, George Washington Papers, Library of Congress.
 1. Letter from Charles Lee not found.
 2. Letter not found.
 3. For the letter concerning the Portland lighthouse, see Benjamin Lincoln to
H, December 1, 1791.

## To the President and Directors of the Bank of the United States [1]

Treasury Department
January 18. 1792

Gentlemen

There are various arrangements necessary to be made between the Government and the Bank of the United States, which will better be treated of in a personal conference than by writing. I request therefore that such proceeding as may appear proper to the Direction, for that purpose, may be adopted.

With great consideration   I have the honor to be   Gentlemen Your obedient servant                    Alexander Hamilton

The President & Directors
of the Bank of The United States

ALS, Historical Society of Pennsylvania, Philadelphia.
1. Thomas Willing was president of the Bank of the United States.

## [To the Gazette of the United States] [1]

[Philadelphia, January 18, 1792]

[Philadelphia] *Gazette of the United States*, January 18, 1792.
1. According to Philip Marsh ("Hamilton's Neglected Essays, 1791–1793," *The New-York Historical Society Quarterly*, XXXII [October, 1948], 289), "The writer . . . [of this unsigned communication to the *Gazette of the United States*] sounds very like Hamilton." No conclusive evidence, however, that H was its author has been found.

## From Tobias Lear [1]

[*Philadelphia*] *January 18, 1792*. ". . . T. Lear has the honor to return to the Secretary of the Treasury General Lincoln's Letter of the 1st of December, respecting the Compensation of the Keeper of the Light House at Portland, and to inform the Secretary that the President conceives from the statement made in Genl. Lincoln's letter, that the addition of twenty dollars, to the annual sum of eighty already established, would be a sufficient compensation for that service, and as much as it would be proper to allow. The letter from the Collector of Alexandria is likewise herewith returned."

ALS, RG 26, Lighthouse Letters Received, "Segregated" Lighthouse Records, Lear, National Archives; LC, George Washington Papers, Library of Congress.
    1. Lear was George Washington's secretary. For background to this letter, see H to Washington, January 17, 1792.

## To Charles Lee

Treasury Department
January 18 1792.

Sir

Sufficient time having been given to the owners and commanders of vessels to provide regular manifests, according to the last collection law,[1] I am of opinion that the clauses you refer to [2] should now be enforced. You will do well to let this idea be communicated immediately among the Gentlemen in Trade, as the season admits of their taking measures to make it known. Their possessing the Pilots of hand bills containing an extract from the law to inform their Captains when they are met with on the coast, or in the Bay, would be an useful step.

I observe your intimations in regard to a table of fees &c which will be under consideration with the new Coasting law.

The Surveyor of your district has written to me upon the subject of a person, who should be authorised by you to aid him in the admeasurement of vessels.[3] This appointment you will perceive is attended with no expence to the United States. No provis⟨ion⟩ for the compensation of such a person being made, the wages he receives will be defrayed by the Surveyor out of his emoluments. It should seem therefore, if he wants such assistance, and the person he recommends to you is unexceptionable, that it might be well to appoint him. But as I do not know particularly how the matter is circumstanced, I should be glad to receive information, if objections occur to you.

The Inspectors of the Customs, on those days when they are actually employed under the Inspector of the Revenue for your port, are to be allowed by you daily pay as in the Customs: but no person is to be compensated for his hire in the Customs on any day in which he shall be engaged in the Revenue business.

I am, Sir, with great consideration, Your Most Obed Servant.

Alexander Hamilton

Charles Lee, Esquire,
Alexandria.

LS, RG 56, Letters to and from the Collector at Alexandria, National Archives; copy, RG 56, Letters to Collectors at Small Ports, "Set G," National Archives.

1. "An Act to provide more effectually for the collection of the duties imposed by law on goods, wares and merchandise imported into the United States, and on the tonnage of ships or vessels" (1 *Stat.* 145–78 [August 4, 1790]).

2. Lee is referring to Sections 9 and 10 of the Collection Law. See Lee to H, January 11, 1792, note 2.

3. The letter which Samuel Hanson, surveyor of the customs at Alexandria, wrote to H has not been found. On March 10, 1792, however, Hanson wrote to George Washington as follows:

". . . About 6 Weeks ago I submitted a part of my Grievance to the Secretary of the Treasury, but, not having been favoured with a reply from that Gentleman, I hope I shall be excused in appealing to your self, as the last Resort.

"Sir, it appears that Mr. Lee, from resentment of my information to you of his neglect of duty, is determined to harass and incommode me, as much as possible in the execution of mine. . . .

"With respect to the Assistant Measurer of Vessels, I beg leave to state that, upon my request, he appointed one about 18 Months ago, without the smallest objection—that this Person was always paid by me—and performed the duty with fidelity and accuracy, untill the said 9th. Jany last, when Mr. Lee thought proper to revoke the appointment, without any complaint against the Assistant. I immediately addressed the Secretary upon the Subject. His reply was as follows: 'The Collector has authority to appoint one; and, if you are willing to be at the expence of such assistance, and recommend a fit Person, as no doubt you will, I presume the Collector will appoint him. This Assistant to the Surveyor is only contemplated when his other duties shall render one necessary; and therefore you will perceive he is left to be agreed with and compensated by the Surveyor out of his fees for Admeasurement.'

"A Copy of this passage I enclosed to Mr. Lee, hoping and expecting he would, upon that authority, reinstate my assistant. But, instead of doing so, he writes to me as follows: 'Whenever it shall be necessary, I shall appoint a Person to measure each and every Vessel that cannot be measured by yourself conveniently with your other official duties. . . .'"

Hanson continues his letter to Washington by complaining that Lee is absent for most of the year and asks if the acts of Lee's deputy are valid and binding upon himself. (ALS, RG 59, Miscellaneous Letters of the Department of State, National Archives.)

# From John Nicholson

[*Philadelphia*] *January 18, 1792.* "Inclosed is one Certificate of each kind granted by the State of Pennsylvania. That Number'd

13768 . . . is the only kind granted for the Debt of the United States, & on which the question arises whether any thereof have been subscribed to the funding system of the United States. The other two kinds No. 1687 for depreciation of the Army and 2506 for all other Debts due by the States, you will find include all that have been subscribed with the loan Officer. I also send you . . . the Laws of Pennsylvania where you will find . . . the Law under which the Certificates were granted mentioned first above. . . ." [1]

LC, Division of Public Records, Pennsylvania Historical and Museum Commission, Harrisburg; copy, Division of Public Records, Pennsylvania Historical and Museum Commission.

1. On February 2, 1792, Oliver Wolcott, Jr., comptroller of the Treasury, wrote to Thomas Smith, commissioner of loans for Pennsylvania, asking whether any "new loan" certificates "have been subscribed to the loan payable in state certificates" (Hogan, *Pennsylvania State Trials*, 278).

On February 3, 1792, Smith wrote to Wolcott: "There has not been any Certificates of the description you allude to in your Letter of yesterdays date & of which you Inclosed a copy subscribed to the U states Loan. The Only Certificates received by me on Loan are those Issued agreeable to the Acts of the Assembly of this state of the 18th Decer. 1780 of the 10th April 1781 & April 1st. 1784, the returns of which are in forwardness & shall be compleated as soon as possible" (LC, RG 53, Pennsylvania State Loan Office, Letter Book, 1790–1794, Vol. "615-P," National Archives).

On February 29, 1792, Nicholson wrote to Governor Thomas Mifflin: "The subject committed to me by your Excellency in Decr last, respecting the claim made by the Secretary of the Treasury to a surrender on the part of the State of the Continental certificates not exchanged having been brought to a close; and being this day informed at the Treasury that all obstacles were removed respecting the transfer & payment of interest quarterly to the State of the residium unsubscribed of this States quota, and orders having gone out to the Loan Office of the District of Penna: consequent thereupon, I hasten to inform you thereof. The subject was an important one, and to have required the Continental Certificates from Pennsylvania, while the New Loans for which they were given were out and the State responsible for; without these means of redemption would have placed her in an unpleasant situation, to take off the appearance of this hardship, it was suggested that in case the New Loans not exchanged would not be subscribed to the United States by the holders (which on the proposed terms of the loan might be done) yet still that the State would by the terms of the same loan, be in the receipt of a sufficient sum from the Union to meet the interest due to these Creditors, but to this it was objected, that this receipt of interest by the State would be temporary, and would cease when the settlement of our Accounts with the United States should be effected and the balances provided for agreeably to Law—whereas the demand against the state would be perpetual, and could only be discharged by payment of the debt. On the whole after much attention to this business it hath been settled to our wish; and the good sense of the Secretary of the Treasury hath led him to a decision under the Act of Congress of Augt 1790, which is equitable and consonant with the scope of the said Act" (LC, Division of Public Records, Pennsylvania Museum and Historical Commission, Harrisburg)

## To William Seton [1]

Philadelphia January
18. 179[2] [2]

My Dear Sir

I have learnt with infinite pain the circumstance of a new Bank having started up in your City.[3] Its effects cannot but be in every view pernicious. These extravagant sallies of speculation do injury to the Government and to the whole system of public Credit, by disgusting all sober Citizens and giving a wild air to every thing. It is impossible but that three great banks in one City [4] must raise such a mass of artificial Credit, as must endanger every one of them & do harm in every view.

I sincerely hope That the Bank of New York will listen to no coalition with this newly engendered Monster.[5] A better alliance, I am strongly persuaded, will be brought about for it, & the joint force of two solid institutions will without effort or violence remove the excrescence, which has just appeared, and which I consider as a dangerous tumour in your political and commercial œconomy.

I express myself in these *strong terms* to you confidentially; not that I have any objection to my opinion being known as to the nature & tendency of the thing.

Yrs. with real regard                    A Hamilton

Wm. Seton Esq

ALS, The Chase Manhattan Bank Money Museum, New York City
  1. Seton was cashier of the Bank of New York.
  2. H mistakenly dated this letter "1791."
  3. H is referring to the "Million Bank," the first of three new banks which were proposed in New York City during one week in January, 1792. On January 16, proposals for the "Million Bank" were published, and during the same day more than twenty thousand shares, or ten times the value of the contemplated capital, were subscribed. On January 17, *The* [New York] *Daily Advertiser* carried the notice of a second bank project, the "State Bank," and by the end of the week still another bank, the "Merchants Bank of New York," was proposed. On Saturday, January 21, the promoters of the three banks agreed on a consolidation (Davis, *Essays,* I, 283; II, 83–85).
  Alexander Macomb, a close associate of William Duer, was an early promoter of the "Million Bank" together with Brockholst Livingston and Melancton Smith, who were both supporters of George Clinton in the 1792 New York

gubernatorial election. The chief promoters of the "State Bank" were Walter Livingston and Richard Platt, who were also connected with William Duer in speculation. Isaac Clason and Jacob Hallet, two New York City merchants, were the promoters of the "Merchants Bank" (Davis, *Essays*, II, 83–85).

A petition for incorporation from the "State Bank" was received by the Assembly on January 20, 1792. On January 23 a similar petition from the promoters of the "Million Bank" was read in the Assembly, and on February 2 a petition was presented for incorporation of the combined projects. On February 4, 1792, Nathaniel Laurence of Hempstead, Long Island, reported on the petitions and brought in a bill, "An Act to incorporate a State Bank" (New York Assembly *Journal*, 1792, 31–32, 46, 49). The bill did not pass the Assembly.

4. The "three great banks in one City" were the proposed "Million Bank," the Bank of New York, and the New York branch of the Bank of the United States. The last, which had been authorized in November, 1791, did not open until April 2, 1792.

5. Section VII of the plan of the "Million Bank" provided: "That the directors of the Bank are hereby empowered to form and conclude on such terms as they may deem equitable and for the interest of this institution, any agreement, association, or coalition, for the space of nine months next ensuing, with the president, directors and company of the Bank of New-York; the stockholders hereby binding themselves to abide by the same" (*The* [New York] *Daily Advertiser*, January 17, 1792).

## From Jeremiah Olney

*Providence, January 19, 1792.* "I have recd. your circular Letter of the 2nd. instant; and will attend to the several Matters therein contained. The Cashier of the Bank of the United States [1] has transmitted to me a description of the Notes, with his and the President's Signatures. My quarterly Accts. have been already forwarded. . . ."

ADfS, Rhode Island Historical Society, Providence.
1. John Kean.

## From Jeremiah Olney [1]

Custom-House,
Providence 19th Jany. 1792.

Sir.

Your Letter of the 8th instant, containing your Opinion on the case of the Brig. Polly, being accompanied by one from Mr. Bourn to Messrs Clark & Nightingale to the same purport; and those Gentlemen being impatient to unload the Vessel, I have given them permission to reland the Provisions and Fish, and have cancelled their exportation Bond. By your taking no notice of the 62nd. section of the *present* collection Law, to which I referred, and by which, alone, I was governed, and supposing me to have recurred to a Section in the *late* Law, which does not exist, there being but 40 Sections in all, induces me to imagine that there may *possibly* be some mistake or misunderstandg. between us: and therefore, lest the Edition of the Law which you have should be sectioned different from mine, I enclose an exact transcript of the 62nd. Section; upon which, had the above mentioned Articles been landed here without permission, I should have thought it my incumbent Duty to have commenced a prosecution for the forfeiture thereof, with the Vessel &c.—no part of the Law appearing to me more clear and possitive as the Bond required in conditioned against *relanding;* But if no mistake has taken place, I am happy that your construction thereof allows an Indulgeance to the Exports of Fish & Provisions, expecting a bounty, which I always thought they should be entitled to under proper restrictions. All Articles of the produce of the United States, which have not been Entered and Bonded for exportation, with an intent to draw back the Duties, or obtain an allowance, I have since the present collection Law took place, permitted when returned unsold to be relanded free from Duty, on the proof required by the 24th Section; those which have been bonded I have uniformly refused upon the 62nd Section; but shall in future permit them also to be relanded, cancelling the Bonds, as I have now done in the Instance of the Brigt. Polly.

I have the honor to be &c.                    Jereh. Olney Collr.

Alexr. Hamilton Esqr. Secy. of the Treasy.

ADfS, Rhode Island Historical Society, Providence.
    1. For background to this letter, see Olney to H, December 29, 1791, and H to Olney, January 8, 1792.

## *From George Gale* [1]

[*January 20, 1792.* On February 1, 1792, Hamilton wrote to Gale: "I have received your letter of the 20th. Ultimo." *Letter not found.*]

    1. Gale was supervisor of the revenue for the District of Maryland.

## To William Short

[*Treasury Department, January 21, 1792.* Letter listed in dealer's catalogue. *Letter not found.*]

LS, sold by Stan V. Henkels, Jr., October 11, 1927, Lot 170.

## To the President and Directors of the Bank of New York

Treasury Department
Januy 22d 1792

Gentlemen,

You will be pleased to furnish Messrs Dannecker and Young [1] with the further sum of Five thousand Dollars upon the same principles as heretofore.

I am with great consideration   Gentlemen   Your most obedient servant,
                                                           Alexander Hamilton

The President & Directors
of the Bank of the United States.

LS, Columbia University Club, New York City.
   1. William Young and George Dannacker were clothing contractors for the Army.

## From William Seton [1]

[New York] 22d Jny 1792

My dear sir

Trusting that Mr King [2] would communicate to you all that has passed between him & me on the subject of coallittion, the New Bankers—& US Bank Paper &ca, I did not intrude on your time by a repetition. Your kind favor of the 18. I recd last night. I had no doubt you would condemn the numerous carrying ons here in the Strongest terms. The folly & madness that rages at present is a disgrace to us.

There is no say where it will end—but it is the strongest proof that could be given, how necessary & usefull a coallition between the Bank of the U S. & this Institution would be in the plan proposed. It is the only thing that can destroy this combination of Speculators. Be assured this Bank will never listen to a Coallition with these madmen. They have aimed too deep a strike at our existence to be forgot or forgiven; for had not the rapidity with which they wanted to carry on their plan defeated their own intentions there is no saying what the immediate consequences might have been to us—for in less than two hours we were called upon for upwards of 500 000 Dollars. Low [3] would not permit them taking entirely Specie, of course they took paper of every Kind and the largest proportion was that of the United States Bank. Their operations being delayed by the over eagerness of every body, as they brought the paper back & wished us to receive it again as a Deposit—self preservation immediately pointed out the imprudence of our allowing these men to increase the balance of their accounts by our ⟨receiving⟩ it, which at any moment they might demand from us in actual Specie. We were therefore obligd to refuse it—not out of any evill intention to that Institution or with a design to affect its Operations you may believe. You will observe that the ⟨funds of all⟩ the large discounts drawn from their Men at Philadelphia, have been ⟨received⟩ by us in the Bank paper—from which & the liberal discounts drawn for them here they had accumulated such large ballances (no doubt with a view to affect what they are now carrying on) that had they all drawn together they might have ruined us at once. Our refusing to take the paper (tho we have still about 100,000 Dollars in hand) has raised a great clamour but I trust you will view the maneuver in a proper light & approve of it. Thus situated there are two or three points, upon which I must request your friendly opinion & advice—for rest assured that our Directors & myself have nothing ever at heart than to pursue such a line of conduct as shall be perfectly agreeable to you. The Collector of the Customs,[4] will no doubt tender to us his payments in National Bank Notes—the purchasers of the last Treasury Bills on Amsterdam which become payable the beginning of augt. will probably do the same & refuse to pay if we do not receive them—how are we to act in such case—for the operation will be thus, our receipts are carried to the credit of the Treasurer, he draws in favor of Mr Kean [5] or Mr

Francis [6]—his checks are passed to their credit—they again draw to individuals, who in consequence have a right to demand Specie from us & (from the existing opperations) will probably do it. The consequence is that our whole Specie is drained from us in payment not of our own circulating paper but for the paper of the Bank of the U S. —& upon the Establishment of the Bank here, it is more than probable, that the Bank will draw upon us for the amount recd for them & that to constitute their Specie Capital, they will not receive their own Notes from us in payment. It is true we can send them to Phia. & then demand the Specie but how unpleasant would that be—in short we are surrounded with difficulties, & with the best intentions in the world shall probably fall short of our wishes.

Pray My Dear sir excuse this lengthy detail, & rest assured of the high respect & esteem of

Your ever obliged ob H Sert

AL, Hamilton Papers, Library of Congress.
1. For background to this letter, see H to Seton, January 18, 1792.
2. Rufus King, United States Senator from New York.
3. Nicholas Low, a director of the Bank of New York.
4. John Lamb, collector of the customs at New York City.
5. John Kean, cashier of the Bank of the United States.
6. Tench Francis, cashier of the Bank of North America.

## From William Ellery

[*Newport, Rhode Island*] *January 23, 1792.* "Yesterday I recd. your Circular Letter of the second of this month, and shall observe your directions. . . ."

LC, Newport Historical Society, Newport, Rhode Island.

## To Benjamin Lincoln

*Treasury Department, January 23, 1792.* "The President of the United States having determined to add to the allowance of the keeper of the light house at Portland head the sum of twenty dollars per annum, you will be pleased to make the same known to him. . . ." [1]

Copy, RG 56, Letters to Collectors at Small Ports, "Set G," National Archives; copy, RG 56, Letters to the Collector at Boston, National Archives.
1. See Tobias Lear to H, January 18, 1792.

## From Jeremiah Olney

*Providence, January 23, 1792.* ". . . I . . . enclose a short Statemt. of the Monies which will become payable into, and of such as will probably be demandable out of, this Office, between this Time and the 14th of May next; by which it will appear that I shall have as much to *pay* as I have to *receive:* I shall therefore omit my weekly deposits in the Providence Bank until I am favored with your determination whether I shall continue them and be furnished with Drafts on the Bank to discharge the principal Sums; or retain all the Money I may receive untill the said 14th of May next, for that purpose."

ADfS, Rhode Island Historical Society, Providence.

## Report on Estimates of Receipts and Expenditures for 1791–1792

[Philadelphia, January 23, 1792
Communicated on January 23, 1792] [1]

[To the Speaker of the House of Representatives]

The Secretary of the Treasury, in obedience to the order of the House of Representatives of the 19th instant,[2] respectfully makes the following, Report:

At the close of the year 1790 there was a considerable surplus of revenue beyond the objects of expenditure, which had required a

Copy, RG 233, Reports of the Secretary of the Treasury, Second Congress, National Archives; copy, RG 233, Reports of the Treasury Department, 1791–1792, Vol. II, National Archives.
1. *Journal of the House,* I, 495. The communicating letter may be found in RG 233, Reports of the Secretary of the Treasury, Second Congress, National Archives.
2. The House "*Ordered,* That the Secretary of the Treasury be directed to lay before this House such information, with respect to the finances of the United States, as will enable the Legislature to judge whether any additional revenue will be necessary, in consequence of the proposed increase of the military establishment" (*Journal of the House,* I, 493).

provision to that period; which surplus, by an act of the 12th. of August in that year,[3] was appropriated to the reduction of the public debt.

The Statement (A.) herewith submitted, will shew, in one view, all the sums, which, according to the establishments heretofore made, and corresponding appropriations have required and will require to be defrayed, from the beginning of the year 1791 to the end of the year 1792, amounting together to seven millions and eighty two thousand one hundred and ninety seven dollars and Seventy four cents.

The Statement (B.) will also shew, in one view, the nett product, of all the public revenues, for the same period, according to the best calculation and estimate, which can now be formed of it, amounting to seven millions and twenty nine thousand seven hundred and fifty five dollars, and twenty six cents.

The Statement (C.) exhibits a Summary of the total annual expenditure of the United States, in conformity to existing establishments, amounting to three millions six hundred and eighty eight thousand and forty three dollars, fifty cents.

The Statement B. includes a view of the probable product, during the year 1792, of the existing revenues of the United States, amounting to three millions seven hundred thousand dollars.

From these Statements will result substantially the information, which is desired by the House of Representatives, as far as it is now in the power of the Secretary to give it.

One or two matters, however, may be proper to be added, with a view to greater accuracy.

There are certain instances, in which the estimates of appropriations have exceeded, and will exceed the sums actually expended. Hence the apparent excess of the expenditure, as exhibited in the statement (A) beyond the product of the revenue, as shewn in the statement (B.) will, probably, not be found real. But the amount of these surplusses or over-estimates cannot be now ascertained, and it is not likely to be very considerable; and because, also, if it should do more than counterbalance the excess, alluded to, it will be safest to set off the surplus against those contingent demands, which from time to time occur.

No deduction has been made from the annual interest on account

3. See "An Act making Provision for the Reduction of the Public Debt" (1 *Stat.* 186–87).

of the debt purchased. This has proceeded from a supposition that it will be deemed expedient by the Legislature to appropriate inviolably the interest of any part of the debt which shall be, at any time extinguished, toward the extinction of the remainder. This point will be more particularly submitted in a report on the subject of the public debt.[4]

All which is humbly submitted,     Alexander Hamilton
                                    Secretary of the Treasury.


Treasury Department. January 23rd. 1792.


## (A)

Statement of Expenditures made, and to be made, pursuant to appropriations heretofore made, in conformity to the existing establishments of the United States from the beginning of the year 1791, to the end of the year 1792. Vizt.


Amount of monies appropriated by an act of the 11th. of February 1791, making appropriations for the support of government during the year 1791, and for other purposes [5] . . . . . . . . . . . . . . . . . $ 740,232.60

Sum appropriated by an act of the 3d. March 1791, towards effecting a recognition of the treaty with the Emperor of Morocco [6] . . . . . . . . . . . . 20,000.00

Sum appropriated by an act of the same date, for raising another regiment, and making a further provision for the protection of the frontiers [7] . . . . . . . . 312,686.20

Amount of monies appropriated by an act of the 23d. of December last past, making provision, among other things, for the support of Government for the year 1792 [8] . . . . . . . . . . . . . . . . . 1,059.222.81

Sums to be advanced, pursuant to the act making provision for defraying the intercourse between the United

4. See "Report on the Public Debt and Loans," January 23, 1792.
5. 1 *Stat.* 190.
6. "An Act making appropriation for the purpose therein mentioned" (1 *Stat.* 214)
7. 1 *Stat.* 222–24.
8. 1 *Stat.* 226–29.

States and foreign nations [9] . . . . . . . 40,000.00
                                                    ————————
                                               $2,172,141.61

Amount of one years interest on the public debt, for-
eign and domestic during the year 1791. . . . . 2,060,861.40
Amount of one years interest on the public debt, for-
eign and domestic, (including that of the respective
States, assumed) during the year 1792 . . . . . 2,849,194.73
                                                    ————————
Total expenditures to the end of the year 1792,
                              Dollars,      7,082,197.74


Treasury department                    Alexander Hamilton
January 23nd. 1792                     Secretary of the Treasury


## (B.)

Estimate of the nett product of the Public Revenues during the years
1791 and 1792

### Import duties for 1791.

| | | |
|---|---|---|
| Quarter ending the 31st March  ⎤ . . . . ⎧ $ | 314,881.11 |
| Quarter ending the 30th June   ⎬ (A) . . . ⎨ | 1,345,303.49 |
| Quarter ending the 30th September ⎦ . . . . ⎩ | 919,570.66 |
| Quarter ending the 31st December    (B.) . . | 600,000.00 |

Total nett product of Imports for 1791 . . . . $3,179,755.26.
Duties on home-made Spirits from the 1st of July
to the last of December . . . . (C.) . . 150,000.00
                                                    ————————
Total nett Revenue, 1791 . . . . . . . . $3,329,755.26.
Duties on Imports for the year 1792 estimated
at . . . . (D) . . . . . 3,300,000.00
Duties on home-made spirits for
the same year, estimated
at . . . . (E) . . . . . 400,000.00    3,700,000.00
                                       ————————    ————————
Total of Nett Revenue, for the years, 1791 and 1792 . $7,029.755.26.

Notes to reference (B)
   (A)   The produce of these three quarters may be considered as

9. 1 *Stat.* 128–29 (July 1, 1790).

ascertained. Though returns have not been returned from all the ports, for the entire period; yet so many have been received (including the principal ports) as to have admitted of a calculation with regard to the rest, not liable to material error.

The produce for the year 1790, has served as a guide, in respect to the ports from which returns have not been received.

(B). The sum here stated, is altogether upon estimate; the time which has elapsed since the end of the quarter not admitting of proper documents. It exceeds the produce of the same quarter for the preceeding year, fifty five thousand seven hundred and seventy three dollars and nineteen cents. If the ratio of increase of any preceeding quarter, during the year 1791, had been applied to this quarter, the sum would have been considerably greater, but it is believed that this would not furnish a just rule. It is understood, that the importations for the last quarter of 1790, were much increased, to avoid the additional duties, which were to take place on the first day of the year 1791, and although the additional duty on distilled spirits, might at first view, be expected to add to the product for the quarter in question, yet it is far from certain, that this was the effect of it. Extraordinary exertions were made to import distilled spirits, prior to July, when the additional duty took effect, which may be supposed to have lessened the quantity afterwards, so as to leave it a question, whether this article was more or less productive in that quarter, than in the same quarter of the former year. Making allowance for these circumstances, it does not appear probable that the last quarter of 1791, will exceed the last quarter of 1790, in so great a proportion, as any of the preceeding corresponding quarters.

(C.) This sum is materially short of the originally estimated product, but from the returns hitherto received, it does not appear likely to be greater; this is owing, partly to a decreased distillation of Spirits from foreign materials, in consequence of a sudden rise in the price of molasses, and partly to the obstacles which have retarded the complete execution of the law.

(D) The sum here estimated, cannot in the nature of the thing be accurate; it includes a compromise of opposite considerations. First, it contemplates an additional sum for the additional duty on imported spirits, which will be fully operative during the present year. Secondly, it contemplates the possibility, that the disturbances in

Hispaniola [10] may tend to diminish the supply of several articles which are objects of considerable duties, and may proportionably diminish the revenue, hence about one third of the probable increase of the duties on spirits is added to the produce of the year 1791, and the aggregate is taken as the produce of the year 1792, abating two thirds of that increase, as an equivalent for the other deficiencies.

(E) The same disturbances in Hispaniola may be expected to diminish the product of the duties on home made spirits, by considerably reducing the supply of molasses; which, added to the obstacles already alluded to (and which it will require yet some time, completely to surmount) cannot fail to render the real product of these duties, in the course of the present year, materially less than the estimated product. Accordingly an abatement of about one third is made in the present estimate.

Treasury Department,                    Alexander Hamilton
January 23. 1792                        Secretary of the Treasury

## C

Estimate of Annual Expenditures, on the ground of existing establishments, Vizt.

| | Dollars | Cents |
|---|---|---|
| For the support of the civil establishments of the government, including 40,000 dollars for foreign affairs | 368,653.56 | |
| Stated expenditure of the War department including 25,000 for Indian affairs . . . . . . | 382,731.61 | |
| Pensions to Invalids . . . . . . . . . | 87,463.60 | |
| Interest on the public debt, foreign and domestic including the amount of the State debts assumed | 838,848.77 | |
| | 2,849,194.73 | |
| Total annual expenditure | $3,688,043.50 | |

Treasury department, January 23d. 1792.

Alexander Hamilton
Secretary of the Treasury

10. H is referring to the slave revolt on the plantations in Santo Domingo which began in August, 1791, and caused widespread property damage in most of the northern plain around Cap-Français.

# Report on the Public Debt and Loans [1]

Treasury Department January 23d 1792.
[Communicated on February 7, 1792] [2]

[To the Speaker of the House of Representatives]

Pursuant to the order of the House of Representatives of the first of November 1791, directing the Secretary of the Treasury, "to report to the House the amount of the *Subscriptions* to the loans proposed by the act making provision for the Public Debt,[3] as well in the debts of the respective States as in the domestic debt of the United States, and of the parts which remain unsubscribed, together with such measures as are, in his opinion, expedient to be taken on the subject": [4] the said Secretary respectfully submits the following Report:

I. The whole amount of the domestic debt of the United States, Principal and Interest, which has been subscribed to the Loan proposed concerning that debt, by the Act intitled "An Act making provision for the debt of the United States," according to the Statement herewith transmitted

DS, RG 233, Reports of the Secretary of the Treasury, Second Congress, National Archives; ADf, Hamilton Papers, Library of Congress; Df, partly in the handwriting of H, Hamilton Papers, Library of Congress; copy, RG 233, Reports of the Treasury Department, 1791–1792, Vol. II, National Archives; copy, RG 39, Reports of Congress, Clerk's Table, 1791–1792, National Archives.

1. Neither the first draft, which is in H's handwriting, nor the second draft, which is partly in H's handwriting, has been printed. Substantive differences between the drafts and the final version have, however, been indicated in the footnotes.

2. *Journal of the House*, I, 503. The communicating letter, dated February 6, 1792, may be found in RG 233, Reports of the Treasury Department, 1791–1792, Vol. II, National Archives

3. Provision for the debts of the United States was made by "An Act making provision for the (payment of the) Debt of the United States" (1 *Stat.* 138–44 [August 4, 1790]) and by "An Act making Provision for the Reduction of the Public Debt" (1 *Stat.* 186–87 [August 12, 1790]), which established the sinking fund.

4. *Journal of the House*, I, 445. This report was debated during March, 1792, and on May 8, 1792, a law concerning the questions raised by this report was passed. See "An Act supplementary to the act making provision for the Debt of the United States" (1 *Stat.* 281–83).

marked A and subject to the observations accom-                    Cts
panying that Statement is  .    .    .    .   Dollars      31,797,481.22
which, pursuant to the terms of that Act, has been
converted into Stock bearing an immediate interest
of 6 ⅌ Cent: ⅌ Annum                                      14,177,450.43
Stock bearing the like interest from the first of
January 1801                                               7,088,727.79
Stock bearing an immediate interest of 3 ⅌ Cent
⅌ Annum                                                   10,531,303.--

              making together .    .    .    .   Dollars   31,797,481.22

of which there stands to the credit of the Trustees
of the sinking fund, in consequence of purchases
of the Public Debt made under their direction the                 Cents
sum of                                        Dollars     1,131,364.76

The unsubscribed residue of the said Debt, according to the statements herewith transmitted
marked B & C and subject to the observations accompanying the statement C appears to amount                      Cents
to                                            Dollars    10,616,604.65

consisting of Registered Debt, Principal & Interest        6,795,815.26
.    .    .    .   Unsubscribed Stock on the books⎫
               of the Commissioners of Loans for  ⎪
               New   Jersey,   Pennsylvania   and ⎬           15,674.62
               Maryland, Principal & Interest     ⎭
.    .    .    .   Credits on the books of the Treas-⎫
               ury for which no certificates have ⎬          107,648.63
               issued, Principal & Interest       ⎭
.    .    .    .   Outstanding or floating evidences⎫
               of Debt estimated ⅌ Statement C at ⎭        3,697,466.14
               making together            Dollars        10,616,604.65

concerning which some further arrangement is necessary.

The greatest part of the registered Debt, hitherto unsubscribed, is
owned by the Citizens of foreign countries, most, if not all of whom
appear now disposed to embrace the terms held out by the act
abovementioned; extensive orders having been received from those
creditors, to subscribe to the Loan, after the time for receiving
subscriptions had elapsed.

A considerable part of the outstanding or floating debt, consists of Loan Office Certificates issued between the first of September 1777 and the first of March 1778, bearing interest on the nominal sum. Many of the holders of this species of debt have come in upon the terms of the act, but others have hitherto declined it; alledging, that the special nature of their contract gives a peculiarity to their case, and renders the commutation proposed not so fair an equivalent to them, as in other instances. They also complain, that the act has had, towards them, a compulsory aspect, by refusing the temporary payment of interest, unless they should exchange their old for new certificates, essentially varying the nature of their contract.

A resolution of Congress of the tenth of September 1777 [5] stipulates in favour of this class of creditors, interest upon the *nominal*, instead of the *real principal* of their debt, *until that principal be discharged*.[6] This certainly renders their contract of a nature more beneficial than that of other creditors; but they are at the same time liable to be divested of the extra-benefit it gives them, by a payment of their Specie-dues; and it may be observed, that they have actually enjoyed, and by accepting the terms offered to them were enabled to realise, advantages superior to other creditors. They have been paid interest by bills on France, from the tenth of September 1777 to the first of March 1782, while other creditors received their interest in depreciated bills of the old emissions; and the terms of the loan proposed put it in their power to realise the benefit of interest on the nominal amount of their respective debts at rates from $62\%_{100}$ nearly to $104^7\%_{100}$ per cent on their real or specie capital down to the last of December 1790.[7] .

It does not therefore appear to have been an unreasonable expecta-

5. The resolution of the Continental Congress to which H is referring reads as follows: "*Resolved*, That the interest which shall arise after the date of this resolution on loan office certificates already issued, or which shall be issued before the 1st day of March next, be annually paid at the respective loan offices, in bills of exchange on the commissioners of the United States in Paris, at the rate of five livres of France for every Spanish milled dollar due for interest as aforesaid, or in continental bills of credit, at the option of the respective lenders" (*JCC*, VIII, 730–31).

6. At this point in the first draft the following sentence appears: "It is true that there is a peculiar ⟨–⟩ in the situation of this class of Creditors; as it respects the nature of their contract; but it is also true that they have enjoyed and in accepting the terms offered would have realized peculiar advantages."

7. At this point in the first draft H wrote and then crossed out the following paragraphs:

"It would be improper to inquire now whether the determination originally made in favour of this class of Creditors was justified by sufficient reasons or

tion, that they, as readily as any other description of public creditors, would have acquiesced in a measure, calculated for the accommodation of the Government, under circumstances, in respect to which, it has been demonstrated by *subsequent events* that the accommodation desired was consistent with the best interest of the public creditors.[8] A large proportion of the parties interested have indeed viewed the matter in this light, and have embraced the proposition. It is probable, that the *progress* of things will satisfy the remainder, that it is equally their interest to concur; if a further opportunity be afforded. But it is, nevertheless, for themselves only to judge, how far the equivalent proposed is, in their case, a reasonable and fair one; how far any circumstances in their claim may suggest reasons for moderation on their part; or how far any other motives, public or private, ought to induce an acceptance. And the principles of good faith require, that their election should be free.

On this ground, the complaint which regards the withholding of a temporary payment of interest, except on the condition of a surrender of the old certificates for new ones importing a contract substantially different, appears to the Secretary not destitute of foundation.[9] He presumes, that the operation of that provision, in the particular case was not adverted to; or, that an exception would have been introduced as most consonant with the general spirit and design of the Act. Accordingly, the further measures which will be sub-

---

otherwise. Respect for an act of Government claims a presumption that it was; unless the contrary were manifest. And the principles of good faith would require at any rate that what has been done should remain unimpaired. Nor is it for any but the parties themselves to judge whether they ought to accept, as an equivalent for their present contract, the terms which were proposed to them.

"It may however without impropriety be observed that considering the superiority of advantages which they have enjoyed and would have realized now in the very act of accepting the forms which were proposed. Under such circumstances It was not unreasonable to have entertained."

8. The material which is printed for the remainder of this paragraph appears on a separate sheet of paper in the first draft and was copied for the second draft. In the margin of the first draft at this point, however, H wrote the following sentences, which he marked for insertion: "But it nevertheless be left to themselves to judge whether it was, & if the proposition be renewed, whether it will be their interest to accept the terms proffered as an equivalent for the ⟨existing⟩ Contract. And the principles of good faith require that their election should be free."

9. In the margin in the second draft opposite this point H wrote and crossed out the following material: "however little room there may have been under

mitted, will contemplate a method of obviating the objection in question.

From the consideration, that an extension of the time for receiving subscriptions, upon the terms of the Act making provision for the Debt of the United States, is desired by a large proportion of the non-subscribing creditors, and from the further consideration, that sufficient experience has not yet been had of the productiveness of a considerable branch of the Revenues which have been established, to afford the light necessary to a final arrangement—It is, in the judgment of the Secretary, adviseable, to renew the proposition for a loan in the Domestic Debt, on the same terms with the one which has been closed, and to allow time for receiving subscriptions to it until the last day of September next inclusively; making provision for the temporary payment of interest to such who may not think fit to subscribe, for the year 1792, of the like nature with that which was made in the same case for the year 1791—Except as to the holders of Loan Office Certificates, issued between the first of September 1777 and the first of March 1778; in respect to whom it is submitted as proper to dispense with the obligation of exchanging their old certificates for new, as the condition of their receiving interest in capacity of non-subscribers; and to allow them, without such exchange, to receive the same interest, both for the year 1791 & 1792 as if they had subscribed to the first Loan. It will not be materially difficult, so to regulate the operation at the Treasury as to avoid in the particular case, that danger of imposition by counterfeits, which was the motive to the general provision for an exchange of certificates.[10]

II. The amount of the subscriptions in the debts of the respective

---

all the circumstances to have expected that a complaint of that nature would have been strenuously urged."

On October 27, 1791, in the Senate "The Memorial of John Nixon and Others, a committee on behalf of certain creditors of the United States was read, requesting that an appropriation may be made for the payment of the arrears of their interest and the annual interest accruing" (*Annals of Congress,* III, 16).

10. In the first draft at this point H wrote and crossed out the following paragraph: "But as it is desireable to decide the nonsubscribing Creditors on a final election whether to remain non subscribers or to become subscribers, it is submitted as expedient to incorporate a provision in the act which shall be passed that any who may receive a payment of interest as Nonscribers pursuant to that act shall be deemed to have made their election and shall be precluded from a right afterwards to subscribe."

States, within the limits of the sum assumed in each, appears by the statement marked D to be Dollars 17,072,334.39 Cents, subject to the observations accompanying that statement. Consequently the difference between the aggregate of the sums subscribed, and the aggregate of the sums assumed, is Dollars 4,427,665.61 Cents. This difference is to be attributed to several causes; the principal of which are the following. First; That the sums assumed in respect to certain States exceeded the actual amount of their existing debts. Second; That in various instances, a part of the existing debt was in a form which excluded it from being received, without contravening particular provisions of the Law; as in the case of certificates issued after the first day of January 1790 in lieu of certificates which had been issued prior to that period, which was reported upon by the Secretary on the twenty fifth day of february last.[11] Third; Ignorance of, or inattention to the limitation of time for receiving subscriptions. It appears, that a number of persons lost the opportunity of subscribing from the one or the other of these causes.

A strong desire that a further opportunity may be afforded for subscriptions in the debts of the States, has been manifested by the Individuals interested. And the States of Rhode Island [12] and New Hampshire,[13] have, by the public Acts referred to the Secretary, indicated a similar desire. The affording of such further opportunity, may either be restricted within the limit, as to amount, which is contemplated by the Act itself; or may receive an extension which will embrace the residuary debts of the States.

The first may be considered as nothing more than giving full effect to a measure already adopted.

11. Report not found.
12. On January 4, 1792, "A memorial of the Legislature of the State of Rhode Island was presented to the House and read, representing the injuries they are subject to from the operation of an act of Congress relative to the assumption of the State debts, and praying a farther assumption of the debt of that State.
"*Ordered*, That the said memorial be referred to the Secretary of the Treasury, for his information." (*Journal of the House*, I, 486–87.)
13. On December 28, 1791, "A memorial of the Legislature of the State of New Hampshire was presented to the House and read, representing the inequality and injustice of a late act of Congress for the assumption of the State debts, and praying that the inequalities thereof may be removed, or the injuries and burthens thereby occasioned to the said State redressed in such other way as the wisdom of Congress shall deem expedient.
"*Ordered*, That the said memorial be referred to the Secretary of the Treasury, for his information." (*Journal of the House*, I, 481–82.)

The last appears to have in its favour all the leading inducements to what has been already done. The embarassments which might arise from conflicting systems of finance are not entirely obviated. The efficacious command of the National resources for National exigencies is not unequivocally secured. The equalizing of the condition of the citizens of every State, and exonerating those of the States most indebted, from partial burthens which would press upon them in consequence of exertions in a common cause, is not completely fulfilled, until the entire debt of every State, contracted in relation to the war is embraced in one general and comprehensive plan.[14] The inconvenience to the United States of disburthening the States, which are still incumbered with considerable debts, would bear no proportion to the inconvenience which they would feel, if left to struggle with those debts, unaided.

More general contentment, therefore, in the public mind, may be expected to attend such an exoneration, than the reverse; in propor-

14. At this point in the first draft H wrote and then crossed out the following paragraphs:

"The states upon which the heaviest burthens would still rest, Massachusettes and South Carolina were certainly among the foremost in exertion during the late war—the latter was second to none in suffering. Georgia also so much and so often the scene of depredation and distress has a considerable debt which must either incumber her beyond her ability or perish in the hands of her citizens.

"There appears to be no comparison between the inconvenience to the United States of exonerating the States which are still incumbered with debt from their remaining burthens and the inconvenience which their citizens must sustain if left to struggle with them unaided. The reflections too, which may be expected to arise in their minds when they not only see the citizens of other states exempt from burthens which they endure; but the governments of some of those States drawing considerable supplies from the National Treasury for their particular use, and when they indulge the consciousness that this disparity of situation has not been occasioned by any defect of effort on their part—cannot be of a nature to promote the harmony and mutual affection or to fortify the confidence which it is desireable to cultivate between all the parts of the Union. With regard to any state the debt of which may have been only *partially* assumed, and that too in a proportion not only short of what has been assumed for some other states but short also of a due proportion of the intire sum assumed, as has been the case in certain instances, the claim of exoneration, by a further assumption has particular force.

"The subsequent reflections of the Secretary have not weakened the strength of his original impression that a complete assumption of the debts of the particular states is a measure of sound policy and substantial justice.

"And the Reception which in the great body of the community has attended the measure as far as it has proceeded affords ground of assurance that the further prosecution of it to the necessary extent will concliliate the general suffrage."

tion as the experience of actual inconvenience would be greater, though only applicable to parts, in the one, than in the other case.[15]

With regard to States, parts only of the debts of which have been assumed, and in proportions short of those, which have prevailed, in favour of other states, and short also of what would have resulted from a due apportionment of the entire sum assumed; the claim to a further assumption is founded on considerations of equal justice, as relative to the measure itself, considered in a separate and independent light.

But there is a further reason of material weight for an immediate general assumption. Monied men, as well foreigners as citizens, through the expectation of an eventual assumption, or that in some shape or other a substantial provision will be made for the unassumed residue of the State Debts, will be induced to speculate in the purchase of them. In proportion as the event is unsettled, or uncertain, the price of the article will be low, and the present proprietors will be under disadvantage in the sale. The loss to them in favour of the purchasers is to be regarded as an evil; and as far as it is connected with a transfer to foreigners, at an undervalue, it will be a national evil. By whatsoever authority an ultimate provision may be made, there will be an absolute loss to the community equal to the total amount of such undervalue.

It may appear an objection to the measure, that it will require an establishment of additional funds by the Government of the United States. But this does not seem to be a necessary consequence. The probability is, that without a supplementary assumption, an equal or very nearly equal augmentation of funds will be requisite to provide for *greater* balances in favour of certain States; which would be proportionably diminished by such assumption. The destination,

15. At this point on both drafts H wrote the following sentence, which he deleted in the second draft: "The contrast would be strong, between the situation of certain parts of the Union, exempted from all burthens except those which they bore in common with their fellow citizens of every other part, and of certain other parts of the Union, which in addition to that exemption enjoyed the advantage of drawing from the National Treasury annually considerable sums for their particular use—when compared with the situation of other parts, which would not only be without the latter advantage but would add the weight of local and extraordinary burthens to their share of those which were common to all."

not the quantum of the fund, will therefore be the chief distinction between the two cases.[16]

It may also appear an objection to a total assumption, that the magnitude of the object is not ascertained with precision. It is not certainly known, what is the sum due in each State; nor has it been possible to acquire the information, owing to different causes. But though precise data are deficient, there are materials which will serve as guides. From the returns received at the Treasury, assisted by information in other ways, it may be stated without danger of material error—That the remaining debts of the States over and above the sums already subscribed will not exceed the amounts specified in the statement D accompanying this report [17]—And that, including the sums already subscribed, the total amount to be *ultimately* provided for, in the event of a general assumption, will not exceed $25,403,362\frac{71}{100}$ Dollars, which would constitute an addition of $3,903,362,\frac{71}{100}$ Dollars to the sum of 21,500,000 Dollars already assumed.[18]

Should a total assumption be deemed eligible, it may still be adviseable to assign a determinate sum for each State, that the utmost limit of the operation may be preestablished; and it is necessary in order to the certainty of a due provision in proper time, that interest should not begin to be payable, on the additional ⟨sums⟩ [19] assumed, till after the year 1792.[20]

16. This and the preceding paragraph do not appear in the first draft. They were inserted in the second draft.

17. In the first draft this sentence reads as follows: "From the returns formerly received at the Treasury and reported to the House of Representatives and from subsequent information in other ways, it may be stated without danger of material error that the sums already assumed for the states of New Jersey Pensylvania Delaware Maryland & North Carolina will cover the whole amount of their respective debts in some instances with an excess; and that the remaining Debts of the other states over and above the sums already assumed will not exceed the amounts specified in the statement accompanying this Report." H revised this sentence in the second draft.

At this point the following paragraph appeared in the first draft and was crossed out in the second draft: "Deducting the probable amount of excesses in regard to some states, from that of deficiencies in regard to others, the additional sum to be provided for in case of a Total Assumption may be computed at      ."

18. This sentence does not appear in the first draft. It was inserted in the second draft.

19. Material within broken brackets has been taken from the second draft.

20. At this point the following paragraph was crossed out in the first draft: "The payments which may in the mean time be made to any state pursuant to

⟨It will oc⟩cur, that provision has been made, for paying to eac⟨h St⟩ate, in trust for its non-subscribing creditors, an interest upon the difference, between the sum assumed for such State, and that actually subscribed, equal to what would have been payable, if it had been subscribed.

In the event of a further assumption, either within the limits already established, or commensurate with the remaining debts of the States, it is conceived, that it will not be incompatible with the provision just mentioned, to retain, at the end of each quarter, during the progress of the further subscription, out of the money directed to be paid to each State, a sum corresponding with the interest upon so much of its debts as shall have been subscribed to that period, paying the overplus, if any, to the State. An absolute suspension of that payment does not appear consistent with the nature of the stipulation, included in that provision; for though the money to be paid to a State be expressly a trust for the nonsubscribing creditors; yet as it cannot be certain beforehand, that they will elect to change their condition, the possibility of it, will not justify a suspension of payment to the State, wh⟨ich⟩ might operate as a suspension of payment to ⟨the creditors⟩ themselves.

A further ob⟨ject⟩ion to such a suspension results from the idea, that the provision in question appears to have a secondary object; namely, as a pledge for securing a provision for whatever balance may be found due to a State on the general settlement of accounts. The payment directed to be made to a State, is "to continue *until* there shall be a settlement of accounts between the United States and the Individual States, and in case a balance should then appear in favour of a State, *until* provision shall be made for the said balance." [21]

This secondary operation as a pledge or security (consistently with the intent of the funding Act) can only be superseded in favour of the primary object, a *provision for the creditors;* and as far as may be necessary to admit them to an effectual participation of it.[22] But

_____

the        section of the Funding Act will of course be to be deducted proportionably from the sums subscribed unless the state shall consent to wave its agency for the Creditors & suffer the money which they are entitled to receive in trust to be reserved for their use."

21. H is referring to Section 17 of "An Act making provision for the (payment of the) Debt of the United States" (1 *Stat.* 143–44 [August 4, 1790]).

22. This sentence and the preceding paragraph do not appear in the first draft. They were inserted in the second draft.

as whatever money may be paid to a State, is to be paid over to its creditors, proportional deductions may, with propriety, be made from the debts of those Creditors who may hereafter subscribe; so as that the United States may not have to pay twice for the same purpose.

If it shall be judged expedient, either to open ag⟨ain, or exte⟩nd the assumption, it will be necessary to vary the description of the debts, which may be subscribed, so as to comprehend all those, which have relation to services or supplies during the war, under such restrictions as are requisite to guard against abuse.

In the original proposition for an assumption of the State Debts, and in the suggestions now made on the same subject, the Secretary has contemplated, and still contemplates, as a material part of the plan, an effectual provision, for the sale of the vacant lands of the United States. He has considered this resource, as an important mean of sinking a part of the debt, and facilitating ultimate arrangements concerning the residue. If supplementary funds shall be rendered necessary, by an additional assumption, the provision will most conveniently be made, at the next session of Congress, when the productiveness of the existing revenues, and the extent of the sum to be provided for, will be better ascertained.

[III] [23] There is a part of the public Debt of the United States, which is a cause of some perplexity to the Treasury. ⟨It is⟩ not comprehended within the existing p⟨rovis⟩ion for the foreign debt, which is confined to *Loans* made abroad; and it is questionable, whether it is to be regarded as a portion of the Domestic Debt. It is not only due to *foreigners*, but the interest upon it is payable, by express stipulation, in a foreign country, whence it becomes a matter of doubt, whether it be at all contemplated by the Act making provision for the debt of the United States. The part alluded to is that, which is due to certain foreign Officers, who served the United States during the late war. In consequence of a resolution of Congress, directing their interest to be paid to them in France,[24] the certificates which were issued to them specify, that "in pursuance of and compliance with a certain resolution of Congress of the third day of February 1784,

23. Material within brackets has been taken from the second draft.
24. On February 3, 1784, Congress "On the report of a committee, . . . *Resolved*, That the Superintendant of finance be, and he is hereby directed to take

the said interest is to be paid, annually, at the House of Monsr. le Grand, Banker in Paris". Interest has accordingly been paid to them at Paris, down to the 31st of December 1788 by virtue of a special resolution of Congress of the 20th. of August in that year; [25] since which period, no payment has been made.

It has been heretofore suggested, as the opinion of the Secretary, that it would be expedient to cause the whole of this description of debt to be paid off, among other ⟨re⟩asons, because it bears an interest at six per centum per annum, payable abroad, and can be discharged with a saving. The other reasons alluded to are of a nature both weighty and delicate, and too obvious, it is presumed, to need a specification. Some recent circumstances have served to strengthen the inducements to the measure. But if it should, finally, be deemed unadviseable, it is necessary, at least, that provision should be made for the interest, which is now suspended, under the doubt that has been stated, and from the want of authority to *remit* it pursuant to the contract.

The amount of this debt, with the arrears of interest to the end of the year 1791 is                    Dollars 220,6468$\frac{1}{100}$ [26]

IV. The Act making provision for the Debt of the United States [27] has appropriated the proceeds of the Western Lands as a fund for the discharge of the public debt. And the Act making provision for the reduction of the public debt,[28] has appropriated all the surplus of the duties on Imports and Tonnage, to the end of the year 1790, to the purpose of purchasing the debt at the market price; and has authorised the President to borrow the further sum of Two Millions of Dollars for the same object.

These measures serve to indicate the intention of the Legislature,

---

measures, as far as may be consistent with the finances of the United States, for remitting annually to the foreign officers of the late corps of engineers, the legionary corps lately commanded by Brigadier General Armand, to Major Segond and Captain Beaulieu, late of General Pulaski's corps and to Captain Pontiere, late aid-de-camp to Baron Steuben, the interest of such sums as may remain due to them respectively, after the payments which shall have been made to them in consequence of the resolution of the 22d of January last" (*JCC*, XXVI, 65–66).

25. See *JCC*, XXXIV, 443.
26. The first draft ends at this point.
27. See note 3.
28. See note 3.

as early and as fast as possible, to provide for the extinguishment of the existing debt.

In pursuance of that intention, it appears adviseable, that a systematic plan should be begun for the creation and establishment of a sinking fund.

An obvious basis of this establishment, which may be immediately contemplated, is the amount of the interest on so much of the debt as has been or shall be, from time to time, purchased, or paid off, or received in discharge of any debt or demand of the United States, made payable in public securities—over and above the interest of any new debt, which may be created, in order to such purchase or payment.

The purchases of the debt already made have left a sum of interest in the Treasury, which will be increased by future purchases—certain sums payable to the United States in their own securities, will, when received, have a similar effect. And there is ground to calculate on a saving upon the operations, which are in execution with regard to the foreign debt. The sale of the Western Lands, when provision shall be made for it, may be expected to produce a material addition to such a fund.

It is therefore submitted, that it be adopted as a principle, that all interest which shall have ceased to be payable; by any of the means above specified, shall be set apart and appropriated in the most firm and inviolable manner, as a fund for sinking the public debt, by purchase or payment; and that the said fund be placed under the direction of the officers, named in the second section of the Act making provision for the Reduction of the public debt,[29] to be by them applied towards the purchase of the said debt, until the annual produce of the said fund shall amount to two per Cent. of the intire portion of the debt which bears a present interest of six per Centum, and thenceforth to be applied, towards the redemption of that portion of the debt, according to the right which has been reserved to the Government.

29. Section 2 of "An Act making Provision for the Reduction of the Public Debt" provided that purchases of the public debt should be made under the direction of the president of the Senate, the Chief Justice, the Secretary of State, the Secretary of the Treasury, and the Attorney General (1 *Stat.* 184).

It will deserve the consideration of the Legislature, whether this fund ought not to be so vested, as to acquire the nature & quality of a *proprietary* Trust, incapable of being diverted, without a violation of the principles and sanctions of *property*.[30]

A rapid accumulation of this fund would arise from its own operation; but it is not doubted, that the progressive developement of the resources of the country and a reduction of the rate of interest, by the progress of public credit, already exemplified in a considerable degree, will speedily enable the Government to make important additions to it, in various ways. With due attention to preserve order and cultivate peace, a strong expectation may be indulged, that a reduction of the debt of the Country will keep pace with the reasonable hopes of its citizens.

All which is humbly submitted [31]          Alexander Hamilton
                                                Secretary of the Treasury

30. This paragraph does not appear in the second draft.
31. The second draft ends at this point.

A.
## Statement of the Debt of the United States, Funded

Agreeably to the Act of Congress of the 4th. of August 1790,[32] at the Treasury and the several Loan Offices, from the 1st October 1790 to 30th September 1791.

| | Funded 6 pr Cent Stock Dollars     Cents | Deferred 6 pr Cent Stock Dollars  Cents | Funded 3 pr Cent Stock Dollars     Cents | Total Amount Dollars     Cents |
|---|---|---|---|---|
| Treasury | 5,184,041.41 | 2,592,018.72 | 3,973,865.10 | 11,749,925.23 |
| New Hampshire | 191,322.44 | 95,661.22 | 147,423.35 | 434,407. 1 |
| Massachusetts | 2,126,062.40 | 1,063,134.94 | 1,984,457.41 | 5,173,554.75 |
| Rhode Island | 279,609.72 | 139,803.55 | 179,577.71 | 598,990.98 |
| Connecticut | 461,644.31 | 230,823.38 | 342,760.99 | 1,035,228.68 |
| New York | 2,204,016. 7 | 1,102,012.12 | 1,643,224.96 | 4,949,253.15 |
| New Jersey | 472,728.51 | 236,358.96 | 271,749.71 | 980,837.18 |
| Pennsylvania | 1,871,455.80 | 935,730.39 | 865,216.21 | 3,672,402.40 |
| Delaware | 26,191.19 | 13,095.64 | 16,242.75 | 55,529.58 |
| Maryland | 717,818.71 | 358,903.15 | 621,188.48 | 1,697,910.34 |
| Virginia | 453,079.69 | 226,996.35 | 343,128.22 | 1,024,104.26 |
| North Carolina | 13,064. 3 | 6,531.77 | 9,398.35 | 28,994.75 |
| South Carolina | 135,366.33 | 67,682.68 | 96,060.87 | 299,109.88 |
| Georgia | 40,149.82 | 20,074.92 | 37,008.29 | 97,233. 3 |
| | 14,177,450.43 | 7,088,727.79 | 10,531,303.— | 31,797,481.22 |

32. See note 3.

The amount of stock funded at the Treasury to 30th. September 1791, has been ascertained with accuracy, but at that time, many subscriptions had been made, which have not yet been adjusted, for want of proper powers of Attorney and other documents. It is therefore, probable, that on settlement of all the loans, the amount ⟨will⟩ be found somewhat different from what is now represented.

The sums funded at the several Loan Offices, it is presumed, are ascertained with accuracy; but as the loans had not been adjusted in all instances, when the returns were made, some immaterial differences will probably hereafter appear.

Joseph Nourse, Register

Treasury Department
Register's Office, September 30th. 1791.

## B.

## Statement of the Registered and Unsubscribed Debt of the United States, which remained Unfunded upon the close of the Loan, on the 30th. September 1791.

### Registered or Unfunded Debt

| | Dollars | Cents | Dollars | Cents | Dollars | Cents |
|---|---|---|---|---|---|---|
| The amount of this Debt, as stated to Congress,[33] on the third of March 1789, was | | | 4,598,462 | 78 | | |
| There were Treasury Certificates issued in exchange for Loan Office and Final settlement certificates cancelled by the Auditor of the Treasury, from the 3rd. of March 1789 to the 30th. of June 1791 | | | 4,716,376 | 45 | | |
| There have been Certificates issued to invalid pensioners and others, entitled thereunto, on final settlement in pursuance of acts of Congress of the present and late government | | | 134,883 | 18 | | |
| | | | 9,449,722 | 41 | | |
| Of the said Debt, there has been loaned, as follows: Vizt. | | | | | | |
| From the opening of the loan to the 31st. of March 1791 | 1,371,978 | 37 | | | | |
| " 1st. April to 30th. June 1791 | 1,088,466 | 60 | | | | |
| " 1st. of July to 30th. Sept. | 1,611,194 | 82 | | | | |
| | | | 4,071,639 | 79 | | |
| Which being deducted leaves a balance, | | | 5,378,082 | 62 | | |
| Principal sum due the several creditors on the Treasury books | | | | | | |
| The interest on said debt to 31st December 1790, is as follows Vizt. | | | | | | |
| Arrearages to 31st December 1787 | 479,677 | 88 | | | | |
| Three years interest from 1st. January 1788, to 31st. December 1790 | 968,054 | 76 | | | | |
| | | | 1,417,732 | 64 | | |
| Registered Debt, principal and interest | | | | | 6,795,815 | 26 |
| Unsubscribed debt. | | | | | | |
| The debt unsubscribed upon the books, New Jersey, Pennsylvania and Maryland Amounts to | | | 12,539 | 70 | | |
| Interest | | | 3,134 | 92 | | |
| | | | | | 15,674 | 62 |

33. For the debt as of March 3, 1789, see "Report Relative to a Provision for the Support of Public Credit," January 9, 1790.

Credits on the Treasury books, to invalid pensioners, and several corps, for which certificates of registered debt are yet to be issued.

## Invalid Pensioners

For the amount due to them under the Act of Congress,[34] providing for the payment of their arrearages — 56,152 76

The following Corps have credit on the Treasury books, being for certain certificates of final settlement, returned to the Treasury and Cancelled, and which certificates had issued to the non-commissioned Officers and soldiers of said Corps, respectively, for their pay

| | | |
|---|---:|---:|
| 4th. regiment, Pennsylvania Artillery | | 846 37 |
| Corps of Light Dragoons | | 1,009 83 |
| Invalid regiment | | 3,803 35 |
| Artillery officers | | 386 28 |
| Willet's regiment | | 2,565 42 |
| Hazen's regiment | | 11,267 49 |
| Baldwin's ditto of Artificers | | 281 28 |
| Corps of Sappers and Miners | | 416 93 |
| Armand's legion | | 834 17 |
| Lee's legion | | 593 17 |
| 4th Pennsylvania regiment, | 487 67 | |
| Captain North's Company | 1,062 97 | |
| " Lacy's | | 1,550 64 |
| Franklin's Company of Militia | | 280 67 |

Individual creditors, of the States of Pennsylvania and Maryland, have credit on the Treasury books, being for certificates of final settlement, returned to the Treasury and Cancelled, and which certificates had issued to them respectively

| | | |
|---|---:|---:|
| By Benjamin Stelle Commissioner of Pennsylvania | 5,436 66 | |
| " John White, Maryland | 693 89 | |
| | | 6,130 55 |
| | | 86,118 91 |

Interest on the foregoing credits — 21,529 72

107,648 63

Dollars — 6,919,138 51

Treasury Department
Registers Office, 30th. November 1791

Joseph Nourse Register

34. The United States had assumed the payment of military pensions to invalids "who were wounded and disabled during the late war" by "An Act providing for the payments of the Invalid Pensioners of the United States" (1 *Stat.* 95 [September 29, 1789]), which provided payment of invalids until March 4, 1790. The payment of invalids for the years 1790 and 1791 was continued in "An Act further to provide for the Payment of the Invalid Pensioners of the United States" (1 *Stat.* 129–30 [July 16, 1790]) and "An Act to continue in force the act therein mentioned, and to make further provision for the payment of Pensions to Invalids, and for the support of lighthouses, beacons, buoys, and public piers" (1 *Stat.* 218 [March 3, 1791]).

## C.

## Estimate of the Outstanding Debt, on the 30th. of September 1791, Vizt.

The amount of the domestic debt of the United States, as stated by the Secretary of the Treasury, in his report of the 9th. January 1790, to the House of Representatives, relative to a provision for the support of the public credit, is as follows:

| | |
|---|---:|
| Liquidated and Loan Office debt, as per Schedule C. | 27,383,917.67 |
| Interest thereon to the 31st. December 1790, pr ditto, D. | 13,030,168.20 |
| Additional sum for sinking the Continental Bills of Credit, and for the discharge of the other parts of the unliquidated debt | 2,000,000.00 |
| | 42,414,085.87 |

| | | |
|---|---:|---:|
| From which deduct amount as per statement A | 31,797,481.22 | |
| Amount of the registered debt, and Credit, with interest, per statement B. | 6,919,138.51 | 38,716,619.73 |
| | Balance outstanding | $ 3,697,466.14 |

Note—The balance above stated to be outstanding, probably exceeds the real sum. In the original estimate, the old emission bills were computed at 40 for 1, but they have been provided for at 100, for 1. There are also loan office Certificates, which were sent to public officers, to be applied to the public service, and which were supposed to have been so applied, but which have since, upon settlements of their accounts at the Treasury, been returned and cancelled.

In addition to this, payments in public securities are expected to be made into the Treasury, which will thereupon be cancelled. And it is presumable that in the course of the War, sums have been lost and destroyed, which are included in the estimate, but as there is some arrearage of interest, not included in the calculation; and as there are certain claims on the Treasury, the event, or amount of which is not yet determined, it is not possible now to make a precise estimate of the difference between the sum computed to be outstanding, and what will be really found so.

Treasury Department
Registers Office, November 30th. 1790

Joseph Nourse, Register.

35. See note 3.
36. In MS the word "unsubscribed" is used. The error was corrected in the copy in RG 39, Reports of Congress, Clerk's Table, 1791–1792, National Archives.

D.

Statement of Subscriptions to the Loan payable in Certificates or Notes issued by the respective States, in the several Loan Offices, from the 1st. of October 1790, to the 30th. of September 1791, Agreeably to the Act passed the 4th. of August 1790.[35]

| States | Amount assumed by the Act | Amount Subscribed[36] | Remaining unsubscribed to complete the amount assumed | Subscribed beyond the amount assumed | Estimated amount of the remaining debt of the State |
|---|---|---|---|---|---|
| | Dollars | Dollars Cts | Dollars Cts | Dollars Cts | Dollars Cts |
| New Hampshire | 300,000 | 242,501.25 | 57,498.75 | | 100,000.00 (a) |
| Massachusetts | 4,000,000 | 4,447,013.81 | | 477,013.81 | 1,838,540.66 (b) |
| Rhode Island | 200,000 | 344,259.49 | | 144,259.49 | 349,259.69 (c) |
| Connecticut | 1,600,000 | 1,455,331.81 | 144,668.19 | | 458,436.52 (a) |
| New York | 1,200,000 | 1,028,238.75 | 171,761.25 | | 195,639.79 (a) |
| New Jersey | 800,000 | 599,703.56 | 200,296.44 | | 207,647.78 (a) |
| Pennsylvania | 2,200,000 | 675,101.33 | 1,524,898.67 | | 500,000.00 (a) |
| Delaware | 200,000 | 53,305.84 | 146,694.16 | | none |
| Maryland | 800,000 | 299,255.40 | 500,744.60 | | 430,000.00 (c) |
| Virginia | 3,500,000 | 2,552,570.88 | 947,429.12 | | 1,172,555.25 (d) |
| North Carolina | 2,400,000 | 1,166,355.57 | 733,644.43 | | 713,192.30 (e) |
| South Carolina | 4,000,000 | 4,634,578.52 | | 634,578.52 | 1,965,756.33 (b) |
| Georgia | 300,000 | 300,000.00 | | | 400,000.00 (f) |
| | 21,500,000 | 18,328,186.21 | 4,447,665.61 | 1,255,851.82 | 8,331,028.32 |

# Notes

1. The sums marked (a) in the column of remaining debts, are inserted upon recent official communications.[37]

2. Those marked (b) are founded upon official statements, some time since received, and reported to the House of Representatives, on the ninth of January 1790,[38] adding interest for the subsequent period.

3. Those marked (c.) [39] are founded on informal information, but such as is deemed substantially authentic and accurate.

The estimate for Rhode Island including a sum not ascertained, which has been cancelled in consequence of former laws of the State, enjoying the creditors to bring in their certificates, and receive payment in paper money, but has been revived by a late law of the State, directing the sums paid, to be liquidated, according to a certain scale, and deducted from the original amount.

4. That marked (d) is founded on a report of a committee of the 11th. November 1791 to the House of Delegates of Virginia,[40] compared with a former return to the Treasury, and other information.

5. That marked (e) is founded upon a statement of the Comptroller of North Carolina, of 20th. May 1790.[41]

6. That marked (f) is founded on a statement of the Treasurer of Georgia, of the 30th. of April 1790,[42] compared with other information.

7. The sums, expressed in round numbers, is not meant to be understood as precisely accurate, but as very near the truth.

8. The foreign, as well as the domestic debt of the States, is included.

Alexander Hamilton Secretary of the Treasury

Treasury Department, January 25. 1792.

37. The official communications from New Hampshire, Connecticut, and New York have not been found. For Pennsylvania, see Thomas Smith to H, October 14, 1791; for New Jersey, see *Votes and Proceedings of the Sixteenth General Assembly of the State of New Jersey, At a Session begun at Trenton on the 25th Day of October, 1791, and continued by Adjournments* (Burlington, 1791), 90.

38. See "Report Relative to a Provision for the Support of Public Credit," January 9, 1790.

39. A committee of the House of Delegates of Maryland reported on December 13, 1792, providing estimates of the outstanding and funded debt of that state (*Votes and Proceedings of the House of Delegates of the State of Maryland. November session, 1791, Being the first session of this Assembly* [Microfilm Collection of Early State Records, Library of Congress], 86-89).

A part of H's information concerning the Rhode Island debt was contained in the memorial from Rhode Island which was referred to H on January 4, 1792 (see note 12). The "late law" of Rhode Island may be found in John Russell Bartlett, ed., *Records of the State of Rhode Island and Providence Plantations in New England* (Providence, 1865), X, 447-50.

40. See *Journal of the House of Delegates of the Commonwealth of Virginia, Begun and Held at the Capitol, in the City of Richmond, on Monday, the Seventeenth Day of October, One Thousand Seven Hundred and Ninety-One* (Richmond, 1791), 46-47.

41. Although no official report of the comptroller of North Carolina, Francis Child, has been found, a letter from Child to Samuel Johnston, Senator from North Carolina, dated May 20, 1790, states that Child enclosed an account of the outstanding state debt in his letter (ALS, Treasurer's and Comptroller's Papers, Correspondence of the Comptroller, 1790, State of North Carolina, Department of Archives and History, Raleigh).

42. Document not found.

## From Maria Reynolds [1]

[Philadelphia, January 23–March 18, 1792]
Monday Naght Eight C, L

Sir,

I need not acquaint that I had Been Sick all moast Ever sence I saw you as I am sure you allready no It   Nor would I solicit a favor wich Is so hard to obtain were It not for the Last time   Yes Sir Rest assuirred I will never ask you to Call on me again   I have kept my Bed those tow dayes and now rise from My pillow wich your Neglect has filled with the sharpest thorns   I no Longer doubt what I have Dreaded to no but stop I do not wish to se you to to say any thing about my Late disappointments   No I only do it to Ease a heart wich is ready Burst with Greef   I can neither Eate or sleep   I have Been on the point of doing the moast horrid acts at I shuder to think where I might been what will Become of me. In vain I try to Call reason to aide me but alas ther Is no Comfort for me   I feel as If I should not Contennue long and all the wish I have Is to se you once more that I may my doupts Cleared up for God sake be not so voed of all humannity as to deni me this Last request but if you will not Call some time this night   I no its late but any tim between this and twelve A Clock I shall be up   Let me Intreat you If you wont Come to send me a Line   oh my head I can rite no more   do something to Ease My heart or Els I no not what I shall do for so I cannot live   Commit this to the care of my maid be not offended I beg

"Reynolds Pamphlet," August 31, 1797.

1. This letter is printed as document No. VIII in the appendix of the "Reynolds Pamphlet," August 31, 1797. It was the first of three letters which Maria Reynolds wrote to H between January 23 and March 18, 1792.

For background to this letter, see James Reynolds to H, December 15, 17, 19, 22, 1791, January 3, 17, 1792; H to Reynolds, December 15, 1791; Maria Reynolds to H, December 15, 1791.

## From Maria Reynolds [1]

[Philadelphia, January 23–March 18, 1792]
Wensday Morning ten of Clock.

Dear Sir

I have kept my bed those tow days past but find myself mutch better at presant though yet full distreesed and shall till I se you fretting was the Cause of my Illness I thought you had been told to stay away from our house and yesterday with tears I my Eyes I beged Mr. once more to permit your visits and he told upon his honnour that he had not said anything to you and that It was your own fault believe me I scarce knew how to beleeve my senses and if my setura-tion was insupportable before I heard this It was now more so fear prevents my saing more only that I shal be misarable till I se you and if my dear freend has the Least Esteeme for the unhappy Maria whos grateest fault is Loveing him he will come as soon as he shall get this and till that time My breast will be the seate of pain and woe.

   adieu


Col. Hamilton

P S.   If you cannot come this Eveneng to stay just come only for one moment as I shal be Lone   Mr. is going to sup with a friend from New-York.

"Reynolds Pamphlet," August 31, 1797.
   1. This letter is printed as document No. IX in the appendix of the "Reynolds Pamphlet," August 31, 1797. It was the second of three letters which Maria Reynolds wrote to H between January 23 and March 18, 1792.
   For background to this letter, see James Reynolds to H, December 15, 17, 19, 22, 1791, January 3, 17, 1792; H to Reynolds, December 15, 1791; Maria Reynolds to H, December 15, 1791.


## From Maria Reynolds [1]

[Philadelphia, January 23–March 18, 1792]
Monday Morning.

   the Girl tells me that you said If I wanted any thing that I should write this morning alas my friend want what what can ask for but peace wich you alone can restore to my tortured bosom and do My dear Col hamilton on my kneese Let me Intreatee you to reade my Letter and Comply with my request tell the bearer of this or give her a line you need not be the least affraid let me not die with fear have pity on me my freend for I deserve it I would not solicit this favor but I am sure It cannot injure you and will be all the happiness I Ever Exspect to have But oh I am disstressed more than I can tell My heart Is ready to burst and my tears wich once could flow with Ease are now denied me Could I only weep I would thank heaven and bless the hand that

"Reynolds Pamphlet," August 31, 1797.
1. This letter is printed as document No. X in the appendix of the "Reynolds Pamphlet," August 31, 1797. It was the first of three letters which Maria Reynolds wrote to H between January 23 and March 18, 1792.
For background to this letter, see James Reynolds to H, December 15, 17, 19, 22, 1791, January 3, 1792; H to Reynolds, December 15, 1791; Maria Reynolds to H, December 15, 1791.

## From Isaac Sherman [1]

Philadelphia 23d. January 1792.

Sir,

I shall not take up your time by assigning particular reasons for my defering paying you the balance due on the money which you lent me in New York; but shall just observe generally, that some circumstances which occurred subsequent to my letter of the 5th of February last [2] that, I did not, neither could I then foresee, rendered a new loan, or a delay of payment indispensibly necessary. I have it now in my power to pay the balance with ease to myself, which is enclosed.

Give me leave to observe, that I feel most sensibly under obligations to you, not only for the money which you advanced, but from other considerations. [3]

I have the Honor to be, Sir with the most perfect Esteem & respect Your most Obedient Servt. Isaac Sherman.

The Honorable Alexander Hamilton Esqr.

ALS, Hamilton Papers, Library of Congress.
1. For background to this letter, see Sherman to H, October 16, 1790. Sherman was employed in the Treasury Department to examine and count various types of Government securities.
2. Letter not found.
3. H endorsed this letter as follows: "Received 30 Dollars inclosed Feb. 8, 92."

## To George Washington

*Treasury Department, January 23, 1792.* Submits "the draft of a Report, pursuant to an order of the House of Representatives of the first day of November last." [1]

LC, George Washington Papers, Library of Congress.
1. See "Report on the Public Debt and Loans," January 23, 1792

## From Otho H. Williams

Baltimore 23d. January 1792

Sir.

The only Brig Hope that I know "which frequents this port" belongs to Stephen Zacharie of Baltimore, a Citizen of the United States, see No. 52, 1790.[1] Mr. Stephen Zacharie is of the House of Zacharie, Coopman & Company. The partners are, *Stephen Zacharie*, resident in Baltimore, who became a Citizen of the State of Maryland, according to an Act of the Legislature for the Naturalization of foreigners, about the Year 1789.[2] *Francis Coopman* a Citizen of France, residing in the West Indies and *John Baptist Vochez*, a Citizen of France, resident in Baltimore. Mr. Gernon resides in Richmond, but whether he is a Citizen of the United States or not I am not informed.[3]

The Brigg hope cleared last from this port on the 22d. of October 1791 for Cape Francois to which place she usually, I believe, constantly runs, and where Mr. Coopman is acting partner. She is now commanded by Mr. Latouch, a Native frenchman endorsed as Master the 7th March 1791 at this office. Whether he is a Citizen or not I do not know, the law of Congress does not authorize a Collector in such a Case to require proof and I am not informed. It is said that the Hope is now at Annapolis, prevented by the Ice from proceeding to this port.

This Brig Hope is the same which formerly belonged to Connecticut, and about which there was a reference to you by Zacharie Coopman & Co. because I refused to grant to her the privileges of an American Vessel on account of some Informality in the instrument of Sale; and the same about which there was lately a petition to Congress to refund the duty upon tonnage exacted here according to law.[4]

Permit me again to suggest to you that the informalities of a bill, of Sale of a Vessel, can be known to no Officers of the Customs except where the new Register is granted, and that, unless it is noted by the Collector on the back of the new Register, the privileges of an American Vessel can not *on that account only* be denied at any other port.

I am Sir   Your most Obedient Humble Servant

Alexander Hamilton Esqr
Secy of the Treasury

ADf, RG 53, "Old Correspondence," Baltimore Collector, National Archives.
1. See Williams to H, December 29, 1790, and H to Williams, April 20, 1791, January 14, 1792.
2. "An Act for the relief of certain foreigners who have settled within this state, and for other purposes, supplemental to the act for naturalization" (William Kilty, ed., *The Laws of Maryland* [Annapolis, 1800], II, November, 1789, Ch. XXIV).
3. See H to Sharp Delany, January 11, 1791, and H to Williams, January 14, 1792.
4. The petition of Stephen Zacharie had been presented to Congress on November 14, 1791 (*Journal of the House*, I, 453).

# From Thomas Jefferson

*Philadelphia, January 24, 1792.* "In consequence of the act of Congress [1] appropriating 40,000 Dollars per annum from July 1. 1790. for our intercourse with foreign nations, I received from the Treasurer [2] a bill, the last spring, on our bankers in Amsterdam [3] for 99,000 florins. As this will be nearly exhausted by this time, and there will be large calls immediately by Mr. Morris,[4] Mr. Pinkney [5] & mr Short [6] for their outfits & salaries, I must ask the favor of a like draught on our bankers in Amsterdam for 40,000 dollars more."

ALS, letterpress copy, Thomas Jefferson Papers, Library of Congress; LC, Papers of the Continental Congress, National Archives.
1. "An Act providing the means of intercourse between the United States and foreign nations" (1 *Stat.* 128–29 [July 1, 1790]).
2. Samuel Meredith.
3. Willink, Van Staphorst, and Hubbard.

4. Gouverneur Morris, United States Minister Plenipotentiary to France.
5. Thomas Pinckney, United States Minister to Great Britain.
6. William Short, United States Minister at The Hague.

## To Philip Schuyler [1]

[*Philadelphia, January 24, 1792.* On January 29, 1792, Schuyler wrote to Hamilton: "Your favor of the 24th instant I received yesterday." *Letter not found.*

1. Schuyler, who was H's father-in-law, had been elected to the short term as United States Senator from New York in 1789 and was defeated for re-election by Aaron Burr in 1791. He was then elected to the fifteenth New York Senate, which met in New York City on January 5, 1792.

## To William Seton [1]

Philadelphia January
24. 1792

My Dear Sir

I feel great satisfaction in knowing from yourself, that your institution rejects the idea of coalition with the new project, or rather Hydra of projects.

I shall labour to give what has taken place a turn favourable to *another* Union; the propriety of which is as you say clearly illustrated by the present state of things.

It is my wish that the Bank of New York may, by all means, continue to receive deposits from the Collector, in the paper of the Bank of the U States, and that they may also receive payment for the Dutch Bills in the same paper. This paper may either be remitted to the Treasurer or remain in the Bank as itself shall deem most expedient. I have explicitly directed the Treasurer to forbear drawing on the Bank of New York, without special direction from me. And my intention is to leave you in possession of all the money you have or may receive 'till I am assured that the present storm is effectually weathered.

Every body here sees the propriety of your having refused the paper of the Bank of the United States in such a crisis of your affairs.

Be Confidential with me. If you are pressed, whatever support may be in my power shall be afforded. I consider the public interest as materially involved in aiding a valuable institution like yours to withstand the attacks of a confederated host of frantic and I fear, in too many instances, unprincipled gamblers.

Adieu Heaven take care of good Men and good views. Yrs

A Hamilton

William Seton Esquire

ALS, Columbia University Libraries
1. For background to this letter, see H to Seton, January 18, 1792, and Seton to H, January 22, 1792.

## To Thomas Jefferson

[*Philadelphia, January 25, 1792*. On January 26, 1792, Jefferson wrote to Hamilton and referred to information "mentioned in your letter of yesterday." *Letter not found*].

## To George Washington [1]

[Philadelphia, January 25, 1792][2]

Mr. Hamilton presents his respects to the President & submits the following alterations in the Letter—

instead of "I shall be *glad*" to say "it is my desire" or "it appears adviseable" that you prepare &c.

Instead of "When *our Constituents*" say

"When the Community are called upon for considerable exertions, to relieve a part, which is suffering under the hand of an enemy, it is desireable to manifest that due pains have been taken by those entrusted with the administration of their affairs to avoid the evil."

It is a doubt whether *our constituents* be a proper phrase to be used by the President in addressing a subordinate officer.

AL, RG 59, Miscellaneous Letters, National Archives.
1. On December 12, 1791, Washington submitted to Congress Major General Arthur St. Clair's report on the defeat which the northwestern Indians had inflicted on American troops under St. Clair's command on November 4, 1791. On January 11, 1792, Washington submitted to Congress two confidential reports prepared by Secretary of War Henry Knox. Washington then ordered Knox to submit to Congress for subsequent publication a statement similar to

the second report of January 11, 1792, which had shown ". . . the conduct which the United States have observed to the neighboring Indian tribes, both during the late war, and since the peace with Great Britain . . ." and that would "enable the mind to form a judgment how far a further prosecution of hostilities against the Indians would comport with . . . justice and dignity . . ." (*ASP, Indian Affairs*, I, 197). Washington also asked both Thomas Jefferson and H to prepare drafts for an introduction to Knox's forthcoming report to Congress. Jefferson's reply to the President's request reads as follows:

"Th: Jefferson presents his respects to the President of the U.S. and subjoins what he supposes might form a proper introduction to the statement prepared by the Secretary at war. The occasion is so new, that however short the letter proposed, he has no doubt it will need correction both as to the matter & manner.

"Jan. 25. 1792.

"Sir

"As the circumstances which have engaged the U. S. in the present Indian war, may some of them be out of the public recollection & others perhaps be unknown, I shall be glad if you will prepare & publish from authentic documents, a statement of those circumstances, as well as of the measures which have been taken from time to time for the reestablishment of peace & friendship. When our constituents are called on for considerable exertions to relieve a part of their fellow-citizens suffering under the hand of an enemy, it is desireable for those entrusted with the administration of their affairs to communicate without reserve what they have done to ward off the evil." (AL, RG 59, Miscellaneous Letters, National Archives; AL letterpress copy, Thomas Jefferson Papers, Library of Congress.)

After seeing Jefferson's draft, H proposed certain changes, which are printed above. Washington then incorporated H's suggestions in the Jefferson draft, and this became the letter he sent to Knox. See *GW*, XXXI, 459. Washington's letter to Knox, in turn, served as an introduction to Knox's report to Congress, which is dated January 26, 1792, and is entitled "The Causes of the existing Hostilities between the United States and certain Tribes of Indians, Northwest of the Ohio, stated and explained from official and authentic Documents, and published in obedience to the orders of the President of the United States" (*Annals of Congress*, III, 1046).

2. In *GW*, XXXI, 459, as well as in *Annals of Congress*, III, 1046, Washington's letter to Knox is dated January 16, 1792. H's notes to Jefferson's draft have been dated in accordance with the January 25, 1792, date that appears on Jefferson's draft.

## From Thomas Jefferson

Philadelphia Jan. 26. 1792.

Sir

It is perfectly equal to me that the 1233⅓ dollars mentioned in your letter of yesterday,[1] be taken out of the 40,000 Dollars now desired, or not.[2] You will observe that the two sums of 40,000 D. each are for the interval between July 1. 1790. & July 1. 1792. and that the act is to continue, even if not renewed, till the end of the next session of Congress,[3] probably the beginning of March 1793. The heavy draughts for Outfits for the late appointments [4] will require a new call in time for the commencements of the 3d. year of the act.

I have the honor to be with great respect Sir   Your most obedient & most humble servt                                    Th: Jefferson

Colo. Hamilton

ALS, letterpress copy, Thomas Jefferson Papers, Library of Congress; LC, Papers of the Continental Congress, National Archives.
    1. Letter not found. Jefferson is presumably referring to warrant No. 780, which was issued on December 20, 1790, in the amount of $1,233.33 in part payment of Gouverneur Morris's expenses on his London mission and John Brown Cutting's expenses in connection with his services in England to impressed United States seaman (ASP, Foreign Relations, I, 131–32, 137).
    2. See Jefferson to H, January 24, 1792.
    3. Section 2 of "An Act providing the means of intercourse between the United States and foreign nations" states: "And be it further enacted, That this act shall continue and be in force for the space of two years, and from thence until the end of the next session of Congress thereafter, and no longer" (1 Stat. 128–29 [July 1, 1790]).
    4. The "late appointments" were Thomas Pinckney as United States Minister to Great Britain, Gouverneur Morris as United States Minister Plenipotentiary to France, and William Short as United States Minister at The Hague.

## From William Short

Paris Jan. 26. 1792.

Sir

I have had the honor of recieving since my return to this place on the 15th. inst. your letter of Nov 1. I have previously acknowleged your others as they have been recieved. Mine to you have been exceedingly multiplied for the reasons which I have repeatedly mentioned. You acknowlege their reciept as low done as the 27th. of July, but do not mention those of the 8th. & 19th. of the same month. I take it for granted however they must have been since delivered to you as they accompanied letters to the Secretary of State, which he mentions having recieved. The dates of my letters since then are Aug. 8. 23. 30. 31. Sep. 3. 23. Oct. 10. Nov. 8. 12. 22. Dec. 1. 15. 23. 28. 30.

My last will have informed you of the then position of affairs at Amsterdam & Antwerp. Nothing new has since occurred at the first, & of course the contract signed by precaution for a second loan at

4 p. cent [1] has not been yet acted under—as soon as the opportunity shall permit itself they will give me notice of it & as the bankers do not mention any changes of circumstances it may be expected ere long—unless indeed war should take place in Europe of which it cannot be denied the proceedings of the assembly here increase the prospect, notwithstanding the aversion to it really entertained by most of the other powers.

I have thought it best to suspend as yet the remittances which I informed you would be immediately made here on the late loan opened there.[2] They would necessarily have been inconsiderable as yet, as a part of the loan is destined to supply the deficiency necessary to answer your draughts (wch. I suppose will amount as you formerly mentioned to 2½ millions of florins)[3] & to discharge the sums now becoming due at Amsterdam on former loans. It was to be feared if this suspension had not taken place, that it would have defeated the plan which I mentioned to you in the two last pages of my letter of Dec. 28. It is much to be desired by us & the mover is sanguine in its success. I cannot help however having strong doubts myself, for the reasons already mentioned to you. The question will necessarily be decided soon one way or another.

I mentioned to you formerly the sums which had been then received on the loan at Antwerp.[4] These reciepts have gone on much more slowly in this month than M. de Wolf [5] had given me assurances of. He still says however that he shall have paid f. 500,000 before the end of the month, & if so we shall have no reason to complain, as he has five months to complete the loan, in equal monthly portions, & this is the only the second. I cannot help doubting however their being carried to that extent as he has only paid about a million in all at the date of my last letters from Antwerp the 18th. inst.

He had been more bold perhaps in his assurances of the reciepts he should make above the terms of the loan, than he was warranted in,

ALS, letterpress copy, William Short Papers, Library of Congress.
  1. Short had signed "a contract for a loan of six millions at 4 p. cent." to avoid "a tax of which the borrower will certainly be obliged to pay the whole or much the greatest part." See Short to H, December 30, 1791.
  2. See Short to H, December 28, 1791.
  3. See H to Short, May 24, 1791.
  4. See Short to H, December 30, 1791. For a description of the Antwerp loan, see Short to H, November 8, 1791, note 4, and November 12, 1791.
  5. Charles John Michael de Wolf, the banker of the United States at Antwerp.

in order to increase my opinion of the resources of Antwerp. As he expected them to remit these sums by bills of exchange, he thought it would be easy to cover the delay if any should arise under the pretext of not being able to find so suddenly bills for so large an amount. If my suspicions should be verified I shall consider him less to be relied on than I had concieved from what Mr. Morris [6] so often told me of him & from the concurrent testimony of people both at Antwerp & at Amsterdam. It is probable however that the same deception & with the same motive would have been practiced by most of those who are in that line of business.

Notwithstanding all the reasons I had for supposing M. de Wolf fully entitled to the extensive confidence which is always & unavoidably placed in those employed to make loans, yet when at Antwerp & about to sign the bonds I could not help for my own personal tranquillity taking the precaution of giving him only a part at a time. He was perfectly satisfied with this desiring only to have such a number as to be sure to be able to deliver them as fast as they should be asked for. On my return from Amsterdam I added 800 bonds to those already given him making in the whole 2000—of wch. as I have mentioned one half was paid at the date of my last letters. The others I brought with me & shall send them to him when wanted—as they will have only my signature there will be no risk, being not complete without his. Although I am persuaded such a caution was unnecessary, yet I could not prevent myself from taking it at the time, as the anxiety from which I have never been free since I have begun to act under the powers given me for making loans (& for which nothing can compensate but the satisfaction you have been pleased to express with what has been done) was increased in this instance, arising from my confidence in M. de Wolf, being not the result of my own experience or that of any other acting for the U.S.— but simply founded on the opinions of others. I hope & trust however that experience will shew that he is a proper person for this kind of business. He presses me much to authorize him to take preparatory measures for making a loan at 4 p cent, assuring me constantly in the most positive terms that the present loan may be considered as absolutely out of the market. I have convinced him however that I will do

6. Gouverneur Morris had undertaken the preliminary negotiations for the Antwerp loan. See Short to H, July 19, 24, 1791.

nothing further until the present loan shall have been actually recieved & paid—& even after that I shall do nothing further until I know your opinion on the subject.

When I communicated to the commissaries of the treasury, as has been already mentioned to you,[7] the intention of the U.S. to make up the depreciation on the assignats, previous to my setting out for Antwerp, they expressed much satisfaction, said they would endeavour to find out some means of fixing the real depreciation in a manner that should be agreeable, & desired me in the mean time to have committed as usual such sums as the U.S. should destine for France. Whilst at Antwerp M. de Wolf began these remittances & carried them as far as about f 100,000. & at that time there came on a crisis which was exceedingly alarming for remittances—two rich banking houses in Brussels failed & it was expected that others would follow them. The assignats went through such a rapid course of depreciation that they had for a moment passed the rate of exchange & it was always uncertain whether between the day of purchasing the bills at Antwerp & that of recieving them at Paris there would not be such a fall as to be a loss to the U.S. who were to find their indemnity in the course of exchange for that they intend allowing France for depreciation on assignats. These circumstances left me no hesitation in proposing to the commissaries of the Treasury to recieve the sums arising on this loan at Antwerp. As they had pointedly refused to give their reciepts in livres tournois agreably to the current rate of exchange, & insisted on the rate being previously paid between us at Paris in consequence of the misunderstanding between our & their bankers at Amsterdam last summer as was then mentioned to you [8] & as the U.S. intended making up the depreciation, I saw no difficulty in consenting that the reciepts for the sums paid should be expressed in florins adding that their value in French money should be hereafter regulated. By this means the payments were made without risk to the U.S. & at the moment of the cash being recieved by M. de Wolf without waiting until bills can be found & also without influencing the exchange to the disadvantage of the U.S. as is inevitable in purchasing them for so large an amount at so confined a market as

7. See Short to H, November 22, 1791.
8. See Short to H, June 19, 1791.

Antwerp. The rate of exchange wch. is regularly marked & the actual depreciation of assignats will furnish the proper data for definitively regulating this business at the close of the account with France.

I have the honor of inclosing you a state of that account as furnished me by the commissaries of the Treasury last month. It is different in some respects from the note you formerly sent to me,[9] viz. as to the commencement of interest on the ten million Loan [10]— & the advances made by individuals to the U. S. These are differences however which there can be no difficulty in settling.

What I have said to the commissaries of the Treasury & the Minister of foreign affairs lies with respect to the making up of depreciation relatively to the future payments, beginning for the Antwerp loan; those on the Amsterdam loan having been made previously to your letter.[11] I saw no inconvenience & even propriety in leaving them open to your reconsideration.

I have said nothing to you lately with respect to London as a place of loans—the persons whom I formerly mentioned to you,[12] thinking since the reduction of the rate of interest that it would be impracticable to effect them under present circumstances. The American stock has become an object of regular sale there & is now quoted by the bankers in their correspondence with this & the other parts of Europe, in the same manner as the English funds. Its price will shew when the U.S. will be able to make these loans to their advantage.

The Minister of Genoa [13] here in consequence of letters from his relation M. Durazzo at Genoa, [14] has resumed the subject with me & seems very desirous that I should open a loan there. M. Durazzo had written under the idea of the U.S. having made their last loan at 4½. p cent. On my observing that it was 4. p cent he agreed that it could not be expected that we should give more there. I told him that I would not decide at present whether I should wish for a loan at

9. See enclosures in H to Short, September 1, 1790.

10. For a description of the 1782 French loan of ten million livres, see Willink, Van Staphorst, and Hubbard to H, January 25, 1790, note 3.

11. See H to Short, September 2, 1791.

12. See Short to H, August 23, September 23, October 10, and November 8, 1791.

13. Christoforo Vincenzo de Spinola.

14. Girolamo D. Durazzo. See Short to H, July 24–25, 1791.

Genoa even at that rate. This will be communicated to M. Durazzo, who will say whether a loan of that sort could be effected there. The propriety of such a loan, after what you have said will depend of course on the prospects at Amsterdam, & on the measures that shall be adopted here in consequence of the proposition of the Minister of Marine.[15]

I have spoken with M. de Brantsen [16] since my return here. He tells me that he has been looking for some person capable of translating into French the observations he has had collected with respect to the mint in Holland. He finds it a difficult task on account of the technical terms. I have enquired also for such a person in vain. He hopes to find one among the Dutch refugees here. I will lose no time in furnishing you whatever I can procure from him.

I subjoin here a list of the vessels which passed the Sound last year as given to the public. I sent you from Amsterdam a list of the American vessels which went to Petersburg.

I have the honor to be most respectfully, Sir, your most obedient humble servant                                    W: Short

The Honble.
Alexander Hamilton Secretary of the Treasury, Philadelphia

15. See Short to H, December 28, 1791.
16. Gerard Brantsen. See Short to H, September 23 and December 30, 1791.


## To Thomas Jefferson

*[Philadelphia, January 27, 1792. Letter not found.]*

Letter recorded in Jefferson's list of letters written and received (AD, Thomas Jefferson Papers, Library of Congress).


## To Wilhem and Jan Willink, Nicholaas and Jacob Van Staphorst, and Nicholas Hubbard

*Treasury Department, January 27, 1792.* "The Treasurer of the United States has been directed to draw upon you a Bill, at ten days, for 95.947½ Guilders, in favor of Mr. Jefferson,[1] the Secretary for the Department of State, to which I request you to pay due honor."

Copy, RG 233, Reports of the Treasury Department, 1792–1793, Vol. III, National Archives. This letter was enclosed in H's "Report on Foreign Loans," February 13, 1793.
    1. See Jefferson to H, January 24, 26, 1792.

## To the President and Directors of the Bank of the United States

Treasury Department
January 28, 1792.

Gentlemen

In order to a final arrangement on the subject, I have the honor to recapitulate to you the suggestions made by me in our late conference.

First I am authorized to make known the wish of the President of the United States, that the provision in the 11th. Section of the Act constituting your institution may be carried into effect, and to take with the Bank the requisite arrangements for that purpose.[1]

It is conceived that it will be for the mutual interest and convenience of the Government and of the Bank, to fulfil the object of that provision by one operation. This may be done by a subscription on the part of the Government of the whole two millions of Dollars, and an immediate loan to the Government of an equal Sum.

The terms of reimbursement are prescribed by the law.[2] The rate of Interest and the time when the arrangement shall be deemed to have taken effect, only remain to be adjusted. It appears equitable, as it relates to the constitution of the Stock of the Bank, that the interest to be paid in this case by the public should be six per Centum per Annum: This however would not be considered as a precedent for any future loan; the prices of the public funds indicating that it cannot hereafter be necessary for the Government to borrow at so high a rate of Interest.

Sparks Transcripts, Harvard College Library.
    1. Section 11 of "An Act to incorporate the subscribers to the Bank of the United States" states that the President of the United States could authorize the Federal Government to subscribe two million of the ten million dollar capital stock of the bank. It also authorized the Government to borrow two million dollars from the bank "reimbursable, in ten years, by equal annual instalments; or at any time sooner, or in any greater proportions, that the government may think fit" (1 Stat. 196 [February 25, 1791]).
    2. See note 1.

As to the circumstance of time it is presumed that it will be thought most adviseable to let it retrospect to the commencement of the operations of the Bank.

If this arrangement shall meet the approbation of the directors, the proper form of a contract, to be ratified by the President of the United States, will be mutually adjusted.

The Treasurer [3] in conformity to directions from me has begun to deposit the Public monies in the Bank of the United States. The sum already there by his return of this date is 464.177 Dollars and 68 cents. Considerable sums still remain and will shortly accrue in the Banks of North America and New York. It is my intention as fast as it can be done without producing any embarrassment elsewhere, to transfer to, and pass the whole of the public monies through the Bank of the United States and its departments.

Second. It will probably be found mutually convenient to the Government and to the Institution under your direction, to carry on through you the negotiations concerning the public Revenues.

Hitherto the following plan has been pursued with the Banks of North America and New York.

The several Collectors of the Customs have been instructed [4] to receive the Notes of those banks in *payment* for the duties, as they became payable, and to *exchange* for them any specie which they should have received, between one weekly return and another weekly return; but not to exchange for them any specie which they had once returned to the Treasury as in hand.

The notes which, in either way, have come to their possession, have been remitted to the Treasurer, in moieties under an agreement and instructions copies of which (A & B) are enclosed.

With regard to the specie sums which have been returned as in hand, draughts have been drawn for them by the Treasurer, and deposited for sale in the Banks with direction to sell those upon Georgia and South Carolina at forty five days credit, on North Carolina and Virginia, and the ports on or southward of Patuxent; on the western shore and on the eastern shore of Maryland; except Baltimore, at thirty days; on Connecticut and Rhode Island at thirty

3. Samuel Meredith.
4. See "Treasury Department Circular to the Collectors of the Customs," September 22, 1789.

days; on Massachusetts forty five, and on New Hampshire sixty days, taking satisfactory Notes for the same, with two good names or two good firms upon them.

It has been lately the practice to pass the draughts deposited immediately to the Credit of the Treasurer as cash; an arrangement of considerable moment to the order of his accounts, with which view it was adopted.

But it has nevertheless been understood that the Credits which were allowed to be given for those draughts, should be at the public risk.

I propose a similar arrangement on this point, with the Bank of the United States; unless the following arrangement in lieu of it should appear preferable to the directors. Viz:

Weekly returns of cash from the Collectors of Customs to be made to the Bank. The monies returned from time to time to be immediately passed to the credit of the Treasurer and of course to be at the disposal of the Bank.

In this case it will be necessary for the Bank to undertake to furnish the monies for all public payments in the several states to the extent of the funds of the Government in their disposal.

The amounts of all Stated payments to be notified to the Bank at certain periods, preceeding such payments, to be regulated between the Treasury and the Bank.

If the first mentioned arrangement should be preferred, it may deserve the consideration of the directors whether they will engage to take the risk of the credits which they shall give, upon themselves on being permitted to take discounts upon the amount of the bills sold for the emolument of the Bank.

Third. The payment of the interest on the public debt at the Bank and its several Departments, by the officers of the institution according to such forms and under such regulations as shall be concerted with the Treasury, will be an accommodation to the Treasury and a security to the public, at the same time that it will probably be also an accommodation to the Institution and to Individuals.

This has been hitherto done by the Bank of North America as to payments on the Spot.

Fourth. The sale of public bills, generally will, if agreeable to the Bank, be committed to it and to its Departments; to be made according to such terms as shall be prescribed from the Treasury.

It will be understood that in every instance, in which public bills or draughts are confided to the disposition of the Bank, the Credits allowed to be given will be at the risk of the Government; (unless where the Bank shall be willing to take that risk upon themselves for the benefit of discounts as before intimated). Nothing more will be required than due discretion as in other cases of agency, and *immediate notice to the Treasury* of any delay of payment, which may at any time happen.

This last requisite will be deemed indispensable. If any delay happens and immediate notice be not given, the Bank will be considered as thenceforth responsible to the Government for the money, the payment of which shall have been delayed, and any interest which may accrue during such delay shall be for the benefit of the Bank.

Weekly returns of the sales of all bills confided to the Bank and its departments for sale will be expected.

It will be considered as a principle in all transactions between the Bank and the Treasury, that the Government is to bear all losses which may happen from the defaults of its own officers.

It will at once occur to the directors that arrangements, which are calculated to repose so great a public trust in the Institution, ought to be accompagnied with every proper precaution for the public satis-faction.

They will therefore permit me to call their attention to the provision contained in the Sixteenth clause of the Seventh Section of the Act which constitutes the Charter of the Bank.[5] If no particular objection occurs a weekly statement will be most satisfactory. To answer the design of the Act it must of course include the several departments of the Institution.

There is but one more point on which I shall at present trouble the Directors.

The distant public officers are put to great inconvenience and

5. The sixteenth clause of Section 7 of "An Act to incorporate the subscribers to the Bank of the United States" reads in part as follows: "The officer at the head of the head of the treasury department of the United States, shall be furnished, from time to time, as often as he may require, not exceeding once a week, with statements of the amount of the capital stock of the said corporation, and of the debts due to the same; of the monies deposited therein; of the notes in circulation, and of the cash in hand; and shall have a right to inspect such general accounts in the books of the bank, as shall relate to the said statements" (1 *Stat.* 195).

sometimes to more expense than they can afford by the necessity of employing Agents to receive their compensations at the Treasury.

If it should be convenient to the Bank to undertake the paying and remitting of these compensations, it would be a great and grateful accommodation to the public Officers.

In this case they will be advised to send the requisite powers to such Officer of the Bank as the Directors shall indicate, and a list of the Sum payable to each person will be made out Quarterly, and deposited with the Bank, in conformity to which a warrant upon the Treasurer in favor of the Bank will issue.

All necessary forms will be so regulated as to occasion as little trouble as possible to the Bank.

With very respectful consideration    I am Gentlemen &c

A. H. Secy

## To William Short

Treasury Department January 28th 1792

Sir

You will find herewith duplicate of my letter of the 30th of November last—Since which I am without any of your favours.

It is with sincere pleasure, I embrace the opportunity of congratulating you on your appointment to the Hague as Minister Resident.[1] This will afford you a better opportunity of watching and appreciating the course of Circumstances. You will consequently be obliged less to rely on others, and I trust by seizing favorable moments, you will be able to reduce the rate of interest on such future loans as may be found necessary.

A bill has lately been drawn upon our Commissioners in favor of Mr Jefferson for 95,947½ guilders for the use of the foreign department.[2]

I send you herewith copy of a report of mine to the House of Representatives on the 23d instant, and of certain statements which accompanied the same,[3] which will give you a view of the present state of Revenue and Expenditure.

Our frontier affairs by occasioning an encrease of the latter will call for an augmentation of the former.

With perfect consideration & esteem   I have the honor to remain
Sir   Your Obedient Servt                                    Alexander Hamilton

William Short Esquire
Minister Resident of the
united States at the Hague

LS, William Short Papers, Library of Congress. A copy of this letter was en-
closed in H's "Report on Foreign Loans," February 13, 1793.
    1. The appointment of Short, United States chargé d'affaires at Paris, as
United States Minister to The Hague had been confirmed by the Senate on
January 16, 1792.
    2. See H to Willink, Van Staphorst, and Hubbard, January 27, 1792.
    3. See "Report on Estimates of Receipts and Expenditures for 1791–1792,"
January 23, 1792.

## From Joseph Whipple

*Portsmouth, New Hampshire, January 28, 1792.* "Herewith I enclose you an account of the expence of Supporting the Lighthouse
for the Quarter ending the 31st. of Dec past. . . . I have no remarks
to make on the Lighthouse respectg its repairs, but its construction
does not admit of its being so usefull as the Situation of it requires. I
enclose a Contract for supples & attendance on the Lighthouse for
6 Months ending the last day of June next for the purpose of its
being laid before the president of the United States."

LC, RG 36, Collector of Customs at Portsmouth, Letters Sent, 1791–1792, Vol.
3, National Archives.

## From Charles Lee

Alexandria [Virginia] 29th. January 1792

Sir!

I have received your letter of the 18th. Instant and I shall act conformably to it with respect to the clauses of the Collection Law,[1] to
which it refers.

As to the appointment of a person to measure vessels,[2] in considering the parts of the Coasting Law, which apply to the subject, more
particularly the third and thirty first sections,[3] I have conceived that
the measurement of every vessel ought to be made by the Surveyor

when it can be done conveniently with his other official duties. Few or none of the duties of that Office are in their natures so confidential. Putting this construction on the Law, I shall consider myself bound to require the admeasurement to be made by the Surveyor in every case, where it shall not be necessary to be made by another person to be appointed for the special purpose: and in every case where it shall be proper or necessary to appoint a measurer it shall be regularly done. This the Surveyor well knew was the proposed plan of my conduct, and also the one directed by Law. I have been led to be more exact and explicit with the Surveyor here, because in my opinion he has not been so attentive to the duties of his Office as he ought to have been; and as he is scarcely ever called by any occasion from Alexandria, he ought to have performed more of the duties of his Office than he has thought proper to do. I did formerly appoint a person to measure vessels indefinitely; and I have been informed that the certificates sent to my Office were signed by the Surveyor generally, yet the actual measurement was made in his absence, by the person thus appointed in almost every instance. This mode of proceeding being in my opinion improper, I thought it necessary in order that the Surveyor may be compelled to perform the duty of admeasurement when he can conveniently do it, to adopt the present mode, of appointing a measurer from time to time in every particular case that shall require it to be done. This latter mode is more troublesome to me but will be attended with a more proper execution of the Surveyors duties, and seems more perfectly legal.

I beg leave to bring your attention to the 31st. section of the Collection Law,[4] because to merchants here have complained of it as inconvenient in requiring the entry to be made on oath by the importer consignee or the known factor or agent of such importer or consignee before the collector of that district where the vessel unladed. The trade of Virginia not being collected to a point, it happens that goods imported by a Merchant at Alexandria are in a Vessel entered in James River, and so vice versa. There is no known factor or agent at the entering port, and the Merchant must go there to take the oath before the Custom House Officer, which inconvenience, it is thought, by altering the Law back to what it was under the first Collection Law,[5] might be removed without any injury to the Revenue. That is to say, by permitting the Oath of Entry to be taken in certain cases before a magistrate, and transmitted to the proper Officer of the Customs.

The Case of Mr. Cuthbert [6] has lately occurred he resides in Norfolk, and has some goods in a ship entered in this district. He has sent the enclosed paper, supposing it to be a sufficient appointment of an agent to make entry of his goods. As the ice has occluded our navigation, no inconvenience will arise to him while I wait for your opinion, and therefore I have submitted to you to direct, whether the oath of entry ought to be admitted to be taken by a person duly appointed by the importer or consignee to be his agent for the particular purpose of entering the goods; or whether the Law does not mean that the agent ought to be a person who previously and in other instances had acted in the affairs of the importer or consignee, and was known as such at the place of doing the business. The former construction might occasion unfair practices if generally admitted; and as the Law has made no exceptions, if admitted in one case it ought also to prevail in every case.

I am Sir! most respectfully   Your most Obedt. Hble Servant

Charles Lee, Collector
at Alexandria

Copy, RG 56, Letters to and from the Collector at Alexandria, National Archives.

1. Lee is referring to Sections 9 and 10 of "An Act to provide more effectually for the collection of the duties imposed by law on goods, wares and merchandise imported into the United States, and on the tonnage of ships or vessels" (1 *Stat.* 145–78 [August 4, 1790]). For the contents of these sections, see Lee to H, January 11, 1792, note 2.

2. For background concerning the dispute between Lee and Samuel Hanson, surveyor at the port of Alexandria, see Lee to H, January 18, 1792, note 3.

3. Section 3 of "An Act for Registering and Clearing Vessels, Regulating the Coasting Trade, and for other purposes" reads in part as follows: "That to ascertain the tonnage of all ships or vessels, the surveyor or other person appointed by the collector to measure the same, shall take the length of every vessel . . ." (1 *Stat.* 55 [September 1, 1789]). For the contents of Section 31, see Lee to H, January 11, 1792, note 4.

4. Lee is mistaken, for he is actually referring to Section 21 of "An Act to provide more effectually for the collection of the duties imposed by law on goods, wares and merchandise imported into the United States, and on the tonnage of ships or vessels," which reads as follows:

"*And be it further enacted,* That the owner or owners, consignee or consignees of any goods, wares or merchandise on board of any such ship or vessel, or in case of his, her or their absence or sickness, his, her or their known factor or agent, in his, her or their names, within fifteen days after report of the master or person having the charge or command of such ship or vessel to the collector of the district for which such goods, wares or merchandise shall be destined, shall make entry thereof with the said collector, and shall specify in such entry the particular marks, numbers and contents of each package or parcel whereof they shall consist, or if in bulk, the quantity and quality, together with the nett prime cost thereof; and shall also produce to the said collector, if any such there be, the original invoice or invoices, or other documents in lieu thereof, and bill or bills of lading; all which shall be done upon the oath of the person by whom such entry shall be made, according to the best of his or her knowledge and belief; who shall thereby also declare that if he or she shall afterwards discover or know of any other goods, wares or merchandise imported in such ship or vessel, belonging or consigned to the person or persons by whom or on whose behalf such entry shall have been made, he or she will forthwith make known the same, in order to the due entry thereof, and the payment or securing the payment of the duties thereupon: *Provided always,* That where the particulars of any such goods, wares, or merchandise shall be unknown, in lieu of the entry herein before directed to be made, an entry thereof shall be made and received according to the circumstances of the case, the party making the same, declaring upon oath all that he or she knows or believes concerning the quantity and particulars of the said goods, and that he or she has no other knowledge or information concerning the same; which entry, as well the first as the last, shall be made in writing, and shall be subscribed by the party making the same." (1 *Stat.* 160–61 [August 4, 1790].)

5. Lee is referring to Section 13 of "An Act to regulate the Collection of the Duties imposed by law on the tonnage of ships or vessels, and on goods, wares and merchandises imported into the United States," which reads as follows:

"*And be it further enacted,* That every person having goods, wares or merchandise, in any ship or vessel, which shall arrive at any port of entry, or of delivery only, shall make entry with the collector of the port or district where the same shall arrive, of all such goods, wares and merchandise, specifying the number of packages, and the marks, numbers and contents of each (or if in bulk, the quantity and quality) together with an account of the nett prime cost thereof; and shall moreover produce to the collector, the original invoice or invoices, together with the bills of loading; and the said collector shall estimate and endorse the duties on the said entry, the party making such entry taking an oath or affirmation, that it contains the whole of the goods, wares and merchandise imported by him, or to him consigned in such ship or vessel, which shall then have come to his knowledge, and that the said invoice contains, to the best of his knowledge and belief, the nett prime cost thereof, and that if he shall afterwards discover any other, or greater quantity than is contained in such entry, he will make due report and entry thereof; and the said oath or affirmation shall be administered by the collector, and the entry shall be subscribed by the person making the same. *Provided,* That in all cases where the party making entry shall reside ten miles or upwards from such port, the affidavit or affirmation of such party, taken before a justice of the peace, and by him endorsed on the original invoices, shall be as effectual as if administered and endorsed by the collector." (1 *Stat.* 39–40 [July 31, 1789].)

6. William Cuthbert was a Norfolk merchant.

## From Philip Schuyler

New York Sunday Jan 29th 1792

My Dear Sir

Your favor of the 24th instant I received yesterday.[1] I shall embrace the first moment which offers and in which I can prudently be absent from hence to pay you a visit.

The bank Mania has somewhat subsided [2] but as in the first paroxism the leaders induced many to subscribe a petition to the legislature for an incorporation, the pride of some and the interested views of others will not permit them to relinquish the object. What fate will attend the application in the house of assembly is problemetical [3]—but I am almost certain that in the senate It will not meet with countenance. It is however prudent to be prepared with every Objection, and I wish you to state those that have occured to you.

I have been pressed by several persons to draft a bill for the future conduct of the commissioners of the land office, in the preamble to which they wish to convey a censure on the board for their conduct in the sale to Mr Macomb.[4] Considering a measure of this kind as a two edged Sword, I have advised that If even It were proper It would not be prudent until matters of much importance to the state had been decided upon, and that the business should be postponed for further consideration. This Advice was acceded to, but with so much reluctance that I am under apprehensions it will be precipatated.

Mr. Rensselaer is arrived, has received the letter you mention before I left Albany.[5] Some intimations were given of the project you mention [6] and I was alarmed as Mr Yates [7] had some little time before observed to me that he apprehended his pecuniary affairs would be injured If he was placed in the chair of Government. I obviated the difficulties he stated, observed that the mere intimation that he doubted of the propriety of being proposed as a candidate would be injurious to his reputation, infinitely distressing to those who had supported him on the former Occassion and who had already committed themselves with great numbers of the citizens. He seemed convinced, and from what he has since said to Mr. Rensselaer and the exertions he makes with the council of appointment in favor of persons who are unfriendly to Clinton; and whom he declares will use their influence to carry the Election in his favor, I am led to believe that he will not yield to Mr Burr's views. I shall however in a day or two bring him to an explicit declaration on the Subject.

As no good could possibly result from evincing any resentment to Mr. Burr for the part he took last winter,[8] I have on every Occassion behaved towards him as If he had never [9] been the principal in the business.

If I cannot speedily visit you I will send on Cornelia [10] who is anxious to be with you & her sister.

My love to Eliza & the Children

Yours affectionately &c                           Ph: Schuyler

Hone Alexander Hamilton Esqr

ALS, Hamilton Papers, Library of Congress.
    1. Letter not found.
    2. For information on the attempt to organize new banks in New York, see H to William Seton, January 18, 24, 1792; Seton to H, January 22, 1792.
    3. See H to Seton, January 18, 1792, note 2.
    4. Alexander Macomb was a wealthy New York businessman and speculator. According to Joseph Stancliffe Davis, from 1789 to 1790 Macomb "concluded negotiations for between three and four million acres, at 8d. per acre, south of the St. Lawrence" (Davis, *Essays*, I, 396). In April, 1792, Governor George Clinton was accused of having profited from the sale of the land (*The* [New York] *Daily Advertiser*, April 14, 1792). Willis Fletcher Johnson states that, after the report of the commissioners of the land office for 1791 had been received, "A long and acrimonious discussion ensued in the Legislature, in the course of which it was pretty directly charged, or at least insinuated, that the Governor and his friends had been personally interested in the transactions and would profit from them. . . . A resolution was introduced into the Legislature by Colonel [Silas] Talbot, of Montgomery county, severely condemning the Commissioners for lack of judgment in the transactions. . . . This was finally defeated, and in its place was adopted by a vote of 30 to 25 in the Assembly, a resolution fathered by Melancthon Smith approving the conduct of the Commissioners" (Ray B. Smith, ed., *History of the State of New York Political and Governmental* [Syracuse, 1922], I, 131–32). The June 16, 1792, issue of *The* [New York] *Journal, & Patriotic Register* contained an affidavit signed by Macomb and Daniel McCormick which exonerated Clinton from any share in the land holdings. At the same time it was implied that Schuyler and H had been interested in the purchase. A reply to this affidavit, signed "Tubero," stated that H's lands had been separately purchased at a higher price (*The* [New York] *Daily Advertiser*, June 21, 1792).
    5. Stephen Van Rensselaer, Philip Schuyler's son-in-law and president of the Bank of Albany, was patroon of the Van Rensselaer estate and an influential New York Federalist. Although it cannot be stated with certainty, it appears that H wished Van Rensselaer to run for lieutenant governor.
    6. With H's letter to Schuyler lost, this "project" remains a mystery, but Schuyler may very well have been referring to the alleged attempts of Aaron Burr to obtain the gubernatorial nomination from the Federalists.
    7. Robert Yates, Chief Justice of New York, had been a prominent Antifederalist during the seventeen-eighties. As a member of the Constitutional Convention of 1787 and of the New York Ratifying Convention of 1788 he had indicated his disapproval of the proposed government. After the adoption of the Constitution, however, his opposition ceased, and in 1789 he ran with Federalist support as a gubernatorial candidate against Governor George

Clinton. At the time this letter was written, the New York Federalists were proposing that he again run against Clinton. Yates, however, declined the nomination for the 1792 election.

8. This is a reference to Burr's defeat of Schuyler in 1791 for United States Senator from New York.

9. In MS, "none."

10. Cornelia Schuyler, Philip Schuyler's daughter and H's sister-in-law.

## From William Ellery

Collector's Office
District of Newport [Rhode Island] Jany. 30. 1792

Sir,

The question respectg. masters of vessels convicted of havg. sworn falsely [1] was the result of a conversation I had with a gentleman on that subject. He conceived that as the credibility of such men must be greatly impaired, it was the intention of the Legislature that they should not be permitted to act in a capacity which would necessarily subject them to take oaths. I had carefully examined the Law, and was satisfied that it did not disqualify them, but as he wished it I proposed the question to which you have favoured me with an answer in your letter of the 13th. of this month.[2]

In a moral view there may be no difference between swearing falsly in a Court of Law, and in a Custom-House—but in the first case false-swearing works a disqualification in the offender to hold an office to the exercise of which his taking an oath is previously requisite, and, to give an evidence &c &c,[3] and in the last, by the 67 Sec. of the Revenue Law, the offender "shall on indictment and conviction be punished by fine or imprisonment or both in the discretion of the Court before whom the conviction shall be had" with a limitation as to the fine and term of imprisonment.[4] This is the only part of the Revenue Law which respects this last case: And by this a master of a vessel would not be disqualified from acting as such although he should have been convicted of having sworn falsly any number of times, and although by repeated shipwrecks of his conscience all ideas of the sacred obligation of oaths should appear to be obliterated from his mind. The frequency of Oaths in Custom-Houses as has been often and I believe justly remarked has a tendency to lessen their force, and may not the admission of those who have been convicted of swearing falsely to take oaths still more diminish their influence? I hope I shall not be thought to have deviated from the path of propriety by having made these few observations.

There are in my office several bonds, conditioned for the due entry & delivery of goods in districts in the State of Connt. for which they were reported to be destined, which were given twelve months ago: and no Certificates have been produced of the entry and delivery of the goods in those districts.

I have not found that the Law [5] has prescribed the time within which Certificates shall be produced, or directed when such bonds shall be put in suit. Where no time is prescribed by law I should suppose a reasonable time is intended, and for producing Certificates from any District in Connecticut may not six months be deemed as sufficient time; but would it be improper to have the time ascertained by Law?

Inclosed is a weekly return of monies received and paid, and a List of a post Note of the Bank of the United States No. 255 dated Jany. 3rd 1792, for 195 dolls. a moiety of which is now transmitted to the Treasurer.

I am Sir Yr. most obedt. servt.                    Wm Ellery Collr

A Hamilton Esqr
Secry Treasy

LC, Newport Historical Society, Newport, Rhode Island.
    1. See Ellery to H, January 3, 1792.
    2. Letter not found.
    3. Section 18 of "An Act for the Punishment of certain Crimes against the United States" provided in part as follows: "That if any person shall wilfully and corruptly commit perjury . . . on his or her oath or affirmation in any suit, controversy, matter or cause depending in any of the courts of the United States, or in any deposition taken pursuant to the laws of the United States, every person so offending . . . shall . . . be thereafter rendered incapable of giving testimony in any of the courts of the United States" (1 Stat. 116 [April 30, 1790]).
    4. Ellery is referring to Section 66 of "An Act to provide more effectually for the collection of the duties imposed by law on goods, wares and merchandise imported into the United States, and on the tonnage of ships or vessels," which provided that masters of vessels convicted of making a false oath were subject to fine and imprisonment (1 Stat. 175–76 [August 4, 1790]).
    5. Section 20 of the Collection Law concerned the procedure to be followed by masters of vessels importing merchandise from abroad into more than one district in the United States (1 Stat. 160).

## From Joseph Whipple

Portsmouth [*New Hampshire*] *January 30, 1792.* Has "exchanged Cash" for "a Note of the bank of the United States No. 314 for two thousand Dollars dated Jany 17. 1792," despite the fact the cash received for the note exceeds "the Amount of Specie received Since the last return." Realizes that this transaction represents "a deviation from the instruction" in Hamilton's circular letter of October 14, 1789,[1] but adds: ". . . having found by consulting the Commissioner of Loans [2] (who alone of late has presented drafts on me from the Treasury) that no inconveniences would arise in his department" because of this transaction. Therefore asks whether "an exact adherence" to Hamilton's instructions of October 14, 1789, "under all circumstances is to be observed."

LC, RG 36, Collector of Customs at Portsmouth, Letters Sent, 1791–1792, Vol. 3, National Archives.

1. In "Treasury Department Circular to the Collectors of the Customs," October 14, 1789, H directed the collectors "to receive in payment of the duties, the notes of the Banks of North-america and New York . . . [and] to exchange any Specie which may at any time be in your hands for them, with this restriction, that you shall not exchange any of the specie which in your weekly return of receipts and payments you state to be in hand; but only the Specie you may receive between one return and another."

2. William Gardner was appointed commissioner of loans for New Hampshire on December 24, 1790.

# INDEX

## COMPILED BY JEAN G. COOKE